CABO

AISLING IRWIN COLUM WILSON
MURRAY STEWART
UPDATED BY DONNA WHEELER

www.bradtguides.com

Bradt Guides Ltd, UK
The Globe Pequot Press Inc, USA

Bradt GUIDES
TRAVEL TAKEN SERIOUSLY

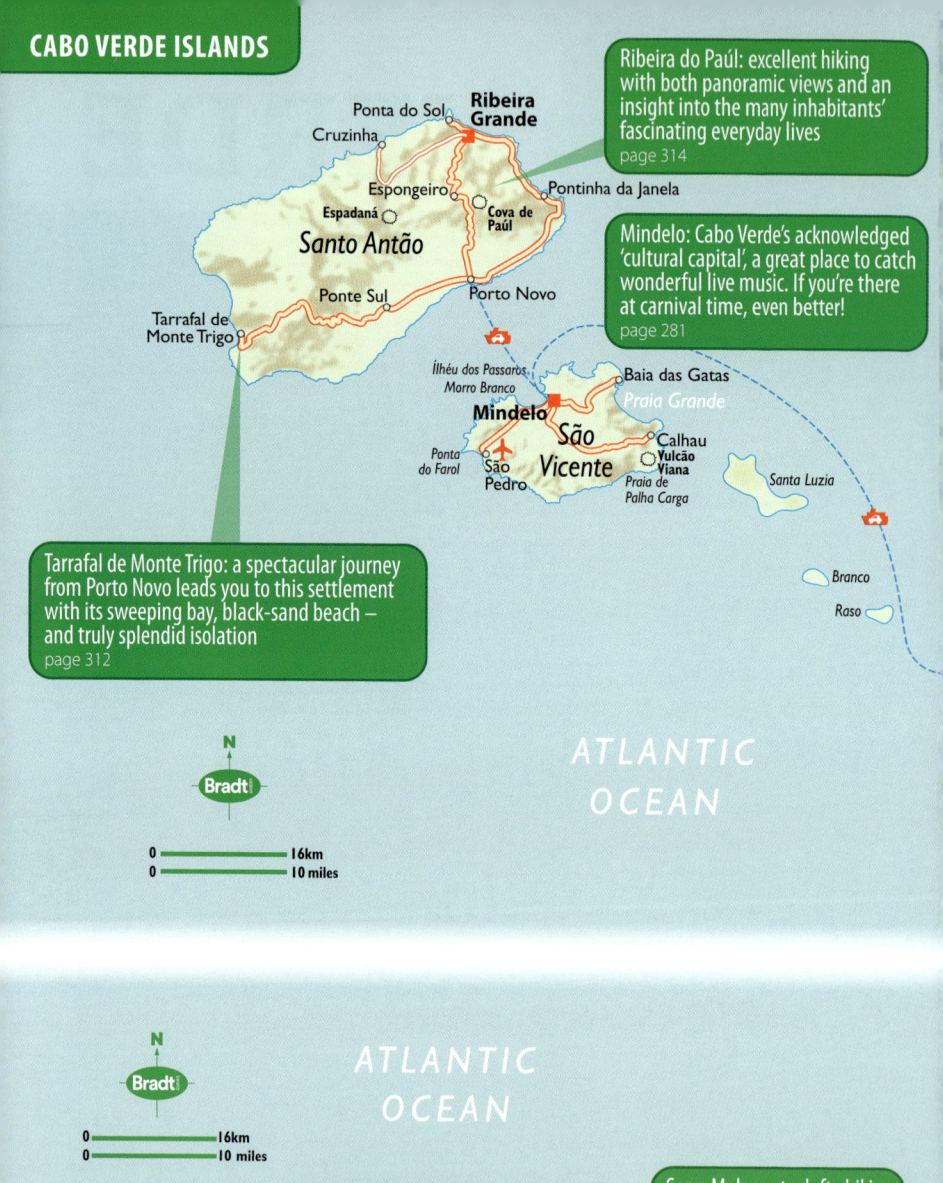

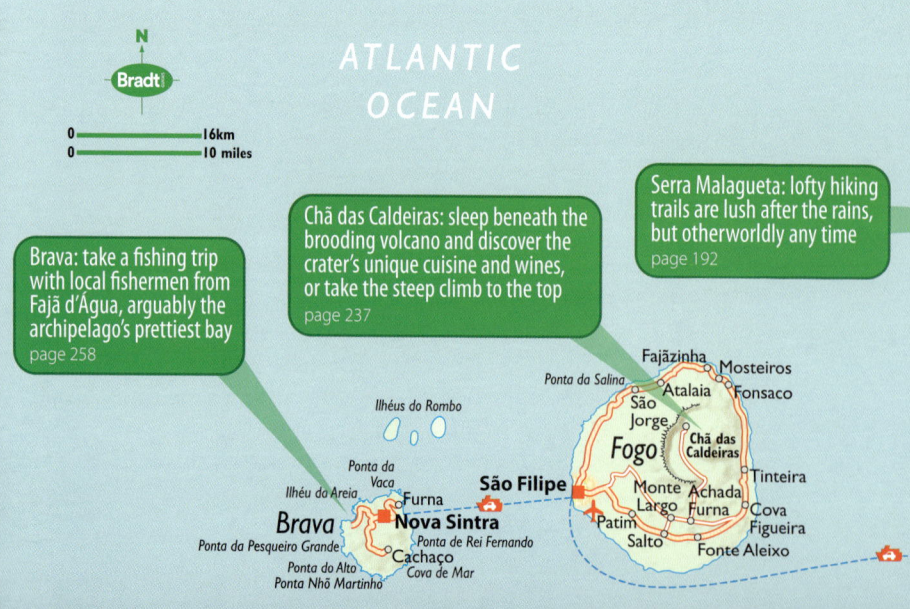

CABO VERDE ISLANDS

Ribeira do Paúl: excellent hiking with both panoramic views and an insight into the many inhabitants' fascinating everyday lives
page 314

Mindelo: Cabo Verde's acknowledged 'cultural capital', a great place to catch wonderful live music. If you're there at carnival time, even better!
page 281

Tarrafal de Monte Trigo: a spectacular journey from Porto Novo leads you to this settlement with its sweeping bay, black-sand beach – and truly splendid isolation
page 312

Santo Antão
- Ponta do Sol
- Cruzinha
- Ribeira Grande
- Espongeiro
- Pontinha da Janela
- Espadaná
- Cova de Paúl
- Ponte Sul
- Porto Novo
- Tarrafal de Monte Trigo

São Vicente
- Ilhéu dos Passaros, Morro Branco
- Mindelo
- Baia das Gatas
- Praia Grande
- Calhau
- Vulcão Viana
- Ponta do Farol
- São Pedro
- Praia de Palha Carga

- Santa Luzia
- Branco
- Raso

ATLANTIC OCEAN

0 — 16km
0 — 10 miles

ATLANTIC OCEAN

Brava: take a fishing trip with local fishermen from Fajã d'Água, arguably the archipelago's prettiest bay
page 258

Chã das Caldeiras: sleep beneath the brooding volcano and discover the crater's unique cuisine and wines, or take the steep climb to the top
page 237

Serra Malagueta: lofty hiking trails are lush after the rains, but otherworldly any time
page 192

Brava
- Ilhéus do Rombo
- Ponta da Vaca
- Ilhéu da Areia
- Furna
- Nova Sintra
- Ponta da Pesqueiro Grande
- Ponta do Alto
- Ponta Nhô Martinho
- Cachaço
- Ponta de Rei Fernando
- Cova de Mar

Fogo
- Fajãzinha
- Mosteiros
- Ponta da Salina
- São Jorge
- Atalaia
- Fonsaco
- Chã das Caldeiras
- São Filipe
- Monte Largo
- Achada Furna
- Tinteira
- Patim
- Cova Figueira
- Salto
- Fonte Aleixo

0 — 16km
0 — 10 miles

KEY

- ■ Capital town
- ○ Other town
- ✈ Airport
- ⛴ Ferry
- ━ Main road
- ═ Other road
- ◠ Crater

Sal
- Ponta Palhona
- Ponta de Casaca
- Praia d'Água Doce
- Palmeira (port)
- Pedra de Lume
- **Espargos**
- Baía da Palmeira
- Pesqueroná
- Murdeira
- Ponta do Morrinho Vermelho
- Baía do Algodoeiro
- Santa Maria
- Ponta do Leme Velho
- Ponta do Sinó

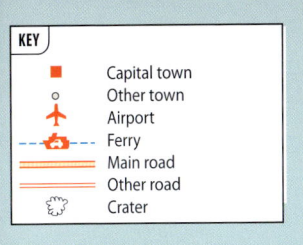

ATLANTIC OCEAN

Ponta Preta: world-class waves for experienced surfers, windsurfers and kitesurfers, and feet-in-the-sand beach bars for the less active
page 104

São Nicolau
- Ribeira da Prata
- Carvoeiros
- **Ribeira Brava**
- Juncalinho
- Barril
- Tarrafal
- Preguiça
- Crater
- Ponta da Vermelharia

Monte Gordo Natural Park: tranquil hiking trails and untouched forest peaks
page 342

Boavista
- Costa de Boa Esperança
- Ponta Antónia
- Ponta do Sol
- Ilhéu dos Pássaros
- **Sal Rei**
- Ilhéu do Sal Rei
- Bofareira
- Baía das Gatas
- Rabil
- Ilhéu de Baluarte
- Ponta do Morro d'Areia
- Cabeço dos Tarafes
- Ponta do Roque
- Ponta Varandinha
- Povoação Velha
- Praia de Santa Mónica
- Praia de João Barrosa
- Ponta Pesqueiro
- Ilhéu de Curral Velho

Praia de Santa Mónica: a long and isolated stretch of stunning sand; watch whales in spring and surfers in winter
page 155

Maio: the 'forgotten island' – a quiet location for seaside relaxation and contemplation
page 205

Santiago
- Ponta Moreia
- Tarrafal
- Baía de Tarrafal
- Porto Formoso
- Mangue de Sete Ribeiras
- Serra Malagueta
- Calheta de São Miguel
- Ribeira da Barca
- Assomada
- Pedra Badejo
- Praia Baixo
- São Domingos
- Milho Branco
- São João Baptista
- São Jorge
- Cidade Velha
- **Praia**
- Baía de São Francisco

Maio
- Ponta Cais
- Ilhéu Laje Branca
- Praia de Santana
- Cascabulho
- Pedro Vaz
- Praia de Soca
- Pilão Cão
- Praia de Morro
- Morro
- Figueira da Horta
- **Cidade do Porto Inglés (Vila do Maio)**
- Ribeira de João
- Praia Preta

ATLANTIC OCEAN

Cidade Velha: Cabo Verde's most renowned historical site is also one of its prettiest and liveliest villages
page 182

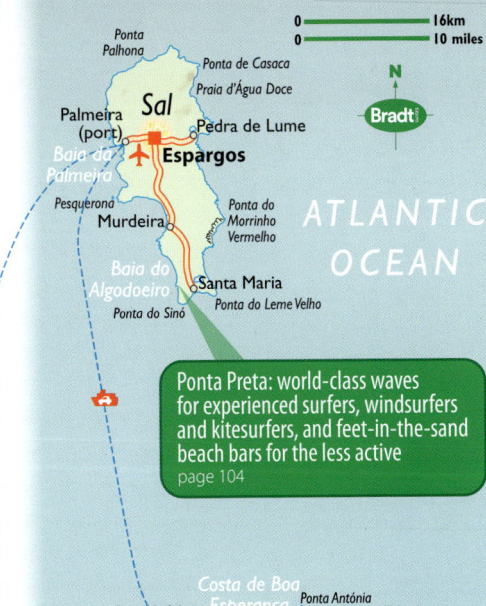

Praia: with a bustling centre perched on a plateau and a trio of city beaches below, Cabo Verde's capital is home to more than a quarter of its population
page 170

0 — 16km
0 — 10 miles

N

Bradt

ATLANTIC OCEAN

CABO VERDE
DON'T MISS...

WATERSPORTS
Perfect winds and plentiful waves have made Cabo Verde a popular destination for board riders of all stripes, as well as a fixture on international championship circuits **PAGE 54**
(MM)

VERDANT *RIBEIRAS*
Precariously perched between mountains and the sea, the fairy-tale village of Fontainhas on Santo Antão can only be reached on foot, via a winding cobbled path **PAGE 322**
(D/D)

PICO DO FOGO
The highest point on Fogo, Pico do Fogo is one of the steepest and most spectacular volcanic cones in the world PAGE 243
(DD/S)

RICH MUSIC SCENE
Music underpins Cabo Verdean life and no visit to the archipelago would be complete without experiencing a *morna* or *funaná* performance PAGE 43
(L/D)

SWEEPING SAND BEACHES
Miles and miles of beautiful white-sand beaches ring the islands of Sal, Maio and Boavista. Boavista's Praia de Santa Mónica, as shown here, is one of the most pristine of them all PAGE 155
(MM)

CABO VERDE
IN COLOUR

above (R/D) Watched over by Brava's ragged peaks, the tiny village of Fajã d'Água fans out along one of Cabo Verde's most beautiful and remote bays **PAGE 258**

below (A/D) Carnival is celebrated across Cabo Verde, including in the capital, Praia, on Santiago island **PAGE 83**

With rows of pastel-coloured buildings, Santa Maria, Sal's lively tourist centre, remains human-scaled and authentic PAGE 111

above (T/S)

Loggerhead turtles, long hunted for their meat, are now doubly threatened by tourist development, although significant conservation efforts have seen nesting numbers spring back over recent years PAGE 8

right (M/S)

Street art is a feature of Cabo Verde's cities and towns; here, a mural highlights Mindelo's status as a crucible of Cabo Verdean culture PAGES 42 & 281

below (P/AWL)

JOIN
THE TRAVEL CLUB

THE MEMBERSHIP CLUB FOR SERIOUS TRAVELLERS FROM BRADT GUIDES

Be inspired
Free books and exclusive insider travel tips and inspiration

Save money
Special offers and discounts from our favourite travel brands

Plan the trip of a lifetime
Access our exclusive concierge service and have a bespoke itinerary created for you by a Bradt author

Join here:
bradtguides.com/travelclub

Membership levels to suit all budgets

Bradt GUIDES

TRAVEL TAKEN SERIOUSLY

AUTHORS

Colum Wilson and **Aisling Irwin**'s first guide to Cabo Verde was published in 1998. Aisling is a journalist and writer, specialising in the environment, the developing world and science. A former *Daily Telegraph* correspondent, she has won several prizes for her feature-writing and has contributed to books on a variety of subjects, including Bradt's guide to solar eclipses over Africa. Colum is a humanitarian worker. He worked for Médecins Sans Frontières and now works for the UK government's Foreign, Commonwealth and Development Office. Colum and Aisling have lived in, and written about, a range of countries including Zambia and Angola. Their other joint book is *In Quest of Livingstone: A Journey to the Four Fountains*, about their retracing of David Livingstone's last journey. See page vi for their authors' story.

UPDATER/AUTHOR

In 2009, with a new-found ambition to become a travel writer, **Murray Stewart** turned his back on a 20-year career in corporate restructuring that included receiving a House of Commons commendation. Drawing on visits to 56 countries, including periods teaching English in Chile and Mexico, he has since been published in national travel magazines, as well as winning prizes for his online contributions. He jumped at the opportunity to update the sixth edition of Bradt's *Cabo Verde*. He spent two months 'speed-dating' the nine inhabited islands of the archipelago, rejoicing in the fusion of cultural influences, the diversity of terrains and the monotony of the weather: warm and sunny. He was happy to repeat the experience for the seventh edition.

Murray has updated other Bradt Guides, including *Azores* and *North Cyprus*. He also wrote from scratch Bradt's first edition of *The Basque Country and Navarre*, the most comprehensive English-language guidebook to the region. This book won the British Guild of Travel Writers' Award for Best Guidebook that year. He speaks French, Spanish, German and passable Portuguese, and three words of Cabo Verdean Kriolu.

Eighth edition published July 2025
First published 1998
Bradt Travel Guides Ltd
31a High Street, Chesham, Buckinghamshire, HP5 1BW, England
www.bradtguides.com
Print edition published in the USA by The Globe Pequot Press Inc,
PO Box 480, Guilford, Connecticut 06437-0480

Text copyright © Bradt Travel Guides, 2025

Maps copyright © Bradt Travel Guides Ltd, 2025; includes map data © MapTiler
© OpenStreetMap contributors
Photographs copyright © Individual photographers, 2025 (see below)
Project Manager: Samantha Fletcher
Copy-editor: Samantha Cook
Cover research: Pepi Bluck, Perfect Picture

The authors and publisher have made every effort to ensure the accuracy of the information in this book at the time of going to press. However, they cannot accept any responsibility for any loss, injury or inconvenience resulting from the use of information contained in this guide. All rights reserved. No part of this publication may be reproduced, stored in a retrieval system, or transmitted in any form or by any means, electronic, mechanical, photocopying, recording or otherwise without the prior consent of the publisher.

ISBN: 9781804692813

British Library Cataloguing in Publication Data
A catalogue record for this book is available from the British Library

Photographs AWL Images: Peter Adams (P/AWL); Dreamstime.com: Alexander Manykin (A/D), Daboost (D/D), Keithpritchard (K/D), Lucian Milasan (L/D), Peter Adams (P/D), Raulrosa (R/D); Marco Muscarà (MM); Martin Haigh (MH); Murray Stewart (MS); Shutterstock.com: africa2008st (A/S), Alicja Magdalena Wojcik (AMW/S), ChrisL30 (CL/S), Curioso.Photography (C/S), Daboost (D/S), Danita Delimont (DD/S), David Thyberg (DT/S), Francisco Freire (F/S), Frank Bach (FB/S), G. Jack'o Berger WWP (G/S), Gail Johnson (GJ/S), German Globetrotter (GG/S), Heidi De Koninck (H/S), Jacob Pinto (J/S), L_B_Photography (LB/S), Lucie.K (LK/S), Manuel Ocen (M/S), Pierre Laborde (P/S), Salvador Aznar (S/S), TravelGirl1981 (T/S)

Front cover Fishing boats in Cidade Velha, Santiago (P/AWL)
Back cover, clockwise from top left A hiking path on Santo Antão (LB/S), women at Praia Carnival (A/D), a turtle in the waters off Cabo Verde (J/S), Santa Maria on Sal (T/S)
Title page, clockwise from top left Pico do Fogo volcano (A/S), Tarrafal Beach on Santiago (C/S), a woman on Santa Maria pier (T/S), the blue church in São Filipe on Fogo (D/S)

Maps David McCutcheon FBCart.S. FRGS

Typeset by Ian Spick, Bradt Guides, and Geethik Technologies, India
Production managed by Imprint Press; printed in India
Digital conversion by www.dataworks.co.in

UPDATER

Donna Wheeler's life in travel publishing began in 2000, when she joined Lonely Planet as a senior editor, commissioning and producing a global restaurant guide series, as well as turning out the odd restaurant review herself. She then spent several years as a producer in that company's nascent digital content arm, before swapping life in-house for full-time travel writing in 2007. Since then, she has written dozens of guidebooks, along with features, photographic essays, hotel reviews and art criticism for various international outlets.

It wasn't until 2019, during an extended stay in Lisbon and a chance encounter with the Cabo Verdean Afrobeat scene in that city, that a new curiosity about the small island nation was unleashed. This was coupled with an old academic interest in the history of the Atlantic slave trade and the politics of postcolonial Africa – plus, as someone born and bred in Sydney, Australia, a lifelong hankering for unpeopled beaches, ocean dips and rugged, remote walks. She recently spent more time getting to know all nine of the inhabited islands in more depth for this eighth edition. It was a trip of discovery and delight, marvelling at the country's staggering natural beauty, its enthralling rural villages and its vibrant, youthful city life but, most of all, the personal warmth and kindness of the Cabo Verdeans.

Trained as a painter and a poet, Donna travels with a sense of wonder and attentiveness to the visual, musical and culinary cultures of place, along with the layers of history of each. She speaks a little Italian, French and Indonesian, sadly only a few Portuguese pleasantries, and now also a growing number of charming, melodic Kriolu phrases.

FEEDBACK REQUEST

At Bradt Guides we're aware that guidebooks start to go out of date on the day they're published – and that you, our readers, are out there in the field doing research of your own. You'll find out before us when a fine new family-run hotel opens or a favourite restaurant changes hands and goes downhill. So why not tell us about your experiences? Contact us on 01753 893444 or e info@bradtguides.com. We will forward emails to the author who may post updates on the Bradt website at w bradtguides.com/updates. Alternatively, you can add a review of the book to Amazon, or share your adventures with us on social:

- BradtGuides & donnawheeler
- BradtGuides
- BradtGuides & donnaelizabethwheeler

ACKNOWLEDGEMENTS FOR THE EIGHTH EDITION   Donna Wheeler

The first thanks must certainly go to all the Cabo Verdeans I met daily during this trip, who were unfailingly helpful, generous, mellow and good-hearted. I was especially grateful for the endless supply of tips and recommendations, not to mention the stories of their lives and such good company.

In the UK, many thanks to Claire Strange for welcoming me into the Bradt family, and to Samantha Fletcher for her kind support. I'm also very grateful to the author/updater of the last two editions, Murray Stewart, for an incredibly thoughtful handover and for generously helping with contacts and other information, as well as all the fascinating insights of the last edition.

In Cabo Verde, many thanks to Dani and Guy at Palmiera Da Cruz, for such a perfect expression of hospitality, and for so much important information about their home of Santo Antao; on Fogo, to David Montrond for both your wonderful winemaking and for your warm welcome to the caldera, and to Aaron and Ellen at La Fora for your flexibility and those great local resources; in Praia, to Elena and her beautiful family for going that extra mile in a crisis and for some wonderful local leads, to Mara too for kindly hosting a last-minute guest and for arranging such a great driver, to Emanuel Sousa and to Bobby for their nightlife tips, to the fabulously efficient crew at Casa Strela in Tarrafal, and to Pascale and Michele for such exuberant and interesting company as well as your excellent Platô suggestions; to Lena Matsuda for her ecological knowledge on Sal and beyond; and finally to Vanessa Monteiro in Mindelo for really pointing me in the right direction.

In Paris, thanks to Eun Lee for your friendship and the lifesaving luggage storage facility, and to the crew at Tony Collective for the kind of night out a travel writer needs just back from a long solo journey. Back in Australia, to Joe, Rumer and Biba Guario for putting up with me when either absent or distractedly desk-bound for months at a time: I again couldn't have done this without your love.

Bradt Guides would like to thank Mark-Anthony Johnson, David Gouldman, Valdir Lubrano Moreira and Sonya Dias of JIC Holdings for their hard work helping to raise awareness of the new edition of this guidebook in Cabo Verde.

ACKNOWLEDGEMENTS FOR THE SEVENTH EDITION   Murray Stewart

Any guidebook is heavily dependent on the generosity of others, particularly generosity of time given to the author or updater in assisting them with their task. Being my second visit, it was no surprise to find people eager to help, though this should never be taken for granted. Thanks go to all Cabo Verdeans for a true kindness of spirit and a hospitable nature that prevents them from being anything other than delightful to spend time with.

Beyond that, special thanks must go to the following: in the UK, to Ian Coates and Susanne Muskita at Archipelago Choice for organising inter-island flights; to Rachel Fielding and the team at Bradt for giving me the opportunity to do my second update to Cabo Verde. Thanks also to Susannah Lord for her editorial expertise. A big thanks to Ana Cassis, who taught me enough Portuguese to get by.

Others I met on my travels and who deserve a mention are: Tommy Melo of Biosfera I and Arnau Teixidor, Elisa Dierickx and Tamas Szekely of FMB for sharing with me their knowledge of the conservation issues facing Cabo Verde; to Marijke Katsburg, firmly part of the Bravan community; Mustafa, who showed me again the fascinating and resilient people of the Chã das Caldeiras crater on Fogo; to Professor

Lucy Durán for her valuable, expert contribution on Cabo Verdean music; Ana Monteiro for her informative pieces on wind power; vista verde (particularly Heike, Simon and Michelle) for their Teutonic efficiency in keeping me up to date with the inevitable changes to internal flights, and for their warm and welcome advice and tips. A big thank you also to all readers of the last edition who came forward with helpful suggestions for this new book; most of these have been incorporated in this edition, all of them have been considered. A special thanks in this respect to Martin Haigh, Livia Pruskova and Lutske van der Schaft.

I must thank Colonial Guesthouse and Casa Marisa on Fogo, KazadiZaza on Brava, Kira's Hotel on São Vicente, the Coração da Ponta do Sol, Musica do Mar and Santantao Art Resort on Santo Antão, Pensão Jardim and the Farinha de Pau Guesthouse on São Nicolau, Hotel Dunas on Boavista, Jardim de Vinho on Santiago and Porto Antigo and the Morabeza Hotel on Sal for providing me with welcome free nights' accommodation. Thanks also to others who helped me with the cost, among these the Solar Windelo in São Vicente. Somewhere, someone will read this and feel they have been left out. I can only apologise. My final thanks go to dear Sara Lister, for doing without me yet again for a couple of months while I bunked off to Cabo Verde and researched the book. And an even bigger thank you to her for having me back afterwards. No-one is indispensable.

CABO VERDE OR CAPE VERDE?

In October, 2013, via a request submitted to the Secretary-General of the United Nations, the island nation commonly known as Cape Verde officially changed its name to the Republic of Cabo Verde – the República de Cabo Verde, in the full Portuguese. Today, Cabo Verde is the name its citizens firmly prefer and universally use – and for that reason is the version Bradt Guides has chosen to use – though Cabo Verdeans, in characteristically generous, no-stress style, won't be offended if you unwittingly revert back to the anglicised form. In the country itself, you will also increasingly hear and see Cabo Verde rendered in its Kriolu spelling: Kabu Verd or Kabu Verdi.

AUTHORS' STORY
Aisling Irwin

When Colum and I first visited Cabo Verde more than two decades ago it was, for the British, an obscure destination. The annual number of tourists was a few tens of thousands, of which Brits were an infinitesimal fraction. Now tourism is in the hundreds of thousands and the development of hotels, apartments and condominiums surges ahead. The country is riding a rollercoaster with the added excitement that no-one knows how safe the structure is. I gaze through the estate agents' windows, at the developers' plans, at the construction sites and I try to extract meaning. Who will be living in these fairy-tale condominiums? What corners of the world will they come from? Will there be any Cabo Verdeans in there? What will it mean if there aren't – and what will it mean if there are?

Now, when I visit, development has made things easier (though the air and ferry connections between the islands are worse than they were a decade ago). But now I am also finding disappointment among tourists. I have heard complaints about sullen service, about the endless wind, flies, the lack of anything to 'do', and the high cost of living. The main reason for their negativity is that they were oversold their holidays. Cabo Verde is – hilariously – being touted as the 'new Caribbean' – when the islands for sale tend to have a barrenness approaching that of the moon.

So I find myself in a strange position now: instead of raving about Cabo Verde, I sometimes advise people not to go. I've even inserted a small section in each island chapter on 'lowlights' so you know what not to expect. Here is my reasoning: I want you to treasure Cabo Verde, and if you're a person who won't find it treasurable, I want you to know beforehand.

So: go, if you love the sea and have a cracking watersports holiday on Sal or Boavista; go, if you love outstanding mountainous landscapes, particularly if you enjoy hiking in them – enjoy Santo Antão; go, if something inside you responds to a barren land with a harsh black coastline pounded by a frothing white ocean; or to a convivial people with the time to strike up a mournful tune over a glass of thick red wine.

I believe, though, that you will have your most fulfilling holiday if a little part of you goes as an anthropologist, interested in whatever the archipelago throws at you. Be like one of my contributors, who responds to notorious Cabo Verdean punctuality with the words: 'It's great how these people refuse to be intimidated by time.'

Cabo Verde is, at heart, a place not to be consumed, but to be understood.

AUTHOR'S STORY *Murray Stewart*

Aisling's words, written opposite, keep returning to me: 'you will have your most fulfilling holiday if a little part of you goes as an anthropologist'. My two months in Cabo Verde demonstrated the inherent truth in those words. Memories reinforce the statement. Cabo Verde does not have a wealth of obvious treasures, few museums, no art galleries, a mere scattering of historical sites. So, travel as an anthropologist and little treasures will appear and quickly turn into big treasures – treasures to store in the memory.

I recall the large, matronly lady in Santo Antão who stood in front of the *aluguer* and refused to let it continue its journey until she had finished an impromptu song she was singing. None of the passengers complained. Then I remember the face of the fisherman on Brava, stretched taut – it seemed – with that island's centuries of loss and longing, his emotion heightened by a few too many shots of *grogue*, singing me a *morna* until the tears spilled down his cheeks and those of his three-person audience. Had I understood Creole, I have no doubt I would have wept, too.

Recollections of shared lunch tables, pick-up trucks groaning with an overfill of people and their purchases from the Assomada Market; an uncomfortable, inter-island journey on a chartered fishing boat during which a local woman sitting on the deck simply wrapped (without asking) both her arms around my leg, to steady herself against the effects of the 4m-high Atlantic swell…

All of these come back to me, finally allowing me to bundle them together and explain to myself why I love Cabo Verde. Yes, the Fogo volcano is stunning. Yes, Santo Antão's craggy peaks steal the breath with their starkness. Yes, the glistening beaches of Sal and Boavista defy you not to curl up your feet and scrunch the white grains gleefully between your toes.

But it is none of these attractions that won me over, rather the gentle patience of the archipelago's inhabitants, their ability to share intimately both time and space with each other (and me), their commitment to live life *communally*. What haunts me is the feeling that the 'developed' countries have lost that ability, and that we'll never get it back. This brings me my own sense of loss and longing, but I can't sing a *morna*.

Contents

	Introduction	xii
PART ONE	**GENERAL INFORMATION**	**1**
Chapter 1	**Background Information**	**3**
	Geography and climate 3, Natural history and conservation 5, History 10, Government and politics 28, Economy 29, People 34, Language 36, Religion and beliefs 38, Education 38, Culture 38	
Chapter 2	**Practical Information**	**51**
	When to visit 51, Highlights 51, Suggested itineraries 56, Tour operators 57, Red tape 58, Getting there and away 59, Health 61, Safety 67, Focus on specific groups 69, What to take 70, Money and budgeting 71, Getting around 72, Accommodation 77, Eating and drinking 79, Public holidays and festivals 82, Shopping 83, Arts and entertainment 84, Opening hours 84, Media and communications 85, Cultural etiquette 86, Travelling positively 88	
PART TWO	**THE GUIDE**	**91**
Chapter 3	**Sal**	**92**
	Highlights and lowlights 92, Background information 93, Getting there and away 98, Getting around 99, Where to stay and eat 100, Excursions and tour operators 101, Activities 102, Espargos 109, Murdeira 111, Santa Maria 111, Other places to visit 125, Hikes 129	
Chapter 4	**Boavista**	**131**
	Highlights and lowlights 131, Background information 132, Getting there and away 139, Getting around 140, Where to stay and eat 140, Excursions and tour operators 141, Activities 141, Sal Rei 145, Other places to visit 153, Hikes 158	
Chapter 5	**Santiago**	**162**
	Highlights and lowlights 162, Background information 163, Getting there and away 166, Getting	

around 167, Where to stay and eat 167, Excursions and tour operators 168, Activities 169, Praia 170, Cidade Velha 182, São Domingos 187, Assomada 188, Serra Malagueta 192, Tarrafal 193, Other places to visit 196, Hikes 198

Chapter 6   **Maio**   **205**
Highlights and lowlights 205, Background information 207, Getting there and away 210, Getting around 210, Where to stay and eat 211, Excursions and tour operators 211, Activities 211, Cidade do Porto Inglés (Vila do Maio) 212, Other places to visit 218

Chapter 7   **Fogo**   **221**
Highlights and lowlights 221, Background information 223, Getting there and away 227, Getting around 228, Where to stay and eat 228, Excursions and tour operators 229, Activities 229, São Filipe 230, Chã das Caldeiras 237, The east-coast road to Mosteiros 242, Mosteiros 242, Other places to visit 243, Hikes 243

Chapter 8   **Brava**   **248**
Highlights and lowlights 248, Background information 249, Getting there and away 252, Getting around 253, Where to stay and eat 253, Excursions and tour operators 253, Activities 253, Furna 254, Vila Nova Sintra 254, Fajã d'Água 258, Other places to visit 260, Drives 260, Hikes 262

Chapter 9   **São Vicente**   **272**
Highlights and lowlights 272, Background information 273, Getting there and away 276, Getting around 277, Where to stay and eat 278, Excursions and tour operators 278, Activities 278, Mindelo 281, Other places to visit 294

Chapter 10   **Santo Antão**   **301**
Highlights and lowlights 301, Background information 302, Getting there and away 305, Getting around 305, Where to stay and eat 306, Excursions and tour operators 306, Activities 306, The East 308, The West 324, Hikes 328

Chapter 11   **São Nicolau**   **339**
Highlights and lowlights 339, Background information 340, Getting there and away 344, Getting around 344, Where to stay and eat 345, Excursions and tour operators 345, Activities 345, Ribeira Brava 348, Around Ribeira Brava 351, Tarrafal 351, North of Tarrafal 353, South of Ribeira Brava 354, The East 355, Hikes 357, Raso and Branco 361

Appendix 1	**Language**	**364**
Appendix 2	**Further Information**	**373**
Index		**378**
Index of advertisers		**386**

LIST OF MAPS

Activities by island	52	Praia, Greater	172
Boavista	132	Praia Platô	176
Brava	249	Ribeira Brava	349
Cabo Verde	1st colour	Ribeira Grande	317
Islands	section	Sal	93
Cidade do Porto Inglés		Sal Rei	146
(Vila do Maio)	213	Santa Maria: centre	116
Cidade Velha	183	Santa Maria: west	114
Espargos	109	Santiago	163
Fogo	222	Santo Antão	300
Fogo crater	237	Santo Antão: hiking	330
Maio	206	São Filipe	232
Mindelo	282	São Nicolau	338
Mindelo: centre	286	São Nicolau: hiking	358
Ponta do Sol	320	São Vicente	273
Porto Novo	309	Vila Nova Sintra	255

HOW TO USE THIS GUIDE

PRICE CODES Throughout this guide we have used price codes to indicate the cost of those places to stay and eat listed in the guide. For a key to these price codes, see page 78 for accommodation and page 79 for restaurants.

MAPS

Keys and symbols Maps include alphabetical keys covering the locations of those places to stay, eat or drink that are featured in the book. Note that regional maps may not show all hotels and restaurants in the area: other establishments may be located in towns shown on the map. On occasion, hotels, cafés, bars or restaurants that are not listed in the guide (but which might serve as alternative options if required or serve as useful landmarks to aid navigation) are also included on the maps; these are marked with accommodation ⌂, café ⌑, bar ♀ or restaurant ✘ symbols.

Grids and grid references Several maps use gridlines to allow easy location of sites. Map grid references are listed in square brackets after the name of the place or sight of interest in the text, with page number followed by grid number, eg: [116 C3].

KEY TO SYMBOLS

═══	Road	☆	Nightclub
======	Track	†	Church/cathedral
----------	Footpath	✿	Garden
	Ferry	※	Scenic viewpoint
✈ ✈	Airport (international/domestic)	🗼	Lighthouse
+	Airstrip	⚓	Beach
🚌	Bus station etc		Diving
🚗	Car hire	★	Watersports specialist shop/hire
P	Car park		Ecotours
⛽	Filling station/garage	➤	Birdwatching
ℹ	Tourist information office		Fishing
🏛	Museum	⁂	Historic site
🎭	Theatre/cinema	▲	Summit (height in metres)
⌂	Historic building	●	Other place of interest
🏰	Historic castle		City wall/fortification
⚐	Statue/monument		Cliff
$	Bank/bureau de change	○	Volcanic crater
✉	Post office	🏟	Stadium
✚	Hospital/clinic/health centre etc		Salt lake/pan
✚	Pharmacy/dentist		Dry river bed
⌂	Hotel		Urban park
✘	Restaurant		Market
♀	Bar		Shopping mall
⌑	Café		Beach

xi

Introduction

The flight to the island of Maio was full. As the tiny propeller plane bounced over Atlantic air currents, I was the only passenger to gaze out with a lick of fear at the mighty mid ocean below. Inside the plane everyone else seemed to have forgotten the sea. All was exuberance, chatter and a roaring laughter. The passengers were young men in polished shoes, expensive trousers and heavy gold jewellery. They spoke in a Creole that was too rapid for me to grasp and I wondered what interest Maio – flat, dry and quiet even by Cabo Verdean standards – could hold for them.

A few days later I was driving through the north of Maio, mesmerised by its endless stony red plains where the goats eat rock and the people eat goats. I reached a village – a single street of dust, two rows of parched, single-storey houses. 'This is Alcatraz,' the driver said. The street was quiet apart from a few of the ragged, wide-eyed children who populate the poorer half of the world. Some of the houses were nothing more than bare concrete carcasses while others were painted in greens and pinks and blues and even had glass in their windows.

From the front door of one of the smarter houses a family appeared. I crossed the street and asked if a man minded if I took a photo.

'Not at all,' the man replied in perfect English. 'But don't you remember me? I was on your flight.'

My perception jolted and suddenly I saw the urbane passenger, representative of a richer world, gold still gleaming at his neck. And then my world altered again and I saw a poor village, forgotten even within Cabo Verde. He must have noticed my perplexity: 'I live in Holland,' he explained. 'I work on the ships…I've come back to see my wife and children.' The woman at his side, uncomprehending, scooped a child on to her hip.

'How long have you been away?' I asked.

'Three years.'

'That's hard.'

'Yes,' he replied. 'But we Cabo Verdeans – we have hard lives.'

That is one of the paradoxes of Cabo Verde. There is a widespread cosmopolitanism that dates from centuries ago, but it lives side by side with poverty and isolation. For generations the young men have gone abroad – to the USA, to Europe, to the African mainland – because the land cannot sustain them, because their families need money. Back at home their relatives mourn not just the loss of their own sons and husbands but the painful emigrations of generations before. They mourn the peculiar lot of the Cabo Verdean, stranded on outcrops in the Atlantic, abused over the centuries not just by the waves but by many nations. They mourn in a particularly beautiful way which I first discovered on Fogo, the volcano island.

I was clinging to the bench in the back of a small truck as it jolted up and down the steep cobbled roads of the old Portuguese town of São Filipe. Every so often the vehicle would halt in front of a house, the driver would shout and a man would appear in the doorway clutching a violin and scramble in beside me.

Soon we had gathered the band back together and we careered up into the foothills of Fogo's dark volcano till we reached the house of Agusto, a blind musician. Inside his white-painted, two-roomed home the men dragged chairs and benches together and I sat in a far corner as the violins made their awakening screeches and the guitars were tuned. Then the music began: sweet melodies and melancholy harmonies. The music was so sad, it was as if the sorrow of generations had erupted in the house.

The Cabo Verdeans express through their *mornas* the sorrow of sons lost to the wider world, droughts, famines and relatives drowned at sea. Their music is exquisite, an Atlantic art form with influences from the four continents that surround it. But soon the sadness was done and there came the lively strains of a *funaná*. Now we were celebrating...what, I wondered? I knew the answer, though. We were celebrating the same notion that had just made us cry – *Caboverdeanidade*, the essence of Cabo Verde.

I absorbed it all in the dim room with its rough furniture and garish crocheted ornaments. Later I stepped outside where the sun was dissolving into the ocean. As I watched, the music still playing behind me, I thought: this is the reason to visit Cabo Verde. There are fine mountains, wildernesses of desert dunes and warm waters. But what makes Cabo Verde take hold of your heart is that rare moment, that flush of empathy, when you begin to understand what they mean by *sodade*.

Part One

GENERAL INFORMATION

CABO VERDE ISLANDS AT A GLANCE

Islands Santo Antão, São Vicente, Santa Luzia (uninhabited), São Nicolau, Sal, Boavista, Maio, Santiago, Fogo, Brava
Location Atlantic Ocean, approximately 1,000km southwest of the Canary Islands, and 460km from the Senegalese coast
Size Ten islands varying in size from 35km^2 (Santa Luzia) to 990km^2 (Santiago), spread over an east–west band of 370km of ocean
Status Independent democratic republic
Government Movimento para a Democracia, or MpD (re-elected 2021)
Population 522,331 (WHO, 2023)
Life expectancy 73.2 years (WHO, 2021)
Capital Praia, on Santiago (population around 160,000)
Economy Tourism an increasing earner; processed fish largest export; continued dependence on remittances and foreign aid
GDP (per capita, 2024) US$4,851
Language Officially Portuguese; everyday language is Creole ('Kriolu')
Religion Roman Catholic (85% of the population, estimated)
Currency Cabo Verdean escudo (CVE, written as $, after the numeral)
Exchange rate €1=110$ (rate is 'fixed' to the euro), £1=131$, US$1=100$ (April 2025)
International telephone code +238
Time GMT −1
Electricity supply 220V AC, 50Hz. Round, European two-pin sockets
Flag Blue with white and red horizontal stripes and a circle of ten yellow stars
National Anthem *Cântico da Liberdade* ('Song of Freedom')
Public holidays 1 January, 20 January, 1 May, 5 July, 15 August, 12 September, 1 November, 25 December; see page 83. Additionally, each island has its own local holidays; see chapters for details.

1

Background Information

GEOGRAPHY AND CLIMATE

Just a few geographical oddities shape Cabo Verde's natural history and economy to a profound degree: a combination of winds and currents that bring heat and cool, dust, dryness and the occasional monsoon. Drought is the key to everything and, as the Cabo Verdeans say, 'the best governor is rain'.

LOCATION AND SIZE The Cabo Verdes are an arrow-shaped archipelago of ten islands, five islets and various rocks and stacks that poke out of the eastern Atlantic on a band of latitude that runs between Senegal in the east and the Caribbean, 3,600km to the west. They stretch between 14°N and 18°N and 22°W and 26°W. The archipelago is the furthest south of the groups of islands collectively known as Macaronesia. Others in that group include the Azores and the Canary Islands, but the distance between them is great. The Canaries, off Morocco, are over 1,000km away while the Azores, parallel with Portugal, are at a distance of about 2,500km. Even within Cabo Verde, its constituent islands are widely spaced. The most easterly is 460km from Senegal and the most westerly is 830km. Santiago, the largest island, is 990km², about twice the size of the Isle of Wight. The smallest is the uninhabited 35km² pinprick of Santa Luzia. Brava is the smallest inhabited island at 64km². The total land area is 4,033km², scattered over 58,000km² of ocean.

The archipelago is popularly divided into two groups. The **Barlavento**, or windward, islands in the north are Santo Antão, São Vicente, Santa Luzia, São Nicolau, Sal and Boavista. The **Sotavento**, or leeward, islands to the south are Maio, Santiago, Fogo and Brava.

TERRAIN Another way of dividing the islands is longitudinally: the easterly islands of Sal, Boavista and Maio are extremely flat, while the rest are mountainous. There is extraordinary variation in height: Fogo's peak reaches 2,829m, and you can walk to the top of it, while Boavista musters only a small hill of 390m.

The variation in height reflects the huge age span of the islands and therefore the time available for erosion to take place. Their geological history is still controversial but the most popular theory estimates the flat ones to be up to 26 million years old, dating from the Miocene era. It has been shown that the central islands of São Nicolau and Maio appeared less than 12 million years ago, in the Pliocene. To the west Fogo and Brava, the youngest, have been around for a mere 100,000 years.

The theory is based on the drift of the African Plate, a section of the earth's crust that stretches well beyond the African landmass as far as the middle of the Atlantic. This tectonic plate began a slow drift to the east about 120 million years ago. Underneath it lies a 'hot spot'. As the plate above has drifted, this spot has periodically erupted, poking a series of holes like molehills through the crust. It is thought that the most eroded volcanoes can no longer be seen, submerged by the Atlantic somewhere between Boavista and the mainland. It is even possible that the basalts of Cap Vert, the Senegal promontory, are remnants of the first eruption of the hot spot into the Atlantic.

But some of the islands are more complicated than that. Not all of the magma that erupted from below actually blasted through to the surface. Some of it became trapped within the crust and cooled there, forming large igneous intrusions. The intrusions swelled up and rose within the forming volcanoes, lifting with them the ancient marine sediments that had been deposited on the ocean floor long before any islands developed. The intrusions and the uplifted sediments remained hidden within the volcanoes for millions of years, but the distance between them and the surface has slowly been shrinking as wind and flash floods have eroded the volcanoes away. Now, like slicing the top from a boiled egg, the sediments are revealed, the yolk within. The result is that the flat land of some islands (Maio in particular) is, very roughly, young volcanic rock around the outside and much older sedimentary rock forming an uplifted ring around the intrusions that are exposed in the heart of the island.

The mountainous islands can be very rugged, sometimes with virtually no flat land. Dunes, both still and wandering, are present mainly in the flat islands, most visibly and beautifully on Boavista, where parts feel like true desert.

CLIMATE Caught in the Sahel zone, Cabo Verde is really a marine extension of the Sahara. The northeast tradewind is responsible for much of its climate. It blows down particularly strongly from December to April, carrying so little moisture that only peaks of 600m or more can tease out any rain. The high peaks, particularly on Fogo, Santo Antão and Brava, can spend much of the year with their heads in the clouds.

Added to that wind are two other atmospheric factors. First is the **harmattan** – dry, hot winds from the Sahara that arrive in a series of blasts from October to June, laden with brown dust which fills the air like smog. The second factor is the **southwest monsoon**, which brings the longed-for rains between August and October. Often half the year's rainfall can tumble down in a single storm or series of storms. Unfortunately Cabo Verde's position is a little too far north for the rains to be guaranteed each year: it lies just above the doldrums, the place where the northeast and southwest tradewinds meet and where there is guaranteed rainfall. The longest recorded time Cabo Verde has gone without being watered by the southwest monsoon is 18 years. For 12 years from 1968 there was also a drought.

ANNUAL WEATHER STATISTICS

	Jan	Feb	Mar	Apr	May	Jun	Jul	Aug	Sep	Oct	Nov	Dec
Temperature °C day	24	25	25	25	26	27	27	28	30	29	28	27
Temperature °C night	18	17	18	18	19	20	22	23	24	23	22	20
Sea temperature °C	21	20	20	20	21	22	23	24	25	25	24	22
Hours of sunshine	8	9	10	10	10	8	7	6	8	8	9	8
Days of rain	0	0	0	0	0	2	3	3	7	4	1	0

In the ocean, the cool stream known as the Canary Current reaches the archipelago from the north and mitigates the heating effect of the northeast tradewind.

Temperature variation on the islands is small – it remains between 22°C and 27°C on Santiago throughout the year. But these figures mask big variations between and even within islands. In the desert centre of some of the flat islands it can reach 40°C between July and September, while on the moist peaks of Santo Antão early in the year it can be as cool as 10°C.

Cabo Verde's rainfall figures tell a similarly strange story. A recurring theme is the wide variation in rainfall even between different slopes of the same island – the northeastern slopes are the wettest. On Fogo for example, the average rainfall over 35 years for the northeastern slope of Monte Velha is 1,190mm, while the average on its leeward side is 167mm. Monte Velha's figures also reveal how precious rain can deluge an island over a very short period. In a single month, 20 years ago, 3,000mm of rain fell there. The lower islands, the flat ones, São Vicente and Santa Luzia, receive much less moisture, leaving them almost totally barren.

These chaotic figures can be processed to give mean average rainfalls in the range 10–900mm. Most regions of Cabo Verde are classified as arid or semi-arid.

NATURAL HISTORY AND CONSERVATION

Many species on Cabo Verde exist nowhere else in the world – the phenomenon known as endemicity. Unlike other islands such as the Caymans, which were once part of a bigger landmass and carry species left over from the greater continent, life here has arrived by chance. Which species completed the extraordinary journey was a lottery and the winners were a peculiar assortment. In addition, these species have had millions of years of isolation in which to branch out on their own, adapting to suit the oddities of the habitat. The grey-headed kingfisher (*Halcyon leucocephala*), for example, in the absence of much inland water in which to live up to its name, dines on insects instead.

The closest relatives of some of Cabo Verde's plants are found in East Africa rather than the west. Scientists think that they were borne here from West Africa, which then itself became so dry that they disappeared from there.

FLORA Cabo Verde has probably never been profusely covered in greenery. Lack of research and poor early records mean we know little about what it was like before humans arrived. The lower slopes were probably grassy and treeless (steppe) or with low vegetation dotted with trees (savannah). There are a few indigenous trees that still survive: the lovely blue-green, gnarled, flat-topped dragon tree (*Dracaena draco*), fast disappearing except on São Nicolau; the tamarisk palms, known locally as *tamareira* (*Phoenix atlantica*), that fill the lagoons and sunken deserts of Boavista (though some believe that it is just a feral version of another palm tree, *Phoenix dactyl*); the ironwood tree; and perhaps a species of fig tree and one of acacia.

The indigenous plants are adapted to dryness (having small leaves, for example) and are small and sturdy to cope with strong winds.

Over the last 500 years, plants have been introduced from all over the world, and people have tried to cultivate wherever they can. Shrubs and trees have been cleared to make way for arable land. Poor farming techniques and the ubiquitous goat have combined with these forces to oust most of the original vegetation. The result is that, of the 600 species of plant growing in Cabo Verde (aside from crops), only a quarter are natural to the islands and about half of those are endemic. Some of the endemic plants, such as *Língua da vaca* (*Echium vulcanorum*) are suited only to ranges of crazily small dimensions, as frustrated botanists will tell you.

ACACIA AMERICANA – A MIXED BLESSING? *Tim Willing*

Acacia americana is not a botanical name. The real name of this thorny tree, which populates the islands of Maio and Boavista, is mesquite (*Prosopis juliflora*), or *espinheiro verde* to the locals. During the 1970s, experts from the United Nations Food and Agriculture Organization (UN-FAO) advocated establishing huge plantations of this Mexican native on some Cabo Verdean islands to provide firewood, charcoal and goat fodder. This plan was duly implemented and in some senses has been a success, such that Maio now exports large amounts of charcoal to Praia. Sadly, this mesquite afforestation programme has created an unforeseen environmental disaster. The pods from the tree have been scattered far and wide – up nearly every *ribeira* (dry river bed), through all the date and coconut plantations and agricultural lands, too. Today, mesquite invasion dominates the landscapes of Maio and Boavista. Owing to the mesquite's incredibly efficient root system, it steals all the available soil moisture, and as a result nearly all the date and coconut plantations are now dying and former agricultural lands are reduced to just thorn thickets. Removing mesquite roots is nearly impossible. This catastrophe has come on top of the disastrous long-term downward trend in annual rainfall, as experienced across the whole Sahel belt of West Africa.

Since independence in 1975, people have been making Herculean efforts to plant trees. The roots form a matrix that traps earth so that heavy rain cannot wash them away, and the branches prevent the wind scattering the precious soil. The trees are also supposed to create a moist microclimate. The reafforestation figures have been almost unbelievable: over some periods about three million new trees have been planted each year, or 7,000 a day. The result is pine trees, oaks and sweet chestnuts on the cool peaks of Santo Antão, eucalyptus on the heights of Fogo, and forests of acacia on Maio.

FAUNA
Birds Cabo Verde has a dedicated following of ornithologists and amateur birdwatchers who can be found wedged into crevices high up mountainsides or, before new restrictions came into force, trying to secure passages with local fishermen across wild stretches of sea to some of the uninhabited islands. Their dedication stems from the fact that Cabo Verde abounds in endemics and some of the seabirds living on cliffs around the islands are particularly important. The archipelago lies on the extreme southwest corner of the western Palaearctic region and is thus the only place in that region where certain species, mainly African or tropical, can be found to breed regularly. There are about 130 migrants for whom Cabo Verde is an important stopping point on their long journeys. Some 40 use the islands for nesting. The archipelago has played host to three threatened marine bird species: the magnificent frigatebird, brown booby and red-billed tropicbird. The previously endangered Cape Verde shearwater has won a welcome reprieve (page 362).

However, as with the plants, much of the natural birdlife has been wiped out, particularly by hungry locals tempted by succulent seabirds or by fishermen treading on their burrows as they search for shellfish along the beaches. Feral cats also pose problems for some species. A more modern threat comes from actual and proposed tourism developments close to important wetland areas, such as Rabil on Boavista and the now-abandoned Salinas development on Maio.

The most prized, rare birds to discover in the islands include the **Raso lark** (*Alauda razae*) and the **magnificent frigatebird** (*Fregata magnificens*), both with extraordinarily restricted breeding areas. The population of the former is thought to be around 1,500 on Raso and up to 600 from the breeding pairs reintroduced to Santa Luzia in 2018–19 (page 361). No such good news for the latter. Their entire eastern Atlantic population was to be found on the islet of Curral Velho off Boavista, but the extinction of the species is now assumed. The **Cape Verde petrel** (*Pterodroma feae*), or *ngon-ngon* bird, is disappearing fast and the elegant **red-billed tropicbird**, or *rabo de junco* (*Phaethon aethereus*), with its red bill and streaming white tail, is also plunging in numbers. More common birds include the colourful **grey-headed kingfisher** (*Halcyon leucocephala*), known locally as *passarinha*. It can be found on Santiago, Fogo and Brava, and has a red beak, and orange, black and blue plumage.

You will also see plenty of **helmeted guineafowl** (*Numida meleagris*) on mountain slopes but the distinctive white **Egyptian vulture** (*Neophron percnopterus*), previously abundant at high altitudes, is also fast disappearing, if not actually extinct. Waders frequent the few lagoons and saltpans, on Sal, Maio, Boavista and Santiago. If you miss the **brown booby** (*Sula leucogaster*) – known locally as the *alcatraz* and also an inhabitant of the islet of Curral Velho on Boavista – take a look at the 20-escudo piece. The **Cape Verde red kite** (*Milvus milvus fasciicauda*) is probably now extinct and the **Cape Verde purple heron**, or *garça vermelha* (*Ardea purpurea bournei*), leads a particularly precarious existence in possibly just two trees in Santiago's interior. There are 25 birds in one tree and even fewer in the other (page 192). The **Cape Verde cane warbler** (*Acrocephalus brevipennis*) (endangered and brownish) lives mostly on Santiago, with about 500 breeding pairs left there, though a significant population was also found in 2004 on Fogo.

Some of the most compelling sites for rare birds in Cabo Verde are the islets. On the Ilhéus do Rombo can be found **Bulwer's petrel** (*Bulweria bulwerii*), known locally as *João-petro*. These are known to breed only on Raso island, which is near São Nicolau, and on Ilhéu de Cima. They are almost totally black with a strip of dark grey stretching along the middle of their wings.

The **Madeiran storm petrel** (*Oceanodroma castro*) is known locally as the *gongon*, the *jaba-jaba* or the *pedreirinho*, and breeds only on these islands and on Branco, Raso and islets off Boavista. It is black apart from a white bit just before the tail. The **Cape Verde shearwater** (*Calonectris edwardsii*), once imperilled by a mass annual culling of its chicks, now thrives again on Raso island, thanks to the sterling efforts of conservationists.

More information can be found on the partially bilingual website of the Sociedade Caboverdiana de Zoologia (w scvz.org) and the English-language website of BirdLife International (w birdlife.org).

Other fauna There are no large mammals and no snakes, but several species of bat can be found, and green monkeys inhabit Santiago and can also be found on Brava. There are also many small, brown, endemic reptiles, geckos and skinks. The Cape Verde giant skink (*Macroscincus coctei*) – delicious, sadly – became extinct in the 1940s (see page 363 for more details). Many interesting endemic insects and beetles live on the islands and there are collections of them in the Natural History Museum in London (w nhm.ac.uk).

MARINE LIFE According to the World Wildlife Fund, we are still ignorant of the riches that may lie in Cabo Verde's waters. But the marine life here is probably globally significant. There is a high degree of endemism, which is unusual for oceanic islands, and the sea is full of corals – not true reefs but slabs, pinnacles and, importantly, coral mountains reaching up from the ocean floor and providing rare mid-ocean habitats at all depths.

One study concluded that Cabo Verde has one of the world's ten most important coral reefs – though that claim has since been disputed by other experts. The highest levels of marine biodiversity are around Boavista, Sal and Maio, which share a marine platform. Meanwhile, despite its aridity, Boavista hosts one of the largest wetlands of the Macaronesia region (page 135).

So far, scientists have catalogued 639 species of fish including mantas and whale sharks. More than 17 species of whale and dolphin have been reported, including the humpback whale, which breeds in Cabo Verde. Five species of turtle frequent Cabo Verdean waters, including the loggerhead (*Caretta caretta*) for whom Cabo Verde is the third most important nesting ground in the world (see below).

Marine life is more tropical than would be found at the same latitude of mainland Africa, on the coast of Senegal. This is because the archipelago is sufficiently far from the mainland to escape the cold 'winter upwellings', in which the turning of the globe causes water from deep in the ocean to surface at the coast. This would otherwise decrease the temperature of the 21°C waters to about 10°C.

There are several threats to the marine heritage of Cabo Verde. One of them is fishing: overfishing by domestic and international commercial boats and the use of destructive fishing methods, such as spear guns, and fishing during spawning seasons, by local fishermen. A second threat comes from coastal development. Many of the most important habitat areas along the coasts are just the places where people want to build hotels and marinas.

The country continues to plan for an ever-increasing number of tourist beds to meet rising international demand. Problems from such developments include pollution, the disappearance of sand as it is siphoned off for construction (entire beaches have already disappeared), the effects of artificial light on turtle nesting and damage from quad bikes and the like roaring across fragile coastal land.

Turtles Marine turtles are some of the most important species on the islands. Cabo Verde is an important feeding area for five species. Research has shown that Cabo Verde is a crucial participant in the life of the loggerhead turtle (*Caretta caretta*), the population being the third largest in the world after the Florida Keys in the United States and Oman's Masirah Island. In the Atlantic, it is the second largest. One estimate states that up to 20,000 breed annually in Cabo Verde, though the figure varies enormously from year to year. The favoured island is overwhelmingly Boavista, probably followed by Maio, then Sal and all the other islands.

Turtles face two threats. The first is hunting. This dates back possibly as far as 1479, when the French explorer Eustache de la Fosse reported that leprosy was treated locally with a diet of turtle meat and by rubbing the affected areas with turtle blood. King Louis XI, who believed he was suffering from leprosy, dispatched his representative to the Cabo Verde Islands to investigate after learning of the cure.

Illegal hunting continues today. Practices vary from island to island: sometimes the meat is cut out of the live turtles, sometimes the eggs are taken, sometimes both. Sometimes the blood is drained and added to wine as a fortifier, while on some islands males are prized for their penises which are added to *grogue* as an aphrodisiac. Meat is often taken from island to island, on fishing boats but also on internal flights. There are nesting beaches where the loss of turtles is 100%.

The threat to habitat has become the greater issue, as increasing amounts of land are used for tourism development and sand is removed illegally for building. A report on the effects of tourism on turtles can be downloaded from the Sociedade Caboverdiana de Zoologia website (w scvz.org).

A report by the secretariat for the Convention on Migratory Species called for urgent attention to conserve West Africa's sea turtles. Klaus Toepfer, Executive Director of UNEP, said: 'In the western Atlantic and Pacific oceans, populations of sea turtles have been falling dramatically in recent years. This makes [recent] findings in western Africa doubly significant, given its now undoubted status as a globally important region for sea turtle species.'

The report recommended that conserving nesting sites for the loggerhead turtle on Cabo Verde should be a priority. The loggerhead is categorised as endangered. The hawksbill (*Eretmochelys imbricata*), which is critically endangered, feeds at the islands. The green turtle (*Chelonia mydas*), which is endangered, calls at the islands, as do the critically endangered leatherback (*Dermochelys coriacea*) and the endangered olive ridley (*Lepidochelys olivacea*).

A national turtle plan was drawn up in 2008 and has since been implemented with various levels of success. There are active turtle campaigns on several of the islands, notably Sal (page 97) and Boavista (page 136), as well as projects run by communities or city halls on all the other islands. In 2009, a coalition of organisations, called TAOLA+, Cabo Verde Marine Turtle Network, was formed to synchronise activities and has had some success raising awareness and lobbying parliament.

Whales North Atlantic humpback whales were driven almost to extinction during the whaling exploits of the 14th century. Now there are 10,000–12,000 worldwide and most breed in the West Indies. A few hundred, however, choose Cabo Verde. This select group makes seasonal migrations between Iceland, Norway and Cabo Verde. The archipelago is where they mate, after which the females travel north to feed, returning around a year later to give birth.

Cabo Verde is the only known breeding ground for humpbacks in the northeast Atlantic. March and April are the peak of the breeding season and also the time when the whales can be sighted – mostly off the west and southwest coasts of Boavista, Sal and most other islands. Individuals can be identified from natural markings (ventral fluke patterns). Males sing songs, at least partly to attract females, and also to maintain distance from other males.

CONSERVATION EFFORTS Marine, coastal and inland areas do have friends in Cabo Verde. The government has signed up to some key international conventions but implementation takes time and money. There are several programmes, including the National Research and Marine Biodiversity Conservation Programme and the Coastal Zone Management Project, which is establishing policies on how to use and manage coastal areas. The two marine-protected areas in Cabo Verde – Baía da Murdeira on Sal (page 111) and the Santa Luzia complex (that island plus the surrounding islets, including Branco and Raso; page 361) – have management plans. The two areas face threats from very different sources: in Murdeira, it's tourist development, whereas in the Santa Luzia complex it's artisanal fishing. Unfortunately, neither area is patrolled nor properly protected, though NGOs have become more active in recent years.

Crucially – not just for marine and coastal areas but also for inland – in 2002 the government established the General Directorate for Environment – a framework from which environmental care can operate. They built on a proposal by Cabo Verde Natura 2000 to create a network of 50 protected areas around Cabo Verde. The areas were declared in law in 2003 but the precise boundaries of most are still not enshrined in law.

Three of the protected areas are part of a United Nations Development Programme/Global Environment Facility project aimed at developing parks with boundaries, services and income-generation activities for local people, including ecotourism. More are in the pipeline, including two on Santo Antão and one on São Vicente.

The government has taken other actions such as banning the removal of sand from the beaches for construction (with patchy enforcement). The Second Environmental Action plan (PANA II) published in 2007, included a proposal that new developments must submit an Environmental Impact Assessment. It's also against the law to build within 80m of the low tide mark.

The Sociedade Caboverdiana de Zoologia (w scvz.org), which was founded with the aim of promoting zoological research in Cabo Verde, publishes a scientific journal, and plans other activities such as organising scientific meetings.

HISTORY

White lives in big house
Mulato lives in shop
Black lives in hut
Sancho lives in mountain:
But a day will come
When Sancho turn all upside down:
Horribly grimacing
Tail curled up
Sancho drag black from hut
Black drag mulato from shop
Mulato drag white from big house
White run to mountain and there he fall
    A *batuque* of Santa Catarina, published in the magazine *Claridade* (1948)
    Translated by Basil Davidson, *The Fortunate Isles* (Hutchinson, 1989)

When the first island of Cabo Verde erupted from the ocean hundreds of kilometres from the African coast, the archipelago's fate was sealed. For, overwhelmingly, the islands' unique and often tragic history has been the result of their position. Their history is one of use and abuse by nations from the four corners of the Atlantic. The world has changed around them and has found fleeting purpose after purpose for them: they have served until they are exhausted and then they have been forgotten until another convulsion in world affairs has produced a new use for them.

The archipelago's story has been a tragic one but it has begun a hopeful chapter. The Cabo Verdeans have shaped their own identity and culture and, perhaps most importantly, govern themselves. Since the 1970s they have been able to act strategically. At the same time, the outside world has changed and has found new uses for Cabo Verde: white beaches to serve the interests of mass tourism, and abundant fish when other seas are severely depleted. Whether the archipelago will be able to exploit these riches for itself, or whether the 21st century will be just another chapter in which it is sucked dry, it is too early to tell.

ROCKS APPEAR AND LIFE ARRIVES According to local lore, when God was satisfied with Creation, and brushed his hands together, the crumbs that fell unnoticed from his fingers into the sea formed Cabo Verde.

The geological explanation for their existence is just as beguiling. Under the plates of the earth's crust lie 'hot spots' of bubbling magma, one of which is several hundred kilometres west of Senegal. Every so often, when the conditions of heat and pressure are right, this hot spot erupts as a volcano, leaving an island in the Atlantic to mark where it has been. In this way, some 15 million years ago, the island of Sal was created. It was a mountain which has since been the victim of the ocean winds and has eroded away until all that remains is flat, brown rock. The hot spot erupted every few millions of years to make another pimple on the Atlantic. Today it is still putting the final touches to youthful Fogo, which lies in the southwest. The island is a geologically youthful 100,000 years old and one senses that brooding Fogo gazes east towards Sal preparing to spend the next ten million years weathering down to a similar fate.

Somehow, plant life found Cabo Verde, carried there on winds from mainland Africa or by the ocean itself. Over such a distance there was only a tiny chance of such a voyage culminating in life reaching the islands – but millions of seeds over millions of years transformed that chance to a certainty. Once they had arrived they were cut off from their relatives and evolved into new species, as island life does.

Next came aquatic life. Washed into the Cabo Verdean shallows by accident, many species remained to evolve their own identity in the same way as the plants. Other, more ocean-going species, such as turtles, have found the islands a useful transit point. The story of the birds is much the same.

Legend shrouds the tales of the first humans to arrive at the islands. They may have been Phoenician sea captains who landed there and left no trace. In 445BC, the Phoenician captain Hanno sailed from Cadiz and reported that he passed some small islands which scholars now believe may have been Cabo Verde. He named them Hesperias. Once, Hanno wrote that he had seen a large volcano off the West African coast: perhaps it was Fogo. West African sailors may have reached Cabo Verde in their sea-going canoes over the centuries, but they, too, left no trace.

And so the islands lay, effectively undiscovered, until the middle of the 15th century. The reason for their elusiveness is also the very reason why, when they were found, they were to prove so useful. For they lie below the latitude of the Canary Islands, a region into which any ship that dared to venture would never return. Myths surrounded the fate of the ships from the north that vanished beyond the Canaries, but their disappearance has a simple explanation. The prevailing northeasterly wind drove them south but then, like a one-way valve, blocked their return. In the 15th century, this barrier to human ambition fell. Then the rig was invented, and allowed mariners to harness the wind so they could sail against as well as before it. It was one of the most significant of all inventions, enabling humans to emerge from their home continents and link every region of the globe. The west coast of Africa was now seen as a prize for whichever nation could reach it first, and it was inevitable that the Portuguese, with the skills and vision of Prince Henry the Navigator behind them, would win.

Several famous mariners pushed ever further south in the 1460s and more than one claimed to have discovered Cabo Verde. The debate will probably never be resolved. Perhaps it was the Venetian, Alvise Ca'da Mosto, who said he sighted the islands first in 1456. More likely, it was the Genoese António de Noli who may have stumbled on them in 1455 or in 1461. Some reports say he was accompanied by the Portuguese Diogo Gomes.

Whatever the truth, all the islands were discovered between 1455 and 1461 and the credit generally goes to de Noli and to Gomes, for discovering Santiago and the other leeward isles. Diogo Afonso discovered the windward islands of Santo Antão, São Vicente and São Nicolau. The archipelago was named Cabo Verde, not because it was verdant, but after the green butt of Senegal that lies across the sea.

It is hard to understand now the value of such a discovery. Venturing over the seas with only the capricious wind for power, with no facility for measuring longitude and with limited water and food, the cry of 'land ahoy' could mean life rather than death.

The Portuguese realised that the islands could be of immense strategic power. And so colonisation began in 1462 when a small group of Portuguese, Spanish and Genoese settled on the most promising island, Santiago. The southern half was allotted to de Noli, who set up in Ribeira Grande on the south coast. The northern half fell to Afonso, who began less successfully in the northwest.

Lisbon wanted to entice talented men to live on the islands and develop them, so Cabo Verde was awarded a valuable advantage over other Portuguese colonies. Settlers were given exclusive trading rights along the creeks and shores of the West African coast between Senegal and Sierra Leone. These rivers thus became known as the Rivers of Cabo Verde, later to be known as the Rivers of Guinea.

At this time the Atlantic was dotted with Portuguese and Spanish ships making prolific forays into the Americas, Africa and beyond Africa's southern tip, as far as India and China. It was the beginning of the expansion of Europe, the spread of its colonisation of the globe and unprecedented mass migration and cultural co-mingling. Over the next 300 years Europeans would emigrate to North and

RAISING CABO VERDE'S HISTORY FROM THE OCEAN FLOOR

Divers investigating the shipwrecks around Cabo Verde say it is the last great unexplored site in the world. They guess there may be up to 600 boats lost on the archipelago's reefs. Through them, it is possible to build up a vivid picture of the islands' trading history.

Already, after several years of exploration, researchers have a warehouse and museum in Chã d'Areia, Praia, which is stacked with treasures brought up from the sea. Coins and clay pipes help to date the wrecks; hoards of goods such as ivory tusks or silver coins testify to the ships' missions; while the odd treasure has been retrieved that is of great beauty or significance.

Perhaps the most spectacular find by the marine archaeologists – from Cabo Verde, Oxford University and the Portuguese company Arqueonautas Worldwide – was a mariner's astrolabe. With the invention of the sextant the astrolabe, which had guided sailors for two millennia, abruptly lost its purpose and many were melted down. The few examples of this marvellous navigational instrument that remain tend to have been found in shipwrecks.

The team found this beautiful example of a bronze and silver astrolabe in a 1650s shipwreck. Despite their detective work, however, they still do not know the identity of the ship. The astrolabe was probably Portuguese, the cannons were Dutch, the coins Spanish.

Sadly Cabo Verde no longer has the astrolabe, but only a copy – in 2001, it was sold at Sotheby's.

South America and Africa. Africans would become a substantial population in the Americas, mostly as slaves. The Portuguese and Spanish had begun nothing less than a global redistribution of people, animals and plants and the beginnings of modern mass trade. Meanwhile, the few resources of Cabo Verde were harnessed, and trading began that would supply the Portuguese Crown with income for centuries.

FROM ROCK TO TRADING POST: THE 1500s The first desire of the colonisers of Santiago was to plant and reap, and to acquire an unpaid labour force in order to do so. They found what they wanted on the mainland coast of Africa: slaves. Over the next century these captives from the great kingdoms of West Africa arrived in their thousands, and were soon put to work growing food crops and cotton in the valleys. By 1582, there were 13,700 slaves labouring on Santiago and Fogo under a regime of 100, mostly Portuguese, men.

The settlers released goats on to the uninhabited islands where they devoured the scrub pasture and provided meat, hides, butter, milk and cheese, and some cattle were farmed. But barren Cabo Verde would never provide enough food for prosperity. Wealth generation was to come from two other activities: resupply of ships, and the slave trade.

Cabo Verde lies at the Atlantic crossroads, not just because of its position in relation to the landmasses of the Americas, Europe and Africa, but because of where it lies in relation to the north Atlantic wind patterns and to ocean currents. Both factors drew America-bound ships towards the archipelago. Increasingly, in the latter part of the 16th century, the Portuguese who stopped there were on their way to take up Crown land grants as part of the colonisation of Brazil. The Spanish were ferrying goods and people to and from the vast new empire they were creating in South America.

Piecing together a ship's history, and matching it with a known vessel, requires all sorts of lateral thinking. The cargo provides clues. Sometimes small collections of coins from a variety of countries – perhaps from the pocket of an individual sailor collecting a souvenir from every port – can help plot the ship's route.

'The quality of the cargoes is amazing,' noted Piran Johnson of Arqueonautas Worldwide. A massive batch of ivory tusks – eaten away like long thin pieces of cheese – was brought up from the *Princess Louisa*, a 1743 ship that was on her way between London and Bombay. An intact bottle of wine 200 years old and, more irresistibly, several bottles of cognac, were retrieved from an unknown wreck in the harbour of Praia. One ship yielded huge copper plates that the Swedes once used as an unwieldy currency – the ship went down in 1781 on her way from Denmark to China.

Another ship – the *Hartwell* – contained a collection of watches: 'They were the Ratner's of the day,' says Johnson. 'Gold filigree on top but cheap tat underneath – they were being shipped out to the colonies to buy off the locals.'

Most of the treasures emerge looking most unpromising, in the form of ugly grey concretions formed by the build-up of iron, sand and other substances over the decades. It takes a professional eye to spot the underlying shape; then it takes weeks of painstaking work to remove the concretion without damaging the valuables inside.

To visit the collection, see page 181.

JEWISH PEOPLE IN CABO VERDE

Anna Ikeda (née Etmanska), Carol Castiel and Murray Stewart

'See these? Old Jewish merchants' homes,' says Jorge Pires, pointing to the dilapidated edifices on the main street in the town of Ponta do Sol, on the island of Santo Antão. The buildings, which are in different stages of decay, line the quiet street that leads towards the ocean. We get closer to examine a faded sign – it reads 'Cohen'. The once-magnificent house stands in ruin, its windows and doors boarded up.

Jorge Pires, an official at the local *câmara municipal*, despairs at the sad state of Ponta do Sol's historical heritage. 'Jews built this town and now our past is left to crumble.'

Mr Pires dreams of turning the old Cohen house into a museum of Cabo Verde's Jewish history, and Ponta do Sol into a heritage tourism destination. This area of Santo Antão has more surviving Jewish sites than any other island in the country. The cemeteries in Ponta do Sol and Penha de França already attract curious visitors, and plans are underway by the Cape Verde Jewish Heritage Project to restore them. The village of Sinagoga is just down the road. And in Ribeira Grande, the green mansion of Ruth Cohen de Marçal still occupies the central position in town.

'The old Jewish lady lived there,' explains a local storeowner. And then he proudly adds, 'My grandfather was Jewish, too.'

Though present-day Cabo Verde does not have an organised Jewish community, or even any practising Jews, the islanders are very much aware of their country's Sephardic heritage.

The two major waves of Jewish immigration left behind them not only names like Benros, Mendes and Levy, or gravestones with Hebrew inscriptions. Thanks to the centuries of intermarriage, the Sephardic culture became an important ingredient in shaping Cabo Verde's modern Creole identity.

The first Jewish settlers came to the island of Santiago in the late 15th century, after Portugal's Manuel I ordered Jews and Muslims to either convert or leave. More arrived after the Lisbon massacre of *conversos* (converts) in 1506. Known as *degredados* (exiles/convicts), they initially lived in Praia, but soon saw opportunity throughout Cabo Verde, married African women, and eventually became an integral part of the brand-new, multi-cultural nation.

Some Jewish traders also acquired the name of *lançados* (outcasts), and quickly became the implementers of the slave trade. Working as intermediaries on the African coast, they traded with whom they pleased and ignored the commercial restrictions imposed on them by Portugal. Yet at the same time, in order to rid Portugal of Jews, the Crown not only allowed, but even encouraged the *lançados's*

In 1580, Spain and Portugal united to create an Iberian Empire with three powerful trade realms: spice in the East, sugar in the south Atlantic, and silver in Spanish America. Iberian vessels often found it useful to stop at Cabo Verde for food and water, for ship repair and for nautical supplies.

Thus, throughout the 1500s, ship supply was the islands' great function, and the most basic commodities – water and food – were its speciality. They charged a high price for fresh water and sold maize, beans and dried or salted goat meat. They also exported horses, donkeys, cattle and goat hides. Cabo Verde's other commodity

activities. Of course not all *lançados* were of Jewish origin: the African trade, just like any other profitable occupation, attracted tough men from varied cultural backgrounds. Some of those traders, be they Jewish, Muslim or Christian, became known as *ganagogas*, which in the African Biafada dialect means 'men who could speak many languages'.

By the end of the 17th century, Jewish presence on the islands was an important factor in the success of the colonial economy. However, with the establishment of a branch of the Portuguese Inquisition in Cabo Verde in 1672, the Crown forcibly confiscated most of the Jewish trading enterprises. As a result, many of the affected merchants hid their true identities until the frenzy of religious persecution died out in the late 1770s.

In the early 1820s, a group of Jews involved in the Liberal Wars fled Portugal and settled in the mountains of Santo Antão. A few years later, they were joined by economic migrants from Morocco and Gibraltar. Following in the footsteps of their 15th-century predecessors, they also engaged in commerce, such as trading salt and hides, and used their skills to rejuvenate the local economy. And as those before them, they took local wives and successfully assimilated into Creole society. As a result, today the great majority of Cabo Verdeans, including the country's former prime minister Carlos Alberto Wahnon de Carvalho Veiga, can claim Jewish ancestry.

Yet the Jewish past of Cabo Verde is also a victim of this assimilation. While Jewish graves remain on Santo Antão, Santiago and Boavista, on Brava and Maio, they are long gone.

Thankfully, the cemetery on Boavista, where the Benoliel family is buried, has been restored through the persistence of one of the descendants, a Lisbon resident by the name of Rafael Benoliel. Similarly, the Jewish graves in Praia's main Christian cemetery were also restored and rededicated in 2013. An additional tombstone was discovered during the restoration work, and commemorative plaques – including one in honour of Morocco's King Mohammed VI, one of the project's main sponsors – were added in 2024.

The initiative of Carol Castiel and her Cape Verde Jewish Heritage Project (w capeverdejewishheritage.org) has been responsible for a great deal of the preservation efforts on the islands of Cabo Verde. Owing to the chronic lack of funds, change is slow, and for now, the ambitious dreams of Mr Pires remain just that – dreams.

Anna Ikeda is an independent filmmaker and a writer who became interested in the history of Cabo Verde Jews after stumbling upon the cemetery in Penha de França on Santo Antão island.

lay in sparkling white lakes on the three flat islands to the east: salt, and enough, it seemed, to supply humans in perpetuity.

Once there were sufficient slaves working on the islands, the Portuguese looked west for new markets. They were in a unique position to sell slaves for labour in South American colonies and so the archipelago became a warehouse for human merchandise. For slave merchants who would otherwise have had to visit the African coast, Cabo Verde was an expensive market but a sanitised one. Forays to the mainland could be dangerous and lengthy. Ships were often delayed, sometimes for months. Payment methods were elaborate: West African vendors often demanded a multiplicity of items – iron bars, cloth, brandy, guns, knives, ribbons and beads. In addition, the land was rife with disease and the creeks and rivers of the coast were tricky to navigate. If a ship became stranded on the shore the local people would claim it for their own.

There were other advantages to be gained from shopping for slaves in Cabo Verde. First of all, they had been 'seasoned'. The sickly and unfit had died, the obstinate and rebellious subdued by constant punishment. They had also learned enough Portuguese words that they would understand orders, and, most importantly, they had been baptised. The Portuguese Church argued that a baptised slave was luckier than a free African because the former had achieved the chance of a place in heaven. Pope Nicholas V had given the trade his blessing in 1455, based on this rationale.

Slavery in some form had been part of West African society for millennia, but the rapid imposition of a European mercantile economy on a wholly different system of trade so remodelled the practice, in both scale and style, that it soon ceased to resemble anything that came before it. The new economic environment also engendered the Mankinka empire's waging of wars to meet the Europeans' ever growing demand for slaves. Soon, the Atlantic slave trade entirely transformed the societies it also exploited.

The business of slavery spawned trade in other goods from the African coast: ivory, wax, hides, gum, amber, musk, honey and gold dust. Cabo Verde took them and became a depot where these products were exchanged for goods coveted by wealthy Africans – Venetian beads and wine from Europe; silver from Spanish America; cloves and coral from the East. Cabo Verde itself supplied the African coast with raw cotton, cloth, salted goat meat, horses and cattle.

The important islands in those first years were Santiago, where the settlers built a capital in the green valley of Ribeira Grande; Fogo, a live but fertile volcano; and the lonely salt island of Maio. Ribeira Grande was the first city built by Europeans in the tropics and became one of the highest-yielding cities of the Portuguese kingdom. Visitors praised its comforts and in 1533, it was elevated from the rank of *vila* to *cidade*. In 1556, the Bishop of Cabo Verde, whose jurisdiction extended to the mainland, began building his cathedral there, and in 1570, the king agreed to the founding of a seminary. All was, for those that weren't enslaved, optimism and prosperity.

ORCHIL DYE

At one time, the mountains of Cabo Verde yielded a single important product – a lichen known as urzela, or orchil (*Litmus roccella*), which could be turned into a blue dye. Together with indigo it was used to colour cloth (page 40). To make orchil dye, lichen was ground to a powder and mixed with stale urine to form a paste. Quicklime was added to make blues, violets and purples, and tin solution for scarlet.

Portugal made a healthy profit from the orchil business, which began as early as 1469. Rights to take the orchil were sold as a Crown Monopoly which was controlled first by a Brazilian group and then, beginning in the 18th century, by the English, because of that country's burgeoning textile trade. An English firm paid over £6,000 for six years' access to the orchil of Cabo Verde, the Azores and Madeira and it was in demand into the 1830s but withered when huge quantities of the lichen were found in Angola and Mozambique, which sent prices plummeting.

Cabo Verde mustered few home-produced goods with one major exception, mentioned above: cotton. It was grown by slaves who then wove it into cloth of the finest quality, which was marketed along the West African coast and in Brazil. Its skilful patterns became outstandingly popular among Africans and the cloth rose to be the chief currency for trading. This gave Cabo Verde a continuing hold on the slave trade even when competition appeared from other nations. English and French ships were forced to stop at the archipelago to obtain cloth for barter on the mainland. Another trade was in the dye-yielding lichen orchil, which was collected in mountainous areas and transformed into a potion of vivid blue.

Thus, positioned between Europe, Africa and South America, slicing taxes from every import and export, and with a monopoly on trade with the mainland, Cabo Verde had become a viable community, with the slave trade its fundamental market and Portugal reaping as much as it could.

During this period the botanical colonisation of the islands was completed as well. As a traffic junction, Cabo Verde received plants from everywhere, particularly maize from Brazil, which became a staple, and cassava, which was later planted on the African mainland.

THE ATLANTIC GROWS BUSIER: THE 1600s

> Driving the defenders before them they entered the City almost without resistance, where they sacked houses and destroyed them. The authorities fled to the hills and the English, carrying away their spoil, departed to Cartagena and San Domingo.
>
> Contemporary account of the sacking of Ribeira Grande

As the 1600s began, rival nations appeared on the seas. The French, English and Dutch spilled into the Atlantic, and aggression on the ocean became more than the sporadic acts of piracy and smuggling that had characterised the second half of the previous century. Cabo Verde became increasingly vulnerable to attack and Portugal foresaw this, responding in 1587 by appointing a governor-general for the islands who was directly responsible to the Crown for Cabo Verde and the Guinea coast.

Now France, England and Holland were becoming serious forces in the Atlantic, founding colonies mainly in the Caribbean and North America. As they began to develop plantation economies in these lands they, too, started to look for slaves. Business across the Atlantic multiplied as the desire for sugar, slaves, salt and fish sent trading ships in a perpetual circle between the four continents.

As international affairs fluctuated so, too, did Cabo Verdean fortunes. They fell for a while when the Dutch seized Portuguese slaving sources in West Africa, and when they were sacked and plundered by nations who were at odds with Spain or Portugal. Their fortunes rose after 1640 when Portugal achieved independence from Spain.

Overall, though, the archipelago still made money because the demand for slaves was rising. It was at its peak for Cabo Verde during the 1600s and 1700s. Numbers are uncertain, partly because many slaves were not measured in whole 'units'. A 15–25-year-old was a *peça*'s worth. A 30-year-old in good health was two-thirds of a *peça*. Records are poor, as most were lost in Lisbon's earthquake of 1755 and were not particularly detailed to start with, but it has been estimated that 3,000 slaves a year left Cabo Verde in 1609 and 1610, although these figures were possibly higher in the preceding decades. These slaves earned Cabo Verde about £6,500 in import taxes and £1,300 in export taxes over the two years. Nearly three-quarters of the revenue the Portuguese Crown received from Cabo Verde was from the slave trade.

RESENTMENT STIRS The question that exercised the people of the archipelago was why so much of its profit should go straight back to Lisbon. It was part of a wider question: what was the purpose of Cabo Verde? If it was merely an overseas warehouse then the Portuguese were entitled to act as they wished. But Cabo Verde was now a place that some called home and they were trying to make a living there in spite of increasingly tight controls from the Crown.

During the first 150 years of colonisation, few Portuguese women or families settled in what was considered an arduous posting. The resulting high levels of European men partnering with both free and enslaved black women produced a remarkably stable society of '*mestiços*' who had nowhere else to call their motherland, but who were unable to truly assert a national identity until the 20th century.

Cabo Verde's Creole origins differed from others around the world for several reasons. The Cabo Verdeans emerged in an empty place where there had been no indigenous population. They were the descendants of a far smaller number of Europeans than is the case with many other Creole cultures and thus its cultural dominance and rigid stratification was not as profound.

It was these 'pre-Cabo Verdeans' – new European arrivals and, increasingly, people of mixed heritage, governing a large number of slaves – who complained bitterly and frequently about the way Lisbon organised the slave and other trades, and in particular about the rise of the Crown monopolies.

THE MONOPOLIES The right to procure slaves from the African coast was awarded by the Crown as a single, monopolistic contract which lasted for six years. The benefit for the Crown was that the contractor paid a lump sum and agreed to supply a few incidentals including slaves for the king, and some money donated to the Church.

Whoever bought this slaving right then subcontracted it to smaller enterprises. The Portuguese Crown received customs duties when contractors deposited slaves at Cabo Verde, and also export duties from those who bought them. The people of Cabo Verde were banned from engaging in other trade with non-Portuguese. This rule was resented and widely flouted.

The islanders began to feel seriously undermined in 1675, when the Crown handed out to various companies a series of crippling monopolistic rights over the West African and Cabo Verdean trades. The terms seemed to bypass the role of the archipelago as entrepôt.

Under the rules of the first monopoly, the contractor possessed the sole right to take international products to the Guinea coast for trading: Cabo Verdeans were permitted to trade only with home-grown products such as cloth and salt. Santiago's access to Africa, therefore, was deeply threatened. Further decrees were issued by Lisbon. Perhaps the most memorable was that of 1687 which banned anyone on Cabo Verde from selling cloth to foreigners, under penalty of death.

The second monopoly was granted in 1690 to a newly formed organisation, the Company of the Islands of Cabo Verde and Guiné (Compania Nacional de Cabo Verde e Guiné). Even more restrictive conditions were included in the new contract, and two seemed almost guaranteed to ensure that Cabo Verde was bypassed in the international slave trade. Firstly, the contractor bought the right to supply the Spanish Indies directly with slaves, so he had no need to find someone to buy them on the archipelago. Secondly, the Governor of Cabo Verde was put in the pay of the new company. By 1700, Cabo Verde felt that it had been ousted by the monopoly companies from its role as a slave-trading depot. It was increasingly left to concentrate on the more predictable business of victualling the hundred ships a year that called at Santiago for supplies in the second half of the 1600s.

CONFLICT: THE 1700s The 1700s began with a bang and the War of the Spanish Succession to prevent France gaining control of Spain. Fears that the fusion of the two countries would give them too much power over Atlantic possessions were typical of the concerns of other European powers at the time. The century was to be one of territorial expansion to the west of the Atlantic, consolidation, and the rise of the British as the supreme naval force.

Cabo Verde would always be prey to the whims of the rest of the world, successful when exploiting the needs of a diversity of countries and unsuccessful when those needs suddenly changed. When Portugal was drawn into the War of Succession, the slave trade with the Spanish Indies came to a sudden end for Cabo Verde but also for the monopoly companies.

That war did not finish until 1714 and was the cause of the sack of Santiago in 1712, a disastrous plunder by the French that robbed Ribeira Grande of all its riches. The people of Cabo Verde urged Lisbon to liberalise its trade and finally, in 1721, Portugal relaxed the rules so that the people could trade with whom they wished. Business was reinvigorated, but the central problem remained – Portugal was not prepared to pour money into a string of rocks which could not guarantee much return. The people of the islands were left to live on their wits.

This conflict was behind many of the background problems of the archipelago. Goats chomped inexorably at the fragile vegetation that had taken millions of years to win a hold in the face of Saharan winds. Without sophisticated, long-term land management it was inevitable that famine would increasingly afflict the islands. Every century there were one or two more famines than the century before and, in 1773–76, 44% of the population died.

Lack of investment in proper military protection also led to raids which were a perpetual drain on resources. Like a fleet of marooned ships the islands were unable to flee marauders of the high seas.

THE END OF SLAVERY: THE 1800s Towards the end of the 1700s the seeds were sown in America and Europe for convulsions that would end the 300-year-old Atlantic slave trade and transform life for most nations bordering that ocean. The changes were partly intellectual. The Enlightenment's faith in rationality and social progress began, slowly to change attitudes about slavery, and was also to spur on the French Revolution. Industrialisation, and the economic concerns of a newly minted middle class, also played a part. Then Napoleon's energies were unleashed on the oceans and Portugal and Spain were cut off from their colonies in South America. The effect of this was profound. A vacuum arose in 19th-century South America into which grew movements for liberation, followed a few decades later by the abolition of slavery.

While slave trading was not to be abolished as a 'business' by the Portuguese until 1854, with private slavery ending in 1876, Cabo Verde's population had already become significantly free and creolised. The census of 1731 indicated that less than 20% were slaves, while *mestiços* made up most of the majority. By 1807, the enslaved population had fallen to less than 10%.

Although slavery continued to form the basis of North America's economy for decades, continuing long after its independence in 1783, it was a land of promise that lured millions of emigrants fleeing starvation or unemployment in other parts of the world. The 1800s also became an era of mass global migration.

During the 19th century the dominance of the sailing ship came to an end, and with it Cabo Verde's prime function as a resupplier. But as Santiago suffered, two other islands began to emerge as arenas where profits could be made.

The first was São Vicente. It has a perfect and generous natural harbour, perhaps the safest place to pause in the entire eastern Atlantic. Other than that it is a sterile pile of stones and so it had been of little interest in previous centuries.

This deep harbour was just the place for the new steamships born of the Industrial Revolution to reload with coal on their journeys along the Atlantic shipping lanes. The British, riding the crest of the invention of the steam engine, flocked to São Vicente to set up coaling stations. Mindelo, its capital, grew at an astonishing rate. The second island where epochal events were taking place was a tiny one: Brava. It was at this insignificant dot at the end of the archipelago that whaling ships from New England began to stop and pick up eager crews of young men. The ships offered the prospect of passage to America and in this way Cabo Verdeans joined the mass migration across the Atlantic.

They went on emigrating throughout the century and on into the next. In the first 20 years of the 1900s, 19,000 Cabo Verdeans began new lives there. Many of them still regarded the archipelago as their home, which would eventually bring great economic benefit to Cabo Verde.

The structure of Cabo Verdean society continued to change dramatically into the 19th century as internal slavery came to an end. In 1834, a rough count yielded 52,000 free or freed men and women, and 4,000 slaves. Yet for most people the formal 1878 declaration that, finally, slavery was abolished did not mean a better life. The enslaved had to serve further years of forced labour which were to continue in various guises until well into the following century.

Another social change occurred as Cabo Verde again became a place of exile for Portuguese convicts, from thieves to political dissidents. Between 1802 and 1882, according to the English historian Basil Davidson, nearly 2,500 such *degredados* arrived at the islands: 'They were at once absorbed into a population increasingly homogeneous in its culture and way of life, if notably various in the colours of its skin.' Portugal ruled by skin colour. A census of 1856 listed 17 distinctions, ranging from shades of 'very dark' to 'almost white'. Many lighter Cabo Verdeans clung to their rank and despised those deemed as darker.

SUFFERING: THE BEGINNING OF THE 1900s The 20th century began with a very different Cabo Verde. The cinder heap of São Vicente, not fertile Santiago, was its chief commercial centre. São Vicente attracted a hopeless migration of the desperate from other islands in search of work. But the island had virtually no natural resources and was incapable of sustaining a rural peasant population. So when the shipping business dipped, as it did from time to time, the consequences of drought became increasingly shocking. Some 17,000 died in 1921. In 1922, the Santiago journal *A Verdade* reported:

> 1921 was horrific...yet now follows this of 1922, equally horrific but with the addition that people have spent all they possess, whether in clothes or land, livestock or trinkets, and today are in the last stage of poverty, while emigration is carrying away all whom the steamers can embark.

The rains came in the end. In the 1930s, they were plentiful and the archipelago turned green. Returned American *emigrantes*, fleeing the Depression in the USA, returned to live with their families. But it did not last, and hunger returned in the early 1940s.

Outside the archipelago World War II began. On the islands, anti-Portuguese sentiment surged when Lisbon decided to garrison over 6,000 men among the islands' starving population. It is possible that Portugal feared that the British or the Germans were planning to seize the archipelago, and their fears were justified. Winston Churchill had well-developed plans to invade Cabo Verde but called them off at the last minute. The matter of who controlled the islands was still of interest to the world.

Peace came in 1945 but for the Cabo Verdeans the worst drought they were ever to face was looming. Some 30,000 people died. The hunger was exacerbated by the return of the *emigrantes* a few years before: they swelled the numbers and decreased the remittances.

This hideous cycle of drought and famine raises the question: could it have been avoided? After all, Cabo Verdeans do not die of hunger today. The answer is still

THE SCHOONER *ERNESTINA*

The schooner *Ernestina*, a beautiful, 112ft sailing vessel over a century old, is one of the most famous of the packet ships that connected Cabo Verde with the USA in the early 20th century.

She was still working as a packet ship in the 1960s, making her last Atlantic voyage to Providence in 1965 in an era that had long been dominated by the steamship, which itself was fast losing trade to the aeroplane.

The *Ernestina* had many lives. After her launch in 1894 she became a Grand Banks fisher and then an Arctic expeditionary vessel. She sank after a galley fire in 1946, and that was when a Cabo Verdean, Captain Henrique Mendes, stepped in. The schooner was raised, restored to seaworthiness, bought by Captain Mendes and then began her new life as a transatlantic packet ship. Her work was to carry passengers and goods between Cabo Verde and the USA. Often she took seasonal workers to New England for the cranberry harvest. Hopeful immigrants would also come. Sometimes she would take successful immigrants on rare trips home; more often it was goods she ferried back to the motherland – bought with hard-won money earned on the bogs or in the textile mills of New Bedford.

For ten years this trade continued between Cabo Verde and Rhode Island. After her last trip in 1965 she continued to work between Cabo Verde and the African mainland. She also worked the islands – one job was to ferry schoolchildren from Fogo and Brava to boarding school in Praia and Mindelo.

But even this work was being eclipsed by other, more modern ships, and eventually it was decided to return the *Ernestina* to the USA. But the trip home, in 1976, was a disaster – a storm dismasted her and she was forced to return to port. There, the government of the new republic had her rebuilt and, six years later, gave her to the USA as a symbol of friendship.

The *Ernestina* then served as a sail training ship, educational vessel and cultural icon until 2005, when the US Coast Guard refused the vessel the certification required to carry passengers, putting at least a temporary end to her many activities on the ocean waves. Fundraising campaigns and legislation were successful, however, and in 2019, she returned as the *Ernestina-Morrisey* to her home port of New Bedford, under the care of the Massachusetts Maritime Academy. She will continue to serve as a training vessel, and as recently as 2023 took part in a tall ships challenge in waters off Florida. For more information on the schooner and a vivid history of the passage of Cabo Verdeans to and from the USA, as well as the current news and community involvement, see w ernestina.org.

contested but it seems certain that an important ingredient of the famines was the way the land was owned and run. It was a system which discouraged peasants from planning more than a season ahead.

Agriculture was mired in a system of inheritance which split land with each generation until people farmed it in splinters in an inefficient way. Land that was not subject to this system was owned in great swathes by a small number of men who rented it out in patches a year at a time. The peasants who farmed this land had no incentive to improve it: they knew that the extra yield would be taken as rent.

TRACING THE ANCESTORS

Romantic stories abound of brave Cabo Verdean men who risked their lives to sail across the Atlantic and find fortune for themselves and their families in the USA. But these days, many Cabo Verdeans in the USA have lost track of their personal family histories. They may have a forgotten great-great-grandfather who toiled on whaling ships on the wild ocean, risking his life to harpoon whales, earn promotion and set up life on the east coast. They may be descended from a couple of lost generations who worked themselves to the bone in the cranberry bogs of New England, returning home with their earnings at the end of each season. Perhaps they are descended from a young man who left his sweetheart on Fogo; perhaps they own a stone cottage or great *sobrado* house, now standing forgotten on Brava.

Of all the Africans who went to the USA in the era of slavery and mass migration, Cabo Verdean Americans are the only ones who can trace their families back to their 'original' villages, according to James Lopes, genealogy expert. This is because there are excellent records of Cabo Verdean arrivals in the USA. Those who have made the journey of rediscovery often find they have relatives, or ancestors, from all over the world, including Europe, Asia and South America.

To decipher your family tree, begin by questioning your immediate family, advises Mr Lopes. Write down everything you unearth – in particular the dates of birth, marriage and death of each remembered person, and how they made a living.

Then, when a particularly dim but fascinating figure emerges from the past, there are several sources to help you investigate. For those whose families went to the USA before 1920 the arrival should have been recorded in the passenger and ships lists of the Port of New Bedford. Most Cabo Verdeans passed through there, though Boston and Providence were other ports of entry. The voyages of all Cabo Verdean whaling ships are also listed, and kept in New Bedford Free Public Library.

One mine of fascinating information is the Old Dartmouth Historical Society at the New Bedford Whaling Museum (Johnny Cake Hill; w whalingmuseum.org). The original logbooks of many of the whaling expeditions that took Cabo Verdeans to the USA are stored here. Details of the trip, including how much your ancestor was paid, might be found.

There are other useful places to begin digging, including the Arquivo Histórico Nacional on Santiago. Staff there will research birth records on request. For general reading, Marilyn Halter's book *Between Race and Ethnicity* (page 374) gives spellbinding accounts of life in the cranberry bogs and other features of emigrant life.

So, at a time when the people could have been producing income for the islands by cultivating cash crops such as coffee for export, agriculture stagnated. This, combined with the dwindling of tree cover, imposed deep poverty. Cabo Verde was becoming an increasingly unsustainable place. Population control was left to the crude device of starvation.

People escaped not just to America but also to work on other Portuguese islands. They left for São Tomé and Príncipe in their tens of thousands: 24,000 Cabo Verdeans worked there between 1902 and 1922; 34,000 laboured there from 1950 to 1970. In this way these *contratados* escaped starvation, though some said the labourers returned more emaciated than when they left.

Soon Cabo Verde's only lingering use, as a coaling station, seemed to be vanishing as well: oil was replacing coal as the fuel for the high seas and, as a result, few ships needed to pause there. When they did stop, resupply with oil was an easier, smaller business than loading coal. There was no need to maintain great companies with armies of staff on the crescent of rock halfway to South America. The world had dumped Cabo Verde.

REVOLT Ideas of independence began to grow in the minds of 20th-century Cabo Verdeans as a result of several world events. The consequences of their uprising, when it eventually came, were momentous. It was probably the first time in Cabo Verde's history that the rocks made a splash of their own, and the ripples spread far. For it was Cabo Verdeans, unique in Portuguese Africa because of their education and cosmopolitanism, who led the foment in other Portuguese African colonies. This in turn weakened Portugal and was the direct cause of the unseating of its fascist dictatorship.

One important force arose from the European 'scramble for Africa', which began in the late 1800s and had allocated most of the continent to colonial rule by the early 1900s. When World War I diverted the colonists' attention, resistance to colonial rule gathered pace, giving rise to the growing feeling that European reins could be thrown away. Cabo Verde, unusual in having been subjugated for long centuries rather than mere decades, absorbed these ideas as they emerged in other European colonies. Allied to this was the rise of communism, which in Africa gave structure to undirected stirrings of antagonism among the people towards their rulers.

Another factor was necessary, however, for Cabo Verdeans to begin to assimilate these ideas: they needed to hear about them and they needed to be educated enough to be able to transform them into action. This impetus came, ironically, from the beneficence of Lisbon. Portugal acknowledged the peculiarity of its Cabo Verde colony and recognised its Creole society as closer to its own than were the populations of their mainland African colonies. As a result of this racist ideology, Cabo Verdeans were granted a form of Portuguese citizenship. Although it is unclear how this benefited most of them, the archipelago was also the intellectual centre of the Portuguese African colonies, with a secondary school which attracted pupils from the mainland, initially as the Seminário-Liceu de São Nicolau, and later in Mindelo.

There arose a small group of urbane Cabo Verdeans whom the Portuguese employed as 'middlemen'. They were considered 'halfway between black and white' and so they could more easily manage the peoples of Portuguese Guinea, Angola, Mozambique and São Tomé and Príncipe, while being an acceptable interface with the 'true' Portuguese. A select group of Cabo Verdeans was thus educated, often in Lisbon, forming a literate class of administrators, and sent to work in diverse outposts of the empire. From this group sprang poets and journalists who first began to express a form of cohesive national identity. Their political objectives were limited: they prized the privilege of Portuguese citizenship and supported enlightened colonialism, defending the fledgling republic that was born in Portugal in 1910.

Perhaps if the liberalism that accompanied the new Portuguese republic had continued, the movement for independence would have come earlier. Perhaps it would have fizzled out. We shall never know, for in 1926, Portugal's republic was overthrown by its own military, inaugurating 50 years of fascist dictatorship. Freedom of speech disappeared.

SOCIAL STRUCTURE: UNTANGLING A TANGLED WEB

Numerous categories defined the different elements of Cabo Verdean society. *Fidalgos* were the noblemen, representing the king and making money for themselves and for the Crown through a system of royal charters, trade monopolies and land grants. They tended to be Portuguese, though there were some Genoese, Venetians and Spanish. *Capitãos* were military governors appointed by the Crown, with a high degree of local autonomy. *Feitors* were powerful private business agents who had won royal trade monopolies and also represented private mercantile concerns.

The pariahs of the slave trade were the *lançados*. They were, by definition, outcasts, but they were essential middlemen, embedding themselves in the tropical creeks of the West African coast where they channelled the trade in goods and humans. Portuguese, they were often political or religious refugees, and a good few of them were Jews who were expelled or had fled the Inquisition. *Lançados* had an ambiguous relationship with the Crown: in theory they complied with royal trade monopolies, but in practice they had a pervasive power that the Crown could not control. They traded with whom they pleased and flouted Portuguese tax and other restrictions. *Ganagogas* were technically Jewish *lançados*, but in practice the term embraced anyone who could speak local African languages.

Tangamãus were the public interface of the African involvement in the trade, and functioned mainly as translators; the name probably comes from *targuman*, the Arabic for translator. The mercenary bodyguards of the *lançados* and *tangamãus* were the *grumettas*.

Banished from Portugal for religious, political or criminal reasons, *degredados* sometimes became galley slaves in rowing boats. They lived either on Cabo Verde or on the African coast, where some became *lançados*. Like the *lançados*, they became an important white presence in the founding of the Creole population. *Pretos* were free black people, while *ladinos* were slaves who had been baptised and given a Latin name.

As slaves escaped or were freed, the peasant population grew. At its core was a group whom the Portuguese despised, as did the later *mestiço* class. These were the Badius, and they clung to their African culture. They were small-scale farmers generally living in the remote central regions of Santiago. *Parcerias* were colonial partnership share-cropping systems; share-croppers usually gave between a half and two-thirds of the crops they grew to their landowner. *Rendeiros* grew subsistence crops for themselves and worked on other people's land, generally for wages.

Later in history came *contratados*, contract labourers who worked in São Tomé and Príncipe and also in the United States.

More visible twitchings of nationhood came with the publication of *Claridade*, a journal that called to the nation to realise the essence of 'Cabo Verdeanness'. It published the work of some gifted writers in three issues over 1936 and 1937, and in another six after the end of World War II, the last in 1960. For 500 years there had been no such notion of the Cabo Verdean. There were Portuguese, there were the enslaved and there were *mestiços*. Yet the Cabo Verdeans were there, incipient, infused with the knowledge of their African and European roots, endowed with a musical and poetic culture. *Claridade* helped them to see this – to define as Cabo Verdean their laments and their poetry, the way they wore their clothes and their craftsmanship. *Claridade* reminded them that they had their own language: Kriolu.

It was those members of the educated class who were teenagers in the early 1940s who made the crucial step in the evolution of Cabo Verdean thought. They were so angered by the mass of deaths in the droughts of that time that they began to believe that the country could be better off if it was independent from Portugal. **Amílcar Cabral** was just 17, and in his second year at secondary school, when the 1941 famine ravaged the people of Mindelo. His later success in rousing the people of Cabo Verde and Portuguese Guinea to rise against the Portuguese, and his effective fighting techniques, have been ascribed by historians to his profound knowledge of these countries and his ability to inspire Africans with a concept of their own nationality.

Born in 1924 of Cabo Verdean parents, Cabral grew up in what is today Guinea-Bissau, then Portuguese Guinea, in great poverty, finding the money to attend school from the small profits of his needleworking mother, whom he greatly admired. His father, Juvenal Cabral, had at least 60 other children. Despite deprivations, Amílcar went on to study agrarian engineering in Lisbon where he graduated with honours. He had a sound colonial career at his feet.

But while he was a student he imbibed from various clandestine sources ideas of communism and liberalism as well as news from the revolutionary intellectuals of other African colonies. After graduating, Cabral's career move must have seemed bizarre to outsiders. He buried himself in the backlands of Guinea, an employee of the farming and forestry service, making the first analysis of its agrarian and water resources. During this time he acquired an intimate knowledge of the country's landscape and social structure.

Cabral's battle was not just against the Portuguese. Cabo Verdeans themselves accepted assimilation, and the cycles of drought and emigration, as an unavoidable consequence of the land. Although an internationalist at heart, Cabral formed a tiny nationalist movement in 1954. He made friends with another product of the Mindelo secondary school, Aristides Pereira, who worked in the posts-and-telegraph office in Guinea. They learned local languages, read literature on uprisings around the world and worked on until Cabral was deported from the country in 1955. The following year, the two formed a tiny party: the PAIGC (Party for the Independence of Guinea and Cabo Verde). Other members were those with administrative jobs in Portugal, Angola and Guinea. The party pursued peaceful means at first, appealing for better conditions. One of their group, Abílio Duarte, returned to Cabo Verde to agitate there among the students and the dockers, while Cabral set up a base in Conakry, capital of ex-French Guinea. The insurrection stumbled forward, manifesting itself publicly through graffiti at first and then through strikes, which inevitably led to sporadic state violence. A wages strike in Portuguese Guinea saw 50 protesters shot dead and the rest sentenced to 15 years' hard labour.

Throughout 1959 and 1960 the activists moved around the world, gaining confidence from news of uprisings outside Portuguese Africa while the islands suffered another drought. This time, however, the loss of life was not of disastrous proportions because of a more in-tune governor. Fighting began in Portuguese Guinea in 1963 and Cabo Verdeans made their way to the mainland to join the army. The war lasted for ten years, with the PAIGC, numerically tiny compared with the number of Portuguese troops, employing brilliant guerrilla tactics to lure the enemy into dispersing into numerous garrisons which it could then besiege. Arms from the USSR eventually arrived and by 1972 the PAIGC had control of half of the country, but not the air, where the Portuguese commanding general, António de Spínola, retained supremacy.

Back in Cabo Verde, nothing had appeared to have happened, even by 1971. Abílio Duarte worked both at the Mindelo school, transforming the aspirations of the next generation, and among the dockers of Mindelo, more open to new ideas than their rural counterparts. From 1966 a band of 30 of the most talented young men of Cabo Verde had been living in Cuba, where they trained for a surprise landing on Santiago and Santo Antão which would begin the war on the archipelago. In fact the landings plan would never be executed, most critically because the group failed to find the transport they needed across the ocean.

It was just as well, because swooping arrests in 1967 eliminated any organised reception the rebels might have hoped for, while the drought of 1968 would have starved any guerrillas trying to survive in the highlands. So, back on the archipelago, there was no war, just the arrests of increasing numbers of suspected revolutionaries. The peasants were waiting with messianic expectation for Amílcar Cabral to come from Portuguese Guinea and liberate them.

But they would never see him. Tragedy struck on 20 January 1973, when traitors from within the PAIGC's own ranks, allegedly spurred on by Spínola, murdered the 52-year-old Cabral on the mainland, just a few months before the victory in Guinea. Anger at his death shook any stagnation out of the guerrilla ranks and this, together with the arrival of ground-to-air missiles from the USSR, triggered the final offensive which was to bring them victory. Guinea-Bissau became a member of the Organisation of African Unity on 19 November 1973.

Cabral had been right when he prophesied in 1961: 'We for our part are sure that the destruction of Portuguese colonialism is what will destroy Portuguese fascism.' Young officers in the Portuguese army in Guinea became convinced that they would never win their African wars and they and their troops were increasingly brutalised by their own actions. Portugal was becoming overburdened, economically and politically. Out of this turmoil came the Carnation Revolution. Just five months after Guinea's liberation, returned Portuguese military personnel formed the Armed Forces Movement and overthrew Salazar's successor, Marcelo Caetano. In a near-bloodless coup in Lisbon, four decades of the Estado Novo dictatorship were over. Independence followed quickly for some Portuguese colonies, though for Cabo Verde it was far from automatic. Spínola, Portugal's new conservative leader, wanted to hang on to the strategically positioned islands.

Meanwhile, all the leading militants on the islands were locked up and the remainder were still on the mainland. All Cabo Verde had won was an agreement that it could have its own National Council.

Returning from the mainland war in August 1974, the Cabo Verdean heroes were given a rapturous welcome. But they arrived in a country where Portuguese authority was not just intact but working overtime under the orders of Spínola. There were those on the islands who thought Cabo Verde should remain with Portugal. Intellectuals from the old *Claridade* movement argued that Cabo Verde could never be economically viable on its own and should remain associated with someone, Portugal or the United Nations. They supported the words of Eugénio Tavares, the poet: 'For Cape Verde? For these poor and abandoned rocks thrown up in the sea, independence? What sense is there in that? God have pity on thoughtless men!'

Most, however, no longer wished to remain allied to the country that had caused them so much ill. Diasporan interests and covert cold war power plays added another layer of complexity to negotiations, but after Spínola's ousting, PAIGC won over those in Lisbon via political mobilisation and diplomacy. After a transitional joint government, a general election was held at the end of June 1975, and the PAIGC became the new National Assembly, proclaiming independence for the archipelago on 5 July 1975. The president was Aristides Pereira, Secretary-General of the PAIGC. Cabo Verde and Guinea-Bissau became 'sister republics', on a path to full unification.

AFTER INDEPENDENCE Cabo Verde was free but it was a wasteland: its resources plundered over centuries, its soil thin and disappearing with every gust of Saharan wind. Drought had come again in 1969 and afflicted the islands for six years. In 1977, the maize and bean harvest was nil. There was no work for wages and exports were almost non-existent. Over half of the islands' imports were of famine food, and emigration surged. The shock of the sudden assumption of responsibility for such a difficult land must have been acute.

One of Cabo Verde's few advantages was that it was not riven with traditional rivalries. In that sense it began rebuilding from a metaphorical, as well as a literal, bare ground. Another advantage lay in its good contacts with the outside world. The new left-wing government of Portugal was on friendly terms with its counterparts in Cabo Verde, a relationship that continues today.

Financial backing came from many countries: once the USA was convinced that Cabo Verde was indeed 'non-aligned' it sent a gift of US$7 million. The World Food Programme dispatched thousands of tonnes of maize, and a variety of countries,

> **FLYING THE FLAG** *Murray Stewart*
>
> When Cabo Verdean cultural icon Cesária Évora (page 44) passed away, one Cabo Verdean restaurant owner mourned that she 'was more important than our flag'. And perhaps it's no surprise that the islands' musical *grande dame* should enjoy more affection: after all, she had been around for a lot longer.
>
> With a blue background, ten yellow stars, two horizontal white bands sandwiching one red one, Cabo Verde's national flag was only adopted in 1992, some 17 years after independence. In those intervening years, the flag was perhaps more 'African' in character: with the continent's traditional colours of red, green and yellow, it was almost identical to that of Guinea-Bissau. But now the flag is altogether more singular, with its details solemnly described in Article 8 of the islands' constitution.
>
> That blue background represents the sea and sky, both of which are plentiful in Cabo Verde. Each island is remembered by one of those yellow stars, so the uninhabited and otherwise neglected Santa Lucia is, for once, not forgotten. The white bands signify peace, while the red one stands for effort and endeavour. Together, the three bands represent the building of the island nation.
>
> In a mark of respect to Cesária Évora, the flags on all public buildings were lowered to half-mast after her death in 2011.

including Sweden, Holland and the USSR, also sent aid. The Cabo Verdean government insisted that the WFP grain was not handed out as charity but was sold to people who did construction work on water-retention and anti-erosion dykes and on barrages in return for wages.

The government was a socialist one which attracted the interest of the USSR, China and Cuba. There are still strong ties with these countries: Cuba and Russia have been the destination of many Cabo Verdean university students, while university links with China are underway. Indeed, the Chinese embassy is the most prestigious building in Praia, and sits opposite Cabo Verde's parliament, and China's economic links with the country are significant. Guinea-Bissau, meanwhile, suffered more turbulence than Cabo Verde, which led to a coup in 1980 that ruptured the link between the two countries. After that 'The Party', for there was only one, renamed itself the PAICV (Partido Africano da Independência de Cabo Verde).

The PAICV had a political monopoly enshrined in the country's constitution and this went unchallenged at first. One person within the party who objected to the lack of democracy, and also to the centralised control of the party and the limits placed on free enterprise, was one Carlos Veiga, who formed the MpD (Movimento para a Democracia) in 1990. Things moved swiftly and by September 1990, Cabo Verde had legally become a multi-party state. Elections the following January swept out the PAICV and handed power to Veiga, who was prime minister from 1991 to 2001. A month later the candidate the MpD supported for president, António Manuel Mascarenhas, was elected. Flagship policies of the government in 1991 were a market economy with less public spending, opening up to foreign investment, and the development of fishing, tourism and service industries. A new national anthem and flag were adopted in September 1992.

A decade later, on 14 January 2001, the PAICV regained control in an overwhelming victory. The people then elected as president (with a margin of 12 votes) Pedro Pires, who had been prime minister of the first government in 1975. More importantly for the PAICV, it won in the National Assembly.

Having previously adopted the Anglophonic version of its name, the country informed the United Nations in late 2013 that henceforward, it wanted to be known as Cabo Verde in all official dealings.

GOVERNMENT AND POLITICS

Cabo Verde is a parliamentary democratic republic with no political prisoners and a clean human rights record. The oldest party is the PAICV, which won independence for the country in 1975, as the PAIGC, and ruled it as a one-party state for 15 years. The MpD (Movimento para a Democracia), running on a neoliberal economic and social reform platform, won democracy for Cabo Verde in 1990 and was elected in 1991 and then again in December 1995. A sliver of the MpD broke away to form the Partido da Convergencia Democratica (PCD) in 1994. In late 2000, the PAICV came to power again and was re-elected in 2006, and again in 2011. The MpD regained power in 2016 and 2021. Their prime minister Ulisses Correia e Silva defeated the PAICV's lawyer and law lecturer Janira Hopffer Almada who, if she'd won, would have been the country's first female prime minister. The current president, meanwhile, is the popular former PAICV prime minister José Maria Pereira Neves. He defeated the MpD's incumbent Jorge Carlos Fonseca, a law graduate, who had been re-elected in 2016. Both parliamentary and presidential elections are next scheduled for 2026.

Elections in Cabo Verde have generally been peaceful and praised by electoral monitors for their legal adherence, though the 2001 election was disputed. (Carlos Veiga, of the MpD, claimed that the results were fraudulent and filed a lawsuit, but international election monitors deemed them free and fair.) The national/municipal split that occurs when differing parties are in power has at times led to a lack of co-operation and stalemates between central government and local government.

ECONOMY

DEVELOPMENT In the 2022 report for the United Nations Human Development Index, Cabo Verde came in at number 131 – not an enviable rank, but after a slump over the last few years, it was, at the time of writing, again 'on the up'. According to the index, GDP (gross domestic product) was US$7,601 per head in the same year. Unemployment has reduced over the last decades but still sits at around 8.4%, according to the IMF. Many of the unemployed are occupied for at least some of the time in fishing or farming.

Also according to the IMF, growth has rallied in recent years in line with a return to pre-pandemic tourist numbers along with low inflation, and is predicted to hit 5.4% in 2025. Remittances from Cabo Verdeans living overseas slowed over the pandemic but, according to a US State Department report in 2024, these remittances still accounted for 15% of Cabo Verde's GDP. Inflation was predicted to remain at 2.1% throughout the year 2024–25.

Cabo Verde forged a special partnership with the European Union in 2007, and current co-operative programmes with them focus on various key competitive clusters. The country is also a member of the World Trade Organization, and has been elevated by the UN to 'middle income' status.

Until 2019, Cabo Verde was considered one of the champions among Sub-Saharan African countries in terms of poverty reduction and, under the United Nations 2030 Agenda, reflected in the new Strategic Plan for Sustainable Development 2022–2026 (PEDS II), the government set the goal of eradicating extreme poverty by 2026. After a slump during the pandemic, this again seems possible, with the proportion of Cabo Verde's population living in extreme poverty (that is, living on less than US$1.90 per day) falling from 22.6% in 2015 to 11.1% in 2022, with greater investment in social protection policies expected to drive the figure down further.

In the long term, Cabo Verde has extraordinary ambition. It hopes to transform itself into an international financial centre and an investment and transport gateway to continental Africa. The first stage in this plan is to get the money rolling

BAROMETER OF A NATION'S PROGRESS

Cabo Verde's transformation since its independence from Portugal in 1975 includes:

- Life expectancy has risen from 57 years to 73.2 years
- GDP has increased from US$134 million to US$2.53 billion
- Illiteracy was 75% in 1975; now, it is less than 10%
- In 1975, the islands had only 13 doctors; the number now exceeds 400
- Whereas a Cabo Verdean woman in 1975 would on average have seven children, this has now decreased to 1.9

in with the rapid development of tourism, on the back of which a healthy service economy can be developed. Other sectors seen as having great potential are the 'blue economy', renewables and digital transformation.

AID AND REMITTANCES Remittances, mainly from the huge diaspora in the USA and smaller groups in Europe, together with foreign aid, still sustain just under quarter of Cabo Verde's economy. The islands were the recipients of one of the highest amounts of international aid, per capita, in the world in the years after independence. Many sources of aid funding were withdrawn from 2007 when Cabo Verde was upgraded by the United Nations to the status of 'middle income country' – one of only a handful that have achieved this elevation. However, there are still substantial amounts of investment, some of it in the form of actual aid, some in the form of mutual business development, coming from other nations. Portugal struck a deal with the nation in late 2024 to 'reinvest' around €12 million of Cabo Verde's €600 million debt in the country's climate change mitigation projects. It also has a number of schemes in place to encourage Portuguese businesses to invest and exchange with those in Cabo Verde.

Small-business owners still form 98% of private firms in Cabo Verde and employ 40% of the workforce. However, they face credit access challenges due to high collateral requirements from banks. To address this, the World Bank is helping to increase availability of finance. Their MSME (micro, small and medium enterprise) project had granted close to 2,200 credit guarantees by 2024, with women-led businesses accounting for 46% of the recipients.

All the aid that went before is however being dwarfed by the agreements Cabo Verde is reaching with China, an ever-increasing influence in Africa, but whose relationship with the country also goes back to the early days of independence. Agreements made in 2008 were so vast, embracing shipping, fishing, communications, electricity and construction, that they were dubbed the 'new Chinese wave'. The key project is with the China Ocean Shipping Companies Group (Cosco), one of the world's largest shipping companies, in partnership with Enapor, which is responsible for Cabo Verde's port facilities. The investments include several port redevelopments and the building of cargo facilities. China built Cabo Verde its first dam (on Santiago) and funded the construction of a national sports stadium with capacity for 15,000 people, completed in 2014.

Since the early 2020s, China has provided assistance and co-operation in the long-overdue transformation of Cabo Verde's energy industry to renewables, including the installation of its first wind farm projects. Meanwhile, the long-mooted Chinese-backed special economic zone (SEZ) in São Vicente offers tax reductions and fiscal incentives to companies also using sustainable methods in fishing and maritime transport, while also backing several housing projects and health initiatives. Another SEZ on Fogo is investigating the island's potential to become a geothermal energy research centre, not to mention a local provider. In early 2025, the Cabo Verdean prime minister and business delegates inked a further €26.3 million package in Beijing, its aims described as further boosting bilateral co-operation, with a special focus on transformation and infrastructure in both existing and new industries.

FISHERIES Fishing contributes a meagre 2–3% of GDP. The archipelago is at the centre of one of the last great underused fishing grounds of the world, a fact that has not gone unnoticed by China's huge fishing fleet.

Tuna and lobster abound, but at present fishing is a trade of artisans, with a fleet of around 1,600 vessels, though there is some export of fish and crustaceans.

Although the continental shelf area is relatively small, the Exclusive Economic Zone of Cabo Verde covers an area of about 734,265km^2, much of which is not exploited by the national fisheries.

In spite of increased fishing efforts during the past decade, landings have reached a plateau at around 9,000–10,000 per year, and catches of some fish have decreased. However, new fishing agreements are on the horizon, particularly with China and the European Union. In 2024, the government approved a plan for a Chinese-backed maritime special economic zone on and around São Vicente, while the European Commission again signed an implementation protocol to the EU's Fisheries Partnership Agreement (FPA) with Cabo Verde in the same year. At the very least, new fish-processing facilities will be built on São Vicente.

TOURISM Tourism is almost entirely responsible for Cabo Verde's recent growth, contributing 25% of GDP in 2023 and quickly climbing its way past the pre-pandemic highs of 2019 over the course of 2024. It thus provides an increasing source of employment – increasing, though possibly not sustainable (while a cleaner at an all-inclusive hotel may be happy to have an income, it's perhaps not the sort of employment they want for their children). The construction boom has also been a major component. Plans for holiday resorts, condominiums and apartments abound, some of them fanciful and some of them halted by economic factors. But there's no doubt that tourism is seen as a cornerstone of the archipelago's future, and visitor numbers are celebrated in the press. In 1991, there were a meagre 19,000 tourist arrivals. Now, over a million people are predicted to visit in 2025, with numbers in the last quarter of 2024 already surpassing the predictions for 2026. Visitors are attracted primarily to Sal and Boavista, which together account for around three quarters of guests, mainly due to the existence of all-inclusive international resort hotels and those islands' white-sand beaches. Inclusive packages operated by TUI account for a huge number of tourists arriving in Cabo Verde, followed by Transavia (from France and the Netherlands), and TAP (Portugal), along with increasingly numbers booking holidays via easyJet. Tourists from the UK make up the largest group of arrivals, at 31.8%, followed by those from Portugal (13.2%) and the Netherlands (7.6%). Arrivals from the USA remain modest if consistent, with a majority of them favouring Santiago as an entry point, perhaps then travelling on to visit family on Fogo and Brava. This may of course change if direct flights from the US East Coast and Brazil resume in the future.

AGRICULTURE 'It is heartbreaking,' says one expat scientist working in Cabo Verde, 'to watch a peasant woman patiently prepare the ground and sow, then wait for months while it doesn't rain, then return to break the ground and sow again.'

Only a tenth of the land, 40,000ha, is suitable for cultivation. Of this, 34,000ha are cultivated and less than a tenth of that is irrigated, although this proportion has been rising (page 32). Some 90% of the crop is maize and beans which are often grown together. The beans grow up the maize stalks which act as trellises and offer some shade. Other major crops are bananas, mangoes, sugarcane, sweet potatoes, manioc and cassava. The only significant exported crop is the banana, although other cash crops are coffee, peanuts, castor beans and pineapples. More than half of the total irrigated land grows sugarcane, most of which is used in the production of *grogue*, the local *aguardente* (page 82).

Historical patterns of ownership have deterred investment in, and maintenance of, agricultural land, but land reform has been very hard to implement. The PAICV's attempts in 1981 were so unpopular that the next government

ENERGY AND WATER IN CABO VERDE *Alex Alper and Murray Stewart*

'Salt, basalt rock, limestone, kaolin, fish, clay, gypsum.' So reads the finite list of Cabo Verde's natural resources, giving insight into the tremendous challenge that existence here has always posed. And yet, in a world where the price of fossil fuels climbs ever higher, Cabo Verde has at least been blessed with the need to innovate. Critical deficiencies in water, agriculture and energy are compelling the country to become an innovator, and maybe a leader, in exciting new technologies, from growing plants without soil to capturing water from the fog.

But the difficulties are formidable, and the lack of water is perhaps the most. Rainfall averages 200mm per year, barely enough to replenish the natural springs that supply much of the rural population with water. As the springs slowly dry up, salt water is seeping into the aquifers, contaminating the sources that remain. Desalinisation technologies provide water to the majority of urban residents but are very expensive.

Agriculture also presents challenges. Throughout Cabo Verdean history, severe droughts have caused epic famines, killing thousands and driving many abroad. Erosion, caused by agriculture, grazing, and wood-gathering in a delicate ecosystem, has decreased the quality of the soil, while much of the country was originally sand and rocky mountain slope anyway. Indeed, only 10% of Cabo Verde's 4,033km^2 of landmass is arable, and home-grown food provides only 10–20% of what is consumed. Nevertheless, a large number of Cabo Verdeans are still involved in agricultural activities, planting corn, beans, peanuts, squash, sweet potatoes, sugarcane, bananas and other crops each year. Some farmers plant corn only for animal fodder, knowing it will not reach maturity.

The rest of Cabo Verde's food is imported, and transportation requires energy – another scarce commodity for a country with no fuel reserves. The country also needs fuel for electricity, for cooking (butane gas) and for desalinisation. Domestic fuel taxes are high compared with other African nations, although there were dramatic reductions in these in 2022 after political pressure. Still, electricity costs here are some of the highest in the world. In the meantime, rural Cabo Verdeans rely largely on dwindling forest resources for their cooking needs to supplement expensive butane gas. This constitutes a great pressure on Cabo Verde's fragile ecosystem. With rising tourism, and annual population growth of about 2%, the demand for affordable, abundant energy will only continue to rise.

Precisely because of the gravity of these challenges, Cabo Verde, with the help of foreign governments and NGOs, is trying to pioneer renewable and sustainable technologies. With 3,000 hours of sunlight per year, Cabo Verde has promoted

reversed them in 1993. Farming on steep hillsides is another challenge to Cabo Verdean agriculture.

There are many devices in the Cabo Verdean hills and valleys designed to keep precious water and topsoil from being flushed away. *Arretos* are lines of small stone walls around the hillsides, designed for erosion control. Although they are not supposed to be used for planting, crops grown behind them are producing double the yield of crops grown before the *arretos* were built. Terraces are much bigger walls, properly designed for the ubiquitous shelved farming seen all over Cabo Verde.

solar energy to pump and heat water, and to illuminate homes in remote areas. The Cabo Verdean government and the European Union have begun a campaign to disseminate solar water pumps to 30 rural communities on Santiago. That will go far to help rural Cabo Verdeans, most of whom make up the considerable part of the population that still lacks electricity.

In one rural community in Serra Malagueta, a pilot project sponsored by the Protected Areas Programme is underway to disseminate more efficient wood stoves. It aims to reduce wood use among residents who can't afford butane gas for cooking, thereby protecting the endangered forests.

Wind energy is another promising technology (page 30). In consultation with the Danish company Wave Star, the government also began exploring the possibility of wave technology for electrical power generation. Still some years away from commercial implementation, Wave Star's machine consists of 20 half-submerged hemisphere-shaped floats that float upward when a wave passes. Ocean waves offer a more potent and constant energy than wind. Still, wave technology must overcome the formidable challenge of keeping costs low while resisting storms and salt damage over the long term.

The government at one stage did give consideration to a floating nuclear island, which would have supplied 70MW of energy, meeting Santiago and Maio's total energy needs. The nuclear material was to have been provided by the Russian company Rosenergoatom, who would also have been responsible for removing and treating the waste. This proposal was controversial and has not progressed.

Cabo Verde is innovating in water, through fog collectors (page 202). Agricultural innovations are perhaps even more promising, with the advent of hydroponics and the spread of drip irrigation. Drip irrigation, called *gota-gota* or 'drip-drip' locally, utilises a series of plastic tubes running the length of the plant bed. They feature tiny holes that allow water to pinpoint the plant roots alone, bringing water use down by 80% and diminishing weed growth. Materials are somewhat expensive and must be replaced after three to five years. However, the technology allows for year-round cultivation, and local governments and NGOs are helping to fund it, with the result that of the 17% of farming families who use some sort of irrigation, 45% use *gota-gota*.

Soil-less culture, or hydroponics, incurs astronomical start-up costs but cuts water use by 90–95%, land use by 90%, and produces much healthier crops. Cabo Verde is still far from the paragon of green technologies it could be, and may need to become, to deal effectively with rising fuel prices and its own historic lack of resources.

Check dams of concrete or stone are built in the *ribeiras* to try and slow the rainwater's progress to the sea. At the moment, when it rains, over 80% of the water is lost. Concreted slopes on the hillside, and sometimes natural rock formations, catch water which then flows into a tank or reservoir at the bottom.

Another major problem for agriculture in Cabo Verde is pests. The millipede on Santo Antão devours potatoes and carrots – as a result the island, which is agriculturally the most productive in the archipelago, has suffered an embargo on exports of its agricultural products for decades, although this was finally, and partially, lifted in 2008. Grasshoppers cause devastation on other islands.

PEOPLE

POPULATION According to the latest official estimates in 2023 (the last census was in 2010), Cabo Verde has a population of 522,331, with projected growth to around 566,135 by 2050. The last time Cabo Verde counted the 'racial origin' of the population was in the 1950 census, when still under Portuguese rule, but suffice to say the great majority of Cabo Verdeans are of Creole/Kriolu ancestry. They are joined by a very small percentage of more recent expat Europeans, including a Portuguese community, and Africans from Senegal, Guinea-Bissau and Nigeria. Women slightly outnumber men because of emigration, although there are now localities where it is the women who are emigrating instead. This demographic inequity, together with the intermittent returns and lengthy absences, are two of the reasons why marriage and the nuclear family are no longer the norm.

Both men and women often have children with many partners and are often married to none of them. As much as that freedom can sound appealing, the responsibility for bringing up children invariably falls to the women.

Population growth has fallen to under 1%, despite a small pandemic-years spike. The government has campaigned hard to bring it down through birth control,

---

THE DIASPORA'S INFLUENCE ON CABO VERDE   *Elizabeth Mistry*

Since the archipelago was first populated, Cabo Verdeans have taken to the seas in search of new opportunities abroad. More than 60,000 emigrated to Portugal, the exodus beginning during the 1968 drought. Italy has up to 12,000 Cabo Verdean immigrants, the first of whom went to work there as domestics in the 1960s and 70s, a route opened up by the Church to single women.

Senegal and Angola each have many thousands of Cabo Verdeans, with up to 10,000 in Angola alone. There are emigrants in Luxembourg, France (25,000) and the Netherlands (13,000). Substantial numbers also live in Brazil, Argentina, Spain and Sweden.

But the largest group by far is in the United States, where there are more than 105,000 Cabo Verdean Americans, and many, many more if distant descendants are also counted.

Today the community is spread right across the US but the strongholds remain the states of Massachusetts and Rhode Island. The US diaspora has representatives in the Legislature in Praia. They represent the interests of the entire Americas, including a sizeable Brazilian population. Regardless of whether they are US-born or fresh incomers, however, diaspora members in the US are fully integrated into the American way of life, with many prominent members of the community working in US state and federal positions as well as at a grass-roots level.

Yet they have also successfully fought to maintain as many traditions from home as possible, not least the use of Kriolu – taught in a handful of schools and several universities, including Harvard – in various media, both print and broadcast, as well as the celebration of all the usual Cabo Verdean festivals. Independence Day (on 5 July, just one day after the host nation's) is one of the most important.

Families still get together to eat *cachupa* and drink imported *grogue*. They listen to *mornas* and also, increasingly, the newer artists who regularly tour the US. This cultural immersion has only increased with the rise of social media

including abortion, although the Catholic Church has campaigned hard against the latter. Life expectancy in 2021 was 73.2 years: 68.8 for men and 77.4 for women. Some 91% of people are literate, and this rises to nearly 98% among the young. Cabo Verde is a young country in more ways than one: less than 8% of the population were over 65 years of age in 2023. Over half the population lives on Santiago, and of these around 160,000 live in Praia, the capital of Cabo Verde. The only other large population centre is Mindelo on São Vicente, though many of the archipelago's other towns now have 'city' status despite being modest in size; meanwhile, the island of Santa Luzia is uninhabited. Visitors to the islands will note that many of the small accommodation options and restaurants are owned and run by immigrants from mainland Europe, including French, Spanish, Italians, Belgians and Germans. Many of the larger hotels are operated by Portuguese, Spanish or Italian chains.

SOCIAL ISSUES

HIV/AIDS UNICEF figures indicate that the prevalence of HIV in the population is 0.6%, a very low rate for an African country. Mother-to-child HIV transmission rates have dropped to below 3% in recent years and 100% of exposed children have access to prophylactic treatment.

and online music and video platforms, as well as the global popularity of Cabo Verdean music.

'The importance of the diaspora's contribution to the islands cannot be underestimated,' said Raymond A Almeida, who lived in the US for many years but who maintained close links with the islands. There is a symbiotic relationship, he suggested, with the remittances from the US a sizeable amount. In addition, the number of charitable associations and friendship groups that provide support, both financial and in kind, is impressive for so small a nation, he said. It is hard to find a school or organisation that does not receive some sort of input from a US-based community initiative.

The political clout, also, cannot be underestimated. It is popularly said that Cabo Verde's legendary cliffhanger presidential election in 2001, won by 12 votes, was decided by the diaspora.

The link works the other way, too. In 2008, Patrick Kennedy, nephew of John F Kennedy and the Congressional representative of Rhode Island, visited Cabo Verde. At the time there were 80,000 Cabo Verdeans in Rhode Island – he joked that he had come from Cabo Verde's tenth inhabited island.

Most American-born Cabo Verdeans who return do so to maintain links with family and friends and, increasingly to invest in business and real estate, especially in the service industries and in small-scale property development.

'We are way behind the Europeans though,' says John Monteiro, who was born on Fogo but went to the US as a six-year-old. 'The only advantage we have over the other developers is that we speak the language and some of us have relatives who can help steer us through the red tape. But we're in it for the long term. Those coming from the Cabo Verdean community in the US want to see the community on the islands benefit too – we want to see improved education and health care and are prepared to help make that happen. We're not just here to make money. I know a lot of people who have come back from visiting the islands and who say, "We've got to help".'

Cabo Verde has a frank attitude towards AIDS, so educational programmes have been able to operate openly and UNICEF is confident that awareness campaigns have almost universal reach.

Drugs When Caribbean and European nations got together to crack down on drug trafficking, they were so successful that the trade along direct routes dropped almost to nothing. Yet, like water, cocaine will always find a way. It continues to enter Europe in abundance because traffickers switched their routes, including 'Highway 10', the 10th parallel transatlantic route from Latin America to West Africa and thence to Europe. A few West African countries are thought to be warehouses for cocaine en route to Europe, and Cabo Verde is one of them. Seizure data in 2024 suggest its role as a transit zone for cocaine on its way to flourishing markets in Europe has picked up substantially since 2019. The country's tiny navy and 965km of coastline – a territory larger than France – have never made the task of combating the trade a simple one. Increasingly, various operations are conducted with the EU and Interpol, including partnering with the EU's Maritime Analysis and Operations Centre (Narcotics) based in Lisbon. Cabo Verde's coastguard, port authorities and policing bodies also work closely with their counterparts from Spain and Portugal's Atlantic islands, along with those in the UK, US and Brazil. The many tonnes of cocaine seized by Cabo Verde since 2020, including more than 5 tonnes in a single sting at sea in August 2024, might be considered a success story, but the fact that it just keeps on coming implies otherwise.

Drug use is far from uncommon in the country, and drugs are freely available, if illegal. The outer suburbs of Praia and Mindelo are affected by drug-related crime and addiction issues. Cartel-fuelled gang violence has calmed down substantially since the 2010s, but is still a problem, and is exacerbated by gang-culture-exposed *emigrantes* returning from disadvantaged neighbourhoods in US and Brazilian cities.

LANGUAGE

In the ethnic mosaic of Cabo Verdean slave communities, the speaking of African languages was actively discouraged. To communicate with each other, slaves were forced to piece together words from Portuguese and a melange of other sources. It was these necessary workarounds that formed the beginnings of the Cabo Verdean mother tongue, Kriolu. It is at root Portuguese, primarily the 15th-century Portuguese of the Algarve, with a simplified grammar. Phonetics, syntactic structure and some words came from the Mande of the Mandinka and Senegambian languages, all members of the large Niger-Congo family of African languages. During the early 20th century, Cabo Verdean writers began to express themselves in Kriolu, not only in order to hide their ideas from Portuguese officials but as a means of cultural definition. Eugénio Tavares of Brava, the legendary writer of *mornas*, was reported by the later luminary Baltasar Lopes to be 'a very mediocre poet in Portuguese but a very good poet in Crioulo'. Above all, Kriolu is the informal, spoken language that everyone understands. It is the language for sharing Cabo Verdean sentiment, the language of intimacy and feeling, of jokes, aphorisms and double-entendres, and of lyrics from *morna* to rap. The soul of Cabo Verde thinks, dreams and speaks in Kriolu.

For more information about Kriolu, Portuguese and English usage, basic words, phrases and hints on pronunciation, see page 364.

KRIOLU'S ASCENDANCE

Portuguese is the official language of Cabo Verde. All official business is conducted in Portuguese as is education. But only very rarely will Cabo Verdeans speak Portuguese to each other. In the bank, the doctor's surgery, or the barber's, at work or after hours, everyone, be they president or goat herder, uses Kriolu. It is the national language, the language of poems, stories, songs, of jokes, banter and everyday life.

Cabo Verde Creole (CVC), or Kabuverdianu, is usually rendered as Kriolu or Criolu – the Sotavento (leeward) and Barlavento (windward) spellings respectively – and sometimes just as 'kriol'. The language is not just a product of Cabo Verdean history, it is an index of Cabo Verdean identity. During Portuguese colonial rule it was forbidden to use Kriolu in public situations, even in the 1960s. This law was, of course, impossible to enforce, and speaking Kriolu became an act of defiance against the Portuguese.

The earliest attempt at a full grammatical description of Kriolu, both in Kriolu itself and in Portuguese by a native speaker, was an 1888 volume written by António de Paula Brito. The most recent was 1994's ALUPEC (Unified Alphabet for the Cabo Verdean Language), which was officially ratified as the standard by the government in 2009, although it is not mandatorily used.

The most common argument against making Kriolu the official language is that it would be a huge task to further codify because of its two branches – Badiu is spoken in the Sotavento islands, Sampadjudu in the Barlavento – and island dialects within those. The other is that, with Portuguese the fifth most commonly spoken language in the world, having a commonality of language with 260 million people is more important, giving Cabo Verdeans entry as it does into a rich, global Lusophone culture.

Those arguments are, however, losing traction and are seen as, even if unconsciously, a reflection of colonial ideas about language and identity, where Portuguese assumes the language of power, prestige and high culture at the expense of a mother tongue. Having an official language that not all citizens speak also is problematic in terms of political participation and the overall quality of democracy.

President José Maria Pereira Neves announced at the UN that Cabo Verde would use a convention of 'Atlantic Creoleness' in 2025, and he has regularly chosen to give official speeches in Kriolu rather than the usual language of officialdom, Portuguese. There are TV shows and radio programmes in Kriolu, and political campaigns and church services are conducted in it. It's also the language of advertising and of social media.

In 2015, the Boston-based teacher and linguist Manuel Gonçalves published a Kriolu-to-English dictionary with 40,000 words; there's now also a language-learning app that you can download for your phone, Speak Kriolu; and an online Kriolu learning portal for English speakers, Kriolish. Musicians continue to sing in Kriolu, and not just in Cabo Verde, but in the thriving diaspora music scenes in Lisbon, the Netherlands, France and the US. A number of schools and colleges in Massachusetts and Rhode Island teach a Kriolu foreign language curriculum which is approved by their education boards. Lisbon's *Mensagem* newspaper is published in Kriolu for the city's large Cabo Verdean community. While Cabo Verde once hesitated, it seems that its diaspora has decided that Kriolu is the only way forward.

RELIGION AND BELIEFS

Cabo Verde is a secular state with freedom of religion enshrined in the post-independence constitution. The islands have unsurprisingly been predominantly Catholic from the beginning and most other denominations have had little chance to win many converts. Some 85% of the nation is ostensibly Catholic, though the priests complain that they have lost their influence. Nevertheless, many churches are standing-room only on Sunday. The largest minority religions are Protestantism (4%), followed by Christian Rationalism, Islam, Nazarene and Adventist (around 7% in total). This last strand is a Protestant grouping introduced to Brava in the early 1900s by emigrants returning from the USA. The Nazarenes collaborated with Sabbatarians, to build two Protestant churches, and they translated the gospels into Kriolu. The islands are seen as fertile recruiting grounds by several other groups, including the Church of Jesus Christ of Latter Day Saints (popularly known as the Mormons). The Church claims around 5,000 members in Cabo Verde. Jehovah's Witnesses proselytise here as well. Also present is the New Apostolic Church, its large churches dotting the fringes of the larger cities. The growing if still tiny Muslim population mostly comprises immigrants from the West African coast, with a mosque or two in Praia. Jews have a fascinating and formative history in Cabo Verde, having fled here to escape persecution (page 14), though today's population is negligible.

EDUCATION

The government provides free education for all children from 6 to 12 years. Education remains compulsory until the age of 11, though take-up is still less than 80%. Upper-secondary education saw a slight drop from 52.5% to 49.1% in the early 2020s, with that statistic skewed downward by the large number of boys that drop out.

Founded in 2006, the University of Cabo Verde is an amalgam of three colleges; the main campus is in Praia, while the Engineering and Maritime Sciences faculties are based in Mindelo. São Jorge dos Órgãos on Santiago is the site for the university's agricultural research centre. It has around 5,000 students.

The archipelago's other main university, Jean Piaget, is named after the famous Swiss theorist and is based mainly in Praia with some courses taught in Mindelo. It was established in 2001, partly from an existing research institution, and has around 2,000 students and 300 faculty. Other private universities have also appeared since 2010, with a total of ten institutions of higher education now in operation.

CULTURE

Cabo Verde's culture is a complex synthesis of its unique geography, history and heritage. Some 500 years in the making, its Creole identity was one of the world's first but, with only 50 years since nationhood, it is one that is also still in the process of definition. Central to this identity is Kriolu, the nation's unofficial language (page 37), along with music and food: these unite the islands with each other as well as the diaspora. The importance of community and family also remain paramount, with celebrations and festivals fostering a sense of belonging.

The concept of *morabeza* is a national paradigm, employed in everything from tourism websites to the names of hotels, radio stations and neighbourhoods. A Kriolu term, it represents hospitality, kindness, an easy-going attitude, good times

BADIU WITH CRACKED FEET, SAMPADJUDU WITH POTATO BELLIES

Alex Alper

Ethnic conflict may affect many countries in Africa today, but the old saying in the title of this passage is perhaps the extent of ethnic rivalry in Cabo Verde. It compares the Badiu, who inhabit the southern islands, with their northern counterparts, the Sampadjudu. Both are descended from the mix of Africans and Portuguese that settled the islands 500 years ago. They speak dialects of the same Creole, root for the same soccer teams, and the Badiu and Sampadjudu vote for both political parties.

Yet there are notable differences. The quaint farmhouses, the lighter complexions, more Lusophone Kriolu, and Portuguese *fado*-tinged *morna* of the north indicate the more 'European' aspect of northern culture. In contrast, the darker complexions, more African Kriolu, and the thriving traditions of continental origin – from the raw beats of the *batuku* dance to the intricate patterns of the *pánu di téra* weaving – denote the vibrant African traditions still alive in the south.

It is said that Sampadjudus look down on their southern counterparts as less 'sophisticated'. Badius would counter this by saying that their culture is more authentically Cabo Verdean, pointing out that singers from both regions usually choose to sing in Badiu. ALUPEC, the current Kriolu alphabet, is modelled on this variant too.

These time-old stereotypes are rooted in the very origins of the names. Badiu most likely comes from the Portuguese word '*vadiu*' or 'lazy'. It is said that the Badiu slaves ran away from their masters to farm their own plots along the steep ridges. When Portuguese masters would demand their labour, Badius would refuse. Their subsequent label '*Badiu*' persists as a proud symbol of defiance, while their alleged 'cracked feet' belie the myth of laziness: in reality there is a truly formidable Badiu work ethic (or lack of sophistication, as the Sampadjudu might say).

The origins of the word 'Sampadjudu' are more obscure. Many think the term comes from the phrase '*são pa' ajuda*' ('they are for helping'). This may refer to those Santiago inhabitants who were convinced to emigrate northward, to populate and cultivate the Barlavento islands. Their 'potato bellies', according to Badiu lore, refer to the only crop that they managed to cultivate.

These stereotypes mostly serve as fuel for good-natured teasing. As Heavy H, a Sampadjudu rapper, sings, '*Sampadjudu ku Badiu, nos tudo, nos e kul*' ('Badiu and Sampadjudu, all of us, we are cool').

perhaps, or, in the words of novelist Gabriel Mariano, a 'super-cordiality'. Joined by the ubiquitous catchphrase 'no stress', it's a pervasive and seductive image of nonchalant joy. That said, fantasy, invention and nostalgia often underpin any national identity, and Cabo Verde is no exception. Many young Cabo Verdean artists and intellectuals reject *morabeza* as a cynical exercise in essentialism and sanitisation, a notion that denies, or at least blurs, difficult histories and cultural complexities in its quest for unity.

That may well be the case, but it's hard to deny the very real, very obvious cultural tendency to be welcoming and friendly, and that it is often this warm, open and accepting attitude that endears visitors to the country. What does unequivocally

CLOTH

The enslaved on Brava, Santiago and Fogo all wove fine cloth using skills brought with them from the African mainland. The cloth was in great demand in the 17th century among the upper classes along the Rivers of Guinea and it was also worn by the elite as far away as the Gold Coast and Brazil. The deep blues and beautiful patterns of Cabo Verdean cloth were superior to what these people could produce themselves but they were familiar, with a West African aesthetic. It became one of the principal currencies underpinning the slave trade, more in demand than European, Indian or African alternatives.

The demand forced English and French slaving vessels that wished to avoid Cabo Verde to call there first for rolls of cloth so that they could barter on the coast. In the late 17th century, a slave was worth 60 *barafulas*, cloths of standard length and width, which in turn were worth 30 iron bars. In the 18th century, Cabo Verde exported 6,000 of the 2m-long cloths a year to the mainland.

The cloth was woven on a narrow loom made of cane, sticks and banana leaves, which produced strips never more than 7in (17.78cm) wide. Dye was made from urzela, a lichen (page 16), and from the indigo plant. Female slaves pounded the leaves of the latter, pressed them into small loaves, dried them in the sun and then left them to ferment in a pot with water and ashes.

The standard design was a six-banded cloth (*pano, pánu*). Within that strict formula there were many variations. *Panos listrados*, for example, were alternating bands of white and indigo. *Panos simples* were simply white. Others interwove silk with the cotton. *Panos de bicho* interwove white, blue and black threads to make intricate geometric designs including the shapes of leopard and snakeskins and also of Portuguese crosses. The most expensive were cloths of a pure deep blue.

The desirability of such cloth continued for hundreds of years, from the 16th until the early 19th centuries. When the wealthy Diogo Ximenes Vargas died in Cabo Verde in 1624, his estate consisted chiefly of hoards of the cloth: 1,800 *barafulas* in 45 large rolls and 840 plain white cloths in 21 rolls. Their value was recorded to be £630.

Today *pánu* are worn by women either as shawls or as sashes tied just below the waist.

---

define Cabo Verdean identity, and may account at least for some characteristics of *morabeza*, is its legacies of isolation and immigration, its history of slavery and colonial erasure, along with the resilience drawn from living in such a harsh, unforgiving and unpredictable environment.

Novelist Germano Almeida, who was born on Boavista in the days of Salazar's rule, grew up understanding he was Portuguese. He tells of how he finally found a sense of who he was in the poem of fellow Cabo Verdean, Ovídio Martins, *Those Whipped by the East Wind*. Almeida evocatively described how in Martins' work 'our national specificity was once again made clear: we were those whipped by the east wind, those whom the she-goats had taught to eat stones in order not to perish'.

LITERATURE 'Caboverdeanidade' – 'Cabo Verdeanness' – is expressed in poetry, the lyrics of *mornas*, folk stories, poems and novels. The emotion that dominates is a sorrowful one, known as *sodade*. It is often translated as 'nostalgia', though that word has pejorative connotations in English and does not convey the depth of feeling or the unsentimentality of expression. 'Longing' is a better word. *Sodade* is the longing of the emigrant looking across the sea to the motherland; the longing of mothers for their exiled children. Much Cabo Verdean poetry focuses on the sea as the bringer of riches, but also of loneliness and sometimes death: 'Oh gold of the sea, you are dearly earned,' wrote Tavares.

The first Cabo Verdean poetry arose in the 1890s and did not directly address the Cabo Verdean condition. It followed Portuguese patterns with their rigidity of meter and verse. The movement began on São Nicolau, then the intellectual centre of the archipelago.

Writers produced a literary annual and a book of poetry. This period, known as the Classical period, continued until the 1930s. Among the writers were a very few who did not remain bound within Portuguese tradition. It was then, for example, that Tavares honed and popularised the art form of the *morna*, a combination of music, dance and poetry that expresses *sodade*. Another militant journalist and poet, whose importance would not be recognised for decades to come, was Pedro Cardoso, who signed himself 'Afro'. He named his journal *O Manduco* (*The Cudgel*), and was the first Cabo Verdean to – in his *Folclore caboverdiano* – systematically collect traditional stories to argue the cultural importance of Kriolu and to begin to articulate and contextualise ideas such as pan-Africanism and Marxism.

With a clarion call in 1936, the Classical period was shattered and a new literary movement began. *Claridade*, a literary review, was published, addressing head-on the nature of Creole culture and the conditions islanders endured. Tales of the lives of Cabo Verdeans appeared in the classic novel *Chiquinho* by Baltasar Lopes, often considered to be the islands' finest. It is a seminal work, one of the first novels from Portuguese Africa, and it was written in Kriolu. Essays on Kriolu culture and language poured from the *Claridosos* in their irregularly published journal whose last edition appeared in 1960. Other leaders were Jorge Barbosa and Manuel Lopes. Barbosa introduced a new style of poetry which he thought reflected better the Cabo Verdean character, a looser verse for a freer spirit. While it reinvented poetic rhyme and meter, and even genres and language, it was also a kind of rooting into the dusty soil of the islands themselves. His book *Arquipélago*, published in 1935 when he was 33, was his pioneering work. It established the central axis of the Cabo Verdean tragedy, the desire to leave while being forced to stay, and the desire to stay while being forced to leave.

From the 1950s, another group of writers emerged. Many of these had studied in Lisbon, and while living in residences with students from other Portuguese colonies discovered common ground that helped forge a new sense of cultural awareness as well as steering them to overt radical action against the Portuguese. This next generation found their voice in the 'cultural supplement', *Cabo Verde – Boletim de Propaganda e Informação*, a photographic and literary newspaper published in Praia from 1949 until 1963. Influence also came from the *Négritude* movement that had emerged from French colonies in both the Caribbean and Africa. Writers like Manuel Duarte and Onésimo Silveira argued that the *Claridade* generation's conceptualisation of the country was a reductive and escapist one. There was much crossover between the seemingly polemic movements, though, with many writers from the *Claridade* days becoming activists and freedom fighters too.

The post-independence generation's greats include Corsino Fortes, João Manuel Varela, Oswaldo Osório, Arménio Vieira, Dina Salústio, Germano Almeida, Fátima Bettencourt, Jorge Carlos Fonseca and Vera Duarte, all born between 1930 and 1960, and José Luís Hopffer Almada, Filinto Elísio Silva, Vadinho Velhinho, José

KNOW YOUR CABO VERDEAN CONTEMPORARY ARTISTS

While brightly daubed amateur canvases can be procured at any market across Cabo Verde, and street art fills the walls of many of its city streets, Cabo Verde doesn't yet have a commercial gallery scene. The best place to see curated shows of its internationally recognised contemporary artists is at Centro Nacional de Arte, Artesanato e Design (CNAD; page 292) in Mindelo and Palácio da Cultura Ildo Lobo (page 181) in Praia. Here are a few names to look out for, both in Cabo Verde and abroad.

César Schofield Cardoso, born in Mindelo but now based in Achada Santo António in Praia, uses photography, video and digital image manipulation to explore memory, history, politics, environmental vulnerability and everyday life in Cabo Verde. His work has been exhibited at the 2017 Venice Architecture Biennale, and in galleries in Europe, the US and Mozambique. He is featured in Phaidon's *African Artists From 1882 to Now* (2021) and *ATLANTICA: Contemporary Art from Cabo Verde, Guinea Bissau, São Tomé and Príncipe and their Diasporas*, published by Hangar Books (2021).

Yuran Henrique, born on São Vicente and now living between Praia and Lisbon, is a figurative painter whose mixed media canvases draw on illustrative techniques (he is also a cartoonist for the Cabo Verdean newspaper *Expresso das Ilhas*), the expressive Postmodernism of painters like David Salle and the immediacy of street art to interrogate the aesthetic stereotypes attached to Cabo Verde and Africa. In 2023, he was described in the international art press as one of the 'Ten African artists to watch'.

Bento Oliveira, originally from Santo Antão but now based in Mindelo, makes sculptural works that incorporate textiles and recycled materials. He is inspired by the lush sensuality of his home island, and often uses raw materials drawn from the natural world. After completing his fine art education at the University of Pará, in the Brazilian Amazon, his work challenges Cabo Verdean's own Eurocentric preconceptions of what constitutes high culture.

Alex de Silva, born in Mindelo, was a sculptor and painter who died in 2019. His best-known work is *Clave* (2013), a monument commissioned to commemorate the 150th anniversary of the abolition of slavery in the Netherlands. The Dutch words stencilled on the base of the sculpture, in English, '*the body of the slave leaves, the free soul stays*', are taken from traditional *morna* lyrics.

Luiz Tavares and Margarida Fontes, born after 1960. Luís Romano – imprisoned for his writing and later exiled to Angola – began to advocate for the use of Kriolu (or as he referred to it, *língua cabo-verdiana*) as the language of literature from the 1950s onwards, although many of his contemporaries still chose to use Portuguese, if playfully and pushing it to its limits, in the Modernist tradition.

Now the elders of the scene, Arménio Vieira and Germano Almeida were winners of the prestigious Portuguese Camões Prize for literature in 2009 and 2018, respectively, and Dina Salústio won the 2018 English PEN Translation Award. The latter's novel *The Madwoman of Serrano* (in its English translation), explores life on her home island of Santo Antão, and notably was, in 1998, the first novel to be published by a woman in Cabo Verde.

Politics and poetry are odd bedfellows in the Anglophone world, but are relatively commonplace in Cabo Verde. Corsino Fortes, the country's first ambassador to Portugal and France, wrote poems of vivid, incantatory beauty. Former president Jorge Carlos Fonseca's 1998 collection, *Porcos em delírio* (Pigs in Delirium), is a groundbreaking work that recalls Joyce, Breton, free jazz composition and the oral traditions of Kriolu. The mellifluous work of Eileen Barbossa, former prime ministerial advisor, appeared in the inaugural *Africa39* anthology in 2014, a collection created to highlight the work of African writers under 40, and she has won several prizes for her poetry and short stories as far back as 2005.

As a postcolonial nation and a diglossic one, Cabo Verdeans instinctively understand contemporary literary concepts such as intertextuality and hybridity, and their writers of the late 20th century can be found in the new canons of world literature. Portuguese publishers such as Rosa de Porcelana Editora and Pedro Cardoso Livraria act as a conduit to the world, publishing work in both Kriolu and Portuguese, as well as in translation, especially for the US market. Writers of Cabo Verdean ancestry in the US, such as Jewelle Gomez and Shauna Barbosa, also evoke a diasporic imagery that continues the dialogue with Cabo Verde in English.

MUSIC AND DANCE Music underpins Cabo Verdean life, gives it continuity and draws meaning from collective, often brutal, experience. In its many forms, it seems to be the oil that allows the Cabo Verde machine to work, or the glue that holds everything together. Cabo Verde relies heavily on its varied musical traditions to project its culture and history, both within the islands and also on to the world stage. No visitor to the archipelago will go far without experiencing some musical accompaniment at some point, and often the experiences will be moving and memorable. These may be simply a radio station playing in a taxi, a band performing in a restaurant, a frenzied and spontaneous session in an unlikely location (page 238) or the beat of the *tambour* at one of the many religious festivals. Any visit to Cabo Verde will be immeasurably enriched by close contact with the islands' music and musicians.

Traditional and modern musical forms With thanks to Dr Lucy Durán, Senior Lecturer in African Music, SOAS University of London, formerly BBC Radio 3

There is some irony in the fact that the dramatic, barren and remote volcanic islands of Cabo Verde have given rise to some of the world's most luscious and accessible musical traditions. But maybe it's not so surprising – the archipelago is on the crossroads of the Atlantic, and has absorbed many different styles over the centuries. Cabo Verde's music, like its language, Kriolu, was born in the particular geographies and histories of the islands, a potent mixture of Portuguese and West African culture. Added to that are elements from the Caribbean, Brazil, and further afield, introduced by sailors passing through the country. Plus, mass emigration of islanders to cities like Lisbon, Paris, Dakar, Boston and Rotterdam has also played a major role in the development of their music.

There is now a vibrant music industry especially on Santiago and São Vicente, with recording studios and festivals, but many Cabo Verdean musicians live abroad. They have contributed to keeping the four main traditions – *morna*, *coladeira*, *batuku* and *funaná* – alive and constantly evolving.

Morna and *coladeira* are ballroom styles that are relatively refined, with their melodies and lyrics written by well-known composers and poets, while *batuku* is a solo-chorus folk style traditionally sung and danced by women. *Funaná* is a rough-and-ready dance music for festive days, with frenetic melodies on accordion and metal scraper, fuelled by the consumption of large quantities of locally produced *grogue*.

Morna is Cabo Verde's best-known music. When I went to the islands in 2009 with BBC Radio 3, in order to record programmes for World Routes, time and again I heard the phrase '*morna* is the soul of our people'. It first became famous in the 1990s through the haunting voice of Cesária Évora, Cabo Verde's celebrated 'barefoot diva'. Her songs like 'Sodade', 'Mar Azul' and 'Miss Perfumado' captivated audiences around the world. *Morna* has a melancholic feel to it, and is often compared to Portuguese *fado*, because of its minor-key melodies and themes of separation and lost love. But it also has a sensual edginess. Its shuffling syncopated rhythms clearly originate in Africa, but are tempered by the encounter with Portuguese, and recall Brazilian styles like samba.

Morna's languorous melodies are traditionally accompanied on an ensemble of string instruments. One or more Spanish guitars (or *violao*), the *cavaquinho* (small four-string guitar), which is strummed, the *viola* (ten-string guitar with five double courses of metal strings), and violin, are woven together into a rich tapestry. Piano and wind instruments like clarinet or saxophone may also be added to the *morna* ensemble. *Morna* orchestras and singers can be found on all the islands, from small villages such as Chã das Caldeiras high up in the volcanic crater of Fogo, to the

CESÁRIA ÉVORA

Cesária Évora, the 'barefoot diva' who died in 2011, had a dedicated international following, particularly in Paris. Her enduring appeal lies in the quality of her voice which, in addition to its mellow elements, is untrained, simple and unaffected – the perfect vehicle for expressing the poetry of the *morna*. It earned her the names 'Aguadente' and 'Red Wine'. Évora is also loved because she sang as if she had just stepped into one of the Mindelo bars – lack of pretension, even bluntness, were her hallmarks. She sang the *morna* accompanied mainly by violin, acoustic guitar, accordion, piano, clarinet and the mandolin-like *cavaquinho*.

Évora was born in 1941. It was a friend of Évora's who remarked on her voice when she was a teenager. She joined a band at the age of 16 and sang in the bars of Mindelo, as well as on Portuguese cruise ships. She made no money from it, apart from a little when she performed at Portuguese official functions – but even that source disappeared with independence in 1975. Her humble career seemed to have evaporated and for a decade she refused to sing.

In 1985, at the age of 45, Évora was invited to Portugal by the Organisation of Cabo Verdean Women to contribute to a record. She went, but the record was not a hit. However, while she was there she met a businessman, José da Silva, who offered to work with her. Three years later she cut a record, La *Diva aux Pieds Nus* (The Barefoot Diva), in Paris. She went on to make several more albums, including *Destino di Belita*, *Cesária*, *Miss Perfumado*, *Mar Azul* (Blue Sea) and *Cabo Verde*. The album *Voz d'Amor* won a Grammy Award in 2003. For a while she lived in Paris, but retained houses on São Vicente. Having already announced the end of her stellar career due to health problems, she died in December 2011, prompting two days of national mourning.

isolated town of Nova Sintra on Brava, shrouded in cloud most of the year. Each place has its own special regional style and composers.

Morna is said to have originated on Boavista in the 18th century, one of the islands that provided salt to the Portuguese Empire. It was popularised by Eugénio Tavares (1867–1930), a poet from Brava, the smallest of the inhabited islands – a place from which many sailors left, never to return. Indeed, *morna* is the perfect soundtrack to this inaccessible spot in the mid-Atlantic whose name means 'wild'. Tavares, who had spent years abroad himself, wrote beautiful songs in Kriolu that are now like anthems for Cabo Verdeans – such as 'Hora di Bai' – about the pain of separation from and longing – *sodade* – for loved ones and the homeland.

The concept of *sodade*, so fundamental to *morna*, resonates deeply with the Cabo Verdean experience of emigration. In the words of one musician: '*morna* expresses the despair of wanting to stay, but having to leave'. The extreme conditions on the islands, the years of slavery, drought and oppressive colonial rule, and the seafaring way of life, have made Cabo Verdean culture what it is. One of the most influential *morna* composers of the 20th century, B Leza (1905–58), whose music is performed by dozens of artists, wrote a song called 'The Sea is the Home of Longing' ('*Mar e mora di sodadi*').

> The sea is the home of longing
> it separates us from our faraway land
> it keeps us from our mothers, our friends
> without certainty of meeting again.

'The ocean is very important to us, as a bridge to the world and also a prison,' commented Mayra Andrade, a hugely popular Cabo Verdean singer/songwriter who is now based in Lisbon, in an interview with British journalist Maya Jaggi. 'Cabo Verdean people need music to feel free.'

However, Cabo Verde's music is by no means only sad – Cabo Verdeans love to dance. This explains the enduring popularity of the country's second national style, *coladeira*, with its infectious rhythms. The name comes from the Portuguese word '*cola*', meaning 'glue', so called because the dancing couple hold each other tightly, hips swinging together to the two-step beat. *Coladeira* developed out of *morna* sometime in the early 20th century, and shares some of its melodic and harmonic features, but it goes at almost twice the speed. Its lyrics are often humorous and satirical, and include sexual innuendo (eg: 'Sangue Beirona', one of the best known *coladeiras*, says 'if you go to the bottom of the hill, you will find the essence of a woman').

Most Cabo Verdean bands have a healthy dose of *coladeiras* in their repertoire, and this is the style you are most likely to hear at clubs and hotel bars whether on São Vicente, Cabo Verde's musical capital, or in Lisbon, which has several popular Cabo Verdean clubs and dance halls, such as B Leza (named after the composer), where many of Cabo Verde's greatest stars have performed. There are also commercialised forms of *coladeira*, such as *cola-zouk* (*zouk* is a syncopated rhythm that was made popular globally in the 1980s by Kassav from Martinique). A much-admired musician from São Vicente who played a tasteful form of *cola-zouk*, was Bius, who died in 2009. A more formulaic and heavily commercialised style, *cabo-love*, was popularised by musicians abroad like Gil Semedo, a Cabo Verdean singer based in Rotterdam.

PALOP musicians (PALOP is an acronym denoting the five former Portuguese territories in Africa) often find themselves working together in bands and studios in the diaspora, and their styles inevitably cross-influence each other. Thus *cola-zouk*

> ## MAKING YOUR CABO VERDEAN PLAYLIST
>
> If you want to search out recordings of modern Cabo Verdean music, here are some ideas to start you off. This list is designed to be a taster: of course there is far more to be discovered.
>
> The *grande dame* is of course **Cesária Évora**, with at least ten albums, including *Miss Perfumado* and *São Vicente di Longe*. **Bau**, a musician who plays regularly in Mindelo, has produced *Djailza*, *Tope da Coroa*, *Inspiration* and *Bli Mundo*. Go for the last if you are buying only one. **Bana** is often referred to as the King of *Morna*, and his death was royally mourned in 2013. The 1972 album *Coladeras: The Best of Bana* provides a suitable introduction.
>
> Other, more recent, artists have one thing in common: mixing traditional Cabo Verdean music with influences from around the world. **Lura**, whom some critics have suggested is Évora's successor, has been well known since her first album release in 2004. Try *M'Bem di Fora (I've Come from Far Away)*. It has a rich mixture of her music, with influences from many of the islands. **Teófilo Chantre**, who composed several of Évora's songs, is a skilled guitarist and has a rich, baritone voice. Try his album *Viaja*. **Mayra Andrade**, who often sings in Kriolu, is one of the country's most beloved daughters for her seductive, sophisticated vocal style, despite being born in Cuba and now living in Lisbon. Start with her album *Stória, stória*, and then the more recent *Manga*. **Tcheka**, a guitarist and vocalist, is said to be able to reproduce the feel of all Cabo Verdean instruments and rhythms on a single guitar. Try *Nu Monda*. **Cordas do Sol** is a band from Santo Antão whose songs are sung in the particular kriol of their home island and mix its traditional

closely resembles *passada*, a popular dance style from Angola. Cuban salsa is also an important strand in Cabo Verde's dance music, as in Cesária Évora's album *Cafe Atlántico*, or Voz de Cabo Verde's album *Voz de Cabo Verde Live*.

Apart from *morna* and *coladeira*, two other genres of Cabo Verdean music are well known and can be considered national, even though they originate specifically on the island of Santiago. *Batuku* and *funaná* are rootsy, vibrantly percussive styles associated with the poorer sector of the population, of African descent. Both genres were forbidden at times by the Portuguese colonial regime, feared for their African sound and their rebellious lyrics. But since independence, in 1975, many artists have taken inspiration from these two traditions.

Batuku is a unique type of music performed by women, who beat out interlocking rhythms of two against three on folded cloth or pillows called *txabeta*, held between their knees. As the pounding of the *txabeta* intensifies and gets faster, women take turns to get up and dance, tying a cloth around their hips to emphasise their hips swaying, while sometimes balancing a bottle on their heads. The songs are organised into solo lines with a choral response in typically African fashion.

The word *batuku* comes from the Portuguese '*batucar*', meaning 'to drum'. It is the oldest form of music from Cabo Verde, dating back, according to oral tradition, to the late 15th century. 'Slave women used to sing these songs in the back yard of the slave houses, when their men were out working the fields. It was our form of protest,' commented a member of Nos Herança, a professional *batuku* group based in Cidade Velha (the first settlement on Cabo Verde, around 1462). Nos Herança is one of many superb *batuku* ensembles from the island of Santiago.

One of the sub-genres of *batuku* is *finaçon*, which features improvised song texts of social critique. The most cherished *finaçon* singer was Nha Nácia Gomi, known

rhythms with modern instrumentation. On Fogo, **Agostinho da Pina**, a violinist with a vision impairment, has an album called *Augusto Cego*.

Kamin di Bedju is a 2012 album by **Michel Montrond** that did well on the world music charts. Anything by **Nancy Vieira** will appeal to lovers of stirring ballads, likewise anything by **Bius** if Latin is your thing. Popular female singers with soulful voices are **Néuza**, who debuted with the upbeat *Flor di Bila* album in 2013, and **Carmen Souza**, with *Protegid* in 2010. For more African-tinged style there's *Gerasonobu* by **Elida Almeida** and **Jennifer Solidade** with *Um Click*. Recently GQ Portugal's Man of The Year in the music category, **Dino D'Santiago** mixes traditional Cabo Verdean rhythms with a dance floor sensibility and is part of Lisbon's electro nu soul scene. Start with his 2020 release, *Kriolu*.

For hip hop, house, Afrobeat and electro sounds, look out for hit single '*Nha Terra Nha Cretcheu*' by **Nissah**, one of Cabo Verde's first female hip hop artists, or her later Afrobeat release '10xaz'. 'Ken Ki Fla' by **Mynda Guevara** is popular on the European festival circuit, while **Nenny**'s 'Tequila' and '*Nha Cidade*' by **Djeison Lumi** might be heard on the dancefloors of Lisbon, Rio or Boston.

Finally, for some compilations try *Funaná*, an album dedicated to that musical form. *The Soul of Cape Verde* features a good mix of some of the bands mentioned here. *Travadinha* is a popular instrumental collection. *Space Echo, The Mystery Behind the Cosmic Sound of Cabo Verde Finally Revealed!*, documents the era when Cabo Verde went electric in the late 70s and early 80s, with some glorious synth and psychedelic sounds, a place where funk and *funaná* meet.

as 'the queen of *batuku*'. Her uncompromising, witty lyrics were much admired by Cabo Verdeans, as was her deeply traditional style, reminiscent of the choral singing of the Manjak from Guinea-Bissau – undoubtedly one of the principal sources of slaves brought to the archipelago.

Other *batuku* groups like Kultura Speransa from Ribeira da Prata, near Tarrafal in the north of Santiago, are seeking to innovate by adding instruments such as drums, guitar or accordion, and referencing global dance styles. Like many *batuku* groups, Kultura Speransa are associated with a community youth programme. Their songs are hard-hitting; for example, 'Droga mau viciu' laments the pernicious influence of drugs on people's lives. *Batuku* in its traditional form is also widely practised among Cabo Verdean expats, both as part of community programmes and as a symbol of female power and solidarity. It was the young Santiago composer Orlando Pantera (who died at the age of 33 in 2001) who first introduced the sounds of *batuku* into popular Cabo Verdean music, influencing many young divas living abroad like Lura, Sara Tavares and Mayra Andrade.

Funaná is the other roots style that has made an impact on contemporary popular music from Cabo Verde. Like *coladeira*, it is a couple dance, but it is more rural, and goes at lightning speed. In its traditional setting it's played on button accordion, called *gaita* – a generic term for bagpipes in Portuguese – and iron scraper, called *ferro* or *ferrinho* (little iron) – a long thin piece of iron with serrated edges scraped with an iron rod. *Funaná* is celebratory music for feast days such as São João (24 June). Its origins are not well known, but it probably pre-dates the arrival of the accordion on Santiago in the early 20th century. The best-known performer was the singer and accordionist Kodé di Dona (died 2009), from São Francisco village in the plateau above Cidade Velha – a charismatic man for whom *funaná* was a family affair, his young son playing *ferrinho* while the rest of the family joined in on the choruses. *Funaná* was frowned upon during colonial rule, but after independence it was popularised and modernised by a band called Bulimundo. Later generations of singer-songwriters such as Boy Ge Mendes, Tito Paris, Mayra Andrade and Nancy Vieira have included *funaná* in their repertoire, though few, except for the group Ferro Gaita, continue the radical roots style of Kodé di Dona.

There are other lesser-known forms of folk music on the islands, mainly associated with religious festivities. *Tabanka* is from Santiago and is a semi-religious folk theatre that involves the ritual stealing of a saint and its return, celebrated with processional dancing and the blowing of conches. On Fogo island, *pilão* and *bandera* are songs with percussion performed to celebrate saint days, especially that of São Filipe, Fogo's patron saint. *Pilão* is accompanied by the interlocked pounding of grain in a mortar by several women, a tradition established there by slaves from West Africa. Tcheka, who lives in Praia, capital of Santiago, is typical of the generation of singer-songwriters from the islands whose music is infused with these sounds, but transformed into something completely new.

The international stage Cabo Verdean music is flourishing. Cesária Évora, barefoot diva with the mellow, unschooled voice, was the figurehead of the *morna* (page 44), and sold albums in the hundreds of thousands, particularly in France. Her enormous popularity has hardly been interrupted by her death in December 2011.

FOOTBALL: EVOLUTION FROM MINNOWS TO BLUE SHARKS

Murray Stewart

Despite the Cabo Verdean Football Federation joining FIFA in 1986, until 2013, any global profile enjoyed by Cabo Verde in the world of football had relied almost entirely on the success of those of Cabo Verdean origin who were able to seek fame and fortune elsewhere. Aficionados of the 'beautiful game' will be very familiar with names such as Nani of Manchester United fame and Henrik Larsson, formerly of Glasgow Celtic and Barcelona, but not so familiar with their connections with Cabo Verde. And why should they be? Despite both players' pride in their Cabo Verdean heritage, Nani played for Portugal's national team, his country of birth, and Larsson won 106 caps for Sweden before his retirement. As the 2013 African Cup of Nations approached, surely a nation with a population of half a million was forever destined to remain as minnows, swimming harmlessly in the vast ocean of soccer obscurity?

Not so. After not even bothering to enter the competition 18 times, withdrawing once and failing to qualify for the finals on seven successive occasions, incredibly the 'Blue Sharks' of Cabo Verde overcame four-time tournament winners Cameroon to reach the finals for the first time. Nor was the fairy tale over, as two draws and a last-minute victory propelled the Sharks into the unknown waters of the quarter-finals. Finally, the Sharks were sunk by Ghana, courtesy of a penalty and a goal 5 minutes into injury time. The streets of Praia and other archipelago towns filled with flag-waving fans, eager to acclaim the team's unprecedented success.

And so, with the 2014 World Cup in Portuguese-speaking Brazil on the horizon, the Blue Sharks set about the task of qualifying. By mid-2013, they topped their

Cabo Verde's various sounds have also become increasingly better known in the Anglophone world through festival performances and compilations with the rise of interest in 'world' music from the 1990s. From the 1960s, the singer Bana – who died in 2013 – and the talented and highly influential Vieira brothers' outfit Voz de Cabo Verde, popularised the *morna* in Europe and were among the key innovators of the form in the 1970s. They were influenced by Latin American and Brazilian rhythms and styles, particularly *cumbia*.

Well-known Cabo Verdean musicians of the late 20th century include Paulino Vieira, Dany Silva, Gabriela Mendes and Tito Paris. The Mendes brothers, emigrants from Fogo, formed a band in 1976 and have worked particularly with the *coladeira*. They also incorporated Angolan music, introduced to them by friends on Fogo returning from their military service on the mainland.

The late Norberto Tavares and bands Bulimundo, Simentera and Finaçon are seen as the 1980s and 90s innovators that transformed the accordion-based *funaná* into the high-energy offspring we have today, as well being a huge part of Cabo Verde's post-independence identity formation. The group Os Tubarões, with superstar lead singer Ildo Lobo, were, though, possibly the most famous of the post-independence musical acts, popularising the various Cabo Verdean sounds internationally and combining them with political, anti-colonial lyrics.

Contemporary Cabo Verdean music often has a symbiotic relationship with the music of Latin America, and today it is also infused with house music, Afrobeat, hip hop, European electro sounds and other hybrid musical forms. For a small smattering of examples of current talent, see page 46, and the artists represented

African qualifying group and seemed set fair to book their place at the world's premier tournament for the first time. But disaster struck. A momentous victory against Tunisia was annulled when it was discovered that the Sharks had fielded an ineligible player. They were duly demoted to second place and an appeal to the authorities failed. But the meteoric rise of Cabo Verde's stars was only temporarily halted, as they qualified comfortably for the 2015 African Cup of Nations. With a succession of draws, they were then eliminated in the group stages without losing a game.

Mirroring Cabo Verdeans' wider tradition of seeking opportunity through emigration, the current squad of players earn their day-to-day livings by playing for teams in many other countries, including those in Portugal, Spain, Belgium, France and the Netherlands. But despite this scattering of talents across the globe, and the tragic administrative blunder that cost them a first World Cup Final appearance, 2013 had demonstrated that, once brought back together to represent their country, the Blue Sharks were capable of swimming with the big fish of football. In terms of FIFA ranking, Cabo Verde hit an all-time high of 39 in 2016, and while they've not returned to that form since, they did make waves in the 2023 Africa Cup of Nations (AFCON 2023). Beginning with a shock 2-1 win over Ghana's Black Stars in their opening game, they went on to an impressive 3-0 victory over Mozambique to reach the knockout stages, eventually pushing Egypt all the way to penalties in the quarter-final.

More national triumph may well be on the horizon. At time of writing, Cabo Verde had snatched a crucial win over Angola and Mauritius in the 2026 World Cup qualifiers, sending them to the top of their group.

by the Lusafrica (w lusafrica.com) label. Purists do fear that true Cabo Verdean musical culture could vanish, but as a musical scene that has flourished precisely because of its ability to absorb and transform divergent influences, Cabo Verdean music can only continue to be distinctive and fertile. That broad remit also means it's increasingly central to both the Lusophone and mainland African industry, with events like the Atlantic Music Expo now having been held in Praia for more than a decade. The event facilitates international connections via a professional marketplace, networking sessions, conferences and musical showcases.

In any case, the purists have little reason to worry. In 2019, *morna* was recognised by UNESCO as an 'intangible cultural heritage of humanity', celebrating it as fundamental to Cabo Verdean social and cultural life. It is taught in workshops across the islands, there are radio programmes dedicated to it and it is performed at weddings, christenings and family reunions. And a televised *morna* competition, *Todo Mundo Canta*, takes place on every island, encouraging a new generation of performers to continue in the tradition.

FOLKLORE Folklore is rich with tales of Sancho, the mischievous monkey who lives in the mountains and causes chaos wherever he goes. He remained in the hills throughout the Portuguese oppression, waiting until it was time to 'turn all upside down', as the poem on page 10 describes. Sancho's threat of confusion is generally a desirable one, a welcome anarchy upsetting those in power. But sometimes Sancho is purely an agent of trouble. He pops up in proverbs, such as the one reminding the lazy or naughty that they will go hungry if they don't till the soil: 'Beans don't grow where monkeys are.' Another character is Nho Lobo, the lazy wolf, who appears in many cycles of tales in the oral tradition handed down through generations. A Nho Lobo story generally conveys a moral for children. Bli Mundo is the ox who broke free from the yoke of the *trapiche*, and symbolises liberty. A charming children's book is *Do Tambor a blimundo*, available as an English translation (page 376).

Speech is also rich in proverbs: 'A scratching chicken will meet its grandmother'; 'A man without a wife is a vase without flowers'; 'A lame goat does not take a siesta'; 'In cooking, eggs show up rotten'; 'Some get the honey, while the working people are left with gall' and 'They'll pay you to climb up the coconut palm but getting down again, that's your affair'.

2

Practical Information

WHEN TO VISIT

The islands are warm and sunny all year round so for many visitors without any special interests, it doesn't really matter when they go. For **windsurfers** the best months are January and February while **divers** will find the calmest waters and peak visibility from June to December; **beach lovers** might wish to avoid the windy winter months. **Fishermen** after marlin should opt for May to October, while tuna fishing is at its best in August. For **hikers**, the mountainous islands are significantly more beautiful during and just after the rainy season of July to December, though flooding can impede some Santo Antão hikes. The heaviest rainfall is usually in August and September. For those concerned about the heat, the peak is in September (with an average daily temperature of 30°C), with the trough being in January (average 24°C). For those who wish to see **nesting turtles** the season is June to October, peaking in mid-July and August. Turtle hatchlings are born from mid-August until the end of November. **Whale-watchers** will find the best opportunities in March and April, particularly off Boavista. **Photographers** should avoid December to March when the harmattan winds dull the light, and leave deposits of sand. **Party animals and music lovers** might choose February for the São Vicente Carnival, or for that on São Nicolau; August for the São Vicente Baía das Gatas music festival; or May for the Gamboa music festival on Santiago. To coincide your visit with one of the more low-key **festivals**, consult the individual island chapters. Those on a **tight budget** will find hotels cheaper from April to June and in October, and should definitely avoid Christmas and Carnival time. **Peace seekers** might avoid July and August, when Cabo Verde is full of both European holidaymakers and *emigrante* families taking their summer holidays back home. As well as Christmas and Carnival times, the whole period from November to March is high season. Unfortunately, this is also the harmattan season, when the occasional sand storm is so dense as to disrupt flights for days at a time, especially those to and from Sal and Boavista.

HIGHLIGHTS

HIKING Cabo Verde is a superb hiking destination – the vistas from the mountains of Santo Antão or from the depth of its gorges, the lonely slopes of Brava and the stunning interior of the brooding volcano crater of Fogo make for a unique experience. Much of the walking on Cabo Verde is on the extraordinary cobbled paths that have been constructed in the most unlikely corners and up the steepest of slopes, making the walking much easier than might be construed from the map.

On Santo Antão the classic walks are up or down the *ribeiras*, taking transport at the beginning or end (page 328). On Fogo, the highlight for many is to ascend the

Pico, the 2,829m spectacular volcano cone and, for some, to spend a night or two in its shadow. On Brava there are endless walks criss-crossing the steep 'flower' island where you are unlikely to meet any other travellers. São Nicolau is a gentle and quiet island with a hidden, green and mountainous heartland filled with beautiful walks, while Santiago has its own mountainous spine with some fine walks between it and the coast.

Most of the walks require a certain amount of fitness because they are steep, and a certain elasticity of knee for the descents. In this book each is rated for difficulty according to a rough scheme:

1 Easy path with little fitness required.
2 Medium fitness, with some bursts of steep ascent and/or the odd slippery stretch.
3 Prolonged steep walking and/or slippery, uncobbled paths.

While we attempt to make our assessments uniform, it is inevitable that our judgements of time lengths and difficulty are a little subjective. Because of this, we have identified the writer of each hike description at the top: CW – fit male, mid-thirties; AI – unfit female, mid-thirties; AH – fit male, 20; HC – unfit female, mid-thirties; MS – fit male, mid-fifties. For those seeking very gentle hikes there are options on Santo Antão and Boavista, but few attractive flat walks on the other islands. You can penetrate quite far by vehicle, however – into Fogo's crater and far up one or two of Santo Antão's *ribeiras*.

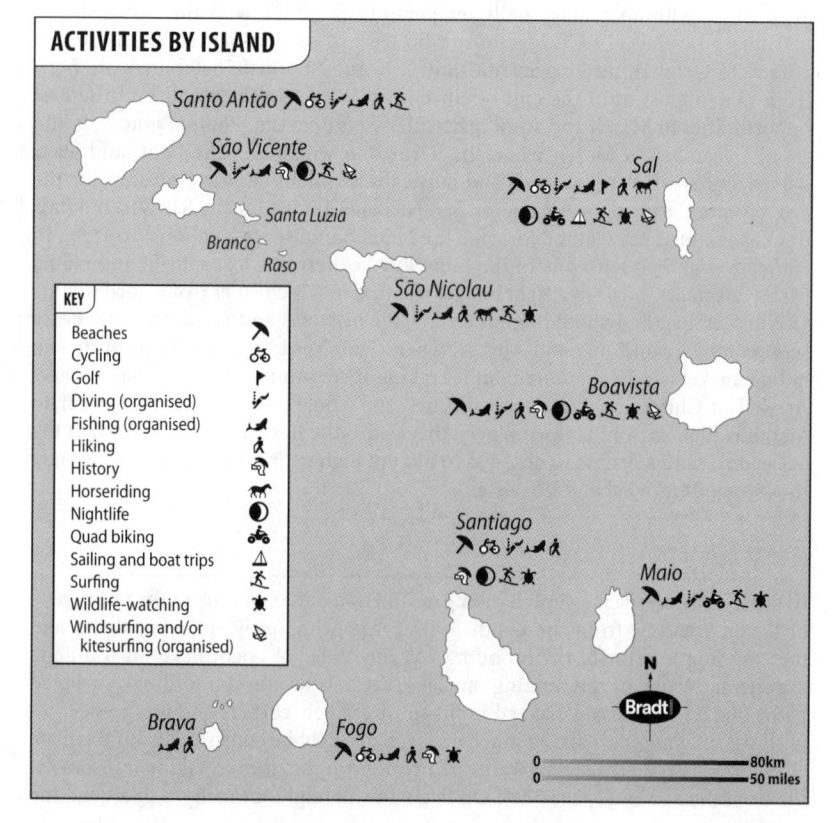

ACTIVITIES BY ISLAND

KEY
- Beaches
- Cycling
- Golf
- Diving (organised)
- Fishing (organised)
- Hiking
- History
- Horseriding
- Nightlife
- Quad biking
- Sailing and boat trips
- Surfing
- Wildlife-watching
- Windsurfing and/or kitesurfing (organised)

0 — 80km
0 — 50 miles

52

TIPS FOR PLANNING YOUR TRIP

- Avoid using ferries (except to Santo Antão and Brava) unless you are on a long trip, enjoy the adventure and aren't prone to seasickness.
- Try to book your internal flights before leaving home, as flight schedules can be less than accommodating.
- Visit no more than two islands (in a week) or three or four (in two weeks).
- Set up your itinerary to minimise the number of flights and unwanted stopovers.
- Select your islands carefully: they differ wildly in character and infrastructure and it can be hard to change your plans.

BEACHES Cabo Verde has miles and miles of virgin coastline – but forget any vision of palm trees. Whether white or black sands, the shores are breathtakingly beautiful – and many of them are remote and desolate too. Sal, Boavista and Maio have the best white beaches, so upmarket holiday resorts are very common in Santa Maria on Sal and there are a few, too, on Boavista. There are more under construction and some seemingly abandoned projects on Maio and São Nicolau. Beware, though, that some beach tourists complain about the wind and some seem to be plagued in the rainy months by flies and mosquitoes, too; others have complained that swimming was not safe in front of their hotel: check before you book. Unless you are confident in rough surf, keen swimmers might want to choose accommodation with a pool, rather than rely on the ocean.

DIVING *with Jacquie Cozens*

Will Cabo Verde soon rival the Red Sea for diving or is it all just hype? The marine life is certainly abundant and there is the novelty of being in the Atlantic yet encountering tropical fish such as parrotfish, angelfish or the occasional whale shark. In addition, flight times from Europe are relatively short, you are never likely to tie up on a crowded dive site and there are exciting seasonal events such as the migration of humpback whales and the breeding of turtles. That said, there are no classic coral reefs, there are occasional strong currents and wind, the water is colder and diving is in its infancy.

Although there are centres on five of the islands, most of the focus is on Sal which has a variety of sites in Santa Maria Bay within 10 to 15 minutes' boat ride, a few along the west coast and some less frequently visited places on the east coast. The underground topography consists of rocky ridges, pinnacles and boulders and underwater arches and caves. On Sal there are a handful of wrecks at between 5m and 30m, including a couple that were purpose-sunk as recently as the 2010s, though actually diving them can be difficult. Sal also offers the opportunity to dive in caves that have been formed by lava in the north of the island. A classic dive is Buracona, a 40m tunnel that emerges at the 'Blue Eye', a pool where you can surface to see the surprised faces of land-based tourists looking down on you.

Dive sites in Cabo Verde are usually ridges with big overhangs smothered in bright-yellow polyps and populated with large aggregations of surgeonfish, goatfish, parrotfish, Atlantic bigeyes, enormous scribbled filefish and metre-long cornet fish. At certain times *papaguia* (Guinea grunts) form huge balls of up to 1,000 fish. The macro life is also abundant, with numerous nudibranchs, tiny coral eels, sharpnose puffers and frogfish. Large marine life you may encounter include dolphins and five species of turtles, including loggerheads which come ashore to nest between June and October. Species such as endangered tiger sharks and bull sharks were once common but are now more often seen being gutted on the pier. Sometimes there are nurse sharks, lemon sharks, reef sharks and manta rays. Humpback whales visit in the spring.

In general the diving around all the islands is reliably good and, compellingly, it is very underexplored. The potential as a diving destination is huge, as the relative isolation in the middle of a vast ocean is likely to lead to exciting and unexpected encounters. Water temperatures range from 21°C to 27°C. Diving and courses are available on Sal, Boavista, Santiago, São Vicente, Santo Antão and São Nicolau. All the centres have rental gear. Be aware that there is no operational recompression chamber on any of the islands.

FISHING Cabo Verde has superlative big-game fishing. Blue marlin, for example, is big both in numbers and in size (fish up to 750lb/340kg have been caught here). There are also tiger shark, sailfish, swordfish, kingfish and striped and white marlin. Closer in to shore there are wahoo, albacore, yellowfin tuna, grouper and dorado. Big-game fishing is best from São Nicolau (page 347) and between São Vicente and Santo Antão (page 279, though it is also possible from Maio (page 212). Hiring a boat for the day for such a trip is around €200–1,000 per day, depending on the size and type of boat, while booking an all-inclusive week's trip is around €1,000–3,000 per person, depending on numbers. Around the archipelago it is possible to join local fishermen on their trips, a great experience whether you personally catch anything or not. Often they go out a few hundred metres, drop anchor, and fish for skipjack, grouper, squirrelfish and many other varieties. Some go night-fishing for moray. The locals use harpoons to catch lobster, octopus and parrotfish. As sport fishing grows in popularity, so do less than ecologically sound practices. Many operators with limited knowledge of marine life take undersized fish and target marginal species such as shark, marlin and other billfish. If you don't want to contribute to this indiscriminate practice look out for a skipper who practises catch and release.

SAILING, SURFING, WINDSURFING AND KITESURFING With the trade winds providing a remarkably steady force 5 to 6 in winter falling to a gentler force 3 to 4 in summer, wind is never lacking, and Cabo Verde has become an international windsurfing and kitesurfing destination.

Sailing Sailing around the islands is still quite unusual. At any one time there might be 20 or more boats moored in the main harbour of São Vicente, and a few more to be found in those of Sal and Santiago. A promised new marina project in Praia has not materialised. Facilities are far inferior to the Azores or Canaries, but there are beautiful anchorages at Baía da Murdeira on Sal, at the remote Fajã d'Água on Brava and at Tarrafal in north Santiago. In fact, each island has some sort of shelter but it may be a long trek to get provisions and an even longer one if you need spare parts.

There are many day excursions in large sailing boats and powerboats on Sal but less available on other islands. Yachts can also be rented, with or without a skipper, on São Vicente. The *Itoma* (w itoma.at) is a 23m (70ft) motor-catamaran with room for 16 passengers; its owners organise cruising, diving and windsurfing tours. (For further information, see page 278.)

Surfing Cabo Verde has 965km of coastline, dotted with reefs and points and steady wind throughout the year, and its reputation as an international windsurfing, kitesurfing and surfing destination is growing. The swell from the open Atlantic, during the winter, can be big – similar to the Canaries and the Azores but it is warmer. The Barlavento – the islands in the north – are in the best position for winter surf, while the Sotavento – southern islands – pick up summer, tropical swells and swells from far away in the south Atlantic. The wind is strongest in the winter and calmest from May to September.

The winter swell season runs from January to March and at this time the average deep-swell height is about 1.8m. The swells tend to hit the western coasts of the islands and wrap around into spots heading south. The result is offshore conditions with northeast winds.

The best-known island for surfing is Sal, whose most famous wave is at Ponta Preta – a long, classic right-hand reef with 200m rides. There are also surfing spots on Santiago – Tarrafal, and the coast in the southeast, south of Ponte de Lobo. The surf is mostly reef breaks but there are some beach breaks. Boards are available for hire on Sal, São Vicente and in Tarrafal on Santiago.

CRUISING IN CABO VERDE *John Abbott and Murray Stewart*

Sailing to Cabo Verde and spending some time sailing between islands is growing slowly more popular. There is a wide variety of scenery and culture and incredibly friendly people. Many find it a convenient location to stop for a while before an Atlantic crossing.

All islands are suitable cruising destinations but the quality and suitability of the harbours and anchorages vary greatly. The Atlantic swell is all-pervasive and can make any of the anchorages uncomfortable, if not dangerous. A good pilot book, such as *Atlantic Islands* by Anne Hammick, is essential for visiting the less-frequented islands and for guidance on working into some of the trickier anchorages.

Given the prevailing northeast winds it is best to cruise from north to south and from east to west. The island of Sal makes a good and friendly arrival destination. The port of Palmeira is well sheltered from all but the southwest winds and there are excellent anchorages further south at Murdeira. Santa Maria Bay and Ponta Sino also offer shelter.

Boavista is an easy day's sail from Sal and has an excellent, isolated anchorage in the shallows between the islet of Ilhéu do Sal Rei and the mainland. A short dinghy ride to the rustic town of Sal Rei allows you to sample the outstanding fish restaurants or, surf permitting, you can land the dinghy on the miles of sandy beach that line the west coast or visit the remains of the fort on Ilhéu do Sal Rei.

Tarrafal on São Nicolau is a pretty anchorage where the water is very clear. The island of Maio in the southern group boasts plenty of fish, birds and deserted beaches; it is possible to anchor at Porto de Maio on the southwest side of the island, though the swell often makes disembarking on the pier a bit tricky.

The country's capital, Praia, on Santiago, has good anchorage. Nearby Fogo is a spectacular island with a good settled weather anchorage on the west coast. Brava is another spectacular and pretty island where it is possible to anchor in the tiny harbour of Furna.

As of 2024, São Vicente hosted the only marina in the island chain, in Mindelo. Shelter is excellent and a good range of facilities, chandlery and insurer-approved repairs are available for those preparing to cross the Atlantic.

Windsurfing and kitesurfing Cabo Verde is a popular spot for windsurfers from Europe to Hawaii, and regularly hosts championships. The two main islands for windsurfing are Boavista (page 141) and Sal (page 102), with São Vicente offering a lot of potential but few facilities as yet (page 278). November to the end of May is the windy season. During this time, the winds range from 18 knots to 22 knots and are good for both intermediate and advanced riders. Even during the windiest times there will be days that are good for beginners. If you want to avoid strong winds, the best time to learn is during the summer. Sal has a dedicated kitesurfing bay and also has Ponta Preta, whose huge breakers, kicked up by a strong offshore wind, led to the venue being added to the World Wave Circuit in 2007 and the Professional Windsurfers Association World Cup (w pwaworldtour.com) in 2008, 2009 and 2010. On São Vicente, in the bay of Mindelo, the average wind speed between January and June is 16 knots, with gusts of up to 30 knots. Round the coast in São Pedro Bay, local windsurfing speed records were set at over 40 knots (although windsurfing here outside competitions is prohibited).

SUGGESTED ITINERARIES

The most important decision the prospective visitor will make is choosing which island or islands to visit. It is difficult to overemphasise the importance of this. There's nothing more tragic than to meet grumpy tourists at the end of their holidays who, in essence, selected the wrong islands for their tastes. If all you want is mountains and greenery you will loathe Sal. If you are after a bit of luxury by a pool, with watersports, you will be frustrated on Brava. You can select islands to suit your interests from the map on page 52 and from the list here, which is followed by a few suggested itineraries. Bear in mind, however, the islands' internal flight system is centred on the hubs of Sal (to get to Boavista or São Nicolau), Santiago (to get to Fogo and thus on to Brava by boat, and to get to Maio) and São Vicente (to get to São Nicolau and Santo Antão – the latter by boat); so it might take two flights to get to your island and occasionally an overnight.

CHOOSING YOUR ISLANDS
Santo Antão Mountain walking; scenic driving; remote ecolodges; a limited amount of adventure sports.

São Vicente Barren; nightlife, music and restaurants in Mindelo, with some buildings of historical interest; interesting small hotels; game fishing; marina with yachts for hire. No real action outside Mindelo city.

São Nicolau Very quiet and undeveloped; beautiful mountain walking; scenic driving; black-sand beaches; game fishing.

Sal Barren, flat interior; superb watersports; beautiful white sands; large, all-inclusive beach resort hotels and a few smaller upmarket properties; nightlife; turtles; wide choice of eating opportunities.

Boavista Flat with desert interior; superb watersports; miles of beautiful deserted beaches; a few beach resort hotels; turtles and whale-watching in season.

Maio Flat, mostly barren interior; miles of deserted beaches; slow pace; few hotels as yet.

Santiago A balanced mix with no extremes; a capital city with some music and restaurants; one or two nice beaches; craggy mountainous interior with a few good walks; and the country's one major historical sight.

Fogo The spectacular volcano for sightseers and hikers; history; *sobrado* architecture; wine.

Brava Very quiet, unspoiled; mountainous with some lovely walks.

SUGGESTED ACTIVITIES
Hiking Make straight for Santo Antão (three+ days) and Fogo (two to three days). If schedules permit, Brava and São Nicolau are also stunning and Santiago has one or two good hikes in its interior.

Watersports Stick to Sal and Boavista. Boavista is quieter and arguably more beautiful but has fewer facilities.

Sightseeing Choose one of the flat islands (Maio, Boavista or Sal) for sunbathing/chill-out time, one of the two extraordinary landscapes (Fogo or Santo Antão) and a day/evening in either Mindelo (São Vicente) or in Praia (Santiago) to sample city life.

TOUR OPERATORS

A growing number of tour operators and travel agents claim to understand Cabo Verde but in reality have only a shallow knowledge. More than for other locations it is essential to choose an operator who understands the islands with all their differences and peculiarities; the large, package-holiday operators generally only cover Sal and Boavista.

UK
Archipelago Choice w archipelagochoice.com. Specialises in tailor-made & activity-focused holidays to all Cabo Verde islands. Company staff are extensively travelled in the islands.
Cape Verde Experience w capeverde.co.uk. Part of Serenity Holidays, with going on 40 years' experience in West Africa.

CABO VERDE
Alsatour CP 33, Paúl, Santo Antão; +238 223 1213; m +238 992 5875; w alsatour.de. Based on Santo Antão for the last 30 years, Alsatour specialises in tailor-made trips including international flights. Particularly good with trekking tours on Santo Antão, including those to remote areas. English spoken.
Nobai [283 G5] Rua Franz Fanon, Mindelo, São Vicente; +238 231 0525; m +238 982 5371; w cap-vert-trekking.com. A Mindelo-based, Cabo Verdean company with walking trips to all the islands. Offers self-guided or guided options, & can organise accommodation ranging from homestays to luxury.
vista verde tours +238 993 0788; w vista-verde.com. Well-established & professional travel agency specialising in social & environmentally responsible tourism. Arranges small-group tours or tailor-made holidays with domestic flights, hotels & excursions. Offices on Fogo, Sal & São Vicente, plus representation on other islands. Part of the Reisen mit Sinnen tour operator group (w kapverdischeinseln.de).

FRANCE AND GERMANY
Nomade Aventure +33 1 46 33 717; w nomade-aventure.com. A French specialist company offering a wide variety of walking trips & Carnival visits.
Olimar Reisen +49 221 20 590590; w olimar.de. A big operator doing mainly package seaside holidays on Sal.

Reiseträume ✆ +49 7512 018458; w reisetraeume.de. English-speaking Gerhard & Sibylle Schellmann live in Calheta on Santiago & have an office in Germany. They offer hiking tours around the archipelago, & specialist tours on Santiago.

Sun & Fun Sportreisen ✆ +49 8933 8833; w sunandfun.com. A good bet for watersports, including diving & kitesurfing, on Sal & Boavista.

RED TAPE

VISAS Visitors arriving from a number of countries around the world are considered visa-exempt for either 30, 60 or 90 days, although they must register online via the EASE portal (e ease-support@cv.zetes.com; w ease.gov.cv), five days before entry. This includes citizens of the EU, UK, US, Switzerland, Norway, Iceland, Canada, Singapore and Brazil, who receive a 30-day permit. You will also be required to pay an airport security fee of 3,400$, either online or on arrival. While Cabo Verde is a member of the Economic Community of West African States (ECOWAS), it doesn't reciprocate total visa-free access. Most ECOWAS countries are, however, able to apply for 90-day entry online.

For those from other countries, including Australia and New Zealand, you can obtain an e-visa online or on arrival, which involves the same requirements as the visa waiver, ie: documentation of your hotel stay (though this isn't routinely checked) and paying the airport security fee. If you're flying on a 'green' passport and not eligible for the visa waiver, it's a good idea to carry all documentation with you – reports have emerged about discriminatory entry policies, even for those with onward or return flights.

Visa extensions can be arranged at the Direção de Emigrantes e Fronteras during your stay (you will need a passport photo, proof of funds, copy of return flight ticket, occasionally a fair degree of persistence, patience and to pay around 3,500$) and it is much easier to do this *before* your visa expires. They have offices in Praia, Mindelo (notoriously difficult), Sal (notoriously even more difficult), and Boavista; the local police will direct you to the office. Fines (around €100) are often levied on departure if you have overstayed.

FORMALITIES FOR NON-TOURISTS Business travellers are encouraged to enter via the visa-waiver EASE portal (see above), unless they intend to stay longer.

A new visa class aimed at digital nomads was introduced in 2020 (see opposite). It simplifies the temporary residency application process (in theory), and retains most of the same requirements. Essentially, this means having your own private medical insurance and a minimum monthly income of €1,500/US$1,750. There is also now a visa called a 'green card' for those buying property in the country. It grants permanent residency and possible tax concessions. These, along with details of the traditional paths to residency, are all outlined on the Direção de Estrangeiros e Fronteiras portal (w e-portaldef.gov.cv).

For those wishing to become Cabo Verde nationals, unless your grandparent was a citizen, it is necessary to have been a (legal) resident for at least five years. This can be waived in the event of substantial investment, as well as for spouses and children of Cabo Verdeans, those of Cabo Verdean ancestry (at least one grandparent), the stateless, or those who have lost their Cabo Verdean citizenship and wish to reacquire it.

In respect of applications for both residence and citizenship, criminal background checks are undertaken.

> **THE ERA OF THE DIGITAL NOMAD**
>
> The Cabo Verdean government introduced a special digital nomad/remote worker visa in 2020, hoping to encourage a more sustainable kind of tourism. It's also part of its focus on developing the country as a start-up hub and innovator in Africa's tech space, building on its reliable Wi-Fi and 4G mobile network coverage, as well as the expanding fibre-optic infrastructure. Its key advantages for travellers are:
>
> - Six-month visa with the possibility to extend up to a year
> - No capital gains or income tax
> - Low visa fees (€20, plus €34 airport tax)
> - No requirement for local registration
>
> The programme's online resource CaboWork (w cabowork.com) has further detail, as well as listings of co-working spaces and recommended laptop-friendly cafés, and helpful news articles.

EMBASSIES AND CONSULATES The Cabo Verde diplomatic missions around the world can be found via the Ministério dos Negócios Estrangeiros website (w mne.gov.cv, with English option). The foreign minister announced in early 2024 that they were planning to open an embassy in the UK.

There is no UK embassy in Cabo Verde. UK and other citizens without diplomatic representation who need consular assistance are usually encouraged to contact their embassies in Portugal. The US, France and various other EU countries do have embassies in Praia; for a list, visit w embassypages.com/capeverde.

GETTING THERE AND AWAY

BY AIR Always bear in mind that the airline industry is a fluid one and the services detailed here may change, sometimes from month to month. There are international airports on Sal, Santiago, Boavista and São Vicente. While all UK-originating flights land at Sal or Boavista, there is increasing traffic into other airports either via Lisbon or direct from European hubs. Internal flight schedules are currently unpredictable (page 73), so it can be an advantage to fly to the airport closest to the island of your holiday destination. For example, travellers making for Santo Antão will have a much shorter onward journey if they fly directly to São Vicente, while those heading for Fogo should choose Santiago.

Cabo Verde Airlines (the consumer-facing name of TACV) connects Praia and São Vicente with Lisbon and Paris-CDG; and Sal with Lisbon, Bergamo (Milan), and Barcelona. Its fleet currently consists of a Boeing 737 MAX 8, an ATR 72-500, a Boeing 737-700, a DHC-8-300, and an ATR 72-600. In 2024, they announced that they would 'soon' reinstate flights to the US and Brazil. Cabo Verde Airlines has an exemplary safety record but, with a small fleet, it also has a reputation for last-minute cancellations. You should, however, check whether the situation has improved, as their flights from Paris and Bergamo are often significantly cheaper than European carriers.

Other scheduled airlines flying to Cabo Verde include **TAP Portugal**, **Transavia**, **Bintercanarias**, **TUI**, **easyJet**, **Luxair**, **Azores Airlines**, **Neos**, **Senegal Airlines** and **Royal Air Maroc**. Direct flights from Europe range from around 6 hours, from the north, to 3 hours from Portugal.

> **KNOW YOUR IATA CODES**
>
> - Nelson Mandela International Airport (Praia, Santiago Island) – RAI
> - Cesária Évora Airport (Mindelo, São Vicente Island) – VXE
> - Amílcar Cabral International Airport (Sal Island) – SID
> - Aristides Pereira International Airport (Boavista Island) – BVC
> - Aeroporto de São Filipe (Fogo Island) – SFL
> - Aeroporto de Maio (Maio Island) – MMO

British visitors to Cabo Verde are easily the most numerous, but they are only serviced by TUI flights to either Sal or Boavista, with most flights originating from London Gatwick, Manchester, East Midlands, Newcastle or Glasgow, along with easyJet direct services from Gatwick to Sal. While these flights are geared towards package tourists heading for all-inclusive resorts, independent travellers can look for 'flight-only' deals.

The best European hubs are Lisbon for regular TAP, Cabo Verde Airlines and easyJet services, Paris for Transavia, or the Canary Islands for Bintercanarias. More roundabout routes include taking advantage of Azores Airlines' sale fares, flying via Porto Delgado from either London, Paris or the east coast of the US; flying with Morocco's flag carrier, Royal Air Maroc (w royalairmaroc.com) to Praia from Casablanca; or using Air Senegal's surprisingly sparse service from Dakar. These can all potentially save money but can involve long stopovers, making a direct flight a far more attractive option.

At the time of writing, mooted direct flights from various Irish airports had not materialised; until they do, the easiest connections remain via Lisbon.

BY CRUISE SHIP Arriving by sea and watching the Atlantic crags materialise from the ocean is an unusual and uplifting way of reaching the islands. An increasing number of larger cruise companies visit Cabo Verde, mostly docking in Mindelo or Praia at either end. There are, though, a few smaller operations that are more likely to be aligned with independent travellers. Noble Caledonia (w noble-caledonia.co.uk) has itineraries that take in three or four islands, as well as visiting the Canaries and/or Morocco. Luxury small cruise specialist Ponant (w ponant.com) has a short, efficient island-hopping cruise of seven days, along with occasionally offering a fascinating combined route that includes the natural UNESCO Biosphere Reserve of Guinea-Bissau's Bissagos islands. Viking (w vikingcruises.co.uk) often includes port visits to Praia and Mindelo in its South Atlantic and African cruises.

BY YACHT Cabo Verde is becoming better known to yachts on the Atlantic run: numbers are increasing, and it is not uncommon to see 20 boats at anchor in Mindelo harbour, a few at Palmeira on Sal and Sal Rei on Boavista, and one or two more dotting bays around the archipelago. One big draw is that pausing in Cabo Verde, rather than the Canaries, can reduce the longest leg of the Atlantic crossing by a week.

There are three good harbours and these are on the best-resourced islands (Sal, São Vicente and Santiago). The other islands all have reasonable anchorages, some of them quite beautiful, but at some the safety or comfort depends on the weather.

Cabo Verde is short on spares and repair skills compared with ports in the Azores or the Canaries. Boat repair facilities are limited: the best and only real maintenance and spares point is Mindelo. This has lifts for quite large craft and a tradition of woodworking and boatbuilding. There is a chandlery here, too, with a lot of high-tech equipment for crossing the Atlantic. Water and diesel are available on the jetty in Mindelo, but otherwise it can be a case of making journeys to the tap. Food is expensive and you won't find pre-prepared meals. Water consumption is also high in this warm climate so you need to plan your route with care unless you have a water-maker.

You don't need a visa unless you plan to sleep onshore, or to stay for longer than three months. You must, however, enter and clear at every island you visit.

In the island chapters, brief information is given as to anchorages and facilities. However, the approaches to many of the islands are tricky and it is best to consult the excellent *Atlantic Islands: Azores, Madeira, Canary and Cape Verde Islands* (page 373). The most detailed charts are pre-1975 Portuguese; there are also British Admiralty charts but these have errors, sometimes dangerous ones. The British Admiralty Africa Pilot has lots of useful information about weather, sea conditions and currents. All these can be obtained from Hammick and Heath's aforementioned guide.

HEALTH   with Dr Daniel Campion

Cabo Verde does not suffer from many of the diseases that are a menace in mainland Africa. There is a limited incidence of dengue fever – and malaria, polio, diphtheria and measles have been eliminated. With increased immigration from West Africa, there have been cases of yellow fever being brought in to Cabo Verde, and hepatitis A and B. Travellers' diarrhoea is common and traffic accidents or other injuries are a threat.

Cabo Verde's tourism is developing faster than its infrastructure. The islands have a good number of **doctors**, trained overseas, and there are **hospitals** on São Vicente and Santiago, and private **medical clinics** on Sal and São Vicente. However, bear in mind that if you are taken seriously ill elsewhere, the correct treatment may be hard to find as facilities on the less-developed islands are more limited.

BEFORE YOU GO   Having a full set of immunisations takes time, ideally at least six weeks. Visit your doctor or travel clinic (page 62) to discuss your requirements. The following points are worth emphasising:

- Don't travel without comprehensive **medical travel insurance** that will fly you home or to another country in an emergency. Cabo Verde does not have an operating hyperbaric chamber, so **divers** should take out proper diving insurance, which will include being flown at low altitude to Europe for treatment of decompression sickness.
- Make sure all your **immunisations** are up to date. The only certificate requirement is for **yellow fever** vaccine for all travellers over one year of age arriving from countries with a risk of yellow fever transmission or from travellers who have transited for more than 12 hours in an airport of a country with a risk of transmission. There is no risk of the disease in Cabo Verde itself, but they do not wish to import it. If there are specific contraindications to having the vaccine, then a yellow fever exemption certificate should be acquired from a qualified medical professional. It is also wise to be up to date on **tetanus**, **polio** and **diphtheria** (usually available as an all-in-one vaccine), **typhoid** and **hepatitis A**. Immunisation against **hepatitis B** may also be recommended. **Cholera** only rarely affects travellers and it has not been detected in Cabo Verde since 1998.
- Anybody travelling away from major centres should carry a **personal first-aid kit**. Contents might include a rapidly drying antiseptic (such as Savlon dry), plasters,

sunscreen, insect repellent, aspirin or paracetamol, antifungal cream, antibiotic eye drops, tweezers, condoms or femidoms and a digital thermometer.
- Bring any **drugs or devices relating to known medical conditions** with you. That applies both to those who are on medication prior to departure, and those who are, for instance, allergic to bee stings, or are prone to attacks of asthma.
- Prolonged immobility on long-haul flights can result in **deep-vein thrombosis** (DVT), which can be dangerous if the clot travels to the lungs. The risk increases with age, and is higher in obese or pregnant travellers, heavy smokers, those taller than 6ft/1.8m, and anybody with a history of clots, recent major operation or varicose veins surgery, cancer, a stroke or heart disease. If any of these criteria apply, consult a doctor before you travel.
- **Malaria** has been eliminated in Cabo Verde (page 65), so anti-malarials are not required.

TRAVEL CLINICS AND HEALTH INFORMATION A list of travel clinic websites worldwide is available on w istm.org. For journey preparation information, consult w travelhealthpro.org.uk (UK) or w wwwnc.cdc.gov/travel (USA). All advice found online should be used in conjunction with expert advice received prior to or during travel.

COMMON MEDICAL PROBLEMS
Travellers' diarrhoea Many visitors to unfamiliar destinations suffer a dose of travellers' diarrhoea, usually as a result of consuming contaminated food or water. Rule one in avoiding diarrhoea and other sanitation-related diseases is to wash your hands regularly, particularly before snacks and meals, and after handling money. Bringing with you an antibacterial handwash to use before meals is recommended. As for what food you can safely eat, a useful maxim is: PEEL IT, BOIL IT, COOK IT OR FORGET IT. This means that fruit you have washed and peeled yourself should be safe, as should hot cooked foods. However, raw foods, cold cooked foods, salads and fruit salads prepared by others, ice cream and ice are all risky. It is rarer to get sick from drinking contaminated water but it happens, so stick to bottled or filtered water.

If you suffer a bout of diarrhoea, it is dehydration that makes you feel awful, so drink lots of water and other clear fluids. These can be infused with sachets of oral rehydration salts, though any dilute mixture of sugar and salt in water will do you good, for instance a bottled soda with a pinch of salt. If diarrhoea persists beyond a couple of days, it is possible it is a symptom of a more serious sanitation-related illness (typhoid, hepatitis, dysentery, worms, etc), so go to a doctor. If the diarrhoea is greasy and bulky, and is accompanied by sulphurous (eggy) burps, one likely cause is **giardia**, which can cause persistent symptoms but is treatable. Seek medical advice if you suspect this.

Insects and ticks
Mosquito and other insect bites It is worth protecting yourself against mosquito bites between dusk and dawn by covering up with trousers and a long-sleeved shirt, and applying insect repellent containing the chemical DEET (50% is the optimum strength); icaridin at 20% is an effective alternative. Ideally you should sleep under a mosquito net. Cabo Verde's waterless climate keeps insects down, but they pop up all year round in odd places where there is stagnant water.

Jiggers or sand fleas Adult female fleas of the species *Tunga penetrans* bury into bare feet where they feed and lay eggs under the skin of the foot, usually at the side

> ### BUFFET BELLY BLUES?
>
> Upset tummies are largely unremarkable among seasoned travellers, but a 2023 spike in severe gastrointestinal illness affecting holidaymakers returning from Sal was alarming enough to hit UK headlines. Testing revealed salmonella, E. coli and giardiasis but, overwhelmingly, results pointed to shigellosis. This was, in fact, the second post-pandemic summer that UK health authorities had traced a rise in shigellosis cases to recent Cabo Verde travel, with similar patterns happening across Europe and Scandinavia.
>
> Shigellosis, often called *shigella*, the actual name of the bacteria, is highly infectious and spread through contact with the faeces of an infected person, most often via contaminated food or water. Its hallmark is watery, blood-tinged diarrhoea, but it can also cause vomiting, cramping, fever and nausea. In most cases, symptoms subside without treatment in a week. Others, though, require hospitalisation for IV antibiotics and rehydration, and it can take months to recover.
>
> African countries currently report a high burden of outbreaks, though the disease is endemic across the world, with up to 165 million cases and up to 600,000 deaths (mostly among children) annually. Since 2023, the number of extensively antibiotic-resistant cases of the infection has also sharply increased.
>
> The Cabo Verdean government announced that hotel health and safety was an 'absolute priority', but, in line with the large UK travel operators and hotel chains, says its most recent investigations in 2023 found only a tiny percentage of visitors to be affected.
>
> By the end of 2024, however, around 1,400 people in the UK began joint legal action after their illness-related compensation claims were rejected, with all alleged cases linked to a handful of all-inclusives. Phase Two trials of a shigellosis vaccine were well underway in 2025; meanwhile, independent travellers should continue to follow usual food safety protocols (see opposite), especially so in the tourist precincts of Sal and Boavista.

of a toenail. This causes painful, boil-like swellings. A local expert must pick them out. If the distended flea bursts during eviction the wound should be doused in alcohol or kerosene to avoid more jiggers infesting you.

Ticks There are several nasty, tick-borne diseases, such as typhus and African tick-bite fever. Avoid ticks by wearing long clothes and repellent, especially if walking in scrubby countryside where you are brushing through vegetation. Ticks should ideally be removed complete, and as soon as possible, to reduce the chance of infection. You can use special tick tweezers, which can be bought in good travel shops; or failing this, with your fingernails, grasp the tick as close to your body as possible, and pull it away steadily and firmly at right angles to your skin without jerking or twisting. Applying irritants (eg: Olbas oil) or lit cigarettes is to be discouraged as a means of removal since they can cause the ticks to regurgitate and therefore increase the risk of disease. Once the tick is removed, if possible douse the wound with alcohol (any spirit will do), soap and water, or iodine. If you are travelling with small children, remember to check their heads, and particularly behind the ears, for ticks. Spreading redness around the bite and/or fever and/or aching joints after a tick bite imply that you have an infection that requires antibiotic treatment. In this case seek medical advice.

Heat and sun

Dehydration It is easy to get dehydrated, especially in the first week. If you wake up in the morning feeling nauseous and tired, that may be the reason. Water requirements depend on temperature, humidity, amount of exercise taken, and the length of time the person has been in the country. Those who get into trouble are people who do not allow themselves to acclimatise, a process that takes up to two weeks. Eager adolescents are particularly vulnerable. In the tropics you need to drink about three litres a day, more if you are exercising. Take it easy for the first week. In Cabo Verde it is very likely you could end up on a long, hot and shadeless hike for a day. In those conditions you will need to have drunk five litres by the end of the day to avoid dehydration. If you are going on a day's hike, drink plenty before you go, try to carry two litres per person, and fill up again in the evening.

Prickly heat A fine pimply rash on the trunk of the body is likely to be heat rash. This prickly heat can be alleviated by cool showers, dabbing (not rubbing) dry and using talc, and sleeping naked under a fan or in an air-conditioned room.

Sunburn Cabo Verde is notoriously lacking in shade, so you must bring your own in the form of a broad-brimmed hat, umbrella, or even a windbreak for a day on the beach. The best solution is to cover up: a light-coloured, loose cotton shirt and long skirt or trousers is also cooler than shorts and a T-shirt. Many visitors don't notice the sun burning them because of the cooling effect of the wind. Try and keep out of the sun between noon and 15.00, and if you must expose yourself, build up gradually from 20 minutes per day. Tanning is not recommended: it ages your skin and can increase your risk of skin cancer. Be particularly careful of sun reflected from water and wear a T-shirt and plenty of waterproof sunscreen, which provides cover for both UVA and UVB (at least factor 30) when snorkelling or swimming.

Heat exhaustion and heat stroke Heat exhaustion develops gradually, caused by loss of salt and water through excessive sweating. It is most common in people new to the heat or new to exercise in the heat and in people who have recently had an illness in which they lost fluids (diarrhoea or vomiting). Sufferers have fast shallow breathing and a rapid weak pulse. They may feel dizzy and sick, be pale and sweating, have a headache and have cramps in the limbs and abdomen. Sit or lie the casualty down in a cool place, raise and support the legs to allow blood to flow to the brain. Give plenty of water.

Heat stroke is less common and is most likely to happen as a result of prolonged exposure to very hot surroundings. This leads to a breakdown of temperature regulation. Symptoms include confusion, swiftly deteriorating to unconsciousness, a strong pulse and slow, deep breathing. The sufferer's skin will be hot, flushed and their temperature will be over 40°C. The essential thing is to cool the person quickly – do this by moving them to a cool place, removing their outer clothing, wrapping them in a cold, wet sheet and fanning them. Call for a doctor immediately.

Skin infections Any insect bite or cut gives bacteria the opportunity to foil the skin's usually strong defences. Skin infections start quickly in warm and humid climates, so they are not such a problem in Cabo Verde. Creams do not keep the wound dry so they are not as effective as a drying antiseptic such as Savlon dry, or any other similar product which dries on the skin. If the wound starts to throb, if it becomes red and the redness begins to spread, or if the wound oozes, then you may need antibiotics and should seek a doctor. Fungal infections take hold easily in moist parts of the body, so wear cotton socks and underwear and shower frequently, drying thoroughly. An itchy and often flaking rash in the groin or between the toes is likely to be a fungus and will require treatment with a cream such as Canesten (clotrimazole). If this is not available, then try Whitfield's ointment (compound benzoic acid ointment) or crystal violet.

SERIOUS ILLNESSES

Dengue fever Dengue fever is present in Cabo Verde, and there was a big spike in cases – more than 8,000 – in December 2024, concurrent with seasonal rainfall. The government declared a state of contingency across Santiago, Fogo and Brava; although there were cases reported on all islands, over 80% were from Santiago. A vaccine against dengue is now available in the UK and Europe. Generally it is recommended only for those who have already had dengue, to prevent a severe second infection. For most travellers, prevention of mosquito bites (page 62) is still the best way to avoid it. The mosquitoes that carry dengue fever fly in the daytime so remember to use insect repellents during the day as well as the evening. Symptoms include strong headaches, rashes, excruciating joint and muscle pains and high fever. Dengue fever only lasts for a week or so and a first infection is not usually fatal. Complete rest and paracetamol are the usual treatment. Plenty of fluids also help. Avoid aspirin and ibuprofen, which may worsen bleeding. Some patients are given intravenous fluids to avoid dehydration. It is especially important to protect yourself and consider vaccination if you have had dengue fever before: a second infection with a different strain can result in the potentially fatal dengue haemorrhagic fever.

Zika virus Zika virus is a flavivirus similar to dengue and is spread by the day-biting *Aedes* mosquito. All travellers to countries where Zika virus is reported, including Cabo Verde, are at risk of infection. The longer you spend in the destination, the more at risk you will be. The infection is often asymptomatic, and in those with symptoms the disease is usually mild with an itchy rash, fever, joint pains and red, sore eyes. Severe disease is uncommon. Travellers are advised to use DEET- or icaridin-based repellents during the day on all exposed skin. In areas where mosquitoes are particularly prevalent, covering up and using a permethrin spray on clothing would also be advised.

Pregnant women need to discuss their travel plans with health-care professionals and should, wherever possible, cancel the trip. Women wishing to become pregnant who are travelling in moderate- to high-risk Zika virus areas should use barrier precautions while travelling and for two months after. If travelling with their partners, then barrier precautions need to be used during the trip and for three months after leaving.

> **MALARIA: FREE AT LAST**
>
> In January 2024, WHO certified Cabo Verde malaria-free. It is the third country to be certified in Africa, joining Mauritius and Algeria, who were declared in 1973 and 2019 respectively. This was the culmination of two decades of public health policy that included expanded diagnosis, early and effective treatment, and the reporting and investigating of all confirmed cases.

Rabies There is no rabies in terrestrial animals in the Cabo Verde Islands, but there may be bat rabies. Pre-exposure vaccination is therefore not routinely recommended. However, exposure to bat saliva or nerve tissue is considered a potential risk and so advice should be sought as soon as possible.

HIV Cabo Verde has a relatively low and stable rate of HIV infection, although despite progress, the number of people on effective treatment could still be improved. Other sexually transmitted diseases are also a risk, whether you sleep with fellow travellers or locals, and the presence of other infections increases the chance of contracting HIV. Up to 20% of travellers will have a sexual encounter with a new partner while abroad and about 40% of HIV infections in British heterosexuals are acquired abroad.

Bring condoms or femidoms with you. If you notice any genital ulcers or discharge, get them treated promptly.

Typhoid This bacterial infection can be transmitted through contaminated food and water. Symptoms include fever, headache, loss of appetite, abdominal pain and sometimes pink spots on the skin. The heart rate may slow. Seek immediate help.

ACCIDENTS Hospitals on the smaller islands are often poorly equipped and have to evacuate you to São Vicente or Santiago, even for the resetting of a broken leg. The hospital on São Vicente is considered the best. The inter-island planes always reserve space for medical emergencies.

On the road Vehicle accidents – not exotic diseases – are often the biggest killers of visitors to Africa. Cabo Verde vehicles are in better condition than those on the mainland and many drivers are careful of their investments. Cobbled surfaces and hidden speed bumps conspire to keep vehicle speeds down. But the roads are vertiginous and damage caused by rains is not always repaired in any great hurry – there is plenty of scope for 100m cliff plunges. Make sure your driver has not been drinking alcohol and try not to travel along precarious roads after dark or during or just after rain, as speed bumps and pot-holes are difficult to spot and landslips a reality.

Swimming Swimming accidents are the other danger. The blue waters may be seductive but they are also the wild mid ocean, abounding with hidden reefs, strange currents and hungry wildlife. The golden rule is to watch what the local people are doing and to ask whether it is safe to bathe (*Não é perigoso tomar banho?* – 'It's not dangerous to take a dip?'), and don't dive from boats that are far from the shore, or you could end up getting nibbled by a shark. In the shallows a pair of plimsolls will protect against coral, sea urchins and venomous fish spines. The trick after being stung by a venomous fish is to denature the poison by heating it – so stick your foot in a bucket of hot water (up to 45°C) until sometime after the pain subsides – perhaps 20–30 minutes overall. If the pain returns, immerse the foot again. Then ask a doctor to check for fish spines in the wound.

Hiking Much of the classic walking on Cabo Verde is through populated areas or at least on paths trodden regularly each day by local people, but some hikes are so deserted you will meet no-one. On Santo Antão in particular, once off the beaten track it is dangerous, with scree, gullies and landslides and no sign of water or food. It can be easy to leave the path in some of the Santo Antão ribeiras, particularly the many tributaries of Ribeira Grande, in which case you could get stuck on a path that has dwindled to a crevice, unable to descend without sliding along the rubble and unable to ascend because there are no footholds – and with the mist approaching. The really remote region is the west of Santo Antão where only experienced hikers should go, and even then, a local guide would be advisable.

Walking accidents are not uncommon. Cabo Verdean terrain – hard, bone-dry soil sprinkled with tiny, rolling bits of grit – can be slippery even for those in good walking boots and even when it is flat. Sometimes you must watch each step, placing the foot on any available vegetation, stone or clear ground and avoiding the mini landslides waiting in the middle of the path. If you break a bone insist on having it set by a qualified doctor rather than another health worker, or you could end up needing it reset later.

If you go hiking don't forget the basic principles: it is essential to wear walking boots with ankle support; plan your route before you set off so that you know which villages to ask for along the way; tell someone who might care where you are going and when you are expecting to be back; drink plenty of water before you go and take two litres of water for a full day away (this assumes you can stock up beforehand and replenish in the evening; bring food – assume you will not find any on the way; take a whistle, as well as a compass or GPS (if you know how to use these tools!); and protect yourself from the sun. In remote areas, you can't always rely on finding a mobile phone signal.

For walks in the Fogo crater and on Santo Antão's peaks, take a jumper – it can get cold. Cuts and grazes can be avoided by wearing long trousers.

Animal bites The only mammals to watch out for on Cabo Verde are village dogs, cats and monkeys. Dogs are everywhere, sleeping, roaming the streets or engaging in cacophonous barking matches when everyone else is trying to sleep. It is rare that they show any aggression. Some people keep monkeys as guards or pets on long stretches of rope. They are accustomed to being fed and may bite.

As above, although terrestrial animals do not carry **rabies**, bats may do (see opposite). Bat bites can be too tiny to see, so if you wake with a bat in your room, consider that you have been exposed. This is another good reason to sleep under a mosquito net if you are not in an air-conditioned room.

Animal bites do, however, pose a risk from a whole host of other bacteria which can infect the wound. This includes tetanus, which can also be caught from soil getting into wounds. Make sure your immunisation is up to date and clean wounds thoroughly. If you see any signs of spreading redness or a collection of pus, seek medical help as soon as possible.

SAFETY

CRIME Although Cabo Verde remains a peaceful and safe place with a very low incidence of crime, theft has increased as a direct consequence of tourism. Sensible precautions should of course be taken, but in this respect Cabo Verde is no different from anywhere else in the world. Theft is most common in Mindelo and Praia, as well as at isolated spots on Sal and Boavista. In Mindelo, tourists can occasionally fall victim to gangs of bag-snatchers, and aggressive begging and pickpocketing are unfortunately common, occurring mostly on the waterfront and on Praça Amílcar Cabral (children and teenagers may follow you asking for money or selling 'tickets', often as a way to access your cash or phone). There have also recently been reports of a spate of violent muggings on the beach between Baía das Gatos and Calhau: go

> **TOURIST GUIDES**
>
> As in many countries across the world, visitors may stumble across people claiming to be 'tourist guides'. Since 2016, local tourist guides in Cabo Verde have been required to carry a photo-ID card issued by the Ministerio da Economia e Emprego. No guide can lawfully operate without the correct authorisation and the supervisory authorities can demand to see their accreditation on request. That's the good news. And the bad? To be properly certificated as a professional local guide, tourist guides have to present qualification documents to the authorities, but some call into question whether the process of certification is sufficiently rigorous. Guiding organisations do exist on most islands, though, with around 300 local guides participating. Some of the larger destination-focused Facebook groups provide up-to-date lists of fully accredited guides and you can also check with Project Biodiversity (page 97) for those on Sal who actively protect turtle and shark habitats.

with a guide. In Praia the speciality theft venue is Sucupira Market, a crowded place and a pickpocket's paradise, but people have had valuables such as laptops snatched from other places in the city. After dark, if you're alone, be careful in Platô, avoid the rainbow stairs from Kebra Kanela to Achada Santo António and exercise a high level of caution in the small streets known as Brasil on Achada Santo António's eastern side, as well as in Varzea, Terra Branca and Tira Chapeú (the latter can sometimes feel threatening in broad daylight too). Reports of armed muggings on the walking trails above Tarrafal have become more frequent, and it's now advised only to do these with a local guide. On Sal it is Buracona, on the west coast, where cars are broken into once their drivers have gone for a walk. On Boavista, in isolated spots, there have been incidents of violent crime against tourists. Other islands remain virtually crime-free, at least with respect to tourists. In the less populous islands, where everyone knows everyone, the perpetrators are also likely to be known to the police and the locals: this is a massive deterrent in itself.

In recent years, Cabo Verde has had to start to grapple with drug-related crime. Drugs have become prevalent as drug-smuggling routes have changed (page 36) and it is also said that tourism has increased the problem. The US's deportation of criminals with Cabo Verdean ancestry back to Cabo Verde is also blamed.

Follow the usual rules. Carry a purse in an inside pocket; when paying, don't open a purse stacked with cash. If you are a victim, make a fuss, as people will come to your aid. Carrying a whistle is also worth considering. Also, it is irresponsible not to report any incident of crime or attempted crime to the police (you'll also need to do this for your travel insurance).

To sum up, the vast majority of Cabo Verdeans you will meet will be scrupulously honest and crime should be no more of a problem than if you were still at home. As a visitor, though, you are slightly more vulnerable to being targeted by the tiny minority of people.

HIKING SAFETY Some of the joys in Cabo Verde are the cobbled paths in the mountains, making some walks easier both underfoot and navigationally than they might appear. Nevertheless there are hazards. Dehydration and sunstroke are two: shade is sparse and, on some islands, non-existent, while water sources are scarce. Another is falls: where the paths are not cobbled they can be shingly, with small loose stones, and it is easy to tumble on the way down. The west of Santo Antão has its own special dangers born of remoteness (page 324). Take the usual precautions: strong boots, several litres of water per person, sun protection, a map, and a message left at your hotel about where you've gone.

FOCUS ON SPECIFIC GROUPS

WOMEN TRAVELLERS Women can travel safely on their own in Cabo Verde and never feel threatened, although they may be irritated by unwelcome attention. Cabo Verdean men will flirt outrageously, and can be casually 'touchy'. The mention of a husband somewhere close makes most men lose interest pretty swiftly, but a firm no can usually also suffice. However, if you reveal that you are childless – whether married, with a partner or single – expect huge sympathy, mystification and interest.

LGBTQIA+ TRAVELLERS Cabo Verde is generally regarded as the most tolerant of African countries when it comes to LGBTQIA+ travellers. Sexual activity between those of the same gender has been legal since 2004. Occasional displays of prejudice can occur, as is the case anywhere in the world, but reports from LGBTQIA+ visitors to the country indicate that there are no particular concerns. That said there are no gay bars or saunas, even in Praia or Mindelo. Dance parties, especially during the summer and Christmas season are 'mixed', so can be a way to meet others in your particular community.

OLDER TRAVELLERS Increasing numbers of older people are holidaying in Cabo Verde, and it poses no particular problems for them. There are a few caveats, though. The elderly may find the undulations of steep islands a little hard – there are one or two hotels that can be accessed only on foot up steep paths and you should check when booking. Make sure you understand about the distribution of medical facilities: if you are taken ill anywhere other than Sal, Santiago or São Vicente it will be a ferry journey or a plane ride to the nearest full-service hospital. Avoid all-inclusive hotels, as there is the risk of shigella (page 63) and other serious food poisoning bugs which can be more serious for people with pre-existing health conditions. Most sights are accessible by car, but do bear in mind, if you are in need of a fairly sedentary holiday, that there are not many cultural 'sights' to go and see – just a tiny sprinkling of museums.

FAMILIES Cabo Verde is increasingly attractive to families as beach tourism develops. Choose your hotel carefully, though: some hotels are built in front of stretches of water in which it is not safe for young children to swim. Some of the resort hotels on Sal and Boavista have dedicated children's facilities, such as playground, swimming pool and even activities, but outside of the all-inclusive complexes there are few ready-made, children-orientated facilities. Many hotels are not near the water and the beaches have no shade. If a beach holiday was not what you had in mind, it's perhaps best only to take children if they are old enough to enjoy activities such as windsurfing or hiking – or be content with bobbing around in the hotel pool.

TRAVELLING WITH A DISABILITY The company **Disabled Access Holidays** (**w** disabledaccessholidays.com) can help travellers with a disability arrange a visit to Sal, although as far as we know there are no operators running specialised trips to Cabo Verde more widely. It would be best to contact a specialist who really knows the islands you want to visit, knows the hoteliers personally and is interested in your quest: they can take the time to craft a journey for you.

The UK's **gov.uk** website (**w** gov.uk/government/publications/disabled-travellers) has a downloadable guide giving general advice and practical information for travellers with a disability (and their companions) preparing for overseas travel. **The Society for Accessible Travel and Hospitality** (**w** sath.org) also provides general information. The website **Wheelmap** (**w** wheelmap.org) has an interactive global map showing accessible and partially accessible properties, including museums, hotels and restaurants.

The local minibuses are generally very crowded and hard to climb into. There are plenty of taxis in the capitals (Mindelo and Praia). In other towns the taxis may take the form of minibuses or 4x4s which may be even harder to get into.

Because many trails, particularly on Santo Antão, are cobbled almost all the way, it is just conceivable that a tailored wheelchair could travel on them. One person who achieved this is Jean François Porret and his account of his experience, with some inspiring photographs, is at **w** bela-vista.net/Wheelchair.aspx.

Travel insurance for those with medical conditions can be purchased in the UK from **Free Spirit** (**↘** 0845 170 7704; **w** freespirittravelinsurance.com). Most insurance companies will insure travellers with a disability, but it is essential that they are made fully aware of your specific needs.

Although the vast majority of people will only want to help you, it is worth remembering that, as a traveller with a disability, you are more vulnerable. Stay aware of who is around you and where your bags are, especially in Mindelo and Praia.

WHAT TO TAKE

Clothing is overwhelmingly casual, though you might want to be smarter for the more upmarket restaurants and if you're going out in Mindelo and Praia. A jumper may be necessary because evenings can turn slightly chilly in the cooler seasons, and are always chilly higher up, for example in Rui Vaz on Santiago, or in Fogo's crater. Take good walking boots and a spare pair of laces if you are planning to hike and walking poles if you use them, as such things are rarely available in Cabo Verde.

Even the cheapest *pensão* is likely to provide towels, loo paper, soap and a basin plug. Those using a homestay might sometimes be thankful they brought a sheet sleeping bag and a pair of flip-flops for washing in. For overnight boat trips, which you may spend on deck, you should consider having a sleeping bag for warmth. The main towns – Santa Maria, Praia, Mindelo – should sell all other basics, including tampons (not necessarily with applicator), hair conditioner, razors, Imodium and painkillers. It's still a good idea to bring painkillers (they will be cheaper at home) and sachets or tablets of rehydrating solution. Shower gel is expensive and also difficult to find in anything other than industrial quantities, and most hotels don't supply it.

Take **sunscreen** – expensive and not so easy to find – and a sunhat. Also: **insect repellent** because there are biters about in the evenings. A few hotels have mosquito nets but if it's very important to you not to be bitten, either take a net, a 'plug-in' repellent available from travel shops, or DEET-level repellent.

Cabo Verde struggles with its **electricity** supply. Some hotels have generators but many hotels of an otherwise good standard do not. Take a torch. Power cuts are far from unknown. The electricity supply is 220V 50Hz, which is standard in western Europe. The plug is a standard European two-pin type so a converter is necessary if coming from the UK, for example.

A Portuguese **dictionary** can be useful if you need to interact with officialdom, and you can download the Speak Kriolu app for your phone. Bring your own reading matter – there is little available in English in Cabo Verde. Some hotels have a book-swap scheme. An ordinary driving licence suffices for car hire.

If you are happy to travel light with only hand luggage you will have the great advantage of whistling through airports much faster. Cabin baggage limits for inter-island flights are however strict at 6kg. Cabo Verde's domestic hold baggage limits are more generous with 23kg for regular tickets, 30kg for flex plus fares.

MAPS Most of the best maps of the archipelago and of the individual islands are produced by German publishers, particularly AB Kartenverlag, as well as by ITMB, and are normally available from specialist bookshops such as Stanfords (w stanfords. co.uk) or The Map Shop in Upton-upon-Severn (w themapshop.co.uk) and also from the website w atlantic-islands.com. AB Kartenverlag's individual island maps, with multi-lingual legend, include hiking trails. As well as the maps listed here, you may also find copies of out-of-print maps of other islands at the map specialists mentioned above. There's also an increasing number of online map apps, like Maps.me, and various online hiking trackers that travellers have reported finding useful.

Boavista, Sal, Maio Hiking map 1:50,000, AB Kartenverlag
Cabo Verde Tourist map 1:150,000, published by AB Kartenverlag
Fogo & Brava Hiking map 1:50,000, AB Kartenverlag
Sal (inc 2 city maps) Tourist map 1:100,000, AB Kartenverlag
Santiago Hiking map 1:50,000, AB Kartenverlag
Santo Antão Hiking map 1:40,000, AB Kartenverlag
São Nicolau Hiking map 1:50,000, AB Kartenverlag
São Vicente Hiking map 1:35,000, AB Kartenverlag

MONEY AND BUDGETING

The Cabo Verdean **currency** is the escudo, represented by the $ sign at the end of the number, or by the letters CVE. The escudo is officially set to a fixed exchange rate with the euro. In practice, banks and exchange bureaux/*cambios* vary the rates slightly. Rates are also varied by hotels charging in local currency. Note that Cabo Verde escudos cannot be taken into or out of the country, so plan accordingly. You will not be able to buy them before departure, nor change any excess escudos after you return home. The euro is increasingly accepted in day-to-day transactions on Sal and Boavista, where prices are often quoted in that currency. This is less prevalent on other islands.

Credit cards are accepted at more upmarket hotels and restaurants, but it is best to assume that most small hotels and casual restaurants will not accept them. **ATMs**

PRICES FOR COMMON ITEMS

water 1.5 litre	80–150$	bread roll/baguette	15–50$
coffee and a cake	250$	chocolate bar	100$
ice cream	200$	banana	30$ each
postcard	100$	litre of petrol/diesel	135/105$
fruit juice	100–200$	small beer in bar/hotel	200/250$
caipirinha	600$		

can be found at the major banks (BCA, BCN and to a slightly lesser extent, Caixa Económica, among others) in nearly all bigger towns and are well lit and reliable. Those on less-frequented islands are occasionally out of operation. ATMs display the Visa, MasterCard, Cirrus and Maestro symbols and both credit and debit cards can be used to make a withdrawal, which incurs a transaction charge, typically of around 200$.

Money transfers can be done very quickly through Western Union to the Caixa Económica and most other banks. High-street banks in the UK will transfer funds to Cabo Verdean banks urgently (within two or three days) for a fee of about £30.

Given the wide availability of ATMs on Cabo Verde, and despite the transaction charges for withdrawals, it's best to arrive with a small amount in euros, then use the ATMs to obtain escudos. Although crime rates are not high, it is foolish to arrive with *all* your trip money in cash and carry it around for the duration of your stay. One apparent anomaly on Sal, Boavista and Maio is that prices are often quoted and payment asked for in euros. If you pay in escudos, however, most vendors will simply convert their quoted euro price by dividing by 100, not the correct exchange rate at the time. A €20 purchase price will usually be satisfied by paying 2,000$, although technically it should be 2,200$. Paying in escudos therefore saves you money.

BUDGETING Many goods and services approach European prices. Better hotels charge €100–200 per night with breakfast for a double room; hiring a vehicle for a day will cost €50–80; a three-course meal in a good restaurant might cost about €40 without drinks. Wine is relatively expensive, costing around €5 per glass in a restaurant, €8–10 a bottle in a supermarket. A guide for a half-day (without car) might cost about €30, €80 with one. At the other end of the scale, a basic hotel might cost about €40 for a double room with breakfast; a more basic restaurant charges around €5 for a lunch *prato do dia* (dish of the day) or €15 for a two-course evening meal; and travelling around in the local *alugueres* will cost anything from €1 to €10 depending on the distance.

Day trips and activities around Sal, Boavista or Santiago tend to cost €60–90, and a driver for the day can cost up to €120 on Santo Antão. Some tourists on package holidays complain that they did not budget for the cost of these excursions and hadn't realised they would be so expensive.

GETTING AROUND

BY AIR The simplest, most convenient, most comfortable, and most reliable way to travel between the islands, is to fly. Anyone with only two weeks in the archipelago should not consider taking a ferry.

Since April 2024, Cabo Verde Airlines (w cvairlines.cv) has been the sole provider of domestic inter-island flights. At the time of writing they were using a minuscule leased fleet, so there are shortfalls in terms of schedules and a 10% cancellation rate of those already limited services. The airline currently serves seven domestic destinations, that is all the islands except Santo Antão and Brava, and its flights are orientated around three hubs. From Sal you can get directly or indirectly to São Vicente, São Nicolau, Boavista and Santiago. From Santiago you can get directly to Fogo, Sal, Maio and São Vicente. From São Vicente you can get directly to Sal and Santiago.

At certain times of the year (during festivals or when *emigrantes* arrive for their holidays), flights get very busy – make sure to book ahead. Booking flights online

INTER-ISLAND AIRLINE WOES

Cabo Verde's domestic aviation sector has always been a volatile one, with a number of airlines having come and gone over the last few decades, including Halcyonair and Binter Cabo Verde, the well-liked Binter Canarias subsidiary. The most recent to be defeated by the logistical and financial demands of providing the sole service to the country's islands with airports – seven in total – was Angola's Bestfly. The latter's tenure was marked with unreliability, and while still selling tickets throughout the early months of 2024, finally suspended all operations in April of that year, effectively leaving the country without reliable inter-island transport, and many travellers without flights or refunds. This came after failing to reach agreement on compliance issues such as operational documentation, pilot licensing and aircraft maintenance records; the split was acrimonious, to say the least.

In late February 2024, when Bestfly was down to a single plane, Cabo Verde Airlines (the new trading name of TACV), who for a few years previously had only operated on the country's international routes, began a vital back-up service using two leased ATR aircraft, as many islands rely on flights for medical emergencies. While they were miraculously able to swing into something approaching a full schedule in April, there followed more than a few hiccups. Some islands' service was reduced to a weekly or twice-weekly flight, there was a pilots' strike in July, and at times, they too were operating across the entire archipelago with just one plane.

The government has repeated promises to establish reliable and regular connections between islands, and to reduce ticket costs on the less touristed islands like Maio and São Nicolau, but at the time of writing had not been able to implement any long-term solutions. In the meantime, Cabo Verde Airlines has been using some of its international aircraft to try to meet demand. For travellers, it's stressful and inconvenient. For an island nation, with an equally erratic ferry service due to Atlantic swells, it is a true crisis.

---

is relatively easy, or any local agent can organise it for you. Costs are reasonable, although they do quickly add up, especially if you need to transit in Praia or Mindelo, as you'll pay for both legs as well as the inconvenience. Short hops start at around €30 per single journey (from Praia to Maio, for example). Flights are often cheaper the further ahead you book and there are sometimes promotional fares.

Journeys take between 15 and 50 minutes. Baggage allowance in economy class for internal flights is 23kg, but hand luggage is limited to 6kg as the planes have limited overhead space.

You are required to be at the airport two hours before your flight when check-in opens. They definitely will reallocate seats of any latecomers, and flights are known to sneak away 15 minutes earlier than stated. You can try calling 12 to 24 hours before your flight to confirm the time. Conversely, if you are told all flights are full it is worth persisting as seats reserved for medical emergencies may become available at the last minute. Once on board, you will find that Cabo Verdeans are not too worried about sitting in the seat actually allocated to them. No stress!

If your flight is cancelled, Cabo Verde Airlines will usually take full responsibility, with stranded passengers put up in hotels where food and drink are provided until a new flight can be scheduled. They will communicate with the hotel about flight times, but don't rely on receiving any emails or texts; it's best to be proactive with reception about any news. Given all of the above, unless things improve, it's important to pad a couple of days around your international exit flight.

BY BUS Outside of Praia and Mindelo (where city buses operate), *hiace* minibuses and open trucks with seating in the back (Hiluxes) constitute the public transport. They are recognisable by the sign '*aluguer*' and on most islands that is what they are called, though on Santiago the preferred term is *hiace* (pronounced 'yazz'). (For more on *alugueres*, see page opposite.) They are often overloaded with people, chickens and packages and trundling along to the sound of happy-go-lucky tinkling music.

Generally, *alugueres* converge at a point in a town or village which anyone can point out to you; often they drive around picking up passengers and few leave town before they are full. You shout ('*para!*' which means 'stop!') when you want to get off and you pay after disembarking. *Alugueres* can be flagged down anywhere along the roads. In Cabo Verde, unusually for West Africa, many of these vehicles are in good condition and consequently most of their drivers are careful and reasonably slow.

The great disadvantage for visitors can be the timings of the *alugueres*. Often they seem to leave outlying villages at 05.00 or 06.00 to take people to town, much to the bewilderment of the visitor. They then leave town for the outlying villages between 11.00 and mid-afternoon. Time and time again tourists pile into the 11.00 *aluguer* only to find they have no way of getting back to town in the evening without chartering a vehicle at ten times the price.

BY FERRY These are not the Greek islands; we are in the middle of rough Atlantic waters with great distances in-between. To reach airport-less Brava or Santo Antão, you have to take a mercifully short ferry ride. For other inter-island journeys, ferry trips are difficult to recommend on grounds of comfort and reliability.

If you are hyper-adventurous, know that ferries *do* operate between most of the islands, although journey times on potentially rough seas are long and schedules are rarely adhered to. It is essential to double-check the sailing times on CV Interilhas's website (see below) and wise to call. Single journeys cost between €15 and €70, depending on the distance. You are unlikely to find a ferry too full to take you, except at Christmas and festival times, but boats can be delayed for days and journeys are long (up to 14 hours!). There are some safety concerns, too. In 2008, two ferries sank and before that, two newly introduced catamarans were withdrawn because they couldn't cope with the rough seas. In 2015, there was a tragic ferry sinking off Fogo, with 11 lives lost. While things have improved, seasickness is still always a huge possibility. Even if you are not a sufferer, it is likely that most of your shipmates will be, and you will be ominously handed a bag upon boarding. It is advisable to keep your bags slightly off the floor and keep an eye on the passengers immediately beside you if you want to escape the consequences.

The services between Fogo and Brava, and between Mindelo on São Vicente and Porto Novo on Santo Antão, however, are rarely as rough, far more reliable and enjoy a much shorter journey time, around 40 minutes and 1 hour respectively.

CV Interilhas (w cvinterilhas.cv) began operations in 2019, and has entered into a 20-year concession contract with the government for the public inter-island passenger and cargo transport service. Their fleet currently has four ships: *Chiquinho BL* and *Dona Tututa* are passenger and cargo ships; and *Kriola* and *Liberdadi* are catamaran ships. Always buy your tickets in advance, either online, via an agent or at the terminal, as ferries do not sell tickets on board. Make sure to take your passport to the office when booking.

Your heavy luggage will usually be stowed in, and in some cases, hurled into, the back of a truck which will lumber on to the ferry when full, so keep your valuables in your hand luggage.

BY CARGO BOAT There are sometimes a few cargo boats travelling between the islands, and the ferry ticket offices sell a few passenger tickets on these for reduced prices – typically about two-thirds of the full price.

BY YACHT AND CATAMARAN There are day trips from Sal to Boavista in various craft (page 102). There are also yachts for charter between the islands.

BY TAXI The term 'taxi' refers both to the cars with meters and taxi signs, found in towns, and to *hiaces* (or *alugueres*; see opposite) that have been chartered by an individual. Chartering costs about ten times the public fare and you may be forced to do it if you want to go somewhere at a different time of day from everyone else. Sometimes the fares for a charter can be bargained down and occasionally an opportunist will try to diddle you, but generally charter prices are fixed – they're just comparatively high. Drivers in general love to be chartered by a tourist so watch out when they tell you there is no more public transport that day – hang around to check and insist that you want to travel *colectivo,* but also accept the possibility that they might actually be telling the truth! Tourists often get together to share a chartered minibus. Note that taxis after dark attract a premium of around 25%.

BY CAR

Hitchhiking Cars are likely to pick you up, except on Santiago. Offer the price of the *aluguer* fare if it seems appropriate, or ask if the journey is free (*buleia*). In remote areas there may be no traffic all day.

However, women travelling on their own should always exercise caution when attempting to hitchhike. It's not recommended.

Car rental This is possible through local chain firms on São Vicente, Sal and Santiago and there are tiny firms on some of the other islands. International firms have opened on Sal and Santiago. For contact details see the relevant island chapters. Book several days ahead if you can and don't expect things to run smoothly – for example, the wrong car might arrive several hours late with no price reduction offered for the inconvenience. Car maintenance standards do not match those you might find in western Europe or North America.

If driving, be on the lookout for speed bumps, which are often poorly marked, wandering dogs, sleeping dogs, meandering goats, careless cows and clueless chickens. Seatbelts are compulsory, though no-one wears them. Your travel insurance may be invalid if you choose not to. The same applies to drink-driving. More than two small beers and you are at risk. Police roadside checks are far from rare. Another dilemma is whether to pick up hitchhikers. As transport on the islands is a communal activity, you may feel guilty whizzing past locals who are genuinely looking for a lift. If you wish to help them, again be aware that your hire-car insurance or travel insurance may not cover you fully if passengers are injured while you are at the wheel.

BY CYCLING Keen cyclists do take their bicycles to the archipelago and return having had a good time. Check if Cabo Verde Airlines currently has the capacity to carry your bike between islands. If it does, you pay by weight, just as with other

TRANSPORT: THE MYSTERIOUS WORLD OF THE *ALUGUER*

Murray Stewart

The undisputed backbone of Cabo Verde's transport system, the *aluguer* can nevertheless be a source of frustration for some visitors to the archipelago, especially if they have no experience of transport in less-developed countries. Understanding the niceties of using these vehicles, which are either minibuses or pick-up trucks, may help to alleviate any confusion surrounding their operation. To understand them completely would take years of intensive anthropological study.

Derived from the Portuguese for 'to hire', the word *aluguer* is written on the side of the vehicle, on a sign on the windscreen, or on its roof. But even the name can confuse the newly arrived tourist, as on some islands they are referred to in conversation as a '*yasser*', which is a (huge) corruption of 'Hiace', the model name of the most common vehicle. With an *aluguer*, you can choose to travel '*colectivo*', thus sharing the cost with other passengers, or to hire them as a private-hire taxi. In the former case, you will pay one-tenth of the price of the latter, so it is important to know which way you are travelling before you set off, to avoid a shock when it comes to payment time at journey's end. The easiest way is to enquire of the driver '*Colectivo?*' and get him to confirm it to you, unless of course it is the private-hire option that you want. If you are the only passenger on board when the *aluguer* sets off, the chances are that you are travelling 'taxi-style'.

Travelling taxi-style means that you are in charge of where you go and you will not have to share the vehicle with other passengers; travelling *colectivo* means that the vehicle will not set off until it fills up with enough passengers to make economic sense for the driver to do so.

Much is made of tourists across the world being 'ripped-off', but most Cabo Verde municipalities issue a printed, laminated list of set fares, from which the drivers should not deviate. Sometimes this is kept in the glove compartment of the vehicle and you can ask to see it if you fear that you are being overcharged. The chances are that you are not: most drivers are honest, helpful and polite. Having said that, they are trying to make a living and so, when business is slow, they will obviously try to persuade you to hire them as a taxi. This way, they are earning money rather than being stuck at the roadside, furiously polishing every part of their vehicle while waiting for their *aluguer* to fill up with passengers. As you almost certainly look like a visitor, you will be targeted more than a local, in the belief that you have more money. And let's face it, you probably have, though

baggage, so carriage is free if it falls within your luggage allowance. Bicycles may also be hired on Sal, Boavista, Maio, Santo Antão and in Tarrafal on Santiago.

However, there are several caveats about cycling in Cabo Verde. Firstly, many of the roads are cobbled, causing ceaseless, tiring vibrations to the hands and sensitive areas, unless you have a bike with good suspension. Pot-holes can also be a problem. Secondly, the bulk of roads in Cabo Verde are utterly devoid of shade and the constant sun can be exhausting. Thirdly, some of the most interesting islands have many stretches that are too steep for cycling – in particular, much of Santo Antão and many roads on Fogo. Fourthly, people trying to take their own bike to the islands have run into problems both with bike damage and with the aircraft unexpectedly refusing to take the bike. Fifthly, the islands are full of dogs. And finally, you are unlikely to find any bike spares easily.

you may not want to spend it on taxis. Local people know when transport to or from is at its most frequent and they time their business in town accordingly, to avoid getting stuck or having to travel 'private hire'.

To varying degrees, drivers are proactive in finding business, often parading up and down the same street several times, interspersing their drive-pasts with U-turns, tooting their horns, slowing down to shout to anyone who looks like a passenger and to persuade them that it's time to take a ride. Of course, as they usually run set routes (which are sometimes painted on the vehicle doors), they will recognise potential passengers and will know exactly where they live and know the chances of them jumping on board. To visitors from abroad, the exchanges between driver and potential passengers defy logic, particularly when, on the third time of asking, the passenger jumps in, having declined to do so on the first two invitations. Surely, you may ask yourself, they either *want* to go home, or they don't?

If you are the first passenger to board an empty minibus, you will have to be prepared to wait, assuming you are travelling *colectivo*. But rather than be impatient, consider some of the advantages of this type of communal transport. Although the driver's motivation for waiting for a vehicle to fill up is monetary, you can comfort yourself that it is also environmentally friendly. Compare this with the 'developed' nations, where car ownership is high and everyone runs around in their own vehicle polluting the atmosphere *ad infinitum*. Travelling *colectivo*-style in an *aluguer* is a lesson in sharing space and time, both of which the Cabo Verdeans do exceptionally well.

I have fond memories of my *aluguer* journey in pre-eruption Fogo, travelling down from the crater to São Filipe. I counted 24 passengers in our 15-seat minibus; everyone seemed to have someone else's baby on their lap, except for me, whose arm was being dribbled on by a two year old. As we left the village, we stopped to pick up three more passengers, as well as four large, blue barrels and two sacks of goodness-knows-what. As well as carrying passengers, *aluguers* also multi-task as delivery vehicles in many areas, supplying food and drink, car parts, medicines and other essentials – Cabo Verde has no door-to-door postal delivery service.

After a well-ordered rearrangement of offspring, some tying of the mystery sacks to the vehicle roof and creative stowing of the barrels into a previously non-existent space, we lurched off again, out of the village. The three latecomers had to stand for the whole of the hour's journey, by the end of which my arm was thoroughly soaked by infant saliva.

ACCOMMODATION

HOTELS The hotel star-rating system is an inflated one, internal to Cabo Verde: if coming from Europe or North America, lower your expectations and go with the flow. The term 'hotel' implies a place of superior quality, though even this cannot be relied upon. The other terms, *pousada*, *pensão* and *residencial*, are interchangeable. Some establishments use the word *casa* to demonstrate a family atmosphere. At the bottom of the range there are some very cheap, grubby places that are not intended for tourists. No-one will mention them, they will not be marked, they are not listed in this book and even the proprietors may discourage you from staying for fear you'll complain about the conditions. Above this level, accommodation is almost invariably clean, if basic, and en-suite bathrooms are the norm. Rooms can vary enormously in quality

> **ACCOMMODATION PRICE CODES**
>
> Price of a double room with breakfast, including tax.
>
> | | |
> |---|---|
> | $$$$$ | 30,000$+ |
> | $$$$ | 15,000–30,000$ |
> | $$$ | 10,000–15,000$ |
> | $$ | 5,000–10,000$ |
> | $ | up to 5,000$ |

within the same hotel. In particular the windows of inner rooms in older buildings in Praia and Mindelo often open only on to a central shaft, which makes them dark and noisy.

There is a tourist tax equivalent to €2 per person per night for all guests, up to a maximum of ten nights. Prices quoted in this book include the tax, but bear in mind that in response to your telephone or email enquiry, hotels often quote their prices *excluding* the tax. There's an increasing number of upmarket hotels in Cabo Verde. At the time of writing, there were many on Sal and Boavista, a few on Santiago, São Vicente and Santo Antão and one on Fogo. Rooms in most three-star hotels will have hot water, telephone, fan or air conditioning, and often a fridge and television (often just local channels, though, and not always working!). If hot water is important to you (and it may be less so in a hot climate), then it is worth enquiring in advance. Sometimes the availability of hot water varies throughout the day, and hotels using solar power often cut the water first. Air conditioning is sometimes offered as an option, with extra charges levied if you say 'yes' – remember, electricity is expensive here. Breakfast is nearly always included in the price. Wi-Fi is commonplace in hotels and other accommodation, though in cheaper places it's still sometimes available in public areas only. Accommodation options are listed in descending order of price, ie: the most expensive first. Note that prices can jump considerably between the winter high season and summer, especially on Sal and Boavista.

HOMESTAYS On the two great hiking islands, Santo Antão and Fogo, as well as on Maio, local people are increasingly opening up their homes to visitors. In general you sleep in a spare (or hastily vacated) bedroom and are fed your evening meal as well as breakfast the next day. Sometimes local people have built concrete annexes on to their houses to accommodate tourists. A few homestays provide better facilities. The system has several advantages. It allows trekkers to do more ambitious journeys safe in the knowledge that they have places to stay along the way. It brings locals and visitors into closer contact – you experience a taste of the rural lifestyle while they derive entertainment and cash from you. An excellent project on Maio is linking up locals with visitors who want a more authentic accommodation experience (page 208).

But rural homestays are not for every visitor. Conditions will be basic: perhaps there will be a room without windows, a very old mattress and some sort of shared washing facility without a huge amount of privacy. Although the price will be lower than that of hotels, it may be higher than you expected it to be. This can be because of the high cost of arranging special food for visitors (for example, some homestay hosts on Santo Antão have to spend a day travelling to town and back to purchase food for their guests). For some visitors, a homestay is the high spot of their trip and even a formative experience in their lives; for others it is a disaster from which they can't wait to escape. The key is to abandon your tourist-as-consumer mindset, accepting what is given and taking an interest in everything you are privileged to witness. You can take comfort from the knowledge that, as you hand over your money, you are directly benefiting the local people. Contacts for homestays are given in the island chapters on Maio, Santo Antão and São Nicolau.

OTHER OPTIONS Camping is permitted on the beaches, but finding a natural water supply may be difficult.

On Sal, Boavista and Maio, as well as in Mindelo and Praia, there are an increasing number of apartments to rent and a few villas.

EATING AND DRINKING

Fish lovers will be in heaven on Cabo Verde. The grilled lobster is superb, as are the fresh tuna, octopus and a multitude of other delicacies. **Vegetarians** may find only omelette on the menu but can always ask for a plate of rice and beans. The very few places that cater properly for vegetarians are mentioned in the restaurant listings.

A Cabo Verdean speciality is *cachupa*, a delicious, hearty dish that comes in two varieties: poor-man's *cachupa* (boiled maize, beans, herbs, cassava, sweet potato) and rich-man's *cachupa* (the same but with chicken and other meat). *Cachupa* takes a long time to prepare: some restaurants put a sign in their windows to indicate when they will next be serving it. *Cachupa grelhada* is perhaps the easiest to find – everything available all fried up together, often for breakfast, and served with a fried egg on top.

An endearing penchant of Cabo Verdean restaurants is a Portuguese legacy: huge mounds of rice *and* potatoes of some variety (chipped, boiled), as well as various other boiled tubers in more traditional places, will arrive with your chosen main. For many, this is too much stodge, but you will have to be very insistent to avoid even one of these carb-laden sides.

Most towns will have local eateries where huge platefuls of rice, chips, beans and fish, or *cachupa*, are served up at lunchtime for 400–600$, but these places may not be open all day. Look out for restaurants offering *pratos do dia*, often at lunchtime. These 'dishes of the day' give you a chance to fill up very cheaply, usually for around 500$. Restaurant prices are defined in the rest of this book by the average cost of a main meat or fish dish. In most places, these go for between 600$ and 2,000$. Lobster tends to cost anything between 2,000$ and 3,000$ and can be much more on Sal and Boavista.

A minor frustration with restaurants can be **opening times** (page 85). Outside the big towns, try to call in at your chosen restaurant about 2 hours in advance to order your meal or you may well be restricted to the dish of the day. Many remote

RESTAURANT PRICE CODES
Price of an average main course dish. Drinks and service charge are extra.

$$$$$	3,000$+
$$$$	2,000–3,000$
$$$	1,000–2,000$
$$	500–1,000$
$	up to 500$

CULINARY GLOSSARY

Cachupa The national dish of Cabo Verde, made from corn and beans. Comes in several forms: *cachupa rica*, with fish or meat; *cachupa pobre*, the simplest, with just the base ingredients; and *cachupa guisado* or *refogada*, a fried 'hash' of the precooked stew, usually served with a fried egg for breakfast, but available all day too.

Cuscus A popular breakfast dish, with 'grains' resembling the North African semolina staple but instead made with sweet bean flour or cornmeal. Steamed into a pudding-like texture, and commonly eaten with butter.

Brinhola (also known as **fidjos**) Banana fritters, which are another breakfast staple.

Gufonginho Fried sweet potato pastries, recalling Portuguese *churros*, usually eaten with coffee.

Pastéis, Rissóis, Croquets, Chamuças Small savoury snack pastries. A *pastel* resembles a mini calzone or empanada, and are fried, the most common variety being *de tum*, with tuna. *Rissóis* are similar but are breadcrumbed before frying, served *de tum* but often also *de camarão*, with prawns. *Croquets*, made with salt cod or potato, are similar to the Portuguese snacks of the same name. *Chamuças* are like samosas.

Mandioca frita Cassava chips/fries; particularly creamy on the inside.

Moreia Eel, most often served crispy fried, but also braised in tomato and onion.

Búzio A conch stew, sometimes made with sea snails or mussels, flavoured, unusually, with soy sauce.

Bafa Another seafood stew, often made with octopus.

Percebes Goose barnacles, usually snap steamed and served in a pile, tasting a little like clams.

Caldo de peixe Hearty fish soup made with white fish, green bananas, root vegetables and herbs, sometimes thickened with cassava flour.

Cozido de piexe Fish stew thickened with coconut flesh and milk, plus beans, rice and eggs.

---

villages have no eating places, but somewhere there will be a shop – often hard to distinguish from an ordinary house. There you can buy biscuits and drinks. Note that on quieter islands such as Maio and São Nicolau, food shops and restaurants may open erratically and only for short periods. To avoid hours of hunger, always have provisions with you.

For a food glossary see above, and for useful food vocabulary, see page 366.

Coffee is often very good, even more so if made with local Fogo beans, but can occasionally be terrible, especially if involving milk. Breakfast coffee in hotels is particularly unreliable and you may need to hotfoot it to a bar or café if your

Jagacida Rice and bean stew.

Canja Portuguese-style chicken soup.

Bacalhau e grão de bico Salt cod and chickpea salad.

Modje Rich goat stew from São Nicolau.

Linguiça Portuguese-style spiced pork sausage, served with drinks or as an addition to other dishes.

Feijão congo Similar to the Portuguese *feijoada*, a pork and white bean stew, but here made with dried pigeon peas and usually eaten with *linguiça* and cabbage. Popular on Fogo.

Xerem Cornmeal porridge, flavoured with bay and served with coconut milk, peppers and sometimes fish.

Doce de papaia Papaya jam, usually served with fresh goat's cheese (the combination widely known as 'Romeo and Julieta').

Pudim Similar to the Spanish *flan*, made with condensed milk and eggs, and sometimes goat's cheese.

Doce leite Milk curds served with a spiced caramel syrup.

Doce de coco Coconut sweets.

Bolinhos de mandioca com mel Sweet baked balls of egg, molasses and cassava flour.

Bolacha and **kamoka** Popular ice cream flavours, the first made with crushed sweet Marie biscuits, the latter with roasted cornmeal.

Grogue and **ponche** *Grogue* (from the English 'grog', also spelled *grog/grogu*), is an artisanal cane *aguardiente* and is the national spirit (page 82). *Ponche* (from the English 'punch') is its liquor offspring, usually flavoured with honey, coconut, tamarind or chocolate.

morning ritual is dependent on it. Most locals drink espresso and asking for a cappuccino usually works, but it's worth trying Portuguese coffee orders such as *meia de leite* (flat white) or *garoto* (*piccolo*). Asking for tea can quite often bring an infusion of camomile or blackberry, so specify you'd like *chá preta*, black tea, if this is what you prefer. Taking your favoured tea bags is a safe option.

A good tip for finding street **snacks** is to search near the town's market, if it has one. There are many women with trays of sweets, monkey nuts, sugared peanuts and popcorn and tiny impromptu barbecues are sometimes set up. Often they will also sell little *pastéis* (fish pastries). Confectionery flavours are local: mainly coconut,

> ## GROGUE
>
> Sugarcane, the sole ingredient of *grogue*, arrived in Cabo Verde with the slaves from mainland Africa. The word '*grogue*' is derived from 'grog' – used by English seafarers. At first, the production of spirit from sugarcane was forbidden on the grounds that it presented a risk to public health. However, restrictive laws simply drove the distillers underground and by 1866 the authorities relented and introduced a brandy tax instead. By 1900, there was even legislation dictating the safe design of sugarcane presses, or *trapiches*.
>
> The *trapiche* is a large machine traditionally made of wood and driven by oxen or mules plodding round in a never-ending circle. Men feed cut sugarcane through heavy metal rollers and sugar syrup runs out and is collected in large wooden barrels where it is allowed to ferment for five to ten days. No water is added, and neither is yeast – there is enough naturally occurring on the cane.
>
> The still is partly buried in a loose stone oven, and the fermented syrup is brought to the boil, producing an aroma that wafts up the valley. After an hour, the steam is run through a curly pipe cooled by water, and the clear distilled spirit starts to flow. A skilled eye can tell from the froth in the distillate the point at which a palatable fraction is being produced. That's the theory, at least.
>
> In practice, the *grogue* drunk in villages will not have been produced under controlled conditions. The rougher distillations of *grogue* cost next to nothing. Distillation is likely to have been carried out in an old oil drum, and the spirit collected in a rusty tin. It will not kill you unless you binge on a particularly dodgy

peanut and papaya. Here and there women fry *moreia* – moray eel – too. Nice, but greasy – just spit the bones out; the dogs or cats will get them.

Cheap **picnic lunches** can be bought from supermarkets, markets and from bakeries. These exist in every town but they can be hard to track down, due to a dearth of signage. Ask for the *minimercado* if you get stuck and don't be too choosy: often they are more *mini* than *mercado*.

Bottled water is widely available and in ordinary shops is reasonably cheap (80–150$ for a 1.5-litre bottle, less in supermarkets); prices are inflated at hotels (200$ or so), although some of the more sustainability-minded small hotels will have complimentary carafes for your room and will refill your water bottle at cost. Some of the **wine** made on Fogo island is distinctive and very quaffable and can be found for sale around the archipelago. Other wines tend to be imported from Portugal or Italy. There are three principal **beer** brands. Strela is brewed in Praia, with Classic, Kriola and dark varieties. The other two are from Portugal: the maltier Superbock and the pils-style Sagres. Costs are typically 150–200$ for local and Portuguese beer and 300$ for other imported brands. On Sal many more familiar brands of imported drink are available, but are usually quite expensive.

The drink that Cabo Verdeans literally live and die for is **grogue** (see above). It is locally produced and abundantly available – in any dwelling carrying a sign above its door prohibiting children under 18 from entering.

PUBLIC HOLIDAYS AND FESTIVALS

Each island has a calendar of festivals, many of which originated as Catholic saints' days and all of which offer a great excuse for music and dancing, as well as the downing of *grogue*. They usually begin with church services and include processions,

brew, but it may upset your stomach. After 20 years of sustained drinking, the accumulated methanol cause you to lose your sight.

For those who are not put off, *grogue* is an exciting and throaty drink. There are, of course, as many subtleties to *grogue* as there are distilleries in Cabo Verde, increasingly including artisan producers. To fully appreciate the eye-watering gaspiness of it, it is quite acceptable to sip it, although you may be left with the strange feeling that much of what you were going to swallow has already evaporated in your mouth.

If you find yourself not up to *grogue*'s rawness, ask for *ponche* (punch). In this amber-coloured liquid the spirit's kick is muffled by honey. It is also available in flavours such as coconut, masking the inherent harshness of the raw spirit, but making it dangerously quaffable in the process. For those who dislike the sweetness or still want extra kick, *coupada* ('cut') is the halfway house – a mixture of *grogue* and punch.

Grogue is close to the hearts of many Cabo Verdeans – an invitation to share a glass in a remote village is not something to be turned down lightly. The drink is an important part of Cabo Verdean culture to the extent that the pressing of the cane, with its steady repetitive rhythm, has proved to be a fertile source of inspiration for music. The most famous ballads sung while at work on the *trapiches* are the *abois* or *kola boi*. They dwell at some length on the socio-economic ills which beset the Cabo Verdeans. It is said the melodies often reduce the oxen to tears.

drumming and the eating of specially prepared foods. On many islands, these have now transformed into popular music festivals. The most renowned is the São Vicente Carnival in February or March. Others of particular interest are described in the island chapters.

All the islands celebrate Christmas, Carnival (February or March) and Saint John (São João, 24 June). The following dates are public holidays, as well as Mardi Gras and Good Friday.

1 January	New Year
20 January	National Heroes' Day
1 May	Labour Day
5 July	Independence Day
15 August	Nossa Senhora da Graça (Our Lady of Grace)
12 September	Nationality Day
1 November	All Saints' Day
25 December	Christmas Day

SHOPPING

Shopping for leisure rather than necessity outside the towns is almost non-existent. The most colourful food market is in Assomada, on Santiago, a true flavour of mainland Africa. Most island capitals have some sort of fruit and vegetable market, and the ones in Praia and Mindelo are particularly atmospheric.

Local crafts can be bought in Mindelo, on São Vicente, where there have been revivals of skills such as the weaving of cloth and baskets. Santo Antão and São Nicolau are also good places to find local crafts and home produce. Locally made souvenirs are becoming increasingly common in the main tourism centres, though they can often be hard to spot when sold alongside crafts imported from the African mainland. For excellent souvenirs of the islands, buy bottles of *grogue* (available in any small shop in a town) or its more exotic (and palatable!) variants (try more touristy shops); Fogo wine and coffee beans; little bags of the abundant local sweets; and ceramics, including glazed *grogue* shot cups. More details are given in the island chapters.

ARTS AND ENTERTAINMENT

MUSEUMS AND HISTORICAL SITES Despite the archipelago's fascinating history there are only a few museums and specific architectural heritage sites. In the capital, Praia, there is a handful (page 181), and a few more scattered about Santiago.

The most important of these is the old city of Ribeira Grande (Cidade Velha; page 182), the first European city in the tropics and a pivotal arena in the transatlantic slave trade. It's an incredibly atmospheric piece of living history. Music legend Cesária Évora has a museum in her honour in Mindelo, which also boasts an exciting art and design museum plus a small maritime museum on the waterfront (page 293). The capital of Fogo, São Filipe, is a fine town full of *sobrado* architecture and has two museum collections (page 236).

Most island capitals have reasonably intact colonial-era streetscapes with a number of different architectural styles. Narrow cobbled streets, ochre-tiled roofs and abundant plantings in well-tended public gardens make for memorable city wandering, even without a checklist to tick off.

MUSIC AND DANCING Music and dancing have long been Cabo Verdeans' principal means of cultural expression. A well-known saying claims that 'eleven out of every ten Cabo Verdeans are musicians'. The music scene is thriving, with an increasing number of bands making the international break and following in the footsteps of the renowned Cesária Évora (page 44), gaining recognition in the Lusophone world and beyond. Music is everywhere in the archipelago: in Fogo crater, in every little village, down the *ribeiras* and of course in the cities of Praia and Mindelo. There are an astonishing number of outstandingly talented musicians for such a small group of islands.

To hear the music in a planned way, spend time in Mindelo (page 288) and Praia (page 178). Many restaurants on Sal have live music in the evenings too. You might pick up different dances on different islands, at local bars, for example. *Possada* is a favourite of Mindelo clubs, danced to zouk music; *funaná*, a fast dance performed mainly to the strains of the accordion, is a more Sotavento dance form, not really accepted in Mindelo; *cola* (which means 'glue') is a slow and amorous pelvic grind.

The contemporary industry is also strong and switched on, in terms of both performers and DJs. Expect to hear Afrobeat, Latin House, electro, hip hop, reggae, soul, R&B, pop and endless mash-ups of all of the above. Nightclubs tend to open at midnight. For more on music, see page 43.

OPENING HOURS

Nearly everything is closed on public holidays and on Sundays, and many shops also close early on Fridays. Opening hours tend to be southern European in style – that is, 08.00/08.30–noon/12.30 and 14.00/14.30–18.00/18.30 Monday–Friday, 08.30–noon Saturday. Banks tend to be open Monday–Friday until 15.00, without a lunch break.

The restaurant listings in the island chapters include opening times only where there is some degree of confidence that they will be adhered to, but even then they are no guarantee. The situation has improved over the last decade, but there is still a laid-back attitude to opening times, one which you may choose to adopt. Especially in remoter places, even if you're told specific opening times, they are often disregarded. One way around this is to pre-order your meal a few hours before. This also often means your meal will be served shortly after your arrival, rather than there being a long wait between ordering and eating. Generally, in the evenings, restaurants operate from about 19.00 to 23.00 (except where specific hours are stated in this guide).

MEDIA AND COMMUNICATIONS

INTERNET All of the international airports in theory have free Wi-Fi. Most municipal free services are no more, due to the availability of cheap unlimited data plans and widespread uptake of smartphones. In Mindelo and Praia, and in the tourist strips on Sal and Boavista, many cafés and bars have (password protected) Wi-Fi for customers.

POST OFFICE Cabo Verdean post offices are well equipped and it is possible to transfer money, send and receive faxes, make phone calls (expensive) and often make photocopies there – as well as buying stamps. Opening times vary somewhat but tend to be 08.00–noon and 14.00–18.00 Monday–Friday; some shut at 15.30.

RADIO AND TELEVISION Local television and radio is provided by RTC (w rtc.cv). RTC's TV arm, TCV, is based in Praia but has offices across the islands. It broadcasts news, entertainment and sports, including football from Portugal, Brazil and other Latin American countries. They also have English-language films at weekends. A wide range of satellite channels is available on the main tourist islands, particularly in upmarket hotels and sports bars. These include BBC, CNN and RAI, French, German, Senegalese and Nigerian stations, and stations showing Portuguese and Brazilian soap operas. Record Cabo Verde is the other main station. Its radio arm, Radio Cabo Verde, RCV, has an office in the cultural centre in Mindelo. Its programmes can be accessed online (w rtc.cv), allowing you to acclimatise to Cabo Verdean music before you visit, and continue to enjoy it after you return. Radio Praia (w praiafm.biz) also has some excellent music programming. The country also has a thriving YouTube community.

TELEPHONE If you're not venturing far and don't need to make lots of calls, you can switch off your phone's data and utilise only Wi-Fi in your hotel and cafés.

If you are likely to make quite a few calls and need consistent data connection for maps, social media and other apps, it's worth buying a SIM card from Alou (formerly known as CV Telecom), or its rival Unitel+. SIM cards, including some initial free credit, are cheap, and can be topped up anywhere where you see the relevant sign. Keep all the information that you are given when you buy your SIM, as you need it to top up anywhere other than the provider's offices. In Praia and Mindelo, you'll usually find an English speaker at these offices, and they are often far more helpful than their European counterparts. Weekly or monthly SIMs can be bought at stalls in airport arrivals on Sal and Boavista, but if you want a data plan that lasts longer than a week, it can be better to buy these at offices in town. These airport stalls have been known to pass off 'unofficial' monthly SIMs which run out a few days to a week shy.

Local calls are cheap but it's very expensive to make and receive international calls on local mobile plans. Almost everyone uses WhatsApp in any case.

At the time of writing, eSIMs weren't available in Cabo Verde.

CULTURAL ETIQUETTE

In many practical ways travelling around the islands is a joy, and in general the people are keen to encourage tourism. As one visitor put it: the people have the carefree approach to life of South America combined with the family orientation of Africa. Culturally there is little corruption and bribery.

Cabo Verde has a history of cosmopolitanism; people know about the outside world because their children, siblings or cousins live there, or because they've had a working life at sea on merchant ships. Nevertheless, tourism always brings with it crime, envy, loss of dignity and hassle. It remains to be seen what impact widespread foreign ownership of land and apartments will have on local people, the usual cost of living hikes aside.

BEGGING In a small but growing number of places in Cabo Verde – the waterfront in Santa Maria, right across central Mindelo, the Museu da Resistencia in Tarrafal – children and teens pursue passers-by with persistent demands for money. Responding to these demands does nothing to alleviate the structural inequalities that lead to poverty. If you would like to help the disadvantaged youth of Cabo Verde, consult page 88 for bodies looking for donations and volunteers. A few local tour companies and some smaller hotels also arrange for school supply donation drop-offs, so enquire about this when booking.

There are some occasionally effective ways of replying to demands for money – firmness of response, smiles and good humour being the best accompaniments to whatever you say: '*Desculpe (deshculp)*' – 'sorry'; '*Não tenho (Now tenyu) dinheiro*' – 'I don't have money'.

HIRING GUIDES Where walks are described throughout the book it is made clear if a guide is required. Where a guide is not absolutely essential, you may still prefer to hire one in order to get to know a local person, embellish your walk with more information and help the local economy. Guide details are listed in some chapters and most hotels also have a list.

LANGUAGE Nearly everyone speaks Kriolu, a creolised melange of Portuguese and several West African languages with vocabulary borrowed from other European languages as well. Kriolu has many island variants but has two main branches: Badiu, from Santiago and the other Sotavento (leeward) islands, Maio, Fogo and Brava; and Sampadjudu, from the Barlavento (windward) islands, ie: Santo Antão, São Vicente, São Nicolau, along with Sal and Boavista. All variants are understandable to most islanders. Portuguese (the official language) is spoken fluently by most townspeople but is not well understood in outlying villages – some people do not speak it at all. Almost everything official and everything written is in Portuguese, however. The most common second European language is French, spoken widely by officials as well as by guides on the smaller islands, but English is widespread too and may soon overtake it.

If you are struggling, keep asking people if they speak English or French (*fala inglês?, fala francês?* – *fowle eenglaysh?, fowle frensaysh?*). Often such a speaker can be found even in the remotest village. For words and phrases and a discussion of

SOCIAL INTERACTION
Steven Maddocks and Gabi Woolf

GREETINGS In social situations, men shake hands with men. Sometimes the handshake lasts for as long as the conversation, so a man may hold on to your hand while he's speaking to you. It takes some getting used to, especially for frigid, contact-shy Brits, but go with it. A man and a woman, or two women, generally shake hands plus a kiss on each cheek, even on first meeting.

SMALL TALK This is the name of the game. Conversations tend to run round in circles. Each person will enquire about the other's well-being, the well-being of each member of the other's family, then their colleagues. Then the questions turn to life in general, work, health. Neither will actually answer any questions – they just keep asking each other. So the response to 'How are you?' is 'How are you?'

'TUDU BON?' There are about 50 variations on *'Tudu bon?'* (which means 'everything OK?'). The *tudu* can be followed by *bon, ben, dretu, fixe, em forma, sabi,* or OK, tranquil, cool, fine, nice, and a million others. If you can master just a few phrases in the local language, make it these ones – it will endear you to the locals and make them smile!

NO The gesture for 'no' is a waggle of the index finger with a 'no' look on your face. It seems rude, but isn't.

HISSING If someone wants to get your attention, they will hiss at you. Sometimes this comes out as 'sss', sometimes more like 'pssssyeoh'! This can strike the newcomer as incredibly rude, but it's not meant to be, and it's a lot more effective than 'Ahem, excuse me…ahem…excuse me! Hello, excuse me?'

'OI' This means 'Hi' and is very friendly.

Kriolu, see pages 37 and 369. Learning a few Kriolu basics, such as greetings, as well as 'please' and 'thank you', will endear you to the locals and make for a better experience for all. Don't be intimidated; many expats who can't speak Portuguese can speak passable Kriolu – the pronunciation is far less daunting.

LOCAL RESOURCES Water is scarce and has invariably taken toil and money to reach your basin. It is very important not to waste it. There are many endangered plant species on the archipelago (page 5).

Ultimately, the goats may get them all. Nonetheless, picking flowers is absolutely out of the question. Don't buy products made of turtle shells, coral or other endangered resources.

SEX WORK There are no laws against any kind of sex work on the islands except for those concerning trafficking and child prostitution. Unaccompanied men may experience some unwanted approaches on the street from sex workers in Santa Maria on Sal, many of whom are from West Africa and often victims of organised trafficking networks. It is not unknown for taxi drivers to offer to facilitate 'meetings' as well, but it's rarely aggressive. Female sex tourism is not as prevalent as it is in the Gambia and Guinea-Bissau, but does occur and can occasionally make interactions with local men hard to read.

SCAMS It may be worth giving suspected 'rip-off merchants' the benefit of the doubt in Cabo Verde. If you think you are being mistreated it could just be a problem with the language barrier, or the local custom (as, for example, with a 2-hour wait in a restaurant), or the fact that prices are genuinely high for everyone (for example, with taxi fares). Do be wary of those claiming to be 'guides' though, especially if it involves wildlife excursions. All guides must be licensed and carry an ID card (page 68).

STREET VENDORS Tourists on Sal and Boavista often complain about aggressive street vendors. Many are recent West African immigrants and do operate very differently from their laid-back Cabo Verdean counterparts (page 122). While they can become annoying, it's worth remembering that they are often in poverty, have few support networks and are often openly discriminated against by Cabo Verdeans as well.

TAKING PHOTOGRAPHS It is respectful to ask people before you take their photo; smile and say hello, pause, ask to take a photo, offer to send them the shot. Never take photos of children unless a parent is present and you can ask their permission. Also ask, and be prepared for a firm no from many older Cabo Verdeans, especially in rural areas. Some unsupervised children, mainly in the cities, will ask to have their photo taken and for payment; Cabo Verdean organisations working to prevent child poverty, exploitation and trafficking see this 'transaction' as a perpetuation of the inequality that creates these conditions in the first place. Also, do not photograph the *rebelados* on Santiago (page 191) or workers in the markets of Praia, unless you have clear consent. In Santa Maria on Sal, there are also a number of people with captive monkeys who will ask for money if you try to take a photograph. The animals are very poorly treated and there have been moves to outlaw the practice; in the meantime, it's wise to avoid entirely. Photographing aircraft may provoke an angry response on the runway due to security concerns.

TRAVELLING POSITIVELY

You can give something back simply by venturing out and about, using local tour operators, staying in the many family-run *pensões*, being mindful of scarce resources and eating in local restaurants.

CHARITIES If you would like to help one of the charities on Sal or Boavista, and are flying from the UK on TUI, you can often organise a 'charity suitcase' waiver with the airline, allowing you to take a suitcase packed with goods for either the stray animal charities or for those dealing with child poverty without the charge for extra hold baggage.

If you would like to contribute to social projects, contact one of the following or ask around about others. Please ensure that the organisation you decide to work with currently complies to the ethical standards and fiscal accountability that you would expect in your own country and is also recognised and accepted by the community they purport to serve.

Associação Nu Bai e associacaonubai@gmail.com; w nobai.wordpress.com; f nubai.caboverde. Nu Bai has been providing practical, hands-on support for solo mothers & disadvantaged children on Sal for more than a decade. This includes organising travel for medical purposes, high-school scholarships & building toilets & bathrooms. Donations of school supplies or new children's clothing can also be left at any Djunta Mo Art shop (page 123) in Santa Maria.

SOS Children's Villages w sos-childrensvillages.org/where-we-help/ africa/cape-verde. This international social development organisation has been working in Cabo Verde for some decades and currently has 2 SOS children's villages, 1 SOS youth facility & 2 SOS kindergartens on Santiago, & focuses on family-based, long-term care of children who are no longer able to grow up with their biological families.

VOLUNTEER AND DEVELOPMENT WORK Many volunteers and other development workers in Cabo Verde have a superb, and life-changing, time. Cabo Verde has retained qualities that some feel that Europe and the USA have lost in the stampede for material success. Returning *emigrantes* from the USA, as well as foreigners, enjoy the peace, the relaxed pace of life, and the high value given to (and consequently time invested in) community, friendships, free time, parties and making music.

Some volunteers arrive with an idealistic notion that the people will greet them with 'outstretched arms, waiting for them to teach, train, and show them a better way of life,' says one volunteer. It can be a shock to discover indifference – or justifiable pride in the current way of life – combined with a reluctance to change.

Adaptability on the part of the volunteer is essential. An invaluable attitude derives from realising that you are in Cabo Verde to learn as well as to teach and give. In this way you will gain a deeper understanding of another culture – one that only comes when you spend time in a place and which will be an asset through life.

Above all you must be able to switch off. This does not rule out caring deeply about your work, and putting in 100%. But it does mean that when things get beyond your control you can shrug, laugh and say: 'I did my best, and the rest is out of my hands.'

Essential characteristics Consider whether you have the following before you go: linguistic ability, especially the ability to pick up a mostly spoken language like Kriolu, but also the wherewithal to learn a formal written language like Portuguese, used for all official purposes; patience (in bucketloads); and sensitivity to other cultures and people skills.

Volunteer programmes Historically, many volunteers in Cabo Verde were sent by the US Peace Corps, but that organisation withdrew suddenly in 2012, perhaps evidence of the islands' advancement up the ladder of development. The United Nations (w unv.org) still sends volunteers to Cabo Verde.

Environmental projects FMB (w fmb-maio.org) and **Project Biodiversity** (w projectbiodiversity.org) accept volunteers for their conservation programmes, especially from June to December (page 208 and page 97). Protecting turtles is a priority. Language skills are especially valued.

ANIMAL WELFARE Treatment of animals in Cabo Verde, particularly cats and dogs, has been a long-standing concern. A lack of veterinarians on all the islands for many years resulted in a large population of feral and free-roaming animals, especially dogs, many of which are in dire need of treatment for a variety of diseases and injuries. Although many dogs do have owners, the culture is to let animals run loose on the streets. The focus of campaigning organisations such as Cabo Verde Cats and Dogs is centred on encouraging government to create a compulsory dog registration scheme to ensure that culling isn't the only solution. All animal welfare organisations are desperately short of funds and will welcome donations of money, medicine, tick and flea treatment and even simple things such as collars and leads. If you are a visiting vet, you could help out for a few days. Even if you have no experience most will welcome your assistance, even for an afternoon. Contact the organisation in question to find out exactly what they need.

OSPA w ospa-cv.org. An organisation that is committed to reducing the number of stray cats & dogs on Sal. Also campaigns on animal welfare issues.

Si Ma Bo w simabo.org. Taking care of stray cats & dogs on São Vicente. Offers the opportunity to adopt a pet. Provides low-cost accommodation for volunteers as well as other animal lovers.

Part Two

THE GUIDE

3

Sal

> You live – sleeping mother
> Naked and forgotten
> Arid, Whipped by the winds
> Cradled in the music without music
> Of the waters that chain us in…
>
> Amílcar Cabral, quoted in Basil Davidson, *The Fortunate Isles* (Hutchinson, 1989)

There can be nowhere on earth as elemental as Sal. Any mountains, streams or vegetation that may have adorned it in the past have been obliterated by the wind over millions of years. Now Sal is just rock, sand and salt, still blasted by the same winds. On Sal the transience of life – animal or vegetable – becomes very clear.

The arrival at Sal on an international flight is a deliciously depressing descent. For hours the traveller has scanned the Atlantic from the aeroplane window, searching for the lost islands of Cabo Verde with a growing sense of their isolation. Then Sal appears: relentlessly brown and featureless, etched with dry cracks through which rain might occasionally flow. Disembarking from the aircraft to cross the heat of the runway you will gaze at the rocky plains in puzzlement, trying to remember why you decided to come. If you've already visited the other less-developed islands, you may think that the airport apron contains more tarmac than exists on the rest of the islands put together, given their penchant for cobbled roads.

Three types of travellers come to Sal: those seeking no more than year-round sunshine, beautiful beaches and blue sea who head for the out-of-town, all-inclusive resorts, the smaller Santa Maria hotels or their own holiday apartments; watersports enthusiasts craving world-class wind- and kitesurfing and diving; and those who use it as a relaxing and comfortable base from which to explore other islands. All three should be satisfied with what Sal has to offer.

HIGHLIGHTS AND LOWLIGHTS

Sal is a top windsurfing, kitesurfing and surfing destination and also offers good diving and fishing as well as Cabo Verde's largest number of organised tourist activities. The beach in Santa Maria is surely world-class and you can sunbathe, snorkel and swim, and enjoy the international hotels with their pools and other facilities. Those based on Sal can get a flavour of other Cabo Verdean islands through day trips by boat or plane.

You can fill a day by visiting the imposing volcano crater and salt lake of Pedra de Lume (a candidate UNESCO World Heritage Site), the foaming lagoon and Olho Azul (Blue Eye) at Buracona or take a boat ride to view whales and dolphins. Other possibilities include taking lonely walks to watch the turquoise sea from its treeless, rugged coastline or crossing the rocky interior with a 4x4 or quad bike. Sal abounds in interesting birds and shells and there are opportunities to watch turtles.

The island's resort, Santa Maria, also has decent restaurants, lively bars, live-music venues and nightclubs – enough to satisfy most party-goers. You will not find the true soul of Cabo Verde here, but you might skim its surface.

Sal is still developing as a tourist destination and some tour operators and travel agents oversell it as some verdant, undiscovered paradise. If the frenzy that arose in the last decade claiming that this was the 'new Caribbean' has not fully abated, then it needs to. It's not any kind of Caribbean: though its beaches are beautiful, its waters crystal clear, and it has the occasional small mountain, its interior is an unrelenting brown desert with very little vegetation. Visitors who book under false impressions sometimes return disappointed with the small number of sights on Sal, relatively high prices and the abundant wind. Many others, of course, have had a happy, sunny holiday.

Those who love Sal tend to be sea lovers rather than land lovers. It is not the place for hikers, those in search of lush scenery or those who seek to immerse themselves in a rustic Cabo Verdean way of life. If your goal is to see several islands you may regret having allocated too many precious days to Sal. Instead, get on with your journey – you can fit Sal into transit times at the beginning and end of the holiday, indulging yourself in this ideal relaxation destination.

SUGGESTED ITINERARY AND NUMBER OF DAYS If you are dedicated to a watersport or two, are a real sun lizard, or enjoy the prospect of the resort hotels you should aim to spend at least a week here. If you are a sightseer, or crave mountains or greenery, go for one to two days, maximum.

If you are passing through Sal between flights, we suggest one of the following, all of which are described in this guide: a walk up and around Monte Curral in Espargos (1 hour); a trip to Pedra de Lume (2–4 hours); and, for those seeking some chill-out time between island-hopping, a few hours on the beach (or at a feet-in-the-sand beach bar) in Santa Maria.

BACKGROUND INFORMATION

HISTORY On Sal the living was always marginal, based on whatever demand could be found for its four specialities: sun, sand, wind and salt. Today, for the first time in its history, it is flourishing as the result of three of those commodities. Sand and sun are in demand from beach-loving tourists. And the wind now catches the sails of delighted windsurfers who have discovered one of the best places in the world for their sport.

For the last five centuries Sal's economy has risen (always modestly) and fallen with international demands for its fourth element, the one from which it takes its name: salt. It is thought that even before the island was sighted by Gomes and de Noli in 1460 it was known by Moorish sailors for its rich saltpans.

The colonisation of the rest of Cabo Verde had little consequence for Sal for hundreds of years – salt was procured more easily from the island of Maio, closer to the capital island, Santiago. Nothing much disturbed Sal except perhaps the offloading of some perplexed goats in the 16th century as part of the archipelago's drive to increase meat production. For much of the time there were probably also a few slaves on Sal, digging for salt. Early reports from passing sailors reveal that people sometimes hunted marine turtles on the island.

Even by 1683 the passing English sailor William Dampier reported the presence of just six men, a governor…and an abundance of flamingos. There are no longer any of the last – it is believed they disappeared with the rise of the salt industry. The men survived by trading with the odd passing ship – salt and goat skins in exchange for food and old clothes.

It wasn't until 150 years ago, when Cabo Verdean businessman Manuel António Martins set up a salt export business, that Sal's population began to grow. A thousand souls came to join the 100 occupants between 1827 and 1882 – 'souls' was the word used by the British businessman from São Vicente, John Rendall, to describe both free men, of whom there were 300, and slaves. The salt business was based at two sites: Pedra de Lume in the east and Santa Maria in the south. Its fortunes fluctuated with the rise and fall of trade barriers in Brazil, the African mainland and even Portugal itself. Eventually the business ceased in the first half of the 20th century and the island returned to desolation. Archibald Lyall, an English journalist who visited in 1936, reported:

> Not even the most rudimentary garden is possible among the shifting dunes, and all the landward windows of the houses have to be kept perpetually shuttered against the penetrating yellow grit.

Sal's 20th-century prosperity began when the Italian dictator Benito Mussolini was looking for a site where aircraft could stop to refuel between Europe and South America. Portugal sold him the right to build an airport on Sal, then bought back the resulting facility in 1945. Since then the airport has grown and the town of Espargos, the island's capital, has developed with it. Mussolini's efforts have ensured that his country's footprint, evidenced by a large number of Italian-owned restaurants and hotels, remains to this day. Another nation also found Sal a useful refuelling point in the past: South Africa. Throughout the years of apartheid, when other African countries refused to allow its planes to land on their ground, the Portuguese permitted South African Airways to stop on Sal. Responding to the need to house airline crews was Sal's first, tiny step towards tourism.

SAL TODAY Sal draws some income from its airport, its petrol-storage facilities, and the fish-processing factory in its harbour, Palmeira. But it is tourism and real estate where the island's economic potential is firmly focused. The wavering fortunes of the tourism infrastructure in Egypt, Turkey and Tunisia, after waves of instability in those regions, saw a rush to build large hotels on Sal, despite the temporary dent

FESTIVALS ON SAL

Festivals, when everything may be closed, are as follows:

19 March	São Jose (Palmeira)
3 May	Santa Cruz (Espargos)
9 June	Santo António (Espargos)
24 June	São João (Espargos)
29 June	São Pedro (Hortela, Espargos)
Early July	Sal Kriol Jazz Festival (Santa Maria)
Last week of July	Santa Ana (Fontona)
15 August	Nossa Senhora de Piedade (Pedra de Lume)
15 September	Nossa Senhora das Dores (Santa Maria)
Mid-September	Sal International Music festival (Santa Maria)

in investment due to the financial crisis of 2008. This sudden lull in tourist numbers and investment was repeated again when the Covid pandemic of 2020–21 hit.

Still, over the last few years, thanks to generous tax concessions and an unquenchable European thirst for fresh destinations, tourism on Sal has followed an upward curve. As on Boavista, the tourist numbers on Sal have given the island a more international flavour than the less-visited members of the archipelago: prices here are often quoted in euros, a currency that is readily accepted. If national development plans are followed, some 17% of Sal's land will eventually be taken up with tourism developments and services.

Echoing this has been a boom in apartment building. The thought of owning a few square metres of real estate on Sal had caught the imaginations of mostly British and Irish nationals who wanted both a place in the sun and a financial stake in what was, at least then, perceived as the 'Next Big Thing'. Following the aforementioned downturns, many inexperienced speculators had their fingers burned and numerous developments still lie unfinished.

Sal today has a purpose, a place in the world. Its population has soared from just 5,500 in 1970 to around 25,000, with two-thirds of its inhabitants in Santa Maria. Wander around Santa Maria today and you will find not just the indigenous inhabitants but their compatriots from most other islands; you will find construction workers, trinket salesmen, artists and musicians from West Africa; estate agents, developers, gardeners, plumbers and furniture importers from Britain and Ireland; restaurant owners from Italy, France and Portugal.

But though Sal may be the crucible of Cabo Verde's economic transformation, it is in some ways its sacrificial victim. It is providing, in the national government's eyes, the quick economic boost thought to be needed in order both to diversify the economy and fund more sensitive touristic development on other islands.

The danger is that Sal will lose its allure in the longer term unless efforts are made to preserve what makes it unique: thick margins of undeveloped beach, dunes, unique birds, turtles and coral mounts in the sea. Even Sal's celebrated windsurfing spots need a custodian, now that they are jeopardised by new buildings blocking the wind. The government has taken some decisive national protective measures: for example, it has banned the use of sand from beaches for construction; it now insists that potential developers make environmental impact assessments and it is supposedly tightening up on what they can build. Sadly, the enforcement of these environmental laws does not yet appear to be vigorously applied.

GEOGRAPHY Sal is the most barren of the inhabited islands. Its highest peak, Monte Grande, in the northeast, reaches only 406m. The island is just over 30km long and nowhere more than 12km wide. Its landscape is of brown, stony plains and desert sands deposited by winds from mainland Africa. The 25,000 inhabitants occupying its 216km^2 live almost exclusively in Espargos, the capital in the centre of the island, and Santa Maria, the tourist resort on the south coast.

FLORA AND FAUNA
Protected areas The Baía da Murdeira is designated a Marine Protected Area – Cabo Verde's first – but little monitoring or patrolling appears to take place, making it an MPA in name only. Known to some as the 'bay of corals' it is home to diverse life, including around 45 types of small fish, many of them endemic (but no big fish). Although Murdeira is rocky it has very small beaches where some loggerhead turtles (*Caretta caretta*) come to nest, but numbers are dwindling due to development and hunting. For both fish and turtles it is a place to hide and feed, and offers perfect conditions as a nursery for fish stocks. Humpback whales can sometimes be seen in the bay, as can melon-headed whales (*Peponocephala electra*). Widespread throughout the world's tropical and subtropical waters, they often go unseen by humans because of their preference for deep water. In 2005, however, a group became stranded here, though human help managed to guide them back to sea.

The salina of Pedra de Lume is a protected landscape and remains on the 'tentative' (candidate) list for designation as a World Heritage Site. Other protected landscapes are the salina of Santa Maria, Monte Grande (the island's tallest mountain) and the lagoon of Buracona. The natural reserves on Sal are Monte Leão (a small hill at the northern end of Baía da Murdeira also known as Rabo de Junco) including the small islet Rabo de Junco behind the hill; the southeastern stretch of coast known as Costa da Fragata; the beaches of Serra Negra and Ponta Sino. Morrinho do Açúcar and Morrinho do Filho are natural monuments.

Birds Birdwatchers will find interesting waders in the saltpans including, in Pedra de Lume and the protected area of Costa de Fragata, the black-winged stilt (*Himantopus himantopus*), known locally as *pernalonga*. This extraordinary, elegant creature has long red legs that extend behind it as it flies, as well as a long, thin beak. It breeds only on Sal. Species you may see all year round include turnstones, sanderlings, Kentish plovers, greenshanks, egrets, kestrels, ospreys, herons and the Cape Verde swift.

Sal is also a nesting ground for several endemic sea birds, including shearwaters, Cape Verde storm petrel and Bulwer's petrel. The highlight for birdwatchers, though, is the beautiful red-billed tropicbird. West Africa's largest nesting colony can be found in the cliffs of Serra Negra and around Monte Leão, part of the protected areas of Rabo de Junco in the north of the island.

Following the rains in August and September many more birds can be seen in the temporary wetlands that are left dotted around the island. Migratory birds such as whimbrels and spoonbills also stop by the island, usually on their way to wintering habitats further south.

Turtles Although it's very difficult to provide accurate figures, one estimate states that around 5,000 endangered loggerhead turtles (*Caretta caretta*) nest annually on Sal (compared with around 15,000 on Boavista island), mostly along the southwestern and southeastern coasts. The numbers fluctuate hugely from year to year.

Turtles have historically faced two major threats on Sal: from tourism and from hunting. Tourists and turtles have the same taste in beaches, so tourism development has been occurring on exactly those beaches that are important for turtles. Illumination from beachfront hotels and apartments disorientates adults and hatchlings. Although the law stipulates that there should be no construction within 80m of the high-tide mark, and no artificial light within 500m of nesting beaches, some developments have flouted this. And the rising number of tourists is leading to more noise, rubbish and adverse types of beach use, particularly as they have not, until recently, been given any advice on how to minimise their impact. One example of the negative effect caused by the increase in tourism is the

SAVING TURTLES ON SAL

For a long time, it seemed as if turtles were doomed on Sal. If the locals didn't get them for supper, the quad bikes would crush their nests; and if the bikes didn't get them, hotel and apartment lights would lure them into a deathly inland wander.

But there is hope, as long as **Project Biodiversity** (354 1959; e info@projectbiodiversity.org; w projectbiodiversity.org) continues its conservation work. In nesting season, a team of employees and a committed body of international volunteers patrol the beaches of the island, warding off the activities of would-be hunters and careless tourists. Sadly, their resources do not allow them to cover all of Sal's beaches every night, and some of the northern sands are unprotected. Here there are a smaller number of sea turtles nesting, but also the highest recordings of poached adults.

A field camp operates on Kite Beach on the east coast, giving the project's night patrols a base. As well as the hunters, beach hotel developments on Sal result in a loss of habitat and there was a huge decrease in turtle nests on beaches where construction work took place. When hotels are complete, the beaches become awash with people, dogs and light pollution.

There are laws already in existence for the protection of turtles, with possession, hunting, consumption and exploitation of sea turtles and their eggs being made criminal offences in 2018. The implementation and enforcement of these laws, however, lags; the willingness is there but shoestring resources don't help.

Ironically, it could be tourists' penchant for the turtles that will help save them, with their appeal mooted as adding over a million euros to the economy. Seeing turtles is a firm part of most tourist itineraries, and this led to the launch of afternoon hatchery visits to safely observe the hatchlings that have been born from relocated nests.

As well as operating the hatchery on the beach in front of the RIU Funana hotel, the Project Biodiversity team campaigns and champions the turtles' cause at local government level. Their initiatives are doing good work to combat the lack of awareness among locals and visitors both structurally and practically, including monitoring visitor numbers and attempting to stop groups without permits (and guides) entering the nesting areas.

Visitors can support the project by visiting the hatchery (mid-January–mid-December), where you will learn more about conservation, can adopt a turtle and donate if you wish. You can also enquire in advance about volunteering opportunities, including taking part in night patrols, and being part of their field camp or homestay teams.

undoubted damage caused by the irresponsible use of quad bikes, 4x4s and horses, which, until being outlawed on dunes and the beach, crushed a large percentage of the turtle nests laid on Sal's beaches. These activities do still continue, though, with even the briefest detour capable of destroying the habitat protecting the nests. Dunes are also often the last barrier protecting the land from ocean storms, as well as acting to block light that lures both adult and baby turtles inland and to certain death by dehydration. The best way to ensure the end of these illegal practices is to refuse to enter the dunes if your tour operator suggests it and report the operator to Project Biodiversity.

Hunting is now only an issue on Sal's northerly beaches. While there has been considerable success in reducing the problem in the south, those committed to saving turtles are still aware of the threat. While some experts believe that tourism will drive every last turtle from Sal, others believe that tourists offer the only hope of salvation – their interest in the matter may convince all parties to change their behaviour. (For more on turtles, see pages 8 and 97.)

SAFETY Take care when swimming: currents are milder than in the UK, but when the wave height is great there can be a powerful undertow. Swimming on the east coast, which has some steep dips, needs care. For unfrequented beaches take local advice.

Theft is common in parts of Sal, mostly of possessions left in unattended vehicles – particularly on Buracona – and on beaches. Violent muggings involving theft are unusual, but have happened. Use common sense if you go to remote places, and don't walk on unlit streets late at night. More prosaically, street vendors and some souvenir shop owners can be irritatingly persistent, but will usually respond to a firm, polite 'no' (page 122).

GETTING THERE AND AWAY

BY AIR Many international flights land on Sal, although there are also international airports on Santiago, Boavista and São Vicente. The arrivals hall at **Amílcar Cabral International Airport** can feel chaotic if there are simultaneous departures or arrivals of tour-group-filled planes, but passport control is becoming increasingly efficient, with automatic passport screening being introduced. See page 58 for details of the visa exemption process. Those taking both international and domestic flights are currently requested to be at the airport 2 hours before travel, when gates open.

The airport has two bank branches: BCA Bank and Caixa Económica. Both have an ATM and Caixa has Western Union facilities. There is also a currency exchange kiosk. Airlines with offices are Cabo Verde Airlines, Bintercanarias, TAP, Air Senegal, Luxair and TUI.

There is a tourist information desk outside arrivals, but its information is fairly limited. Tour agency representation comes and goes but **Morabitur** (often unmanned, but with emergency numbers; m 918 7307/7366) is a perennial fixture. The airport has a café/restaurant, phone company outlets, a rental-car agency, several good souvenir shops, a branch of the music store Harmonia, and a left-luggage office (150$ per item).

International departures from Sal If you're flying with TUI or easyJet to a UK airport, it can be wise to ensure you get there before the group buses arrive from the all-inclusive hotels; otherwise it can take well over an hour to get to the head of the check-in queue. If you do this you will have time to kill airside: there are some decent souvenir shops selling local products, as well as a branch of Ocean Café (page 120) and the upmarket Cabo Verdean chain restaurant Américo's (page 119), with signature Portuguese-style *prego* sandwiches.

In transit through Sal If you are in transit to Praia Airport on Santiago with Cabo Verde Airlines then your baggage may well have been checked all the way through. You will, however, have to go through immigration and customs yourself, after which you should check in immediately for your onward flight. If you are in transit to any island other than Santiago you may have to collect and re-check in your baggage. If you have a long wait you can leave your luggage at the airport and take a 5-minute taxi ride into Espargos or a 15-minute one to Santa Maria.

Domestic flights Cabo Verde Airlines flies from Sal to all the other islands with airports, though this may involve transiting via Praia. At the time of writing the timetable was in flux and not particularly accommodating of island-hopping travellers. Bookings can be made online or with agencies such as Barracuda Tours or vista verde tours in Santa Maria (page 101). Flights are limited and book up quickly; fares can also increase dramatically the closer to departure you are. It is advised to pre-book internal connections before leaving home.

From the airport Most of the big, all-inclusive tourist hotels meet international charter flights with their own buses, but there are also plenty of **taxis**. Santa Maria is a 15-minute journey (1,500$, or 1,800$ at night), Murdeira 10 minutes (1,200$), and Espargos less than 5 (400$, or 500$ at night). You probably won't find **public transport** (an *aluguer*) waiting at the airport, but if you walk out of the airport and stand on the main road you can catch an *aluguer* (150$ to Santa Maria); be aware that you may wait some time as most *alugueres* leave Espargos full. Alternatively take a taxi only as far as Espargos and pick up an *aluguer* there. Relying on finding an *aluguer* is not recommended if your flight lands late at night.

BY FERRY CV Interilhas (w cvinterilhas.cv) ferries connect Sal with Santiago, Boavista and São Vicente via São Nicolau, leaving from the port of Palmeira on the island's west coast. It would be misleading to describe them as running to a regular schedule, or as being reliable or comfortable. They are, therefore, not advised if you are on a tight schedule or liable to seasickness. They can be booked online (with a Visa card only), via any local travel agency or at the CV Interilhas office in Espargos. For more on ferries, see page 74.

BY YACHT Sal is the most upwind of the islands. There is a very good anchorage in the western harbour of Palmeira and it is a useful place for making crew changes because of the international airport. Yachts generally need to fill up with jerry cans. There is a small shipyard where they can do welding. If this is the first island you visit you will be dispatched in a taxi to the airport for an immigration stamp – an easy enough process. Other anchorages lie in the broad Baía da Murdeira in the west; just south of the promontory of Monte Leão; and in the southern bay of Santa Maria, except in southerlies.

GETTING AROUND

A tarmac dual carriageway road links the airport to the capital, Espargos, and runs down the spine of the island between Espargos and Santa Maria. The journey takes

20 minutes by car. The other paved roads run from Espargos to Pedra de Lume, and Espargos to Palmeira. There are many tracks, some of them pretty rocky, criss-crossing the island, and one can drive straight across much of its inland terrain in a 4x4.

BY PUBLIC TRANSPORT *Alugueres* run regularly between Espargos and Santa Maria (150$) and between Espargos and the airport; less regularly from Espargos to Palmeira (100$) and very infrequently to Pedra de Lume. A taxi is probably best for this last route. In Espargos the *alugueres* have two main departure points in the centre, the easiest to find being on Rua 5 de Julho near the entrance to the town; in Santa Maria they depart from near the BCA Bank at the entrance to the town.

BY TAXI Taxis (or public *alugueres* chartered as taxis) from Espargos or the airport to Santa Maria cost 2,000$, usually quoted as €20, occasionally with a €5 surcharge at night; and from Espargos to the airport 1,500$. Taxis may also be chartered for a half- or full-day's sightseeing (page 108).

BY CAR Hiring on arrival at the airport is costly and not to be relied upon because cars get booked up quickly. There are several car-hire firms of varying standards: use the list below or get a personal recommendation and check the car's tyres, brakes and lights before setting off.

Prices start at about €50 per day for a micro-car to around €75 for a Nissan Navara or similar, sometimes with a distance limited to 100km, with a surcharge per kilometre thereafter. You're unlikely to need a car for more than a couple of days, at most. Many firms require a deposit by credit card. It's a good idea to discuss your itinerary with the hirer, as they can assess if you'll need a 4x4 or not. Take care not to leave valuables unattended in the vehicle as smash-and-grab is not unknown in quieter parts of Sal. The police sometimes stop vehicles on Sal, checking front-seat passengers are wearing seatbelts, documentation is correct (proof of ownership or hire; driving licence), and lights are working. Cars do break down more frequently than in Europe so take basic precautions: water, a hat, relevant telephone numbers and a mobile phone.

Car-hire companies

Caetano [116 A1] Based at the fuel station, Santa Maria; 241 3636/354 2262; e geral@caetanorenting.cv. Professional, good cars & often the cheapest.

Hertz Offices in Santa Maria are located at the entrance to the Hotel Morabeza [116 A3] & opposite the Oásis Atlântico Belorizonte Hotel [114 B5], with another at the airport; m 977 4009; e hertz-sal@cvtelecom.cv

Mendes & Mendes [116 A2] At the Ouril Hotel Pontão, Santa Maria; 242 8060; e mendesemendes@cvtelecom.cv

BY BIKE Sal's flat terrain makes it an easy place to navigate by bike, though it's important to ensure you have enough water. See page 107 for hiring information.

WHERE TO STAY AND EAT

There are two main places to stay: Espargos (page 109) and Santa Maria (page 111). Most travellers limit stays in Espargos to emergencies caused by flight delays or changes to schedules. The island capital may be cheaper, near the airport and almost entirely unaffected by the tourism in the south, but the commute to Santa Maria carries the added inconvenience and cost of transport. The lure of Santa

Maria's beaches, watersports and nightlife are most likely what have brought you here in any case.

The third option is to stay in Murdeira village, halfway between the airport and Santa Maria (page 111). It's an attractive hideaway with some facilities, but it's isolated and still a vehicle trip to the action in Santa Maria or to anywhere with Cabo Verdean character.

With the explosion in apartment-building, there are many self-catering options in and around Santa Maria. Renting an apartment can be a much cheaper option than staying in a hotel, especially if you are in a group. Self-catering in Santa Maria has become easier in recent years with a few supermarkets offering a reasonable selection of fresh produce, including meat. Renting an apartment for a week starts at around €350 in low season, though longer stays can be substantially cheaper.

There are always enormous development plans for Sal in the offing, with multitudes of apartments, villas, townhouses and resorts being built in and around Santa Maria. Many however stay unfinished; it can make the outskirts of town feel rather bleak.

Eating out is a pleasure all of its own in Sal, and those who only experience all-inclusive buffets really do miss out. There's a very broad range of places catering for all budgets, from upmarket tourist restaurants and hotel beach clubs offering up steak and lobster to bustling backstreet grills where a *plato do dia* will cost you 500$. Pizza, poke bowls, sushi, gelato and smoothies are ubiquitous and often of good quality.

EXCURSIONS AND TOUR OPERATORS

Island excursions and activities can be booked via the following companies, all of them offering island tours, boat and sport fishing trips, horseriding, diving and snorkelling, and quad bike and car rentals. Prices between them are fairly consistent, starting at around €30 for a short walking tour to €220 for a round-island private tour. There were no 'day trip' flights between islands on offer at the time of writing, although this will hopefully change so is worth enquiring about. Smaller-scale operators may approach you either personally or on social media; many are well respected but do always ensure that they are licensed.

Barracuda Tours [116 B3] 242 2033; m 983 1225; e geral@barracudatours.com; w barracudatours.com; 08.00–13.00 & 14.30–18.30 Mon–Fri, 09.00–13.00 Sat. Long-established Cabo Verdean operator situated just east of Santa Maria's pier.

Explore CV [116 A2] Rua 1 de Junho; m 590 1549; e jonathan@explorecv.com; w explorecv.com. A range of eco-conscious & nature-related tours, including family-friendly turtle walks, birdwatching, sharks, stargazing & guided bike tours. Also offers bike hire.

Logan Tours On the far eastern side of Espargos, past the 2 roundabouts; m 924 5810; w loganislandtours.com; 09.00–19.00 Mon–Sat. Young multi-lingual team which offers all the usual tours along with guided walks of Espargos & Palmeira.

Morabitur [114 B5] Rua 1 de Junho, Santa Maria; 242 2070; e morabitursantamaria@morabitur.com; w morabitur.com; 08.30–16.30 Mon–Fri. Well-respected agency for both Sal & Boavista.

No Limits [114 A6] m 582 4474; e incoming@nolimitsadventure.com; w nolimitsadventure.com; 09.00–12.30 & 15.00–18.00 Mon–Sat. Offering adventure-orientated & Segway excursions from Santa Maria.

Porto Seguro Tourist Office [116 A3] On the walkway running along the main beach in Santa Maria, near the west side of Hotel Morabeza; m 959 2030; 09.00–17.00 daily. A private company offering a friendly, helpful service in English & other languages for both land & sea excursions.

vista verde tours [116 B2] `242 1261;
m 952 5458; e info@vista-verde.com,
office@vista-verde.com; w vista-verde.com;
⏲ 10.00–13.00 & 16.00–19.00 Mon–Fri,
10.00–noon Sat. In the Patio Antigo complex
behind the Caixa bank in Santa Maria, this
well-established & multi-lingual travel
agency specialises in social & environmentally
responsible tourism. Also good for pre-booking
tailor-made holidays with accommodation,
flights, hiking & excursions. Additional offices
on Fogo & São Vicente.

ACTIVITIES

SAILING AND BOAT TRIPS There are many ways to get out on the sea from Sal. Boats including catamarans, yachts, and powerboats offer whale-watching, cruising, snorkelling and fishing. They leave from either the pier in Santa Maria or the dock in Palmeira. If it is the latter, transport to Palmeira is usually included. Boats come and go so check with a local booking office or your hotel when you arrive. A half-/full-day sailing trip will cost around €50/90. Catamaran trips to Boavista are also possible and start at around €135 per person. These usually involve a very early morning departure and a late evening return back to Sal.

Always Sailing m 951 0606; e sail@
alwaysailing.com; ⓕ Alwaysailing. Sailing trips for
up to 10 passengers. Full-day trips including lunch,
snorkelling & fishing.
Cuba Libre Sailing m 953
4954; e cabosurfclub@gmail.com;
w cubalibresailingtrips.com. All aboard a 40ft
yacht for sailing & snorkelling trips around Sal. Also
available for charter.
Sea Warrior Sailing Tours
e seawarriorsailingtours.com. Half- or full-day
trips which include time for snorkelling or SUPing.
Full days include lunch on board; private hire is also
possible, starting at €500 for a half-day.

WINDSURFING AND KITESURFING For a discussion of Cabo Verde's wind- and kitesurfing potential, see page 56.

Sal is a great destination for these sports and Cabo Verde is included in the Professional Windsurfing Association's competition circuit. Winds can be strong from November to May, however, and beginners need to be careful. For surfers, the best surf comes between November and the end of March. All kite, wind and surf locations are deep-water locations; there are no shallow areas for kitesurfing here. Many of the more than 20 schools have rescue boats and a rescue will cost you upwards of €50.

Sal is favoured by many because it has five major locations all within a 15-minute drive from Santa Maria. There are several schools offering equipment hire and/or tuition. Sample prices are: kitesurfing introductory lessons €80, full course €450 (12 hours), one day's rental €65–80; windsurfing lessons: 90-minute introduction course €60, one day's rental €80, one week's rental €450.

A wide range of conditions can be found between locations, including waves, flat water, offshore winds and onshore winds. There are a number of places along the west coast for more advanced surfers and windsurfers. Spares and items such as leashes, helmets and fins are not usually available, so bring your own. The main spots are:

Santa Maria Bay Some 3km of white sandy beach and no rocks. The most convenient spot because it's likely to be walking distance from your accommodation and it's where the kite- and windsurfing schools are. The water is generally flat with gentle swells but the wind can gust a bit close to shore. Near the pier is suitable for beginner windsurfers, the middle of the bay for all levels of windsurfers, and the far end (Ponta Sino) is popular with kitesurfers. Ponta Sino also has a lovely wave when the swell is right. Schools teach kite- and windsurfing in this area, where the wind is more side offshore at the start of the bay and side onshore at the end. Further out, the wind becomes stronger and steadier; nowadays, the wind closer in to shore is gustier due to the increase in construction. For this reason, more advanced windsurfers prefer Lembje Beach or round the corner in front of the RIU Palace Hotel.

SAL'S KING OF THE KITE: MITU MONTEIRO

Growing up in Sal may have its many challenges, but the island also bequeaths those born there with a profound and joyful relationship with the sea. Pioneering kitesurfer Mitu Monteiro, born in 1981, is no exception. Monteiro's childhood fascination with the ocean began when, as a very young child, he would head each day to Santa Maria's *pontao*, the famous pier, to watch the fishermen and their boats while his mother worked to support the family. Soon he was fashioning small craft from driftwood and garbage bags, and by 12 was both surfing and windsurfing on old boards discarded by travellers.

Ultimately though, it would be Monteiro's venture into kitesurfing at 17 that would change the course of his life, not to mention transforming the sport both in Cabo Verde and across the world. After his first competition at Sal's legendary reef break, Ponta Preta, in the early 2000s, he began practising with a normal surfboard and a kite. While this was down to simply using what he had on hand, Monteiro's discovery of the freedom and creative movement the lack of bindings allowed saw him forge a new 'strapless' discipline – one that demands exceptional timing, balance and precision, not to mention a certain fearlessness.

This innovative 'shred' earned him the World Championship title in 2008, making him the first-ever Cabo Verdean champion. Many of the characteristic 'air-time' moves – the jumps where tricks are performed – now commonly seen in the sport's peak competition, the GKA Kite-Surf World Tour, were first conceived and executed by Monteiro. In 2016, he was to become a different sort of 'record man', becoming the only person to ever kitesurf solo between all the islands of Cabo Verde, an epic journey of over 740km. Fast forward to 2023 and 2024, and Monteiro was still placing second against much younger riders: no wonder he is widely known as the sport's GOAT – the greatest of all time.

In addition to Monteiro's competitive achievements, he is also deeply committed to giving back to his community, teaching children and teenagers across the country about the potential of kitesurfing, as both passion and business.

The GKA tour's 2024 season saw Cabo Verde serve up the best conditions ever witnessed in competition. Its reputation as one of the sport's best wave locations in the world is only made sweeter when it is also home to some of kitesurfing's most gifted and successful athletes. Mitu Monteiro has inspired and nurtured Cabo Verde's next generation of stars, including recent champions Airton Cozzolino and Matchu Lopes. They may one day be joined by Monteiro's eldest son Michael, who has recently joined the competitive ranks. A great legacy indeed.

In front of the RIU Palace Hotel A 3-minute taxi ride from Santa Maria, this west-coast beach is popular with kitesurfers and windsurfers. The area in front of the hotel offers some of the strongest side offshore winds on the island and the sea becomes wavier the further out you go. More advanced kite- and windsurfers enjoy this location as the wind is more consistent, but from January to March there can be a strong shorebreak. Surf Zone has a base there and can take you there or rent you equipment once you are there.

Punta Lembje (or Punta Leme) Many windsurfers start out in the bay and make their way to this point at the eastern end of Santa Maria. Lembje is great for more advanced windsurfers; the water is flatter on the inside of the bay and wavier outside. There are some rocks (more in the wintertime) when entering the water, so shoes are advisable. When there are waves at this beach, they are great clean waves. It is also a good spot for more advanced kitesurfers, as it is difficult to enter the water from this beach, because of the rocks and the gusty wind (once you are out in the water the wind is more constant). A mini hurricane exposed some more rocks in 2015, so caution is advised.

Kite Beach Formerly known as Shark Bay, this 2km stretch of nature reserve on the southeastern coast has stronger and more constant side onshore winds but gentler waves. It's shallow for hundreds of metres out to sea. There is a small reef providing a stretch that is useful for beginners and intermediate wave riders, and a deeper area further south for the more advanced (but watch for the occasional rock). It is growing in popularity with windsurfers, but at present mostly kitesurfers are seen here.

It's a bit too far to walk but you can get there in 15 minutes by taxi from Santa Maria (€15 round trip), or cycle. There are no schools at Kite Beach but the schools in Santa Maria will often allow you to rent equipment to take there. There is a bar/restaurant, the **Kite Beach Club** (⊕ 09.00–17.00 daily) and a turtle field-camp and hatchery in nesting season.

Ponta Preta Firmly on the world wave-jumping circuit, Ponta Preta is suitable only for the experienced, with huge, hollow, perfectly formed waves that can reach 6m in height. Ponta Preta presents a number of challenges including an offshore (or side offshore) wind, waves breaking mostly on to sharp rocks (though finishing on sand), and strong undercurrents. There are no schools here or rescue boats and it is rare that a school elsewhere will rent you equipment to take there, since the risk of damage is so high. Ponta Preta has a couple of casual beach bars/restaurants (page 125).

SURFING Surfing in Cabo Verde is discussed on page 54. Sal's surfing is mostly done on reef breaks but there are some beach breaks too, and there are breaks suitable for all abilities. Most are, however, more suited, and particularly good, for advanced surfers, especially when the big waves arrive in January–March. In Santa Maria Bay the area beside the pier is home to a mellow, beginner-friendly beach break as well as lefts on the reef near the old harbour. These waves, like all the waves on the island, are dependent on an ocean swell and trade winds, but when the waves do come in they average in size from 1m to 2m. Other reliable-enough waves are at Ponta do Sinó, at the far end of the bay; a consistent zippy left, south of the harbour at Palmeira, and the world-class if treacherous long right at Ponta Preta. Kite Beach is often blown out but if the wind dies down it's also good. Note the east coast is considered 'sharky'. The kite and wind schools usually hire boards; prices for board rentals are around €20/35 (half-/full day) and for wetsuits €5 a day, with much cheaper weekly deals.

Surf and kite schools

Angulo Cabo Verde Surf Centre [116 G4] Praia António de Sousa; ╲242 1580; e joshangulo@mac.com; w angulocaboverde.com; ⊕ 08.00–17.00 daily. East of Santa Maria, Angulo offers windsurfing, kite rentals, SUPs (stand-up paddles), private tuition & island trips. The website has good location information.

Kite Verde [116 F4] Praia António de Sousa; m 916 1420; e kiteverde@gmail.com;
w kite-verde.com. On the east side of town, offering kite, surf, SUP, bodyboarding & snorkelling excursions.

Surf Hub Cabo Verde [116 C3] Rua 15 de Agosto; m 595 5794; e surfhubcv@gmail.com; w surfhubcapeverde.com. English/Cabo Verdean-owned surfing & kitesurfing operation, based in a shop near the main square.

FISHING For a description of Cabo Verdean fish, see page 54. Fishing is best done between July and October, but wahoo is available almost nine months of the year. There is a good wahoo fishery about 20 minutes away, by sea, from Santa Maria. Big-game fishing (for tuna, shark and blue marlin; €600–1000 per boat for half a day), trawl fishing (for wahoo, tuna, barracuda and bonito; about €400 for a boat), bottom fishing (bonita, sargo and more), pier fishing, and surf casting (about €40 per person for 2 hours) are available from a number of Santa Maria-based companies and can be booked through the tour agencies (page 101) or your hotel. In addition, local fishermen at the pier might be recruited more cheaply for interesting fishing trips, though you should check the safety of the vessel first.

DIVING Diving in Cabo Verde is discussed in detail on page 53. There are some exciting dives on Sal, however, not all schools dive the island's wrecks. There is the 1966 freighter *Santo Antão* sitting at a depth of only 11m but full of large, colourful fish, and the Russian fishing trawler *Kwarcit* (known locally as 'Boris' as its real name is difficult to pronounce!), which was confiscated after being caught transporting illegal immigrants from Africa, and which now sits at 28m. Ships, including a decommissioned Cabo Verdean naval vessel, have also been sunk to create artificial reefs as a means of increasing fish life and developing diving as a form of sustainable tourism and marine environment awareness. These reefs are also hoped to have a role in improving aquatic biodiversity.

Within the bay of Santa Maria and along the west coast there is a range of reef dives suitable for all levels. A highlight is Cavala (40m), a dramatic wall dive ending in a large cave. There are several cave dives in the north, including one at Buracona where, 25m down, you swim into lava tubes and journey through caves for about 80m until the tunnel turns upwards, revealing a chink of light. Following it further you reach a huge, open-topped cave, 10m in diameter, where you can surface to the surprise of land-based tourists looking in from the top. There are also good dives at the many other small caves and inlets north of Palmeira (10–15m drops). Salão Azul, 200m off Pedra de Lume, is a reef with a wall that stretches to a depth of 45m, peppered with recesses full of marine life, but the northwesterly winds mean it is rarely dived.

Dive centres based at Santa Maria's hotels are also open to non-guests and all the dive centres offer PADI (Professional Association of Diving Instructors) courses including try dives. All have equipment to rent. Prices are around €45 for single dives, €90 for a try dive, and €400 for an Open Water course.

Cabo Verde Diving m 997 8824; e info@caboverdediving.net; w caboverdediving.net. PADI operation located at Melia Tortuga [114 B1], Robinson Club [114 C3] (page 115) & VOI Vila Do Farol hotels. Italian-run, offering PADI courses & guiding in English & other languages. Will help find accommodation.

Scuba Caribe [114 B4] RIU Palace Hotel; 242 1002 (town office), 242 9060, ext 8235 (dive centre on beach); w scubacaribe.com. Offers a full range of diving excursions, & has a kids' PADI course.

Scuba Team Cabo Verde [116 B3] On Santa Maria Beach near Hotel Morabeza; m 991 1811; e info@caboverdescubateam.com; w caboverdescubateam.com. More than 25 years of experience on the island. Offers guided dive trips in small groups & PADI courses, as well as equipment rental. French-owned; English spoken.

SWIMMING There are plenty of lovely swimming areas on Sal, but it's not by any means uniformly safe. The swell and the shore breaks vary depending on the time of year, so ask at your hotel for advice. The *câmara municipal* has employed members of the civil guard to work as lifeguards on some beaches. The beaches east of the pier including Praia António de Sousa are often calm when the west is rough. Igrejinha, at the far eastern end of Santa Maria, is a 20-minute walk or a few minutes in a taxi (750$) and has a small lagoon and a lovely beach which is perfect for children. Ponta Preta has a wide beach and stunning dunes as well as a restaurant. Calheta Funda, north of Santa Maria, is favoured by locals and is good for swimming when it is calm (see opposite for directions). The small coves north and south of the residential complex at Murdeira usually offer calm conditions and clear water.

SNORKELLING There are a couple of good spots for snorkelling but the sea floor off the main beaches is mostly sandy. Look for areas that have rocky outcrops but take care if there is surf. The area directly east of the pier and around Porto Antigo and Papaia's Restaurant in Santa Maria are good spots (there is an underwater statue 50m straight out from Papaia's). Further out of town Calheta Funda and Cadjatinha are local favourites. Some of the boat excursions will also include snorkelling, but it can be a good idea to ask to view the equipment before booking, unless you've brought your own. Other boat excursions may take you to Baía da Murdeira (a Marine Protected Area) where the fish life is good, but they often anchor in a deep part and you will have to swim to the reef – ask where to go before you jump in or you might be disappointed. You can also snorkel here from the shore; there are good beaches north and south of the residential complex 10 minutes' drive from Santa Maria.

SHARK-WATCHING South of Pedra de Lume is an area where it is possible to see lemon sharks (*Negaprion brevirostris*) in 2–3m of water. You can get in the water with these relatively docile, toothless species which have more in common with stingrays than great white sharks. Some tour companies organise excursions for around €35, including the €3 entry fee, but you could drive yourself there or catch a taxi and ask them to wait. Ensure your guide is licensed and is not feeding the sharks to attract more of them.

CYCLING Some people say that Sal is an excellent place to train for cycling or for triathlons. You could do a fairly relaxed trip from Santa Maria past the RIU Palace Hotel and up to the restaurant at Ponta Preta, all on good roads. If you wanted to carry on you could cycle on the main road until you reach Murdeira and then turn off and follow a small road and then a track around the bay to Monte Leão (a half-day trip), though an off-road bike would be required.

A trip following the road through Santa Maria to the east, past the Art Kafé, will take you on a good track that follows the coastline to Igrejinha (little church), a favourite barbecue spot for locals. You will find a small lagoon protected from big waves by a line of rocks. Carrying on from Igrejinha you could find the track behind the dunes and pass by the old salina on the way to Kite Beach (less than 1 hour). After Kite Beach there is a dry, dusty, rocky, red sand track that will take you all the way to the beach at Serra Negra (approx 2 hours). Follow the coastline so you don't end up on the track heading to the town dump.

On the west coast, a trip to Calheta Funda, where you could swim and snorkel in the protected cove, could make a pleasant half-day excursion. Alternatively you could visit Calheta Funda and then head a little further north to the residential complex of Murdeira where there is a restaurant, bar and pool. To get there, head north from Santa Maria towards the airport until you reach the roundabout with Calheta Funda signposted to the left. Head west along the dirt track (you will appear to be going through private property; it is in fact a cement factory and the road is a public road). Keep heading straight on until the road turns to the left to run alongside the coast. Calheta Funda is a small bay that is signposted.

Electric bikes and cruisers can be rented from **Electrica** [116 B3] (just by the Morabeza; m 528 8491; w electricabikes.com) or from **Gus Adventures** (m 997 6735; w gusadventures.com), who have either electric or mountain bikes and do hotel drop-offs. Both of these companies also offer guided bike tours. There may be other operators; ask at your hotel and check with other cyclists. Prices start from €10 per day, accessories included.

BOTANICAL GARDEN AND ZOO A botanical garden seems as unlikely as a zoo on an island as barren as Sal, especially as there are no wild animals. But at **Pachamama Eco Park–Viveiro** (w pachamamaecopark.com; e pachamamasal@gmail.com; ⏰ 10.00–18.00 daily; €5), situated 3km north of Santa Maria, you can have both, well, after a fashion. Lower your expectations – think exotic garden centre and petting farm – and it's a sweet diversion from Sal's monochromes. Using grey water recycled from the nearby hotels, the garden sets out to showcase many of Cabo Verde's indigenous plants, as well as some spectacular cacti, while the 'zoo' contains ducks, peahens, rabbits, rescue donkeys, goats and a peacock. The animal poo is used as fertiliser and recycling is the philosophy here. There is a bar selling natural juices and snacks.

GOLF Sal is home to the country's first golf course, Viveiro (at Pachamama Eco Park–Viveiro; ✆ 986 6031; w viveiro.golf), created in patchwork style to use the least water possible, as well as retain the visual impact of its moonscape surrounds. The greens utilise a grass that can be tended with a large percentage of sea water. These factors, along with ocean views and high wind, make for a unique golfing experience. Fees start at €70 for nine holes, club hire from €30.

HORSERIDING Horseriding has become increasingly popular and can be organised through **Santa Marilha Horse Excursions** (m 589 8121; e sevenhorse. info@gmail.com; w horseexcursionsal.com; ⏰ 09.00–18.00 Mon–Sat; from €50/ hour). Located a few kilometres north of Santa Maria, behind the Viveiro botanical garden, this well-regarded operation offers rides of various duration for all levels of experience. Helmets (mandatory) are provided and insurance is included. Do ensure your guide will not take you anywhere that may endanger turtle habitats, though (page 97).

> **HIKING**
>
> You can go for lonely long walks virtually anywhere on the island. See page 129 for details of suggested hikes.

YOGA If you fancy something a *tiny* bit more energetic than sunbathing, there's the opportunity for indoor or outdoor yoga in Santa Maria.

Odjo d'Água (page 117). Hosts open ocean-view classes at 08.00 on the beach near their pool on Mon, Wed & Fri for guests; call m 934 8814 to reserve your mat.

Yoga Cabo Verde [116 E3] m 580 1121; e surfsheena@gmail.com; w yogacaboverde.com ⊕ often closed Sep; check website for class times as they vary during the year; 1,500–2,000$ for a 75-minute class. The studio is within the Porto Antigo complex, on the main thoroughfare from the Odjo d'Água hotel. Small group classes run by a highly trained teacher; private & healing sessions are possible too. WhatsApp message the number to reserve, as classes can fill up quickly. Clean mats are provided.

TURTLE-WATCHING Many people will claim to be specialist guides offering turtle walks. In fact, only a few guides are officially approved each year, so caution is required, as many others do not follow best practices. Laws have also been introduced only permitting the observation of nesting turtles from 15 July to the end of September. You can volunteer with **Project Biodiversity** (page 97), an NGO committed to conservation, for a minimum of a week, or take a shorter turtle walk with a government-approved company. Project Biodiversity will be happy to recommend appropriate operators, including Explore CV (page 101). From mid-August to the end of November, there are also conservation hatchery visits on the beach outside the RIU Funana hotel, where a talk is given and you can see nests being excavated and hatchlings being given a second chance of life. You can also adopt a turtle or a nest through the project. Note that all dates are approximate and rely on the turtles themselves.

SIGHTSEEING BY CAR OR QUAD BIKE There are organised island tours by vehicle for a half day (approx €35) or full day including lunch (approx €50). These take in the two key sights of Buracona and Pedra de Lume, and other points of interest. Contact one of the local tour operators (page 101). To see the island you have a number of options: rent a car and see the island in a day without a guide, taking in Pedra de Lume, Buracona, Espargos and perhaps Palmeira and one or two remoter locations described from page 125 (for information on car hire, see page 100); charter a taxi for €100 for a full day; or take a round-island tour in a pick-up – the local guides are popular and usually receive good reviews. The pick-ups are normally marked *Volta ilha* and can be found outside your hotel (from €35 per person for a half-day). If you don't fancy bouncing around in the back of a pick-up, go for a minibus tour or take the private taxi option.

Some tour operators offer a tour of Santa Maria, but the village is so small and safe it hardly seems worth it.

You can rent a quad bike (€80/day, €50/half-day) or take an organised tour (€45–100 per person) from most of the tour operators. It is possible to take a quad-bike tour around the southern part of the island through some interesting terrain that would not be possible by car. It is illegal to drive on any beach or dune: the laws are in place to protect turtles and their fragile habitats (page 97).

ESPARGOS

Poor Espargos has a reputation for dreariness. In fact, it is just an ordinary town of middling size, with no great attractions but no major hassles for the visitor either. There is no reason to visit it but then it didn't invite you: you are meant to be in Santa Maria. Still, Espargos has benefited slightly from Sal's economic growth. It

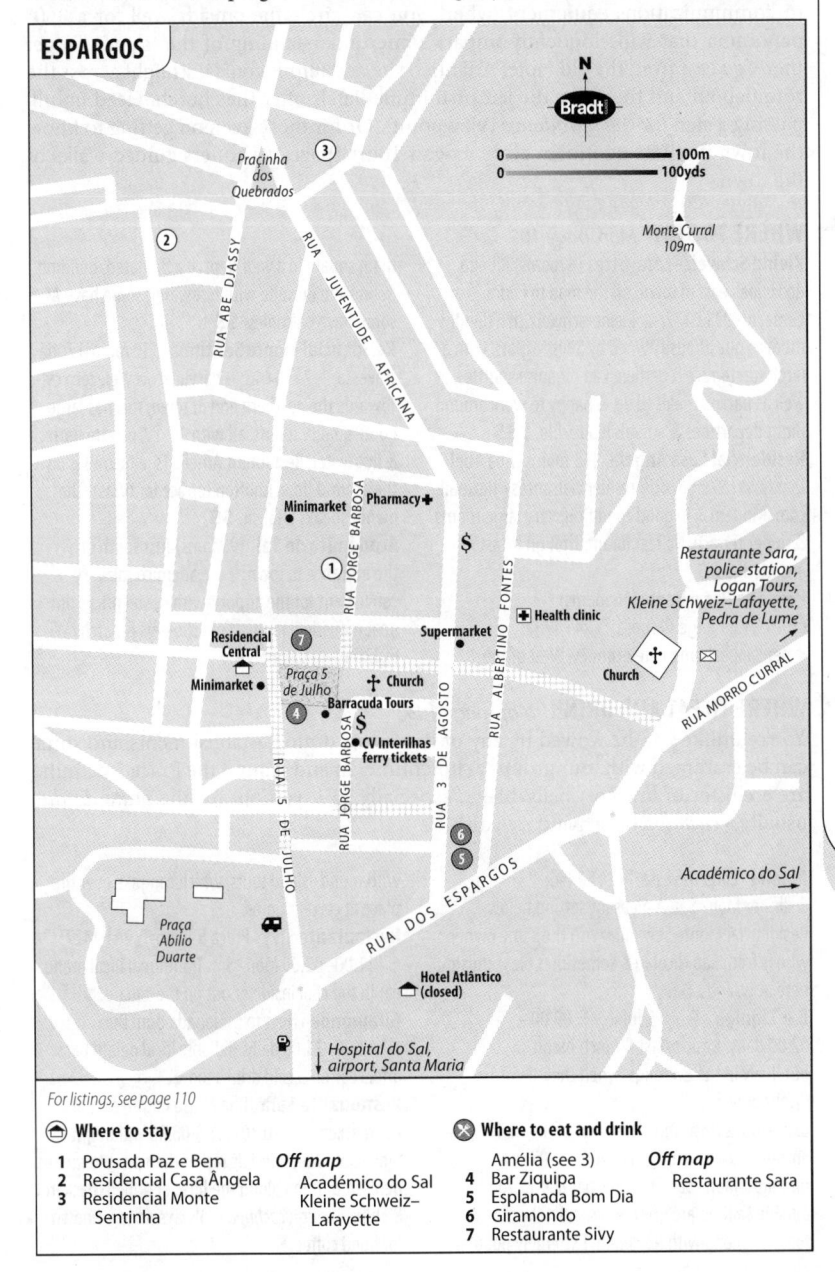

For listings, see page 110

Where to stay
1. Pousada Paz e Bem
2. Residencial Casa Ângela
3. Residencial Monte Sentinha

Off map
Académico do Sal
Kleine Schweiz–Lafayette

Where to eat and drink
Amélia (see 3)
4. Bar Ziquipa
5. Esplanada Bom Dia
6. Giramondo
7. Restaurante Sivy

Off map
Restaurante Sara

has a few good restaurants and at night it is pleasantly lively with locals in the main square; perhaps its main interest is the stark contrast of its African flavour compared with visitor-orientated Santa Maria.

Espargos draws its unlikely name from the wild, yellow-flowered, red-berried asparagus bushes that are said to grow on sandy parts of the island. There is nothing 'touristic' to do in town except perhaps walk up Monte Curral, the mound covered in communications equipment, where you can circle the outside wall for a 360° panorama that will eloquently impart some understanding of the island. To get there, go east from the old Hotel Atlântico site and tennis courts, straight across the roundabout and then take the left turn immediately after the church. Head uphill, passing a sign for the *miradouro* (viewpoint). Or for those keen on getting to know the town in all its quotidian glory, Logan Tours (page 101) offers guided walks of the town.

WHERE TO STAY *Map, page 109*

Kleine Schweiz–Lafayette (4 rooms) Ribeira do Feijoal, east of town, off the road to Pedra Lume; m 931 6137; w kleine-schweiz.ch. Friendly, modern guesthouse owned by Swiss expats, with a large sun terrace & garden. Can organise shuttles, as well as packed meals to go, & happy to work around flight departures & arrivals if possible. **$$$**

Residencial Casa Ângela (15 rooms) Rua Abel Djassy; m 979 6676; e residencialsantos@hotmail.com. Modern & in good condition; very large rooms & upper terrace. No restaurant, though b/fast included. **$$$**

Pousada Paz e Bem (16 rooms) CP 161, Rua Jorge Barbosa; 241 1782; e pensaopazbem@cvtelecom.cv. West of the main square in a well-kept, if a bit dated, building. Rooms are en suite with hot water; some have AC, some have balconies. **$$**

Residencial Monte Sentinha (10 rooms) Zona Travessa; 241 1446; e barviolao@cvtelecom.cv. Towards the northern end of town, this has large, good-quality rooms, all with AC, TV, private baths & hot water. Restaurant Amélia (see below) is on the ground floor. Rooftop terrace for b/fast. The owner speaks English. **$$**

Académico do Sal (9 rooms) Just south of the entrance to town; academico.sal. Very convenient for the airport, with hostel prices but neat individual rooms. Cold showers & patchy Wi-Fi, but there's a pool. **$**

WHERE TO EAT AND DRINK *Map, page 109*

You're unlikely to be wowed by any of the town's dining establishments and some can be crammed with tour groups at lunchtime. In and around the Praça 5 de Julho are a cluster of low-cost belly-fillers, especially so if you opt for the *prato do dia*, usually a *cachupa* or fish and rice dish.

Amélia Zona Travessa; 241 1446; lunch & dinner Mon–Sat. A pleasant setting below Residencial Monte Sentinha with the same owner, who is from São Nicolau & sometimes plays music here at w/ends. **$$**

Bar Ziquipa Praça 5 Julho; 09.00–02.00 daily. Basic b/fast & lunch menu, but lively in the evenings, when they serve drinks only. **$$**

Esplanada Bom Dia Just east of the main entrance into town; 241 1400; 07.00–midnight Mon–Sat. This café-bar has a large outside seating area & serves snacks like cheese toasties, along with ice cream. Extremely popular with round-island tours, which can take over the place at certain times. **$$**

Restaurante Sivy Praça 5 Julho; 241 1427; 11.00–02.00 Mon–Sat. Traditional local menu; eat in the cool inside or out on the square. **$$**

Giramondo Next to Esplanada Bom Dia; 08.00–21.00 daily. Reliable local gelato bar; offers coffee & cold drinks too. **$**

Restaurante Sara Rua Morro Curral, east of the market; m 970 3077; 08.00–midnight Mon–Sat. Daily specials rather than printed menus here, something along the lines of grilled mackerel & chips, though *cachupa* is always on too. Known for good coffee. **$**

OTHER PRACTICALITIES
Health care The Hospital do Sal (✆ 241 1130) is just out of town on the road towards Pedra de Lume, although most travellers opt for the private clinics in Santa Maria. There is a small government-run clinic on Rua Albertino Fontes (✆ 241 1130; ⊕ 08.00–17.00 daily). There's also a pharmacy, Farmácia Ivete Santos (Rua 3 de Agosto; ✆ 241 1417; ⊕ 08.00–20.00 Mon–Fri, 09.00–13.00 Sat).

Police Call ✆ 241 1132. To find the police station, with your back to the desolate Hotel Atlântico site, follow the main road to the right for 10 minutes (going straight on at the roundabout). The police station is on the right almost at the bottom of the road.

Shopping *Minimercados* are to be found opposite the church, just off the main square, and a block further north on rua 5 de Julho. There is a supermarket on the main square, under Residencial Central and another on the east side of Rua 3 de Agosto, halfway up.

The rest
Ferries
CV Interilhas Rua 3 de Agosto; ✆ 241 2279; w cvinterilhas.cv; ⊕ 09.00–17.00 Mon–Fri

Tour operators
Barracuda Tours Praça 5 de Julho; ✆ 241 2383; ⊕ 09.00–noon & 14.30–19.00 Mon–Fri, 09.00–13.00 Sat; page 101
Logan Tours Page 101

MURDEIRA
With an increasing number of apartments available to rent here, Murdeira may favour those who don't want or need to be in the hubbub of Santa Maria.

WHERE TO STAY AND EAT
Murdeira Village Resort (40 suites) ✆ 241 5220; e reservas@murdeiravillageresort.com; w murdeiravillageresort.com. Pleasant, practical rooms feature AC, TV, kitchenette & sitting area. Saltwater pool & swimming pool, plus small beach with usually calm waters. Restaurant & shuttle to airport & Santa Maria. $$$

O Ninho Dos Piratas North of the town, along the beach road; m 599 9937; ⊕ 09.00–22.30 Sun–Thu, 09.00–02.00 Fri, 09.00–midnight Sat. Unabashedly touristy, this jolly restaurant is housed atop a rusting hulk, right on the beach. Great views & good-value fish dishes, as well as lots of snacky-type options for under 1,000$. $$$

SANTA MARIA
For all the international hype about Cabo Verde, Santa Maria das Dores – 'Saint Mary of the Sorrows' – its key tourist town on the main tourist island, remains small and unassuming. Its coastal road and those just behind it are lined with low pastel-coloured buildings housing restaurants, bars, hotels and souvenir shops and the occasional home – lively, but nevertheless often considered in the shadow of the giant, all-inclusive resorts that lure most of Sal's visitors. In 1938 Archibald Lyall, the English journalist, reported:

> Never was a place better named than these two or three dozen little houses by the sad seashore. There is no vegetation and nothing to do but steel oneself against the

unceasing wind which blows the sand into food and throat and clothes. At night, when the red-eyed people retire to their shuttered, oil-lit houses, the great white crabs come out of the sea and march through the streets like a regiment of soldiers.

But Santa Maria is considerably more cheerful these days (and has all but dropped its mournful epithet). The big thing has happened: tourism, and Lyall would struggle to recognise it. And instead of crabs it is tourists that walk the streets at night.

HISTORY While the bay at the south of the island was probably frequented over the centuries by salt diggers and sailors, Santa Maria only officially came into existence at the beginning of the 19th century, when Manuel António Martins of Boavista arrived to exploit the saltpans that lie behind the village.

Martins's workforce scraped away the sand to the rock beneath. They guided seawater inland along little trenches and then pumped it by means of wooden windmills into the rows of broad shallow pans. The water would gradually evaporate leaving white sheets of salt which were dug into pyramids. These were loaded into carts which were pulled by mule, along the first railway tracks to be built in Portuguese Africa, to a newly built harbour. Around 30,000 tonnes of salt were exported each year from the port of Santa Maria and much of it went to Brazil until the late 1880s when that country imposed a high customs tax to protect its own new industry.

In the early 1900s, several new ventures with European companies collapsed, forcing the people of Sal to leave in search of work on other islands. Just a few peasants were left, making a living from salting fish and exporting it to other islands.

Santa Maria's fortunes surged again in the 1920s, when a new market for salt opened up in the Belgian Congo and some Portuguese companies revived the business. By the mid-1900s, Sal was exporting 13,000 tonnes a year and there was enough money to build the Santa Maria of today but, as always, international events were to snatch away whatever prosperity they had bestowed. Independence for the Congo, changes in Portugal and then independence in Cabo Verde brought an end to the business. By 1984, even the routine maintenance of the saltpans ceased. The lure of Santa Maria's golden sands were to change the town's fortunes forever though, when, spurred on by the growing popularity of the Hotel Morabeza (page 115), the Cabo Verdean government opened the Hotel Belorizonte in 1986, thus paving the way for mass international tourism.

Testimony to how tourism has wrought changes in recent times, the town's modest 1990 population of 1,343 has now grown to an estimated 17,000.

ORIENTATION The bay of Santa Maria takes up most of the southern coast of Sal. The town of Santa Maria begins roughly at a point in the middle of this coastline, and extends to the east. To the west of this midpoint is a line of bigger hotels and the casino, connected together by a cobbled dual carriageway. The hotel district extends to the southwest coast.

Santa Maria town has three 'circles': hotels and restaurants make up the first, along with the odd villa belonging to affluent locals and expats; self-catering apartments and smaller hotels cluster on the parallel streets behind, where there are also many restaurants, bars and shops; beyond that the more workaday part of Santa Maria stretches inland. To the east, Zona António Sousa, also known as the Zona Tanquinha, mostly consists of apartment buildings built for the European market, along with a handful of good restaurants, a couple of hotels and a hostel; while its infrastructure still seems incomplete, it is improving.

The heart of the town itself consists of three main roads running east to west and centred on the main *praça* and the pier.

WHERE TO STAY All of the big, upmarket and mostly all-inclusive resort hotels lie on the road running parallel with the beach, west of Santa Maria centre, or around the corner on the southwest coast. The latter are quite isolated from the town itself, especially since short cuts through the all-inclusive hotels are forbidden. The beach promenade from the Hilton onwards, though, makes the walk a far more pleasant proposition for those on the southern coast. Santa Maria's other hotels, ranging from budget to upmarket independents, are in town, at varying distances from the beach, though Santa Maria is still so small that none are much more than 5 minutes' walk from the sea. The weekend nightspots around the pedestrian street back from the beach can be late and noisy, so bear this in mind when choosing your accommodation if you go to bed early. Santa Maria's many apartment blocks largely lie immediately to the east of the town centre in the Zona António Sousa and offer a quieter alternative. Cheaper options are harder to come by than elsewhere, though there are a few, especially for longer stays. For would-be

---

ACCOMMODATION IN SANTA MARIA

Santa Maria's accommodation options split into three distinct sectors, both in terms of what is on offer and (roughly) geographically. To the east of the town centre are a wide range of apartment buildings; in the centre are a range of good-quality top-end and mid-range hotels; to the west are an increasing range of all-inclusive, internationally owned chain hotels. While recognising the appeal of the all-inclusive option, this book concentrates largely on the first two sectors. We have, however, listed a handful that may suit independent travellers, either because of relative flexibility of terms or overall ambience and size.

As we say elsewhere, you will not find the true soul of Cabo Verde on Sal and you will certainly not find it in the all-inclusive establishments. What you might find is an opportunity to put the children in the Kids' Club, order an already-paid-for beer from the swim-up bar and start your suntan. Often they will provide buffet dining; their evening entertainment of Cabo Verdean music will be a lifetime away from the wailing violins or raw, sensuous singing found elsewhere in the archipelago. That said, many of the resorts employ a cohort of very talented musicians and dancers, and everyone will be having a ball.

Most people wanting an all-inclusive holiday will book through a large tour operator or travel agent, such as **TUI** (w tui.co.uk) or **Thomas Cook** (w thomascook.com) in the UK, or **Transavia** (w holidays.transavia.com) for example, if coming from mainland Europe. It's sometimes also possible to book via the websites of the companies that own the hotels themselves, such as **Melia** (w melia.com) or **RIU** (w riu.com). Some all-inclusive hotels have exclusivity agreements in place with the large tour operators and airlines, and some also don't allow walk-up clients to make bookings. Since 2023, there have been an increasing number of reports of various gastric illnesses circulating in a handful of the larger resorts (page 63), though the main tour operators still say the numbers are very low. For many, all-inclusives are a dream holiday; for others a worst nightmare.

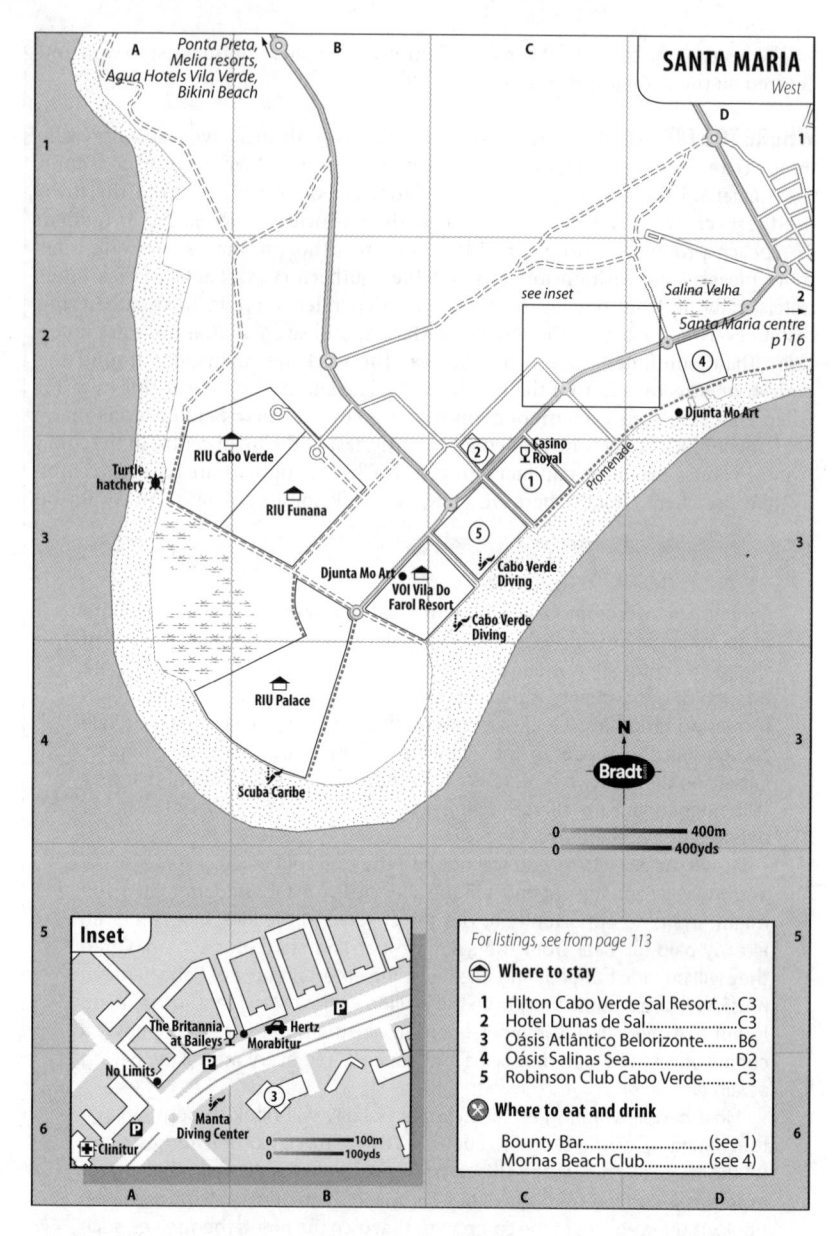

SANTA MARIA
West

Map labels:
- Ponta Preta, Melia resorts, Agua Hotels Vila Verde, Bikini Beach
- Turtle hatchery
- RIU Cabo Verde
- RIU Funana
- Djunta Mo Art
- VOI Vila Do Farol Resort
- RIU Palace
- Scuba Caribe
- Casino Royal
- Cabo Verde Diving
- Salina Velha
- Santa Maria centre p116
- Djunta Mo Art
- Promenade

Inset: The Britannia at Baileys, Hertz, Morabitur, No Limits, Manta Diving Center, Clinitur

For listings, see from page 113

Where to stay
1. Hilton Cabo Verde Sal Resort.....C3
2. Hotel Dunas de Sal..........................C3
3. Oásis Atlântico Belorizonte..........B6
4. Oásis Salinas Sea..............................D2
5. Robinson Club Cabo Verde..........C3

Where to eat and drink
- Bounty Bar..................................(see 1)
- Mornas Beach Club..................(see 4)

---

self-caterers, bear in mind that food shopping in Santa Maria can be expensive and the range is limited, though perhaps better than on other islands.

West of Santa Maria village/ Avenida dos Hoteis

Hilton Cabo Verde Sal Resort [114 C3] (241 rooms) ℅ 334 4444; e caboverde.reservations@hilton.com; w hilton.com/en/hotels/sidcvhi-hilton-cabo-verde-sal-resort. Despite a blandly monumental exterior, the Hilton is by far the most elegant & easy-going of the upmarket hotels. It's cut through with a diagonal sweep of emerald pool, a calm place to while away a few hours or days. Rooms are large, luxurious but unfussy; all have balconies or terraces & baths. Easy access into town via the beach promenade. Restaurants & bars welcome non-guests & have good happy-hour deals. **$$$$$**

Robinson Club Cabo Verde [114 C3] (307 rooms) 334 22 00; w robinson.com. Pick of the adults-only all-inclusives. Favoured by Europeans, it has a full range of activities like daily aqua aerobics & yoga, but also works for quiet relaxation. Rooms are large & light with extras such as coffee machines. Fantastic beach bar with sunset DJs & beanbags on the sand. Supposedly has the best food of the all-inclusives. **$$$$$**

Oásis Atlântico Belorizonte [114 B6] (363 rooms & bungalows) 242 1045; e belorizonte@oasisatlantico.com; w oasisatlantico.com. Just beyond the Morabeza, this is an all-inclusive with a mixture of rooms – cute wooden bungalows or pleasantly simple doubles arranged around 3 pools. Bathrooms however are dated. Kids' club/children's activities & children's pool. Note, the FB drinks package does not include wine. **$$$$**

Oásis Salinas Sea [114 D2] (337 rooms) 242 2300; e salinassea@atlantico.com;

A HOTEL WITH HISTORY   *Murray Stewart*

As you walk down the pedestrianised path from the CV Telecom building in Santa Maria, heading towards the start of the pier, you will be met by a short column bearing the bust of one Georges Vynckier. Look to your right and you'll notice that the street is named after him too.

In fact, you've already passed the Vynckier family's most lasting legacy: the Hotel Morabeza. It was back in the 1960s when Georges's father Gaspard and his wife Marguerite Massart decided to overcome their dislike of their native Belgium's weather by constructing a house in the then sleepy fishing village of Santa Maria. The house was finished in 1967, and soon afterwards it became accommodation for aircrews whose planes were making stopovers on Sal. In particular, South African Airways used the island, due to the embargo on their planes landing in the African mainland. Eventually, thanks to the drive and determination of Georges's wife Geneviève, the 'house' became an acclaimed 140-room hotel with an excellent reputation. As global events unfurled – and aircraft became more capable of longer flights – the Sal stopover became less popular, but the dwindling needs of aircrew were quickly replaced by the increased accommodation demands of tourists, first from Portugal and Germany, then France and Belgium. Today, many visitors favour the elegant hotel as *the* hotel to stay at on Sal, if not *the* hotel in Cabo Verde.

But there is more to the Vynckier dynasty than just managing hotels. The family were true pioneers in the use of renewable energies, making use of two of the few natural resources in Cabo Verde, namely sun and wind. Gaspard Vynckier installed a solar-powered seawater distiller on Sal; his son Georges introduced the first solar panels for producing hot water, as well as wind-harnessing equipment that at one time produced 60% of the hotel's electricity needs. The electricity produced by the wind ran a desalination operation through the process of reverse osmosis, the wind supplanting the sun as the energy-giver for the desalination process. Sadly, time has moved on again, and water and electricity are now simply bought from the local suppliers.

So, doff your sunhat to Georges Vynckier's noble bust, before your feet touch the white sands of Santa Maria. The management of the elegant hotel has been passed down to his daughter, Sophie Vynckier Marcellesi. Likewise, many of the existing staff members are the grandchildren of some of Gaspard's very first collaborators – a true dynasty in a young country.

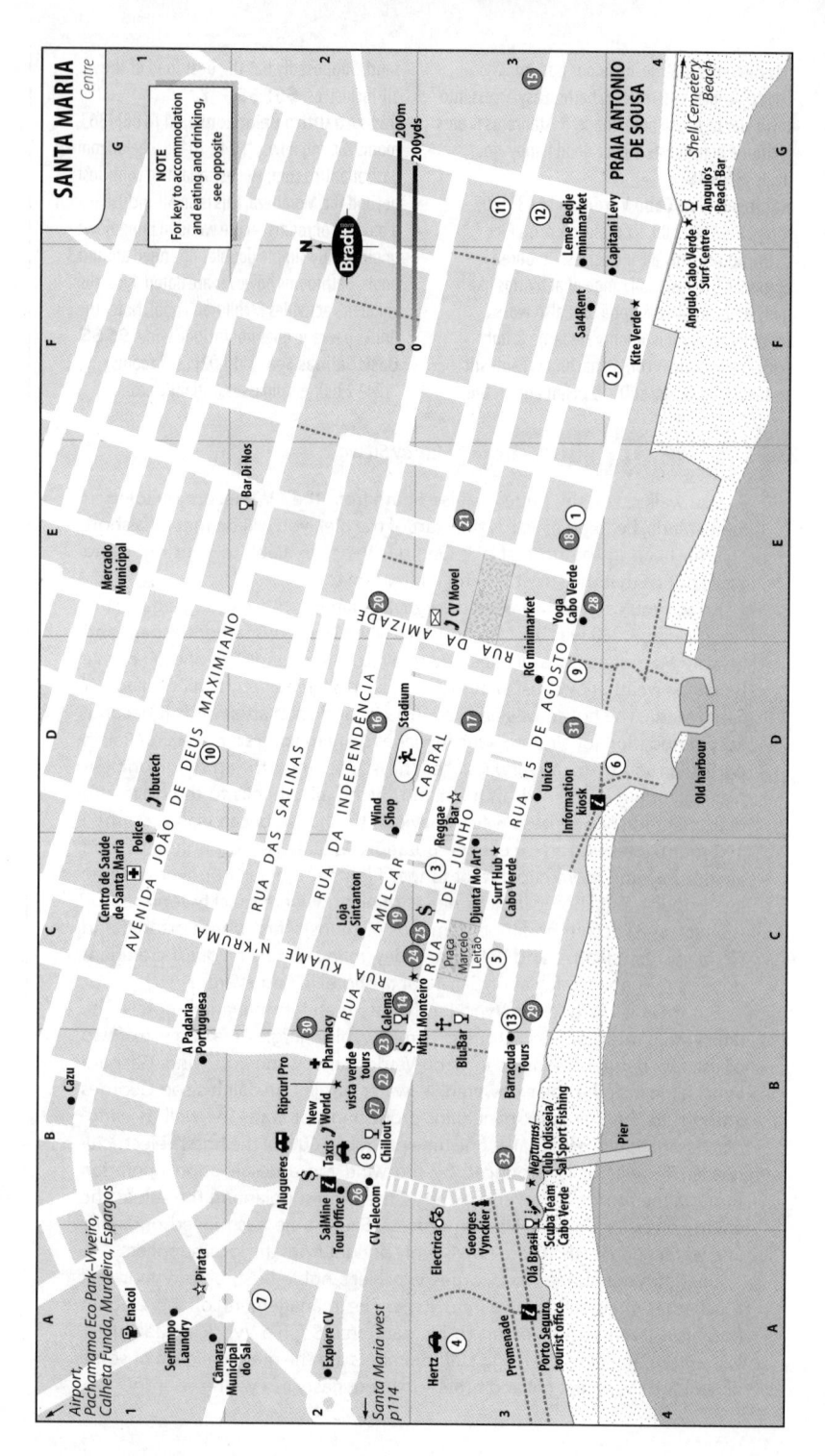

SANTA MARIA
Centre

w oasisatlantico.com. Another full-service resort, but with B&B, HB & FB options. Standard rooms are like suites, with sitting area. All have balconies, some with sea view. Modern & airy, if beginning to look a little bit tired. Avoid the cheapest 'garden view' rooms as these can be on a lower-ground level. **$$$$**

Hotel Dunas de Sal [114 C3] (49 rooms) On the landward side of the road that runs west of Santa Maria, behind the Hilton; ☏ 242 9050; e geral@ hoteldunasdesal.com; w hoteldunasdesal. com. This mid-size, low-key hotel has a large central pool, massage & beauty centre, gym, yoga & Pilates classes. Superior rooms come with kettles & coffee machines, cheaper ones don't. **$$$–$$$$**

Santa Maria village

Hotel Morabeza [116 A3] (120 rooms) CP 33; ☏ 242 1020; e info@hotelmorabeza.com; w hotelmorabeza.com. Built as a private house in the 1960s, long before tourism hit Sal. Centrally positioned, a 4-star, low-rise hotel with long-serving, loyal & affable staff. Combines low-slung Portuguese-style architecture, a genteel ambience & the advantage over other top-end hotels of having the town on its doorstep. Elegant reception with pleasant artwork. Attractively laid out, each room has a veranda with sea or garden views. The facilities include 3 pools, a games room with full-size snooker tables, massage, archery, minigolf, watersports, table tennis, tennis, yoga & even traditional dancing & Kriolu language classes. There are 3 restaurants & 3 bars, including a rooftop venue serving international dishes & Cabo Verdean cuisine, & an attractive beach bar. **$$$$**

Hotel MiraBela [116 C3] (10 rooms) ☏ 242 1446; e contact@hotelmirabela.com; w hotelmirabela. com. In the centre of Santa Maria, in a traditional, peach-daubed Cabo Verdean building, this welcoming hotel has attractive rooms, each with a balcony, TV & fan. B/fast on terrace overlooking rooftops to the sea. Judith & Ron, the Dutch owners, are English speakers & gradually endeavouring to make the hotel as eco-conscious as possible. **$$$**

Ocean Suites [116 C3] (10 rooms) w oceancaboverde.com. Overlooking a busy square, a short walk from the beach, these spacious, contemporary & nicely quirky rooms are big on comfort, with extras like coffee machines

& AC. Staff are friendly. There's a popular bar-restaurant downstairs (page 120): great if you're here to enjoy the nightlife, but can be noisy around midnight if not. **$$$**

Odjo d'Água [116 D4] (46 rooms) Down on the shore to the east of the pier; ☏ 242 1414; e reservas@odjodagua-hotel.com; w odjodagua-hotel.com. A rambling, lushly planted & pretty hotel with a personal feel & a restaurant practically on the waves There's a small but attractive pool above steps leading down to what feels like a private beach, & a terrace bar provides an all-day venue for admiring the view. All rooms have balconies, although only some face the sea. Locally owned, many satisfied guests & a popular alternative to the all-inclusives for first-time Sal visitors. **$$$**

Ouril Hotel Pontão [116 A2] (84 rooms) At the western edge of Santa Maria; ☏ 242 8060; w ourilhotel.com. A few mins' walk from the beach. Superior rooms are good value with

---

SANTA MARIA Centre
For listings, see from page 113

🛏 **Where to stay**

1	Angulo House	E3
2	Aparthotel Santa Maria Beach	F4
3	Hotel MiraBela	C3
4	Hotel Morabeza	A3
5	Ocean Suites	C3
6	Odjo d'Água	D4
7	Ouril Hotel Pontão	A2
8	Pensão Nha Terra	B2
9	Residencial Porto Antigo	D3
10	Sakaroule	D1
11	Surf House Cabo Verde	G3
12	Surfhouse Hostel	G3
13	Villa ao Mar	C3

✴ **Where to eat and drink**

14	Américos	C2
15	Art Kafé	G3
16	Bar Di Nos	D2
	Beach Club	(see 4)
17	Café Criolo	D3
18	Cape Fruit	E3
19	Chez Pastis	C3
20	Coconut Room	E2
	Farolin	(see 6)
21	Flor d'Sal	B2
22	Giramondo	B2
23	Leonardo's	B2
24	Meky's Burgers	C3
25	O Caranguejo	C3
	Ocean Café	(see 5)
26	Papaya Café	B2
27	Pizza Art Food & Drinks	B2
28	Sabores Livros	E3
29	Sal Beach Club	C3
30	Simple Bar & Grill	C2
31	Snack Bar Bilu	D3
32	Sol Doce	B3

balconies, AC & TV. Some are looking a little tired but are gradually being refurbished. There's an unexpected, leafy courtyard with a pool of reasonable size. $$$

Pensão Nha Terra [116 B2] (25 rooms) Rua 1 de Junho; 242 1109; e hotelnhaterra@gmail.com; hotelnhaterra. Conveniently positioned at the western edge of town, this airy family-run hotel is bright & well cared for, with balconied rooms, all en suite & with AC & TV. Sea view rooms extra. It has an attractively planted pool, if in full view of passers-by on the main street. Bar & restaurant. $$

In the eastern district (Praia António de Sousa and Zona Tanquinho)

Angulo House [116 E3] (2 rooms, 3 apts) One street back from Praia António de Sousa; w angulohouse.com. Part of Angulo's watersports empire, 'ten steps' from the beach. Smartly furnished rooms & large, well-equipped apts, all with balconies. Pool & 24-hour reception. $$$

Aparthotel Santa Maria Beach [116 F4] (31 rooms) Praia António de Sousa; 242 1450; m 994 3410; e santamariabeach@yahoo.com. East of the centre, newish yet still a bit old-fashioned. Pleasant, spacious rooms with AC & TV, some with sea view. $$$

Sakaroule [116 D1] (7 rooms) Just east of the police station; +33 6 24 28 02 55; e sakaroule1999@yahoo.it. Tucked away at the back of Santa Maria, this colourful Italian-owned *residencial* is a traditional Cabo Verdean building with an atmospheric interior courtyard. Some of the rooms have kitchens & balconies. Has a place to store wind- & kitesurfing equipment & an evening bar in high season. An excellent price because of its location; some love it exactly because it's not in the tourist zone. $$

Surfhouse Hostel [116 G3] (24 beds/6 dorms) Zona Tanquinho; m 915 4412, 3493 394 028; e surfhousecaboverde@gmail.com. Classic & charming hostel that's a firm favourite with kiters given its proximity to Kite Beach, but all guests made welcome. Clean & bright dorms, some with ocean views. Barbecues & outings organised at guests' request. $

Apartments

Residencial Porto Antigo [116 D3] (90 apts) 242 1815; e portoantigoreservas@hotmail.com; w portoantigohotel.com. A pretty, beautifully planted apartment & villa complex on the edge of the sea. Smart 1-, 2- & 3-bedroom apartments with living room, kitchenette & balcony, plus AC & TV. The complex is run like an upmarket hotel, with daily cleaning services. B&B, HB & FB are available, though not recommended given the proximity of good dining-out options. Attractive pool, & the scenic old harbour in front provides a small, almost private beach with snorkelling opportunities. Weekly or daily rentals. $$$$

Villa ao Mar [116 C3] (14 apts) e info@villaaomar.com; w villaaomar.com. Located just off the main square & thus very central. Spacious, with beachy interiors & beautiful sea views if you book 1 of their penthouses. Options with up to 4 bedrooms. $$$$

Surf House Cabo Verde [116 G3] (5 apts) m 915 4412; e surfhousecaboverde@gmail.com.

APARTMENT AGENCIES

The following Santa Maria agencies all let holiday apartments by the night as well as offering long-term rentals, property management, keyholding service & commercial units.

Bobbywashere m 591 8254; e info@bobbywashere.com; w bobbywashere.com. Good range across all budgets; also offers excursions & kitesurfing.

Capitani Levy Lda 242 2717; e leniselevy@gmail.com; w capitanilevy.com. More than 100 properties to let, & sales too. English, Italian & French spoken, though website only in Portuguese.

Sal4Rent 242 1715; e info@sal4rent.com; w sal4rent.com. Good-value long-term rentals, & well-regarded staff.

If 'Surf House' conjures an image of a rush-roofed hut, think again. Instead, these are modern apartments, with full kitchen, AC, fans, balcony, TV with international channels & excellent showers. Some apartments can accommodate 6 people, making it very good value. **$$$**

✖ WHERE TO EAT AND DRINK You can find many international cuisines in Santa Maria, but fresh fish and seafood have the constant presence they do everywhere in the archipelago. There is a strong Italian influence too, which means some reasonable-quality pasta and pizza and excellent coffee. Although on some of the other islands you can find nothing but local fare, here you'll actually have to search beyond Rua 1 de Junho and the beachfront places. While overall prices might be higher on Sal, you can still find a *prato do dia* for around 650$, making it worth heading further back from the beach to eat, especially at lunchtime.

Most of the upmarket hotels that aren't all-inclusive have restaurants that welcome non-residents, including the Hilton and the Morabeza. If you wander along the beach west of town you will find several of the hotels also have beach bars that serve food, along with a few independent operations.

Bars right across the town have happy hours, and the hours are staggered. Those in the know can drink cheaply for most of the early evening. The Morabeza's chic upstairs bar has a particularly appealing, if short, session between 18.30 and 19.30 when *caipirinhas*, Fogo wine and beers are an absolute steal. Later, the popular tourist restaurants and some hotels have live music, especially in high season. The sports bars in Santa Maria are geared towards European football fans, and there is always somewhere to watch a game. Apart from the national TV station, sports can be watched on three Portuguese channels as well as British satellite, African, French and Brazilian services. **Sal Beach Club** [116 C3] (page 120) is a British favourite, with pints, breakfasts and all live sports shown on multiple screens. For those not keeping score, a well-chosen spot on the beach will let you watch the endless live beach volleyball or beach football matches taking place. Or you could join in.

Fresh bread can be bought from early morning at **A Padaria Portuguesa** north of Simple Bar (page 121).

Best for vegetarians Santa Maria's internationally geared kitchens mean there are usually at least a few vegetarian options on most menus, though omelettes, plates of rice and beans, pizza or pasta can start to get monotonous pretty quickly. A few places do something different.

- **Art Kafé** [116 G3] Page 120. Vegetarian standouts include *xauxau* rice with peanut sauce and fried banana, or an eggplant and goat's cheese lasagne.
- **Cape Fruit** [116 E3] Page 120. Serves up veggie crêpes and generous salads.
- **Flor d'Sal** [116 E3] Page 121. Meat-free joy from breakfast to dinner, and happy to make your mocktail of choice too.
- **Papaya Café** [116 B2] Page 120. Chia cups, beet burgers, mushroom soup and dairy-free cheesecakes will make homesick vegans smile.

Restaurants and cafés

Américos [116 C2] Rua 1 de Junho; ✆242 1011; ⊕ noon–22.30 Mon–Sat. A big-night-out choice for many, with lobster, Algarve-style seafood & steak cooked on a hot rock. Smart, simple upstairs dining room. There's also a branch in international departures at the airport. **$$$$$**

Beach Club [116 A3] Hotel Morabeza, page 117; ✆242 1020; ⊕ lunch 12.30–15.00 daily. 1 of the hotel's 3 restaurants, it's on the beach, with beach shack seating & sunloungers, along with an open grill where you can watch your meal being prepared. Excellent service & unexpectedly cheap drinks. $$$$$

Bounty Bar [114 C3] Hilton Cabo Verde Sal Resort, page 114; ⊕ 07.30–22.00 daily. Lovely stepped seating areas mean this beach bar/restaurant is equally appealing for a leisurely lunch or for snacks & drinks on the sand-side sofas. Steaks & lobster are popular & they do a reasonable vegetarian risotto. $$$$$

Farolin [116 D4] Odjo d'Água hotel, page 117; ✆ 242 1414. A wonderful, invigorating location overhanging the rocky headland at the centre of this well-loved hotel. Specialises in grilled fish & seafood. Weekly live music. Good place for a romantic dinner (which is perhaps why they've been known to baulk at seating solo diners). $$$$$

Leonardo's [116 B2] Traversa Pousada, off Rua Amílcar Cabral; m 981 0057; ⊕ 18.30–22.00 daily. This cosy Italian restaurant has mixed reviews. Some expats swear by it, others claim it's too pricey for the quality. $$$$$

Chez Pastis [116 C2] Rua Amílcar Cabral; m 984 3696; ⊕ 18.30–23.00 daily. This atmospheric, well-respected place is not the French bistro of your dreams, but instead offers up pan-European seafood & meat dishes, Brazilian beef & homemade pasta. Book ahead. $$$$

O Caranguejo [116 C3] Rua 1 de Junho; ✆ 242 1231; ⊕ 18.00–23.00 daily. Dingy corridor entrance opens up into a courtyard bedecked with fairy lights. Mixed reviews, but good vegetarian pizza under the stars. Take-aways available. Booking sometimes necessary. $$$$

Mornas Beach Club [114 D2] Oásis Salinas Sea, page 115; ✆ 242 2300; ⊕ 10.00–midnight daily. On the beach in front of its parent hotel. Buffet lunches, barbecue dinners & bar menu, too. $$$–$$$$$

Art Kafé [116 G3] Rua Praia António de Sousa; m 994 9211; w artkafesal.com; ⊕ 09.00–22.00 Tue–Sun, sometimes later on Fri & Sat. A short walk east of the centre, this fun & brightly decorated day-to-evening place is one of Santa Maria's best places to try well-priced regional cooking, be that *cachupa* or peanut- & coconut-embellished *xauxau* rice (with your choice of grilled banana, fish or seafood). Conch & fried sweet potato or fish stew offer a good alternative to the ubiquitous grilled fish, though they do that too, along with vegetarian pastas & crêpes. The b/fast deals & sandwich menu are very good value. Reservations recommended for evening. $$$

Cape Fruit [116 E3] Rua 15 de Agosto; m 982 2205; ⊕ 08.00–16.00 Thu–Tue. Recommended for its laid-back vibe, great smoothies & juices. A relaxed, healthy b/fast & lunch place in a quiet part of town. $$$

Ocean Café [116 C3] On the beach side of the main square; ✆ 242 1895; ⊕ 07.30–01.00 daily. Lively bar/restaurant popular with visitors. Live music every night (see opposite), & tasty pizzas. Also serves burgers, omelettes, etc. Plush suites to rent upstairs (page 117). $$$

Papaya Café [116 B2] Behind Hotel Morabeza; m 976 8181; w papayacafecaboverde.com; ⊕ 07.00–23.00 daily. Homemade cakes, fresh juices & an unusually broad menu of vegetarian, vegan, gluten-free & dairy-free options, along with fish dishes like tuna tataki. Good for a coffee stop too. $$$

Sabores Livros [116 E3] Rua 15 de Agosto; m 970 8453; ⊕ 11.00–23.00 Mon–Sat. A rare Portuguese restaurant, although the menu veers more towards the international: sushi, poke bowls, tuna tartare & the like. A lending library, good cocktails, friendly staff & a hip-hop sound track make it somewhere special. $$$

Sal Beach Club [116 C3] On the beach just east of the pier; m 995 9308; ⊕ 08.00–midnight daily. Pints, b/fasts, reliable big-screen sports – unashamedly a sports bar. Has free sunbeds & acceptable pub food. A favourite with Europeans. $$$

Café Criolo [116 D3] Rua Patrice Lumamba; ✆ 242 1774; ⊕ 07.30–22.00 Mon–Sat. A friendly & pleasant snack bar, offering great-value b/fasts including *cachupa*, & dishes of the day, as well as salads & options as fancy as lobster. Cash only. $$–$$$

Coconut Room [116 E2] Just north of the post office; m 915 0796; w thecoconutroom.com; ⊕ noon–23.00 Tue–Sat, 15.00–23.00 Sun. Baromie & Adeyemi, originally from Sierra Leone, champion West African & Caribbean flavours here, including Sal's most authentic jerk or peppered fish or chicken, served, naturally, with jollof rice. Mains are on the expensive side, but there are plenty of good-value, high-flavour snacks to be had too. Some live music (see opposite). $$–$$$

Bar Di Nos [116 E2] Av João De Deus Maximiano, just before the market; ⊕ Mon–Sat. Recommended budget choice. Grilled meat & fish at outdoor tables, popular with residents & good value in a rough-&-ready setting. $$

Flor d'Sal [116 E3] Rua lombinha, on the Praça do Presidente; m 982 0000; 🌐 flordsal.cv; ⊕ 07.30–23.00 daily. Start the day with fresh fruit bowls, avo on toast or *cachupa* with the lot. Or drop in later for a great-value burger, salad or *bitoque* (Portuguese-style steak & egg) on their large terrace. Coffee is good, as is homemade ice cream. Live music Fri–Sun nights as well as an extended (& more expensive) grill menu on Sun. $$

Meky's Burgers [116 C3] Rua 1 de Junho 23; ⊕ 11.00–23.00 daily. Modern burger joint that also serves hot dogs & Portuguese *prego* sandwiches. More expensive than burgers elsewhere but consistent quality, including brilliant chips. Take-away available. $$

Pizza Art Food & Drinks [116 B2] On the western end of Rua 1 de Junho; f pizza.art.cv; ⊕ 09.30–midnight daily. Family-friendly pizza place, with seating on the street, & always buzzing. Also serves pasta, poke bowls & fish dishes. $$

Simple Bar & Grill [116 C2] On the same street as the Farmácia, a block north; m 951 1536; ⊕ 18.00–midnight daily. Expats rave about the brimming mixed seafood or meat platters at this relaxed off-strip grill restaurant. Simple, yes, but also very good value with mains all under €10. Bookings advised. $$

Sol Doce [116 B3] Beside the pier; ⊕ 07.00–19.00 daily. Fish grill in a great, if busy, location. Also known for their tuna tartare. $–$$$

Giramondo [116 B2] Rua 1 de Junho; ☎ 242 2111. Proper gelato, including locally inspired flavours like *kamoka* (roast corn). Also serves coffee, smoothies, crêpes, waffles, pastries, b/fasts & cocktails. A popular meeting point. Cones from 270$. $

Snack Bar Bilu [116 D3] Down the side road as you leave the Odjo d'Água hotel; ⊕ daily (daytime only). This almost unmarked restaurant serves Cabo Verdean food & continues to be popular. Very good value for the budget-conscious. $

ENTERTAINMENT AND NIGHTLIFE You can opt to chill out in a beach bar, enjoy early-evening Cabo Verdean music to accompany your evening meal, or party all night. Events are generally advertised at the venues themselves, and on social media.

Angulo's Beach Bar [116 G4] Praia António de Sousa; ⊕ 07.30–midnight daily. An open-air chill-out bar & restaurant at the eastern end of Santa Maria, on quieter Praia António de Sousa. Come for sunset, then stay for the friendly staff & live music.

The Britannia at Baileys [114 A5] Djadsal Moradias; m 951 4761; ⊕ 09.00–22.00 daily. Offers pints, football, quiz nights & other themed evenings for homesick Brits, as well as British food ($$$) – inc curry nights – in the western part of town.

Calema [116 C2] Rua 1 de Junho; ⊕ opens late & closes early (the next morning) daily. Famous, popular nightspot with live music. Note the upstairs bar is a strip club, not an upmarket chillout area.

Casino Royal [114 C3] Av dos Hoteis; ☎ 242 1970; w casinoroyal.cv; ⊕ 18.00–04.00 daily. Small, modern casino; nothing much to offer unless you're an enthusiast, apart from a late place to drink near the big hotel strip.

Chillout [116 B2] At the end of Rua 1 de Junho; ⊕ 10.00–midnight daily. Tourist favourite with *kizomba* dancing, pop DJs or live music.

Coconut Room [116 E2] (see opposite). This happy, bustling restaurant has African drumming & the occasional dance fest on Fri & Sat nights. Also good for an early-evening drink.

Ocean Café [116 C3] (see opposite) This all-day café morphs into a fun bar & live venue in the evening.

Olá Brasil [116 B3] On the beach in front of Hotel Morabeza; m 923 5654; ⊕ 11.00–21.00 Thu–Tue. This feet-in-the-sand beach bar is where locals, expats & visitors in the know gather for sunset drinks. The *caipirinhas* are punchy, the crowd & staff friendly & the soundtrack on the money. Beach volleyball or football provide the entertainment.

Reggae Bar [116 D3] Rua 1 de Junho; ⊕ 18.00–02.00 daily. Booms out loud, exclusively reggae music from its rooftop location. Gradually becomes a disco as the night progresses. Take ample change for drinks.

SHOPPING Souvenirs can be bought at shops dotted all over town, at hotels and at the airport. The vast majority of these are imported from Senegal and other parts of West Africa, but if you look around you can find a few places selling products made in Cabo Verde. **Djunta Mo Art**, with three locations (see opposite), is a good place to start.

Surf clothes, accessories and a few boards are for sale at **Angulo's** [116 G4], at **Ripcurl Pro** [116 B2] and **Mitu Monteiro** [116 C5] (w mitumonteiro.net), the Sal local and world champion kitesurfer's place, as well as a few other operations on the street leading down to the pier. Sunscreen and other toiletries can be found in often unmarked Chinese stores (*lojas chineses*), where you can also find cheap clothes, shoes and household items. If you want snorkelling equipment, ask the dive clubs if they have stock (page 106); overall, it's better to bring your own as those sold in some of the souvenir shops tend to be poor quality and overpriced.

By archipelago standards, there is a wide range of good-quality food available in *minimercados* on Sal but availability varies. Many of the *lojas chineses* have also started selling fresh produce and other food. **Loja Sintanton** [116 C2] has a decent selection of Cabo Verdean wine while **Cazu** [116 B1] is the largest and best-value supermarket (that said, don't expect any bargains). It has the usual shelf goods, plus bread, pastries, fresh fruit and vegetables and occasionally some European imports. The mid-size **Mercado Vila Verde** [114 B1] in the Agua Hotels Vila Verde apartment complex, near the Melia hotels, is convenient to the big resort hotels north of town and has fresh bread and wine.

> **STREET VENDORS**
>
> 'Cabo Verde – No Stress!' adorns many a T-shirt and is the motto of nearly every souvenir shop in Santa Maria. But for the unwary who venture into one of these emporia, stress could be exactly what you *do* get. Tourism has attracted souvenir vendors from mainland West Africa whose tactics can be disconcerting for Europeans. Their methods differ greatly from the laid-back approach of local Cabo Verdeans, who at times seem indifferent to selling you *anything*. You will need to practise the art of saying 'no' without getting upset or wound-up. If staying in an all-inclusive, ask reception to cut off your wrist tag before venturing into town, otherwise you will be targeted by the most persistent of the curio sellers, and they may follow you for some time.
>
> If you are approached and not interested in buying the wares, you will need to give a firm but polite 'no', perhaps accompanied with a smile, and avoid being drawn into conversation. Keep walking and resist invitations to follow them to their stall at the local market or into their shop. If you do succumb, then once inside the shop, you may feel intimidated, especially at the point when you decide you really don't want to buy anything. Some vendors' tactics can include blocking the door and offering a furious reduction in the price of anything in which you have expressed the slightest interest. Do not allow anyone to adorn you with a sample piece of jewellery: some pieces don't unfasten. Even if you are interested, these shops and stalls are one place where you should definitely bargain down the price initially quoted.
>
> There are alternatives: see opposite for details of the delightfully local **Djunta Mo Art.**

> **GENUINE CABO VERDE**
>
> Fed up with the lack of local products available and growing tired of street vendors claiming that their imported Chinese knick-knacks are from Cabo Verde? Try **Djunta Mo Art**, which has branches at Rua 1 de Junho [116 C3]; on the beach promenade just past Mornas Beach Club [114 D2]; and in the VIA Vila Do Farol Resort. It stocks only Cabo Verdean-made products, including *grogue*, jewellery, hand-woven pouches and other soulful souvenirs.

Fruit and vegetables can often be bought from street vendors along Rua Amílcar Cabral, or head to the **Mercado Municipal** [116 E1] in the north of town near the murals. It's open daily except Sunday, and also has a small restaurant, along with the usual souvenir stalls. Don't bargain too hard at the latter, but do bargain.

OTHER PRACTICALITIES

Banks There are banks around town [maps, pages 114 & 116], all with ATMs (all ⊕ 09.00–15.00 Mon–Fri).

Health care Most hotels either have their own **clinics** or provide an English-speaking doctor call-out service for €70; if it's not too urgent ask for a cheaper in-clinic appointment. The newish, modern **hospital** just outside Espargos (page 111) has few specialists available, and very few doctors speak English; it's best to try the private clinics below first. Note that if it's a serious emergency you may need to be airlifted to Praia, Mindelo or even the Canaries.

There's a large **pharmacy** just north of the main square [116 B2], on Rua Amílcar Cabral, which is open daily (⊕ 08.00–20.00 Mon–Sat, 08.00–13.00 Sun). As well as usual pharmacy goods, they sometimes stock the Italian gluten-free Schär brand of breads and biscuits.

Centro de Saúde de Santa Maria [116 C1] Next to the police station; ☎ 242 1130. Consultations are €25.
Clinitur [114 A6] On the road from Santa Maria to the resort hotels; ☎ 242 9090; m 988 7075 for emergencies; ⊕ 08.00–18.00 Mon–Fri, 09.00–13.00 Sat & Sun. Consultations at this large private clinic cost €70; treatments such as X-rays are extra. Some hotels have special arrangements with them, which make it cheaper.

Spas and therapies The Morabeza and Hilton hotels (pages 117 and 114) both have well-respected spas open to non-guests, but expect prices to be higher than elsewhere. Otherwise, try:

Beauty Room de Marcella Colombo [116 C3] In Villa ao Mar; m 528 9379; ⊕ 09.00–19.00 Mon–Fri, 09.00–14.00 Sat. Mani/pedis, lash lifts & a range of massages, including lymphatic drainage, at very reasonable prices.

Unica [116 D3] Rua 15 de Agosto; m 950 2960; ⊕ 09.00–20.00 Mon–Sat. Beauty therapy, massage & hairdressing.

Telephone SIM cards can be bought at the airport, but it is more reliable, and cheaper, to buy them in town. Try **CV Movel** [116 E3] (Rua da Amizade, near the post office; ⊕ 08.00–19.30 daily; English spoken) or **Ibutech** [116 D1] (⊕ 08.00–19.30 Mon–Sat, 08.00–13.00 Sun), across from the police station, or you can also buy smaller MB limit cards at supermarkets if you know what you're doing.

SANTA MARIA FESTIVAL *Beverley Chadwick, saxophonist*

During the summer months, from August onwards, each Cabo Verdean island celebrates its music with a lively festival. Each festival is different; some featuring international bands, others just concentrating on the extraordinary talents of local musicians. Perhaps the most famous of the festivals is the Baía das Gatas on São Vicente, which grew from a tradition of a few musicians jamming annually around the August full moon.

But Baía das Gatas is by no means unique. On Sal, the Santa Maria festival is held annually, in early September – but in true Cabo Verdean fashion, no-one knows the exact date until a couple of weeks in advance, and the line-up is usually announced only a week or so before the event. In the past, the festival has featured top international artists including Alpha Blondy, Youssou N'Dour, Steel Pulse, Ky-mani Marley and Turbulence, plus Cabo Verde's own legendary Cesária Évora and many highly talented musicians from Sal island itself.

When I first heard about Santa Maria festival, I was cynical as to whether our sleepy little village would actually get a music festival together, but I have to say I was hugely impressed when a stage with full PA systems and lighting – which would easily compete with Glastonbury – was built on the beach a week beforehand. The beach gets completely transformed, and lots of tiny little stalls are rented out to anyone who wants to sell food and drinks, and create their own 'music' between festival sets. As a result there is a marvellous mix of eager vendors, from individuals selling cold beer and local drinks and delicacies – including *ponche*, *grogue* and *moreia* (moray eel) – right through to the more upmarket town bars, who set up on the beach for the weekend. All around you will be the eclectic music of Cabo Verde, West Africa, Brazil and elsewhere, escaping from the many sound systems all over the festival site.

Everyone comes to the festival, pouring in from the island's three main towns and further afield. Whole families will turn up for the weekend, some with tents, and children and babies will sleep contentedly on the beach. Most hardcore festival-goers will arrive on the first day and not go home until the end. Fishermen – perhaps too full of *grogue* – will be found asleep under the stage and the many local characters come out in force to entertain and amuse. It really is a wonderful community event not to be missed.

Depending on which way the wind is blowing, local residents and tourists in hotels may (or may not) get any sleep for the duration, but that is the whole point...after all, it is festival time!

Up to 20,000 people can attend the Santa Maria festival, so it's wise to book accommodation ahead; tickets can be bought in town and should cost around 500$ per day.

Tourist information There is a **booth** operated by the Câmara Municipal do Sal [116 A1] at the entrance to Santa Maria, slightly inconveniently located near the roundabout and seemingly never open. More central is the reliable **SalMine Tour Office** [116 B2], on the pier street between Rua 1 de Junho and Rua Amílcar Cabral. Although this is an agency for many tour operators of all types, they only deal with properly licensed companies and also act as a helpful, multi-lingual, informal tourist office. You will also find another agency-run information kiosk on the beachfront by the Odjo d'Água hotel [116 D4].

The rest

Laundry Serilimpo, [116 A1] Rua Amílcar Cabral; m 995 3494; ⊕ 08.00–20.00 Mon–Fri, 08.00–17.00 Sat. On the left-hand side of the roundabout as you come into Santa Maria from the airport.
Police [116 C1] Av João de Deus Maximiano, in the northern part of Santa Maria; ☏ 242 1132. The new building on the tarmac road.
Post office [116 E3] ⊕ 08.00–15.30 Mon–Fri. The large, pink building to the east of town.
Taxis [116 B2] There is a usually well-attended taxi rank on the street running to the pier, between Rua 1 de Junho & Rua Amílcar Cabral.

WHAT TO SEE AND DO Santa Maria is a base for the surfing, windsurfing and fishing that are the chief sporting activities of the island (page 102). Beach basking on its stunning white sands is equally popular, as is joining a workout at the beach gym, or a game of beach football or volleyball. Impromptu drumming sessions also spring up in the early evenings on the foreshore just before the Odjo d'Água hotel. You can also visit Santa Maria's own saltpans – walk inland through the northern part of town, and they are on the other side. And at the town's far eastern end is the odd tourist attraction of 'Shell Cemetery Beach', where innumerable discarded shells take the place of sand.

OTHER PLACES TO VISIT

These are arranged in clockwise order beginning at Santa Maria, to be of use to those doing a tour of the island.

SANTA MARIA SALINA Located behind Costa Fragata, the salina can be found by walking directly north from the closed Sab Sab Hotel. The salina is still worked by hand by a small community; unfortunately they cannot sell the fruits of their labour since it does not meet required regulations for quality and sanitary control. You can walk between the saltpans and early in the morning it is possible to see a variety of wading birds.

PONTA PRETA AND PRAIA ALGODOEIRO Ponta Preta is a stunning beach with only two well-spaced restaurants from which to appreciate it, and a favourite of windsurfers and surfers. It is possible to reach the beach by walking for well over an hour around the coast from Santa Maria. Alternatively, walk or drive along the road that goes west from Santa Maria by the resort hotels, turn right at Robinson Club and go straight ahead for approximately 1.5km. You will then find a rough track leading towards the water.

There is also a little wooden hut, where a man can be seen making handicrafts from fish bones and sandstone. (Some of his other products are imported from mainland West Africa.)

Just north of Ponta Preta, the Melia Group has a host of all-inclusive hotels on and around Algodoeiro Beach; the Melia Tortuga is home to **Cabo Verde Diving** (m 997 8824; e info@caboverdediving.net; w caboverdediving.net). This is also the location of the massive Agua Hotels Vila Verde apartment complex.

✕ Where to eat and drink

Bikini Beach Praia Algodoeiro, just north of Ponta Preta, in front of the Melia hotels; w bikinibeachclub.com; ⊕ noon–midnight Wed & Thu, noon–03.00 Fri & Sat, noon–20.00 Sun; bookings online. Built on a pier jutting into the sea, this is a European-style beach club with large

sunloungers & shaded beds around a central pool. The daily fee (€45–60) is redeemable on food & beverages. You can also just drop in for a drink & bite to eat if you're not up for a day of house music, sun worship & indulgence. Menu includes sushi, seafood & pasta. $$$$–$$$$$
Ponta Preta 242 1774; m 991 8613; 10.00–17.00 daily. Large, rustic, wooden building overlooking the beach with a wide deck & sunbeds, serving salads, snacks, fish, seafood, meat & spaghetti. Slightly more expensive than in town, but there is that view… $$$$
Bo Beach Bar 282 380 222; 10.00–17.00 daily. Run by Água Hotels at nearby Vila Verde, but open to non-guests. Well-priced food & cocktails or sangria, with a spectacular view & surfer-friendly vibe. Mostly escapes the tour crowd onslaught next door. $$$

BAÍA DA MURDEIRA This bay lies about 8km north of Santa Maria. The coast here is quite rocky, with some smaller sandy areas and a fine, quiet beach and sheltered cove just to the south. There is a resort here – Murdeira Village (page 111). It is gated but you can enter and use the beach, pool and so forth if you are a customer of the bar or restaurant.

CALHETA FUNDA A favourite with locals at the weekend, this lovely little beach is usually deserted and is a fine place for a swim, snorkel and picnic. See page 107 for a description of how to get there.

MURDEIRA TO PALMEIRA A few places of interest or beauty (and sometimes both) lie hidden within the land that stretches, like a vast natural car park, between Murdeira and Palmeira.

At the far northern end of Baía da Murdeira there is a dead-end track to the west, which leads to the coastal foot of **Monte Leão**, the unmistakable 'lion' gazing out to sea. It is known on the maps as Rabo de Junco. Drive with caution; a 4x4 is recommended.

At **Ponta da Parede**, there is a small, secluded beach, about 0.5km before the end of the track to Monte Leão. There's a small blowhole and some pretty rockpools.

After visiting Monte Leão, about 2.5km back along the track, there is another track branching to the north, which later joins a bigger track to the left that leads to a **viewpoint** which stands some 45m above sea level. There's a good view over Monte Leão and down to Santa Maria.

Fontona is a pretty, tree-filled oasis that lies about 3km south of Palmeira. It can be reached by following the track from the viewpoint for a further 2.5km, in a northwesterly and then northerly direction. Alternatively, it can be reached from Palmeira (take the signposted turning to the left off the road into Palmeira).

PALMEIRA Palmeira is a little place, defined by its role as Sal's port for cargo and passengers, and it features on the route of many round-island tours. It is a peaceful village with a couple of well-frequented restaurants, plus a weekly village gathering for dancing and drinking on Sundays, with things really getting going from around 19.00. You could also idle away an hour or two here waiting for a ferry, lounging at the bar overlooking the water with the locals, frolicking in the sea, or chatting to visiting yachties taking a break on their passage across the Atlantic. There are a couple of souvenir shops selling the usual trinkets. Get there by *aluguer* from Espargos (70$) or by walking or hitching.

✕ Where to eat and drink Restaurants can get packed with tour groups at lunchtime, but there are a few more options scattered back from the beach if the following options are full: just ask around.

Capricornio Near the port & church; ⊕ 09.30–21.30 daily. Octopus & fish grills, with outdoor seating. $$

Esplanada Rotterdam ⊕ 11.00–22.00 daily, though hours can be a lottery. Towards the beach, centred around a brightly painted sea container. Serves tuna steaks, lobster & snacks. $$

Gilda Pastelaria A couple of streets back from the port; ⊕ 07.00–midnight daily. Reliable bakery, handy if you're on an early or late departing ferry. $

BURACONA This is a small exhilarating natural swimming pool encased in black lava rock over which white foam cascades every few minutes. Nearby is the **Olho Azul**, the Blue Eye, an underground pool reached through a large hole in the ground. Divers can swim along an underground tunnel out into the sea.

If you are not in a car or taxi, you'll have to walk the hot and dusty 6km from Palmeira. Follow the main road into Palmeira and as the road swings round to the left, follow the sign off to the right, just after the Mercado Municipal, for Buracona. The terrain is about 25 shades of brown (including chocolate, wine-stain and rusted) covered with a few bent-over trees. Superimposed on this is a disused wind farm, industrial storage, a few scavenging goats and the odd anti-litter sign with plastic bags caught round it. The coastline itself is wildly beautiful, a jumble of black lava rock and waves. You pass a lesser pool but go the full 6km to reach Buracona, which is just before **Monte Leste** (263m). It's a great place for a swim and a picnic (but don't leave belongings unattended).

Go early if you want to avoid large tour groups, which can be relentless right throughout the day. There is also a restaurant (⊕ around 09.00–15.00 daily).

PEDRA DE LUME This is a spectacular place, and best appreciated in silence, so the poetic should rise early to reach it before anyone else. Inside a ring of low mountains lies a sweeping geometry of saltpans in blue, pink and green depending on their stage of salt formation, all separated by stone walls. You can sit here, listening to the water lapping in the lakes below and the cry of an occasional bird circling the crater rim.

There is nowhere to stay in this area, and a long-ago planned development is but an ugly half-finished monstrosity marring the previously beautiful vista from the small town.

History Manuel Martins, who developed Santa Maria, had a business here as well. Bags of salt were strapped to pack animals, which had to climb up the slopes of the volcano and down the other side to reach the port. In 1804, a tunnel was cut through the volcano wall, and in 1919 transport was made easier when a businessman from Santa Maria and a French firm bought the salt company and built the tramway, the remnants of which can be seen today. They could then transfer 25 tonnes an hour to the port, from where it was shipped to Africa. But markets shifted and the saltpans fell into disuse by 1985: today they do not even produce enough salt for Sal. Pedra de Lume is still inhabited but it feels like a ghost town except on public holidays.

There is disagreement about how salt water rises into the bottom of this crater – some believe it comes from deep in the earth, but the most orthodox explanation is that it infiltrates through the natural holes in volcanic rock along the kilometre distance from the sea.

Getting there and away The village is off the main Santa Maria to Espargos road. There are no *alugueres* running here, so unless you're on an island tour, a taxi is the only option unless you have your own rental car or quad bike. A taxi here and back from Espargos – the driver will wait as you look around – could cost you as little as 1,000$, including waiting time, but Espargos's taxi drivers may try to charge 2,000$ or more. It depends how much time and effort you are willing to spend on bargaining or waiting around for the cheapest option. You can try hitching but you might just end up walking all the way.

✕ Where to eat and drink Located inside the crater, the **Café/Restaurant** (⊕ 09.00–17.45 daily; $$$) serves drinks, snacks and main dishes.

What to see and do

Salina (Saltpan) (⊕ 09.00–17.45 daily; adults 600$, children – under a certain height – free) When you have looked around the village with its important-looking housing blocks and its little white church you can examine the relics of the pulley system for taking salt from the crater and loading ships. Then turn inland, along a track that lies just after the church, and follow the old overhead cables uphill. After a few minutes the track arrives at a car park. Ahead is the tunnel into the crater.

Once you pass through the entrance tunnel, there is a café, as well as a shop selling 'the white stuff' and a few other souvenirs. You can take a dip – more a leisurely float – or book a reasonably priced massage or other treatment such as thalassotherapy; antioxidant treatment to face and feet; or an application of water, salina salt and aromatic oil, said to be draining and nourishing. Showers and toilets are available. If you don't fancy paying the entrance fee to go down into the crater, follow the path off to the right of the ticket kiosk and after about 100m you can scramble up the slope for a free look down. You can sit here, listening to the water lapping in the lakes below and the cry of an occasional bird circling the crater rim.

The old wreck Head south from Pedra de Lume briefly back towards Espargos and after passing the cemetery on your right, you can turn right (unmarked) and follow a wide dirt road towards the coast. A 4x4 is preferred for this trek. Soon you will see the remains of a wreck sticking out of the sea. It is possible to snorkel here although it is a bit of a walk across slippery rocks. Take care as the sea can be very rough on this side. A little further on you will see a small sandbank. At certain times it is possible to spot the fins of schools of lemon sharks (*Negaprion brevirostris*) that swim into this area which is less than 1m deep. Further south are some pleasant bays and coves but, ultimately, a dead end.

SERRA NEGRA This is a stunning stretch of coast. Beaches alternate with black rocks lashed by white waves and the cliffs of Serra Negra rise behind them providing a touch of topographical grandeur unusual for Sal. This is a good place for a peaceful day away from the crowds. You can swim here, but note that the northern end of the beach gets cut off by high tide so, in common with the whole of the eastern coast, you should take care. It's a lonely spot, except on public holidays, so take the usual precautions against opportunistic theft. There are no facilities.

Getting there requires a 4x4 or quad bike and is hard (but not impossible) to navigate, over slightly tricky terrain, if you've never been there before. The driver must negotiate the sparse network of rough tracks and rocky ground that lies between the main road and the east coast. Coming from Santa Maria, turn right at the roundabout just before the chapel on the hill on to a dirt track. Follow the track as it forks to the right; there will be another fork to the right, marked with painted rocks, which you should follow (going straight on will bring you to the town dump). Turn left and follow the coast. You will cross some dry *ribeiras* which look steeper than they actually are. You will see a sign when you have reached Serra Negra. (See also page 107.)

PONTA DA FRAGATA This wild coast is hardly visited, most people preferring the calmer western and southern beaches. Its designation as a nature reserve should ensure some degree of protection for the important dune ecosystem. It is home to many native plants and an important turtle-nesting area. (See below for a description of where to start and finish.)

HIKES *Jacquie Cozens (JC)*

Although not really an island for walkers, hikers can go more or less anywhere on Sal – the important thing is to take plenty of water and a hat. Even on the very quiet beaches it is rare for muggings or theft to take place, but take minimal possessions and ask for advice. For more details on hiking in Cabo Verde and abbreviations used below, see page 51.

1 ART KAFÉ–IGREJINHA
Distance: 2km (circuit); time: 1 hour; difficulty: 1
Follow the instructions for the bike trail (20 minutes; page 107). You can make this a circuit by continuing north to the start of the beach on Costa Fragata, turning left and walking through the dunes back to Santa Maria (20 minutes).

2 COSTA DA FRAGATA
Distance: 6km (circuit); time: 1 hour; difficulty: 1
Costa da Fragata is a natural reserve and in theory is protected from development. Along the wildest coast, subject to strong northwesterlies and with attractive dunes and some birdlife, walking one-way will take around 1 hour. In the summer you will see many turtle tracks, and in the winter dozens of sails of kitesurfers flying in the sky. Start at the eastern end of Santa Maria, where the development peters out or take a taxi to Kite Beach (500$) and walk southwards along the coast to Santa Maria. Don't rely on getting a taxi back from Kite Beach unless it is during the windsurfing season; better to make an arrangement with the driver to be picked up.

3 SERRA NEGRA
Distance: 1km (one-way); time: 30 minutes; difficulty: 1
To many, this is the most beautiful beach on Sal. It consists of three secluded bays surrounded by tall cliffs. Other than at weekends in the summer it is deserted. The area is home to many types of birds including the red-billed tropicbird (*Phaethon aethereus*), known locally as Rabo de Junco, and is an important turtle-nesting beach. It is possible to walk to Serra Negra from Santa Maria but it is a dry, dusty and rocky walk. Much better to drive to the start of the beach and then take a walk to the end (30 minutes) – to reach the last bay you need to walk over a rocky area. You can also drive along a track around the back of the cliffs, park and walk to the top for a magnificent view of the coastline. There is a bit of scrambling to get to the top, so you need to be in reasonable shape to do this. At the top you will see cairns and tributes built from stones and shells to friends, family and lost loves.

4 SANTA MARIA PIER–PONTA PRETA
Distance: 4km (one-way); time: 1½ hours; difficulty: 1
A big favourite with locals and resident expats alike, this is a delight first thing in the morning. Heading west out of Santa Maria, this takes you past all the big hotels and on to Ponta Sino, a long, unspoiled nature reserve with Sal's only lighthouse. Turning north you will pass the RIU Palace Hotel; continue up past the dune until you reach the Ponta Preta Restaurant. You can either return the same way or walk beside the road directly inland from the restaurant, where you can easily stop a taxi or *aluguer*. The alternative is to take transport towards Espargos, asking the driver to drop you on the main road nearest to Ponta Preta and do the walk in reverse.

5 MONTE LEÃO
Distance: 2km (circuit); time: 1½ hours; difficulty: 2
Follow the trail to the top of Monte Leão at the northwestern end of Baía da Murdeira for an amazing view of the surrounding area (1 hour). Eagles and their nests are frequently seen here. You will need a rental car or hire a taxi driver to reach Monte Leão.

4

Boavista

> Mornas Dancing
> In the sensuous bodies of the sensuous girls
> In the dyspnoea of the brave waves
> Dying in the sand
> In the rolling of the
> Languid and gentle waves,
> Boavista,
> The unforeseen
> Scenery
> Of sands marching on the village
> > Jorge Barbosa

Boavista is the siren island. For many seafarers down the years, it was the first sight of land for months. The white dunes, like cusps of icing, must have been an alluring sight but Boavista's beaches have drawn many to a watery grave. It is ringed by reefs and its iron-rich rock formations send ships' compasses spinning. Over 40 ships have foundered here, within sight of land.

Beyond the idyllic beaches another story unfolds. The bleached land has a terrible beauty but it can leave you feeling parched and a little crazed by the sun. The only forests are petrified remnants on the shores: eons ago, Boavista was a moister place. In many parts the struggle for existence has become too much, the lure of the bigger towns too much. Villages are abandoned, and sand drifts across the floors of now empty houses.

HIGHLIGHTS AND LOWLIGHTS

Go for walks along deserted, searingly beautiful beaches, drifting dunes and desert oases; go for wind- and kitesurfing and go for game fishing. There is diving, though currents and wind can make it hard to explore many of the shipwrecks and can impair the clarity of the water. Go for fledgling ecotourism centred on birds, turtles, corals and whales. Or just go for unashamed sunbathing on pristine white-sand beaches, cooling yourself with some swimming in crystal-clear waters.

However, don't expect any mountain walking. If the landscape or the watersports do not appeal then the only other reason to come here is sunbathing: there is little in the way of conventional tourist 'attractions'.

SUGGESTED ITINERARY AND NUMBER OF DAYS You can see Boavista in a day by 4x4, although you will be hot and exhausted by the end of it. Three full days would be an ideal period in which to do a more relaxed vehicle tour that encompasses some of the remoter beaches; do a hike, perhaps to the north and/or a quad-bike expedition, maybe to the Viana Desert, with a watersports session or an eco-focused trip thrown in as well. Add a few more days if you want to relax on those gorgeous beaches.

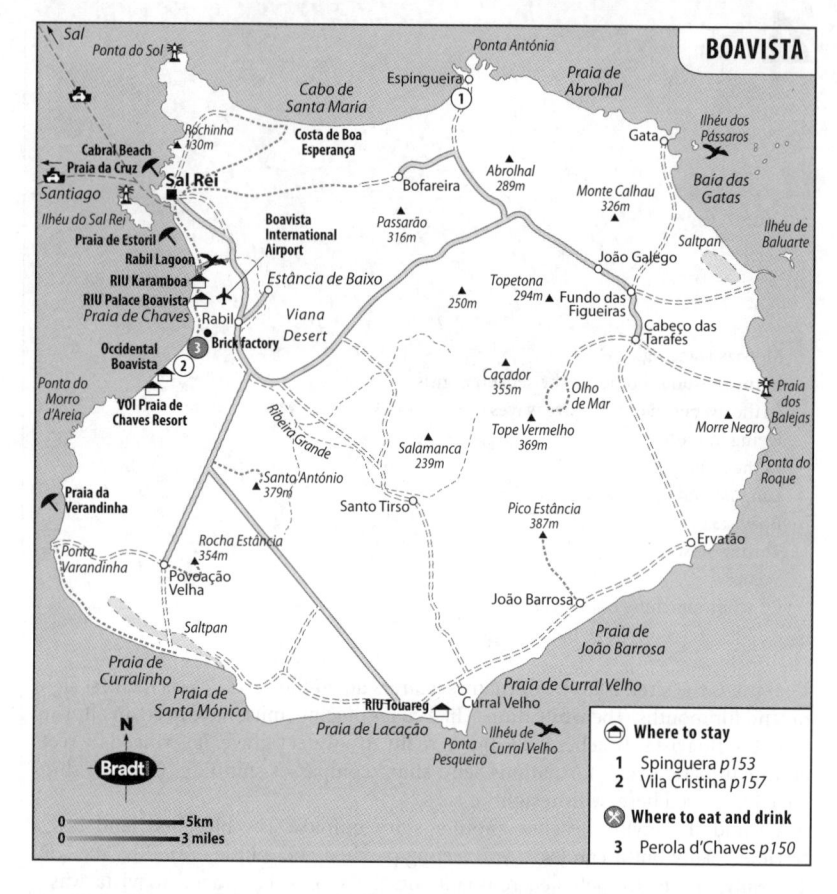

BACKGROUND INFORMATION

HISTORY With little to offer but salt, Boavista, like Sal, did not receive much attention after its discovery on 14 May 1460. It was named São Cristovão until, it is said, a storm-tossed sailor's triumphant cry: *'Boa vista!'*, the equivalent of 'Land ahoy!', led to its present name.

Island life has been punctuated by shipwrecks – tragedies that were often fortuitous for the starving islanders who would clamber over the rocks after a stormy night to retrieve food and goods from the debris. It is said that in times of starvation the people would tie a lamp to a donkey's tail and send it in the darkness along the coastal reefs in the hope of luring ships to their doom.

Most ships were wrecked by a strange conflation of circumstances. A strong and gusty trade wind combined with a powerful current pulled sailing ships towards the island. Flat, and often shrouded in a dusty haze, Boavista could be invisible until those boats rammed into the hidden rocks of its northern and eastern coasts. Meanwhile, maps and charts consistently placed Boavista several miles to the west of where it actually is.

Against this background, modern life began very slowly. It was visited early in its history, in 1498, by Christopher Columbus on his third voyage. By then the island already had a few inhabitants and was also used as a leper colony for well-to-do Europeans. After three days Columbus left, made a brief stop at Santiago and went on, reporting that the islands had: 'a false name...since they are so barren that I saw no green thing in them and all the people were infirm, so that I did not dare to remain in them.'

Apart from that, little happened on the island for the first 150 years after its discovery except desecration by goats. In 1580, there were only 50 people living there and by 1619, there was just a group of hunters chasing the goats.

Then English sailors discovered Boavista's high-quality salt and a mining and trade settlement was established in around 1620, based at Povoação Velha – its first village. By 1677, Boavista even had a priest, but periodic sackings shook its economy. English sailors attacked the island in 1684, taking chalices from the churches to trade on the African coast. There was another attack in 1697, and by 1702, the population of Povoação Velha was routinely armed.

Nearing the 1800s, Porto Inglês (now Sal Rei) became the most important town on the island and salt production was increasing, reaching its zenith in the first half of the 19th century. But the pillages continued in 1815 and 1817. The final desecration came in 1818 when the town was razed. As a result a fort was built on the Ilhéu do Sal Rei, and with this protection Boavista began an era of relative prosperity, becoming an important cultural centre. In 1834, it was even argued that the town should become the capital of Cabo Verde. The anti-slavery Luso-British Commission made Boavista its base in 1843.

The fortunes of even the prosperous dwindled, however, when the building of the port at Mindelo transformed the island of São Vicente into the new trading centre. When Charles Thomas, chaplain to the American Africa Squadron (an anti-slavery police) visited in 1855, he found the inhabitants to be starving and the cattle 'with sad faces and tears in their eyes, walking solemnly in cudless rumination over grassless fields'. The chief amusements of the people, he reported, were 'fishing, salt-making and going to funerals'. Fortunes changed again towards the end of the 19th century with increasing business in lime, clay tiles and castor oil. Over the last hundred years or so the island has been the victim of drought, famine and grasshopper infestation, all of which has led to mass emigration.

Perhaps the island's most famous son is Aristides Pereira, the 12th son of the priest of Boavista, who became the first president of Cabo Verde in 1975 and who now has the island's international airport named after him.

BOAVISTA TODAY Boavista is an island marked by tragedy and struggle. There is little in its history, though, to guide it through the pressures it faces today. On the one hand it is poised to participate, for the first time, in international prosperity, through mass tourism. On the other it seems ready to fall headlong into destruction – plundered by the same industry and with little to show financially as a result.

Boavista's beaches have an almost traumatic beauty. In these days when so many bewitching landscapes have been consumed by tourism, and the European palate is jaded, Boavista has allure. Exploiting this, most people seem to believe, means to build, build, build massive hotels and streetfuls of apartment blocks and condominiums, filling the coast from Sal Rei to Curral Velho. Some voices have questioned Boavista's develop-at-all-costs direction. There is the economic question: how much does an all-inclusive resort hotel under foreign ownership, built under generous tax concessions, actually make for the island? Then there is

FESTIVALS ON BOAVISTA

1 January	New Year (whole island)
6 January	Twelfth Night (João Galego and other northern villages)
3 May	Santa Cruz (Rabil slave liberation) Parades, drumming and whistling
4 May	Pidrona (Rabil)
8 May	São Roque (Povoação Velha)
Last weekend of May	Cruz Nhô Lolo (Estância de Baixo) Horse racing, *coladeras*, goat fighting
13 June	Santo António Procession to a church near the deserted Rock of Santo António
24 June	São João Baptista (northern area) Procession and offerings
4 July	Santa Isobel (Sal Rei) Boavista's most important feast day, attracting visitors from around the archipelago
15 August	Nossa Sra da Piedade (João Galego)
16 August	Saint Roque (Rabil) Praia da Cruz festival A week after the Baía das Gatas festival in São Vicente, this beach festival attracts national and international musicians.
8 December	Imaculada Conceição (Povoação Velha)

the more complex question: might Boavista's 'progress' destroy its very capital and thus, ultimately, extinguish itself? And of course, there are urgent environmental questions. The very least of these being, where do they put the waste from the hotels and how do they keep their lawns watered and pools full?

Given the significant impact the 2018 opening of a huge all-inclusive RIU hotel had on an important turtle-nesting beach in remote Lacação, further building phases could potentially mean there is no untouched land on this section of the southern coast. Today, though, apart from the strip of flourishing all-inclusives on the north of Praia de Chaves, the outskirts of Sal Rei are dotted with the half-built, slowly decaying dreams of long-departed investors. One Italian hotel owner blamed it all on climate change, suggesting that northern European travellers, who can now rely on hot summers at home, are no longer the year-round visitors they once were, further diminishing numbers. The pandemic and the subsequent economic downturn did mean that, at least for a while, the pace had slowed. For the meantime, at least, many kilometres of stunning beaches remain, for the most part sublimely unpeopled.

GEOGRAPHY Boavista is the closest island to the African mainland, and 50km from Sal. It is the third largest, at 620km^2, sparsely populated, despite its population more than doubling since the 2010s to more than 14,000 inhabitants and consolidating around its capital, Sal Rei. The island is very flat with the highest point, Pico Estância, at only 387m. The barren, stony landscape is covered in many areas with white sand and drifting dunes, which pile up on its western coast. The dunes have swallowed various buildings and covered the once-busy saltpans just outside

Sal Rei, as well as at one time infiltrating one of the all-inclusive hotels – without an identity wristband, would you believe.

There are 55km of white beaches and, in the centre, Sahara-like oases filled with date palms. Since independence, environmental measures have been taken such as the building of catchment dams and planting of trees.

FLORA AND FAUNA Boavista's biodiversity is of global importance as it includes endemic species of plants, birds and insects, as well as marine species. Its shores provide important nesting sites and feeding grounds for endangered marine turtles. Humpback whales come here to breed. A broad swathe of eastern Boavista is a hugely important coastal ecosystem, encompassing wetlands and nesting sites for thousands of loggerhead turtles. It is scattered with temporary wetlands all the way from Curral Velho at its southern tip to Ponta Antónia in the north. There are breeding colonies for a variety of seabirds along this shore and its offshore islets (Pássaros, Baluarte and Curral Velho). Corals grow in small bays and coves of the north and northeast coasts, protected from high swell and strong currents. These quiet and warm inshore waters are often frequented by nurse sharks (*Ginglymostoma cirratum*), juvenile hawksbill turtles (*Eretmochelys imbricata*) and green turtles (*Chelonia mydas*).

Protected areas In 2003, a law was passed approving a number of protected areas across the archipelago, including 18 on Boavista. The technical work carried out to delineate these areas has still not been approved, which has left them vulnerable.

After 2003, the government published its zones for integrated tourist development (ZDTIs). Land that was part of the protected areas was reallocated to ZDTI areas – most notably the coastal part of the Morro de Areia area in the southwest of the island and much of Praia de Lacação, the beach to the east of Santa Mónica: an ominous sign, perhaps, of future priorities.

The protected areas are Curral Velho, Monte Caçador and Pico Forçado. There are nature reserves at Boa Esperança in the north and Ponta do Sol at the northwest tip, Tartaruga, and Morro de Areia on the southwestern coast. An expanse of the northwest has been made into a natural park. Many of these areas will be affected by roads designed to link the island's villages. National monuments are: Monte Santo António, Monte Estância, Rocha Estância and Ilhéu do Sal Rei (the islet opposite Sal Rei). The islets of Baluarte, Pássaros and Curral Velho are Integral Nature Reserves (RNIs).

UNEP-GEF and the Ministry of Environment of Cabo Verde have committed to support and co-finance a project named 'Consolidation of Cabo Verde's Protected Areas System'. This project is being implemented over a period of four years, with the focus on Boavista primarily on the island's east coast which contains marine reserves, integral reserves, a natural reserve, a natural park and landscape protected areas. The east shore of Boavista harbours the most important loggerhead turtle nesting beaches in the whole country, several feeding habitats for juvenile green and hawksbill turtles, as well as other significant natural resources of the archipelago (seabird breeding colonies, coral areas, etc).

Ramsar sites Given the aridity of much of the island, it may seem counterintuitive that Boavista has one of the largest wetlands in the Macaronesia region. It stretches from Curral Velho, at its southern tip, up to Ervatão, and this region has been designated a 'Ramsar site' – that is, a wetland of international interest.

It's not wet all the year round – just over the rainy season and during extreme spring tides. But this is enough for it to be an important host to many migratory birds coming from Europe and West Africa.

A second Ramsar site is Rabil Lagoon, which acquired this status in 2005 and is also categorised by BirdLife International as one of Cabo Verde's Important Bird Areas. This site – however precarious with its proximity to the airport, quad bikes tripping through the area, nearby quarrying and coastal development – still sees a wealth of birdlife, including up to 16 species of wintering migrant waders, along with migrant herons and terns.

Marine life Boavista shares with Maio and Sal a single large marine platform that harbours the country's highest levels of marine biodiversity. The nearby João Valente seamount, an underwater mountain between Boavista and Maio, hosts a particularly rich biodiversity. Seamounts are known to fishermen for high concentrations of fish, and to researchers as rare and unique habitats.

Turtles Thousands of loggerhead turtles (*Caretta caretta*) nest on Boavista's east coast and especially its southeastern beaches annually, making it the second most important nesting site in the Atlantic Ocean and the third most important in the world, after the Florida Keys and Oman's Massirah Island. The key stretch for turtles is from Curral Velho in the south to As Gatas in the northeast.

The mother turtles crawl up the beaches between mid-June and late October. Once they have laid their eggs they disappear, leaving the hatchlings to fend for themselves. When the baby turtles emerge from their eggs in late August to late December, they make a frenzied dash for the sea. It is thought that the glimmering surface of the ocean is what attracts them – hence the problem that lights from houses and hotels could lure them in the wrong direction.

But development is not the only threat to turtles. There remains a strong local culture of turtle consumption, and dead turtles, the relics of this, sometimes litter the beaches. This is not done out of hunger, says Professor Luis Felipe Lopez Jurado, who has studied turtles on Boavista since 1998, including for the NGO Cabo Verde

WORKING WITH TURTLES ON BOAVISTA

Around 70% of the archipelago's loggerhead turtle nesting takes place on Boavista. The number of nests fluctuates each year according to climatic factors such as water temperature. In 2009, around 20,000 nests were recorded on Boavista; two years later there were a mere 5,000. Promisingly, an average figure today would be around 15,000. The nesting season takes place primarily between June and October and researchers gather on Boavista to study the loggerhead turtles (*Caretta caretta*) that nest at Ervatão Beach. (The most important beaches are on the east coast.) They want to understand the status, distribution and numbers of the turtles. It's a night job, and as soon as volunteers spot a turtle coming ashore they lie on the ground and crawl towards her. After she has laid her eggs and is on her way back to the sea, they put a chip in the turtle and ID attached with tags on the flippers. Turtles equipped with satellite transmitters send information about their migratory routes and feeding areas back to scientists. Meanwhile, hatchlings are counted, weighed and measured before being released into the sea.

A history of under resourced law enforcement has allowed the threats to loggerheads to continue, despite the full protection afforded to all turtle species by the Cabo Verde environmental legislation. But progress has been made, with the approval of the Marine Turtle National Conservation Plan and the

Natura 2000. 'The people killing turtles have big cars and jobs,' he says. 'They come down on a Friday night. Nobody needs the meat of the turtle to survive.'

Whales Sal Rei is the bay of choice for many humpback whales as a place to give birth and nurse their young. They arrive from December onwards, although March and April are probably the best months for sightings, which can sometimes be experienced as late as June. The giant mammals nurse their calves in a shallow haven free from waves, and then depart for the deep ocean (for more on whales, see page 138).

Sharks The quiet bays and coves of the north are often frequented by nurse sharks (*Ginglymostoma cirratum*). Lemon sharks (*Negoprion brevirostris*) can also be seen close to shore. Both species are relatively harmless to humans.

Birds The emblematic species of Boavista are the white-faced storm petrel (*Pelagodroma marina*) and the magnificent frigatebird (*Fregata magnificens*). The latter is monitored only sporadically and is now considered extinct in Cabo Verde. Other sought-after birds are the cream-coloured courser (*Cursorius cursor*), and the Egyptian vulture (*Neophron percnopterus*), the latter of these also approaching extinction. There are also breeding colonies of red-billed tropicbirds (*Phaethon aethereus*). The Cabo Verde sparrow (*Passer iagoensis*), one of four endemic Cabo Verdean birds, is found in Rabil Lagoon.

Overall there are more than 20 species of bird breeding on Boavista. The areas of most interest are perhaps Ilhéu de Curral Velho, Ilhéu dos Pássaros, and the wetland areas, both fresh water and salty.

Flora The *tamareira* (*Phoenix atlantica*) and the date palm (*Phoenix dactilifera*) fill the lagoons and *ribeiras* of the island (for more information on palm trees in Cabo Verde, see page 5).

---

establishment of TAOLA+ – from the Kriolu *tartaruga kriola*, 'Creole turtle' – as the umbrella organisation for turtle protection being significant achievements. Ana Liria Loza, President of CV Natura 2000, reported in 2016 that they had success in reducing the number of turtles killed for meat, at least according to the data they can collect from carcasses on the beaches. They then also turned some of their attention to the illegal 'fishing' of turtles, caught by boats even before they reach the shores. The effects of incidental catch ('by-catch') by industrial and artisanal fishing is still undergoing further research and assessment. Data for that is, however, harder to monitor than land-based slaughter.

Since 2008 another group, Fundação Tartaruga Cabo Verde (w turtle-foundation.org), has also become active on five beaches, concentrating on preventing the slaughter of the turtles as they nest. Patrols by international volunteers are made through the night on Canto, Boa Esperança, Norte and Lacação. Another NGO, Bios (w bioscaboverde.com), is also now involved, as is the Varandinha Community Association.

The growth of tourism is bringing increasing problems for the endangered loggerhead species through loss of habitat, light pollution and increasing numbers of cars, quad bikes and dune buggies. With the developers on one side, and hard working local NGOs on the other, battle has well and truly been joined.

> ## WHALES
> Interest is growing in the whales that frequent the waters around Boavista and other islands, and a consolidated team of international whale researchers has been created, supported and funded by various organisations. Over the last decade Beatrice Jann, a biologist from the University of Basel in Switzerland, has been documenting sightings of humpbacks and other species. Sometimes Pedro López Suarez, a naturalist who has been living on Boavista for a decade, gathers what information he can for her during the whale-watching trips he organises for tourists. Other groups such as the Irish Whale and Dolphin Group have organised research trips to try to uncover a link between the Cabo Verdean whales and the whales sighted around Ireland. Their website (w iwdg.ie) has a useful report on humpbacks off Cabo Verde.
>
> Whales are identified by the undersides of their tail flukes, each underside being unique to that whale. Their shifting patches of black and white look like an ink-blot pattern. The shape and scarring of the dorsal fin is also used in the photo-identification process. The photographs are sent to a store at Bar Harbour in Maine, USA, where there are now 'fingerprints' of 5,000 whales. 'It's sort of an Interpol of the humpbacks,' says Beatrice. By matching observations, scientists can piece together the whales' migrations. They have found whales photographed in Norway turning up in the Dominican Republic, and whales from western Canada appearing in Japan. For the visitor, Boavista presents great opportunities to see these mighty mammals, with over 5,000 people taking whale-watching trips annually. In season, sightings are almost a certainty.

ECONOMY Apart from the growing tourism sector, there is some business exporting dates and fishing (limited because of lack of investment in the large boats needed to withstand the stormy seas). An unusually poor soil thwarts agriculture. Villages across Boavista are supplied with water by tanker from a desalinisation plant in Sal Rei. Some water is drawn from the ground by windmills, but this is brackish and not suitable for drinking. It is used for washing, and also for agriculture, although the salt content constrains the type of vegetable that can be grown. Salt production ceased in 1979.

SAFETY
Crime Unfortunately robberies, some of them violent, became increasingly frequent on Boavista as tourism advanced in the early 2000s. Most of these incidents took place out of Sal Rei, on remote beaches, the dunes along Chaves Beach or in the vicinity of the wreck of the *Santa Maria*.

The City Hall of Boavista responded by calling in the army to work with the police. Locals say that this stabilised the situation and those levels of crime have not been reported for over a decade. Do still take basic precautions, however. Don't go walking alone on remote beaches, and if dining after dark at the beach bars south of Sal Rei, returning by taxi is advisable.

Visits to Boa Esperança, the *baraccas* on the outskirts of Sal Rei are safe during the day, but not advisable at night.

Ask around about the current security situation at restaurants and bars, as crime waves come and go, and it would be a shame to restrict yourself unnecessarily.

Hiking Boavista is a parched landscape, bereft of shade, which could cause serious dehydration or sunburn for the unwary, particularly hikers. Kit must include several litres of water (as many as five for a full day's walking); boots for dealing with the stony ground and frequent, short hilly scrambles; and sun protection. The interior is empty: most folk gave up on the possibility of living there many years ago. Learn from them and take at least a map and preferably a compass or handheld GPS. Some parts of Boavista have, however, no mobile-phone coverage. This includes much of the north coast.

Driving If you rent a 4x4 or quad bike remember that it is illegal to drive on beaches and dunes; stick to the tracks. If you become stranded, help may be hard to find. Carry food, water and a spade – and leave details of your journey at your hotel. Quad biking on your own in remote areas is not recommended.

Swimming Offshore winds and swells in the north make swimming periodically hazardous. In places (for example stretches of Chaves Beach or north of Espingueira) the beach slopes steeply and there can be a strong undertow. Check before you dip. The calm water off Praia de Estoril, just south of Sal Rei, is generally a safe place to swim, with the island offering protection.

Near the wreck of the *Santa Maria*, the beach attracts debris which can cut an ill-placed foot, so keep your shoes on.

GETTING THERE AND AWAY

BY AIR There are direct international flights from the UK with TUI. You can also fly direct from Paris, Luxembourg, Milan, Barcelona or Lisbon. Airlines servicing the island include Cabo Verde Airlines, TAP, Transavia, Luxair, Neos and Royal Moroccan. There is at least one daily flight, sometimes two, to and from Sal with Cabo Verde Airlines. As with all internal flights it is best to book well in advance in order to get a seat.

The **airport** (Aristides Pereira International Airport; BVC; ⟩251 9000) is 6km south of the capital, Sal Rei, near the town of Rabil. It's an attractive place, as airports go, with laid-back open-air architecture and an endearing welcome notice in the arrivals hall: 'This airport loves you. We hope you love us too.' Facilities include a bar/café, bank and two ATMs, souvenir shops, and car hire through Mendes & Mendes (m 991 8622) and tour operator Morabitur. Cabo Verde Airlines (⟩251 1415) and TAP (⟩241 3647) both have desks. There is also an information desk for tourists, which opens to coincide with international flight arrival times. There is free Wi-Fi access, though it is not reliable.

Some hotels meet their clients with a minibus. *Hiaces* and *hiluxes* wait outside and can be hired as taxis. The charge to town is 1,000$.

Transport back to the airport from Sal Rei can be found by loitering in the main square, though getting a collective *aluguer* is a hassle and risky if your flight is imminent. Better to bite the bullet and go 'private hire'. You can also ask your hotelier to arrange a vehicle.

BY FERRY CV Interilhas (w cvinterilhas.cv) has twice-weekly services to Sal and Santiago. The journey times – assuming they run – are 4 and 9 hours respectively. The cost at the time of writing was 2,500$ to Sal and 5,000$ to Santiago. They often run late, and currently leave late at night.

The other ocean option is a day trip to Sal by catamaran.

BY YACHT The waters off Sal Rei offer a very good anchorage. Most people anchor between the southern end of the islet and the shore. Harbour officials are generally on the pier. There are few facilities for yachts, but you could ask around at the port.

GETTING AROUND

BY PUBLIC TRANSPORT *Alugueres* run frequently between Sal Rei and Rabil (150$). To other destinations they generally leave Sal Rei in the afternoon, and do not return until the following morning, arriving in Sal Rei at about 07.00. Information is particularly difficult to come by from anyone in town: don't get stranded. Minibuses for the northeast leave from the west side of the main square in Sal Rei at about 13.00. Those heading south depart from the south of the square.

BY TAXI In the form of chartered *alugueres*, these can be hired for about ten times the public fare (eg: to Rabil 10,000$; to Santa Mónica 7,000$; to Morre Negro 10,000$; around the island 9,000–15,000$). To do a thorough tour of Boavista it is essential to have a 4x4.

BY CAR Most of the hotels can put you in touch with a car-hire firm or driver. A 4x4 is recommended. Prices start at around 7,500$ per day, self-drive.

La Perla [146 C5] Largo Santa Isabel, Sal Rei; \251 2293; m 997 4863; e info@laperlaboavista.com; w laperlaboavista.com

Mendes & Mendes [146 C5] Rua dos Emigrantes, Sal Rei; m 955 8889; e mendesemendes@cvtelecom.cv
Olicar [146 B3] Largo Santa Isabel; \251 1743. On the main square.

BY SCOOTER AND BIKE A cheaper option, worth considering given the price of cars. The **KatlantiK** apartment complex (page 148; w katlantik.com) rents bikes from 4 hours (€15) to a week (€100).

WHERE TO STAY AND EAT

Unless you have opted for an all-inclusive, most accommodation, including all of the cheaper places, is in the capital Sal Rei. The five-star Barceló Marine, opened in 2025, is one of the few options on the town's northside, plus there are a few rental apartments stretching a few kilometres to the south, along Chaves Beach. There is also one very remote, upmarket ecolodge in Espingueira. The massive RIU Touareg is in the far south and there are plans for many more hotels along Chaves Beach and behind Santa Mónica Beach, though at the time of writing these had not come to fruition. As on Sal, hotels on Boavista are more expensive than in the rest of the archipelago. There are an increasing number of apartments available for long- and short-term rental. Try asking tour operators or rental agencies such as Blue Banana or Boavista Apartments (for contact information, see page 148).

To be within walking distance of any external facilities, such as local restaurants or the watersports establishments, it's best to stay in Sal Rei. If you are staying at one of the options along Chaves Beach, this is isolated and too far (and, after dark, potentially dangerous) to walk to Sal Rei, so you will be reliant on the hotel shuttle or taxis.

Boavista is known for its excellent dining, with a terrific amount of choice across all budgets. You'll find a pervasive Italian influence, so pizza, gelato and coffee are reliably good. Sodade (page 149) is one of the first upmarket day-to-night places, with a particularly evocative Italian, local and West African culinary melange. There's also a unique café-restaurant, Bowlavista (page 149), where almost all the produce is hydroponically grown on the island.

EXCURSIONS AND TOUR OPERATORS

The companies listed in the following sections can assist with tours and activities on the island.

Barracuda Tours [146 C7] Av 4 de Julho, Zona de João Cristovão, Sal Rei; 251 1907; e geral@barracudatours.com; w barracudatours.com; 09.00–13.00 & 15.00–18.00 Mon–Fri, 09.00–13.00 Sat. Southwest of town on a road running towards the beach from opposite the fuel stations. Offers half- & full-day trips around the island, quad tours & buggy tours, as well as a day trip to Fogo.

Clamtour [146 C5] Av 4 de Julho, Sal Rei; 251 2121/1982; m 918 7351/7352. Offers walks, 4x4 tours, boat tours & transport-booking services.

Giggling Gecko Adventures m 978 6926; e info@gigglinggeckoadventures.com; w gigglinggeckoadventures.com. A highly rated tour company, run by an enterprising Scottish couple who support local charities. Offerings include island tours, BBQ tours, whale-watching & turtle tours (both seasonal), Sat night sunset tours & many more.

Morena Travel Agency [146 C2] Largo Santa Isabel, Sal Rei; 251 1445; e boavistapoint@cvtelecom.cv; w boavistamorena.com. 09.00–12.30 & 15.00–18.30 Mon–Fri, 09.00–12.30 Sat. In the north of the main square. It offers day trips to the dunes & further afield to Santa Mónica Beach, & other activities.

Naturalia 355 2221; m 953 6408; e naturaliabooking@gmail.com; w naturaliaecotours.com. Offers whale-watching, snorkelling among corals & nurse sharks, turtle-watching & birding trips. The company, set up in 2008, is one outcome of the EU's Naturalia Project to restore ecosystems & test whether they can be used sustainably & profitably in ecotourist activities.

Sea Adventures Boavista m 985 7286; e info@sea-adventures-boavista.com; w sea-adventures-boavista.com. Fishing tours & whale-watching in season on a motor yacht.

ACTIVITIES

DIVING See page 53 for a discussion of diving.

Boavista Diving Near the Alisios restaurant, Estoril Beach; m 588 81 74; e info@dcriamar.com; w dcriamar.com; 08.00–17.00 daily. Multi-lingual PADI centre, offering dives, lessons & a kids' programme. Has a 'no feed, no touch' policy in regard to the maritime environment. Offers hotel pick-ups for €10.

WINDSURFING AND KITESURFING The excellent windsurfing potential of Cabo Verde is discussed on page 56. Boavista has many great spots but not everywhere is suitable: rescue facilities are non-existent in many places so beaches like Santa Mónica, with a strong offshore wind, are not recommended. The northern shore has a heavy wind swell, and though wind- and kitesurfing are possible there are better places elsewhere. The island is good for independent and advanced kitesurfers, windsurfers and surfers looking for a variety of conditions, but beginners should stick to Sal Rei Bay. For many of the other spots you will need a hire car or arrange a pick-up or taxi. Key locations are:

SHIPWRECKS ON BOAVISTA

A few years ago, divers plunged into Cabo Verde's waters on a hunt for shipwrecks, and surfaced clutching a gold coin bearing the date 1760. They believe they discovered the remains of the *Dromadaire*, a French trading ship that sank in 1762, carrying more than £3 million of gold and silver. It is said the crew of the *Dromadaire* only realised their plight when they saw the reef surf under the prow. Some 17 miles south of Boavista lies the notorious reef, Baixo de João Leitão: it has wrecked many a vessel. One man who spent tormented hours battling (successfully) to avoid it was Captain James Cook on his third and last voyage to the South Seas, in 1776.

Old people on Boavista still tell of a legendary cargo of gold brought to their ancestors by shipwreck. This may have been the wreck of the English vessel *Hartwell* on 24 May 1787. The ship suffered a mutiny while on the seas and in the confusion the crew let the boat stray to Boavista's shallows. The reef that sank her is now called the Hartwell Reef and lies at the northeast side of the island – it is partly above water, and extends for about 6km.

Cabo Verde's version of the *Titanic* disaster occurred in the 19th century – the tragedy of the *Cicília*. It was the night of 5 November 1863, and the Italian ship was carrying emigrants destined for South America. Their spirits were high and there was a dance going on in the ballroom when the ship foundered near Boavista. When the captain realised what had happened he commanded the door of the ballroom to be locked. He made a great error. According to the poet José Lopes de Silva: 'There inside was true horror…a dance of life was transformed into a macabre dance of death…' Passengers were later found dead in the act of struggling to get out of the portholes; in all 72 died.

The *Santa Maria* was wrecked in August 1968 on the northwest coast. She was en route from Spain to Brazil with a cargo of cars, drink, melons, cork and cheese. The year 1968 had until then been a bad one for Boavistans: they spent the next 12 months salvaging booty.

Sal Rei Bay A long white sandy beach stretching south of town, with the wind increasingly stable as you move south, and the ground increasingly sandy once you have left town behind. The wind is offshore, so make sure you know how you will be rescued. There's a reef with small break waves. Apart from that the water is flat.

Chaves You can windsurf or kitesurf on the beach outside the RIU Karamboa but in the winter this often has a large shorebreak and to find a good place to enter the water you will have to go much further down the beach.

Baía Varandinha Reached by 4x4 overland, this remains a lonely place with stable, side-shore winds, beach break waves and sand below. Not suitable for beginners.

East coast Outside the turtle season (page 136) it should be possible to windsurf and kitesurf on many of the beaches here. Again the wind is stable and side-shore to side-on. There is some wind swell out of the protected bay areas. Not suitable for beginners.

Kit hire and lessons are available from the following:

Kitekriol m 994 3487/984 7630; e KiteKriol@hotmail.com; w kitekriol.com. The furthest south of the operators on Praia de Estoril has a good reputation.

Wind Club François Guy Praia de Estoril, just south of Sal Rei; m 972 0107; e info@boavistawindclub.com; windclubfg. This long-established club offers windsurfing & rents windsurfing, kitesurfing, kayaking, SUP & surfing kit. Also offers surf safaris to 'secret' surfing spots on the island.

SURFING Cabral Beach, where the swell is greatest, is the most popular venue for surfers. Surfing is best from November to March in terms of waves and swell, but calmest in May to September. Boards can be hired from the Wind Club François Guy (see above).

BEACHES AND SWIMMING The vast, wild strands of Chaves, Curralinho, Santa Mónica, Curral Velho and many others encircle Boavista as one huge, dazzlingly beautiful beach. There are endless opportunities for sunbathing and swimming. Praia de Estoril opposite Ilhéu do Sal Rei is a lovely option – the water is never more than 2m deep and it is only 1,000m to the island, which gives protection from large waves nearly all the time. Another possibility close to Sal Rei is Praia da Cruz, just before the private beach of the Barceló Marine hotel, and divided from it by a little spit of land. There are also many protected coves around the island – for example Praia de Ponta Antónia in the north (page 153).

FISHING Both line fishing and deep-sea fishing are available. Try **Sea Adventures Boavista** (m 985 7286; w sea-adventures-boavista.com), who offer catch and release for blue marlin, with all other fish divided among the crew, and part of the catch given to locals in need.

WHALE-WATCHING Humpback whales come to Boavista to have their young and to nurse their calves until they are strong enough for the open ocean. A report in 2016 declared that the Cabo Verdean population of humpbacks is endangered. Journeying out on a catamaran in search of them, watching their great masses surging and looping effortlessly through the water, and catching glimpses of their signature tail flukes, is a magical experience, as is taking a dip on the way back to shore. You may be accompanied by scientists photographing, recording and collecting skin samples, which adds even more interest to the trip.

Naturalia Page 141. Available Mar–May most days of the week, depending on the wind & swell; price depends on boat & number of passengers.

Sea Adventures Boavista Page 141

BIRDWATCHING Local fishermen can be recruited to take tourists to the various islets. **Naturalia** (page 141), offers half- and full-day tours for €50–80, depending on the number of participants.

TURTLE-WATCHING Watching nesting loggerhead turtles is a night-time experience, with August the peak of the nesting season. There is an 80-minute journey to the southeastern coast. A guide gives a briefing on turtle biology and conservation work in Cabo Verde as well as the basic rules to follow to minimise disturbance to the animals. Seeing turtles is guaranteed; witnessing their egg laying is more hit-and-miss as it depends on their finding a suitable nesting site. Visit **Naturalia** (page 141; available Jul–Oct 20.00–01.00 approx; adult/under-12 €60/35, hotel transfer included; book directly or via travel agent).

There are three NGOs currently involved on Boavista in turtle conservation: **Turtle Foundation, BIOS.CV** and **Cabo Verde Natura 2000**.

CORAL SNORKELLING Snorkelling takes place at Gatas Bay, on the northeast shore of Boavista, where, in the summer, you may find yourself nose to nose with nurse sharks as well as exploring the corals. Contact **Naturalia** (page 141; available at high tide; adult/under-12 €60/30, min 4 people; price includes equipment & transfers).

QUAD BIKING Motoquad is popular and a compelling way to see the sights. It is, however, frowned upon by some who wish to preserve the peace of Boavista's beaches as well as the island's significant turtle habitats. Because of the latter, it is illegal and irresponsible to take vehicles, including quad bikes, on to the beaches or the dunes. If you're on a guided tour, ensure the company is 'turtle aware' before setting off. Try **Quadzone Boavista** (m 924 2727; e info@quadzone-boavista.com; w quadzone-boavista.com; tours from €75 for 2hrs up to a whole day for €170; also quad-fishing tours).

HIKING Although Boavista lacks the verdant mountainous scenery of the more traditional hiking islands, its white deserts, pretty coastline and serendipitous oases, combined with its emptiness, make it a rewarding place to explore on foot (provided the hiker is properly shod, hatted and watered; see page 66 for potential hazards). There are several short hikes around the north of Sal Rei, and three of these can be joined together to make a full-day excursion. There are a couple of short hikes up small peaks in the southwest, near Povoação Velha, and a charming hike down Chaves Beach and around Rabil Lagoon.

For hike descriptions, and further hiking ideas, see page 158.

CULTURE The Morabeza restaurant (page 150) has weekly displays of drumming and fire-eating. Sal Rei has three interesting small museums exploring the history of the island, as well as the charming domestic collection on view upstairs at Sodade (page 149). While the craft traditions of palm weaving and ceramics can be glimpsed in Povoação Velha and Rabil respectively, the latter is highly commercialised.

SIGHTSEEING BY VEHICLE For self-drive vehicles, see page 140. You can pick up 4x4 taxis at the east end of Largo Santa Isabel.

> **THE BOAVISTA ULTRATRAIL**
>
> Running for three days through the dunes, beaches and oases of Boavista, testing themselves in the bone-dry heat and under the desert night skies, is the experience of a lifetime for many of the contestants in the annual ultratrail (formerly ultramarathon). Launched in 2000, the 150km race, held in December, lasts for up to 60 hours, with a hefty entry fee (€400 in 2024) but an equally hefty prize fund. Sleep as you go. For more information, including details of two shorter courses, contact Boavista Ultratrail (e info@boavistaultratrail.com; w boavistaultratrail.com).

A popular activity is to join a half- or full-day tour of the island, using one of the tour operators listed on page 141. You can also hire your own car, scooter, bicycle or taxi with driver, for the day. The latter option, of course, has the advantage that you can dawdle where you please, but will still more or less take the same form, and you'll find you are on the same circuit as other individuals and groups. Getting drivers to do anything out of the box, say cherry-picking attractions from the north and south, can be a little difficult, but not impossible.

Another option is to hire a quad bike and set out on your own, but if you are new to quad bikes take advice on how to extract yourself from the sand. A possible route is to go south from Sal Rei, northeast along the main road after Rabil, branch off north to see Espingueira and Bofareira and then return to the main road; follow it to Fundo das Figueiras and Cabeço das Tarafes; take the track south to Curral Velho, northwest back up to the main road, then southwest on the main road to Povoação Velha, where a new road has now been built. Most of the sights along this route are described from page 153. Exercise extreme caution if travelling alone as there have been incidents of mugging on deserted beaches. Ask for advice about the current situation before venturing to remote places. Remember that it is illegal to drive on the beach anywhere in Cabo Verde; unfortunately, you will still see it done.

Take local advice about the state of the track directly linking Curral Velho to Povoação Velha and, if you are using a driver, check with them beforehand that they are happy to follow your route. Don't embark on the venture on your own without a good map.

SAL REI

There is a charm about this town that seeps in slowly, as you sit with a beer watching life go by, or drink coffee in thankful shade overlooking the beach. The water is a glorious turquoise and the mounds of sand are a true, desert-island yellow. Men maintain their painted boats and children shout and play around them or hurl themselves into the water from the old pier. From the town, the modest hillocks of Boavista appear like craggy mountains. At night, you may become aware of a canine sub-culture, characterised by ferocious barking matches and brawling in the empty streets.

Sal Rei is laid back, but there's a gentle business too. Town planners made the cobbled roads wide and planted acacias, their trunks painted a tidy white. The main *praça*, Largo Santa Isabel, is vast, with bandstands, children's play areas, benches, a café and an ice-cream stall. At the time of writing, it was, however, heaped with stones waiting to become fresh pavers, and a great dusty mess, but with any luck during the life of this book, the upgrade work will be completed and it will be returned to its bright, austere grandeur.

So far the influx of visitors to the all-inclusive hotels has made little impact on Sal Rei, which has not experienced the sudden boom in restaurants and late-night bars as the neighbouring island, Sal. There is, however, obvious money and care being invested in a handful of new restaurants, bars and cafés, and these give the town a quiet sophistication. Chinese shops are still the mainstay when it comes to groceries, with a couple of large ones that are open daily.

WHERE TO STAY Those not staying in one of Boavista's massive all-inclusive hotels on Chaves Beach will find accommodation is available across all price ranges. That said, the cost tends to be higher than on the other islands, apart from similarly tourist-orientated Sal. There are options in the town and on

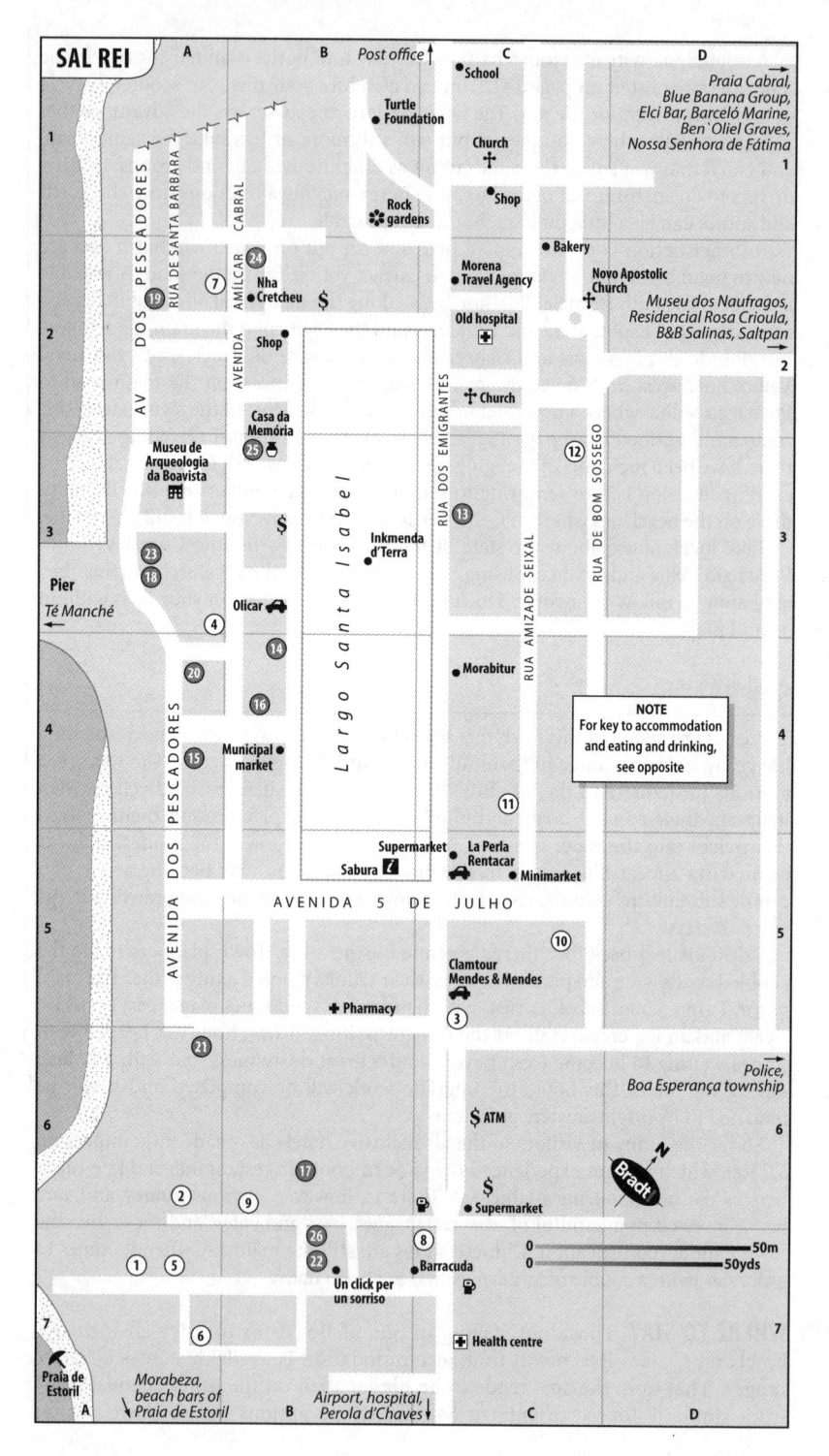

SAL REI

A — AV DOS PESCADORES / RUA DE SANTA BARBARA / AVENIDA AMÍLCAR CABRAL

B — Post office ↑

- Turtle Foundation
- Rock gardens
- (7) Nha Cretcheu
- (19)
- Shop
- Casa da Memória (25)
- Museu de Arqueologia da Boavista
- (23) (18)
- Olicar (4)
- (14)
- (20)
- (16)
- Municipal market (15)
- Largo Santa Isabel
- Inkmenda d'Terra
- Supermarket
- Sabura
- AVENIDA 5 DE JULHO
- Pharmacy
- (21)
- (2) (9) (17)
- (26) (22)
- (1) (5)
- (6)
- (8) Barracuda
- Un click per un sorriso

C

- School
- Church
- Shop
- Morena Travel Agency
- Bakery
- Novo Apostolic Church
- Old hospital
- Church
- RUA DOS EMIGRANTES
- (12)
- (13)
- RUA AMIZADE SEIXAL
- Morabitur
- (11)
- La Perla Rentacar
- Minimarket
- (10)
- Clamtour Mendes & Mendes
- (3)
- $ ATM
- $ Supermarket
- Health centre

D

Praia Cabral, Blue Banana Group, Elci Bar, Barceló Marine, Ben'Oliel Graves, Nossa Senhora de Fátima

Museu dos Naufragos, Residencial Rosa Crioula, B&B Salinas, Saltpan

RUA DE BOM SOSSEGO

NOTE
For key to accommodation and eating and drinking, see opposite

Police, Boa Esperança township

N ↗ Bradt

0 ——— 50m
0 ——— 50yds

← Pier
Té Manché

↙ Praia de Estoril

↙ Morabeza, beach bars of Praia de Estoril

↓ Airport, hospital, Perola d'Chaves

146

its southern edge behind Estoril, with most apartments clustered around the latter. Cabral Beach, north of town, also has a few mid-range and budget places, though apart from the upmarket Barceló Marine hotel further along at Praia de Cruz, this stretch can feel a little desolate.

Hotels

Guest House Orquidea [146 A6] (10 rooms) At the start of Estoril; 251 1041; e domorquidea@hotmail.com. A charming, elegant guesthouse of grey stone only a few metres from the sea featuring delightfully decorated rooms, each with balcony, fridge, TV & safe. There is also a gym, internet & laundry service. Upstairs rooms have a wonderful sea view. Buffet b/fast is served in a shady, bougainvillea-edged courtyard & the welcoming owners, long-term residents of Sal Rei, will arrange all the excursions you could want. A brilliantly located & comfy place to base yourself while exploring Boavista. **$$$$**

Hotel Dunas [146 A3] (20 rooms) Av Amílcar Cabral; 251 1225; e saradunashotel@gmail.com. Great location, overlooking the sea but also with the town's best places to eat, drink & hang out on your doorstep. Rooms are well maintained, compact but comfortable. Courtyard restaurant serves b/fasts & there's a rooftop for catching the breeze. **$$$$**

Migrante Guesthouse [146 A2] (5 rooms) Av Amílcar Cabral; 251 1143; m 995 3655; e info@migrante-guesthouse.com; w migrante-guesthouse.com. On a road to the west of the main square, an atmospheric guesthouse with appealing colonial-era architecture. Set around a courtyard, it's tastefully, if rather eccentrically, decorated. Rooms are en suite with fans, which you'll need. Italian owner speaks English. Only open Nov–Mar, but subject to change. **$$$$**

Oásis White Hotel [146 C7] (67 rooms) On the main road at the start of town coming in from the airport; w oasisatlantico.com. A newcomer in 2023, with fresh & comfortable rooms, rooftop and sea vistas, great staff & a rooftop pool. Its location is a busy one though, so check the room when booking to avoid the service station view. **$$$$**

Hotel Boavista [146 C5] (34 rooms) Rua dos Emigrantes; 251 1145; e hotelboavista@cvtelecom.cv. Positioned on the right as you enter Sal Rei from the airport. Large, mostly balconied rooms with AC, TV & fridge are good value but a little tired. Avoid the back rooms that have no sea view & can be dark. **$$$**

Hotel Estoril/Residence Cardeal [146 A7] (45 rooms & apts) To the southwest of town, close to Praia de Estoril' m 955 2116; e estorilboavista@gmail.com; w estorilboavista.com. Mix of hotel rooms or units with kitchen areas & multiple bedrooms, some with terrace. Fans, sat TV & an easy-going atmosphere for a relatively large complex. Restaurant next door. Will arrange activities. **$$$**

Ouril Hotel Agueda [146 B6] (14 rooms) Just behind Guest House Orquidea; e ourilagueda@ourilhotels.com. Friendly, proactively helpful staff & a fantastic rooftop bar with hot tub will make

SAL REI
For listings, see from page 145

Where to stay
1. Aparthotel Ca' Nicola..........A7
2. Guest House Orquidea......A6
3. Hotel Boa Vista....................C5
4. Hotel Dunas.........................A3
5. Hotel Estoril/Residence Cardeal................................A7
6. KatlantiK...............................A7
7. Migrante Guesthouse.............A2
8. Oásis White................................C7
9. Ouril Hotel Agueda..................B6
10. Residencial A Paz B&B...........C5
11. Residencial Boa Esperança....C4
12. Residencial Bom Sossego......C3

Off map
B&B Salinas....................D2
Blue Banana Group......D1
Residencial Rosa Criola................D2

Where to eat and drink
13. Bar Naida...............................C3
14. Blu Marlin..............................B4
15. Bowlavista.............................A4
16. Ca' Baby.................................B4
17. Cachupa Café........................B6
18. Caffé del Porto.....................A3
19. Casa Rosa..............................A2
20. Cremositos............................A4
21. El Mirador..............................A6
22. Pastelaria Doce Vida............B7
23. Porton de nos Ilha................A3
24. Rosy Bar/Café.......................B2
25. Sodade....................................B3
26. Spazio 51................................B7

Off map
Elci Bar....................D1
Té Manché..............A3

> **BOAVISTA'S ALL-INCLUSIVE LINE-UP**
>
> These upmarket hotels stretch down the coast a few kilometres from Sal Rei, with the exception of the Barceló Marine, to the north of town, and the RIU Touareg, which is in the far south of the island. All have hundreds of beds and full facilities from spas to multiple pools to kids' clubs. UK tourists tend to favour the RIUs, the Occidental is a European favourite and VOI is almost exclusively Italian.
>
> - Barceló Marine
> - RIU Karamboa
> - RIU Palace Boavista
> - Occidental Boavista
> - VOI Praia de Chaves Resort
> - RIU Touareg

you overlook creaky balcony doors & other minor maintenance issues here. Rooms are spotless, light & generously sized, with king beds. Right on the sand, too. Great value. **$$$**

Residencial A Paz B&B [146 C5] (9 rooms) Av 5 de Julho; m 914 0372; e info@apazboavista.com; w apazboavista.com. Near the main square, this small Italian/Cabo Verdean-run house has been decorated with some charm & much bamboo. Comfortable enough, all rooms are en suite with hot water & fan, & some have a balcony & sea view. B/fast is on a roof terrace. Free Wi-Fi only in public areas. **$$$**

B&B Salinas [146 D2] (14 rooms) Rua Bom Sossego; 594 0504. Simple, clean rooms with large bathrooms, fans & TVs near the salinas in the northern part of Sal Rei. Sun terrace & a bar & restaurant downstairs. Well-respected budget option with friendly Italian owners. **$$**

Residencial Bom Sossego [146 C3] (7 rooms) Rua de Bom Sossego; 251 1155. In the block behind the church – the lively, English-speaking owner lives at Bar Sossego around the corner. Basic, but reliable, a couple of bedrooms have verandas, all with TV & fans. Communal roof terrace. **$$**

Residencial Boa Esperança [146 C4] (8 rooms) Rua Tavares Almeida; 251 1170. In the road east of the main square. Proud to be by far the cheapest in town, this establishment is definitely just a place to lay your head: it's basic & tatty around the edges. No b/fast. Some rooms have shared bathrooms. **$**

Residencial Rosa Criola [146 D2] (7 rooms) On the northern edge of town; m 992 7854; e rosacriolaresidence@hotmail.com. Good-value budget option with private bathrooms, balconies, TV & fan. No Wi-Fi. **$**

Apartments

KatlantiK [146 A7] w katlantik.com. Smartly furnished complex on Praia de Estoril & a selection of separate apts & villas further south on Chaves. The main Estoril apt building has roof terrace & 24hr reception. Can organise excursions, vehicle rentals & lobster BBQs on the beach. **$$$$**

Aparthotel Ca' Nicola [146 A7] 251 1793; e info@canicola.com; w canicola.com. Earthily decorated 1- or 2-bedroom apts in stone building 50m from Estoril Beach. All fully equipped, some with terraces or balconies. **$$$**

Blue Banana Group [146 D1] 251 2698; m 974 2349; e sabine.vileyn@gmail.com; blue_bananaholidayrentalsbv. Offers spacious, well-equipped apts as well as maintenance & management. At Cabral Beach, where they manage some units, guests have use of a good-sized pool & children's pool. **$$$**

Residence Cardeal [146 A7] (See *Hotel Estoril*, page 147) Apts which can sleep up to 5 people. **$$$**

Boavista Apartments [not mapped] m 529 9013; e boavistaapartments@yahoo.com; w boavistaholidayrentals.com. Wide choice of apts, from 1 to 4 bedrooms. British-owned. **$$–$$$**

✕ WHERE TO EAT AND DRINK Island specialities include *chicharro assado* (saurel fish coated in olive oil and roasted); *canja de capado* (boar broth); and *botchada* (sheep or goat stomach). You may be lucky to come across those, but, with fresh fish in abundance and a strong Italian community, you're more likely to find menus of fish grills, pasta and pizza. For something more local, try Bar Naida, listed on page 150, or the street behind Rua de Bom Sossego, which has a few other budget possibilities. While the town *praça* undergoes its interminable upgrade, a few old favourites like Esplanada Municipal Silves remain closed: once it's complete, check for reopenings.

On Praia de Estoril and the northern end of Chaves Beach, several of the beach bars have sunbeds and parasols for the use of their clients. Some are free, some are not, so it's worth asking before you order your meal. A couple also have special barbecue nights, which should be booked ahead.

You can buy fresh bread from the busy *padaria* east of the Bom Sossego Bar in the mornings, focaccia and pastries from the small cluster of cafés in the backstreets of Estoril, and cheese and vegetables from the women at one corner of the square or in the Mercado Municipal.

Blu Marlin [146 B4] 251 1099 09.00–23.00 Mon–Sat. This small restaurant & bar is on the main square & popular with locals & expats, serving freshly caught tuna, carpaccio & seafood pasta. Advance booking essential. $$$$

Casa Rosa [146 A2] Rua de Santa Barbara; 983 1889; w luxury-beachvilla.com/casa-rosa-restaurant-bar; noon–23.00 Thu–Tue. Cosy downstairs restaurant & surprisingly inner-city-feeling rooftop terrace that's perfect for an afternoon or evening drink. Surprisingly expensive menu ranges across the usual burgers, pasta & fish grills, with a few more European options like meatballs & mustard. Live music Thu & Sat from 20.00. $$$$

El Mirador [146 A6] m 530 4188; 12.30–15.00 & 18.30–22.30 Mon, Wed & Fri, 18.30–22.30 Sat & Sun; closed Jul/Aug. An outpost of Spanish-ness among the many Italian restaurants, this place serves paella & other old-school Iberian favourites. Spanish wine by the glass. $$$$

Ca' Baby [146 B4] Just off Largo Santa Isabel; 594 4901; 08.30–23.00 Tue–Sun. On a side street running towards the bay, this cosy shopfront is known for its pizza, as well as serving pasta, *tatakis* & seafood dishes. $$$

Caffé del Porto [146 A3] 08.00–22.00 daily. Serving pasta, pizza & fish & meat dishes in the evenings. Outdoor tables on an expansive terrace, with welcome umbrellas, overlooking the pier. Expat favourite, but no longer gets rave reviews. $$$

Elci Bar [146 D1] m 992 3244; 10.00–20.00 Tue–Sun. Along Praia Cabral, 10 mins' walk northeast of town. Wide variety of snacks, b/fast dishes (inc waffles), full meals & cocktails all served around a good-size swimming pool. A pleasant, quiet alternative to Estoril, with friendly Belgian owners & sport on the sat TV. May close during May or Jun. $$$

Porton de nos Ilha [146 A3] Rua Marginal; m 991 9331; noon–15.00 & 19.00–22.00 Mon–Fri, 19.00–22.00 Sat. A well-favoured & busy seafood restaurant with large upstairs terrace. Occasional special sushi nights, lobster, prawns & octopus are specialities here. $$$

Sodade [146 B3] Av Amílcar Cabral; m 581 2200; e info@sodadeboavista.com; w sodadeboavista.com; 08.00–14.00 & 17.00–midnight Mon–Sat, 17.00–midnight Sun. *The* Sal Rei place to have morning coffee, with excellent espresso, pastries & fresh juices in a bustling social milieu. A ramble of rooms & colonial-era artefacts are also fabulously atmospheric. At night, book a table for very reasonably priced mains (most under 1,000$), good wine & music by candlelight. The small, thoughtful menu includes West African-style *yassa* chicken, a few Italian favourites like vegetarian parmigiana & local specialities such as *buzio* – sea snail – stew. Fish or vegan *cachupa* or lobster for 2 can be preordered. $$$

Té Manché [146 A3] On the pier; m 991 8784; 08.00–midnight daily. No better spot for a grilled tuna & chips than this casual restaurant's beautiful terrace looking directly out to the *ilhéu* & with the pier jumpers' joyful hubbub as entertainment. Standard big serves, good *caipirinhas* & very sweet, friendly service. $$$

Bowlavista [146 A4] Av dos Pescadores; 977 5137; w goodgreens-cv.com; 08.00–22.00 Mon–Sat, 08.00–15.00 Sun. From b/fast bowls & smoothies to salad bowls at lunch or dinner, almost all the produce used here is sourced from their own sustainable hydroponic farm in Rabil. Fish tartares, skewers & veggie soups washed down with Cabo Verdean craft beer from Cervejaria Afreecana are other fresh options. Take-aways available & they also sell housemade chutneys & jams; useful if you're self-catering. Lovely space overlooking the bay. Music on Thu nights from 18.00 & at Sun brunch. $$–$$$

Bar Naida [146 C3] 251 1173; m 993 4804; ⏰ 12.30–14.00 & 19.00–21.30 daily. A venerable establishment on the north side of the main *praça* (it may just be the oldest restaurant in Sal Rei). Varied menu served in a whitewashed yard with a banana-leaf roof. More authentic than most. Book in advance. $$

Cremositos [146 A4] Av dos Pescadores; 355 2422; cremositos_boavista; ⏰ 07.00–midnight daily. Excellent gelato (200$ a scoop) might be the most compelling reason to come here, but there are many others. Good coffee, an easy-going, breezy courtyard to hang out in & a shifting menu ranging from pastries, omelettes & crêpes in the morning to grills, spritzes, cocktails & live music at night. $$

Rosy Bar/Café [146 B2] Av Amílcar Cabral; 251 1242. Close to the Migrante Guesthouse. Not much menu choice, but popular, homely & authentic. Advance booking advisable. $$

Spazio 51 [146 B7] 981 0145; ⏰ 11.00–midnight daily. Simple diner décor in a street back from the northern part of Estoril Beach sets the scene for great-value dining. A lunchtime *prato do dia*, perhaps lasagne or stuffed pork rolls, will set you back 500$. Mains like pasta, roast chicken or fish & salad are more expensive but well prepared. Service usually quicker than in many other more tourist-orientated places. Does take-away pizza. $$

Cachupa Café [146 B6] Between Rua dos Emigrantes and the beach; ⏰ 06.00–19.00 Mon–Fri, 06.00–15.00 Sat. Busy hole-in-the-wall café for excellent coffee & pastries, or b/fast like a local *cachupa* with sausage & egg. Fresh orange juice, too. $

Pastelaria Doce Vida [146 B7] Near Praia de Estoril; 251 1533; ⏰ 06.30–19.00 Mon–Sat, 07.00–13.00 Sun. Good coffee & b/fast option. Top-value pizzas & sandwiches, croissants, & Italian cakes & focaccia. Feels like you've joined a secret club. Wi-Fi. $

Beach bars The following are listed in geographical order beginning closest to town and heading south. All of these have sea views and many also have feet-in-the-sand dining. Locals recommend catching a taxi back at night if you end up reasonably south.

Boavista Social Club m 936 4627; ⏰ 08.30–late daily. Low-season hours may be shorter. Pleasant outdoor venue on Praia de Estoril. Bar/restaurant during the day, when it's a popular stop-off for adventurous AI-ers. Free sunbeds for diners. Lobster dinners available. $$$

Tortuga Beach Club/Café m 993 0811; ⏰ 09.00–18.00 daily. An open-air, Italian-run restaurant serving mainly Italian dishes, meat & fish cooked on the alfresco grill. Free sunloungers & parasols on the sand, with food or drink purchase (or €5 per day). $$$

Toca da Garoupa ⏰ 09.30–17.30 daily. Owned by an Italian/Brazilian couple. Without electricity, they manage to conjure up fresh fruit salads, grilled fish, vegetarian options & b/fasts. $$$

Alisios m 972 1716; ⏰ 08.00–21.00 daily. Spacious, cheerfully tatty café on the beach with a large deck. Features b/fasts, snacks, lunch & dinner. $$$$

Wind Club François Guy Page 143; windclubfg. Part of the board-hire operation of the François Guy school, this elevated wooden pavilion is one of the liveliest bars during the day. Food options are limited to burgers, sandwiches & chips but you're here for the music, G&Ts, cheap beer & banter anyway. Pull up a lounge chair, put your feet up & enjoy the view. $$

Bahia, The Beach m 910 3535; ⏰ 09.30–18.00 daily, kitchen noon–15.00 daily. Beautifully located & friendly, with imaginative fish dishes, *carpaccios* & pasta. Sunloungers free if you have a drink or food. $$$$

Morabeza m 952 4513; ⏰ 09.00–late daily. A sprawling place with a great vibe both day & night, this is a recommended stop if you're heading along Chaves Beach. Lobster dinners & sunset parties. $$$

Perola d'Chaves [map, page 132] Praia de Chaves. The most southern of the beach clubs, just south of the RIU hotels, & possibly the friendliest. Gorgeous setting on what feels like a private beach, in front of the old brickwork chimney. Whether it's a simple grilled tuna salad at the bar or a slap-up special-occasion table on the sand on their popular BBQ night, it's a memorable experience. $$$$

ENTERTAINMENT AND NIGHTLIFE Particularly in high season, a few restaurants in town feature live music. Also try the southern beach bars – there will be some action in at least one of them most nights.

Cremositos See opposite. The town's much-loved gelateria morphs into a laid-back, open-air music venue on Wed, Fri & Sun nights.
Morabeza See opposite. Reggae nights, Cabo Verdean nights, African drum nights – a full programme in high season. Locals also favour it for w/end dancing, but never before midnight.

Museu dos Naufragos Page 152. Music, drinks & focaccia (yes, focaccia) on Fri nights from 18.30.
Sodade Page 149. Relaxed live acts play in the pretty courtyard from around 20.00 most nights.

SHOPPING Traditional Boavistan crafts include hats made from palm leaves (a speciality of Povoação Velha) and ceramics (from Rabil). There are a few small craft and souvenir shops in the backstreets of Sal Rei, for example one street north of Rua dos Emigrantes, near the old hospital. Also try **Nha Cretcheu** [146 B2] (⊕ 10.30–13.00 & 14.30–18.00 Mon–Fri, 09.00–13.30 Sat), where everything is made on Boavista (though the material used may come from elsewhere in Africa). They sell clothes, bags and other bright, colourful souvenirs.

A good, ethical option for your souvenirs is the rather quirky shop of **Un click per un sorriso** [146 B7] (Unclickperunsorrisoit), an Italian project which supports various good children's causes on Boavista. The crafts they sell are all made in Cabo Verde, including pottery, straw hats, flip-flops, clothing, fridge magnets, etc, and all the items sold make a contribution to the project, which helps a nursery school and a kindergarten. You can find their shop open weekday mornings (and maybe 17.00–19.00 in high season), next to Pastelaria Doce Vida. The town's largest **supermarket** [146 C6] is diagonally opposite the Oásis White Hotel.

OTHER PRACTICALITIES
Banks BCA and BCN (⊕ 08.00–15.00 Mon–Fri) are both on the main square. Caixa Económica and Banco Interatlantico are near the fuel stations on the road to the airport. All have ATMs.

Health care The hospital is out of town, on the way to the airport. There is a pharmacy in town [146 B5] (Farmácia Dias; ☏ 251 8094; m 995 6693; ⊕ 08.00–20.00 Mon–Fri, 09.00–18.00 Sat), in the street that faces the Hotel Boavista.

Police The police station [146 D6] (☏ 251 1132) is a little out of the town, close to the Boa Esperança township.

Post office The post office is located up the hill to the north of town [146 B1] (⊕ 08.00–15.30 Mon–Fri).

Tourist information and tour operators
Barracuda Tours Page 141
Clamtour Page 141
Mendes & Mendes Page 140
Morabitur [146 C4] m 918 7328; e morabitur.boavista@morabitur.com; w morabitur.com; ⊕ 09.00–12.30 & 14.30–18.00 Mon–Sat. Flight tickets & excursions.

Morena Travel Agency Page 141
Sabura [146 B5] ⊕ 09.00–13.00 & 15.00–18.00 Mon–Sat. Not quite an official tourist office, this kiosk in the main square sells excursions & dispenses information. English spoken.

WHAT TO SEE AND DO For activities, see page 141. In Sal Rei itself the joy is all in soaking up the atmosphere, or basking or swimming on Estoril or Chaves beaches, south of town.

However, there are a few interesting small museums to break up leisurely days. There are also a handful of places to visit within walking distance of Sal Rei. These are listed below and can be visited individually or put together into hikes.

Museums

Casa da Memória [146 B3] (Av Amílcar Cabral, above Sodade, page 149; ⏲ 08.30–13.30 & 17.00–21.30 daily; adult/child €4/free) The upper floors of this busy café and restaurant re-create a typical wealthy colonial home of the mid 19th century with a collection of furniture and objects. There's an audioguide that can be used on your phone. Downstairs you can see shows of photography and crafts (free).

Museu de Arqueologia da Boavista [146 A3] (Av dos Pescadores; w museus. cv; ⏲ 08.00–12.30, 14.00–17.00 Mon–Fri, 08.00–13.00 Sat; adult/child 300$/free) Sal Rei's Portuguese-era Customs House was reopened in 2023 as an archaeological museum, housing a significant part of the national collection. Much of it was recovered from shipwrecks that surround the island, dating back to 1770. It also has artefacts from the Forte Duque de Bragança site on the Ilheu de Sal Rei.

Museu dos Naufragos [146 D2] (Rua do Museu, a few streets up from Rua bom Sossego; m 528 1173; e museudosnaufragoss@gmail.com; w museudosnaufragos. com; ⏲ 09.15–12.30 Mon & Wed–Sat; adult/child €7/5) This private museum uses highly crafted interpretive displays to tell the story of trade winds, slavery, piracy, the independence struggle, famine, and the importance of music to Cabo Verdean identity. The guides are highly knowledgeable. There is a rooftop café and Friday-night music sessions (from 18.30).

Ben'Oliel graves [146 D1] These lie directly in front of the main entrance to the Barceló Marine hotel at the far end of Cabral Beach. Happily, they have survived several attempts to be relocated, and have been restored with a wall built around them, and their future in the present location looks assured. Follow the signs out of the northeast of Sal Rei and along the road that runs the length of Cabral Beach. The walk is perhaps 2km in total, with only the Elci Bar (page 149), halfway, to provide refreshment.

The graves are of the Jewish Ben'Oliel family, who fled here from the Moroccan persecution of the Jews in 1872. There is also the tomb of a young Englishwoman, Julia Maria Pettingall, daughter of Charles Pettingall, who was one of the administrators of the Luso-British Commission. Julia was the 19-year-old victim of a plague of yellow fever that struck Boavista in the 1840s. She left with her family to the safety of another island, but her father later decided the threat had receded and returned to Boavista. He was wrong. Julia died in November 1845. While on board the boat returning to São Nicolau after her death, Pettingall himself died, and later his daughter's fiancé died too.

Igreja Nossa Senhora de Fátima [146 D1] This is a little hike (page 159) – 45 minutes from the centre of Sal Rei.

Ilhéu do Sal Rei This islet is nearly 2km at its longest, and up to 700m wide. It was the site of the fort of the Duque de Bragança, though all that remains of the

19th-century construction is some circular stonework and a few cannons. In the north of the island there are also some ruins and a lighthouse. It is uninhabited apart from crabs, lizards and litter left by previous visitors. Along the western side are little sandy coves, while to the east there are views over the anchored boats. Looking back, there are beautiful views of Sal Rei and down Chaves Beach.

You should be able to persuade a fisherman to take you out there for a fee (about €20 or 2,500$). Alternatively, if you are a strong swimmer, you could swim the 1,000m: locals say the water is never deeper than 2m.

OTHER PLACES TO VISIT

The rest of the island is described here in a clockwise order, beginning at Sal Rei.

COSTA DE BOA ESPERANÇA This long and beautiful, windswept and deserted beach stretches from the lighthouse in the northwest (Ponta do Sol) to Ponta Antónia in the northeast. Along it is the unmistakable wreck of the *Santa Maria* (page 142). At its western tip is Ponta do Sol, where there is a lighthouse reachable on foot (page 158). This area is usually deserted, there's no phone signal, and it has been the scene of muggings. Be wary and preferably go in a group.

BOFAREIRA AND ESPINGUEIRA These villages can be reached by 4x4 along a road from Rabil. After leaving Sal Rei, bear left at the fork south of Rabil and take the road to João Galego. After about 11km turn left at the small shrine to the Virgin Mary at the side of the road. Stay on the cobbled track and after 20 minutes you will emerge at the tiny village of Bofareira. This place is serviced by a daily *aluguer* and it's a picturesque, if everyday, place. There's a shop, a couple of bars and a telephone box, but apart from the occasional tour-bus group traipsing around, not much else.

From the Bofareira road it is possible to get to the shore: about 4km from the village take the rough track, signposted to Spinguera, which resembles the bed of a river. This leads to the coast and the ruined village of Espingueira, now partly transformed into a hotel. There is a small fishing camp out on the Ponta Antónia and, just east of the point in a semicircular cove, lovely snorkelling – if you're lucky, among nurse sharks (*Ginglymostoma cirratum*). Looking west along the beach there is a good view of the hulk of the *Santa Maria*.

Where to stay and eat Map, page 132

Spinguera (12 rooms) 251 1941; m 997 8943; e info@spinguera.com; w spinguera.com. The ruined cottages of an abandoned village inspirationally transformed into chalets in a small ecolodge. This is a deeply quiet, lonely & evocative stretch of coast & the hotel has been created in a sparsely elegant style that echoes its environment. Wi-Fi in lounge bar & reception (sometimes available in rooms, depending on which way the wind blows); no mobile-phone reception. The 2 larger villas can be self-catering. A bar & restaurant are both open to non-guests for lunch & in the evening. Dinner, a 3-course set menu (€30) that must be booked in the morning, can be a little hit & miss. Unless you're seeking utter relaxation & intend to stay put, or have a hire car, figure in a €30 each-way taxi fare to Sal Rei, more at night. The hotel is about 25 mins' walk from the water's edge. Swimming is not recommended in winter. **$$$$**

JOÃO GALEGO, FUNDO DAS FIGUEIRAS, CABEÇO DAS TARAFES Accessed along the road that leads south and then east from Rabil, these three villages are strung out at the fertile end of a *ribeira*. After the flat, dry plain you have crossed from Rabil, reminiscent of a Wild-West movie set, it is refreshing to be near vegetation again.

The villages are centred on the most agriculturally productive part of Boavista and enjoy modest renown as the source of delicious goat's cheese. João Galego has a smattering of shops; in Fundo das Figueiras, a few kilometres further on, there are shops and a few restaurants, among which are **Mansão** (m 985 4568) and the **Reencontro** (m 992 9556). At most sensible hours, you will find something to eat in the village, or call ahead.

What to see and do

Baía das Gatas The bay is a 15-minute drive by 4x4 along a reasonable track 7km from Fundo das Figueiras. It is named after the tiger sharks that have been seen from the point. There is a small, semi-permanent fishing camp here, with racks of salted fish hung out to dry. The fishermen will let you have a piece very cheaply – it is probably best to strap it outside the vehicle on the way home. You can see dolphins here. The largest of the islets in the bay is Ilhéu dos Pássaros, home to the white-faced storm petrel or *pedreiro-azul* (*Pelagodroma marina*). Travel to the islets is prohibited.

Morro Negro Lighthouse The most easterly point of Cabo Verde, this lighthouse sits on a 150m-high promontory accessed along a track southwest from Cabeço das Tarafes. It offers a great panorama of the east coast.

A SIP OF THE SEA *Alex Alper*

Salt water is fast becoming a widespread source of drinking water for Cabo Verdeans. Desalination plants on Sal, Boavista, Santiago, Maio and São Vicente – managed by Electra, the state-owned energy company, and Águas da Ponta Preta, a private enterprise – produce roughly 4 million cubic metres of water annually. That supplies almost 30,000 Cabo Verdeans.

The most common technology used in Cabo Verde is reverse osmosis (RO). Osmosis is a natural phenomenon in which the substance dissolved in the water (in this case, salt) naturally moves from an area of high concentration to an area of lower concentration through a semi-permeable membrane, equalising its distribution between the two. During reverse osmosis, the salt water is pressurised so that the salt moves towards an area of high concentration. What's left behind is clean water. RO is cheaper, but more high-tech, than vapour-compression distillation and multi-effect distillation, two other technologies used in Cabo Verde. Still, it is far more expensive than other water-collection methods, such as drilling or rainwater harvesting. The most energy-efficient RO plants still require between 2kWh and 3kWh per cubic metre of water.

Moreover, it is possible that the highly saline leftover 'brine' dumped back into the ocean is harmful to marine life.

Other forms of desalination are being tested to address these problems. Two volunteers are working with students at Assomada's technical school to develop solar stills that use sunlight alone to convert sea water into fresh water through evaporation. Construction costs are low and materials readily available – but so far the prototype produces only about two litres a day.

Nevertheless, Cabo Verde is counting on desalination for the future. If all goes according to plan, underground water sources will be left exclusively to agriculture and Cabo Verdeans will drink sea water every day.

Oasis of Santo Tirso This is the greenest part of the island, where you will find coconut palms, acacia and baobab trees. If rains have been good in the previous few years, it is a nice shady spot for a break.

Olho de Mar A small natural pool overlooked by a cliff with a remarkably human face. It lies to the southwest of Cabeço das Tarafes, along a track and then a path. It's particularly nice in August or September if it has rained.

Ponta do Roque and Praia dos Balejas From the lighthouse, the path continues to the south to this point and to the dolphin graveyard. Here lie the bones of nature's equivalent of the Boavista shipwrecks. They litter the sand near Morre Negro, which is alleged to have magnetic properties that draw the creatures to their deaths.

PRAIA DE CURRAL VELHO This beach is glorious but exposed and remote. Come prepared for a day in the desert. At 15km from the nearest civilisation, it's probably too far to attempt on foot for most people. Curral Velho is, however, accessible by 4x4 from Povoação Velha, from Cabeço das Tarafes, or directly across the heart of the island from Sal Rei. This last route is 43km from town and takes just over an hour by jeep. On the road south from Rabil, bear left at the fork towards Fundo das Figueiras, and after about 1.5km, strike right on a track. For the next hour or so, you will feel as if you are driving across the surface of the moon, and then at last you will reach a T-junction near the coast. Turn right and, after about 300m, take the rough track down to the left through the deserted village of Curral Velho. Then head round to the right of the salt lagoon until the track runs out at the back of the dunes. Beyond is a blindingly white beach, with extensive, Sahara-like dunes to your right, providing the unwary motorist with ample opportunity to get stuck.

There are only two islets in the whole of the eastern Atlantic where, until recently, the magnificent frigatebird or rabil (*Fregata magnificens*) deigned to breed. You can see one of those islets ahead: Ilhéu de Curral Velho. The last of the males perished in 2015, leaving only two ageing females. Sightings of them continued to be made across Boavista for the next couple of years, but most often here, as they habitually returned to their old breeding ground. Probably in vain, watch out for the bird with its long, slim, black wings that have a span of around 2m. The female has a white breast and the male's is red. It may be a 'vagrant' bird from the Caribbean you've spotted, but you never know, perhaps those two elder females have persisted. Much more likely is a sighting of some of the pairs of brown booby (*Sula leucocaster*), which still breed on the islet.

PRAIA DE LACAÇÃO This can be reached by following the track from Santa Mónica. This impossibly beautiful beach is also the location of the RIU Touareg. This massive development occasioned the building of a new tarmac road and has changed this remote area into a destination for all-inclusive mass tourism. If you can get past the imposition of the hotel's faux Africana sprawl, the beach is still stunning. There are no facilities, apart from a couple of souvenir stalls.

PRAIA DE SANTA MÓNICA AND PRAIA DE CURRALINHO These contiguous beaches are well worth a visit, but do come prepared, particularly if you are walking. You will need food, sunscreen and loads of water – it's around 2 hours from Povoação Velha to Curralinho and further on to Santa Mónica. In a 4x4, turn right by the bright-green school in Povoação Velha and follow the cobbled road until you reach the sand. This is not the beginning of the beach – you are still about 3km away. Beyond the dunes there is dusty flat land, pockmarked with a reafforestation programme. Then, at last, is the sea. For Santa Mónica, go through Povoação Velha, then take the very rough track. This will deposit you on the beach after a very bumpy ride. The beach is named not for a saint but after the famous Californian strand. The Boavistan version is undeniably more magnificent and a good deal less populated. Swimming is possible here because of the southern aspect, though rips are not unheard of and the drop-off is steep. Bring your own shade for beach days. A half-built, abandoned hotel is set back from the dunes at its southern end. Just past here you'll find 'destination' bar, **Boca Beach** (m 956 7904; bocabeachsantamonica; ⊕ daily, occasional closures usually noted on their Facebook page). They serve the usual fish grills and snacks, as well as icy cold Strela beer and *caipirinhas*. It's a rustic, rush-roof, feet-in-the-sand sort of place. Most half-day tours of the south will make a stop at Boca Beach, or you can book a meal and pick-up/drop-off from Sal Rei or your hotel direct with the bar.

POVOAÇÃO VELHA In the words of a Povoação Velha landlord: 'It's a slow place, this.' It doesn't look much, but a settlement has endured here for almost 500 years, and it's a toss-up as to whether it was here or the southern town of Curral Velho that was the birthplace of the *morna* (see below). Whichever it was, *morna* superstar Maria Barba, and the subject of the song of the same name, was born here in 1910. There's a monument to her at the town's entrance.

Today it has a sleepy appeal: old folk ruminate on doorsteps, dogs scratch in the sun and donkeys twitch their ears on street corners. There are two main, parallel streets with a handful of rather kooky souvenir shops. If you'd like to see a traditional palm weaver at work, or perhaps buy a hat if his inventory has not already been packed to send off for sale in Praia, ask around if 'Frank' is in. He lives in the bright blue house, just past the *praça*. Central **Bar António** will prepare food on request; they need about 2 hours' notice so you could place your order before you ascend Rocha Estância, or drive out to Santa Mónica, and return to the village as the meal arrives on the table. Another similar option, open for lunch only, is **Ka Fabiana**, a standalone building on the outskirts of town.

> **THE ORIGINS OF THE *MORNA***
>
> The origins of the *morna* are obscure but it is said to have emerged on Boavista, named after the English word 'mourn' or perhaps the French word '*morne*', meaning 'sad'. There are a multitude of theories as to how its characteristic melodies arose. According to the Cabo Verdean historian António Germano Lima, one theory is that it came from the sound of fishermen's oars hitting the water on their long journeys, and their marking of the rhythm of the rowing with the call 'vo-ga...vo-ga'. Others say it came from a mixture of musical types, such as the medieval Portuguese ballad, the *cancioneiro*, the Portuguese–Brazilian *modinhas* and the priests' liturgical chants. Lima himself favours the idea that the melancholy music must have been born from the hearts of slaves longing for home.
>
> The modern *morna* was developed by Eugénio Tavares (page 257). Boavistan *mornas* are much livelier than Tavares's tearful versions. They can be full of satire, caricature, ridicule and dreams of revenge.
>
> If passing through Povoação Velha, look out for the monument to Maria Barba, one of the most influential of early *morna* singers who gives her name to one of the most-sung *morna*, still sung today.

You can reach Povoação Velha from Sal Rei by *aluguer* – there's one at 13.00 and another at 16.00 – but be aware that *alugueres* from Povoação Velha to Sal Rei only go very early in the morning. A taxi will cost you around 3,000$ return from Sal Rei, but make sure you organise the return trip when booking to avoid getting stuck. For further details on the ascents of Rocha Estância or Pico Santo António, see page 160.

PRAIA DE VERANDINHA An exposed beach with fantastic conditions for wind- and kitesurfing (though not for beginners). Another attraction is the caves behind the beach. Reach them along a track heading west from Povoação Velha. Much to the locals' dismay the area has become a racing track for quad tours, ripping through the village of Povoação Velha and destroying crops on the way to the beach. If you drive yourself there, take care as the dunes constantly change and require a 4x4. There are also caves here, but no facilities.

RABIL This was the capital of Boavista until the early 19th century. It is a bit short on attractions, but has the **Escola de Olaria pottery** (⊕ 09.00–17.30 Mon–Sat), which gives employment to nine locals and also acts as a school, training children in the potter's art. The workshop has some long-dormant Portuguese-era tile presses that are quite magnificent pieces of machinery to behold. To find it, follow the 'Artesanato' sign up on to the ridge, past the **Chaminé** restaurant (⊕ 09.00–20.00 Wed–Mon) and it's at the end of the road. The restaurant itself offers fish grills, *cachupas* or pasta lunches, and occasional music in the evenings. Look too inside the imposing church of São Roque, built in 1801, the oldest church on Boavista. You can visit Rabil by *aluguer* (page 140) or as part of a hike described on page 159. You'll have to ask to include the town on an island tour, as drivers won't expect you to want to visit. The canyon east of town is very Saharan in scenery, with palm trees and the dunes to the northeast enhancing the atmosphere.

A much-praised desert to the northeast of Rabil, **Viana Desert** is beloved for its fine white sands and its oasis filled with coconut and date palms. This is a vast, unique, if rather overwhelming, place covering about a quarter of the island and extending for about 15km north–south and 10km east–west.

PRAIA DE CHAVES One of the most exhilarating beaches of Cabo Verde, Chaves lies to the south of Sal Rei and stretches seemingly forever down the coast. The walk from Sal Rei is wonderful and although the return journey can often be a bit sand-blown, is well worth doing. Its dunes are gasp-inducing.

Where to stay and eat *Map, page 132*
Chaves Beach is dominated by the string of huge all-inclusive hotels, which at the time of writing, comprised the RIU Karamboa, RIU Palace, VOI Praia de Chaves Resort and the Barceló group's Occidental (page 148). There are also a few villa complexes tucked between the behemoths, including **Vila Cristina** [map, page 132] (m 982 4213; e info@vila-cristina.com; w vila-cristina.com) with three studios and one one-bedroom apartment to rent. The only place to eat here for non-guests is the delightful **Perola d'Chaves** (page 150), which would be a destination in itself, even if the beach were not as extraordinary as it is.

What to see and do The **brick factory** is an eerie building that is slowly being submerged by the dunes. It takes just over an hour to walk to it from Sal Rei down Praia de Estoril to the south, crossing Rabil Lagoon after about 35 minutes and continuing towards the chimney, which you will see poking out of the sand. There is a track leading inland from the factory to Rabil from where you can travel back to Sal Rei. Ribeira do Rabil is the main watercourse on the island and its water content varies through the year – sometimes dry, sometimes brackish pools, sometimes a good stream.

Rabil Lagoon itself has water all year round. It's a pretty lonely place, surrounded by shifting sand dunes, but popular with birdwatchers for its wintering migrant waders and for the Iago sparrow (*Passer iagoensis*). In fact, BirdLife International has designated it one of 12 Important Bird Areas in Cabo Verde and it is a Ramsar site – a wetland of international importance. The area stretches from the airport road to the sea. The quickest way to reach it is to take an *aluguer* destined for the airport and ask to be deposited at the bridge (*ponte*), after about 3km. But from the road, the lagoon looks rather uninviting, so it is better explored from the beautiful beach end. You can do this by walking down from Sal Rei (see opposite).

HIKES Aisling Irwin (AI); Colum Wilson (CW)

In the northwest of the island is a triangle of hikes: Sal Rei–Ponta do Sol Lighthouse (7km); Ponta do Sol Lighthouse–wreck of the *Santa Maria* (5km); and Sal Rei–wreck of the *Santa Maria* (7km). Combining them yields a satisfying hike of 21km, which should take at least 6 hours and requires several litres of water per person as well as hiking boots and sun protection.

1 SAL REI–PONTA DO SOL LIGHTHOUSE (FAROL)
Distance: 7km; time: 2 hours; difficulty: 1 (AI)

The first part of this walk is not particularly scenic. Walk along the road to the Barceló Marine hotel until you are 200m from it, at which point fork right along a road that runs for just over 2km to the cemetery. Just after the cemetery the road becomes an ascending track and bends to the left. Continue for 500m until you reach a fork: straight on leads to the church of Nossa Senhora de Fátima; branch to the right instead, and continue uphill. The view of old rubbish dumps is not edifying – but look on the bright side: they enhance the magnificence of the end of the walk. Stick to this track even, after 2.5km, when you pass another that forks to the left and appears to be a more direct route. Less than 1km after that fork you will come to Chã de Água Doce where the path turns left for the lighthouse (or right for the wreck of the *Santa Maria*). Continue for another 2km, through Curral Preto and its further litter dumps. Finally, you ascend to the etiolated structure that passes for a lighthouse. It's a lonely, atmospheric place.

2 PONTA DO SOL LIGHTHOUSE–WRECK OF THE *SANTA MARIA*
Distance: 5km; time: 1½ hours; difficulty: 2 (AI)

The first 2km of this walk are a reversal of the final 2km of the previous walk. Follow the track from the lighthouse, through Curral Preto, and on to a fork. The right track leads back to Sal Rei. The left track takes you down, past lime kilns and on to the beach. You have a choice of following this track to its bitter end – it bends inland and then out again in a 'U' shape – or descending to the beach as soon as you have reached white sand. The two routes take about the same amount of time. After this the hulk of the wreck can be your guide.

3 SAL REI–WRECK OF THE *SANTA MARIA*
Distance: 7km; time: 2 hours; difficulty: 1 (CW)

The old hulk of the *Santa Maria* dominates the beach to the north of the island, though the wreck is now crumbling so badly that it is becoming barely recognisable as a ship. It is within walking distance of Sal Rei. Looking northeast out of town from a high point you will see a ridge – it lies over that.

Head south out of town towards Rabil and just past the small houses at the edge of town you will see the old road to Rabil (signposted Via Pitoresca) branching off on your left. Follow the old road for about 2km until a left turning. Take this rough track for about 7km. You will pass through Floresta Clotilde, an oasis filled with various species of palm including the endemic *tamareira* (*Phoenix atlantica*), and then through Boa Esperança. At times now the road is almost entirely obscured by sand but the route is straight. About 1.5km after leaving the oasis the paving gives way to sandy track. Just keep going until you hit the beach where you cannot miss the wreck – though due to deterioration, this may change.

Following this route in the other direction (ie: starting at the wreck), the track is signposted; in the oasis avoid a track branching off to the left: keep right.

4 SAL REI–BARCELÓ MARINE HOTEL–IGREJA NOSSA SENHORA DE FÁTIMA
Distance: 2.5km; time: 45 minutes; difficulty: 1 (Al)
Walk northeast out of Sal Rei on the straight road that leads to Praia de Cruz and continue along the beach. Once at the front of the Barceló Marine hotel, follow the little path that takes you around the coast, at first on a nicely crafted passageway. At the end of this walkway it becomes a rough little path and then a track along a pretty coastline including a sandy beach that would fit perhaps one person. By this time you will be able to see the chapel and the path towards it. Beside it there was once a house with steps leading down to the beach.

5 SAL REI–PRAIA DE ESTORIL–RABIL LAGOON–ESTÂNCIA DE BAIXO–RABIL
Distance: 10km (18km if done as circular walk); time: 3 hours (circular walk: 5 hours); difficulty: 1 (Al)
This walk begins down the beach and over high dunes with views over the sea, inland up a bird-filled lagoon and up a silent *ribeira* filled with *tamareira* trees and surrounded by sand hills. There's a hill to ascend to Rabil but in general it is a flat and easy walk. At Rabil it should be possible to organise transport back to Sal Rei – the alternative is to walk. (Guard against sun and theft, however – see page 138 for information on hazards.)

Go to the beach at Sal Rei and turn left (south), following the coast. After 10 minutes you'll pass Tortuga Beach Club, where you can pick up a drink and watch people skidding across the bay.

Set off again south, walking up the dunes until you reach a disorientating world composed of nothing but expanses of hard-packed white sand. From those high dunes there is a vertical drop to the beach below and superb views of the cobalt sea and the islet of Sal Rei. There are often whales in the bay, in season, and you may spot turtles on the beach. Half an hour from the windsurfers is the lagoon. All you can hear is the waves, the wind on the dunes and, increasingly, the tweets of a multiplicity of birds who thrive on the salty water. The mud is covered in millions of their footprints.

Walk inland up the side of the lagoon. If you choose the left side then ascend a great beer-belly of a dune and after that follow your instinct – there is no path and sometimes you must leave the lagoon edge out of sight in order to find a way between the thick trees. After 20 minutes there is a rough track to the main Sal Rei–Rabil road. Follow the road south as far as the bridge and then clamber down into the *ribeira* on the landward side and follow it inland. It is a broad, dry riverbed full of *tamareira* trees (*Phoenix atlantica*), a speciality of Boavista. After the rain it

> **MORE HIKING IDEAS**
>
> Armed with a good map (page 71), downloads from a reliable hiking app or fresh local advice, it is possible to walk to remote Bofareira in the northeast. There is a round-trip hike from Povoação Velha west to Varandinha and then southeast along the coast to Praia de Santa Mónica, followed by a northern leg back to Povoação Velha. Finally, you can create another trip by hiking from Cabeço das Tarafes west and then southwest, first along a track and then a path, to the pool at Olho de Mar.

is lush, full of grass and small plants. The *ribeira* is hauntingly quiet except for the sounds of goats and the occasional child on a donkey collecting water.

The *ribeira* broadens and turns to the right; at times it must be 200m wide. Soon you are between two ridges – inland the hills look as if they are covered in snow with just the tips of plants poking through. Always stay where the trees are thickest. To the left appears a cliff with the village of **Estância de Baixo** on top. Keep well away from that side of the *ribeira* and stick to the right until, eventually, you see Rabil Church, on the ridge; tracks lead up to it.

From Rabil you may find transport back to Sal Rei or you can walk down to the airport (look for the windsock), before beginning the 8km trek back to town, hopefully picking up a lift on the way. If you want to walk back to Sal Rei, it's more scenic to take the old road (now called the scenic route), which begins after the main road crosses the *ribeira*, and goes straight on where the main road bends to the left.

6 SANTO ANTÓNIO (379m)
Distance: approximately 8km round trip; time: approximately 2½ hours; difficulty: 2 (CW)
From the waterfront at Sal Rei, Santo António can be seen on the left. Take an *aluguer* towards **Povoação Velha** and disembark at the point which seems closest to the mountain. The castellation near the summit means that it cannot be ascended from this side, so cross the rough ground to the mountain (past the men breaking rocks) and skirt round its north side, past some small ruins, before beginning the ascent from the east, which is straightforward.

7 ROCHA ESTÂNCIA (354m)
Distance: 3km round trip; time: 1 hour; difficulty: 2 (CW)
From the waterfront at Sal Rei, Rocha Estância is on the right, with the antennae on top. There are two routes to the summit. The first involves a scramble. Go straight out of the back of the village of **Povoação Velha** and strike slightly up to the right towards the saddle. Once on the saddle, head left towards the summit. Alternatively, go towards the church on the low ridge to your right as you are looking north at the mountain, and then follow the shoulder up to the left. It is longer this way but gentler.

For a less arduous walk around the base of the mountain, continue past the church and go around the *rocha*'s north side. It is not possible to reach the summit from this side.

5

Santiago

> The sea
> You enlarge our dreams
> and suffocate our desires
>
> Jorge Barbosa, born on Santiago island, 1902

Among the extremes of the Cabo Verdean archipelago – the desert islands and the islands so mountainous there is barely a scrap of level ground – Santiago stands out as the normal relation. It is more balanced, more varied – it has a bit of everything. At its heart are craggy mountains cut into exotic outlines and afforested on their lower slopes. Sliced in-between are green valleys, alive with agriculture. To the south lie irrigated plantations; to the southwest a sterile and gravelly landscape where nothing grows; and in the north and southeast there are pretty beaches of both black and golden sands.

On Santiago the varied ingredients of the archipelago's past are at their most vivid. On its far southern shore is the old capital of Cabo Verde – Ribeira Grande, now known as Cidade Velha ('Old City') – the first European city in the tropics whose pivotal importance in the Atlantic slave trade is still being uncovered. Up in the mountains, a few villages still hold on to the traditions of the escaped slaves from the city below.

And of course, this island is where you'll find the majority of the Cabo Verde population, in Praia, the capital city of the archipelago.

HIGHLIGHTS AND LOWLIGHTS

Cidade Velha, the 500-year-old city, is the most important historic site in the country and is of such international significance that in 2009 it became a World Heritage Site. The landscape in central and northern Santiago, and down much of its east coast, is stunning and worthy of exploration by vehicle and if time permits, with a couple of hikes as well. Santiago also gives a good overall sample of what Cabo Verde has to offer if you are very limited in time, and is the only island that offers the combination of white sand beaches, mountainous interiors and urban culture.

Santiago is maybe not the island for those who seek idyllic beaches though, nor for the best diving, surfing or windsurfing. It has some beautiful hikes but if that is your only priority, and you are stuck for time, it's best to head straight for Santo Antão or Fogo.

Praia is far from a tourist city and some people find it hot, unattractive and – at night, at least – threatening. Yet its heart, Platô (also traditionally spelled Plateau), has an utterly distinct personality. Named for its lofty position on a plateau with sheer sides overlooking the sea, there are a couple of interesting museums to

SANTIAGO

Where to stay
1 Kaza di Marli *p188*
2 Pousada Vassora *p189*
3 Strela Mountain Lodge *p192*

discover, along with plenty of busy restaurants and bars, many with live music. A trio of urban beaches offer swimming opportunities and breezy waterfront bars.

SUGGESTED ITINERARY AND NUMBER OF DAYS You could 'do' Santiago in a day and a half – half a day for Cidade Velha and a full day for an organised, round-island excursion. But for a richer and more relaxing experience, take two days for the round-island tour, spending the night in either Assomada and visiting its lively market, or by the coast at Tarrafal. Those with more time and inclination could easily find two or three good hikes to do in and around the Serra Malagueta, spend a day on the beach in Tarrafal taking in its coastal ambience, or take advantage of some of the excellent remoter accommodation options like Kaza di Marli or Strela Mountain Lodge (pages 188 and 192); and then finish with an afternoon and evening getting to know the capital.

BACKGROUND INFORMATION

HISTORY Santiago *was* Cabo Verde for hundreds of years. It was here that the two discoverers of the islands, António de Noli and Diogo Gomes, together with a small group of settlers from the Algarve in Portugal, set up in 1462. Their town grew and the business of resupplying ships and trading in slaves flourished. The other islands, except for Fogo, remained unexplored or were exploited merely for salt or grazing. Even today, inhabitants of Santiago refer to the island as Cabo Verde – as if it were the mainland – and to the other islands as just that: '*as ilhas*'.

Yet from early on Santiago was also a centre of dissent. Its links to West Africa were strong. The *rebelados* and other African renegades escaped forced intermarriage and lived isolated lives in the interior where they remembered their ancestral tribes. In the 20th century, rebellion stirred primarily on São Nicolau and São Vicente, yet Santiago too had its uprisings – and produced the islands' first great poet and dissenter, Jorge Barbosa.

The Portuguese spelling São Tiago (St James) died out early on in favour of the Spanish spelling used today. (For more on Santiago's history, see page 12.)

SANTIAGO TODAY Praia, the political centre of Cabo Verde, continues to expand in all possible directions, while its infrastructure struggles to keep up. Much of the economic development projects of the country are based here. The south of the island is changing quickly, with a new ring road, a few enormous condominium developments, shopping centres and hotels, together with the general spread of the city and its attendant services, including a number of universities.

New roads also connect many towns in the north but the island still feels very much at times like rural Africa. Here there is a slower pace of life, permeated with donkeys and carts, pigs, hens, dogs and goats.

GEOGRAPHY The largest island in the archipelago, at 990km², Santiago has two mountain ranges: the Serra do Pico do António, which rises to a peak of 1,392m, and the more northern Serra Malagueta, rising to a height of 1,064m. There are lush valleys in the centre and several permanent sources of water. Just under 300,000 people live here, well over half of Cabo Verde's population, with around 160,000 in Praia, the capital.

The volcanic rocks on Santiago are 4–5 million years old while the rocks from the sea floor are even older, at 8.5 million–9.5 million years. An important and

FESTIVALS ON SANTIAGO

15 January	Municipality Day (Tarrafal)
Late-January	Nhu Santu Nomi festival (Cidade Velha)
2 February	Nho Febrero festival (São Domingos)
Wednesday after Carnival	Ashes Day
13 March	Municipality Day (São Domingos)
15 days after Easter	São Salvador do Mundo (Picos)
Early April	Atlantic Music Expo (AME)
April	Kriol jazz festival (four days, exact dates vary)
23 April	São Jorge
1 May	São Jose A three-day festival celebrating Municipality Day
8 May	São Miguel Arcanjo Feast (Ribeira Calheta de São Miguel)
13 May	Nossa Sra de Fátima (Assomada)
Around 19 May	Music festival (Gamboa Beach, Praia)
31 May	Imaculada Conceição
June and July	*Tabanka* processions
15 August	Nossa Sra do Socorro
Mid-September	Festival Pela Paz (Tarrafal)
25 November	Municipality Day (Santa Catarina area)

distinctive feature of Praia's landscape is the *achadas* (elevated plains) on which the different districts of the city are built. Santiago is the principal agricultural producer of Cabo Verde.

FLORA AND FAUNA
Protected areas There are two protected areas on Santiago: Serra Malagueta and Serra do Pico do António, both of which are natural parks. Serra Malagueta is one of three protected areas in the archipelago where there is a team (the Cabo Verdean government working with the United Nations Development Programme, the UNDP, and with funding from the Global Environment Facility, GEF) working to combine conservation measures and development of local economic opportunities.

It boasts a large number of endemic plant species, including erva-cidreira (*Melissa officinalis*), used to treat a wide range of illnesses, aipo (*Lavandula rodindifolia*) and losna (*Artemisia gorgonum*).

Birds There are five Important Bird Areas on Santiago, as designated by BirdLife International. Three trees – a huge kapok tree in Boa Entrada and two mahogany trees near Banana – constitute two of them. The first tree, a single, huge, 25m-high kapok tree (*Ceiba pentandra*), lies at the heart of a valley near Boa Entrada village. The two mahogany (*Khaya senegalensis*) trees are of moderate height, and also stand at the valley bottom in Santa Catarina.

Here are the only two breeding colonies of the endemic Cape Verde purple heron (*Ardea purpurea bournei*), although it is said that the occupants of the mahogany trees have moved north to Serra Malagueta. Some 8km of rugged cliffs along the southwestern coast of the island of Santiago, from the fishermen's village of Porto Mosquito to Baía do Inferno (Baía de Santa Clara), make the third area, which is known for its brown booby (*Sula leucogaster*) and red-billed tropicbird (*Phaethon aethereus*) populations, among others. The fourth site is made up of two lagoons and their environs south of Pedra Badejo on Santiago, where about 20 species of wader have been recorded.

The final site is the central mountain range including Pico do Santo António, a breeding haven for many endemic birds including Cape Verde little shearwater (*Puffinus assimilis boydi*), Cape Verde buzzard (*Buteo 'buteo' bannermani*), Alexander's kestrel (*Falco tinnunculus alexandri*), Cape Verde peregrine (*Falco peregrinus madens*), Cape Verde swift (*Apus alexandri*), Cape Verde cane warbler (*Acrocephalus brevipennis*) and the Iago sparrow (*Passer iagoensis*).

SAFETY Bag-snatching, pickpocketing and break-ins are far from uncommon in Praia, but violent crime tends to be either drug-related or the settling of local scores and well away from most parts of the city where visitors linger. To avoid *kasubodi*, a Kriolu rendering of the English demand 'cash or body', take the usual precautions (no visible or accessible laptops, cameras, purses, phones, etc). Sucupira Market is notorious for thefts and Achada Santo António (especially the group of small streets on its east known as 'Brasil'), Varzea, Terra Branca and Tira Chapeú all have bad reputations after dark, as do the steps leading up to Achada from Kebra Kanela. A high level of care should be taken in Tira Chapeú and any of the outer areas during the day as well. Taxis are everywhere and relatively inexpensive: it's worth hailing one if you're not sure about where you're going, and absolutely advisable after dark. Restaurants and bars are usually happy to call one for you if there are none about.

GETTING THERE AND AWAY

BY AIR
International flights There are direct Cabo Verde Airlines flights between Praia and Paris or Lisbon, on TAP to the latter, and between Praia and Casablanca (Morocco) with Royal Air Maroc. There are also direct flights to Ponta Delgada in the Azores, from where you can connect to east coast cities in the USA with Azores Airlines. Flights also go directly to Senegal and Guinea-Bissau on both Cabo Verde Airlines and Air Senegal. At the time of writing there are no direct flights to Brazilian cities such as Fortaleza and Recife. For full information on international flights and relevant airlines, see page 59.

Domestic flights There are Cabo Verde Airlines flights to and from all the islands that have airports. Don't expect a daily service to all of them, though.

Praia International Airport (Nelson Mandela International, RAI; w vinci-airports.cv) The airport and terminal building are reasonably modern and well equipped. There are ATM and money-changing (⊕ 09.00–18.00 & 20.00–last arrival/departure Mon–Sat, though times may vary); international and local car-hire firms (see opposite); an underwhelming and sometimes unmanned tourist information kiosk; a tour operator (Orbitur) and free Wi-Fi. Coffee and snacks are available at the café beside domestic departures. There is a larger café and several well-stocked shops airside for international departures. Prices in these are often no higher than in local supermarkets, making them a good place to pick up Fogo coffee, *grogue* and *ponche*.

For details regarding entry requirements, see page 58.

Taxis from the airport wait in a mostly orderly queue, though some drivers will approach you inside the arrivals hall. A taxi from the airport to town costs around 1,000$, or 1,500$ after dark; add 500$ extra to the Palmarejo neighbourhood, west of the city.

BY FERRY
CV Interilhas services connect Praia with nearby Maio, and to Fogo and on to Brava three times a weekly. Even for these relatively short trips, flying is still the recommended option. There are also twice weekly ferries to Boavista and from there on to Sal, and a twice weekly service to São Vicente.

The port is at the northern end of the harbour. Taxis to the port or back from Praia cost 300–750$, depending on where your journey begins. The national office is located in Plató (CV Interilhas; Correios de Cabo Verde Bldg, Rua João Cesário de Lacerda; ℡ 350 0330; w cvinterilhas.cv; ⊕ 08.00–18.00 Mon–Fri, 08.00–13.00 Sat) but there is also an office at the port itself.

BY YACHT
Praia provides a well-sheltered harbour where yachts are asked to anchor in the west between the two jetties. It is essential to follow all the entry procedures with the port captain and immigration office, whether or not this is your first stop in Cabo Verde; on departure get clearance again from the port captain. Yacht facilities are poor, though a world-class marina development was earmarked for Gamboa in 2021 and may yet eventuate. In the meantime, ask the port captain for a watchman.

The next-best anchorage is Tarrafal, at the north of the island. Visit the harbour office on arrival. Another anchorage is at Ribeira da Barca, but there is swell and northeast winds funnelling off the island.

GETTING AROUND

BY PUBLIC TRANSPORT *Alugueres* (on this island, more commonly referred to as *hiaces* and pronounced 'yazz') travel up and down the spine of the island – the road between Praia and Tarrafal – all day and evening. Villages down the west coast are reached on roads extending from this central spine, so catch one of these *alugueres* and change at the relevant junction. *Alugueres* are also frequent along the slower, eastern coastal road between Praia and Tarrafal. They all leave from the chaotic Sucupira Market west of Platô. For Cidade Velha there are regular *alugueres* leaving from the far side of the main street across from the Sucupira Market, and from Terra Branca in Praia, southwest of Platô. Sucupira Market is a noisy melée of drivers and their assistants trying to get you to choose their vehicles. Pick the one with the most people inside, as they don't leave until they are full.

Many of the roads are relatively new, making travel on Santiago more comfortable and faster as well as improving the lives of the residents by providing small communities with better links to main towns. Old adage: a grey-haired driver is the safest bet. Around Praia itself, *colectivo* transport is available in numbered, half-size buses, though there is no timetable as such and no very obvious bus stops. Best to ask at your accommodation: a single journey in these buses costs 50$.

BY TAXI The taxis in Praia are everywhere, clearly marked and cream-coloured. Some are comfortable, others in an unbelievable state of disrepair. They will gently beep their horns at anyone vaguely tourist-like, in the hope of a fare, but can also be helpful if they sense you've wandered into a neighbourhood you shouldn't. A journey within town costs 150–500$, sometimes more, especially after 23.00. A taxi for the day costs about 10,000$. There are no taxi companies, just individual owners/drivers, so get your hotel to book you one or flag one down in the street.

BY CAR There is plenty of choice in Praia and a walk around Platô can scarcely avoid the numerous tour agencies which will happily arrange a rental vehicle. Remember that only a 4x4 can take you on some of the dirt tracks down to the west coast: anything less may limit your ambitions, though a standard car is enough for a standard island circuit. One day's hire should cost around €50–90, the usual deposit by credit card or in cash is required. It is cheaper to hire a car in town (many companies are in the Praínha area), but not as convenient as picking one up at the airport. There are two rental kiosks at the airport – **Intercidades** and **Hertz** – but note they are closed on Saturday afternoons and all day Sunday. Be aware there are parking meters in Praia's Platô – an unwelcome 'first' for Cabo Verde, but hopefully collecting some helpful revenue for the city.

Hertz At the airport; 261 2858; m 991 7907; e hertz-praia@cvtelecom.cv; w hertz.pt
Intercidades Rent-a-Car [173 E6] Rua Uccla, Achada Santo António, Praia; 261 2525;
m 918 9961; e comercial@intercidadesrentacar.cv; ⏰ 08.00–noon & 14.30–18.00 Mon–Fri, 08.00–13.00 Sat. A local company that covers most of the islands.

WHERE TO STAY AND EAT

People often stay in the capital Praia because anywhere on the rest of the island can be reached in a day trip, unless, like many Europeans, they are heading straight to the beach at Tarrafal. The capital has four large hotels with pools and various levels of other facilities, all fine but not exactly to international luxury standard. There are then many others encompassing a wide range of quality, though none of those are places in which to laze for a day. Airbnb lists a number of apartments to rent, many of them in the upmarket suburbs of Palmarejo and its western neighbour Ciadadella, which can be a safe and tranquil alternative to Platô. Just outside the city, Cidade Velha has few good hotel options but does have the possibility of Airbnbs and homestays.

There are two other main towns on the island with hotel rooms on offer. The expanding city of Assomada has a couple of acceptable hotels, and is a growing staging post – a departure point for hikes, with a craft centre and a vibrant market. In Tarrafal, meanwhile, in addition to budget hotels and apartment rental, there are a number of excellent choices for those who want to enjoy this quiet seaside town and its beach in more comfort.

If you prefer to get away from it all, there are a few interesting choices in the deep interior, most notably Quinta da Montanha, Kaza di Marli and Pousada Vassora. If you have a vehicle you could comfortably base yourself at these locations and make day trips to other parts of the island.

Santiago has a huge range of restaurants, including many upmarket and international options across Praia catering to the city's professional class. You'll also find an interesting assortment of Brazilian and West African places in the city's inner neighbourhoods. Supermarkets will feel miraculously well stocked if you arrive here from another island. Tarrafal's collection of bars and restaurants are firmly in the easy-going beach mode and mostly geared for tourists, with one excellent upmarket, waterfront restaurant and bar to be found at the King Fisher Village resort (page 193).

EXCURSIONS AND TOUR OPERATORS

Try the following operators for guided tours to highlights of the island.

G and S Schellmann Esplanada Silibell, Ponta Calhetona, Calheta de São Miguel; 273 2078; w reisetraeume.de. Gerhard & Sibylle have lived in the islands for years now & specialise in individual & small-group hiking holidays on Santiago. They also operate on an international level, organising your entire holiday in the archipelago including international flights. At their base in Calheta de São Miguel (page 196), they offer an open-air, sea-view restaurant, bar & information centre & can direct you to hard-to-find accommodation options or to finding out more about the weaving of *pánu di téra*.

Girassol Tours Rua Serpa Pinto 47, Platô [176 C2] & Av OUA, Achada Santo António [173 D6]; 261 289; e girassoltours@cvtelecom.cv. Offers transfers around the island, excursions to Cidade Velha or Achada Leite & a round-island tour, as well as the usual hotel reservations, car rental & national & international air tickets.

Praiatur [176 B2] Av Amílcar Cabral, Praia; 261 5746/7; e online@praiatur.cv;

w praiaturcaboverde.com; 08.00–noon & 14.00–16.30 Mon–Fri. This established agency has been running for decades in Praia. It offers Tarrafal transfers & bookings, Santiago excursions including a Charles Darwin tour, Praia street art walks & a guided Cidade Velha trip, & can also organise itineraries on other islands for you.

Soul Tours Ponta d'Atum, Tarrafal; e contact@ soultours-caboverde.com; w soultours-caboverde. com. Can assist with excursions, guided hikes & exploring other islands. Great local team.

vista verde tours [173 E7] Located in the reception, Hotel Oásis Atlântico Praiamar, Praia; m 989 2841; e santiago@vista-verde.com; w vista-verde.com; 09.00–13.00 & 15.00–17.00 Mon–Fri, 09.00–13.00 Sat. Multi-lingual agency, can organise excursions, walking guides, etc.

Zebra Travel [176 C2] Av Amílcar Cabral, Praia; m 262 5010/11; e info@zebratravel.net; w zebratravel.net. Based primarily on Fogo island, but with an office in Platô organising excursions, car rentals, hotels & other services.

ACTIVITIES

HIKING The interior of Santiago is filled with towering, craggy mountains, *ribeiras* and plantations. Though it does not have the breathtaking drama of Santo Antão, or the sheer spectacular drama of Fogo, it has walks that are both beautiful and rewarding, for which it is definitely worth putting aside some time. Many walks consist of finding a point along the spine of the island and walking down a *ribeira* to the coast (or vice versa). The two, perhaps classic, hikes are to descend from Serra Malagueta down towards Tarrafal (about 6 hours – you could get yourself dropped off and your luggage taken on to a hotel in Tarrafal) and the hike down Ribeira Principal, towards the east coast.

The biggest hike is to the top of Pico do Santo António – a twin peak that protrudes from the landscape like a canine tooth. Unfortunately the path to the Pico is not clear, the final ascent borders on the hazardous and knowledgeable guides are hard to find on the spot – organise one via your accommodation. One option is to stay a few days at Kaza di Marli (page 188), as the owner, Etienne, is a keen hiker and can either advise or accompany you. A network of trails in the Serra Malagueta area represents the best opportunity for walkers. See page 192 for more details.

FISHING You can link up with local fishermen in almost any coastal village (try Tarrafal or Pedra Badejo) – pay them about 10,000$ per boat for 2 hours to a half day to take you out on one of their trips. See page 54 for a discussion of fishing.

DIVING Most diving is done in Tarrafal where there are several interesting diving spots all reachable within 15 minutes by boat. There is also diving off Cidade Velha, particularly interesting for the relics of centuries of ships that anchored there.

Divecenter-Santiago Tarrafal; \266 1118; m 993 6407; e divecenter-santiago@email.de; w divecenter-santiago.de. The website gives a good description of diving spots off Santiago.

King Bay Tarrafal; \266 1007; e hrolfs1@gmx.net. At the King Fisher Village (page 193). 4 languages spoken. €38/dive.

SURFING There are some reasonable surfing spots on the island, though it is not worth coming to Santiago especially for them. The swell is best between January and March.

In Tarrafal, a short walk southwest from the main bay, there are some reef breaks, in particular at Ponta do Atum and at Chão Bom. The other well-known spots are in the southeast of the island: the coast south of Ponta do Lobo Lighthouse which marks the easternmost point of Santiago (accessible only by 4x4) and the local bodyboarding beach at Praia itself, just in front of Platô. See page 54 for general surfing information.

BEACHES Santiago's beaches fade into insignificance compared with the exhilarating expanses of Boavista and Sal, and the beaches on Maio. Nevertheless there are some to enjoy: Tarrafal has perhaps the best, a pretty cove and white-sand beach, busy at the weekends with local day trippers. Also try Ribeira da Prata, a short journey south of Tarrafal, a long black-sand turtle-nesting beach set in front of lush green palms. The *câmara municipal* (town hall) operates a turtle hatchery on this beach during the summer. São Francisco is another, but currently hard to get to except at weekends when locals head down there from Praia and *aluguer* services are more frequent. There is a beach at Praia Baixo and there are several, including the small and popular Quebra Canela, now more commonly rendered in its Kriolu spelling, Kebra Kanela, in Praia. You may well find other undiscovered gems if you explore the island in depth.

CULTURE The whole city of Cidade Velha is a museum, and one of the country's most compelling historical sites. Praia has a small ethnographic museum in Platô, another devoted to Amílcar Cabral and an interesting one with an archaeological focus, which includes many wreck-diving trophies. Heading north, in Chão de Tanque, near Assomada, there's the Tabanka Museum documenting this fascinating traditional dance and music form, while Tarrafal has its more sombre Museu do Campo de Concentração, the site of a former concentration camp near there. You can enjoy traditional and modern Cabo Verdean music at Quintal da Música, which has done so much to shepherd and nurture the country's musicians. Praia has many other music venues, too.

SIGHTSEEING BY VEHICLE A one- or, less often, two-day tour of the island by vehicle is a popular thing to do and well worth it, though it leaves a tantalising amount unseen off the main roads. If you hire your own vehicle or taxi for exploration try to get a 4x4 so you can go down some of the quieter roads, though an ordinary car will easily take you on the main island circuit and to and from Cidade Velha.

CYCLING Santiago has become a mountain biking destination over the last decade, partly encouraged by the facilities provided by the King Fisher Village (page 193) in Tarrafal, who hire out high-quality full-suspension bikes (Genius 930), electric mountain bikes, and hardtails, but also because of the exciting trails its natural topography provides.

PRAIA

Praia has continued to grow at pace since Independence and the current estimated population is in excess of 160,000. Infrastructure – from sewage treatment to electricity generation – hasn't always kept pace with this relentless expansion. However, journey to Cidade Velha to the west and you'll see how far and fast the city has grown.

Built on a tableland of rock, with the city overflowing on to the land below its steep cliffs, Platô, the traditional centre of Praia is attractive, if disorientatingly removed from the rest of the city. During the day, people from throughout Praia go about their business in Platô but then it can seem empty after dark. To its south rises another level plain, the Achada Santo António, where the affluent live in apartment blocks and where you'll find the huge parliament building and busy shopping strips. Between the two lies Chã d'Areia, and, in front of Achada, Praínha and Kebra Kanela, where there are embassies up on the hill, and upmarket hotels, beach bars and nightlife by the coast.

Other districts include Terra Branca just west of Platô and Fazenda district to the north. On the west, Palmarejo, stretching from the coast to its elevated main *praça*, and beyond to the university, is a middle-class residential area, relatively recently developed with apartment blocks, shops, restaurants and cafés running down its Avenida de Santiago.

HISTORY From the early 1600s, Portugal tried both to entice and to force its citizens to make Praia da Santa Maria their capital instead of Ribeira Grande (now Cidade Velha). But the colonisers ignored instructions and stuck to their preferred settlement, 13km away. By ignoring Praia, they left themselves open to attack from behind: Praia, with its poorly fortified beaches, was a place where pirates could land. From there it was an easy overland march to attack the capital.

This happened on two disastrous occasions. Francis Drake used the tactic in 1585 and the Frenchman Jacques Cassard did exactly the same more than a century later in 1712. After the first assault the population built the fort, which survives to this day just outside Cidade Velha. The second sacking signalled the demise of Ribeira Grande as investment was made in the fortification of Praia. Praia's shacks were replaced by permanent buildings and it grew. By 1770, it was the official capital achieving, in 1858, the rank of *cidade*.

One of Praia's most distinguished visitors was Charles Darwin, who anchored there at the start of his famous voyage on the *Beagle* on 16 January 1832, and spent some time examining the flora and fauna, as well as making forays to Cidade Velha and São Domingos. He reported that he 'feasted' upon oranges and 'likewise tasted a Banana: but did not like it, being maukish and sweet with little flavour'. He wandered through a valley near Praia:

> Here I saw the glory of tropical vegetation: Tamarinds, Bananas and Palms were flourishing at my feet. I expected a good deal, for I had read Humboldt's descriptions, and I was afraid of disappointments: how utterly vain such fear is, none can tell but those who have experienced what I today have. It is not only the gracefulness of their forms or the novel richness of their colours. It is the numberless and confused associations that rush together on the mind, and produce the effect. I returned to the shore, treading on Volcanic rocks, hearing the notes of unknown birds, and seeing new insects fluttering about still newer flowers…It has been for me a glorious day, like giving to a blind man eyes, he is overwhelmed with what he sees and cannot justly comprehend it.

He also wrote about the more barren slopes of Cabo Verde:

> A single green leaf can scarcely be discovered over wide tracts of the lava plains; yet flocks of goats, together with a few cows, contrive to exist. It rains very seldom, but during a short portion of the year heavy torrents fall, and immediately afterwards a light vegetation springs out of every crevice. This soon withers; and upon such naturally formed hay the animals live. It had not now rained for an entire year. When the island was discovered, the immediate neighbourhood of Porto Praya was clothed with trees, the reckless destruction of which has caused here, as at St Helena and at some of the Canary Islands, almost entire sterility.

Today Praia remains the administrative and financial centre of the country, although cultural organisations tend to gravitate towards Mindelo.

THE LINDBERGHS

Charles and Anne Morrow Lindbergh, the famous aviators, arrived in Praia while trying to circumnavigate the north Atlantic. Their plane was named the *Tingmissartoq* ('big flying bird' in a Greenland Inuit language). They took 6 hours to come from Morocco, arriving on 27 November 1933. They were not impressed with the island, which Anne said was 'boring'. On Santiago they recalculated their course and returned to the African mainland, deciding instead to attempt the transatlantic leg to Brazil from The Gambia.

For listings, see from page 174

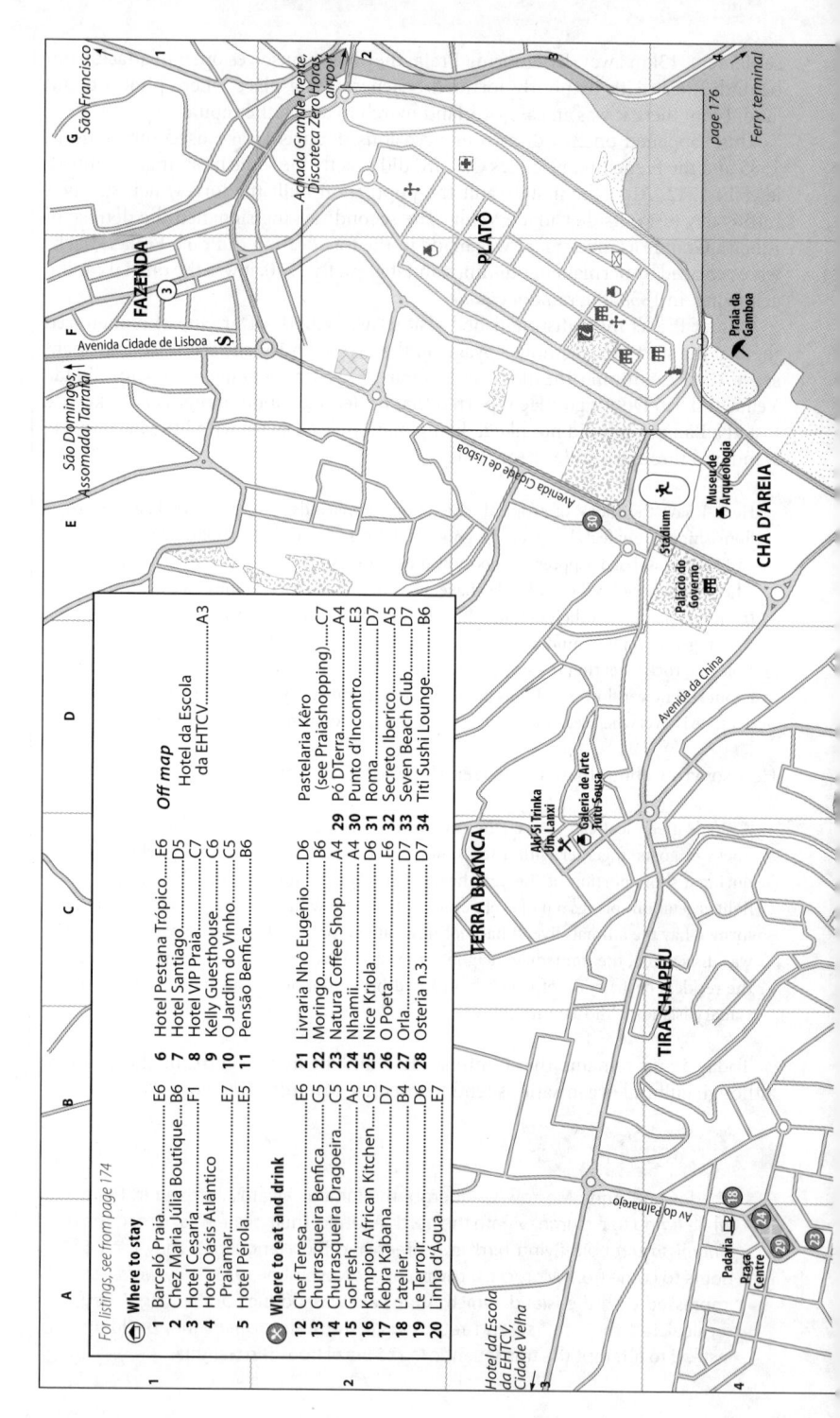

Where to stay

1. Barceló Praia...................E6
2. Chez Maria Júlia Boutique....B6
3. Hotel Cesária....................F1
4. Hotel Oásis Atlântico
   Praiamar........................E7
5. Hotel Pérola.....................E5
6. Hotel Pestana Trópico........E6
7. Hotel Santiago..................D5
8. Hotel VIP Praia.................C7
9. Kelly Guesthouse...............C6
10. O Jardim do Vinho............C5
11. Pensão Benfica................B6

Off map

Hotel da Escola
da EHTCV......................A3

Where to eat and drink

12. Chef Teresa....................E6
13. Churrasqueira Benfica.......C5
14. Churrasqueira Dragoeira....C5
15. GoFresh........................A5
16. Kampion African Kitchen...C5
17. Kebra Kabana.................D7
18. L'atelier........................B4
19. Le Terroir......................D6
20. Linha d'Água..................E7
21. Livraria Nhô Eugénio........D6
22. Moringo........................B6
23. Natura Coffee Shop..........A4
24. Nhami..........................A4
25. Nice Kriola....................D6
26. O Poeta........................E6
27. Orla............................A5
28. Osteria n.3...................D7

29. Pastelaria Kêro
    (see Praiashopping).........C7
30. Pó D'Terra....................A4
31. Punto d'Incontro.............E3
32. Roma...........................D7
33. Secreto Iberico..............A5
34. Seven Beach Club...........D7
    Titi Sushi Lounge............B6

GREATER PRAIA

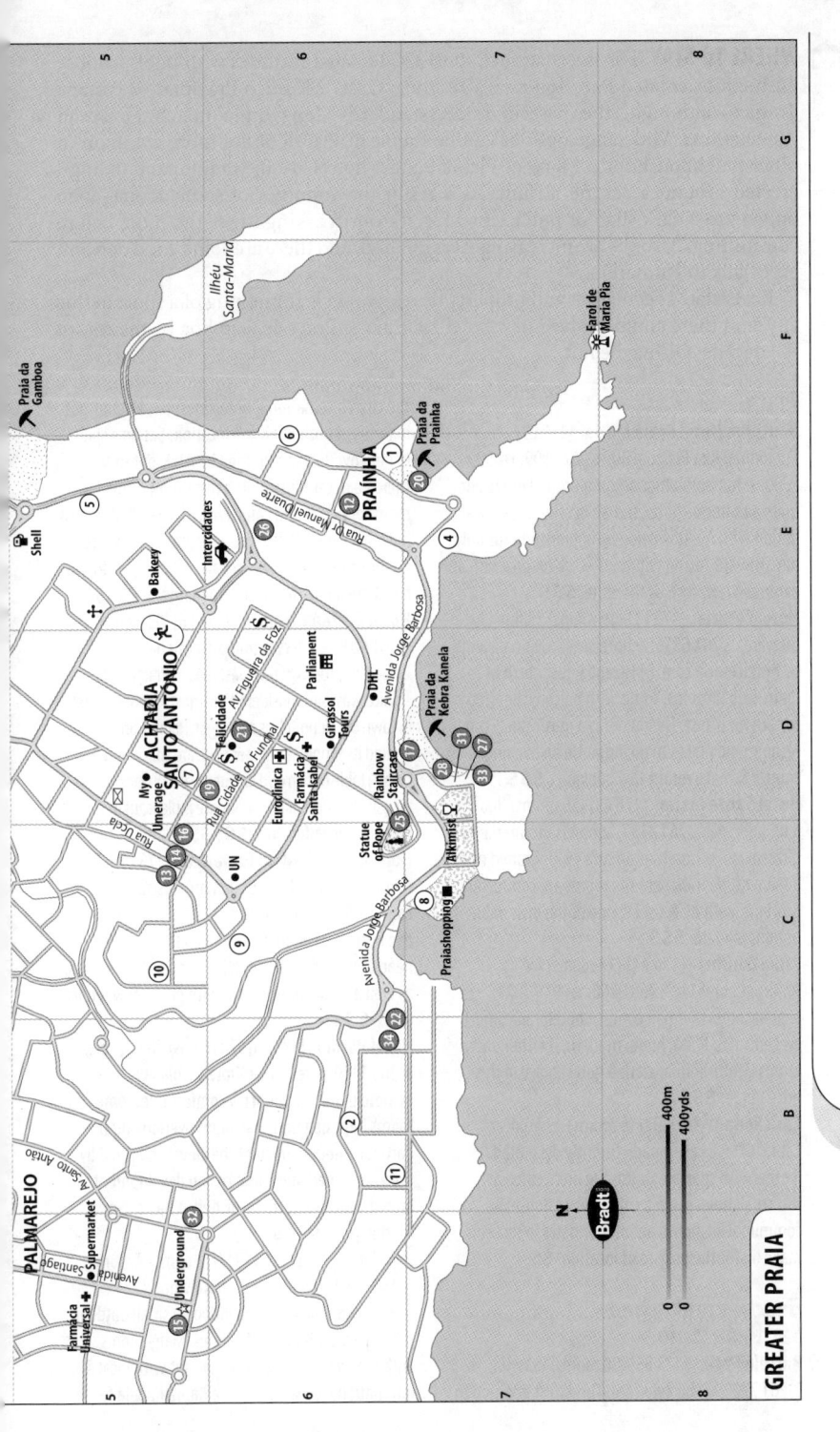

PALMAREJO

Farmácia Universal
Supermercado
Avenida Santiago
Underground

ACHADA SANTO ANTÓNIO

Shell
Bakery
Interdidades
My Umerage
Rua Ucdá
Felicidade
Av. Figueira da Foz
Rua Cidade do Funchal
Eurocínica
Farmácia Santa Isabel
Parliament
Girassol Tours
DHL
Avenida Jorge Barbosa
Rainbow Staircase
Statue of Pope
UN
Alkimist
Praiashopping

PRAÍNHA

Rua Dr Manuel Duarte
Avenida Jorge Barbosa
Praia da Kebra Kaneia
Praia da Prainha
Farol de Maria Pia

Praia da Gamboa
Ilhéu Santa-Maria

Av Santo Antão

N

0   400m
0   400yds

Bradt

Santiago PRAIA

5

173

WHERE TO STAY For international, tourist-orientated facilities with pools, choose business-orientated Barceló Praia, VIP Praia, Oásis Atlântico Praiamar or Pestana Trópico, although, the Barceló aside, standards don't quite match European expectations. Mid-range options can be found in Platô but are more common in other neighbourhoods. Many of Platô's budget hotels are in traditional buildings, erected around a central atrium. As a result the windows of some rooms open only on to a dark shaft or public corridor: it's worth asking to see the room before committing. Airbnbs are increasingly easy to find, and there are some good options, especially in Palmarejo.

Real estate speculation and property development is something of a sport in this city, and there could yet be a new hotel zone along Praia de Gamboa by the end of the decade. Or maybe not.

Platô

Boutique Hotel Praia Maria [176 C3] (12 rooms) Rua Pedonal 30; 262 2099; m 999 7850; e hotelpraiamaria@gmail.com. Perhaps not quite a boutique hotel, but an excellent & central option with AC. Downside is that most rooms only have inward-facing windows – ask for one with an external view, such as the suite. **$$$**

Hotel Cesaria [172 F1] (19 rooms) 33 Rua Che Guevara; 261 6556; e hotelcesaria@gmail.com; w hotelcesaria.com. In Fazenda, just north of Platô. Bright rooms, some with balcony. Rooftop terrace for b/fast. The owner is a music fan & can recommend places to go, organise an evening shuttle & make return taxi bookings. **$$$**

Hotel Santa Maria [176 C3] (36 rooms) Rua 5 de Julho 42; 261 4337; e hotelsantamaria@girassol.cv; w hotelsantamaria.cv. Upgraded from a mere *residencial*, here the rooms are comfortable & bright, with AC & sat TV; one of the best-value options in Platô. **$$$**

Praia Confort [176 A4] (17 rooms) Av Amílcar Cabral 11; 260 0200; m 919 7721; e praiaconfort@gmail.com; w hotelpraiaconfort.cv. Central to Platô; huge, modern, if rather dark, rooms. Multi-lingual staff. A good choice in this price range. **$$$**

Casa Sodadi [176 B2] (6 rooms) Av Amílcar Cabral 67; casasodadi. Brightly decorated, if otherwise spartan, rooms are great value at this small hotel set in a colonial-era house. AC, communal kitchen & an interior patio to relax on make up for the busy road location. **$$**

Beaches and Achada Santo António

Barceló Praia [173 E6] (80 rooms) Praínha; 261 7700; w barcelo.com. This latest addition to the city's international hotel line-up is a stand-out in terms of both quality & location. Set on a spit of land overlooking Praínha beach & out to sea, there's a decent fine dining restaurant & good room service. Rooms are stylish, large & light; most have sea views. Deluxe options are more akin to junior suites, with sofas & balconies. Hopefully will be a benchmark for future openings. **$$$$$**

Hotel Pestana Trópico [173 E6] (93 rooms) 261 4200; e reservas.tropico@pestana.com; w pestana.com. On the coast road in Praínha, the Trópico was long considered the most luxurious hotel in town but definitely is no longer. Rooms, arranged around its simple sea-water pool, are spacious & comfortable but an odd layout means privacy is an issue for most of them. Service is pleasant if occasionally perfunctory. **$$$$$**

Hotel Oásis Atlântico Praiamar [173 E7] (123 rooms) 260 8440; e praiamar@oasisatlantico.com; w oasisatlantico.com. Attractive, low-rise hotel bookending Praínha on the opposite headland to the Barceló, with terraces & balconies, as well as a swimming pool with pool bar & tennis court. **$$$$**

Hotel Pérola [173 E5] (20 rooms) Chã d'Areia; 260 1440; e reservas@hotelperola.cv; w hotelperola.cv. Smart & comfortable, some rooms have generous balconies overlooking the harbour (though much of the view is blighted by the abandoned Macanese casino development on the waterfront). Refurbished, it has a gym & rooftop pool. **$$$$**

Hotel VIP Praia [173 C7] (75 rooms) Av Jorge; 260 3280/1; e booking@hotelvippraia.cv; w hotelvippraia.cv. Large indoor & small outdoor pools, jacuzzi, & fitness facilities. Many rooms with sea view & there's a restaurant with local & international cuisine. Close to Kabra Kabala for sunset drinks, w/end concerts or a morning dip in the sea. $$$$

Hotel Santiago [173 D5] (22 rooms) Av Figueira da Foz; 260 4980; e hotelsantiagocv@gmail.com; w hotelsantiagocv.com. Handy for government offices, or neighbourhood shopping in Achada Santo António. Bar & lobby lounge. The few front rooms are a good option, the rest are claustrophobic & more than a little run-down. Great b/fast, though. $$$

O Jardim do Vinho [173 C5] (5 rooms) Achada Santo António; 262 4760; m 970 6849; e ojardimdovinho@gmail.com; w ojardimdovinho.com. A good-standard, good-value, secure establishment with spacious rooms & shared bathrooms. Run by a knowledgeable French couple: they may offer you a glass of wine on the leafy patio & offer tips on where to see some live music. $$$

Kelly Guesthouse [173 C6] (5 rooms) Achada Santo António; m 919 1817; w kelly-guest-house.cape-verdehotels.com. On the edge of the embassy district in Achada Santo António, this gated townhouse has 5 super-comfortable (if not particularly stylish) guest rooms. Many repeat guests, who rave about attentive service, the rooftop terrace for b/fast & garden nooks to curl up in with a book. $$$

Palmarejo

Chez Maria Júlia Boutique Hotel [173 B6] (12 rooms) 262 7770; w chezmariajulia.cv. Down towards the seafront, this small hotel is attached to a cooking school. B/fasts are therefore great & served in a large, stylish space. Rooms are modern, large & have TVs & AC, but lack personality. Peaceful neighbourhood. $$$

Pensão Benfica [173 B6] (24 rooms) 262 9313; e pensaobenfica@cvtelecom.cv. Situated in the west of Palmarejo, this is one of the few hotels with proper ocean views. Basic rooms but with AC & TV. Downstairs restaurant. $$$

Hotel da Escola da EHTCV [172 A3] (50 rooms) 260 2230; e hotelescola@ehtcv.edu.cv; w ehtcv.edu.cv. The hotel is used for giving hands-on experience to the students of the tourism school next door, so your stay here will benefit Cabo Verde's next generation of hospitality professionals. Some rooms have AC, others fans, but do ask for one with a balcony or patio. A good, clean budget option, despite the vaguely desolate location. Particularly handy for those with a rental car, as there's parking. A good bit out of town & the facilities of central Palmarejo (accessible on bus route no 12, or by taxi). $

✕ WHERE TO EAT AND DRINK
Platô

Café Sofia [176 B3] Rua Visconde de São Januario, on Praça Luís Camões; ⊕ 07.00–23.00 daily. One of the places in Platô to sit under a parasol & watch life go by. Popular venue for chess matches. A standard menu plus large assortment of desserts. Service maintains its reputation for being notoriously slow & serving food that's average, but it remains an institution. $$$$

Quintal da Música [176 C2] Av Amílcar Cabral 70; 261 2608/1679; ⊕ from 19.00 to around midnight Mon–Sat, with live music every night. One of the iconic places to spend an evening in Praia, this restaurant was founded by musician Mario Lucio along with the Cabo Verdean band Simentera to promote traditional music & stimulate local musicians. It's an evocative place & the food is good. Some purists now claim it's a bit 'touristy' but that's forgetting it's a locals' favourite too. Booking required. $$$$

Restaurante Panorama [176 B3] Rua Serpa Pinto; ⊕ 08.00–15.00 & 19.00–22.00 Sun–Thu, 08.00–15.00 & 19.00–23.00 Fri & Sat. Above the defunct Hotel Felicidade, but with its entrance in Rua Serpa Pinto, not Av Corvo. Climb the unpromising stairs to discover a rooftop restaurant – an escape from the noise & heat below, with plenty of seating including an open-air terrace. Better during the day: lunchtime buffet is popular with office workers for its speed, conviviality & price. $$$

Restaurant Flor de Lis [176 C2] Rua 5 de Julho; ⊕ 07.30–23.00 Mon–Sat. Friendly staff & a bright interior, plus some outdoor tables on the pedestrianised street. Service can be relaxed. Changing menu of meat & fish dishes. B/fast *cachupa* is the one constant & the coffee is better than average. $$$

Esplanada Morabeza [176 A4] Praça Alexandre Albuquerque; ⊕ 09.00–23.00 Mon–Sat. In the middle of the square, an outdoor cafeteria-style option. The setting outdoes the food; still, there are good-value daily dishes, pizzas, burgers & snacks. $$

For listings, see from page 174

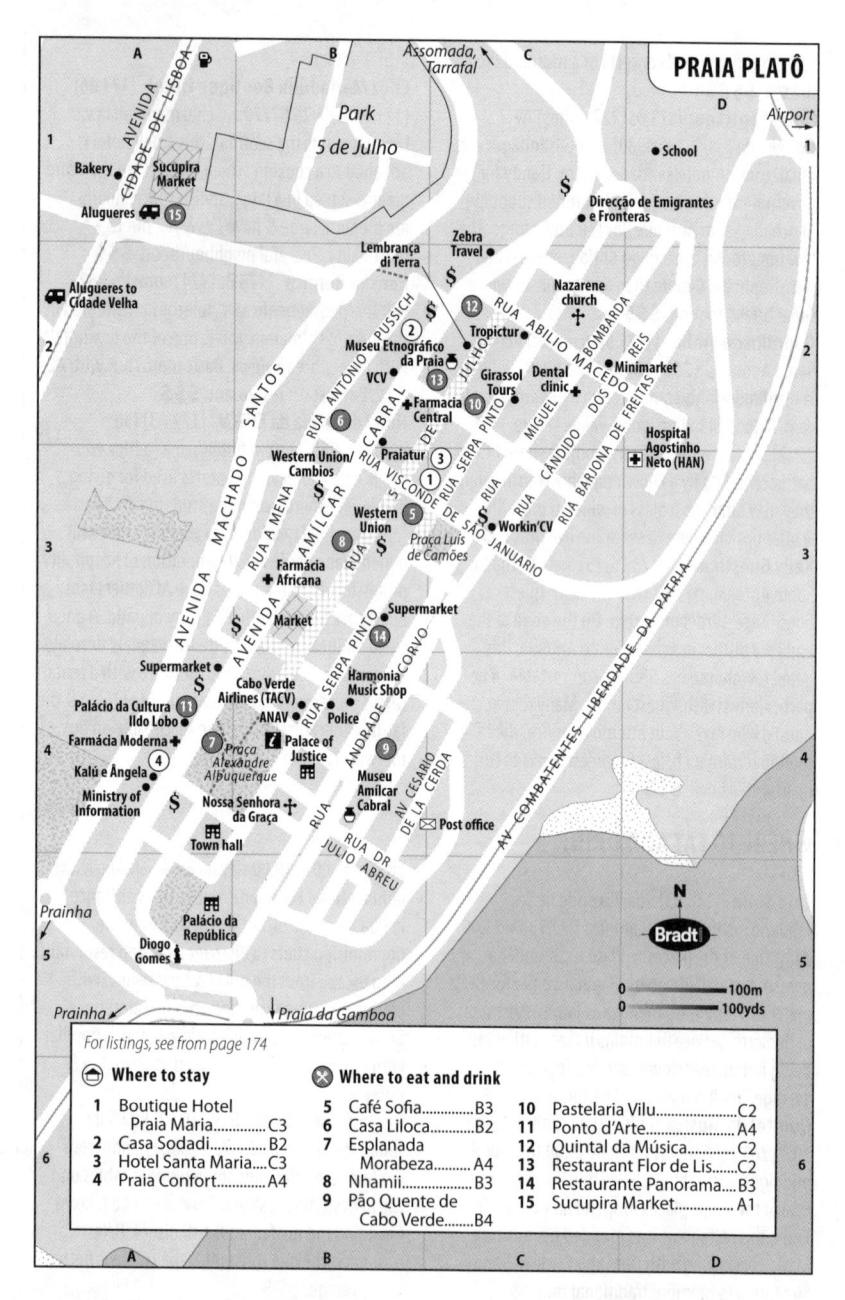

🏠 **Where to stay**

1. Boutique Hotel
   Praia Maria..............C3
2. Casa Sodadi...............B2
3. Hotel Santa Maria....C3
4. Praia Confort............A4

❌ **Where to eat and drink**

5. Café Sofia..............B3
6. Casa Liloca............B2
7. Esplanada
   Morabeza..........A4
8. Nhamii..................B3
9. Pão Quente de
   Cabo Verde........B4
10. Pastelaria Vilu......................C2
11. Ponto d'Arte........................A4
12. Quintal da Música.............C2
13. Restaurant Flor de Lis.......C2
14. Restaurante Panorama....B3
15. Sucupira Market...............A1

Pão Quente de Cabo Verde [176 B4] Rua Andrade Corvo; ⏱ 06.30–21.30 daily. A wide variety of delicious cakes, snacks & sandwiches in a busy, spacious European-style café. Part of a small chain; look out for other branches around town. $$

Pastelaria Vilu [176 C2] Rua 5 de Julho; ☎261 9743; ⏱ noon–16.00 & 18.00–midnight daily. Savoury snacks & cool drinks, served inside or out. Cheap & very cheerful. $$

Casa Liloca [176 B2] Rua Visconde de São Januario 3–5; ⏱ noon–17.00 Mon–Sat.

176

Formerly an unofficial dining room in a family home, this place has now acquired a name. Run by two sisters, informality still reigns, however, with excellently cooked & inexpensive daily dishes, including Cabo Verdean specialities. This is a real gem. $

Nhamii [176 B3] Rua 5 de Julho; m 938 7010; nhamiicv; ⊕ 09.00–23.00 daily. Excellent gelateria, cute design. Flavours change daily, but bissap, kiwi & mango are stayers. Also crêpes, waffles & toasted panini. There's another branch in Palmarejo [172 A4] (page 178). $

Ponto d'Arte [176 A4] Palácio da Cultura Ildo Lobo (page 181). Casual café/bar that's great to just hang out in, with its dual street & courtyard frontage. Hosts occasional performances (page 179). $

Sucupira Market [176 A1] ⊕ daily (daytime only). Great platefuls of cheap lunchtime eats can be found in the kiosks of the market, round the back in the covered area. $

Beaches and Achada Santo António

Chef Teresa [173 E6] Just off Rua Dr Manuel Duarte; Praínha; 263 8632; ⊕ 12.30–15.30 & 18.30–23.00 daily. Possibly the city's most intimate dinner option, with white tablecloths & a dining room stacked with European wines. Meticulously prepared seafood dishes & Portuguese saucing, with extensive wine list. Note that the cold seafood entrées that grace your table are not complimentary (& yes, you can say no). In a residential side street; book ahead, arrive at your appointed time & wait to be admitted. $$$$$

Nice Kriola [173 D6] Achada Santo António; 262 0870; NKrestaurante; ⊕ 07.30–23.30 Mon–Fri, 09.30–23.30 Sat & Sun. Super-slick panoramic restaurant on the headland above Kebra Kanela. Known more as a place to come for a drink & the view rather than for its food. $$$$

O Poeta [173 E6] Achada Santo António; 261 3800; ⊕ 10.00–midnight daily. One of the oldest restaurants in Praia & remains a firm fixture. Its clifftop position gives its outdoor terrace splendid views over the port, the island & the coast. Food is adequate. $$$$

Punto d'Incontro [172 E3] Av Cidade de Lisboa, opposite the old football stadium in Chã d'Areia; 261 7090; ⊕ 13.00–23.00 daily. Italian bar & restaurant serving pizzas, pasta, seafood *carpaccios* & beef. $$$–$$$$

Churrasqueira Benfica [173 C5] Achada Santo António; 262 2195; ⊕ 08.30–midnight daily. Piles of barbecued meats, popular at w/ends. Smaller than its nearby competition. $$$

Churrasqueira Dragoeira [173 C5] Rua Uccla, Achada Santo António; 262 3335; ⊕ 08.30–midnight daily. The place to go for towering piles

KEBRA KANELA: TAKE YOUR BEACHSIDE PICK

Perched up above one of the city's beloved beaches are a handful of open-air restaurants. It can be hard to choose: everyone in Praia has their favourite. While menus do vary from reasonably local to deferentially Italian, they all serve seafood, steaks, pasta and snacks, along with cocktails, beer and wine. All also have music on the weekends. Opening hours are usually 10.00–midnight during the week, with Orla and Seven kicking on until around 02.00 on Friday and Saturday nights.

They are listed below from east to west.

Kebra Kabana [173 D7] 585 3489. The beachiest vibe of the lot, with rush ceiling & steps to the sand.

Osteria n.3 [173 D7] m 976 0661. Upmarket Italian food & cocktails.

Roma [173 D7] m 996 3300; w roma.daidze.com. Smart-casual place, specialising in pizza.

Orla [173 D7] m 976 9999; e oquebracanela@gmail.com. Earthy & fun, the most authentically Cabo Verdean both in terms of ambience & crowd.

Seven Beach Club [173 D7] m 975 0957; sevenbeachclub_cv. Glam, gleaming white interiors, but relaxed, friendly crowd & excellent seafood.

of barbecued chicken, pork kebabs & beefsteak. Indoor & outdoor seating. It's hectic, & as basic a dining room as is possible, but staff are sweet & the grills justifiably famous. $$$

Linha d'Água [173 E7] Praínha; m 938 7009; linhadaguapraia; ⊕ 09.00–midnight daily. City beach bar right on the sand, below the Barceló hotel. Sleek minimalist pavilion seating or shaded tables & sun beds for hire. Burgers, pizza & nicely plated fish grills. $$$

Pastelaria Kêro [173 C7] Praiashopping, Av Jorge Barbosa; f keroartesebolos; ⊕ 09.00–23.00 Wed– Mon. Tucked away at the back of the shopping centre. A Platô *pastelaria* famous for their donuts; at this branch you can sit on the enclosed terrace with a slice of passionfruit cheesecake and the well-to-do locals, while the Atlantic crashes on the rocks directly below your table. Or lunch on seafood, a *bitoque* or big salads & a glass of Fogo white. $$$

Le Terroir [173 D6] Av Figueira da Foz 21, Achada Santo António; m 994 0411; f leterroircv; ⊕ 07.30–22.30 Tue–Sat, 08.30–15.00 Sun. Don't come expecting a proper French wine bar, & you won't be disappointed. Neighbourly café by day for b/fast *cachupa* & simple 500$ *prato do dia*. In the evening there's a more expensive menu of dips, entrées & fish dishes. Jazz on w/ends. $$–$$$

Kampion African Kitchen [173 C5] Cnr Av Figueira da Foz & Rua Uccla, Achada Santo António; m 939 3227 ⊕ 09.00–midnight daily. Bright corner restaurant with Nigerian home cooking & a few Senegalese & local favourites thrown in too. Jollof rice is naturally a speciality & there's also *fufu*, pepper or *egusi* soups & *yassa* fish. Very good value, plus a hearty West African welcome. $$

Livraria Nhô Eugénio [173 D6] Av da Europa, Achada Santo António; \262 3550; nhoeugenio; ⊕ 08.00–20.30 Mon–Fri, 08.30–14.00 Sat. This bookshop has sofas inside or a collection of tables on the terrace facing the square. Known for its good coffee & herb-strewn toasted sandwiches, but it has a more extensive menu too. $$

Palmarejo

Pó DTerra [172 A4] Praça Centre; t 261 7900; ⊕ 08.30–23.30 daily. Tapas, seafood, cocktails & reasonably priced lunches. $$$$

L'atelier [172 B4] Cnr Av do Palmarejo & Praça Centre; m 586 2065; ⊕ 08.00–23.00 Tue–Sun. Popular corner spot to watch the world go by with a coffee or cocktail or two. B/fast pancakes or lunchtime pasta, & burgers; same in the evening plus a few traditional dishes. $$$

Moringo [173 B6] Condominio Ondas do Mar; m 991 5253; ⊕ 08.00–21.00 Tue– Sat. A Palmarejo stalwart for traditional b/fast on the sea-facing veranda, with some claiming it's Praia's best *cachupa*. Short blackboard menu for other dishes for lunch or dinner. Don't miss their fresh passionfruit juice. $$$

Secreto Iberico [173 A5] Av Santo Antão; m 922 8531; ⊕ 17.30–23.30 Mon–Sat. Sit in the fun, atmospheric interior or chose one of the footpath tables at this favoured Fri night out venue. The secret might be more the menu and wine list are not particularly Spanish than any reference to Spain's most prized cut of pork, but dishes are interesting & tasty nonetheless. $$$

Titi Sushi Lounge [173 B6] Around the corner from Condominio Ondas do Mar; m 587 0256; f TitiSushiLounge; ⊕ 17.00–23.00 Mon–Sat. Sushi, *tatakis* & other basic Japanese dishes served on a terrace in this tranquil neighbourhood spot. Does take-aways, useful if you're staying nearby. $$$

GoFresh [173 A5] Cnr Av São Vicente gofreshcv; ⊕ 06.30–21.00 daily. Grocery shop with terrace & courtyard tables. Join locals for great b/fasts, easy lunches or pre-dinner drinks. Good range of local products. $$

Natura Coffee Shop [172 A4] Av Santiago; f naturacoffeeshopcv; ⊕ 07.00–22.00 daily. B/fast dishes, cakes, coffee & healthy Cabo Verdean cooking for lunch & dinner. Friendly staff & excellent value. Also has grocery shelves with hard-to-find health food items & good local produce. $$

Nhamii [172 A4] Praça Centre; m 938 7008; ⊕ 09.00–23.00 daily. Branch of Platô gelateria (page 177). $

ENTERTAINMENT AND NIGHTLIFE Praia has some excellent nightlife but uncovering it can be tricky. Firstly, because locals will automatically send you off to **Quintal da Música** and not understand that you might want to dig a little deeper. Secondly, because of the city's after-dark edge, it's not somewhere you can easily bar-hop, hoping to find a place that is happening on any particular night. This list represents a good starting point, and you can ask around for more spontaneous happenings at any of these places.

Kebra Kanela is by far the easiest place to begin a night out, with a shift in mood after 22.00 when people finish eating. For the more adventurous, the small streets that run down the hill on the western edge of **Achada Santo António**, including Rua Brasilia, are home to bars which kick off late. Don't go here alone and prebook a taxi to pick you up at the end of the night. There are clubs in **Achada Grande Frente**, but you'll similarly need to prearrange transport home unless you are with locals who can do that for you.

Discoteca Zero Horas [172 G2] Achada Grand Frente; ⊕ midnight–06.00 Thu–Mon. One of the city's longest-running clubs, in a neighbourhood also known for its street art. Open air. DJ styles vary depending on the night. Doesn't really get going until after 02.00.

Kebra Kanela [173 D7] Down on the waterfront, a stage is often set up for live music on Fri & Sat. The mostly outdoor **Alkimist** [173 D7] (Av Jorge Barbosa) bar here, a local's favourite, often has live music too & is open to 04.00 on w/ends. Most of the Kebra Kanela beach bar restaurants listed on page 177 have live music on w/end nights, it's worth checking on other nights too. Orla & Seven in particular tend to attract a local crowd keen to party, with the latter also a favoured spot for Afrobeat fans & diplomatic staff.

Ponto d'Arte [176 A4] Palácio da Cultura Ildo Lobo (page 181); m 996 9719; f CafePontodArte; ⊕ show usually around 19.30, but often open till midnight. Cultural centre café hosting a calendar of music acts, with a very local & welcoming feel.

Quintal da Música [176 C2] (page 175) If you're not up for the whole dinner & a show thing, you can have drinks in the tiny courtyard at this venerable music venue. You can't see the stage but you can definitely still hear the music (& you won't be alone). Pop in earlier & let them know to keep you a seat.

Underground [173 A5] Av São Vicente, Palmarejo (Universidade Lusófona); ⓘ underground_praia; ⊕ 21.00–02.00 Thu–Sun. An intimate, easy-going club dedicated to growing the city's contemporary music scene. Upcoming acts are listed on the club's Instagram, or DM owner Bob for details.

SHOPPING Music shops include the Harmonia Music Shop [176 B4] (ᒥ 261 6561) and Quintal da Música [176 C2] (page 175) in Platô, or you can buy lots of things you probably don't really need at Sucupira Market [176 A1]. This is also the place for buying clothes: great mounds of them await you inside and the motto could be 'the deeper, the cheaper' as prices seem to drop as you penetrate further into the market's middle. Garments laid out flat, rather than those displayed on hangers, cost less. Gentle bargaining is acceptable here. There are also a couple of stalls near the entrance where clothes can be made to order.

Achada Santo António has a few small independent shops dotted about as well as the more prosaic ones lining the main *praça*. **My Umurage** [173 D5] (just off Av Figueira da Foz; ⓘ myumurage; ⊕ 10.00–18.30 Mon–Fri, 10.00–15.00 Sat) showcases Cabo Verdean-made fashion and accessories, including printed silk scarves and artisan *grogue* and *ponche*, alongside perfumes and candles evoking various African cities. The expat owner Ariana Fernandes spent her childhood in the island's rural town of Fonte Lima and also sources ceramics from women makers there. On the northern corner of the *praça*, **Livraria Nhô Eugénio** (see opposite) is a lovely place to lunch but you can also browse their bookshelves and occasional collections of local crafts.

There are many *minimercardos* in Platô for food shopping, including **Felicidade**. There is also a large supermarket [176 A4] by the main square on Avenida Amílcar

Cabral. On the same road, to the south, is a branch of **Kalú e Ângela** [176 A4], with a wide range of groceries. The main outlet of that same company (a megastore by Cabo Verdean standards) is in the suburb of Achadinha; any taxi driver will take you there.

Santiago has one 'mall', the breezy **Praiashopping** [173 C7], scenically perched on the shore it shares with the VIP Praia hotel (page 174). It incorporates a cinema, a smart café/restaurant (page 178) overlooking the water, a medium-size **Kalú e Ângela** supermarket in the basement and a few other local shops and outdoor food stalls. The long stretch of **Avenida Santiago** in Palmarejo is home to a string of medium-size but very well-stocked supermarkets and there are also a couple of organic cafés that sell groceries and fresh produce (page 178) in the same neighbourhood. Both of these also have good wine selections. A padaria and café, Padaria [172 A4] on Palmarejo's main *praça* has a huge selection of bread and pastries.

OTHER PRACTICALITIES
Banks You will not walk far before passing a bank with an ATM. Most neighbourhoods have several banks and ATMs and, on the Platô, there are various *cambios* along Avenida Amílcar Cabral.

BAI Banco Av Amílcar Cabral, in the middle; ⊕ 08.15–15.00 Mon–Fri
BCN Rua 5 de Julho, at the very northern end; ⊕ 08.30–15.00 Mon–Fri

Caixa Económica Av Amílcar Cabral, at the northern end; ⊕ 08.00–13.00 & 14.00–15.00 Mon–Fri. No ATM.

Police The office [176 B4] (❧ 261 3205) is on Rua Serpa Pinto, opposite the large TACV Building.

Post office In Platô, behind the Palace of Justice [176 B4], and in various other districts. For delivery services, contact DHL (Av OUA, Achada Santo António, CP 303A; ❧ 262 3124).

Tourist information A privately run information kiosk can be found on Praça Alexandre Albuquerque [176 B4], providing maps of the city & of Santiago & Fogo, & selling a small range of souvenirs.

The rest
Co-working
Workin'CV [176 C3] Rua Visconde de São Januario, Platô; w workincv.com; ⊕ 08.00–18.00 daily. The largest & most central of the capital's current crop of co-working spaces with 30 workspaces & a range of facilities. Day passes 1,650$, with monthly rates cheaper per day, at 18,200$.

Health care
Euroclinica [173 D6] Rua Largo da Europa, Achada Santo António; ❧ 262 3734; m 991 7512. A respected private clinic, although with limited hours.

Farmácia Africana [176 B3] Opposite the Mercado Municipal square, Platô; ❧ 261 5955; ⊕ 08.00–12.30 & 14.30–17.00 Mon–Fri
Farmácia Moderna [176 A4] Av Amílcar Cabral, Platô; ❧ 261 2719; ⊕ 08.15–12.30 & 14.30–17.00 Mon–Sat
Farmácia Santa Isabel [173 D6] Largo di Europa, Achada Santo António; ❧ 261 3747 ⊕ 08.00–20.00 Mon–Fri, 09.00–13.00 Sat.
Farmácia Universal [173 A5] Av Santiago, Palmarejo; ❧ 262 9337; ⊕ 08.00–20.00 Mon–Fri, 09.00–13.00 Sat.
Hospital Agostinho Neto (HAN) [176 D3] Rua Barjona de Freitas; ❧ 261 2462; w han.gov.cv.

Situated at the northeastern edge of Platô, overlooking the airport road, this has a mixed reputation though it is well equipped & has had a recent upgrade of facilities. There is a 24-hour emergency department & you can check waiting times on the hospital's website.

WHAT TO SEE AND DO Praia's richest cultural offerings may be more those of lived experience, but there are a couple of interesting museum collections, as well as some contemporary cultural organisations. Football fans should ask around about fixtures, as a couple of tournaments are played in the city.

Museu Etnográfico da Praia [176 C2] (Rua 5 de Julho, Platô; \ 262 3385; w museus.cv; ⊕ 09.00–17.00 Mon–Fri, 09.00–14.00 Sat; 200$, students/children free) Small but well-curated display in a restored 18th-century building in Platô, with some interpretations translated into English. One of the few places you will see the beautifully woven pánu cloth that was so important in Cabo Verde's history (see also page 40). There is also a collection of artefacts that illustrate various practices of traditional rural life.

Museu de Arqueologia [172 E4] (Rua Cabo Verde Telecom, Chã d'Areia; \ 261 8870; ⊕ 08.00–16.00 Mon–Sat) Tucked away behind the football stadium. Interesting if modest display of treasure retrieved by the companies Afrimar and Arqueonautas from various shipwrecks around the islands, with exhibits demonstrating the detective work done in piecing together the histories of the various wrecks and their painstaking restoration. Information in Portuguese, English and French. (See also page 12.)

Museu Amílcar Cabral [176 B4] (Rua Dr Júlio Abreu; \ 261 3370; ⊕ 08.00–noon & 15.00–18.00 Mon–Fri; free) A modest, one-room tribute to Cabo Verde's most significant hero in the struggle for independence and one of the world's most influential anti-colonial thinkers. Information is in English. Outside, don't miss the iconic mural around the corner.

Praça Alexandre Albuquerque [176 A4–B4] In Platô, this main square is lined with 19th-century architecture, including the Neoclassical Nossa Senhora da Graça, the old Palace of the Council and the Presidential Palace, joined by the mid-century Palace of Justice. In the centre, there is a pleasant café, Esplanada Morabeza (page 175), allowing you high-quality people-watching. If you're here on a Sunday, check mass times at the church to hear some beautiful choral work. Behind the square is the statue of Diogo Gomes, one of the two discoverers of the southern islands. Wander a little further and enjoy the views off the plateau down to the sea.

Palácio da Cultura Ildo Lobo [176 A4] (Av Amílcar Carral; \ 261 8018; e palaciodaculturaildolobo2021@gmail.com; f palaciodaculturaildolobo; ⊕ 09.00–16.00 Mon–Fri, café until 21.30 or later depending on performances) This wonderful, rambling collection of colonial-era rooms hosts talks, performances and other cultural events, and you can visit anytime to see contemporary art shows in its exhibition space, plus a small collection of historical objects and some rare views from the rooftop. There's also a calendar of additional emerging artist shows on the walls of its friendly café, Ponto d'Arte (page 177).

Terra Branca street art [172 C3] The low-rise, working-class neighbourhood Terra Branca, just north of Achada Santo António, has, over the last decade, become home to the country's most concentrated collection of street art. Begin at **Rua d'Arte** with a visit to the eponymous **Galeria de Arte Tutu Sousa** [172 C3] (◉ art_gallery_tutusousa; ⊕ 10.30–18.30 Tue–Sat) founded by the scene's pioneer muralist; the gallery and Sousa's studio are set in what was once his family home. From there you can explore other densely daubed streets. Circle back for a cheap bite to eat or a drink at friendly **Aki Si Trinka Um Lanxi** [172 C3] (Rua d'Arte; m 918 8254; ◉ akisitrinkaumlanxi; ⊕ 08.00–23.00 daily), an integral part of the community and happy to provide directions to any new mural sites. To the east of Platô, the more industrial **Achada Grande Frente** [172 G2] neighbourhood is also known for its street art. Both these neighbourhoods can be visited on a tour with Terra Terra Tours (◉ terraterratours).

Beaches Praia's citizens make good use of their clutch of sandy curves, heading there to exercise, to meet up and to grab a meal or a drink. Gamboa is the largest but has been overshadowed by the failed Macanese casino project. The beach of upmarket Praínha is, however, a pleasant little yellow-sand cove, popular with locals, tucked between the Oásis Atlântico Praiamar and the Pestana Trópico hotels. There's a beach bar/restaurant here but no other facilities.

To the west of the Hotel Oásis Atlântico Praiamar, you can find pretty **Kebra Kanela** [173 D7], which is larger and less busy, if still lively. Beach bars loom behind the sands, most of them featuring live music on weekend evenings.

Other places of interest The wild and windswept **lighthouse**, Farol Dona Maria Pina, has a good view of the town; the caretaker might let you climb to the top.

CIDADE VELHA

This once-proud town, formerly known as Ribeira Grande, has had more than 300 years to decay since the French robbed it of its wealth in 1712. Now it is a laid-back village by the sea, set among the ruins of numerous churches, the great and ultimately useless fort watching over all from a hill behind. Its inhabitants' lives are much like those in any Cabo Verdean small town, though there is also a palpable sense of pride, and there have been efforts to develop some tourist potential. It is indeed a delightful place, with bars lining the shore, a lively outdoor restaurant at the start of its beautiful original street, Rua Banana, and bright fishing boats in the harbour. It is magical to wander through the vegetation in the *ribeira* and in the surrounding hills to discover the ruins of what was once a pivot of Portuguese Empire. It's also popular as a Sunday day-trip destination for city dwellers, which makes it fun for travellers too.

HISTORY Ribeira Grande is where the history of Cabo Verde began – where the first Cabo Verdeans were born. It was chosen by António de Noli as the centre of his portion of Santiago and it flourished. It had a reasonable and defensible harbour that was the second safest in all of Cabo Verde, Madeira and the Azores. It had ample fresh water and a stony landing beach. One of its early illustrious visitors was Vasco da Gama, in July 1497, who sailed to India later on the same journey, a milestone in European maritime exploration and imperial plunder. Just 70 years after the *ribeira* was settled it was granted the status of *cidade*, and by the late 1500s, it had 18 churches and chapels, and was the bishopric seat for West Africa. It even had the region's first hospital, and some 1,500 people walked its streets. Many of these were slaves whose captivity underpinned the city's wealth and perished in high numbers.

CIDADE VELHA

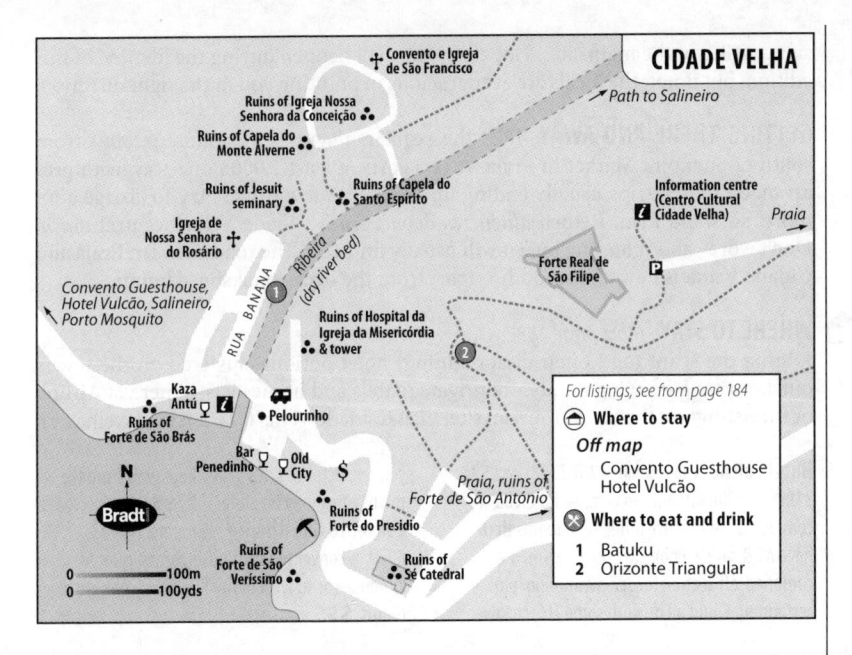

Map labels:
- Convento e Igreja de São Francisco
- Ruins of Igreja Nossa Senhora da Conceição
- Ruins of Capela do Monte Alverne
- Ruins of Jesuit seminary
- Ruins of Capela do Santo Espírito
- Igreja de Nossa Senhora do Rosário
- Path to Salineiro
- Information centre (Centro Cultural Cidade Velha)
- Praia
- Ribeira (dry river bed)
- Forte Real de São Filipe
- Convento Guesthouse, Hotel Vulcão, Salineiro, Porto Mosquito
- RUA BANANA
- Ruins of Hospital da Igreja da Misericórdia & tower
- Kaza Antú
- Ruins of Forte de São Brás
- Pelourinho
- Bar Penedinho
- Old City
- Praia, ruins of Forte de São António
- Ruins of Forte do Presídio
- Ruins of Forte de São Veríssimo
- Ruins of Sé Catedral

For listings, see from page 184
- Where to stay
- Off map: Convento Guesthouse, Hotel Vulcão
- Where to eat and drink
  1 Batuku
  2 Orizonte Triangular

0 — 100m
0 — 100yds

The upper valleys tended by the slaves were planted with 'vast groves…of oranges, cedars, lemons, pomegranates, figs of every kind, and…palms which produce coconuts', according to one 16th-century account. Although there are still plantations in the valley it is hard to imagine such bounty there today.

But this was an isolated outpost, helpless under attack and victim of any country that happened to have a grudge against its colonial masters. In 1585, forces supporting the Prior of Crato, fighting for the succession to the throne of Portugal, attacked.

When Francis Drake's force later landed, in mid-November 1585, his 1,000 men found the city deserted. Everyone had fled into the mountains, where they remained for two weeks while the Englishmen were below. Drake marched 600 men inland to São Domingos but they found it too deserted. They torched the settlement, went on to Praia and did the same and then left, having acquired food and water but none of the gold they were after. Two weeks later a fever contracted on the island killed hundreds of Drake's crew.

Nevertheless, Ribeira Grande continued to grow. By the end of the 1600s, it had a population of around 2,000. The grand cathedral was completed in 1693, but little did the people know that the demise of their city was imminent. The French raid of 1712, led by Jacques Cassard, began the drain to Praia. The city's fate was sealed by the decision of a new bishop in 1754 not to live at Ribeira Grande. Soon it was to be known only as Cidade Velha.

CIDADE VELHA TODAY Archaeologists today are still trying to piece together what the city was like. They are finding a rich buried history that could shed light on the origins of Cabo Verdean culture, the history of slavery, and Jesuit history as well. This, the first European city in the tropics, is more than just a national treasure. In recognition of its importance, in June 2009, Cidade Velha became Cabo Verde's first UNESCO World Heritage Site. It seems that very little has changed since this status was bestowed, although funds were assigned in 2023 to address the lack of signposting of the main sites. Hopefully this will happen during the lifetime of this edition, but if not, the locals are ever gracious in pointing you in the right direction.

GETTING THERE AND AWAY Take the regular *aluguer* (30 minutes; 200$) from south of Sucupira Market in Praia. A taxi costs at least 2,000$ one-way, with pre-arranged return trips usually ending up cheaper; a few drivers try to charge a lot more, so stand firm. Return *alugueres* depart from Cidade Velha's central *praça*. Don't worry about finding one: it will usually find you. The road between Praia and Cidade Velha is new and smooth – apart from the occasional speed bump.

WHERE TO STAY Map, page 183
Joining the scant (and often disappointing) hotel options clustered on the town's outskirts are a growing number of private rentals and homestays, either via Airbnb or the listings on the town's tourism site, Visit Ciadade Velha (w visitcidadevelha.cv).

Hotel Vulcão (58 rooms) 267 3198; m 958 3198; e info@hotelvulcao.com; w hotelvulcao.com. A seafront 'resort' hotel, with rooms that have AC & sat TV. Pool, kids' pool & gym, & a cordoned-off section for sea-swimming, plus a restaurant. Could all do with some TLC, so lower your expectations. It's a half-hour walk from the town; a taxi may be preferable. **$$$$**

Convento Guesthouse (5 rooms) m 923 6929; e conventoguesthouse@gmail.com. A kilometre or so west of town, with decent, clean rooms. **$$$**

WHERE TO EAT AND DRINK Map, page 183
There are several busy, casual restaurants and bars, including **Bar Penedinho** ($$), **Kaza Antú** ($$) and **Old City** ($$) right on the Esplanade, where you can watch locals fishing and swimming as the waves crash over the rocky beach. They are all open daily, but the kitchens may be closed in the late afternoon for a few hours.

Batuku Rua Banana; m 976 1869; restaurantebatukuruabanana; ⏱ noon–23.00 Tue–Sun. Cidade Velha's outstanding place to eat, good enough a restaurant to warrant a trip from Praia on its own account. Outdoor seating is atmospherically shaded by trees & a collection of rush-topped huts. Dishes are simple but elegantly presented renditions of Cabo Verdean standards. Don't neglect to try the housemade chilli relish with your tuna steak & tomato peach salad. Good wine-by-the-glass options & live music from 14.00 on Sun & some evenings. The amiable owner can also arrange homestays, hikes & fishing trips, & advise of any events going on in town. **$$$$**

Orizonte Triangular In between the fort and town; ⏱ 09.30–19.30 daily. This small, prettily decorated bar/restaurant is a welcome sight if you're on foot up or down the winding road to the town from the fort: stop for cold drinks & snacks (or lunchtime grills), plus a wonderful view. **$$**

OTHER PRACTICALITIES There's a **bank** just east of the main square. For the **police**, call 267 1132. At the start of Rua Banana, **Centro Cultural Cidade Velha** (267 1247; e centroculturalcv@gmail.com; ⏱ 08.00–17.00 daily, though these are optimistic) is more a craft shop than an information centre, but does also have a small library and hosts occasional poetry readings and concerts along with giving directions.

WHAT TO SEE AND DO
Key ruins in Cidade Velha
Forte Real do São Filipe (Guided tours, in English, ⏱ 08.00–18.00 daily; 500$, students/children free) Most easily reached from the main road from Praia, where there's a makeshift car park at the top of the site; the information centre here, if it's

open, offers multi-lingual information boards, a 15-minute multi-lingual video and cold drinks.

The fort was built after the 1585 sacking and was intended to guard primarily against attack from overland. Its extraordinarily thick walls were built with brick from Lisbon; its turrets with their little windows give a wide view over the Atlantic and the village. Behind are long views over flat-topped hills and lonely, rocky moors, and also deep into the canyon of Ribeira Grande with its sprinkling of plantations spreading up the valley floor. Inside the fort are some of the old cannons.

Sé Catedral Open to the elements (and visitors), with basic information boards to assist. Inside are the remains of its 1m-thick walls, begun by the third bishop of Cabo Verde, Francisco da Cruz, in 1556. After his initial impetus, the work was half-hearted and construction funds were diverted elsewhere. In 1676, the ambitious original plans were scaled down and it was proposed to build only a sanctuary about 24m long. But the energetic Bishop Vitoriano Portuense, who arrived in 1688, returned to the original design and it was completed in 1693. Its life was short, however: in 1712, it was attacked and virtually destroyed by French pirate Jacques Cassard. It serves as a popular playground for the local children, a joyful contrast to its melancholy old bones.

Archaeologists have done occasional digs here and these have revealed the gravestones in the floor; the balustrade between the central nave and the transept; the baptistry, with red-tiled floors and the foundations of the font; and the tomb of António José Xavier, first bishop of Cabo Verde. Their research also points to the cathedral having had a gabled façade, a tower on either side and a flight of steps which led down to the square.

Pelourinho This ornate 16th-century column was built as a pillory for the punishment of slaves. It is an arresting symbol of colonial inhumanity, the intricate workmanship and exuberant Manueline-style decoration rendering its terrible purpose all the more shocking.

Igreja de Nossa Senhora do Rosário Named for the patron saint of the town's black populace, this is the earliest documented church in the tropics still in use. With sections built as early as 1495, it contains wonderful examples of late Gothic and Manueline architecture. It was the settlement's principal place of worship until the cathedral was built. Still full every Sunday, its touching parochial clutter makes its long history seem more compelling. Heavily researched and restored over the years, the latest round was completed in 2020, when an original small side chapel was discovered and excavated. Laid in the floor are 17th-century tombstones of noblemen from the time of the reign of Philip of Spain. There are some beautiful Portuguese azulejo tiles, but most affecting is the baptismal font overlooked by early painted vaulted ceilings.

Convento e Igreja de São Francisco Built in about 1640, this was first a Jesuit monastery and later passed to the Franciscans who also used it as a training centre. Another victim of Jacques Cassard, it was all but destroyed in 1712, and then further damaged by storms in 1754. Restoration work took place in the 2000s, and while it has little detail or decoration remaining, it has a haunting and austere grandeur.

> **TAKE THE HIKE**
>
> Hike 8, page 203, finishes at Cidade Velha.

A CHURCH GIVES UP ITS SECRETS

When archaeologists first started work on the Igreja Nossa Senhora da Conceição, all that was visible were some foundations protruding into the neighbouring track and some walls that had been incorporated into dry-stone terracing. Between 2007 and 2015, the team, led by Konstantino Richter of Cabo Verde's Jean Piaget University, along with Christopher Evans and Marie Louise Stig Sørensen from Cambridge University's Archaeological Unit, exposed the church's foundations and reconstructed its outline. Thought to have been begun in the city's first decade, though only completed in the mid-1550s, it was 26m long and 11m wide with, on its north side, a Gothic-style side chapel. They have also found some very early 'relief-style' tiles dating from about 1500 nearby, which they believe were the first tiles used in the church. An early 16th-century inscribed grave-slab set into the church's floor was also uncovered, along with an enormous tombstone, dating to the mid 16th century, laid into the floor of the side chapel. Late 16th–17th-century tiles have been found in the nave – presumably the result of a later recladding job.

'All this indicates that we certainly have found a very early church here,' say the researchers. It is quite likely that there is an even earlier phase of the church still buried underneath: the archaeologists estimate that they have found the remains of over 1,000 bodies sealed below floor, as well as collections of amber and ivory beads, and iron nails that could have once held together the coffins of those buried. According to the archaeologists, this number of burials in light of the population demonstrates 'just how high the mortality was during the first half century of the settlement's history'. Isotope analysis of the teeth has suggested that the remains are of two or three distinct populations, at least one of West African origin, pointing to the early conversion to Christianity of the enslaved population.

Chinese porcelain, Portuguese earthenware and what is most likely West African pottery have only added to the fascinating historical narrative prompted by these ongoing discoveries.

A walk through Cidade Velha Start at the fort, then walk down into town either along the main road or via the zig-zag path down the mountainside. The **cathedral** is on the right of the main road. Returning to the road and descending into town you will find the *pelourinho* (pillory) at the far left of the square.

Leave the square at the pillory end, by the coastal road, and turn right into the wide and dry *ribeira*. This was once a great stream, which, before it reached the sea, formed a wide pool which was dammed at the mouth by a maze of pebbles through which the water trickled out slowly to the ocean. Fresh water was loaded from it into small boats and brought out to the ships, for which a huge charge was made. You can walk up the *ribeira*, past the football pitch and turn second left on to a track that joins it about 100m after a tall ruin. The track bends round to the right and climbs some rough steps and cobbles to first reach the dusty excavation site of **Igreja Nossa Senhora da Conceição** (see above) and the more impressive and somewhat intact **Convento e Igreja de São Francisco** (page 185), before petering out.

Partly renovated, this church and convent hides among the trees. It has been restored with help from Spain and thus a plaque commemorates the visit of that country's queen in 2006. Returning to the *ribeira*, you can continue to walk up among the trees of the valley, past pig pens and chickens to reach, after 15 minutes, a small water tank in which the local people bathe and which used to supply water to Praia. Return to the bottom of the *ribeira* and stroll up the hugely atmospheric **Rua Banana** with its thatched-roofed stone houses and a streetscape dating back to the 15th century, then the parallel road where you'll find **Igreja de Nossa Senhora do Rosário** (page 185). If you have time you can also wander further up Ribeira Grande among the plantations. The road beyond the town continues up the coast, reaching the listed accommodation options, then heads on for about 20km as far as the small village of Porto Mosquito.

SÃO DOMINGOS

The main reason to stop here is for drives or walks up to the west into the hills.

GETTING THERE AND AWAY *Alugueres* leave Sucupira Market all day for São Domingos (80$). Any Tarrafal or Assomada *aluguer* will stop there. They run back to Praia into the early evening. By hire car from Praia, take the road north, signposted São Domingos, Assomada and Tarrafal, passing through the urban sprawl and into the countryside. About 12km later there is a sharp bend to the right at which you take the main road to São Domingos.

WHERE TO STAY AND EAT There is little in the way of worthwhile accommodation and eating options in São Domingos itself, but nearby Rui Vaz offers a hilltop hotel; otherwise it is probably best to stay in Praia.

Quinta da Montanha (18 rooms) Rui Vaz; 268 5002/3; m 992 4013; e quintamontanha@cvtelecom.cv; w quinta-da-montanha.cape-verdehotels.com. Adults only. Enjoys an imposing position high in the mountains, with a dramatic view of the lush plantations below. Good base for visits to the botanical gardens, hiking & birdwatching. The owner, a returned *emigrante*, is an agriculturalist, so the hotel grows its own vegetables & fruit, including strawberries in season. There is a telescope for stargazers. Rooms are en suite with TV, hot water &, unusually for Cabo Verde, baths. Wi-Fi in public areas only. FB possible; hiking excursions arranged. Its restaurant ($$$$) is often packed with day trippers from Sal so booking is advisable. Take a jumper for the evenings. Can arrange airport transfers. $$$

WHAT TO SEE AND DO
Rui Vaz and Monte Xota The road up into the mountains to this village and up to the peak is magnificent. Take a left turn among the shops, towards the end of São Domingos, then take the first right at an ill-defined roundabout. *Alugueres* go as far as Rui Vaz fairly regularly – the rest of the journey can be completed on foot. Alternatively, charter an *aluguer* in São Domingos (around 750$ one-way). At the top it is sometimes possible to enter the antennae complex and go up to the viewpoint for a panorama of the interior of Santiago, or there is another viewpoint around a kilometre before the antennae. The park office has maps of this trail, as well as one finishing in Hortelão. (See also page 198.)

Barragem Poilão Just before João Teves, in São Lourenço dos Orgãos at the roundabout where there is a large, modern school, turn right and follow the road down to reach a reservoir and dam. This 26m-high dam cost 38 million Cabo Verdean escudos to build and has a potential capacity of 1.7 million cubic metres. This was the country's first official dam project, funded by the Chinese, and was inaugurated in 2006. It quickly became popular with birdwatchers from Europe, and although swimming was never allowed, it is something of a weekend destination for locals too. Its capacity has been affected by sediment over the years, and low rains since the early 2020s have also meant that it can often be completely empty: do check with locals about its status before setting off.

São Jorge dos Orgãos and botanical garden Cool, verdant and pretty, this tiny village is reached by going up the main road as far as the village of João Teves (*aluguer* from Praia 200$; 1 hour) and turning left a few hundred metres after the post office for São Jorge. Above you tower the mountains of the Serra do Pico do António.

Here, houses rise up the crevices between the mountains, all relying on a single little mountain spring for the watering of their many crops. The agricultural research station here, known as Inida, became part of the then newly established University of Cabo Verde in 2007. It is located near the blue church and has a national **botanical garden** (Jardim Botânico Nacional; ⊕ 09.00–15.00 Mon–Fri; free), which lies up a turning to the left just beyond its main buildings.

Here they study endemic species and are working to conserve those threatened with extinction. The research station, meanwhile, selectively breeds plants in the quest for ever hardier species and develops more efficient irrigation techniques. If the researchers are not busy they sometimes show visitors around the garden, though you can visit on your own. Look out for 'cow's tongue' *língua de vaca* (*Echium vulcanorum*), though note that this is a different species from the one that is endemic to the Fogo volcano, and the purple flowers of *contra-bruxas-azul* (*Campanula jacobea*).

Where to stay and eat Up in the high wilderness in the middle of the island, half an hour's 4x4 drive from São Lourenço dos Orgãos itself, you can stay in true isolation. It's impossible to find it on your own, so the owner will come and collect you, or you can follow him up the bumpy track if you have your own sturdy 4x4. This place is **Kaza di Marli** [map, page 163] (2 rooms, 2 safari tents; São Lourenço dos Orgãos; m 921 0488; e info@caboned.com; w caboned.com; bookable daily or weekly, on B&B, HB or FB basis; **$$$**). Built on the childhood home of one of the owners, it is ideal for hiking. Activities also include birdwatching, photo-safaris and day trips. The guesthouse has two bedrooms (accommodating up to five guests), living area and terrace with stunning views, while tents accommodate up to 5 and have balconies, their own bathroom facilities and fridges. English and Dutch are spoken.

ASSOMADA

Recently granted the rank of *cidade* (city), and sporting a traffic light on its main intersection, Assomada nevertheless still feels like a country town. It is, however, the capital of the region of Santa Catarina, the grain basket of Santiago. It is an ancient settlement, as old as Cabo Verde's human history, and was at times more highly populated than Cidade Velha. It certainly is nowadays.

GETTING THERE AND AWAY By public transport, the journey from Praia takes 1½ hours (300$). *Alugueres* leave all day from Sucupira Market, returning to Praia until late at night.

The drive to Assomada is spectacular, particularly after João Teves, when jagged clifftops rear into view and there are vistas into valleys on both sides of

> ### OLYMPIC VICTORY: THE MOUSE THAT ROARED
>
> 'I'm the first one to write this story, and I've shown the world we are small, but we are strong,' proclaimed flyweight boxer Daniel David Varela de Pina. His 2024 Paris Olympics defeat of Zambia's Patrick Chinyemba, the recent African Games champion and Commonwealth Games medallist, in boxing's 51kg division, indeed represented a historic sporting win for Cabo Verde. Despite losing to Hasanboy Dusmatov of Uzbekistan a few days later, De Pina's hard-won bronze happened to be the country's very first Olympic medal.
>
> The thrilling athletic and intelligent boxing style of de Pina wowed fans in Paris, but it was his endearing hairstyle and million-watt smile that made him front-page news around the world. Instead of the braids favoured by many African boxers, de Pina chose to sport two neat bunches on either side of his head, which saw him immediately likened to cartoon character Mickey Mouse. The look quickly had a stadium of fans affectionately emulating his style in support.
>
> With his eyes on Los Angeles 2028, de Pina first plans to finish his degree in physical education at the University of Cabo Verde, on his home island of Santiago. He's also hoping his victory will secure enough sponsorship to ensure he won't have to go back to working on construction sites in Lisbon to support his young family while he trains to secure his, and Cabo Verde's, golden goal.

the road. A rock formation that looks like the profile of a recumbent face has been christened the Marquês de Pombal rock, after a statue of that nobleman in Lisbon. Other rocks are said to look like a man on a horse, though locals say that the resemblance depends on how much *grogue* you've consumed. Climbing out of the Pico you can, on a clear day, see the island of Maio to the east, before the descent into Assomada.

WHERE TO STAY AND EAT There are a few places to stay in Assomada itself, should you get stuck. The two below are probably the best town-centre options. As there is usually a good wind blowing through town, the hotels' lack of air conditioning is not a major problem. Pousada Vassora provides an out-of-town alternative. For cheap eats in town, try the market where you can find fresh fruit and goat's cheese.

Pousada Vassora [map, page 163] (5 rooms) Cabeiça Carreira Vassora, Assomada; 265 3800; m 912 7536; e pousada.vassora@gmail.com; pousadavassora. Countryside location, about 3km north of town. Tasteful, spacious rooms have private bath & balcony, some with TV. French/Cabo Verdean-owners are warm, helpful & great cooks. Min stay 2 nights. **$$$**

Hotel Avenida (16 rooms) Av Amílcar Cabral; 265 3462. Clean, large, if basic, rooms. Not all have views – ask for a top-floor room looking over to the mountains. No Wi-Fi. **$$**

Residencial Cosmos (9 rooms) Opposite the market, right in the middle of town; m 530 8460. Up 2 flights of stairs. Large, basic rooms with fans, en suite (some with baths) & ornate doors. Very spacious suites available if you fancy an upgrade. No Wi-Fi. **$$**

Restaurante Asa Branca Portãozinho; 265 2372; 08.00–22.00 daily. A popular stop for local walking guides & their groups. Usual beef dishes & some fish options, good-quality home-cooking style. If you're short of cash & options, they also have a few large, clean, if old-fashioned, rooms upstairs. **$$**

OTHER PRACTICALITIES There are many **banks**, including BCA, Banco Interatlantico (both with ATMs), and Caixa Económica. Assomada also has a hospital (✆265 1130), on the main road a little north of the centre and a **pharmacy** (Farmácia H Camacho; ✆265 1819), just off Avenue Amílcar Cabral in the centre, while the **police** station (✆ 265 1132) is near the Palace of Justice. The **tourist information office** is in the main square – a small wooden kiosk with limited information and sporadic opening hours. There is also free **Wi-Fi** here.

WHAT TO SEE AND DO

Centro Cultural Norberto Tavares (In the main square; ✆ 265 2800) On the former site of the museum, this attractive cultural centre has a good selection of locally made crafts, including dolls, clothes, ceramics and modest jewellery. Named in honour of a well-known musician who was born in the town and died in 2010. A small display cabinet contains mementoes to him.

Museu de Tabanka (100$) In the village of Chão de Tanque, located on the left of the main road, 15 minutes' drive from Assomada. Ask directions at the Centro Cultural (see above). The museum has extensive coverage of the musical form of *tabanka*. There are also interesting displays of pictures, instruments and other objects, though the information is in Portuguese only. Only snag…you may need to ask in the village to find someone with the key, as it is often closed and there's no indication of when it officially opens.

African market With all the mesmerising colours, smells and noise of a West African market, this is held in the town centre every day, but ramps up a notch on Wednesdays and Saturdays. You can buy a chicken, dead or alive, whole or in pieces; you can buy a dog, step on a dog or simply be barked at by a dog. On the two busy days, near the schools in the southernmost part of town, there is a livestock market. Pigs, cows, goats and the smell of freshly cooking *chouriço* makes this a unique experience. At the end of the day, logic is defied as small pick-up trucks are crammed to bursting (and beyond) with villagers and their purchases, before trundling off home.

On Saturday evenings, the hustle and bustle moves to the main square, where hundreds gather to hang out and chat.

Porto Rincão This little fishing village is reached by turning west at Assomada (or catching an *aluguer* from beside the market or from the road junction) and following a fantastic road to the coast. There are deep red canyons and a stunning view of Fogo sitting on its cloud cushion across the water. Halfway along, the cobbled road turns to dirt. It's a 24km round trip, but if you have time for just one foray down to the west coast, the more northerly one, to Ribeira da Barca is recommended in preference.

Boa Entrada North along the main road from Assomada, just slightly out of town lies a signposted turning to this village, which lies in the green valley that meanders down to the east. You can walk down to Boa Entrada from Assomada. Dominating the valley is a magnificent, centuries-old kapok tree, in which once nested one of the few known colonies of the Cape Verde purple heron, known locally as *garça vermelha* (*Ardea purpurea bournei*). You may have more luck seeing them nowadays at Banana de Ribeira Montanha, near Pedra Badejo or around the Serra Malagueta – see page 192. This impressive tree might be the biggest you will ever see and is said to have been there when the island was discovered.

The valley can be reached by several obvious paths. One leads down to a white church with pinnacles and a green door and from there to the tree. There is also a cobbled road that leads down from the main road about 100m further on, but if you are driving down, you'll need a 4x4 to get there – and back. See also the walk described on page 200, which includes a 'visit' to this mighty specimen.

BADIUS AND REBELADOS

The Badius were at the heart of the Santiago peasant population. Whenever there was a pirate attack, or drought caused some social chaos on the island, some of the slaves would seize the opportunity and flee into the mountainous interior. There, though in exile in a restricted and infertile area, they had freedom. The Badius form the African core of Cabo Verdean society, reflected in their music, which harks back to the African coast for inspiration, and in other aspects of culture. Because of this they were despised by many. It was from the Badius that the Rebelados movement arose as a reaction against the arrival in the 1940s of the Portuguese Catholic priests of the Holy Spirit Congregation. They wished to purify Catholicism, eliminating the many syncretic practices which were based on a clashing personal spiritualism. It is said that those who stuck to the old methods in regard to baptisms, marriages and other rituals were imprisoned or persecuted.

Ultimately the movement coalesced around practices such as the communal farming of land, the refusal to deal with money and a prohibition on killing living creatures. As their rebellion centred on treasuring traditions and rejecting change, they also renounced many of today's 'luxuries' such as television and radio – though this has now changed. Leaders were arrested and dispersed to other islands after refusing to allow the fumigation of their homes as part of an antimalarial campaign.

Some communities still live in the Santiago highlands in distinctive rush-and-clay *funco*-style dwellings; some of these houses can be seen from the main Tarrafal–Calheta road, principally around the village of **Espinho Branco**. The villagers welcome visitors and sell craft work made from local materials such as acacia, shells and skins, as well as paintings using stretched T-shirts for canvas at their **Rabelarte** gallery. As the older generations die out and many of the younger generations distance themselves from the traditions, the all-natural *funcos* are being replaced by concrete block housing. This has happened more and more, as the cane straw has become a far more precious resource in years of low rain. A fire also sadly swept through the village in March 2024 and while no-one was hurt, many buildings were destroyed. Rebuilding has been aided by both the government and online support groups, the former showing a new spirit of reconciliation with the community.

Coming from Tarrafal down the east-coast road, look out for the 'Rabelarte' sign on the right-hand side of the road. Do not attempt to take photos unless you ask precise permission. It's also possible to visit with a small group, which can be a more engaged and respectful way to discover this unique part of Santiago. Caboverde Green (w caboverdegreen.com) hosts village picnics in Espinho Branco and Terra Terra Tours (terraterratours) has good connections with the community too. Note that the separate village on the other (seaward) side is *not* open to visitors: a sort of 'breakaway' faction lives here who do not wish to be disturbed by outsiders.

House of Amílcar Cabral National hero Amílcar Cabral lived as a child in a yellow-walled, red-roofed house set back from the main road that leads north from Boa Entrada, on the left-hand side. However, he spent most of his short life on São Vicente, Portugal and the African mainland. The house is not open to the public, but anyone in town will be able to direct you here to pay your respects.

Ribeira da Barca and Achada Leite It should be possible to reach this village by *aluguer* but there may be some long waits at the road junction. It's a 6km walk so it could make a pleasant day trip.

As you leave the vicinity of Boa Entrada start counting churches that possess separate bell towers. After the second one on the left there is a fork in the road – turn left and follow the cobbled track as it swings past a dramatic canyon on the left and continues past deeply carved *ribeiras* all the way to this beachside village. Sadly, most of the black sand that characterised the beach has long since been removed for house construction, but it still has character.

✘ Where to eat and drink Try **Restaurante Riba Mar** (Ribeira da Barca; ✆ 265 9017; m 991 6764; $$), about 200m up the *ribeira* to the right as you enter Ribeira da Barca town. This is a pleasant place for a meal of fresh fish or a drink, and there's occasional live music on Saturdays.

SERRA MALAGUETA

Situated in northern-central Santiago, Serra Malagueta is an important area ecologically and one of the last remaining forest resources on Santiago. It is the starting point for some classic Santiago hikes.

The heart of the area is now a natural park, which spans 774ha and reaches a height of 1,064m at the peak of Monte Malagueta. The park shelters important threatened and endemic species (page 165), including one ultra-local endemic, the *carqueja de Santiago*, a small shrub that lives between 500m and 800m. The ecotourist facilities offered are not quite as well advanced as those on Fogo or São Nicolau but there is a new-ish centre and the management has marked out (on a map and information boards) some suggested hikes covering in total 55km and with a wide range of difficulty and duration. They are also best placed to know of any changes to tracks.

While hiking in the area, watch out for (introduced) vervet monkeys and for the rare endemic Cape Verde purple heron or *garça vermelha* (*Ardea purpurea bournei*), which can sometimes be seen in the trees near the visitors centre. Santiago is its only home.

⌂ WHERE TO STAY AND EAT The only reliable accommodation option here is a good one. **Strela Mountain Lodge** [map, page 163] (8 rooms; m 972 5511; e reservation@casastrela.com; w mountain-lodge.strela-travel.com; $$) is a beautifully sited, soulfully decorated guesthouse care of the same crew behind Tarrafal's Casa Strela (page 194). All but one of the rooms has extraordinary views of either the mountains or the sea, some both. Half board is 1,500$ on top of the reasonable room rates and full board can be arranged.

WHAT TO SEE AND DO
Casa do Ambiente (Serra Malagueta Visitors Centre; ✆ 265 3707; e ecoserramalagueta@gmail.com; ⊕ 08.00–17.00 Mon–Fri, 08.00–15.30 Sat &

Sun; park entrance 200$) Look for the bright yellow building. This is the place to have a drink or buy handicrafts, or simply get an information pamphlet, and small maps, available in Portuguese or English. There is also a useful wall map. Call ahead to arrange homestays and meals. The view down into the valley from the ridge is spectacular.

TARRAFAL

A cobalt sea, a string of little sandy coves and a flat land under forbidding mountains are what make Tarrafal. Don't be deterred by the shabby entrance to town and the streets of half-built villas between you and the sea. The beach beyond the main square is of lovely soft sand and there's a jumble of life going on there: fishermen, local sports fanatics, sunbathers, mojito-sippers and lots of dogs. There's a second little beach, Mar di Baxu, that's almost always safe for swimming and has an amphitheatre-like collection of stone steps and rocky places to find shade. Both beaches become packed at weekends (though not unpleasantly so) but are quieter midweek. It can be windswept during the harmattan period from December to March.

Tarrafal is a good base for doing some of the walks the island offers and it is easy to laze away a few days here – the beach is cosier and more lived-in than Santa Maria on Sal, though it has none of the awesome splendour of beaches on the flat islands. Activity opportunities here are on the sharp increase, with surfing, diving, snorkelling, kayaking and biking all available.

The town's mention in the history books comes from its notorious Portuguese political prison, 3km before town on the main Praia road, on the west side (page 196).

GETTING THERE AND AWAY The 80km trip from Praia along the central road takes 2 hours and *alugueres* leave all day from Sucupira Market (600$); you may have to change in Assomada. To return to Praia on the same, inland road catch an *aluguer* from where the Praia road joins the main square of Tarrafal. They run until around 16.00. To return along the coastal road find an *aluguer* behind the church in the main square along with women returning from their early forays to Tarrafal Beach to buy fish. *Alugueres* on this road rarely go all the way to Praia so you will have to change where necessary (250$ to Calheta; 300$ Calheta to Praia).

Most Tarrafal hotels can arrange private pick-ups from Praia or the airport. This should cost around 7,000$ during the day, or 8,000$ at night.

WHERE TO STAY

King Fisher Village (21 rooms & 7 apts) 266 1007; e info@king-fisher-village.com; w king-fisher-village.com. In western Tarrafal, a good walk from town, this is an imaginatively conceived set of lodges built into the rocky promontory of Ponta d'Atum. Each has a terrace or balcony & its own surprises (one, for example, is built over a wave-washed grotto). Options from standard rooms to 2-bedroom apts. At some times of year there is a minimum booking period. A restaurant & bar, set back from the sea-water pool & looking out over the rocks, is open to non-guests, with an impressive cocktail list & friendly service (page 194). The German owner has plenty of information for guests, as well as a dive centre & cycling shop on site. For ocean swimmers, there's a ladder leading directly into the sea; always romantic, but no actual beach. **$$$$–$$$$$**

Oásis Tarrafal Alfândega Suites (22 rooms) 266 1245; w oasisatlantico.com. The only true beachside option, the bright, light modern rooms here have views over both beaches & the Bay of Tarrafal. All have kitchenettes; downstairs family rooms have large terraces. Excellent location means everything in town is only steps away. **$$$$**

Casa Strela (6 rooms) Ponta de Atum; ✆ 266 1071; m 917 0292; e reservation@casastrela.com; w strela-travel.com. Surely the best value in town; find it along a track from the King Fisher Village. A good vibe is generated in this warm, relaxed place. Roof terrace, with honesty bar. English spoken. Can organise hiking, fishing, diving island tours, excursions & transport to & from Praia, all with excellent local drivers. Also rents surfboards, & there's a surf shack a short walk away. They serve food, too (see below). $$$

Pensão Mille Nuits (12 rooms) ✆ 266 1463; e pensaomillenuits@hotmail.com. At the heart of town with respectable, budget-type rooms arranged around a bright atrium. The cheapest have shared bathrooms. All have fans, only some with hot water. Has a restaurant serving basic lunch & dinner but it's a little overpriced. $

Pensão Tátá (5 rooms) ✆ 266 1125; w pensaotata.cv. Simple guesthouse with smallish rooms in the centre of town. Has a restaurant serving lunch & dinner. Good budget value. $

Tarrafal's Meeting Point (Ponto de Encontro) (8 rooms, 2 6-bed dorms) Rua dos Correios; m 931 6763; ◉ tarrafalsmeetingpoint. Tarrafal's 1st backpacker option is a friendly place with private & shared bathroom options & (non-bunk) beds in a couple of dorms. Also runs interesting social projects. $

✴ WHERE TO EAT AND DRINK

King Fisher Village Page 193; ⊕ daily. Small but smart à la carte menu for lunch & afternoons, or book for 3-course fine dining in the evening, usually featuring fish delivered by fisherman that morning & vegetables grown in the resort's own garden. Great wine list too, with good European labels to splash out on. Or just call in for a signature Tarrafal spritz, with prosecco & tart passionfruit. All this in an extraordinarily pretty setting. $$$$$

Altomira Rua Macaco; ✆ 266 2251; m 996 3865; w altomirarestaurant.com; ⊕ 17.30–23.00 Mon–Sat. Through an unprepossessing doorway is a little courtyard with a bamboo roof, where you'll find a very good restaurant run by a Frenchman, François. Come for his pizza or fish & seafood cooked over a wood-fired grill. Sometimes closes for a month in off-season (May). $$$$

Casa Strela see above; ⊕ 18.00–20.30 daily. Book ahead for good-value set menu dinners on the roof terrace of this welcoming small hotel. If you're dining alone, ask them to book you a taxi back into town. $$$

Maracuja Rua Macaco; m 913 8854; e restmaracuja@hotmail.com; ⊕ 10.00–23.00 Mon–Sat. Fresh fish, including signature tuna & onions, homemade ice cream & huge stuffed crêpes. Local specialities can be ordered in advance. Interesting woody interior, or plentiful terrace seating. $$$

Restaurante Riba Mar m 989 7530; e xarxalda@gmail.com; ⊕ 11.00–23.00 daily. Right on the water, at the end of the main beach. Authentic Cabo Verdean b/fasts are a speciality, including cuz cuz, cachupa & doce de papaia-daubed pancakes. $$$

Sol e Luna ✆ 266 2339; m 997 9535/925. Breezy beach restaurant overlooking Mar di Baxu, the town's smaller beach. Serves fish & pasta. Reasonably priced & good food. $$$

Vista Mare Mar di Baxu; ✆ 356 6123; ⊕ 08.30–23.45 daily. Above Tarrafal's fishing harbour, a popular place with a blend of Italian & Cabo Verdean cuisine. International b/fasts served, & good coffee. Live music on Sat. $$$

Churrasqueira Mangui Baxo 3mins' walk from Mar di Baxu, just over Rua Centro; m 994 1404. Pre-order your BBQ or be prepared to wait a while. Buzzy on w/ends. $$

Sucupira Market In & around the new market hall are several small restaurants & snack bars that offer simple local dishes & cakes at very low prices. Best budget lunch spot. $

ENTERTAINMENT AND NIGHTLIFE Locals gather on the beach for sunset. Head to **Sol e Luna** (see above) overlooking Mar di Baxu, where there are often impromptu sound systems set up at weekends, or sit feet in the sand at **Kabungo Beach Bar** (◉ kabungobeachbar; ⊕ 11.30–20.30 daily) right in the thick of it at the main beach. The *caipirinhas* and mojitos at the latter come in many fresh fruit flavours but are universally strong: bring your own chips or nuts for stomach-lining snacks. There is also occasional live music at **Restaurante Riba Mar** (see above) from about

19.00, or Afrohouse nights, while festivals and holidays bring crowds to Plaça de Tarrafal. There used to be a couple of discos, but if you really want to dance, you'll have to head down the road to nearby Chão Bom.

OTHER PRACTICALITIES The **banks** BCA and Caixa Económica are both near the main square and both have ATMs. The **hospital** is on the main road to Assomada, on the left, opposite the football stadium (⚲ 266 1130). The **police** station is also on the main road to Assomada, on the left (⚲ 266 1132), while a **post office** is on this road, on the left (⊕ 08.00–15.30 Mon–Fri). The **tourist information office** is in the middle of the main square (⊕ 08.00–18.00 Mon–Sat), a helpful place, with information on activities nearby; English-speaking staff are usually available.

WHAT TO SEE AND DO

Cycling Trips by mountain bike can be organised through **King Fisher Village** (page 193), either guided or self-guided using their expert trail maps. They rent full-suspension bikes, electric mountain bikes and Scott hardtails, all meticulously tuned, and have servicing facilities for your own bike. They are multi-lingual, and speak English.

Boating Local fishermen may take you out fishing or down the coast to Ribeira da Barca and on to Achada Leite (page 192). A good option for a boat trip is Sety Martins (m 951 7716), based in Ribeira da Barca: good reports have been received. Otherwise, you could ask around at the Mercado de Peixe at the start of the main beach or over at the small beach on the far side of Restaurante Riba Mar. Negotiate, but expect to pay around 10,000$ per boat (*not* per person) for 2–3 hours.

Diving The diving operates from the King Fisher Village; it's well respected and good value at around €50 per dive. They also rent SUPs.

Mercado Municipal Artesanat Cultura (⊕ 09.00–18.00 Mon–Sat) In a courtyard (formerly the main market) next to the main square, this houses a selection of stalls selling handicrafts and souvenirs. The number of stalls varies from day to day. Some of the wooden items, though attractive, are from mainland Africa rather than from local artisans.

Snorkelling Snorkelling is available with **Kabungo** (e kabungosurfschool@gmail.com; 📷 kabungo_surfschool_tarrafal), on the main beach, with 2 hours costing from 3,000$.

Surfing Before midday, the break to the west of the bay is good and extends all the way down to Ribeira da Prata. Many locals favour the water near the King Fisher Village, but newcomers should head further south as this area is less rocky. Casa Strela has a few boards to rent to those staying there, as well as offering lessons (€39 for 2 hours, with equipment rental) or try **Kabungo** (see opposite), which offers lessons starting at 3,000$ per person.

Hiking Tarrafal is a good base for a few hikes or forays into the Serra Malagueta, but note that the short walk from town to the lighthouse is no longer recommended without a guide, as armed robberies have occurred.

THE CONCENTRATION CAMP AT TARRAFAL

It was known as the Campo da Morte Lenta (slow death camp) to some; Aldeia da Morte (death village) to others. The low-slung, sprawling complex just outside Tarrafal (to the left of the main road as you exit the village of Chão Bom, 2km before Tarrafal; w museus.cv; ⏰ 08.00–18.00 daily; 200$, students/children free) had at its centre a cemented building whose temperature would soar during the day. Each cell was a completely enclosed cement box about 3m long by 2.5m wide. At one end was the iron door. The only ventilation was a few holes of less than 1cm in diameter in the door, and a small, grilled hole up near the ceiling.

Completed in 1936 at the behest of the PVDE – Polícia de Vigilância e de Defesa do Estado, that is, the secret police of Salazar's Estado Novo regime – 157 Portuguese anti-fascists were first imprisoned here. The prison continued to house hundreds of political prisoners until 1954, when it closed after international protest. But it was reopened in the early 1960s, this time to incarcerate independence fighters, militants and intellectuals from Cabo Verde, as well as Portugal's other African colonies, Angola and Portuguese Guinea.

The camp's history as an active prison came to an end on 1 May 1974, a few days after the Carnation Revolution in Lisbon, which ushered in democracy and decolonisation (page 26). The gates were thrown open and out tottered a bewildered group, many of them crying. Waiting for them was a crowd of thousands who had rushed from Praia in cars, trucks and on bicycles as soon as they heard of the telegram ordering their release.

The bleakness of the place is emphasised by the wind that gusts around the compound; there is still some barbed wire, and you can walk along the top of the prison walls. Officially named the Museu do Campo de Concentração, it's often referred to deferentially as the Museu da Resistencia or, more starkly, simply by its location, Chão Bom. There's multi-lingual information panels but the camp's horrors need little explanation. Given the modest entry fee, it is well worth a visit.

OTHER PLACES TO VISIT

CALHETA DE SÃO MIGUEL There's no particular reason for stopping the night here, although it is a pretty enough coastal town. It is a useful starting and end point for some hikes to and from the interior. To get there from Praia take an *aluguer* from Sucupira Market that is travelling up the coastal road; from Tarrafal catch an *aluguer* from behind the church in the main square. From Assomada you can catch an *aluguer* that takes an interesting route down a cross-country road to Calheta.

Where to stay and eat

Hotel Edu Horizonte (32 rooms) m 594 3003; e emanuelsantos_2@hotmail.com. Near the Shell petrol station as you enter town from the north. Spacious rooms, en suite, with TV & fan. Useful if you miss the last transport back to Praia, perhaps. Good, busy restaurant ($$$) downstairs. **$**

Esplanada Silibell Ponta Calhetona; \273 2078; m 996 7930; e info@silibell.com; w silibell. de; ⏰ 09.00–21.00 Mon–Sat. Situated at the southern end of Calheta, on the right as you head south, this is an open-air restaurant & bar with a sea view. It's the place to recover from the heat of the day & mull over what you have seen with Gerhard & Sibylle Schellmann, the German owners. The Schellmanns have been in Calheta for years & willingly offer tourist information as well as tour operator services, specialising in hiking in the hinterland (see also page 168). They will also give sound advice on local accommodation choices. $$$

PEDRA BADEJO This growing coastal settlement is located a little north of Praia Baixo along the northeast coast. Some people love it, but it can be hard to see beyond the sprawl, rocks, litter and cement-block buildings, many unfinished. Admittedly, the large black-sand beach at the southern end is quite impressive, but it is often dirty with refuse. The southern wetlands are an important destination for birdwatchers, but it's probably better to stay in either Praia or in the interior and day trip back here.

PRAIA BAIXO Located on the northeast coast of Santiago about 20km from Praia, this spot is noted for its safe beach. Sir Francis Drake is thought to have made a landfall here. Right on the beach, **Big Lanche** (m 996 9457; ⊕ 10.00–22.00 Tue–Sun) serves seafood and fish.

SÃO FRANCISCO With superb beaches and deserted coves, this is the best place near Praia for a day in the sun.

Alugueres leave approximately every 30 minutes from Paul, behind Fazenda in Praia and cost about 100$. They drop you in the village of São Francisco, but from

> **ROUND-ISLAND DRIVE**
>
> This is highly recommended: the interior of Santiago is a drama worth making the effort to see. The drive could be accomplished in one day but this would be pretty exhausting. It would be better to travel from Praia to Tarrafal, Assomada or another location with accommodation on the first day and return down the coast road on the second. If you have time, take the left turn after Assomada (just before Fundura) and visit Ribeira da Barca for a vivid glimpse of the terrain leading to the west coast. There is a cursory description of the landscape below; for more information see the individual entries for towns and places in this chapter.
>
> The drive begins through the urban sprawl of Praia, ever expanding as people move from the villages to the city. As you reach the countryside you should see the long yellow flowers of aloe vera lining the roadside, along with, at the right time of year, maize and haricot beans. About 12km from the centre of Praia, where you take the left turn, you begin to gaze down into a green valley. The road passes through São Domingos and Assomada – springboards for visiting all the places described above. After marvelling at the Pico do Santo António and its surrounding craggy peaks, you will later come to the Serra Malagueta, the other high point of Santiago.
>
> From Tarrafal, the journey to Praia along the coast is 2½ hours. There is less to stop for than on the inland road but the drive is spectacular, tracing hairpin bends that take you into verdant creeks with compact black-sand beaches, waves crashing over brooding rocks and out again into the dry mountainsides. The houses have hay piled high on their flat roofs and sometimes goats live there too. Wires stick out of the top of every house in anticipation of the building of the next storey. Pigs forage round the houses and the dry landscape.
>
> After Calheta the land becomes almost lush with great banana plantations, coconut trees and the yellow of aloe vera poking up from cactus-like leaves.

there it is a walk of several kilometres downhill to the beach. A more convenient taxi from Praia costs about 2,000$ each way.

HIKES Alexander Hirtle (AH); Aisling Irwin (AI); Murray Stewart (MS)

1 SERRA MALAGUETA–HORTELÃO–RIBEIRA PRINCIPAL (LONGER ROUTE)
Distance: 13km; time: 4½ hours; difficulty: 3 (AH)

This is a beautiful walk, and the peak time for it is between mid-August and early December (late October is probably the greenest and most picturesque). Beware, though, that during the rainy season that usually starts mid–late July and ends mid-October, trails can be slippery and, in a good year for rain, wiped out with streams rushing through them. Visibility can also be limited due to cloud cover and the rain itself. The walks are mainly downhill, but continual downhill jaunts can be very stressful on knees and ankles. You need to get transport up to the area of Serra Malagueta. From Assomada, an *aluguer* costs 100$. Tell the driver to drop you off at the secondary road with the gate (*portão*), before the primary school (*escola*).

Follow the secondary road, which is clear and wide with generally good footing, up several hundred feet; it makes winding turns, some so sharp and steep you'll wonder how vehicles get up there. There are some excellent views of the *ribeira* off to the left. As you continue upwards, the flora changes. You'll see groups of pine trees, part of a continual reafforestation project in which the locals participate. It is a necessary programme, because local residents are always collecting firewood from the area (you may pass several people coming down the road carrying loads of wood on their heads). Continue up the road and it begins to level off. You are near one of the highest points on the island, **Serra Malagueta**. There are spectacular views to the right; you may even be above the cloud cover, depending on the day. Watch the sides of the cliffs though: a misplaced step will send you hundreds of feet down. Continue on the road, and past a small clearing where at times vehicles are parked.

Stay to the right, along the drop-off, but not too close to it. The paths to the left lead to somewhat dangerous wooded areas. You will begin to descend, as the path takes a left turn and leads you into very green and beautiful woods: thus begins the decline to Ribeira Principal.

The path switchbacks several times; it is important to stay on the main path that generally goes to the left of the ridge and eventually to the bottom of the *ribeira*. If you find yourself going down to the right of the ridge, you will need to retrace your steps and find the correct path again. You will descend to an area with some enclosed animal pens and houses. Most residents here are very friendly, but it's wise to respect their privacy and property as on occasion you may meet a local who is not always happy with foreigners passing by. After entering the first area of houses, continue through another area with sets of houses and, as the path veers to the right, walk along an area that is a small ridge where the drop-off is steep to the left, shallow on the right. You will reach an area where the path quickly drops down, makes a slight turn to the right, and then a sharp turn to the left. This place can be dangerous when it is wet, so take it slow and steady. The path then takes you along a lower terrace that brings you to the left side of the *ribeira*. You will descend further to more houses, again staying along the lower ridge that overlooks the *ribeira*. There are very good views here: you can see the terracing of the agricultural areas, and the isolated *vilas* below. In several places there are diverging paths, so you need constantly to ask the locals the way to Hortelão, the *vila* just past Ribeira Principal.

You will come to a converging area that will bring you across to the right side of the *ribeira*. You may not notice it at first, but once you leave the denser areas with houses, you will be following the lower ridge on the right side of **Ribeira Principal**.

Continue to descend, past some fantastic rock structures on the right including a keyhole in one part of the ridge. Your final climb down is full of tricky switchbacks. The path eventually takes you to the bottom of the *ribeira*, to **Hortelão**. Waiting vehicles can take you to Tarrafal, or Calheta, where you can change vehicles to return to Assomada, or Praia. Alternatively, you can walk the extra 30–40 minutes along the road to the main road, but it is not the most scenic part of the trip, and may take longer if you are tired and hungry.

2 SERRA MALAGUETA–RIBEIRA PRINCIPAL (SHORTER ROUTE)
Distance: 8km; time: 3½ hours; difficulty: 2 (MS)

The second, and shorter, way down the pretty Ribeira Principal starts 100m from the visitors centre, across the road at the end of a bridge on the main road towards Tarrafal. (Just beyond the bridge is a minimarket, Marcilino's, where you can stock up with drinks, etc.)

Start down some rough-hewn stone steps and descend a narrow dirt track along a ridge. Soon you will see the houses of Ribeira Principal village away down to your left. Ignore the narrow path off to the left. Your descent takes you through agave plants; in the rainy season, look out for the yellow-and-black spiders who make their home in them. About 0.5km after leaving the main road, take a path that leads down to your left as the ridge continues off to your right. The path is visible ahead, winding its way along the side of the mountain. Descend to a Y-shaped junction, at which you veer left on to a narrow path with a distinctive, sharp pinnacle as your 'sighter'. Continue down towards the base of the pinnacle, noting ahead how the narrow path continues on the other side of the short valley. Now follow the path as it continues through the first houses of the extended settlement to reach a junction with a dirt path where you turn right, continuing downwards with a stone wall now below you on your left. After a few hundred metres, take a left at a fork in the path, again heading downwards. After a further few hundred metres of descent, you will reach a riverbed, usually dry. There is some welcome shade here. Cross this and continue with the riverbed now down to your left. You will probably see locals coming and going, carrying water from the tank, or maybe sugarcane: give them passing space with their heavy loads. As you follow the path, you will pass several *grogue* distilleries. Many owners enjoy demonstrating how their distillery operates; feel free to enquire, but you may find they are at a tricky moment and can't take a break just now. Soon you will reach the centre of the village and its welcome bar, which is the location for any available transport; if there is none there or imminent, you have to continue along the road for around 40 minutes to reach the main Tarrafal–Calheta road, where you should find an *aluguer*.

3 CHÃO BOM–RIBEIRA DA PRATA–FIGUEIRA DAS NAUS
Distance: 9km; time: 3½ hours; difficulty: 2 (AI)

This is an attractive, if lonely, walk that begins on the level, following the coast as far as Ribeira da Prata. It then toils uphill along a remorselessly shadeless track, relieved by the drama of the canyons and the vista back towards the sea. The walk is on road and track and there are no problems with slipperiness or steep slopes, but the 1½-hour upward slog from Ribeira da Prata requires a certain amount of fitness if it is to be enjoyable. To get to the beginning of the walk at Chão Bom (pronounced 'shambome'), travel for about 5 minutes by *aluguer* from Tarrafal along the Assomada road. The turning to Ribeira da Prata is signposted, on the right, at the beginning of Chão Bom.

From the Tarrafal side of Chão Bom, take the road signposted **Ribeira da Prata**, passing initially through slums. Leaving habitation behind, the lonely road passes in and out of the coastal fractals for about an hour, revealing eventually the black-sand beach of the *ribeira* with acacia and coconut palms offering a bit of shade. The bottom of the valley is where people pause in the shade to rest. Follow the road out, up, into the village and out of the other side after which it will do a great loop backwards and upwards to ascend into the hills.

This is an extremely quiet road and, as it ascends, there are views back to Tarrafal, to the harshly bright sea and over the rocky ground that characterises the western side of Santiago. There is a huge amount of reafforestation here. Some 1½ hours after leaving Ribeira da Prata the track begins to pass through a series of villages, including Figueira Muite and Marmulano, most of which have bars tucked away – all you have to do is ask for them. Some 2½ hours from Ribeira da Prata you reach **Figueira das Naus** with its pretty church. Here the road divides and you can wait for an *aluguer* (there are three to four per day) to take you along the right fork and back to the main Tarrafal–Assomada road.

Alternatively, if you have a taste for more of this rocky, inland drama, you can walk the 8km to the main road. Just take the right fork and remain on the same track, ignoring a single right turn.

4 MONTE XOTA ANTENNAE–SÃO DOMINGOS
Distance: 5km; time: 2 hours; difficulty: 1 (Al)

Spectacular views accompany this downhill walk from the antennae station at the peak of Monte Xota to the town of São Domingos on the main road, or if this is not possible, from a point around 1km before you reach the barracks. The road is cobbled throughout and navigation is simple: just head downwards. If you become tired at any point, you can just sit and wait for the next *aluguer* – these are frequent enough from Rui Vaz downwards. To reach Monte Xota for the beginning of the walk either take a public *aluguer* as far as the Rui Vaz turning and walk, or charter an *aluguer* in São Domingos, which should cost around 700$.

Try to kick off the walk by gaining entry to the grounds of the Monte Xota telecommunications station and climbing the knoll to the right. The soldiers there may let you in if you ask nicely and they are not too busy. From the knoll you can see, spread before you, the heart of Santiago. Retracing your steps, join the road and enjoy the greenery and the sharply scented, cool air before it fades as you descend. The magnificent cobbled road takes you through sheer cliffs and craggy rock formations with occasional glimpses of Pico do Santo António, the canine tooth poking up behind them. Watch out for Pico de João Teves, one of many raw, majestic shapes, which looks like the top of a submarine. You will also pass the president's holiday home, on the left.

Further on, the road descends towards the valley and runs parallel with it before a left and a right turn deposit you on the main road in the north of São Domingos.

5 ASSOMADA–GIL BISPO–BOA ENTRADA
Distance: 7km; time: 2 hours to the kapok tree, 2 hours 40 minutes to the main road at Boa Entrada; difficulty: 1 (MS)

This is a shortish, pleasant walk with plenty of contact with the rural population and their daily lives. If you're lucky, you may pick up transport just after you reach the kapok tree, saving you 40 minutes of uphill at the end. To find the starting point, get your *aluguer*/taxi driver to drop you off 100m after the Assomada town sign, coming from Praia. The walk begins from the main road, directly opposite the Minimercado Bar Lindinho Ebethe, where you can stock up with drink. Across the road from the shop, climb steeply for around 20m and then turn left on a wide, rough road. This winds first right, then left along the side of a building then right again through some houses. Between the last two houses, turn left and follow a path (ill-defined at first), rising steeply. Below and to your left are the houses of Assomada, Santiago's second-largest city; behind you is Pico do Santo António, the island's highest point at 1,392m. After a climb of around 5 minutes, you reach a ridge. To continue, turn right (though you could briefly turn left along the ridge for a better view of the city sprawl, and possibly a sighting of Fogo island, before retracing your steps to the junction) and take a path that descends diagonally with the village of Gil Bispo directly in front of you. The path leaves the mountainside and takes you down to the first buildings of the rambling village, then through these with the distinctive three-pointed peak directly in front of you. After a further descent, the path joins a cobbled road section where you turn left. Follow the cobbles as they then take you sharply uphill to the right and through more village buildings. After a few hundred metres, you pass on your left a small, white shrine with a cross on the top. In times gone by, these shrines were the only places where coffin-bearers could rest their load! Around 20m after the shrine, leave the road, taking a rough path on your left with two buildings on the skyline. Now ahead of you in the distance is a distinctive, sharp cone of a mountain, with a mast on the top. Descend a short path and turn left as you rejoin the cobbled road and descend gently past more buildings with a plateau off to your right. A few hundred metres later, take a sharp right, cutting back on another cobbled road which descends towards the plateau and into the valley. Continue to descend, with the plateau now off to your left. When the cobbles end, turn left (but not sharp left!) to follow a rough dirt road which heads first towards the plateau and then swings right, descending towards the valley floor. When the path levels out and turns sharply right, at the end of a concrete building look out on your left for a rough-hewn staircase leading down. Take these stairs and descend carefully to find lush vegetation and then the public washing area, which may be a centre of activity as women do the laundry and men wash themselves here. Turn right and cross the concrete floor of the washing area to find a large water tank. Continue along the top of the concrete wall of the tank, turn right along the top of the next wall and towards the end, leave it to turn sharp left and continue downwards with the water tank wall now above you to the left. Reaching a narrow stream bed, turn right and now continue between two stone walls. Eventually you reach a narrow, concrete water channel; ignore the steep wide path that rises up to your left, and with the channel on your left and banana trees on your right, go forward to continue along the stream bed as before. Reaching a junction, you now turn left on to cobbles which take you gently upwards. At the junction do take time to note, up to your right, the giant, ancient kapok tree (page 190). If you're in luck, you may find transport here; if not, it's 40 minutes up the rough road to reach the main road, though there is a tiny shack selling drinks after a few hundred metres and a working *trapiche* opposite, to distract you.

6 CALHETA–FLAMENGOS DE BAIXO–RIBEIRETA–CALHETA
Distance: 11km; time: 3¼ hours; difficulty: 1 (Al)

This is a pleasant little walk with no great ascents or descents, although it is quite rocky underfoot. It is not a walk of great drama but it shows off plenty of Santiago rural life on the way: from *trapiches* to terracing, and water extraction to traditional stone housing. The middle of the walk, up in the verdant hills, is very pretty.

Walk south out of Calheta along the main road as far as the big bridge across Ribeira dos Flamengos. Descend the rocky track into the *ribeira* and turn inland, among the palm trees. Wander up the *ribeira* for 1½ hours, past three windmills in total, until you confront an earth road that crosses the *ribeira* and heads up to the right, becoming cobbled very quickly. Now you are walking uphill in pretty countryside. Some 15 minutes after joining the road, you reach a 'crossroads'. Go straight across, and then turn right, down the riverbed, disturbing clusters of butterflies as you go.

The descent down this second *ribeira* involves negotiating your way round several barrages. See the tiny, drystone terraces and hear the dogs, cockerels, goats and people, whose echoes help to make *ribeira* life a noisy experience.

Some 15 minutes after passing a pumping station on your right you will reach the main road. Turn right and walk for another 15 minutes through Calheta to reach the bridge again.

7 TARRAFAL–LIGHTHOUSE–TARRAFAL
Distance: 6km; time: 2½ hours; difficulty: 2 (AI)
Note: there have been muggings on this route, so only go with a guide.

This walk will take you from the Tarrafal cove to the lighthouse at the foot of the big headland to the north of Tarrafal, which you can see from the beach. It involves a steep scramble at the end and there is no shade – take at least 1.5 litres of water and a hat.

HAVE YOU EVER DRUNK A CLOUD?   *Alex Alper*

High along the jagged cliffs of Serra Malagueta Natural Park, green nets billow in the wind like a half-erected modern art installation. They are, in reality, fog collectors, harvesting water from the clouds that shroud the park in almost year-round mist. The technology is simple: water vapour condenses along the mesh surface, forming droplets that fall into a gutter below and on to a holding tank. How much water could that possibly provide? More than you might think. Fog contains 0.05–3ml of water per cubic metre. Serra Malagueta, which receives only about 900mm of rainfall per year, has a semi-permanent layer of 'stratocumulus' – low-lying clouds – pushed upwards from the coast by the mountains themselves. Thanks to these clouds, Serra Malagueta's 120m of netting (suspended on eight separate frames) produce approximately 1,440 litres per day, with production reaching 75 litres per metre of net per day in the rainy season. That's a big help for the park's 488 families, who rely principally on local springs, wells, and private cisterns for their water. Rainfall is decreasing and underground sources are drying up, but 80% of Serra Malaguetans still earn their livelihood in agriculture.

Fog water is free from the microbes that contaminate ground water, requiring no treatment. Construction materials – mesh, plastic tubing, and wood or metal poles – are cheap and readily accessible worldwide. The most challenging aspect is positioning the nets accurately, and scientists say that fog harvesting will not damage the microclimate.

Despite these benefits – and while 1,133ha of Cabo Verde's territory are considered suitable, yielding potentially 14 million cubic metres of water per year – fog harvesting does not yet constitute a major source of water in Cabo Verde. While Santiago leads the way, São Nicolau, Brava and Santo Antão are also gearing up to implement the schemes developed here and on other Atlantic islands such as the Canaries.

Go to the north end of the most northerly cove of the beach and follow a little sand path up through the rocks and past the last of the holiday bungalows. You can see the path cut into the cliffside ahead. Keep an eye on it as it often disappears underfoot. After 30 minutes clinging to the headland, the path turns inland to face an inhospitable ravine strewn with huge boulders from a landslide. There is a path, though it turns to a scramble at times. When you have reached the end of it, follow a path out along the big bulge of land, past deserted drystone walls built to keep cattle.

Instead of turning to the lighthouse you can continue up the coast and walk for hours, even as far as a distant cove (about 3 hours). It really is empty and there are exhilarating views down green stone canyons and up the coastline.

8 SALINEIRO–CIDADE VELHA
Distance: 4km; time: 1½ hours; difficulty: 2 (AI)

This walk plunges you from a dry, impoverished village up on the escarpment down into the verdant *ribeira* of Cidade Velha and past a few of the old city's important ruins before depositing you in the main square. This *ribeira* is quite lush with a wide variety of trees and the canyons on either side are magnificently striated. It's not hard but the initial descent is steep and shingly underfoot.

Take an *aluguer* from the old town up to the village of Salineiro for 100$, or charter a taxi for around 500–600$. At the village, ask to be set down as close as possible to the *caminho* to Cidade Velha, a path that lies a little beyond the village's water source. The path is inauspicious, rocky, steep and rubbish-strewn, but persist as it winds into the canyon, and watch the greenery of the acacias and palm trees below.

After about 10 minutes of descent you reach a T-junction of paths, more or less at the treeline. Turn right towards the sea. Some 5 minutes later you will pass piping and a barrage across the *ribeira*: there are several ways down to the *ribeira* floor.

As with many *ribeira* walks, the path emerges and fades and walkers have to negotiate themselves around the great barriers erected against the rain. Here there are mango trees, a stream and an unusual sensation of humidity. Keep heading seaward, passing a mighty baobab, and finally the route becomes a track, about an hour after the start of the walk. Some 10 minutes later you will round a bend and the fort will be in sight, and a few minutes later you will pass a *grogue* distillery on your left. After another 5 minutes you will find yourself in the main square of Cidade Velha.

JOURNEY BOOKS
CONTRACT PUBLISHING FROM BRADT GUIDES

DO YOU HAVE A STORY TO TELL?

- Publish your book with a leading trade publisher
- Expert management of your book by our experienced editors
- Professional layout, cover design and printing
- **Unique** access to trade distribution for print books and ebooks
- Competitive pricing and a range of tailor-made packages
- Aimed at both first-timers and previously published authors

"Unfailingly pleasant"... "Undoubtedly one of the best publishers I have worked with"... "Excellent and incredibly prompt communication"... "Unfailingly courteous"... "Superb"...

For more information – and many more endorsements from our delighted authors – please visit: **bradtguides.com/journeybooks**.

Journey Books is the contract publishing imprint of award-winning travel publisher, Bradt Guides. All subjects are considered for Journey Books, not just travel. Our contract publishing is a complement to our traditional publishing, not a replacement, and we welcome traditional submissions from new and established travel writers. Please visit bradtguides.com/write-for-us to find out more.

JB
JOURNEY BOOKS

6

Maio

> Huge heaps of salt like drifts of snow, and most fine and perfect in nature, the abundance whereof is such, and the daily increase so exceeding great, that they serve all countryes and lands about them, and is impossible to be consumed.
> Sir Francis Drake, British sailor, pirate and slave trader, 1578

Maio was, and some would say still is, the forgotten island. Its quiet dunes and secret beaches have been overshadowed by the more boisterous Sal and beguiling Boavista. It has been waiting to be thrust into the tourist mainstream, and fleetingly it seemed that its time had come. But plans for a massive increase in accommodation have, at least for now, been thwarted and development projects stand gathering dust. How the transport and other infrastructure were ever intended to keep pace is unclear. For many, this is a blessing, as it leaves undisturbed this island backwater. With uncertainty over Maio's future as a mass-market destination, restaurants and tourism-related businesses are susceptible to frequent changes of ownership or closure. Visitor footfall is light.

Those who live on Maio or visit it frequently justifiably claim that the island is overlooked in other ways. Flight times are often changed, cargo boats fail to materialise and as a consequence, the shops sometimes run short of supplies. But visitors may revel in the authentic feel that Maio possesses, the genuineness of the island and the seemingly gentle and welcome indifference of the inhabitants to grabbing hold of your hard-earned holiday spending money.

HIGHLIGHTS AND LOWLIGHTS

Much of Maio is flat, desolate brown desert, broken by unexpected patches of acacia forest and, in the east, relief for the eye from the odd fertile valley planted with crops and palm trees. In the rainy season, the landscape is transformed into a carpet of green, *ribeiras* are full and the fragile roads can be washed away. The main town of Cidade do Porto Inglés (formerly Vila do Maio, and still often referred to locally as the *vila*) is charming and quaint with a slight spaghetti western feel, narrow cobbled streets and brightly painted houses. But it is not Clint Eastwood who will step out of the shadows; more likely a chicken or a dog. There is little traffic to run you over and few taxis to stalk you.

Maio lacks the development of Sal or as generous a supply of beautiful dunes and oases as Boavista. It has little gripping walking. But it is this very quiet that attracts some people – there are some lovely, lonely white-sand beaches. There is the biggest acacia plantation of the archipelago – and the trees are mature and green although they make surprisingly little impact on the eye, perhaps because the soil itself remains dry and bare. For naturalists there are turtles in the summer and some interesting birds, particularly seabirds on Ilhéu Laje Branca off the north of

MAIO

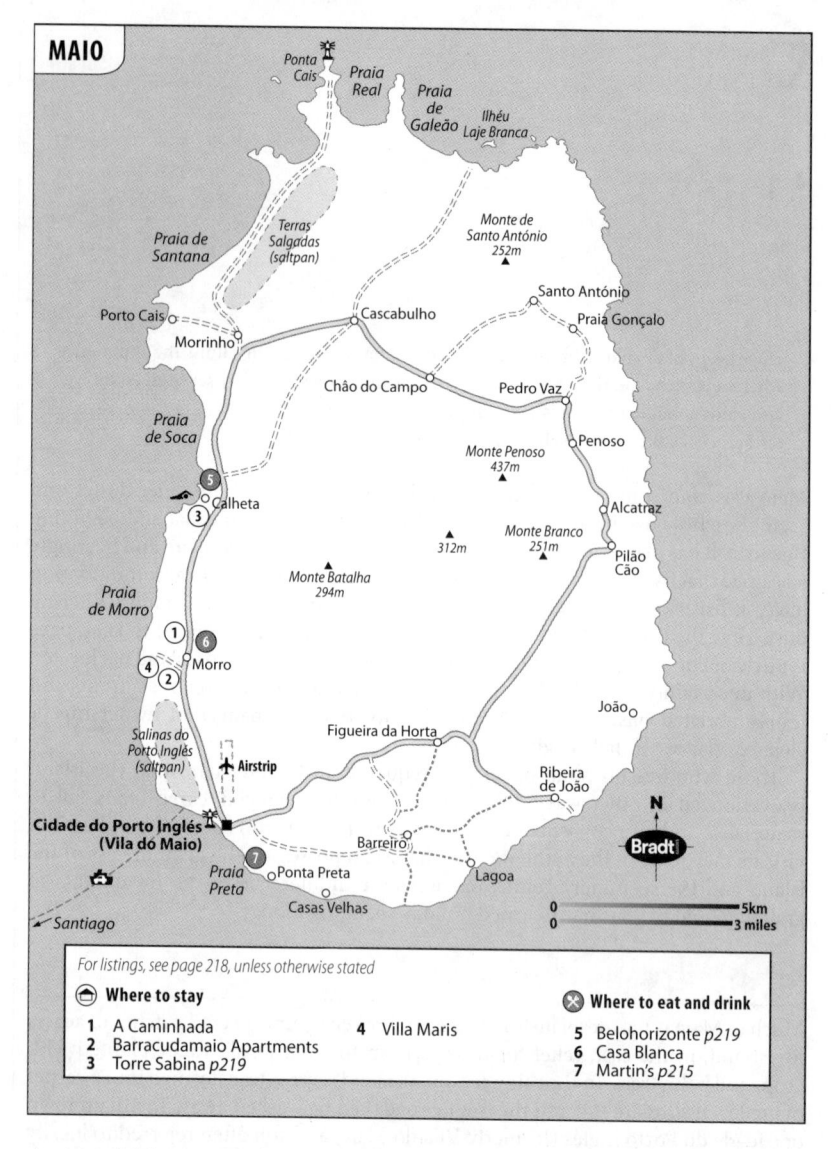

For listings, see page 218, unless otherwise stated

🛏 **Where to stay**
1 A Caminhada
2 Barracudamaio Apartments
3 Torre Sabina *p219*
4 Villa Maris

🍴 **Where to eat and drink**
5 Belohorizonte *p219*
6 Casa Blanca
7 Martin's *p215*

the island. There are a few options for diving and fishing, and several good and good-value restaurants in the capital. Maio's treasures are small and hard to find for the visitor, yet it remains an island with its own considerable charm.

SUGGESTED ITINERARY AND NUMBER OF DAYS There is little point in visiting Maio if your goal is to tick off the sights of Cabo Verde. There's so little here, but combining it with a trip to Santiago could be the perfect combination of islands: Santiago for hiking and mountains, a strong African flavour and a bustling capital city, and Maio for the old Cabo Verde, peace and tranquillity, beautiful empty beaches and a selection of reasonable restaurants. A day to visit the town and a day to undertake an island tour will be enough for most. Beyond that, Maio is really a place to flee to for a quiet retreat, a place with few distractions or competing demands. It's a destination for wandering and musing among the dunes and beaches. This could take half a day to a lifetime.

BACKGROUND INFORMATION

HISTORY Maio's one resource is its prolific salt and for this reason it was a bustling island from the late 16th century until the 19th. In a good year it exported 11,000 tonnes. Before this treasure was discovered, Maio was a grazing ground for cattle and goats, producing 4,000 head a year at its peak. But soon the fragile vegetation was eaten and there was little left to sell but salt and lime.

It was the English who commandeered the salt production because the Portuguese never had much interest in Maio. One Englishman even made a profit by loading salt at Maio and bartering it at Santiago. The salt was shovelled into sacks at the salt lake, fastened to donkeys and carried to the beach where it was loaded into boats specially designed to cope with the heavy swells in the bay. They would travel out to the boats belonging to the big ships which would themselves be anchored away from the shore.

The English ships, each laden with about 200 tonnes of salt, would leave for Newfoundland to pick up cod, salt it, and take it to Europe. Other ships took salt on journeys between Europe and the West Indies and between America and Africa. Maio's neat, tiny fort was built by English sailors left behind by Sir Francis Drake in 1588.

All through the 17th century, about 80 English ships a year called at Maio for salt; there was usually a battleship standing by to guard English interests. The Maio people were paid with some money but also with old clothes and food. It is said their houses were full of English ornaments.

By the 19th century, the principal market for salt switched to Brazil, where thousands of tonnes were sent annually. That business was killed when Brazil introduced protective tariffs at the end of the 19th century.

Maio did not escape plunder or hardship. In 1818, a pirate ship from Baltimore sacked the port, and a South American ship sacked it in 1827. In the 20th century, there were repeated droughts and emigrations.

MAIO TODAY Farming and fishing occupy some people, but still probably less than 20% of the population. The people use their now plentiful wood to turn to charcoal in underground ovens for export to other islands. There are large lime reserves

FESTIVALS ON MAIO

The religious festival of Santa Cruz on 3 May, and the saints' days in June, are the biggest celebrations. There is a music festival at the beginning of September.

2 February	Nossa Sra do Rosário
19 March	São José (Calheta)
3 May	Santa Cruz (Maio)
13 June	Santo António (Santo António)
24 June	São João (Ribeira de João)
29 June	São Pedro (Pedro Vaz)
26 July	Santa Ana (Morrinho)
1st week September	Music festival (Cidade do Porto Inglés)

MAIO BIODIVERSITY FOUNDATION (FUNDAÇÃO MAIO BIODIVERSIDADE; FMB)

With thanks to Elise Dierickx and Arnau Teixidor

Energising the sleepy island of Maio, FMB is an NGO committed to both avian and marine conservation and combining that with initiatives in sustainable tourism development. This last aspect of their activities involves bringing visitors and local Cabo Verdeans closer together through a fledgling homestay project.

FMB works closely with the University of Bath in the UK, among other institutions, and uses the services of volunteers from various countries to monitor bird and marine species. Very importantly, FMB is a Cabo Verdean NGO and locals are actively involved, with some engaged in monitoring birds such as the Kentish plover or the cream-coloured courser, while others are employed during the turtle-nesting season to patrol the beaches against those hunting turtle meat.

With the homestays, the intention is to give visitors the opportunity to experience life with a Cabo Verdean family for a night or two, and maybe share some of their everyday activities. If you've never fed chickens and ducks, then this could be your chance; if your host happens to be a fisherman, you would be welcome to join him. For open-minded guests, sharing the same roof and meals with Cabo Verdeans is a rewarding experience, one which may alter your perceptions of the local lifestyle. As you're feeding your host's chickens at six in the morning, you may be surprised to see the large number of young men weeding and planting in the neighbouring fields. Maybe those are the same young men that you've seen apparently 'lounging around' in the village centre at lunchtimes; perhaps they've just finished working the land before the heat of the day kicks in.

For details of volunteering opportunities or how you can help or donate, join a walk to see nesting turtles or to organise a homestay, see the FMB website (w fmb-maio.org).

---

and there is some gypsum. A co-operative, launched in 2003, gathers a little salt from the salina at Porto Inglés. Although several low-key holiday complexes have successfully opened since the 2010s, sadly it is the half-built Salinas Beach resort that dominates the western part of the capital from the air, giving the entirely false impression of a thriving beach complex. The premature publicity of the early 2010s promised a hotel, apartments, restaurants, shops and even a golf course. Instead, there is a modern ghost town, perhaps in future destined to become an unusual tourist attraction in its own right.

But for some, the failure of the project is welcome, keeping Maio as the peaceful place it always has been, its character unchanged. A few accommodation options have presented themselves in Calheta – which is good for swimming – and Morro. Initiatives are underway to protect the avian and marine biodiversity. The island has potential; the question is simply how it will be realised.

GEOGRAPHY Maio, like the other islands, is an old volcano that has slowly been eroded by the wind. But Maio is unusual because beneath the volcano that welled up out of the ocean floor was ocean sediment that ballooned up behind it. Subsequent erosion of the volcanic rock has exposed vast amounts of marine sediments that are 190 million years old, which is why some texts refer to it as the oldest island.

Maio is small, at 268km^2, with a population of about 6,000. It lies 25km to the east of Santiago, visible across the ocean. Its terrain is similar to Sal and Boavista with one big difference: it has been heavily reforested in parts, almost exclusively with acacias, which can survive for years without rainfall. The highest peak is Monte Penoso at 437m. There are saltpans in the southwest and northwest and there is more fertile, agricultural land in the east.

FLORA AND FAUNA Terras Salgadas, Casas Velhas, Lagoa Cimidor and Praia de Morro are natural reserves. Barreiro e Figueira is a natural park and the Salina

A BIRD'S-EYE VIEW OF LOVE

Some birds stay faithful for life, some have a roving eye – and it was always thought that this varied according to their species. Now researchers have discovered that even within the same species you get different types of behaviour. Just as with humans, some look after their kids and some are too busy elsewhere. What intrigues scientists is what makes one bird's attitude to its eggs or chicks so different from the next. 'The classic situation is who (mother or father) should go to the disco and who should provide care for the young,' says Tamas Szekely, Professor of Biodiversity at the University of Bath, UK. 'If they both go to the disco then the babies die.'

Maio may be the place to answer this question because it is home to the Kentish plover (*Charadrius alexandrins*), the object of this research. Unlike elsewhere in the world, the Kentish plover stays in Maio all year round. Wander down to the salinas outside the *vila* and you might find Szekely or one of his students or volunteers manning their mobile hide, documenting behaviour, ringing birds, counting nests and taking genetic samples.

So far, it appears that the birds are remarkably good at varying their behaviour depending on what's going on around them. In Saudi Arabia, where they lay their eggs in the heat of the desert, it takes two parents to run the show: one to sit on the eggs to keep them cool and the other to fetch food. In less demanding environments like Maio two parents may not be so vital – might this liberate one, and if so is it mum or dad who gets to play around? Even more intriguingly, it looks as if even one individual bird may behave differently from one relationship to another. 'If you are a good mother in one family it doesn't mean you will be a good mother in a different family,' says Szekely.

Kentish plovers nest on the ground and start to breed after the annual rains (usually from September onwards). This is when Szekely and his team start their work. In addition to the plovers, the salina harbours breeding populations of cream-coloured courser (*Cursorius cursor exsul*) and the greater hoopoe lark (*Alaemon alaudipes*). It also hosts migratory waders and waterbirds and easy sightings could include black-winged stilt (*Himantopus himantopus*) and sanderling (*Calidris alba*). The common kestrel (*Falco tinniculus*) is the island's most common bird of prey. Protection of the salina is an issue, because both the research and the habitat were briefly threatened by the massive Salinas construction site right on the edge of the salina. The future of the two seem inextricably interlinked.

do Porto Inglês, Monte Penoso, Monte Branco and Monte de Santo António are protected landscapes. A marine reserve stretches east of Praia Preta. For the natural history of Maio's great salina, see page 216.

Turtles Maio has the second-largest nesting population of loggerhead turtles (*Caretta caretta*) in the archipelago. Its long sandy beaches and limited amount of development have, in the past, made it an ideal habitat. Their survival, as elsewhere in Cabo Verde, is threatened by the hunting of females for food, nest poaching and new beachfront development. There are programmes for their protection and in season it may be possible to take a guided walk to see them nesting. Ask around for information when you are there.

SAFETY Maio boasts that it is crime-free. Many northern beaches are unsafe for swimming, as is Praia Preta to the south of the capital. There is a strong current at Ponta Preta which has claimed the lives of the unsuspecting. Follow the advice, and more importantly, the actions of the locals.

GETTING THERE AND AWAY

BY AIR There's a 10-minute Cabo Verde Airlines flight from Praia, the frequency of which varies enormously. At the time of writing, this was three times a week. Even more than the other islands, it is vital when travelling to and from Maio to check and recheck that your flight has not been rescheduled. Any sudden shortage of aircraft seems to target Maio first, before it impacts on the other more-frequented islands. *Hiaces* wait at the airport and can be chartered as taxis for the 5-minute trip to town. It is easy enough to walk the few kilometres into the centre with a modest backpack, though tiring if laden with luggage. Facing the sea, the town can be seen to the left. Take the only road, towards the sea, and turn left at the T-junction. Pass the saltpans and in about 40 minutes you are in town. On departure, ask your hotel to organise transport back to the airport.

BY FERRY CV Interilhas (w cvinterilhas.cv) operates a service direct from Santiago. At the time of writing, there were two services per week. With flights around €35 each way, and ferries 2,300$, the price difference isn't enough to make up for the ferry's lack of comfort, frequency or reliability – but sometimes the schedule may be more convenient.

BY YACHT There is good anchorage in the rocky, sandy bay in front of the *vila*, but it can be difficult to disembark on the pier on account of the big swell. (After a few scary landings in Maio, the old fast ferries gave up their proposed route to the island, never – thus far – to return.)

Clear all landing formalities with the police (page 216) on arrival.

GETTING AROUND

BY PUBLIC TRANSPORT It is just about possible to do a circuit of the entire island in a day by picking up *alugueres* and hitching. But there is always the small chance of being left stranded, and the desire not to end up in this situation will prevent you from exploring off the main road, especially given the lack of accommodation options. Hitchhiking is an option and if there is passing traffic it will normally stop for you.

Tumbling cliffs, crashing Atlantic waves and villages frozen in time draw hikers to this trail on Santo Antão's north coast PAGE 328
above (CL/S)

The fluid, undulating rock formations of Carbeirinho on São Nicolau are considered one of the country's 'seven wonders' PAGE 354
below left (H/S)

The 'Blue Eye' at Buracona on Sal is an azure underground pool connected to the sea by a tunnel PAGE 127
below right (LK/S)

above (F/S) Maio, the 'forgotten island', is a quiet, easygoing retreat with beautiful beaches and simple, small hotels PAGE 205

below (G/S) Despite Boavista's volcanic origins, much of the island's interior is now flat and reduced to desert PAGE 134

Spot a red-billed tropicbird (*Phaethon aethereus*) on the rugged coast of Santiago PAGE 7 above left (DT/S)

Each spring, humpback whales travel to the sheltered waters around Boavista, Sal and Maio to breed PAGE 9 above right (AMW/S)

The emblematic *dragoeiro*, or dragon tree, is one of Cabo Verde's few surviving endemic plants PAGE 5 right (MH)

The endangered Cape Verde shearwater (*Calonectris edwardsii*) is thriving on the uninhabited island of Raso PAGE 7 below left (K/D)

The striking grey-headed kingfisher (*Halcyon leucocephala*), known locally as *passarinha*, is considered the national bird PAGE 7 below right (GG/S)

above left (MS) On Maio, fishing is often a family affair, with children helping out after school PAGE 205

above right (FB/S) Santo Antão has the largest cultivated area of any of the islands, its slopes lined with steep terraced plots PAGE 303

below (P/S) From impromptu street performances such as this scene in Mindelo, to heaving international festivals, music is an integral part of Cabo Verdean life and identity PAGE 43

Locals make good use of the many paths that criss-cross the beautiful Serra Malagueta on Santiago island PAGE 192

above (MH)

Cabo Verde has produced some of the world's most revered and innovative kitesurfers, many of whom honed their craft at Sal's Ponta Preta break PAGE 56

right (MM)

Bustling Assomada, in Santiago's mountainous interior, hosts what is arguably the country's most vibrant and authentic market PAGE 188

below (P/D)

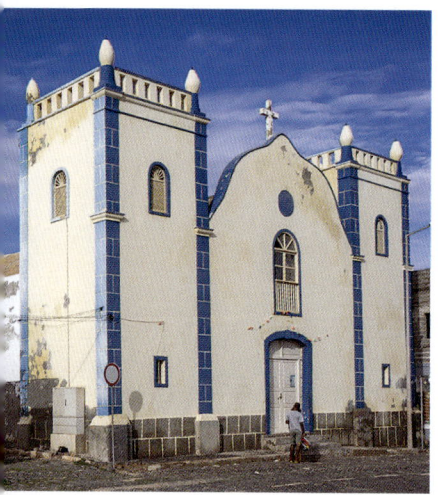

above (GJ/S) Surrounded by lush, fertile *ribeiras*, Santiago's Cidade Velha was Cabo Verde's first settlement; at its centre, pretty Rua Banana is considered the oldest surviving Portuguese-built street in the tropics PAGE 182

left (S/S) The carefully renovated church of Santa Isabel, in Sal Rei on Boavista, adds colour to the town's main square PAGE 145

below (MM) A mural commemorates Cabo Verdean revolutionary Amílcar Cabral on a historical house in Praia's original heart, Platô PAGE 25

A national collection of art and craft is displayed in a restored 19th-century villa and an architecturally striking contemporary wing at Mindelo's Centro Nacional de Arte, Artesanato e Design (CNAD) **PAGE 292**

above (GJ/S)

SANTA CRUZ
FEEL THE RHYTHM, TASTE THE FLAVOUR

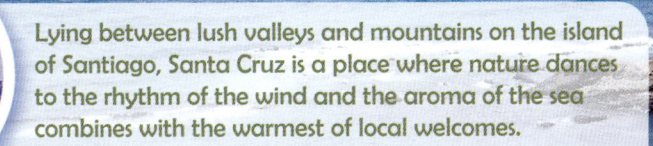

Lying between lush valleys and mountains on the island of Santiago, Santa Cruz is a place where nature dances to the rhythm of the wind and the aroma of the sea combines with the warmest of local welcomes.

Its cuisine is rich with fruits from the fertile land and fish from the sea, while the funaná echoes in the alleys and squares. Relax on the beach, enjoy a festival, strike out along mountain trails and explore a landscape that's perfect for ecotourism and adventure tourism.

Santa Cruz will embrace you when you arrive and create memories to cherish when you leave.

Discover Santa Cruz. www.cmscz.cv

MORABEZA
Since 1967

Where tradition meets hospitality

88 Rooms & 33 Suites, Beach Club, 3 Bars, 3 Restaurants, 3 Pools, 2 Tennis Courts, Pétanque, Fitness Trail, Archery, Mini Golf, Fitness Room, Game Room, Trimaran Excursions, Diving Club, Jet Ski Club, Kite & Wing Centre, Car Rental, Massage, and Boutique.

Hotel Morabeza, Santa Maria, Sal - Cabo Verde
info@hotelmorabeza.com I +238 242 10 20
www.hotelmorabeza.com

Several of the good beaches lie within walking distance either of the *vila* or of Figueira da Horta, which is easy to reach by *aluguer*. For other sights take a chance, hire transport, or ask your hotel owner to come and pick you up late in the day, if they have a car.

Alugueres depart from villages such as Ribeira do João and Alcatraz very early in the morning to come to the *vila*. From the little square northeast of the post office, they return to Barreiro at around 11.00, Figueira, Alcatraz and Ribeira do João around midday, coming back again from Figueira and Barreiro an hour later. For Morrinho, they leave the capital mainly between 08.00 and 10.00, from the stop on Avenida Amílcar Cabral near the fish market. One-way fares are 150–200$.

BY CAR Find a 4x4 – a minibus or car will substantially restrict where you can go. A vehicle can be rented for about 6,000$ a day, and one day is usually enough. A car plus driver will cost a little more – about 7,500$, and you probably should tip, if they'll let you. Distances are short, but your average speed will be slow: you'll be driving on cobbles most of the way. Try **MaioCar** (Av Amílcar Cabral; m 995 9681; ⊕ 08.00–13.00 & 14.00–17.00 Mon–Fri, 08.00–noon Sat).

BY BICYCLE A great way to see Maio is by bicycle, but you need to be able to ride the cobbles. There are currently no formal bike hire places on Maio but many apartment and villa rentals have bikes for guests, including A Caminhada and Wave Maze, while Residêncial Porto Inglês offers e-trikes. Check when booking what might be on offer. Take several litres of water and remember that every village has a shop somewhere, often indistinguishable from a private home – so ask.

WHERE TO STAY AND EAT

There is a growing assortment of apartments and condominiums in the *vila*, some of which are very pleasant, as well as a few small hotels or *pensões*. There is little choice outside the capital, though, apart from in Calheta. Likewise, restaurants are clustered in town, with one also popping up overlooking the beach at its very southern outskirts, along with a couple of options in Calheta. Italian dishes are often the default, as is seafood.

EXCURSIONS AND TOUR OPERATORS

Maio is a place for resting and taking early-morning walks along the beaches and around the saltpans. Most of the accommodation options offer a simple round-island excursion and will have preferred drivers, while vista verde in Praia (page 168) may be able to help you out with transport hiccups.

ACTIVITIES

HIKING Maio is not really the island for hiking but it is still possible to go for a couple of pleasant walks. In particular, you can head out from Morro towards Monte Batalha or try the more challenging walk to the top of Monte Penoso for which you almost certainly need a guide. Ask around in the *vila* for more information when you arrive.

BEACHES Maio has many accessible beaches, some of them breathtakingly deserted and remote. Near the *vila* are Ponta Preta and the delightfully named

Praia de Bicxe Rotcha, but caution is required due to a powerful tow: take your cue from the locals. Up the west coast it is sandy way past Morro until just before Calheta. Calheta itself has probably the best accessible beach for swimming, one that slopes gently and is usually safe. The beautiful half-moon-shaped Santana Beach, northwest of Morrinho, is often deserted. Porto Cais, directly west of Morrinho, is a remote and beautiful beach. You will make your own enchanting and personal discoveries.

CAMPING If you are self-sufficient you will find many quiet places to pitch a tent. You can arrange with an *aluguer* driver to be dropped off and, more importantly, collected.

DIVING French-run, friendly dive operation **AAA Maio** (m 951 8102; e maio. plongee@laposte.net; ⏰ year-round), offers one-on-one discovery dives for €70, experience dives for €65 and equipment rental from €20.

KAYAKING/SUP/WINDSURFING There are currently no hire facilities, but ask around.

SURFING There is exceptional surfing at Praia de Ponta Preta and Calheta, but currently no formal board hire. Ask at Wave Maze (page 215) for rental possibilities and for tips on breaks and conditions.

WHALE-WATCHING Winter and spring are the times when humpback whales pass by with their newborn calves. Ask around if there are any boats that will take you to see them – you may even be lucky enough to see them from the shore.

FISHING Big Game Maio (m 971 0593; e biggamemaio@gmail.com) organises both big-game fishing and options closer to shore.

A day trip for up to six passengers will cost around €600, depending on what type of fishing you fancy; furthest from shore, fishing for marlin may cost more.

Wave Maze (page 215) can arrange hire of a Boston Whaler for up to eight people.

QUAD-BIKE RENTAL Big Game Maio (page 215) can organise rentals. Quad bikes are not allowed on any beaches in Cabo Verde. Expect to pay around €50 per day.

CIDADE DO PORTO INGLÉS (VILA DO MAIO)

Now officially renamed Cidade do Porto Inglés – it was previously known as Vila do Maio – and bestowed with city status, the capital has a tranquil town centre. It features a large town square endowed with extra drama because it rises up a small but steep hill to a huge, white neo-Baroque church, built in 1872. As the principal streets reach the edge of town, the *vila* becomes a little more scruffy with half-built construction projects.

At the southern edge of town is a pretty 18th-century fort, now restored and including some cannons. A nearby local may offer to get the key and let you in, but you can see as much from outside the locked gate. In front of the town stretches the long and wide expanse of pristine white sand of Praia de Bicxe Rotcha, with a couple of beach bars.

WHERE TO STAY *Map, below*

There are a few mid-range options in the town centre, including Big Game Maio and Flashback Hostel, but most travellers choose to stay in apartment and villa complexes such as Stella Maris (its beachfront location and infinity pool make it by far the most popular choice) or Wave Maze. These can be booked direct or via various holiday rental sites, travel agents or Airbnb. The latter also lists a couple of good private room options, mostly hosted by expat families. A social project

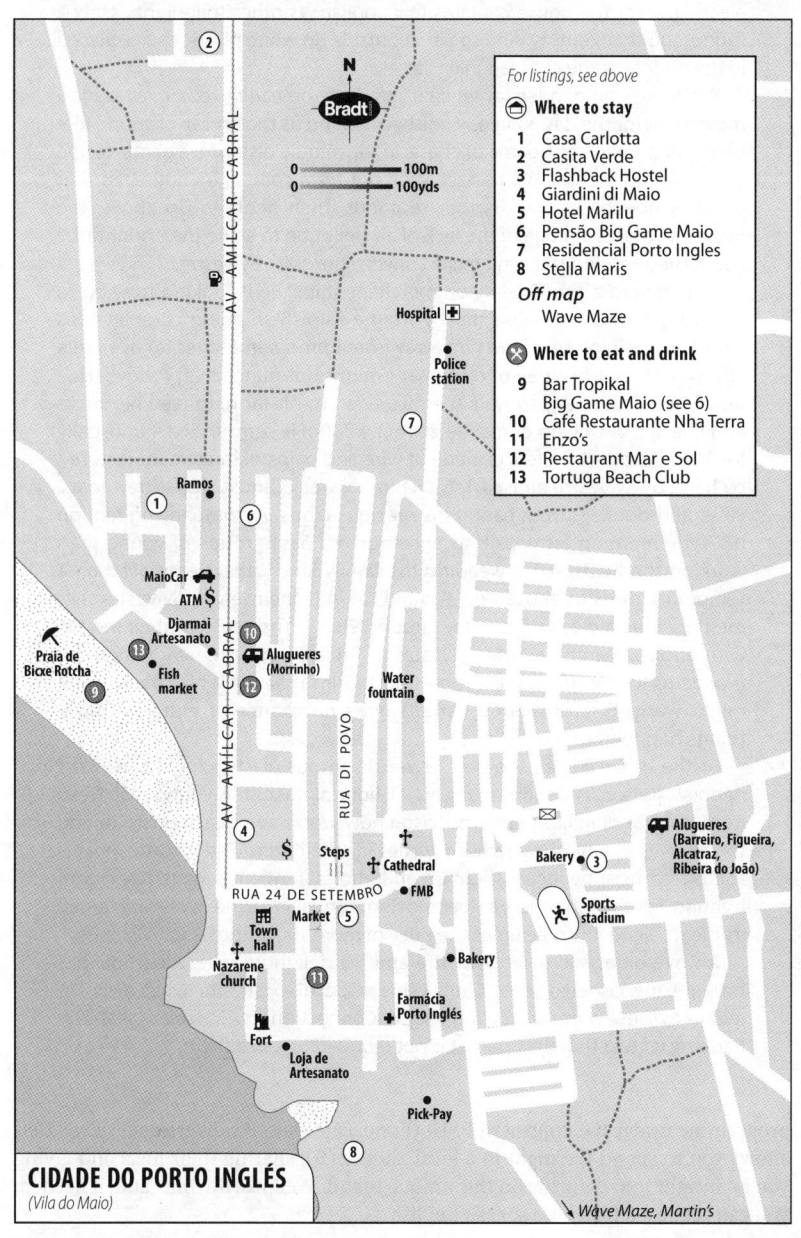

CIDADE DO PORTO INGLÉS
(Vila do Maio)

For listings, see above

Where to stay
1. Casa Carlotta
2. Casita Verde
3. Flashback Hostel
4. Giardini di Maio
5. Hotel Marilu
6. Pensão Big Game Maio
7. Residencial Porto Ingles
8. Stella Maris

Off map
Wave Maze

Where to eat and drink
9. Bar Tropikal
    Big Game Maio (see 6)
10. Café Restaurante Nha Terra
11. Enzo's
12. Restaurant Mar e Sol
13. Tortuga Beach Club

A HOMESTAY ON MAIO   *Murray Stewart*

'No connections are available,' my computer is telling me, as I search for non-existent Wi-Fi in the village of Barreiro, on peaceful Maio island.

A few minutes later, the electricity goes off, for the second time that evening and it won't be coming back. *'Não tem luz,'* says Albertina ('There is no light') and her choice of words provides some insight. Not 'there is no electricity', for the house contains few appliances other than lights. Only a fridge, and that's empty. And so we sit outside on white plastic chairs, placed in the middle of the cobbled main street.

But there's no danger, for while it may only be early evening, all vehicle movement for the day is already finished. Behind us the tip-tap of young feet on cobbles indicates a game of chase; in the middle distance, a gentle fusion of guitar and accordion squeezes itself out from someone's house. Further afield, a dog barks and another responds, then another. Up above, the heavens take advantage of the lack of air pollution to shine their brightest. I count the shooting stars and make conversation with Sylvestre.

Now retired after 30 years on merchant ships, he is looking forward to receiving his pension, due shortly from a Danish shipping company. His career on the high seas kept him away from home, sometimes for five years at a stretch. But his idea of retirement might not match everybody's. He's up at 06.00 every day to walk the mile or so to his farm, to feed his ducks and chickens. His land of maybe 200m by 200m is surrounded – unusually for Maio island – by a fence, made of wire and painstakingly manufactured by hand by Sylvestre himself. It took him six weeks and it stops stray goats, cows and donkeys from eating his precious crops. Accompanying him on his early-morning farm visit, to my surprise I pass groups of young men working the fields, some weeding the family land, others employed on a temporary basis by those now too old to do it themselves. Sylvestre tells me they are paid 1,000$ per day (around €8.50). They sustain their morale with endless banter, asking Sylvestre to bring them some early-morning *grogue* to fortify them and suggesting to him that 'his white friend' (me) might want to lend them a hand. There's no chance of either of those things happening.

At the other end of the day, as we sit on our plastic chairs, Sylvestre's nephew, Kelson, is departing for his 11-hour nightshift. A young man fresh from his year of military service, Kelson now works as a beach guard during the months in which loggerhead turtles lay their eggs. Sadly, turtle meat is still prized here by local fishermen and efforts are being made to prevent hunting. For the fishermen, a slow-moving, egg-laying turtle is an easy target, its meat selling for three times the price of more-difficult-to-catch fish.

An overnight stay with Sylvestre and his delightful wife, Albertina, has brought me close to some Cabo Verdeans, a glimpse into what daily life means to these warm and giving people. Connections *are* indeed available in Barreiro; it's just that the internet is not required to make them.

---

programme under the control of FMB (Fundação Maio Biodiversidade; page 208) allows you to spend the night in a local's house (**$**), sharing their meal and giving you an insight into daily life on this unique island. Well worthwhile: and, if needed, you can request a host who speaks English.

Hotels and *pensões*

Casa Carlotta (9 rooms) Just up from Praia de Bicxe Rotcha; w caboverdegreen.com. Sweetly decorated rooms with pops of colour, spread over 2 floors. Try to book an upper room, as they are larger, lighter & more private. There are also a couple of apts. with fridges & basic kitchenettes. B/fast can be taken in a nearby café. Staff are famously kind & happy to accommodate early & late check-ins/-outs if possible. $$

Casita Verde (2 rooms) 5mins' walk along the airport road; m 996 0633; e info@casita-verde.de. Private, German-owned house. Comfortable rooms are both en suite with hot water, fan, mosquito net & fridge. Sit on the shaded terrace admiring the garden & the sea view. Excursions offered. $$

Giardini di Maio (5 rooms) Av Amílcar Cabral; 255 1199; e giardinidimaio@gmail.com. Friendly Italian host, rooftop terrace facing the ocean, pleasant courtyard. Restaurant is for guests only. Free airport transfer. $$

Hotel Marilu (10 rooms, 2 suites) Rua 24 de Setembro; 255 1198; e mariluhotel_cv@hotmail.com. Central location & friendly staff. Rooms have balconies, AC & TV, & a colourful charm. Can occasionally be noisy. $$

Pensão Big Game Maio (10 rooms) Av Amílcar Cabral; m 971 0593; w biggamemaio.com. A modernised place with a bright, maritime theme. All rooms have private bath, terrace & balcony, & TV. A good choice at this price. $$

Residêncial Porto Inglês (7 rooms) 202 Rua di Povo; 255 1698; e rportoingles@gmail.com. An orange-striped building just northeast of the centre, this has some decent rooms with AC. Try for an upper-floor room. Wi-Fi in the lounge area only. $$

Flashback Hostel (2 twin rooms, 1 4-bed mixed dorm, 1 6-bed female dorm) m 334 2254; e flashbackhostels@gmail.com; w flashbackhostels.com. A 5-min walk from the beach, in a large candy-pink building. New in 2024, this gently 80s-themed place is the smart, fun hostel Maio needed. Fully equipped kitchen, friendly communal areas & welcoming staff. All rooms have fans & mosquito nets. Bunks have individual sockets & lamps, & some have privacy curtains. $

Apartments

Stella Maris On the beach, south of town; w stella-maris-maio.com. Large gated apartment complex with cliffside pool & a good variety of simple, comfortable apartments. B/fast can be included in some deals. Can be booked via the contact form on the website or via various other booking sites. $$$

Wave Maze m 982 3472; e booking@wavemaze.com; w wavemaze.com. Located on the southern edge of town, around 10 mins' walk to the beach at Ponta Preta. Simple, atmospheric apartments for 2 to 4 people spread over a few villas. Has bicycles and scooters for hire. $$

✘ WHERE TO EAT AND DRINK *Map, page 213, unless otherwise stated*

For a small, unfrequented island, Maio has some very decent restaurants, many of them Italian. A peculiarity of the town is a number of unmarked Senegalese establishments which informally serve meals at lunchtime. Usually just comprising a kitchen and a table or two, these serve tasty traditional West African dishes based on chicken and fish, usually with tamarind rice, and are very cheap. They come and go: ask around or go for a hungry wander and sniff one out.

Big Game Maio At Pensão Big Game Maio (see above); m 971 0593; ⊕ 07.30–15.00 & 18.00–23.00 daily. A highly regarded Italian restaurant, popular with expats. Fish, meat, pizza & pasta dishes. Plus a lauded tiramisu. $$$

Martin's [map, page 206] South of the centre, overlooking the beach at Ponta Preta; m 592 7046; ⊕ 08.00–20.00 daily. Great-value snacks, starters & fish plates such as catch of the day cooked in coconut milk with sweet potato purée.

Other seafood & meat dishes on offer at higher prices. Fabulous location for escaping the midday heat after a swim or for scenic sunset drinks. Friendly service. $$–$$$

Bar Tropikal On the main beach; m 597 7268; ⊕ 08.30–23.00 Tue–Sat. This casual bar is popular for its prime beach location. Specialities are *carpaccios* & *caipirinhas* at sunset. It also serves omelettes, hamburgers, *cachupa* & fresh fish. Live music from 21.00 on Sat. $$

Café Restaurante Nha Terra On the main street looking over the port; m 970 6391; nhaterracafemaio; ⊕ 08.30–23.00 Thu–Tue. Colourful, casual local place with good fish & chicken dishes, as well as mammoth plates of pasta, if rather forgettable pizza. Drop by early to put in your order for lobster spaghetti. Homemade cakes & pastries during the day too, plus music some nights. $$
Restaurant Mar e Sol Off Av Amílcar Cabral, north of the centre; ℡255 1455; ⊕ 09.00–22.00 daily. Well-kept, pleasant restaurant/bar that does a good grilled tuna. Reasonable prices. $$

Tortuga Beach Club On the main beach, just before Bar Tropikal; m 972 1967. Simple grills, snacks & drinks. Sunloungers, umbrellas, toilets & showers plus Wi-Fi mean you can settle in. $$
Enzo's Inside the market hall; ⊕ 07.00–16.00 daily. Run by an amiable Italian, the place to run to if you've had enough fresh fish. Espresso coffee & homemade quince-jam-topped muffins in the mornings, then authentic & inexpensive pizza the rest of the day, all on high stools overlooking the kitchen. Take-away too. $

ENTERTAINMENT AND NIGHTLIFE Not too much happens outside of festival times, but **Bar Tropikal** on the *vila*'s main beach (page 215) often has Saturday night music from around 21.00, or try **Café Restaurante Nha Terra** (see above).

SHOPPING Whether the market has produce depends on when the last boat arrived from Praia, but there are several **food shops**: Pick-Pay (close to Stella Maris) and Ramos (on the way to the airport) are the largest and probably have the best choice. There are a number of unmarked bakeries; you could ask at your hotel for their preferred choice, but they are not hard to spot. The fish market is situated at the start of the main beach and the best time to buy fresh fish is when the boats return, between 11.00 and midday.

For souvenirs, **Loja de Artesanato** (⊕ 09.00–noon & 14.00–17.00 Mon–Sat), next to the fort, features pottery, artwork and figurines made from banana leaves, among other things. **Djarmai Artesanato** (⊕ 09.30–18.00 Mon–Sat), in the pink building just where Avenida Amílcar Cabral hits the beach, also has crafts made from driftwood, as well as hats and totes.

OTHER PRACTICALITIES There are no Cabo Verde Airlines or CV Interilhas offices in town. For tickets, try Loja de Artesanato (see above). There's a choice of two **banks**, both with ATMs and Western Union: one on the square and one close to the cathedral (Rua Principal; ⊕ 08.00–15.00 Mon–Fri).

There is a fairly modern, if basic, **hospital** (℡255 1130), just outside the centre, to the northwest and a **pharmacy** (Farmácia Porto Inglés; m 974 4066) in the south of the town.

The **police** station (℡255 113) is now housed in a new HQ near the hospital. The **post office** (⊕ 08.00–noon & 14.00–18.00 Mon–Fri) is just north of the square on the road heading east of town.

WHAT TO SEE AND DO
Salinas do Porto Inglés This extraordinary lake of salt is, at 5km long and 1.5km wide, the largest salina in Cabo Verde, stretching almost as far as the village of Morro. It no longer produces the vast supplies it once did, but it is a poetic reminder of Maio's historical significance and thus an island treasure.

The salina is still in use: from April to June, endless little conical piles of salt appear around it as local women work to make salt for the local market – just 1.5 tonnes a year. Inside the small co-operative building at the salina's southern end, women sort the salt by hand before it is ground and packed. The United Nations funds the operation, providing local women with employment.

> **PROTECTING THE SHARKS FROM THE SHARKS?** *Murray Stewart*
>
> Sharks are not prone to attracting good publicity: they usually only make the news when they choose someone's leg for dinner. But in Cabo Verde, it's far more likely that they will end up as someone's dinner – someone abroad, that is. According to Tommy Melo of environmental organisation Biosfera I, sharks are in danger of disappearing from Cabo Verdean waters. Under an agreement with the European Union, up to 75 boats from the EU were allowed to fish those Cabo Verdean waters for tuna, but if other species were caught as a 'by-catch' (ie: incidentally), then that was permitted, too. And as the fishing method is trawling, it is no wonder that other species are regularly netted.
>
> What was surprising is that in one year, more than 12,000 tonnes of shark were caught…and only 600 tonnes of tuna, according to Melo, a man with a wise old head on his young shoulders. Ignoring the value of the shark meat, the annual revenues to the Europeans for just the fins of the sharks – a popular ingredient in some cultures' soup – are estimated at a staggering €200 million. And the annual price paid by the EU for the right to fish? Just €435,000.
>
> Recognising the mismatch between the tuna catch and the shark catch, an agreement is now in place, but it specifically *permits* the catching of sharks, so the situation has deteriorated. Although certain species of shark are protected in theory, in practice what is actually caught is not monitored.
>
> The Cabo Verde government are aware of the issue, but the threat if they don't sign up to such agreements is that Cabo Verde fish exports will not be given access to the lucrative EU market. In the cut-throat pool of international negotiations, it seems that 'big fish eats little fish', while it seems that from the ocean around Cabo Verde, those same big fish eat the big fish (the sharks) – and profit from it handsomely, as well.

Between the pans and the sea is a raised beach over which the seawater rises during spring tides and at times of high swell. Seawater also infiltrates underground, while rainwater trickles in from mainland streams between August and October. For the rest of the time the intense heat, wind and lack of shade allow the water to evaporate, leaving crusts of salt behind.

But the salina is not just Maio's biggest piece of heritage and a source of local income – it has important natural history as well. As a wetland it is visited by migrant waders. Its situation, surrounded by dunes and desert, make it an important breeding and feeding habitat for a wide variety of birds, including the cream-coloured courser (*Cursorius cursor exsul*) and the Kentish plover (*Charadrius alexandrinus*; page 209). Alexander's kestrel (*Falco alexandrii*) and the Iago sparrow (*Passer iagoensis*) are the two endemic birds to be found in the salina. Loggerhead turtles (*Caretta caretta*) nest here, though in smaller numbers than in Boavista.

The salina and its inhabitants face several threats. Firstly, sand extraction for building on both Maio and Santiago threatens to remove the barrier between the salina and the sea. Secondly, it was threatened by burgeoning tourist ambitions – though, as it is in itself a tourist attraction, one would assume that the salina will eventually be ring-fenced rather than destroyed and the town hall is developing a conservation plan.

Ponta Preta From the *vila* walk east along the coast, across the refuse tips and past the cemetery on the left – after about 15 minutes there is a small, pretty bay.

A further 30 minutes will take you to the beach at Ponta Preta. Ask in town for further directions. This beach is not safe for swimming, due to a strong current. Behind the beach lies one of the island's two desalination plants, which use sea water and the process of reverse osmosis to provide water for the entire island.

OTHER PLACES TO VISIT

MORRO Morro is a small, everyday village but its beach is well regarded. In common with many beaches in Cabo Verde, it fluctuates in size with the seasons' changing currents; in winter about 3m depth of sand vanishes, and the sea as a result comes many metres further in. It's usually safe for swimming here apart from the odd day when the waves come from the south. It is quite a long walk to the beach from the village, so make sure that you ask to be dropped off at the beach.

There is a 2-hour walk up the nearby hill with good views at the top and a walk along the stunning beach to Calheta.

Where to stay and eat *Map, page 206*
Although Morro has been earmarked for tourist development, at the time of writing there are still only a handful of places to stay, and few places to eat beyond the accommodation options. There is a surprisingly large supermarket in the settlement, though, along with a smaller shop and a bar hidden away behind the village's water fountain.

A Caminhada (4 apts) On the outskirts of the village; m 987 8890; w maio-cap-vert.net. A French-owned *chambre d'hôte*; all meals can be catered by request. Simple, well-cared-for bungalows with kitchenettes & outdoor space. Pool & free bike rental. Happy to arrange anything you need, from airport pick-ups to fishing trips. **$$**

Barracudamaio Apartments (2 apts) Boca de Morro; m 972 5213; e monachrisbarracuda@gmail.com. A couple of well-fitted apartments, with kitchen, fan, Wi-Fi, etc, just outside Morro village. Also a villa near the *vila*. Will collect from the airport & can organise fishing trips with locals. **$$**

Villa Maris (21 studios & apts) Beachfront; m 595 7968; villamarisecolodge. Large, low-slung apt complex right on the beach. Make sure you upgrade to a sea-facing option, though. Best for the self-sufficient: while the manager & staff are friendly & eager to please, there's not much in the way of guest interaction or help with excursions or transport. On-site restaurant & basic kitchenettes. **$$**

Casa Blanca Behind the village water fountain; m 956 4149; 07.00–midnight daily. Also known as Mariama's, in reference to the owner & cook. Try her 'pasta africana', a spiced, herbed vegetable spaghetti that showcases the flavours of her Gambian roots. Attached is the shop Loja Bert. **$$**

CALHETA About 3km north of Morro is Calheta, divided into the inland town which is clustered around the main road, and the pretty fishing village, reached by turning left off the main road towards the sea. It is only 5 minutes' walk between the two. Unusually for Cabo Verde, the small fishing community here still use sailing boats, called *faluchos*, to bring in the catch, rather than the more common motorboats. You can swim here, though it is probably cleaner away from the settlement itself. Bashona (Baxona) Beach is one of the calmest on the island. Calheta is also the place to buy locally woven bags: look for the **Centro de Artesanato da Calheta**, in the (inland) town centre; its opening times are at best random, but if you ask around in the town, they'll find the key. Inside is a weaving loom and a small collection of crafts for sale.

Where to stay and eat There are few formal restaurants in Calheta. The bar **Belohorizonte** [map, page 206] on the beach has great views but can be overpriced. **Vanuza** (✆ 979 1096; **$**) in the village is, however, great value and very welcoming. There are also a few basic bars and a grocery store. You may also find someone willing to cook for you if you ask around and give advance notice. Book your food, go to the beach, come back and *voila*, dinner is served. In terms of accommodation, **Torre Sabina** [map, page 206] (2 villas; ✆ 256 1299; m 985 5585; e torresabinacv@gmail.com; w inseltraum.biz; **$$$**) is an unmissable establishment down on the seafront. Quirky, but tasteful, one 'villa' is a tower, the other is a chapel. Each sleeps two people. The price includes the use of the owner's kayaks and fishing trips are possible with the local fishermen. Meals by arrangement for residents.

MORRINHO About 4km north of Calheta is Morrinho. A couple of local men manufacture souvenirs here, though you'll see no signs to help you find them and handicrafts are now more easily sourced in the designated shop in the *vila* (page 216). Still, if you want to find them, stop on the main road in the village centre and ask for either Itelvino – who makes boxes and photo frames from *tamara* grass – or Wilbert, who uses banana leaves to make bags and other items. There is a rough track that leads from Morrinho west to Porto Cais – keep heading towards the already visible sand dunes. As you leave the village on this track, off to your left you may see a few smoking pits, covered over with arched metal covers and surrounded by upright plastic sacks. This is where charcoal is made, using the plentiful supplies of replanted acacia. Much of this charcoal is 'exported' to the other islands and is sold there for twice the price it fetches in Maio, a valuable source of income. Continuing along the track, stop your vehicle on firm ground before the track becomes too sandy, and continue on foot. Look for the dune with the footprints on it. On the other side is the beautiful beach of Porto Cais, popular with locals at the weekend and usually safe for swimming. Back at Morrinho, a further track heads northwest from town and takes you to Praia de Santana, a wild and desolate beach that remains invisible from the long road, hidden by a ridge of dunes. These endless, evocative dunes are well worth exploring. In the middle of them is a patch of palm trees which the locals think of as an oasis. It is possible to drive along the track by the beach for a few kilometres, after which it peters out: if you want to go further you must walk. Eventually, you reach Praia Real: bear in mind that northern beaches are not safe for swimming. There is a further track from the settlement of Cascabulho that leads north to Praia Real.

CASCABULHO AND PEDRO VAZ This area in the north is filled with more green and mature forest followed by a landscape that feels like an abandoned opencast mine.

> **MAIO'S MYSTERIOUS BEACH BOULDERS**
>
> On the beach at Praia Real are a series of boulders that have intrigued visitors for years because they do not originate from anywhere in the archipelago. Some thought they harboured clues to the whereabouts of Atlantis – it was once argued that the islands of Cabo Verde might be the tips of a submerged continent. The mystery was solved by a vulcanologist who demonstrated that the boulders were from Brazil and were used as ballast – thrown on to the beach when the boat was loaded with salt.

Pedro Vaz feels like it could be the end of the earth but it's not – there's another two rough kilometres to the beach, possible by car. This is perhaps the loneliest and wildest beach, enlivened occasionally by women who come to meet the returning fishermen. There is a bar and a shop in Pedro Vaz. Food may be available if you ask around and are prepared to wait. On the road north of Pedro Vaz, towards Santo António, you can see a number of low-level dams, built to slow the flow of water in the rainy season and let the water penetrate the ground.

PENOSO This is an old village where all that remains is a little white church. They hold a service here on the last Sunday of each month. Just after the church you can walk up the slopes of Monte Penoso. Even a short stroll will be rewarded with good views.

ALCATRAZ The land between Pedro Vaz and Alcatraz feels increasingly isolated – abandoned stony plains and lifeless land. Alcatraz lies 4km from Pedro Vaz – a single wide and dusty street.

FIGUEIRA DA HORTA AND RIBEIRA DE JOÃO Ribeira de João is reached by a turning to the south, east of Figueira da Horta. It's a road past pretty oases, though take care as the road is sometimes washed away in the rainy season and not repaired in a hurry. On arrival, turn right off the main street, down a footpath, and it is a 10-minute walk past the football pitch and along an enormously wide *ribeira* to find a magnificent beach with unbearably turquoise water. Look behind you – the village nestles on the top of the bare brown hills. There is a bar up there which can serve food if given notice – order it before going to the beach, eat it on your return. Ribeira de João is also home to a goat's cheese factory, set up by the EU and the local town hall.

BARREIRO AND LAGOA Barreiro is a neat settlement built on two sides of a valley. It is possible to drive from here to Lagoa and on to the beach. Locals say they walk to the beach from the *vila* (about 9km along the coast) if you want to give it a try.

7

Fogo

> It is all of it one large mountain of a good height, out of the top whereof issues Flames of Fire, yet only discerned in the Night: and then it may be seen a great way at Sea.
> William Dampier, 1683

Fogo rises steeply from the ocean, pokes through the clouds and towers above them. From the coast of Santiago or the peaks of São Nicolau it looks as forbidding as a fortress. And this is no sleeping giant. Fogo is a volcano, still active, and proved its credentials as such as recently as 2014, when a violent eruption wiped out the two villages in the Chã das Caldeiras crater. Fortunately there were no fatalities, something which perhaps explained the almost complete lack of reporting in the world's press.

To some visitors, Fogo is a menacing place: dark lava rivers from centuries of eruptions reach down its eastern side to the ocean. But it has a soft heart. Among the clods of cold lava that have covered much of the floor of the crater are fertile fields. Spilling over its northeast side are woods of eucalyptus and cool valleys in which grow coffee, fruit trees and vines.

The resilient community of people who inhabited the crater villages before the 2014 eruption returned, building new houses before the lava even finished cooling. Nothing new, perhaps; after all, after the earlier 1995 eruption, they defied government orders to relocate and soon moved back to live and farm below the smouldering peak.

HIGHLIGHTS AND LOWLIGHTS

A unique landscape, the crater with its curious villages and tough inhabitants were a true highlight of the Cabo Verde archipelago even before the 2014 eruption. And it remains so today. Different in character from the mountains of Santo Antão, Fogo is still one of the principal hiking islands, but it is also fascinating for its unique culture and natural history. Staying overnight in the Chã das Caldeiras continues to be an option, and at least visiting for lunch or dinner is a must. This area and other parts of Fogo have caves to explore if a summit doesn't suffice. For island touring and visits to the crater area, you can engage one of the established tour operators based in São Filipe, hire a vehicle, or simply use *alugueres* or taxis to ferry you around.

Apart from the simmering volcano, the second attraction of Fogo is the town of São Filipe itself, a neat and attractive island capital peppered with handsome Portuguese-era houses. It has a small but lively market, a reasonable range of decent-quality restaurants and a couple of quirky museums. The town's lively multi-night festival in late April draws many US expats home, as well as talented musicians from the diaspora and the rest of Cabo Verde.

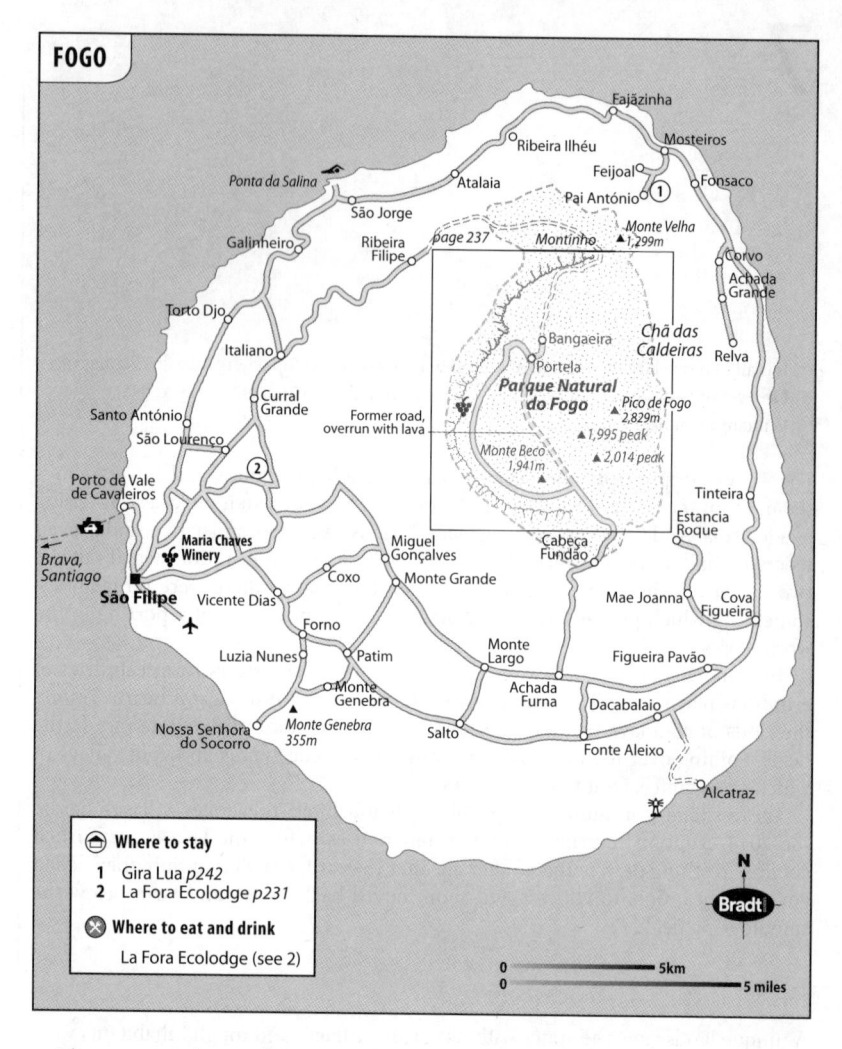

There are only modest opportunities for swimming and no white-sand beaches, but the sea pools at Ponta da Salina are appealing for keen ocean swimmers. Apart from the vague possibility of doing some fishing, there are still no organised watersports.

SUGGESTED ITINERARY AND NUMBER OF DAYS Many visitors spend two nights on Fogo, wandering round the pleasant town of São Filipe on their first afternoon, spending their one full day travelling to the crater for an ascent of the Pico, and departing the next day. The fascination of the crater and its relatively recent eruption is rewarding enough to merit a little longer than this. We suggest four nights, with at least one of them up in the crater, the rest based in São Filipe. Perhaps add in a trip to one of Fogo's lesser-visited sights such as the sea pools at Salina. On day two head to the crater and climb the Pico. Day three, another of the crater walks or lunch and a wine-tasting back down in Chã das Caldeiras. Day four, a descent to the northeast, to Mosteiros. After a night in Mosteiros an early *aluguer* or booked taxi should be able to take you back to São Filipe or to your flight. Unfortunately, day trip flights from Sal, Santiago or Boavista appear to be a thing of the past.

BACKGROUND INFORMATION

HISTORY Geologists have done intricate work to piece together the volcano's history by extrapolating from the directions of lava flows of different ages and combining that information with literary descriptions of the appearance of the volcano at different times.

Fogo erupted from the sea a few hundred thousand years ago, a single volcano reaching a mighty 3.5km high. Its walls were steep and unstable and so, sometime within the last 10,000 years, a great section in the east collapsed towards the sea – reducing the height of its walls by about 300m in one giant avalanche. After the first eruption there were numerous smaller ones, all making craters in the floor of the original large crater, which is now about 10km long and 7km wide.

Volcanoes are fertile places and Fogo's agricultural potential was harnessed from early on – it had acquired a population of 2,000 within the first 120 years of its discovery. It was the second island of the archipelago to be settled and was populated with slaves who grew cotton and developed a weaving industry – the island was famed for its *pano preta*, or deep indigo cloth (page 40). The cloth was shipped to Santiago, and because of this the island remained remote from the trans-oceanic ship trade. But it did not escape attack: the Dutch had a four-day spree there in 1655. Lisbon's response to the ensuing plea for more Portuguese settlers was to dispatch convicts. Fogo was regarded as a hardship posting and, though it is only 50km from Santiago, it was the threatened place of exile for the people of the greater island.

For much of this time the volcano in the background was growing: it appears to have put on several hundred metres between 1450 and 1750, and in the early 1600s, black clouds swathed its heights. An eruption in 1680 was savage and gave the island its name, which means 'fire' – before that it had been called, as usual, after the saint's day on which it was discovered. Much fertile land was ruined in that 1680 eruption and many people emigrated permanently to neighbouring Brava. From the end of the 1600s well into the 1700s, the fire of Fogo could be seen from afar and was used by ships to aid their navigation.

It was into the open space left by the giant ancient collapse that, in 1785, Pico do Fogo erupted. Lava spewed down the northeastern slopes creating the bulge on which the town of Mosteiros is situated today, and the Pico became the highest point of the archipelago.

Against this tempestuous background the people of Fogo welcomed the crews of American whaling ships who came ashore in search of supplies and personnel, as they were doing on Brava. Thus began the emigration to the United States and the creation of the great Cabo Verdean diaspora.

Since 1785, all eruptions have been inside the old crater. There was one in 1799 and three in the following century, in 1847, 1852 and 1857, after which there was a century's gap. Each eruption leaves cones in the crater floor, which is how it earned its name, Chã das Caldeiras or Plain of Craters. In 1847 there were fatalities caused not by lava flows but by the associated earthquakes. The eruption of 1852 created the cone known as Monte Preto de Baixo.

In the 20th century there were two eruptions, in the 21st so far, just the one. Lava spewed from one of the two chimneys on the southern side of the volcano in 1951, and also created cones to the north and south of the Pico – such as

Monte Orlando, Monte Rendall and Monte Preto de Cima. These eruptions all began along a line of volcanic fissures extending from the flank of the Pico do Fogo summit cone across the floor of Chã das Caldeiras. The lava flows that issued from these vents spread over the northern and southern parts of Chã das Caldeiras and down the eastern flank of the island.

The second eruption in the 20th century occurred on the night of 2 April 1995. For a week before, the villages had been shaken with small but increasingly powerful earthquakes. Just after midnight the flank of the Pico split apart as a line of fissures opened. It was as if the Pico had been 'cut by a knife', said one villager. The eruption began and a curtain of fire issued from the volcano and poured down into the crater. Thousands of inhabitants fled. By daylight the whole island was covered by a thick cloud of dark ash extending 5km into the sky; lava bombs up to 4m wide landed half a kilometre from the eruption and a day later lava fountains were spurting 400m high: it is estimated that at its height the volcano ejected between four and 8.5 million cubic metres of lava per day.

One month later the lava had thickened but was still flowing at 15cm per hour. It was another month before the flow stopped. Miraculously nobody died; perhaps the luckiest escape was made by two guitarists who are said to have climbed the Pico the day before the eruption, to make music and enjoy the view.

The 1995 eruption was different from the others. Unusually, it occurred southwest of the Pico, through a system of fissures that lay in a broadly south–west orientation. As a result the lava flows spread west and then north, covering an area of fertile volcanic soils and ultimately much of the small village of Boca Fonte. Today, shells of its houses remain, invaded by monstrous clumps of lava as high as their roofs. One house was even spun around on its axis by the lava flow, but remained standing.

Alternative housing was quickly built on the southern slopes – it can be seen from the road as you ascend to the crater. It was assumed that the people would move there permanently but most of them defiantly returned to their crater homes to cultivate whatever land escaped the lava flow. The road across Chã was then rebuilt.

For most of the duration of the eruption (from 10 April to the end of May) the only active vent was at the northeastern end of the fissure system and it is here that the largest volcanic cone of the eruption grew.

After 19 years of hopeful rebuilding, the volcano erupted again on 23 November 2014. Rivers of molten lava left two villages destroyed – with only five out of their 234 houses spared – plus 120 hectares of agricultural land wiped out along with the road and a thoughtfully designed and painstakingly built new visitor centre. Almost a thousand people were evacuated. The area's booming winemaking industry, both its vines and its production facilities, were also hit hard. But it was only a matter of weeks before some villagers returned, preferring to live in tents as long as they were home. Building began again too, in some cases on lava that was still so hot that shoes were needed on the new floors to protect against the heat. In under a year, a third of the residents had returned. A new road, soon built by villagers from Portela and Bangaeira with little mechanical help, rejoined Portela and the vineyard area of Montinho. It was christened the *estrada da coragem*: the road of courage.

FOGO TODAY Fogo has long benefited from foreign investment and development work, much of it funded by Germany, Switzerland and Japan. In the last few decades, this has given the island a new harbour, and acres of terracing, catchment dams and reafforestation.

Agriculture, along with tourism, remains the island's main activity, though fishing occupies a small number of people too. There's plenty of water underground

FESTIVALS ON FOGO

The end of April/early May is the time for Fogo's big party, Bandeira (Flag) de São Filipe, also called Festa Nhô São Filipe. The island has a distinctive music known as *pilão*, a bit like *batuku*, a chanting and beating of drums that forms the background to the grinding of corn in the run-up to the festival. The multi-day event features horse racing, processions, children's rides and activities, food trucks, and a main stage hosting musical acts each night that last into the early hours. This remains a joyful, easy going locals' festival, but it also attracts *emigrantes* from the US and city slickers from Praia in large numbers. Many of the headline bands are internationally known. Accommodation during the entire festival period is scarce and prices rise. Flights and ferries also can get booked up.

20 January	São Sebastião
Late April/early May	Bandeira de São Filipe/Festa Nhô São Filipe
24 June	São João
29 June	São Pedro
2nd Sunday in July	Santa Rainha de Cabo Verde (Chã das Caldeiras)
5 August	Nossa Sra do Socorro
10 August	São Lourenço
15 August	Municipality Day (Mosteiros)
Late November	DjarFogo International Film Festival
24 November	Santa Catarina (Cova Figueira)

but hoisting it to the surface is expensive, and directing it higher – to the slopes that carry much of the agriculture – is even more costly. Some rainwater catchment tanks have been built to address this, with every village now possessing at least one of these communal resources. The islanders grow coffee and – to the delight of many a visitor to Cabo Verde – produce wine. Grapes are grown in the crater by digging pits among the little black pieces of basaltic rock known as *lapilli* and planting a vine in each: at night the moisture condenses on the rock and dribbles into the holes. There is a more traditional vineyard near São Filipe (page 236) and another co-operative in the far north. The results are some really very quaffable wines, and there is also production of juices and various liqueurs.

Fogo is thought to have potential for geothermal energy for electricity production, though the investment needed to kick-start this is currently not a priority. Rainwater filters through the permeable volcanic rock and reaches underground reservoirs. The water samples taken during investigations have reached as high as 200–300°C. In the meantime, some of the more progressive commercial establishments are installing solar panels to harness the 320 days of sunshine.

GEOGRAPHY Fogo is the fourth-largest island, with an area of 480km^2. Its highest point is the Pico do Fogo which reaches a towering 2,829m. The island has a population of around 35,000 and São Filipe, with just over 8,000 residents, is the third-largest town in Cabo Verde – though a long way shy of Praia and Mindelo.

FLORA AND FAUNA

Flora There are eight plant species endemic to Fogo. Two to watch out for are *língua de vaca* (*Echium vulcanorum*), a white flower with a broad leaf, which is

> **CONSERVING THE CRATER**
>
> The crater was designated a natural park in 2003. The park extends over a large part of the landmass of the island: its 8,469ha include a margin around the south and north of the crater and a western section that extends quite close to the coast at some points. Some areas are under greater restrictions than others: for example any land use is banned on the Pico and on the inner wall of the crater, but some uses are permissible elsewhere. A project to conserve and develop the crater has been in progress, in one form or another, for some years. It is said that the true value of the crater is geological, rather than to do with its flora and fauna, and so the priorities lie with conserving its rocks. 'Geological tourism' is said to be the focus.
>
> Since the crater houses two villages still under reconstruction and there are increasing numbers of visitors, some activities threaten the crater while others do not. The areas where people are growing vines are just ash, and thus this causes no problems. Conversely, large quantities of ash and sand in the crater have been shovelled away and used in the construction boom. These are valued because, compared with sand from the shore, they have a low salt content. And lava stone is used for roof tiles. On a small scale this would be no problem, but the expansion of the crater population from 500 in the year 2000 to over 1,000 by 2014 resulted in significant construction, and this has increased during the rebuilding seen over the last decade.
>
> Conservation plans extend to the crater slopes. On the outer northern slopes of the volcano, there are eucalyptus, pines and acacias, planted during job-creation activities in the 1940s after the famine. In an area of the southwest, the project has planted fruit trees watered by drip irrigation and by reservoirs which fill over two to three months and then are used over the rest of the year.
>
> To deal with an out-of-control goat problem, the original project did a deal with local people: they were offered 'beautiful, big' goats from the Canaries that produced a lot of milk, if they agreed to build stables for them and prevent them roaming the countryside.

confined just to Fogo volcano and might be encountered on a Pico ascent; and *cravo-brabo babo* (*Erysimum caboverdeanum*), a delicate pink flower with long pointed leaves, which is found only inside the crater.

Birds The crater is designated an Important Bird Area by BirdLife International. Fogo is one of four islands in Cabo Verde where the endemic Fea's petrel (*Pterodroma feae*) is known to breed, and it likes the inner walls of the crater best. There are at most 100 pairs of this monogamous bird in the crater, and there could be only half that. The Cape Verde little shearwater (*Puffinus assimilis boydi*) breeds on the outer slopes of the crater and it has the largest population of Alexander's swift (*Apus alexandri*). Other breeding species include the grey-headed kingfisher (*Halcyon leucocephala*), the spectacled warbler (*Sylvia conspicillata*), a small population of the Cape Verde cane warbler (*Acrocephalus brevipennis*) and probably the Cape Verde peregrine (*Falco madens*). (For more on birds, see page 6.)

Turtles As with all the Cabo Verdean islands, Fogo is home to nesting loggerhead turtles (*Caretta caretta*) from June to October. There are no facilities at present for tourists to observe, but guards patrol the beaches during nesting season.

SAFETY You should take care if **swimming**: the land drops steeply away and the removal of vast quantities of sand for construction has not helped this. Take local advice. **Hikers** should be aware that the Pico is pretty challenging and some walks, like the crater rim, are dangerous without a guide, with jagged rocks and still hot fissures on the crater's terrain.

Tour agencies warn against going solo or taking any valuables down to the black-sand beaches around São Filipe, as thefts have been reported.

GETTING THERE AND AWAY

BY AIR Flying over the flanks of the volcano and landing on a sliver of flat land between the grey slopes and the blue sea is one of the most spectacular experiences you will have on the archipelago. There is usually a daily flight with Cabo Verde Airlines from Santiago, which takes 30 minutes. Sit on the right-hand side, for the view, though volcano sightings are often thwarted by low cloud shrouding its peak.

Fogo's airport was in the midst of renovation at the time of writing, but currently has a shady kiosk in the car park, serving drinks and welcoming slices of cake. It's 2km from the airport into the capital, a 20-minute walk downhill into town. A shared *aluguer* from the airport to São Filipe should not cost more than 100$ (taxi 500$), though most hotels collect their guests if they have booked in advance. At least one *aluguer* for Mosteiros meets every São Filipe flight. On Sundays, the taxis that have been stalking you all week can mysteriously disappear, so if you have a flight to catch, best organise your trip to the airport in advance.

BY FERRY The situation with ferries to Fogo, once volatile, has been somewhat stabilised with CV Interilhas (w cvinterilhas.cv) running the service. At the time of publication there was a connection with Brava twice weekly and somewhat more frequent connections with Praia (Santiago). Note that timetables are published only one month in advance and it is essential to check the website beforehand – or better still, check with one of the tour operators, as they are often better informed. This is especially true if you are relying on returning to Fogo (from Brava) or to Santiago (from Fogo) by ferry to get an onward flight. As on any of Cabo Verde's longer sea routes, the voyage to and from Praia can be very rough.

Fogo's port (Barca Balêro, or Vale de Cavaleiros) lies a few kilometres to the north of São Filipe and a taxi to or from town costs 500$. At present, ferry tickets can be bought online or in advance from the CV Interilhas office or via many of the tour operators listed, but not at the port or on the boat. Take your passport when booking. There's a modern terminal building with smart waiting room but it's not beside the dock, and considered a bit of a white elephant by locals.

BY YACHT Fogo is bathed in a swell that can only be avoided by anchoring at the harbour to the north of the capital, the development of which has improved matters for yachties. Nevertheless, the user-friendliness of the port is questionable, with reports of the tie-ups next to rubber bollards designed more for large ships resulting in chafing and wrecked fenders. The approach of any vessel will be noted by the Delegaçao Maritimo (Port Authority) and you will be required to present the usual identification documents.

GETTING AROUND

BY PUBLIC TRANSPORT *Alugueres* leave Mosteiros, the villages in the crater and other outlying villages as early as 04.00. They generally head north, travelling anticlockwise down the west coast to profit from the tarmac surface, and arrive in São Filipe about an hour later. They depart from São Filipe mid-morning and also at midday and at 14.00 for the crater (700$): don't get stranded. There are no communal *alugueres* to and from the crater on a Sunday, so a private hire is usually the only option; ask around at your hotel in case other guests would like to share. An *aluguer* leaves São Filipe for São Jorge sometime between 09.30 and 11.00 and one returns to São Filipe around 13.00.

Alugueres for the crater and for Mosteiros leave São Filipe from beside the block that houses the town hall (*câmara municipal*) and the market. Those for São Jorge, the salina, the airport and the port leave from outside Pousada Belavista.

BY TAXI The bright-yellow taxis or chartered *alugueres* will go most places. The main taxi rank in São Filipe is down behind the market, with another just north of the Colonial Guesthouse. In practice taxis also roam the streets of the town incessantly and are likely to find *you*, except on Sundays. Fares are relatively fixed – for example, to the crater 8,000$; around the island 9,000$; to Mosteiros 6,000$; to São Lourenço 1,000$; to Curral Grande 1,500$. For longer trips, it's advisable to book via your accommodation at least 24 hours in advance. You can struggle to find an English-speaking driver – there is currently only one – but a further handful do speak excellent French. Note, these multilingual drivers all usually charge around $1,000 extra for tours and can be somewhat unreliable due to their popularity.

BY CAR The going rate is from €75 to €86 for a one-day hire, though the choice is very limited and advance booking is advisable. Mileage limits may apply, but you can't really go too far on this small island. The usual deposit will be requested, by credit card or cash. Most tour operators will find you a car, but there is only one car-hire firm operating on the island [233 F5] (Intercidades; São Filipe; \ 281 3334; e sucursalfg@intercidadesrentacar.cv; w intercidadesrentacar.cv). Several individuals in São Filipe also offer cars, but the vehicle quality is suspect and the existence of adequate insurance is questionable.

WHERE TO STAY AND EAT

Almost all the major accommodation is in São Filipe where you have a choice between the comfortable Bamboo Xaguate Hotel and the atmospheric Colonial Guesthouse as well as a full range of *pensões* of varying price and quality, some of them tastefully renovated and situated in traditional *sobrado* houses and some with views of the ocean. Away from the capital, a US expat couple have opened La Fora, a small ecolodge around 15 minutes' drive above the city, and there's also the charming Pensão Christine in Monsterios. But the most unique and unforgettable place to overnight is up in the crater, beneath the brooding volcano: a handful of *pensões* have been built, and/or rebuilt, in the decade since the lava flow. São Filipe has an exuberant little restaurant and bar scene, with plentiful options across all budgets, along with reliably good pizza, gelato and coffee. That said, don't miss out on experiencing the hyperlocal and unique dishes of the crater. Most restaurants in the Chã villages operate on a 'call ahead' basis – give them a couple of hours' notice and they'll have a pre-negotiated dish of the day ready for you.

EXCURSIONS AND TOUR OPERATORS

The operators listed here are established, experienced and usually multi-lingual. They more or less offer the same kind of tours. Sample prices are: trip up to the crater, with a guide, trip to the winery, a walk between the two villages, return transport, plus stops on the way – 8,000$, or 9,000$ for an English-speaking driver. Lunch is not usually included in this fee, and note that these prices do not include a guide for the climb to the top of the volcano. An organised trip to the salina for one to four people would cost around the same as a round-island tour, but a return taxi would be a third of that.

You may well be approached by unofficial 'guides' in São Filipe. All guides must be licensed and carry ID. Whoever you use, agree exactly what the tour will include and the price, in advance.

If you prefer to plan your own day trip, speak to a taxi or *aluguer* driver – they'll usually be happy to oblige even if at first they keenly try and get you to follow one of the usual itineraries.

Qualitur [232 C5] Praça Câmara Municipal, São Filipe; 281 1089; m 997 1142; e qualitour@sapo.cv; w qualitur.cv. An efficient outfit organising tailor-made individual & group trips to Chã das Caldeiras, the salina, Monte Genebra, island tours & a variety of walks in & around the crater, with guides. English, German, French & Italian spoken.

vista verde tours [232 C6] Close to the blue church, in a square-towered building, São Filipe; m 993 0788; e office@vista-verde.com; w vista-verde.com; ⏱ 10.00–noon & 15.00–17.00 Mon–Fri. Well-established, efficient travel agency specialising in socially & environmentally responsible tourism. Arranges small-group tours or tailor-made holidays for individuals incorporating accommodation, flights, hiking & excursions. Also offices on Sal & São Vicente.

Zebra Travel [232 D3] On the main square, São Filipe; 281 3373; m 919 4566; e info@zebratravel.net; w zebratravel.net. Can arrange flights, tours & excursions; also rents cars. Connected to the Colonial Guesthouse & Zebra Corner Tapas Lounge, & within the guesthouse complex (236). Business centre also available.

ACTIVITIES

HIKING This is *the* great activity of Fogo. As well as the big hike up to the Pico in the crater, there are still several delightful, and arguably more rewarding, walks from various points in and around the crater, and those exploring the island's diverse bioclimates below (page 245).

FISHING The game fishing around Fogo's waters is high quality, with plenty of blue marlin, sharks and tuna. Zebra Travel (see above) is currently the only operator who can organise big-game fishing trips, though you could always try and strike a deal with one of the local fishermen if you are happy with smaller fish. Cost will depend on the number participating and advance notice is required.

CYCLING Fogo is steep and cobbled, and cycling anywhere but along contours or downhill can be unbearable without a good, comfy, mountain bike. Only for true lovers of discomfort. Qualitur (see above) and Casa Marisa 2.0 (page 239) have limited numbers of rentals available.

BEACHES AND SWIMMING It is often dangerous to swim off Fogo, but when the sea looks really calm it is safe at the beach at the port, and at Praia Nossa Senhora.

The best place to swim, however, is Ponta da Salina – a stunning cove with black rock formations smothered by white sea-spray and riddled with grottos and reefs. There are ladders to get you back to dry land after you've plunged into the sea, as well as a small curve of black pebble beach. Sundays here often take on a festive air, with locals bringing picnics and sound systems. It can be reached on the São Jorge *aluguer* – ask to be dropped off and do check when, and if, the *aluguer* is returning before setting off. A return taxi can be negotiated for around the same price or a little less than an island circuit (page 243).

CAVES There are a few volcanic tubes to explore on Fogo, including the Gruta da Fonte do Monte Inhuco and the Gruta do Monte Preto, and the Parque Natural do Fogo is slowly opening more to visitors. The tubes are lava flows that solidify on the outside, after which the inner liquid flows away leaving them hollow inside. Inside they are beautiful, with frozen lava in streams down the inner walls like melted chocolate.

Gruta do Monte Preto is only 500m from Casa Ramiro in Chã das Caldeiras (page 240) and has newly built entrance ladders and other safety structures. Others are to be found around the interior of the Bordeira, the scarp that lies above the villages. None of these is for amateurs, with crawling involved and uneven ground. Bring a good head torch and don't go without a guide unless you are an extremely experienced caver and have consulted with equally experienced locals.

CULTURE The *sobrado* architecture of São Filipe could make the capital a destination in itself for some, and a wander around the pretty streets can be complemented with a visit to Casa da Memória and the municipal museum. The Casa has occasional outdoor screening of films in its courtyard; São Filipe also has an annual film festival each November focusing on African cinema. Live music can usually be found around São Filipe and up in the crater, especially at weekends. The line-up at the annual Festa Nhô São Filipe in late April will also impress music fans.

SIGHTSEEING BY VEHICLE A round-island trip can be done in a hire car or set-price taxi, at 8,000$ with a Portuguese-speaking driver or 9,000$ for an English- or French-speaking one. You could attempt this by public transport, but given the very real chance of getting stranded overnight on the far side of the island, a taxi is the most sensible option. Note that the island's few English-speaking drivers tend to get booked up quickly.

SÃO FILIPE

São Filipe is large by Cabo Verdean standards, a pretty landslide of a town, with its houses seemingly tumbling down steep cobbled streets towards the narrow black-sand beach and the ocean below. It is on the 'tentative' list as a UNESCO World Heritage Site, hardly surprising given the many Portuguese-era squares, esplanades and *sobrado* houses (page 236) of the Bila Baxo, the historic centre, and its equally historic counterpart up the hill, Bila Riba. It's far from pristine, with some buildings lovingly restored and others in various states of disrepair, but the town has a proud and prosperous, and friendly, feel to it. Colourful façades are topped with terracotta tiles, and vegetation springs from pots on every fragile wooden balcony. Bougainvillea abounds and trees are a healthy size.

The town could do with some more outdoor cafés from which to enjoy its architecture and views of Brava (we've included some good options in the listings from page 234). There is, though, a promenade, adorned with busts of Portuguese heroes, which lines the clifftops and from where you can gaze down upon the harsh drop to the black sands and the occasionally violent sea below. There's also a large terrace where you can sit, halfway up the hill at the top of a flight of steps.

WHERE TO STAY Some hotels raise their prices threefold in late April to capitalise on the island's annual festival, and most places in the centre get booked up far in advance of that week. While there is a full span of budget options, there's not really a commensurate difference in price between the top-level options and the mid-level ones. Note that a couple of the properties listed here are located out of town: although taxis are plentiful, you'll need to factor in the extra cost of these.

Fogo Boutique Hotel [233 H1] (5 rooms) ` 281 3131; e fogoboutiquehotellda@gmail.com; markaslda. On a headland just north of the centre, staying at this boutique place feels more like staying with well-to-do local friends. All rooms have views, but it's worth spending the small amount extra for one of the larger ones, at almost twice the size. Beautifully prepared dishes, including a bountiful seafood pasta, are served on a spectacular terrace by the pool at on-site Tony's restaurant. TV, AC, minibars. **$$$$**

The View [233 H1] (10 rooms) m 989 6169; the_view_cv. North of town, right on a cliff overlooking the ocean. Fabulous rooftop dining space, outdoor pool, nightclub & large suites. **$$$$**

Bamboo Xaguate Hotel [233 G1] (39 rooms) ` 281 5000; e reservas@hotelxaguate.com; w hotelxaguate.com. Set in a spectacular position on the headland. Views can be enjoyed from the balconies of some of the rooms, or from the swimming-pool terrace. This is the largest hotel in town, if not exactly the 4-star establishment that's claimed; nonetheless, it's good value. AC, sat TV & most mod cons, including notably strong & hot showers, though Wi-Fi is only in public areas. **$$$**

Colonial Guesthouse [232 D3] (10 rooms) ` 281 3373; e info@zebratravel.net; w casacolonialguesthouse.cv. This undeniably elegant colonial building dates back to 1883, & has been tastefully restored, including the addition of a small rooftop swimming pool. Tatty-chic décor & high ceilings add to the charm, as do pretty views. While all rooms have their own bathroom, not all are en suite. Sea breezes often suffice, but there's AC too. Rates include airport transfers. Zebra Travel (page 229) is on site, making it simple to arrange guides, excursions & transport. **$$$**

Hotel Santos Pina [232 D6] (20 rooms) ` 281 4225; e hotelsantospina@gmail.com. Friendly staff & views, but tired bathrooms. A dependable option, though lacks the character of the converted *sobrado* hotels. Small covered swimming pool. Rooms have AC, TV & minibar. **$$$**

Hotel Savana [232 D4] (16 rooms) ` 281 1490; e reservasavana@yahoo.com. A beautifully restored traditional *sobrado* house with great sea views in a quiet location. AC, TV, hot water & fridge. Plunge pool in courtyard. **$$$**

La Fora Ecolodge [map, page 222] (10 rooms) m 985 9230 e info@laforaecolodge.com; w laforaecolodge.com. Around a 15-minute winding drive from town. Tile-roofed bungalows, all with private verandas & en suites, are dotted down a lushly planted hill. Up here, the sea views, atmospheric rural surrounds & cooler evenings are lovely, while pops of West African textiles & comfortable beds soften otherwise austere interiors. The US expat owners can recommend tours & guides, as well as call taxis. Good bar/restaurant (page 234). No AC, fans or minibars, but there's a small pool. **$$$**

Melissa's Guesthouse [232 D4] (12 rooms) ` 281 4035; e reservas@melissasguesthouse.cv; w melissasguesthouse.cv. A very central, elevated position, friendly staff & spotless, modern rooms make this a good choice. The guest-only rooftop pool & terrace bar, with spectacular views across the rooftops to the sea, make it even better. The downstairs restaurant is also inviting & has its own airy terrace overlooking one of the town's lively squares. **$$$**

Arko Iris [232 C5] (8 rooms) Rua da Biblioteca Municipal; ` 281 2526; e arkoiris.fogo@gmail.com; w caboverde.com/pages/812526.htm. Don't expect stunning views here; just a good-value, modest hotel. Vibrant & colourful with modern fixtures & a welcome roof terrace. Rooms have AC & TV. Above the café of the same name. **$$**

Casa Beiramar [232 A5] (5 rooms) Opposite the cathedral; ` 281 3485; m 979 2322;

SÃO FILIPE

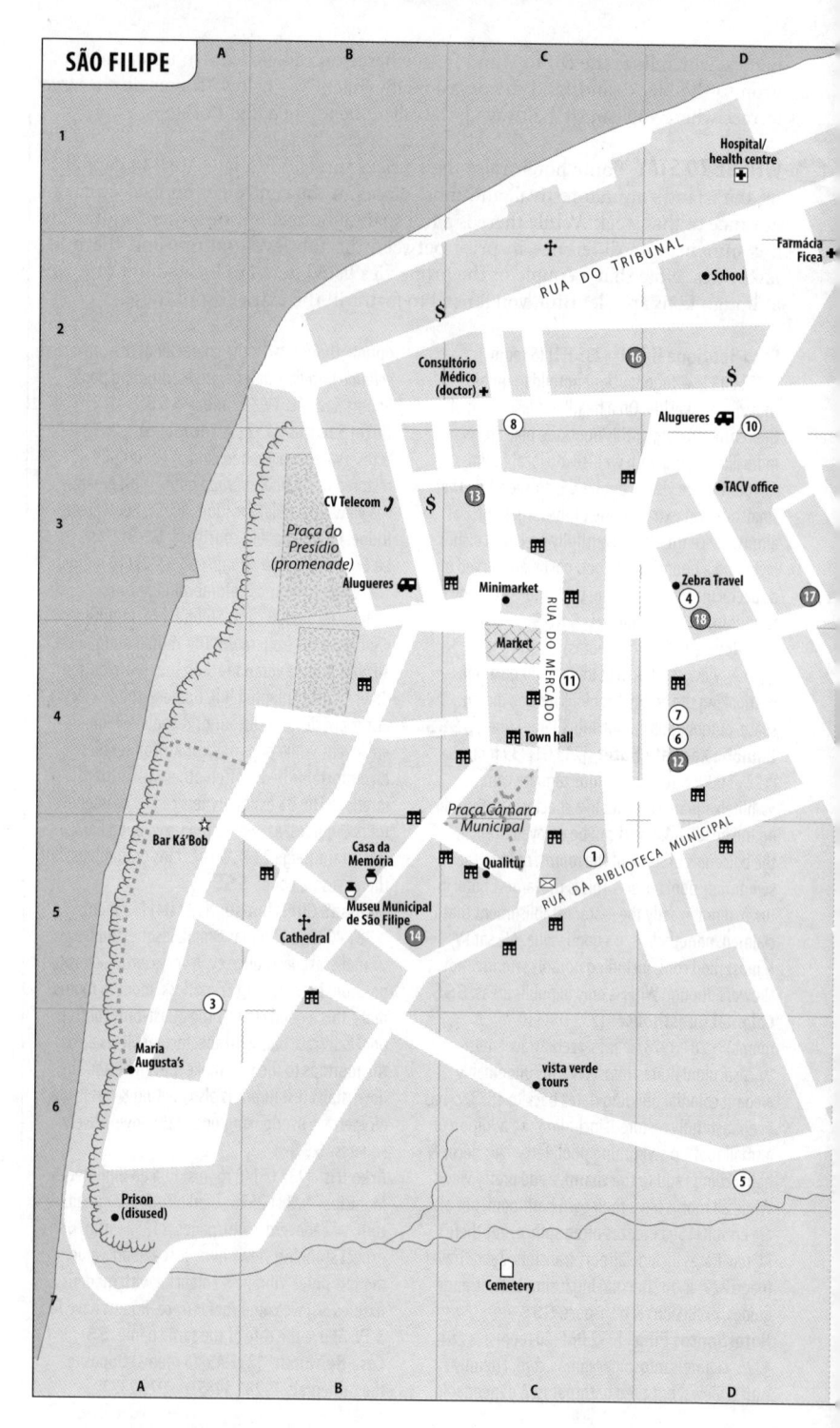

- Hospital/health centre
- Farmácia Ficea
- RUA DO TRIBUNAL
- School
- Consultório Médico (doctor)
- Alugueres (10)
- (16)
- (8)
- CV Telecom
- Praça do Presídio (promenade)
- (13)
- TACV office
- Alugueres
- Minimarket
- Zebra Travel
- (4)
- (18)
- (17)
- Market
- RUA DO MERCADO
- (11)
- Town hall
- (7)
- (6)
- (12)
- Praça Câmara Municipal
- Bar Ká'Bob
- Casa da Memória
- Qualitúr
- (1)
- RUA DA BIBLIOTECA MUNICIPAL
- Cathedral
- Museu Municipal de São Filipe
- (14)
- (3)
- Maria Augusta's
- vista verde tours
- (5)
- Prison (disused)
- Cemetery

232

KEY

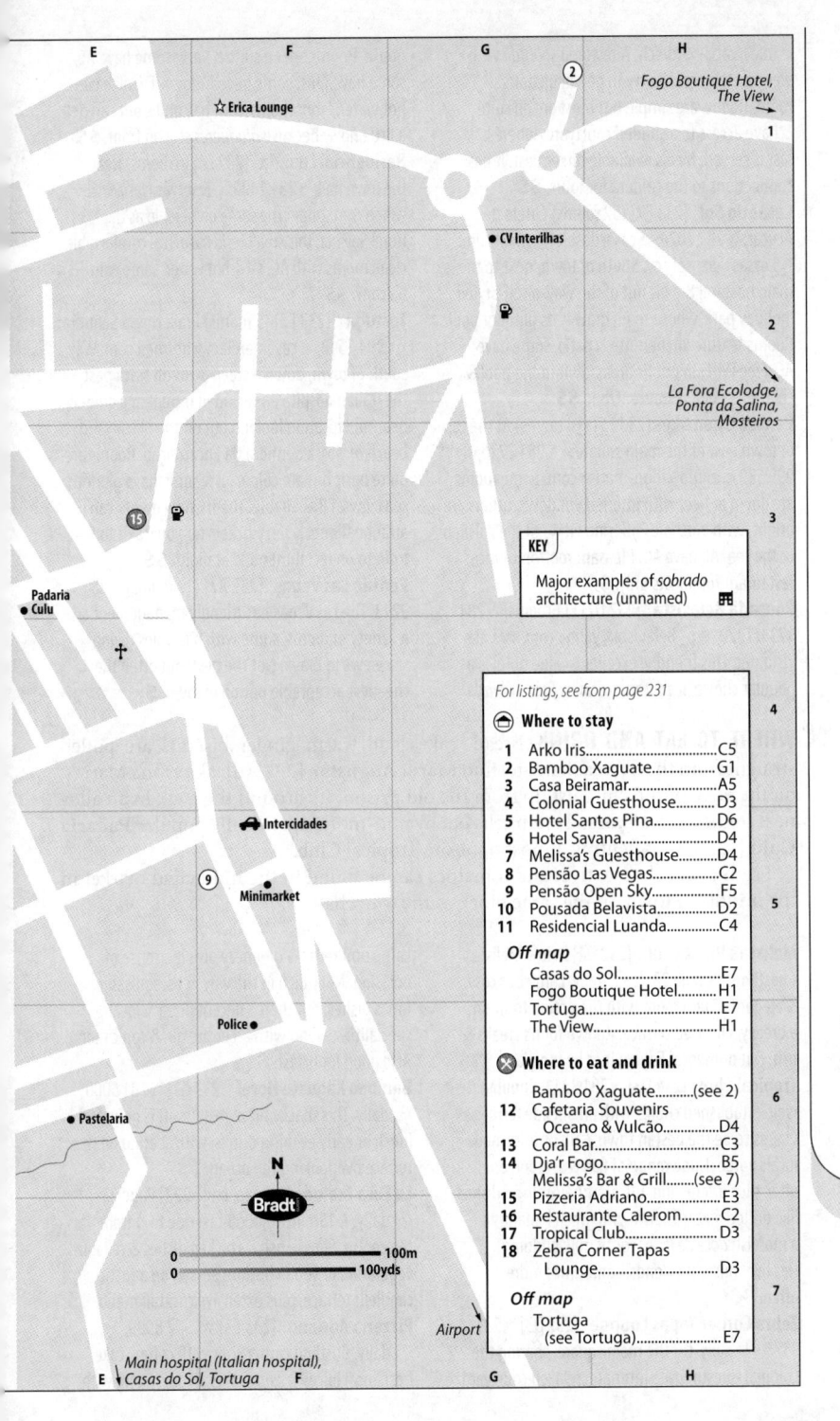

Major examples of *sobrado* architecture (unnamed)

For listings, see from page 231

Where to stay
1. Arko Iris....................................C5
2. Bamboo Xaguate................G1
3. Casa Beiramar.....................A5
4. Colonial Guesthouse.........D3
5. Hotel Santos Pina...............D6
6. Hotel Savana........................D4
7. Melissa's Guesthouse.........D4
8. Pensão Las Vegas................C2
9. Pensão Open Sky.................F5
10. Pousada Belavista...............D2
11. Residencial Luanda.............C4

Off map
   Casas do Sol..........................E7
   Fogo Boutique Hotel..........H1
   Tortuga...................................E7
   The View.................................H1

Where to eat and drink
   Bamboo Xaguate...........(see 2)
12. Cafetaria Souvenirs
    Oceano & Vulcão..............D4
13. Coral Bar................................C3
14. Dja'r Fogo.............................B5
    Melissa's Bar & Grill.......(see 7)
15. Pizzeria Adriano..................E3
16. Restaurante Calerom........C2
17. Tropical Club.......................D3
18. Zebra Corner Tapas
    Lounge..................................D3

Off map
   Tortuga
    (see Tortuga).......................E7

Fogo SÃO FILIPE

e info@cabo-verde.ch. A restored *sobrado* with views of the ocean – try to get an upstairs room. Rooms are simple but most are en suite & have access to a shaded courtyard, where b/fast is served. Meals available on request. It has connections to the caldera for tours. **$$**

Casas do Sol   [233 E7] (32 rooms) Cutelo de Acucar; ✆ 281 2024; e casasdosolcv@gmail.com; 📷 casas_do_sol_cv. South of town, next to the main hospital & a bit out of the way, a self-styled 'holiday park' whose main draw is its outdoor pool. Rooms feature kitchenette & patio, some have AC. Free Wi-Fi in public areas. Swimming pool & children's pool, restaurant/bar. **$$**

Pensão Open Sky   [233 F5] (10 rooms) At the top of town east of the main square; ✆ 281 2726; m 999 5392; e info@fogo-marisa.com. Some rooms are down at heel with internal windows; others are bright, with balconies offering views of the volcano or the sea. All have AC. Pleasant rooftop terrace; restaurant for guests only. **$$**

Pousada Belavista   [232 D2] (11 rooms) ✆ 281 1734/1220; e p_belavista@yahoo.com; w bela-vista.net. This friendly, excellent-value hotel is a popular choice in an immaculately kept *sobrado* house. Rooms are en suite & vary: some have AC, some have fans; some have fridge & TV; all have hot water. Front rooms have balconies but can get a little noisy because *alugueres* stop in front. **$$**

Residencial Luanda   [232 C4] (6 rooms) Near the town hall; ✆ 281 1490; e reservasavana@yahoo.com. Under the same ownership as the Hotel Savana, this small *residencial* has comfortable clean rooms with AC, TV & hot water, some with balcony. **$$**

Tortuga   [233 E7] (5 rooms) Praia Nossa Senhora; m 994 1512; e casamarelacv@hotmail.com. Way south of town, down a steep & rough track past the Italian hospital, a secluded retreat in a quiet & beautiful location looking out on the black-sand beach of Nossa Senhora da Encarnação. Rooms are quite basic but are colourful & some have glorious sea views. FB available. The friendly owner can arrange flights & ferry tickets for you. Taxis to & from town recommended at night. **$$**

Pensão Las Vegas   [232 A2] (12 rooms) ✆ 281 2223. The Las Vegas has friendly management & a variety of rooms, some with balconies giving sea views to Brava. Not the best, but often the cheapest acceptable option in town. **$**

✘ **WHERE TO EAT AND DRINK**   Bread, cakes and warm ginger biscuits are pulled straight from the oven at hard-to-find **Maria Augusta's** [232 A6], aka Dona Maria's, on the edge of the cliff, just up from the old prison. It's around the back in an alley next to the sea wall. Bread often sells out by mid-morning. Equally popular **Padaria Culu** [233 E3], is central, almost opposite Tropical Club.

Fresh goat's cheese, fruit and tomatoes can be found in the municipal market in the middle of town, in the same block as the town hall.

Melissa's Bar & Grill   [232 D4] Below Melissa's Guesthouse (page 231); ⊕ daily. Large but cosy & elegant dining room with the option to sit on a breezy, elevated terrace. Known for its steaks & fish, & it does local Fogo wines by the glass. **$$$**

Tropical Club   [232 D3] ✆ 281 3311. Popular, well-established choice with an outside terrace. Claims to be the best in town & many informed locals agree. Huge range of fish & seafood on offer, plus interesting, ultra-authentic local dishes like grilled gizzards, fish with green bananas & a moreish *doce de leite* (confit milk pudding). Has live music at w/ends, sometimes more often. **$$$**

Zebra Corner Tapas Lounge   [232 D3] ✆ 281 3373; ⊕ daily. Off the main square, sharing the Colonial Guesthouse's intimate, relaxed courtyard. Large umbrellas & greenery give it a sense of occasion. Not much in the way of recognisable tapas dishes, but there's decent pizza & local specialities, along with an entire gin & tonic menu. Also good for b/fast. **$$$**

Bamboo Xaguate Hotel   [233 G1] ✆ 281 5000; ⊕ daily. This snacky hotel restaurant is good for lunch or early evening drinks, with seating on the terrace overlooking the ocean. **$$**

La Fora Ecolodge   [map, page 222] Page 231; ⊕ daily. A 15min, 10,000$ taxi ride to & from the centre. Simple fish & chicken dishes & reliable vegetarian or vegan options served on a rustic candlelit terrace, plus extensive cocktail menu. **$$**

Pizzeria Adriano   [233 E3] m 957 8999; ⊕ daily. Bustling corner spot with coffee, cake, fresh local juices & *caipirinhas* all day, along with queue-worthy gelato. From 18.00, there's proper pizza & pasta in the airy upstairs dining room, care of the Venetian owner & a top-of-the-line pizza oven imported from Italy. $$

Restaurante Calerom [232 C2] ⊕ 07.00–late Mon–Sat. A rollicking open-air place for b/fast *cachupa*, barbecued chicken & other basics in huge portions. Live music from 22.00 Sat, sometimes until very late. $$

Tortuga [233 E7] See opposite; ⊕ daily, by appt. Simple dishes in a unique seaside spot; essential both to book & to arrange transport. $$

Cafetaria Souvenirs Oceano & Vulcão [232 D4] ⊕ 10.00–19.00 Tue–Sat, 15.00–19.00 Sun. Homemade cakes & coffee, along with plates of goat's cheese, fruit & wine. Also sells locally made jewellery, T-shirts & postcards. $

Coral Bar [232 C3] ⊕ daily. A watering hole & good-value eatery in the centre of town, with outside tables in an inner courtyard. $

Dja'r Fogo [232 B5] ✆ 281 2879; ⊕ daily, or by appt. Coffee at this gallery/coffee shop is roasted & ground by the owner from local beans. $

ENTERTAINMENT AND NIGHTLIFE In high season, other restaurants and bars in São Filipe may also offer live music.

Bar Ká'Bob [232 A5] Down the hill, towards the Praça do Presídio. Reggae or rap soundtrack, with a young crowd throwing back Strela beers & shots of *grogue*.

Erica Lounge [233 F1] North of the centre. This rooftop terrace restaurant strung with fairy lights morphs into a live music venue later in the night.

Restaurante Calerom [232 C2] See above. Live music on Sat evenings & big matches on the courtyard TVs.

Tropical Club [232 D3] See opposite. Traditional live music every Fri & Sat night.

SHOPPING Souvenirs, including Fogo wine and coffee, and crafts, are on sale at **Qualitur** [232 C5], coffee roastery and gallery **Dja'r Fogo** [232 B5] and **Cafetaria Souvenirs Oceano & Vulcão** [232 D4] (see above). You can also pick up some souvenirs from the museum. Food supplies can be found at the various minimarkets or the Mercado Municipal.

OTHER PRACTICALITIES

Banks BCA, BCN and Caixa Económica; all have ATMs. See map, page 232, for locations.

Health care The main hospital facilities are located in what locals refer to as the 'new' Italian hospital [233 E7], which has A&E, an operating theatre and a reasonably good reputation, located to the south of town. There's also a health centre [232 D1] (✆ 281 2685) and a pharmacy, Farmácia Ficea [232 D2] (✆ 281 1206); ⊕ 08.00–19.00 Mon–Fri, 08.00–13.00 Sat), up the hill north of the main *praça*.

Tourist information There is no tourist office, but the tour operators (page 229) are very helpful.

Water use Water is an even more scarce resource on Fogo than on the other islands, so be sparing with your usage.

The rest

Ferries CV Interilhas [233 G2]; m 970 6948; ⊕ 08.00–13.00 & 15.00–17.00 Mon, Wed & Fri, 08.00–13.00 Tue, Thu & Sat. It's easier to book online, via local tour operators or your hotel.

Police [233 F6] ✆ 281 1132

Post office [232 C5] Down in the town hall square; ⊕ 08.00–15.30 Mon–Fri

WHAT TO SEE AND DO
Architecture Wander the streets of Bila Baxo, the town's historic centre, admiring the *sobrado* architecture. A good number of these houses remain, many of them restored. Built by wealthy merchants and farmers in the late 19th century, they are decorated with fine wood and colourful tiles imported from West Africa and Portugal. If you can peek into one of them, do take the opportunity. A central courtyard would have been planted with trees and vines for shade, and around it, on the ground floor, were the working rooms for servants. The next floor, that of the owner's family, was more decorative, lined with an internal balcony that overlooked the courtyard on three sides. On the street side there would have been another balcony of carved wood. During the summer the townhouses would be closed as families relocated inland to oversee their coffee plantations, vineyards and farms. See map, page 232, for the location of some more prominent examples, which include the town hall [232 C4], and others that have been converted to hotels, such as the Colonial [232 D3], Belavista [232 D2] and Savana [232 D4].

Casa da Memória [232 B5] (House of Memory; 281 2765; e moniquewidmer@yahoo.com.br; w casadamemoriafogo.wixsite.com/biblioteca; 10.00–noon Tue & Fri or by prior appointment; free) A private museum in a restored family house, run by a Cabo Verdean team together with Monique, who has lived in Cabo Verde for many decades. Through many hundreds of exhibits, many of which have been catalogued in an impressive book, it depicts Fogo's history from the early 1800s to 1950. It is full of photos and domestic objects; its patio, which housed Fogo's first cinema, has been restored and screens a programme of open-air movies. Cultural events are held here, as well as occasional conferences. Browse photographs that document the 2014 eruption from beginning to end and explore a library packed with interesting literature about the islands, some in English. There are also books for sale. Although admission is free, donations, which go towards the upkeep, are gratefully received.

Museu Municipal de São Filipe [232 B5] (São Filipe Municipal Museum; 281 1295; e camaramunicipal@yahoo.com.br; 08.00–16.00 Mon–Fri; 150$, students/children free) You'll find excellent displays explaining the everyday life of Fogo's inhabitants at this quirky municipal museum, with exhibits on the island's unique gastronomy and wine, festivals and agriculture, and a shocking video of the 2014 eruption. There is also a reconstruction of a *funco*, a traditional Fogo house made out of volcanic rock, while the museum itself is housed in a nice *sobrado* mansion. A small selection of crafts and Fogo wine is available for purchase.

Adega de Monte Barro (Winery) [map, page 222] 281 2000; e adegamontebarro@gmail.com; by appointment only; free, though tastings will incur a charge) Also known as the Maria Chaves Winery, this Italian-run social project produces around 65,000 bottles of wine per year from Italian grape varieties. You can visit, but you'll need to get your hotel to arrange this at least one day in advance, especially if you'd prefer an English-speaking guide. The winery is substantially funded by Italian donations, with profits directed to support the local hospital, agricultural schools and other ventures throughout Cabo Verde.

The beach and swimming A walk down the ramshackle *ribeira* road to the beach of Fonte Bila below is a must, if not a conventional tourist attraction (and best not done alone or at night). This strip of black sand lies under the ominous Fogo cliffs, which are lashed by relentless Atlantic breakers. As you begin your descent you will see the prison. Perched on the cliff, with a view of both the ocean and the cemetery, it must have afforded many a prisoner an inspirational setting in which to reflect on his misdemeanours. Take your cue from the locals as to whether swimming is safe – the surf can be powerful, as can the unseen currents.

The large, square pool at the Bamboo Xaguate Hotel [233 G1] is an alternative if the sea proves too treacherous or black sand isn't your thing; a day pass for non-guests is 1,500$, including lunch and a beer or soft drink.

CHÃ DAS CALDEIRAS

The road to the volcano passes first through pleasant countryside dotted with abandoned Portuguese farms, old volcano cones and swathes of cashew, banana and papaya trees. Just after a left fork, where the sign says '14km to Parc Natural de Fogo', is the 1951 lava spill down the right-hand slope.

Later the road becomes a series of terrifyingly steep hairpin bends with views down the massive ancient lava spills to the coast. Then it enters the echoing silence of the crater. Its sinister dark walls, and the vast clods of lava scattered over it, make one feel very small.

You'll notice quite quickly that some of the people here, with their striking fair hair and blue or green eyes, look quite different from the already diverse Cabo Verdean mix throughout the archipelago. These are the relatively recent

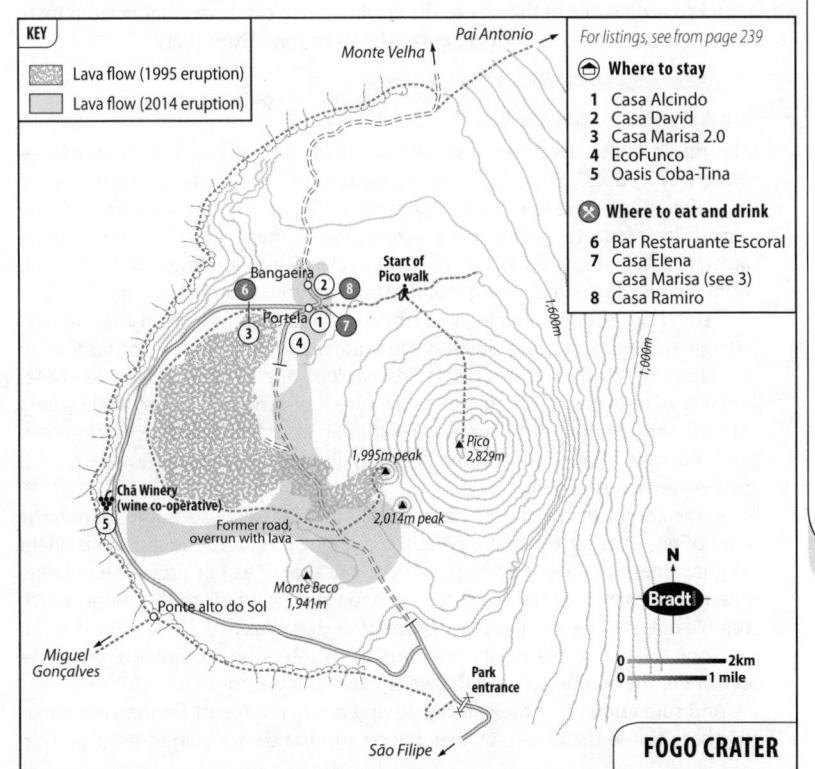

FOGO CRATER

KEY
- Lava flow (1995 eruption)
- Lava flow (2014 eruption)

For listings, see from page 239

Where to stay
1. Casa Alcindo
2. Casa David
3. Casa Marisa 2.0
4. EcoFunco
5. Oasis Coba-Tina

Where to eat and drink
6. Bar Restaurante Escoral
7. Casa Elena
   Casa Marisa (see 3)
8. Casa Ramiro

descendants of the Duc de Montrond (page 241), a French nobleman who came here in the 19th century and is thought to have brought the vines that began Fogo's wine production. More than half of the Chã villagers still bear the Montrond name, and, presumably, his DNA.

There have been many attempts to improve the crater's fragile ecology and geology, and to develop an economy (page 226). One step has been to define the crater as a natural park; another has been to set up small-scale tourism, with bed and breakfasts, restaurants and a network of hiking trails and guides to accompany walkers, and even a via ferrata. Of course, the volcano has not always been a willing accomplice in this, but reconstruction has continued apace.

The crater settlement is traditionally split into two villages: Portela (upper) and Bangaeira (lower), though there is actually very little to distinguish them from each other. Nevertheless, that does not diminish the rivalry when the two meet in local football matches, on a pitch which must be almost unbeatable for its stunning volcanic backdrop.

In many places in Chã das Caldeiras the electricity is turned on in the early evening and off at 22.00.

GETTING THERE AND AWAY There is a midday *aluguer* from São Filipe (700$). The return journey starts very early: listen for the horn which sounds loudly in the village at about 06.00. Better to let your *pensão* proprietor know the night before that you want transport, and they should make sure that the *aluguer* doesn't leave without you. For a small supplement, you can ask to be dropped at the airport. If you prefer to walk some of the way to the volcano, then catch an *aluguer* from town to Achada Furna; it takes 3 hours to cover the steep road from there.

CHÃ DAS CALDEIRAS MUSIC NIGHT   *Murray Stewart*

The music is due to start at Ramiro's at 18.00, so we joke that it should be underway by 20.00. But an unexpected busload of Cabo Verdeans has turned up mid-afternoon from São Filipe, hell-bent on having a party, and the occupants are already jammed into the tiny space in front of the grocery store's counter when we arrive at 17.00. It's chaos as the party-goers clamour to buy more wine: it's clear from the swaying and clapping that these are far from being their first bottles.

Behind the counter, Ramiro is combining some mournful violin-playing with customer service, putting down his instrument to sell a packet of biscuits or some olives. António strums his tiny *cavoquinho* one-handed as he passes over a bottle of red wine; in charge of the till, Jose is playing percussion while taking money and handing out change. An old man in a distinctive white cloth-cap and probably in his eighties, who keeps asking me if I am from '*A-mer-ee-ca*', is playing an acoustic guitar.

In the corner sits Kevin, son of an emigrant to Massachusetts and visiting the land of his roots for the first time at the age of 25. He tells me that he is fluent in Kriolu, despite never having been here, but that does not prevent him being relentlessly teased by the locals for not knowing the words to the songs, which tumble out from behind the counter one after the other.

'Soon, we go to my brother's house. He is returning to America. Soon. We celebrate!' the octogenarian in the white cap tells me earnestly.

And sure enough, as the smiling, waving bus party depart for the vertiginous trip back to the island capital, their happy and somewhat blurred faces pressed

A day trip to the volcano is tricky by public transport, though you might find a car in the crater which could be chartered as a taxi for the trip back to São Filipe in exchange for several thousand escudos. Most people organise their day trips through agencies (page 229).

WHERE TO STAY Map, page 237

You will not find luxury up in Chã das Caldeiras. But the locals don't live in luxury and the minor hardship of a cold shower and unreliable electricity are small things to suffer when set against the stunning landscape and unique ambience. Meanwhile, things are constantly improving, especially with the installation of solar panels and other sustainability projects. Book your accommodation in advance, as places do fill up in the busy season.

Casa Alcindo (9 rooms) m 992 1409; e alcindo6@gmail.com. Simple, spacious rooms, all with private bath. Good food, including picnic provisions. The owner Alcindo is also a well-respected guide for Pico climbs. **$$**

Casa David (2 rooms) m 991 4262; e davidtchan87@gmail.com. This is an absolutely unique place to stay, with a lava flow incursion into the dining room retained as part of the décor. There are volcano views from the roof terrace. Will also host wine tastings. **$$**

Casa Marisa 2.0 (15 rooms, 7 bungalows) 282 1662; e info@fogo-marisa.com; w fogo-marisa.com. Staying here, the quickest place to rebuild after the eruption, is a special experience. It's built defiantly on top of the lava flow, so the temperature inside the individual *funcos* – traditional round bungalows – hovers at around 26 degrees, even on chilly nights. All accommodation types are relatively spacious, including the budget rooms in the main building, though the *funcos* also have their own rooftop terraces. Proprietors Marisa, a local, & her partner Mustafa, are well connected in the village

against the windows of their crowded *aluguer*, Ramiro's grocery store/music venue is closed up and we pile into a dual-cab pick-up for the short drive down towards the only light left shining in Bangaeira village. Inside the house are maybe 20 people, most of them seemingly living there; three generations, maybe four. I am introduced to the 'brother', a man in his seventies with a Boston Celtics sports cap on his head.

'So,' I enquire, conscious of the stated reason for this party, 'is it tomorrow that you're leaving for the States?'

'No,' comes the reply, as he picks up his guitar. 'I'll be going back in about 35 years.' I estimate that, by then, he'll be about 110 years old. Perhaps these volcano-dwellers have discovered the secret of immortality.

At this point, the electricity goes off, but the wail of the violin, the frenetic strumming of the guitars and the tinny resonance of the *cavoquinho* have only just begun. These guys might still be playing in 35 years.

A pot of food is produced by the womenfolk of the house, a delicious stew accompanied by some rice. We are encouraged to eat, the Fogo wine flows a lot quicker than lava.

Towards midnight, we say our thanks and leave, despite protestations that we stay. Amazingly, it is us who are thanked profusely, and we depart feeling as if we have done these incredibly warm, generous people some kind of favour. Outside in the cold and the dark, the giant, brooding volcano seems to point upwards to a star-spangled sky.

& have great tips for adventure-seeking travellers. They also promise 24hr electricity. **$$**
EcoFunco (3 rooms) m 997 9935; e ecofunco@ ecofunco.com; w ecofunco.com. Léa & João's collection of brightly decorated *funcos* have great views of the volcano & the couple are known for their warm hospitality. **$$**
Oasis Coba-Tina (13 rooms) m 981 4792. Next to Chã winery, 2km before reaching Portela. It has a large restaurant. **$$**

WHERE TO EAT AND DRINK Map, page 237

Bar Restaurante Escoral m 977 1233. Serves basic dishes, including great homemade chips, directly opposite Casa Marisa & with an outside terrace & view. **$$**
Casa Elena m 9898 2127; ⏰ by appointment. Looking out over Bangaeira from Portela's high point, this family-run dining room serves beautiful dishes that are unique to the caldera, such as braised chicken & piquant gooseberries or tuna in a blanquette-style sauce. They also have rooms; the hosts are super attentive. To eat here, call ahead (or get your driver or hotel to do so). **$$**
Casa Marisa Page 239 Offers daily dishes such as chicken in sauce, pork & a fish dish, in a roomy dining hall. **$$**
Casa Ramiro m 587 2778; ⏰ daily. Grocer's store & wine bar at the midpoint between the 2 villages (notably one of the few buildings to survive the lava flow). You can do Chã wine tastings, buy a bottle, or sit down with a glass & a plate of fresh goat's cheese. **$**

ENTERTAINMENT AND NIGHTLIFE There is often wine, music and impromptu dancing at Casa Ramiro (see above). An evening there is unforgettable, if something that can't be planned.

WHAT TO SEE AND DO

Hiking The highlights are the walk up and down the big Pico (which can take anything from 3 to 6 hours, depending on your fitness and your proficiency at running back down through the lava powder), the walk down to Mosteiros and the hike to see the smaller 1995 peak and the 'new' peak of 2014. Some of these walks are described from page 243.

For some walks it is essential to have a guide and the use of one is strongly recommended. Most of all, for climbing the Pico do Fogo, because the path shifts with the movements of the ash. The crater rim, to be negotiated at times by clipping oneself to a cable handrail, should also involve a guide, as should any trip to the new peak.

There are several English-speaking guides conversant with the natural history of the volcano, having worked with botanists and geologists. The guides have formed themselves into an association, which should guarantee a good level of training and regulate pricing, as well as regulate group sizes. The current cost for a guide is 6,000$ to ascend the big Pico; 1,000$ for the small volcano. Best bet is to book through Casa Marisa or a tour operator, as this should ensure you get an official, reliable and English-speaking guide. For walks where a guide is not essential, you might still consider employing one to embellish the experience and contribute to the fragile local economy. Your hike will be greatly enriched by finding out at first-hand what it's like to have experienced a volcanic eruption and its consequences.

Wine It may seem extraordinary to most visitors to the crater that anything is grown here at all. But walking around, you'll quickly encounter apparently randomly planted vines. Each of these belongs to someone, however. Each year the planting of the vines creeps higher up the mountain. The humidity is trapped by the ash and a bit of animal manure is used to encourage the vines' growth. There is no watering of the vines, the trapped humidity and any rainfall providing the only moisture. Harvesting takes place in June.

> **THE DUKE OF MONTROND**
>
> The sudden preponderance of blue or green eyes, light skin and fair hair among the people of the crater can come as a surprise, even in ever-diverse Cabo Verde. This is, however, no mystery: you'll soon discover that over half of the residents here share the same French surname – Montrond.
>
> These families can trace their ancestry back to one François Louis Armand Fourcheut de Montrond, an eccentric French duke who, after setting off for Brazil, instead made Fogo his home in 1872. After travelling the islands and fixing on Fogo he spent the rest of his life here, only ever returning to France for visits. The duke had at least 11 children by a few wives and has over 300 descendants in the USA alone.
>
> His legacy exists in far more than the intriguing appearance of the crater's residents, however: he put to use his background in engineering and medicine in his new home. He oversaw the construction of a road from São Filipe to Mosteiros, and he sank wells, some of which are still in use today. Trained as a doctor, he also imported medicinal herbs along with, it is said, the vines that kicked off wine production on the volcano slopes. The duke died at age 56, after falling off his horse, breaking his leg, and sustaining a deadly infection.
>
> The duke was not credited for his achievements during his lifetime, because the Portuguese felt he showed them up, claims Alberto Montrond, a great-great-grandson who lives in the USA and regularly visits Fogo. 'He did great things for the people on the island,' he says. Alberto's work tracing the Montrond ancestry and investigating the duke's story was the subject of a French documentary film, **Odjo Branco**, released in 2011.

Post-eruption, government investment helped found the Adega Cooperativa de Chã das Caldeiras, opening in 2016 on a site that had recently been destroyed by lava. It has nearly 100 members and currently produces up to 300,000 litres per year, though production can vary. The grapes grown include Sabro, a white grape usually found only in the Canaries, and Baboso Negro, also now mostly cultivated in the Canaries, though it's originally from the Alentejo region in Portugal, and known there as Alfrocheiro. Its reds, whites and rosés, as well as a sparkling and a Passito-style sticky, can be found in restaurants throughout Cabo Verde. The production is all consumed domestically, though the odd bottle or two might by 'smuggled' back to the United States by homesick *emigrantes* after their holidays in the archipelago, says the co-operative's president. All the wine from the co-operative is sold under the 'Chã' label, and given its improbability, is very good indeed. In addition to wine, liqueurs made with pomegranate and herbs are also made here.

Casa Ramiro and other outlets sell wine with the Manecom label too, which is not part of the co-operative's production. You can also find unlabelled wine, but it's unlikely to have the same quality as the Chã label. With advance notice, you can visit and do tastings at the Chã **cellar door** (m 991 4262; e pedraburkan@gmail.com). Your tour may be in either French or Portuguese, but ask if the charming winemaker David Montrond is on site, as he speaks English.

Shopping At the high point between Portela and Bangaeira, Ramiro's shop/bar/restaurant sells an array of wines as well as groceries and various spirits, fruit juices and simple crafts. You may also be approached by children selling articles made from the few materials locally available, as well as little packets of pink peppercorns, coffee beans or raisins.

THE EAST-COAST ROAD TO MOSTEIROS

The journey up the east coast to Mosteiros is on a narrow, cobbled road and is spectacular. The points of interest here are the lava flows created by the 1951 eruption, a succession of jagged, dark intrusions on the landscape. Over 60 years on and still nothing grows on this unforgiving terrain. The road stays high above the sea: there are no swimmable beaches and little fishing for locals until the terrain flattens just before Mosteiros. Anyone driving this route will have their speed tempered by the usual suspects: the cobbles, speed bumps, all manner of animals and pedestrians. Turn off left just before Mosteiros, signposted to Pai António, on a short, steep detour to find a lookout point with views down over the lava flows and the beach. After Mosteiros, the road rises again away from the ocean, cutting across the middle of steep *ribeiras* as they plunge seawards. Eventually you reach tarmac which will return you to São Filipe.

MOSTEIROS

The town, also known as Vila da Igreja, is a useful stopping-off point for lunch during trips around the island but otherwise is not worth a visit on its own account. It has a pretty centre, squashed between the mountain and the sea, and a depressing suburbia of black, lava-block houses built on lava rock.

GETTING THERE AND AWAY The cobbled southern *aluguer* journey to and from São Filipe is a fantastic journey along the precipitous eastern slope of the island but since the opening of the tarmac road around the north and west, that is understandably the direction that most of the public transport prefers. If you are overnighting in Mosteiros, the proprietor of Pensão Christine will arrange for one of the drivers to call at the hotel for you early for the 06.00 run to São Filipe. Invigorating. The alternative is to take a later *aluguer* to Atalaia and change for transport to São Filipe. *Alugueres* leave São Filipe for Mosteiros at about midday.

WHERE TO STAY AND EAT Fogo coffee is excellent, and **Lava's Coffee Spirit** (991 7484; e lavascoffee@gmx.com; ⊕ by appt, Mon–Sat), on the road parallel to the main road through the southern part of Mosteiros, can arrange tastings in their lush courtyard, from the beans grown just above. Call ahead or ask your round-island taxi driver to do so. Packaged coffee is also for sale.

Pensão Restaurante Christine e Irmãos (11 rooms) 283 1045; e pensaorestaurantechristine@hotmail.com. In a rambling green building on the main road through town; airy & thoughtfully furnished rooms include some freshly updated ones with AC. Christine's excellent cooking & warm welcome make the restaurant & its big terrace a reliable lunch stop. **$$**

Pensão Tchon de Café (12 rooms) 283 1610; e gennybarbosa@hotmail.com. Rooms are pleasant, en suite with hot water, in this *pensão* nestled at the foot of a hill. The small restaurant with courtyard is well regarded. **$$**

Gira Lua [map, page 222] (2 rooms) Monte Borro, Pai António; m 953 4145; e giraluacv@gmail.com. Take the Pai António turn-off to the left, when entering Mosteiros from the south. Offers rooms with balcony & patio. Wi-Fi in public areas, restaurant & bar. Uses all local products, & serves some of the best coffee on the island. Superb views from its promontory high above Mosteiros. Popular with hikers on their way to the Chã das Caldeiras, 3hrs' walk away. **$**

OTHER PRACTICALITIES Both **BCA** and **Caixa** banks have ATMs in town. The hospital (**Centro de Saúde dos Mosteiros**; \ 282 1130) is a 5-minute drive north of Mosteiros. The **post office** is in the central square (⊕ 08.00–noon & 14.00–16.00 Mon–Fri).

OTHER PLACES TO VISIT

Nothing else on Fogo matches a crater visit, but all of the visits below are pleasant alternative ways of filling spare days on the island.

PONTO DA SALINA This is one of the few swimming spots on Fogo, and is darkly enchanting, the lava having formed a natural pool and rocks that protect bathers from the incoming waves. There are ladders to get you back to dry land after you've plunged into the sea, as well as a small curve of black pebble beach. Weekends here often take on a festive air, with locals bringing picnics and sound systems. It is located on the northwest coast, not far from the village of São Jorge. Take an *aluguer* bound for São Jorge, ask for the salina and walk the 20 minutes down to the sea. Do check about the return journey before setting off, though. A return taxi there can be negotiated for around the same price or a little less than an island circuit, and in a car, you can drive all the way there down the cobbles. A *pensão* and bar, **Hotel Salinas São Jorge**, opened late in 2024 and offers simple rooms with panoramic sea views, hearty seafood lunches and dinners, and has friendly English-speaking staff. There are no other facilities, other than lock-ups for the fishermen who depart at 04.00 each morning.

SÃO LOURENÇO Visiting this large church and peaceful graveyard, with clusters of white crosses all with stunning views of Brava, is a pleasant way of enjoying the green Fogo lowlands. It is a 12km round trip but you will probably find lifts for parts of the way. Leave São Filipe from the roundabout opposite the Bamboo Xaguate Hotel, and, with your back to the hotel, take the second turning on the left (the first leads down to the port).

MONTE GENEBRA AND NOSSA SENHORA DO SOCORRO Find an *aluguer* (or drive) to Forno and from there walk to the village of Luzia Nunes, then take the left fork to Monte Genebra, the light-coloured hummock down towards the sea. German development workers helped to build the gardens here in 1976. Pumping stations take hundreds of cubic metres of water from a natural spring near the sea, to water tomatoes, potatoes, cabbages and fruits. You can go to the top of Monte Genebra, while down towards the sea is the little chapel of Nossa Senhora do Socorro.

HIKES *Aisling Irwin (AI); Hannah Cruttenden (HC); Jacquie Cozens (JC); Murray Stewart (MS)*

1 THE PICO
Distance: 9km; time: return trip between 4 and 7 hours; difficulty: 2 (MS). A guide is essential.
Note that it requires energy and fitness particularly because there is no easy way of going back: to return halfway along requires a guide, but so does continuing to the top and there is generally only one guide per group.

From Portela, you will take the dirt road towards the left side of the big peak. First there is a gentle, flat meander through scattered fig trees, vines, apple and pear trees, as well as mustard plants and the odd lavender bush. After 10 minutes, the route goes off the main track and you face the volcano head-on. For the following half-hour, the slope is gentle, before ramping up steeply through ash and then on to a shoulder of stones, where occasionally you may have to scramble on all fours. Walking in ash is often a case of taking two steps forward and one back, making the calves protest. From the village to the summit will take most climbers between 3 and 5 hours. You may well come across examples of *lingua de vaca* (cow's tongue), an endemic plant, but you may be too focused on avoiding a fall. You will be grateful for any breeze. Away to your left, you will see the sea, bordered by the white of waves crashing on to the shore. At around two-thirds of the climb, you may catch the first whiff of sulphur, then it's gone on the wind, only to return again, this time perhaps stronger. From the summit, gazing down into the crater, the twin villages are like dust specks below. Marvelling at the crater in front of you and pondering the *via ferrata* for the more adventurous, you will no doubt conclude that all the effort has been worthwhile. This is one of the steepest and most spectacular volcanic cones in the world and you have just conquered it. Now, the real fun is about to begin.

The first part of the descent involves 15 minutes of picking your way back down over the stony descent. Then, your guide takes you across to the top of the slope of ash scree. Staring down maybe 600m of steep descent, off he sets with giant strides, each ending in his front leg sinking knee-high in *lapilli*. Perhaps tentatively at first you follow him, but quickly you realise that you can't fall and your confidence and speed increase accordingly. You have to focus on what's in front of you, as the odd rock will appear, threatening to derail you and halt your rapid return to the villages. This is better than any fairground rollercoaster, surely. Your guide will have done this many times before, so is likely to be more fearless and quicker than you, however much of your inner daredevil you release. Eventually the ash becomes thinner and you have to return to a more conventional descent, as the depth of ash is no longer enough to cushion those giant strides. As long as your knees have held up, you'll have a giant smile on your face. As well as dirty black legs, you will have socks that will need several washes and boots that will be spewing out bits of ash for weeks to come.

2 PORTELA–1995 PEAK–2014 CRATER–PORTELA

Distance: 9km; time: 3 hours; difficulty: 2 (MS). A guide is recommended.

You will never have done a walk like this. Walking across the dusty *lapilli* that seems to muffle sound and life, then up to the 1995 peak, before making the short ascent to peer down into the colourful, smoking crater created in 2014. It still throws out sulphur and nearby fissures are red-hot: drop in a tissue and they will combust. A guide is recommended, but if you are going solo, your 'sighter' is the right-hand side of the big peak, where its steep slope levels out with three little peaks to the right. Leave Portela on a traceable path with Casa Alcindo behind you on your left, passing through sporadically planted fruit trees and vines, your path pushing gently upwards. As you approach, you will see that you first ascend the 1995 peak, on a steep but fairly short path; once at the top, down to your left is the 1995 crater, now losing the chemical colours from its interior rockface – weather has taken its toll. Now proceed to climb again, once more short and steep, to find yourself by the new, slightly higher, 2014 craters. A small one to your left, where you will also find a couple of fissures, still widening, while to your right are a chain of larger craters which were responsible for the destructive lava flows which wiped out the villages.

The largest of these still emits sulphur and the rocks are tinged with the colour of chemicals. A narrow ridge – not to be attempted – extends along the edge of the crater chain. High above you towers the high Pico. Away down below to your left you can see where the lava truncated the cobbled road that once led into the wider crater, and the secondary dirt track that now curves around below the *caldera* wall and serves as the primary route in its place.

You must return more or less the same way you arrived, but the descent is much easier and should take about 45 minutes. The buildings of Portela provide you with guidance.

3 BANGAEIRA–CRATER RIM–BANGAEIRA
Distance: approximately 14km; time: 5 hours; difficulty: 2 (AI)
This trip takes you up to the rim of the volcano for a stunning bird's-eye view of the crater. Parts of the path are steep and slippery.

From the centre of Portela, walk the 5km north along the road to the barrier that marks the protected forest. Continue down the road for 15 minutes to a fork. The road to the right leads to Mosteiros. Follow the left-hand road which becomes a dirt track, quite precarious in places. It winds its way up the side of the volcano. Soon you find yourself above the low cloud, gazing at a superb view of Santiago, if the weather is clear. The road eventually climbs steeply upwards to a large white building used to store rice and grain: this is where cars must stop. Walk past the front of the storehouse and on to a path running along the left-hand side of the building and up towards the volcano rim. It's a steep climb and the path is slippery in places but it shouldn't take longer than half an hour to get to the top.

This part of the crater is very green and you will see women from the villages gathering firewood. Recent eruptions are 'mapped out' in the vast area below, covered by lava. The darker the lava, the more recently it has been spewed out. Closer to you, the slightly lighter-coloured lava is from 1951; the lightest-coloured lava, directly in front of you, is oldest of all. It is possible to continue walking round the rim – but take a guide.

4 PORTELA–1995 LAVA FLOW–BOCA FONTE–*COOPERATIVA*
Distance: 5km; time: 2 hours; difficulty: 1 (HC)
This 2-hour walk starts in the centre of Portela. From there, follow the road that goes to your right and skirts the foot of the crater wall (your transport will have arrived on this road). The track leads you towards the west walls of the crater and continues round the edge of the 1995 lava to the former village of Boca Fonte – now destroyed except for the colonnaded façade of a *Cooperativa* which still stands at the edge of the flow. About 100m further on, climb up on to the lava and clamber across it to get a view of a house marooned in the flow. A short walk later you arrive at the vineyards, straggling along the ground like weeds. Next, after curving round to the left and on to the southern side, you'll see several small agricultural and fruit farms and off to your right, the wine co-operative. The agricultural produce goes to the market in São Filipe. While formerly you would have had the chance to turn left on to the cobbled road back towards the Pico and Portela, now you will have to retrace your steps as the road is blocked by lava.

5 CRATER–MONTEBARRO–PAI ANTÓNIO–MOSTEIROS
Distance: approximately 10km; time: 4–5 hours; difficulty: 2 (AI)
This delightful walk takes you out of the crater and down the volcano's steep northeastern side, with views across the sea to Santiago, and a host of pretty

plantations, in particular oranges and coffee. The hike involves some steep descents likely to produce aching and shaking knees, and those who find such descents difficult could find the walk takes 5 hours. Navigationally it is pretty easy.

Begin with a 5km walk north along the road through Bangaeira and the crater which takes you out, past a road barrier that marks the protected forest and on past a road to the left that goes to **Montinho**. Two minutes after this turning there is a steep little path down to the right. You can stick with the road or follow this short cut, in which case you will rejoin the road after 10 minutes, turning right. Some 15 minutes past this point you arrive in Monte Velho. The road bends to the right over the bridge where there are a few small houses. After crossing the bridge leave the road and turn right, down the right-hand side of the first house. The path takes you down the side of a ravine, across which can be seen the president's house. Giant *carapate* plants stack the sides of the path. Descend through **Pede Pranta**, after which the ban on farming expires. You enter little valleys planted with coffee, mango and orange plants.

Mist drifts upwards and the view of the ocean through the vegetation is beautiful. After a while, descending past little dwellings built on terraces of lava rock, you reach the first region of Mosteiros – **Montebarro** – and the air is filled with the scents of oranges and fires and the noise of children and cockerels. Three hours into the walk you reach **Pai António**, with a steeply cobbled street, from where it is a 40-minute walk down the cobbled road (ignoring the left turning to Feijoal) to the centre of Mosteiros. Alternatively, it should be possible to pick up a lift in Pai António to save your knees that last steep descent.

6 THE CRATER RIM
This is probably the longest walk available as it could take as long as two days, but a shorter version is possible. Stretches of the rim are so precarious (Ponte Alto de Norte and Ponte Alto do Sol are the worst sections) that the park staff have erected cable handrails to which you can clip yourself with a hoop available from the park offices. It is essential to have a guide. Contact Casa Marisa in advance (page 239) for more details and to organise a guide.

7 MOSTEIROS–FEIJOAL–MOSTEIROS
Distance: approximately 5km; time: 2 hours; difficulty: 2 (AI)
There are various strolls up into the lower slopes of the volcano. To walk up to **Feijoal** for a drink, leave Mosteiros on the south road and, a little after the big Delegação de Fogo, take the cobbled road on the right (ignore a turning up to the left just before Feijoal). After a drink at the *mercado*, find a little footpath (*caminho para Igreja*) back into the centre of Mosteiros: with your back to the *mercado* turn right and the path is a few metres along on the left, running between two buildings. It's a bit slippery and the less sure of foot may prefer to return by the road.

8 CAVES
Distance: approximately 1km; time: 1 hour; difficulty: 1 (JC)
A simple walk to see some caves that you can look inside, but you will need a guide to explore properly.

WALKING ROUND THE NORTH From the Mosteiros end, the first 2km north along the coast are dismal – save your legs and hitch if you can. Just before the disused airport, there is a left turning uphill. This is the beginning of a spectacular road, which goes up to Ribeira Ilhéu and then continues as a 9km track to São Jorge.

From there you have to try and hitch back to São Filipe – there is supposed to be an *aluguer* at 13.00. The better alternative is to take a mid-morning *aluguer* to São Jorge from São Filipe and walk in the other direction, staying in Mosteiros at the end of the walk.

8

Brava

Swallows of the wide seas
What wind of loyalty
Brings you on this bitter journey
To our land of *Sodade*

Eugénio Tavares, quoted in Archibald Lyall,
Black and White Make Brown (Heinemann, 1938)

Brava is the most secret of the islands – a volcano crater hides its town, rough seas encircle it and the winds that buffet it are so strong that its airport has been closed for years. Brava lies only 20km from its big brother, Fogo, but many visitors to Cabo Verde will merely glimpse it from the greater island's western slopes.

Brava – or 'wild' island – appears at first to live up to the meaning of its name. Approaching by boat, the dark mass resolves itself into sheer cliffs with painted houses dotting the heights above. A few fishing hamlets huddle at sea level.

But its unpromising slopes hide a hinterland that is at times fertile and moist, filled with hibiscus flowers and cultivation. At least that is how it was: today, after years of drought, its flowers are less visible and its food more likely to be imported than grown.

This tiny, westerly island, dropping off the end of the archipelago into the Atlantic, seems to always look towards where the sun sets – it is dreaming of the possibilities of America. Perhaps that is no surprise. For Brava is the island where the great 19th-century American whaling ships called to pick up crews and spirit hopeful young men away to new lives on another continent (page 268). The legacy is an island full of empty houses waiting for the return of the *Americanos* who have built them for their retirement. Meanwhile, a big container ship from Boston visits several times a year and American goods appear in the streets. Brava Creole is peppered with American expressions; those who speak English do so with a transatlantic twang, their words emerging from beneath a Boston Red Sox baseball cap. For some visitors and the few expats who have chosen to live here, Brava is the most 'authentic' of the islands. There are few concessions to tourism and the inhabitants get on with their everyday lives regardless. Having said that, those visitors who choose to engage with the locals will find a friendly, welcoming and gregarious people, more than willing to share their time and space with tourists. At times you may feel that *you* are the real attraction.

HIGHLIGHTS AND LOWLIGHTS

Go for the walking, for the peace and for the sheer authenticity and intrigue of a place that is so out of the way. Contemplate the gentle, communal way of life, appreciate the challenges the locals face with transport and water supply. Don't go for beaches or watersports, don't expect any conventional tourist attractions, and don't go if you are pushed for time. If you have just arrived from Praia or São Filipe, with their comparative bustle of taxis gently tooting their horns for your business, you will find Brava's capital, Vila Nova Sintra, to be a quiet alternative. With little traffic, cobbled streets and a sense of space, it is a pleasant town in which to stroll, though with few outright attractions as such.

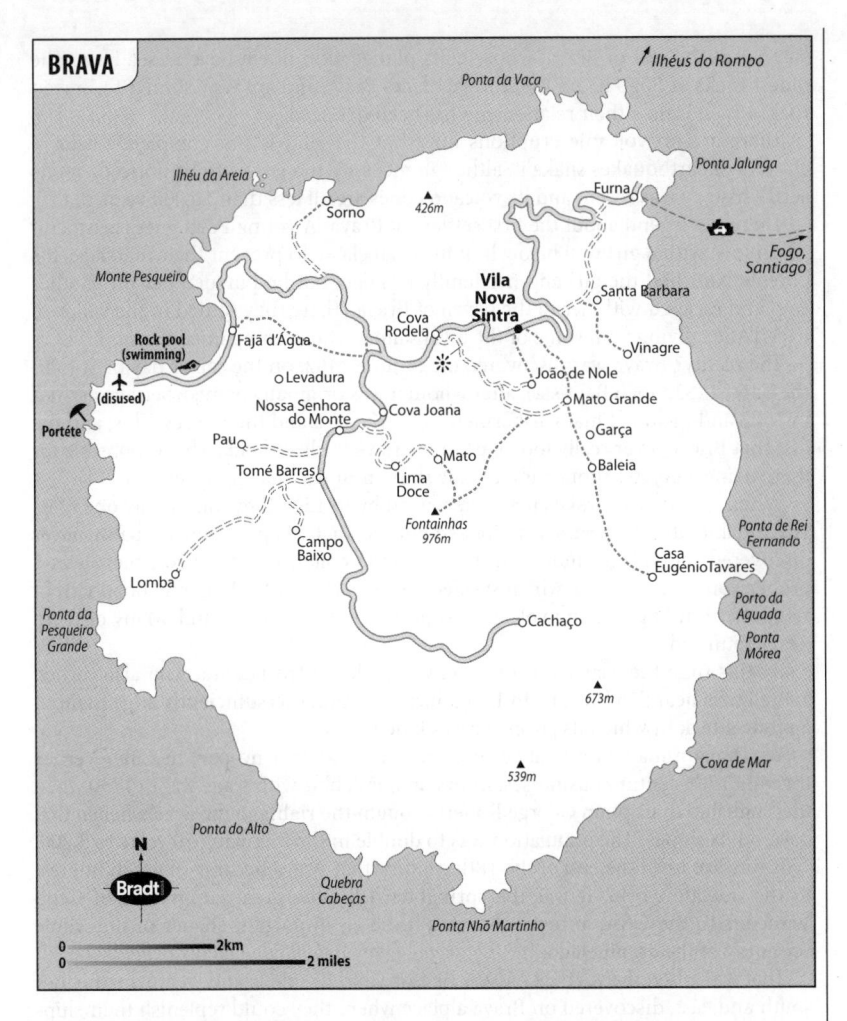

SUGGESTED ITINERARY AND NUMBER OF DAYS Brava is small. While it would be physically feasible to see all the island in less than a day by vehicle, it would be a shame (as well as impossible, with current ferry timetables) to leave it at that. Fajã d'Água is a beautiful place to relax for a few days, perhaps taking a fishing trip, while keen hikers will find several days' worth of enchanting walks to undertake.

BACKGROUND INFORMATION

HISTORY Brava is, geologically speaking, part of Fogo. The channel between them is just a few hundred metres deep – shallow compared with the ocean floor that surrounds the rest of Brava, whose cliffs plunge 4km down beyond sea level. The oldest rocks of Fogo lie on the side that faces Brava and are very similar to Bravan rock, which is how their relationship has been deduced.

There are no volcanic eruptions now, but the land is not completely calm – clusters of earthquakes shake it, although most are too gentle to be noticed. Yet its active history was recent and its volcano cones are all less than 10,000 years old.

There is a legend about the first settlers of Brava. A young Portuguese aristocrat fell in love with a girl well below him in social class. To prevent their marriage, his parents banished the girl and her family to Fogo, but he pursued her on another ship and escaped with her to the haven of Brava. There they settled in the valley of Fajã d'Água, living with some of the loyal sailors who accompanied them.

The reality? Brava was discovered on 24 June 1462, on the saint's day of St John the Baptist (São João Baptista), after whom it was originally named. Settlers arrived in 1573 and included many fishermen from Madeira and the Azores. This, and the fact that Brava never really took part in the slave trade, is held to be responsible for there being a greater proportion of pale skin on Brava than anywhere else.

When Sir Francis Drake's mariners passed by in 1578 they found only one of its 100 inhabitants – a hermit who looked after a small chapel. They probably never discovered the villages hidden in the volcano's crater. By the 1620s, there was a proper community there, which swelled 60 years later with desperate boatloads of refugees from Fogo fleeing volcanic eruptions on their own island. Many of them never returned.

By this time the island was owned by Luis de Castro Pereira, who also owned Santa Luzia near São Vicente. In 1686, the population was sufficiently large to merit a pirate attack in which its governor was killed.

Yet Brava remained a relative secret and took almost no part in Cabo Verde's thriving 17th-century businesses. Its first major dabble with trade was in 1730 when the Englishman Captain George Roberts bought the rights to the urzela lichen that covered its slopes. The population was to double in the following 50 years to 3,200.

It was not until the end of the 18th century that Brava became of much interest to the outside world. It was the springboard for the great emigration of Cabo Verdeans to the USA: an exile that was to be an important shaper of the whole economy of the archipelago.

That was when the whalers of New Bedford and Rhode Island, venturing further south and east, discovered on Brava a place where they could replenish their ships and recruit eager new crews. English whaling boats recruited there as well – it was easy for the ships to land in Brava's small but secluded harbours. Many of the young men disembarked at New England and set up new lives there (page 268).

Withstanding an attack in 1798 by the French, who were trying to oust the Portuguese from the islands, Brava continued to prosper into the first decades of the 19th century. Intellectually, Brava became the place to be. The parish of Our Lady of the Mountain was created, an American consul arrived in 1843 and a secondary school opened in the 1850s to which students came from throughout the archipelago and from Portuguese Guinea. It was into this environment that the poet Eugénio Tavares was born in 1867 (page 257).

By the late 19th century, Brava was considered one of the most pleasant islands in which to live and its population rose to 9,200. Income surged into the 20th century, as American *emigrantes* sent their money home. But the prosperity was not to last. The depression came; remittances from abroad dwindled and, confident that the rainy years of the 1930s would continue, many *Americanos* returned home.

It was a mistake. A drought was looming that was to prove the worst catastrophe in Brava's history. It squeezed the island just as World War II caused foreign remittances to dry up completely. Hundreds died in the ensuing famine.

Brava's ageing population peaked at 10,000 in the 1960s and then fell back again. Some predict it may fall to 3,000, less than half of its current level. Other more recent disasters were Hurricane Beryl, which destroyed much of the infrastructure in 1982 and earth tremors in August 2016, which prompted the evacuation of Cova Joana village. Luckily, the residents returned unscathed within a few days.

BRAVA TODAY On the surface not too much has changed on Brava and the march of developers and property speculators has left it unspoiled. What changes have occurred are welcome: the square in the principal town has been further prettified and new small hotels have sprung up. Land prices underwent a surge in the mid-2010s. This may partly have been in anticipation of what has happened on other islands, or because Cabo Verde's prosperity is attracting more *emigrantes* from Brava to return from the US and elsewhere. Also, there is anecdotal evidence that the building of schools on Brava has combined with general optimism about the future to reduce the flow of emigration, though people are still leaving. The population now hovers around 7,000. In 2024 plans were announced for a Marriott hotel resort in Vila Nova Sintra, with nearly 200 rooms, a conference centre, spa, gym and transport fleet. Aimed at the US *emigrante* market, it might not end up being of much interest to independent travellers, but will help the island's economy

FESTIVALS ON BRAVA

The festival of São João is held on 24 June and many emigrants return for it. Several days before the festival the women begin a ritual pounding of the corn, joined by others who sing with a high-pitched chanting and clap to a complex beat until the preparation is finished. Another preparation for the festival is the dressing of the mast of *Cutelo Grande* – decorating it with intricately woven breads and also cakes, fruit and drinks and guarding it against pilfering by children. On the day, the mast – all greenery and red flowers and edible ornaments – is raised with a pulley. At the right moment the pulleys are cut, the mast comes plummeting to the ground and the children run to grab what plunder they can. In Vila Nova Sintra, a number of temporary bars are constructed in a designated space opposite the market, and music, drinking and dancing take over. The heaviest imbibers can be seen sleeping off their excesses in the streets. Other festivals are as follows:

5 January	Twelfth Night
20 January	São Sebastião
1 May	São José/Labour Day
24 June	São João (Brava's main festival)
Late June	Miss & Mister Brava Quest
1st Sunday in July	São Paulo
2nd Sunday in July	São Paulinho
Last Sunday in July	Santaninha de Baleia e Mato Grande
	Santa Ana
1st fortnight in August	Nossa Senhora do Monte (Fuma)
15 August	Nossa Senhora da Graça

with an influx of jobs. Meanwhile, many people depend on government aid and the island relies heavily on fruit and vegetables imported from Fogo, Praia and Portugal. Maize is planted every year but often turns brown and dies. In better times the islanders can grow coffee, sugarcane, cassava, maize, potatoes and bananas, as well as papayas, mangoes and other fruits. Finding enough fodder to fill the cattle can be a struggle. Fishing forms the base of the economy, with some of the catch exported to other islands.

GEOGRAPHY The archipelago's smallest inhabited island, Brava is 64km^2 and just 10km across at its widest point. Much of the coastline is steep cliffs, which rise to a dry central tableland with some mountains rising out of it. In the west there is a spectacular valley – Fajã d'Água – which previously enjoyed the benefits of a small, semi-permanent stream, now long gone. Nevertheless, it is still green in parts. The valley between Lomba and Tantum is fed by a stream which creates something of an oasis. Offshore in Fajã's beautiful bay, photo opportunities for visitors are presented by the many jagged, wave-battered rocks and stacks. The highest point of the island is Monte Fontainhas at 976m, and often swathed in mist. Even a little lower down, within the crater, there is generally moisture and coolness.

FLORA AND FAUNA Brava hosts none of Cabo Verde's 47 protected areas but the adjacent Ilhéus do Rombo are a protected reserve. There are 24 endemic species on the island. The Cape Verde warbler (*Acrocephalus brevipennis*) once made Brava its home but is thought to have gone now, with dwindling agriculture. However, it was also thought to have disappeared from São Nicolau but was later rediscovered, so keep a lookout. The previously endangered Cape Verde shearwater is most famous for its occupancy of Ilhéu Raso, but also dwells within the Ilhéus do Rombo. Up in the valleys above Fajã d'Água and Lomba, carefully nurtured crops of fruit can be swiped by the mischievous monkeys who live there. Wild goats also pose a problem. Offshore, you may spot a pod of dolphins or the occasional whale passing by.

Flowering garden plants found on Brava include plumeira, bougainvillea and jasmine. Vila Nova Sintra abounds with planted dragon trees (*Dracaena draco*). It is cold between December and April in the *vila* and in higher zones. Rains normally fall from late June to September and at times these are heavy and cause rockslides.

SAFETY Swimmers should ask locals about any hazards before taking a dip. The natural rock swimming pool near the disused airport is a good bet and reasonably accessible from Fajã d'Água.

GETTING THERE AND AWAY

Historically, Brava has been very hard to reach. There is no air service to the island because of dangerously strong crosswinds. The history of the ferry service to Brava has also been patchy, with ferry companies appearing and disappearing, amid cancellations and delays due to bad weather. The CV Interilhas ferry today is comparatively comfortable, but is still susceptible to significant delays and cancellations. At the time of writing, there were only three crossings to and from Fogo a week, and as the ship returns immediately to Fogo, then on to Praia, day trips are impossible. It is always necessary to confirm departure times in advance, either at the local CV Interilhas office, by checking on their website or with one of the travel agencies, as the schedule can change. Trying to leave Brava with an international flight looming from Sal or Santiago is stressful and also fairly certain to end in trouble: it is advisable to give yourself at least a few days' leeway to get back to Fogo, though if bad weather persists, even that may not be enough. Take seasickness tablets and accept the offer of the plastic sick bags cheerfully handed out on board by the ferry staff!

BY FERRY Ferry tickets to Brava can be bought online, or in São Filipe on Fogo either from the CV Interilhas office or from Qualitur, Zebra Travel or other travel agencies (page 229). In Vila Nova Sintra on Brava, go to Brava tur [map, page 255] for your ticket. The price is 1,500$ one-way from Fogo, or 4,450$ from Praia. Some agencies advise purchasing return tickets in advance (a return is no cheaper than two singles but ferries do get booked up during festival periods on both Brava and Fogo). Ferry timings are subject to last-minute changes, so do check the day before.

BY YACHT Some of the best anchorages in the archipelago are here. Fajã d'Água is secure and beautiful, as is Furna, except during southeasterly winds.

GETTING AROUND

On arrival at Furna, get to Vila Nova Sintra either by chartered **aluguer** (1,500$) or shared *aluguer* (350$), which will be waiting for you quayside. Alternatively, you could walk the steep 3km up the old road, the reverse of the hike described on page 269 though with luggage it will seem a long, long way. From Vila Nova Sintra to Nossa Senhora do Monte a charter is around 1,500$, to Fajã d'Água about 2,000$. From Furna to Fajã d'Água is 2,250$. If these seem expensive, ask around to see if you can share the cost with fellow travellers.

The island's road network is so small that even one day's **car hire** is unnecessary. There is one local car-rental company, DT Servicos de Transporte in Nova Sintra (285 1136; 08.00–18.00 daily, though these hours are highly speculative) but actual cars are very scarce. You might also find a car by asking at one of the tour operators on Fogo or at O Poeta restaurant (page 256).

WHERE TO STAY AND EAT

There are few options around the island, but Vila Nova Sintra, naturally, has the biggest choice. For something even more remote and relaxing, a seaside stay in Fajã d'Água is recommended. There are a number of restaurants in the capital, with a few more options in Fajã d'Água and Furla. Hotels and guesthouses usually offer meals as well. Note that in Fajã d'Água you usually have to order ahead, and that most places on the island will only accept cash.

EXCURSIONS AND TOUR OPERATORS

If you want something organised on your behalf, do it from Fogo with **Zebra Travel** or **Qualitur** (page 229).

ACTIVITIES

HIKING Brava is a superb hiking destination, with numerous circular walks, many of which can start and finish at the *vila* (page 262). Hikes from Fajã d'Água or Cova Rodela are plentiful.

SIGHTSEEING BY BOAT AND FISHING From Fajã d'Água, it is possible to hire a fisherman and his boat, for a trip along the coast, a spot of fishing, or both (page 260).

SIGHTSEEING BY VEHICLE You could probably see Brava in half a day by vehicle.

SWIMMING Brava is not really a place for swimming, but there are a few safe lagoons, including the natural sea pools between Fajã d'Água and the disused airport.

FURNA

Furna is the main port and lies in an extinct volcano crater, encircled with rocks on three sides. The bay is just a few hundred metres in diameter – sailing ships used to find it easy to get in but trickier to escape. It is more bustling than the *vila* but not as attractive.

From Furna the road winds up the slopes of the mountain. The sea and the harbour sink far below until after endless hairpins, it drops suddenly over the rim of a small depression and into Vila Nova Sintra.

There are modest restaurants and bars near the waterside in Furna, should you get stuck waiting for the ferry, but there is no real reason to linger. Note the town currently has no ATMs.

VILA NOVA SINTRA

> ...an enchanted garden hanging by invisible cords from the clouds
> Archibald Lyall

Named after the Portuguese town of Sintra, the *vila* is 520m above sea level. For weeks it can labour under a *Brigadoon*-like fog, inspiring melancholy in the visitor. On a clear day, though, there is a view across the ocean to Fogo: it is said that if you have good eyes you can see the women in São Filipe cleaning rice.

Nova Sintra is a quaint town, nestled among wild volcanic rocks but with a well-kept feel to it. Pretty and planted, hibiscus trees line many of its streets, scarlet against the ancient cobblestones. In wet years its gardens are jumbles of blue plumbago and bougainvillea, almond trees and jacaranda. The houses of the town – all Portuguese whitewash with red tiles – are covered in flowering vegetation, and fruit trees intersperse with fields of corn and cabbage. A good deal of renovation work has taken place over the years and the result is pleasing on the eye. Statues fêting Eugénio Tavares and São João Baptista add to the palpable sense of civic pride.

The *vila* is very quiet and sometimes you can be the only person in the pretty square. But before mealtimes the fish vendors arrive, crying '*Nhos cumpra peixe*' – 'You all buy fish'. Each of the three fishing communities has its own signature cry so that potential customers will know where their dinner is from before they make their purchase.

WHERE TO STAY *Map, opposite*

Hotel Brava Tur (10 rooms) 285 1919; m 972 7878; e bravaturbrava@gmail.com. Large rooms, some suites, with tiled floors & high ceilings. $$$

Hotel Cruz Grande (11 rooms) 285 1222; e cvol.brava@caboverdeonline.com. Modern building in colonial style, with good-size rooms, decent hot water. Friendly, helpful staff. Restaurant. $$$

Hotel Pousada Brava (8 rooms) 285 1222; e cvol.brava@caboverdeonline.com. A neatly

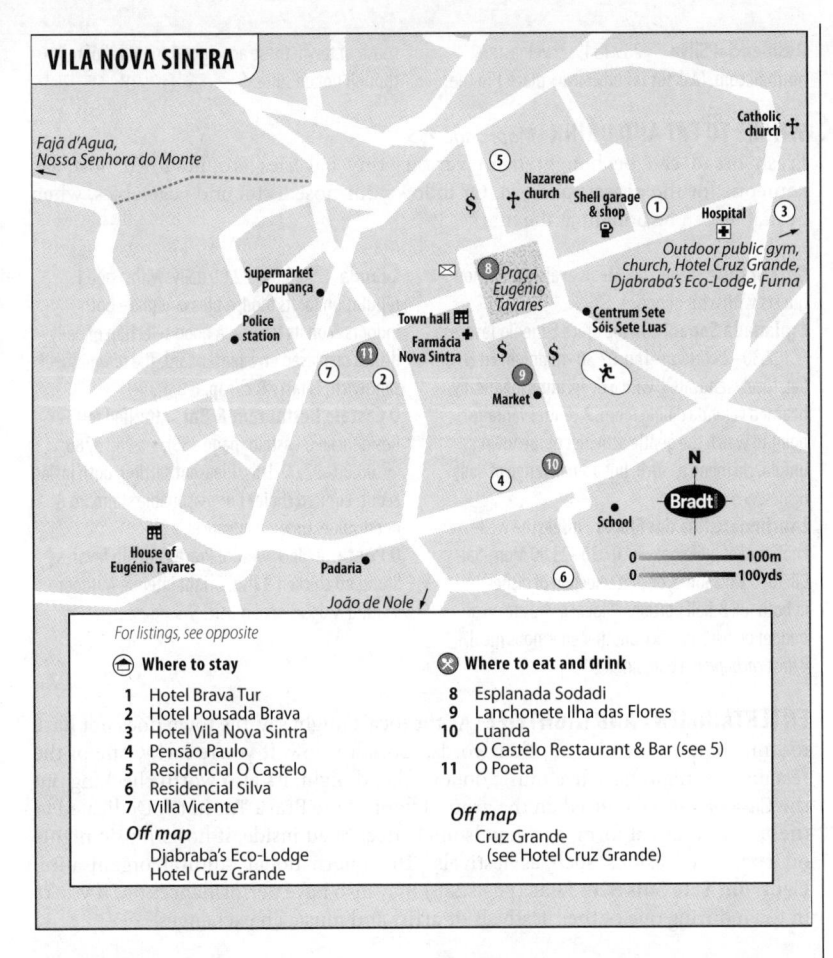

VILA NOVA SINTRA

For listings, see opposite

Where to stay
1. Hotel Brava Tur
2. Hotel Pousada Brava
3. Hotel Vila Nova Sintra
4. Pensão Paulo
5. Residencial O Castelo
6. Residencial Silva
7. Villa Vicente

Off map
   Djabraba's Eco-Lodge
   Hotel Cruz Grande

Where to eat and drink
8. Esplanada Sodadi
9. Lanchonete Ilha das Flores
10. Luanda
    O Castelo Restaurant & Bar (see 5)
11. O Poeta

Off map
   Cruz Grande
     (see Hotel Cruz Grande)

---

renovated colonial property, offering good-standard, simple rooms. Under same ownership as the Cruz Grande, but with colonial character. **$$$**

Djabraba's Eco-Lodge (8 rooms) 285 2694; m 979 4934; e marcogiandinoto@gmail.com; w djabrabaeco-lodge.cv. Italian-run place east of town, overlooking Furna. Good en-suite rooms, if a hostel-like vibe, some with great mountain views. Also 2 self-catering suites. Mario, the owner, is hugely helpful with local advice, including hikes, & can arrange charity donations to local schools too. **$$**

Pensão Paulo (20 rooms) 285 1312; e pensaopaulo@hotmail.com; w pgbspensao.cv. Dark wood furniture, ornate bedspreads & the like make this old-fashioned guesthouse feel like you're staying with your long-lost Cabo Verdean granny. Rooms are en suite & have TVs. **$$**

Residencial O Castelo (10 rooms) 1 block north of Praça Eugénio Tavares; 285 1063; m 982 5786; e eugenia.martins@yahoo.com. The owner, Eugenia, lived in the US for years & speaks English. A comfortable, well-established B&B, some rooms with private bathroom. Try to get a top-floor room, as these are brighter with big windows. Bar & restaurant downstairs. **$$**

Villa Vicente (3 rooms) m 958 3532. A 5-min walk from the *praça*, this small guesthouse is welcoming & pristinely renovated. B/fast is generous & there's a shared rooftop for evening drinks. **$$**

Hotel Vila Nova Sintra (18 rooms) 285 2037; m 973 0852; e pensao_novasintra@yahoo.com. Spacious rooms in a large building, clean but with rather dated décor. At the lower end of the price scale though, & good value. Some rooms supposedly have minibars: it's worth asking. **$**

Residencial Silva ✆ 285 1349; e velnastar@hotmail.com. (Ask for Johnny Silva's place.) To the south of town, these are a good standard of room though not en suite. **$**

✖ WHERE TO EAT AND DRINK *Map, page 255*

Fresh bread can be bought from various tiny bakeries around town: just ask someone for the nearest *padaria*. Or follow your nose. Fruit and vegetables, when available, can be bought at the market.

Cruz Grande Page 254. Meals available for non-guests with a bit of notice. **$$$**

Esplanada Sodadi On the Praça Eugénio Tavares; ⊕ 07.30–22.00 Sun–Thu, 07.30–midnight Fri & Sat. Nicely renovated, with a deep, atmospherically beamed veranda dining room. A central vantage point to watch the gentle activities of the town unfold. No menu as such, but a small range of daily dishes. **$$**

Lanchonete Ilha das Flores Inside the well-kept market building; ⊕ 07.30–23.00 Mon–Sat, 08.30–23.00 Sun. A decent selection of dishes in both full & half portions – ideal if you are on a budget or just can't face another enormous meal. B/fast *cachupa* is a bargain. **$$**

Luanda ⊕ 08.00–22.00 daily. With a good reputation for its food, a pleasant place both indoors & on its terrace. A good selection of daily dishes displayed on a blackboard. The *bifana* (beef sandwich) is tasty & cheap. **$$**

O Castelo Restaurant & Bar Attached to Residencial O Castelo (page 255); m 982 5786; ⊕ 08.00–22.00 daily. Pleasant setting, both inside & out. Limited choice but reasonable standard & good value. Order in advance! **$$**

O Poeta A block west of Praça Eugénio Tavares. Standard chicken & fish. Bright interior, outdoor seating & occasional music. **$$**

ENTERTAINMENT AND NIGHTLIFE As the locals might say, the town does not have too much 'movement' – in other words, footfall is low. If you're lucky, one of the restaurants might have live music on a weekend night; it's also worth checking out the **Casa di Morna**, housed on the ground floor of the Brava Tur hotel. Dedicated to the *morna* musical form, and handsomely decorated inside, it hosts music nights on special occasions such as festivals. The international cultural organisation **Centrum Sete Sóis Sete Luas** (page 258) may also have performances on, if you're in town during one of their festivals or artist and musician exchanges.

OTHER PRACTICALITIES

Banks Caixa, BCA and BCN banks are all close to the Praça Eugénio Tavares, all with ATMs (⊕ 08.00–15.00 Mon–Fri).

Health care Brava's medical outpost is on the Furna road out of the *praça*, on the right (✆ 285 1130). There is no capacity for complex interventions like transfusions or surgery. There is now a well-stocked official pharmacy, Farmácia Nova Sintra, also just by the *praça* (✆ 285 1309; ⊕ 08.30–15.00 Mon–Fri, 08.30–noon Sat); the pharmacist Evaldina Gonçalves, known as Edna, can arrange emergency supplies outside opening hours – ask your hotel to make contact.

Police On the main road, west of the Praça Eugénio Tavares (✆ 285 1132).

Post office On the Praça Eugénio Tavares (⊕ 08.00–15.00 Mon–Fri).

Shopping *Minimercados* are often better stocked than those on Fogo because of the American connection. For Fogo wine, *grogue*, certain food and drink products that are unavailable elsewhere, and items like sunscreen, try the impressively large

Supermarket Poupança (⊕ 08.00–20.00 daily) just off the main road that leads from the *praça*.

Tourist information There is no formal tourist information in town, but staff at the town hall (*câmara municipal*; ℡285 1314) are very helpful to visitors looking for guidance, as are hotel owners.

WHAT TO SEE AND DO A house once occupied by Eugénio Tavares (see below) is southwest of the centre, just off the main road and has been transformed into a modest **museum** (⊕ 09.00–noon & 13.00–16.00 Mon–Fri, though these are very unreliable), honouring one of Brava's favourite sons. There is also a bandstand with a plaque commemorating Tavares on the main *praça* that bears his name. In English, it translates as:

EUGÉNIO TAVARES

Eugénio Tavares was born in 1867 and spent his life writing music and in particular developing the art of the *morna*. He wrote in Creole rather than Portuguese, which was one reason for his immense popularity. Tavares lived on Brava where the sense of parting was particularly strong. Perhaps his most famous work is 'Hora di Bai' ('Hour of Leaving'), which was traditionally sung at Furna dock as relatives boarded the ships bound for the USA. The first verse is as follows:

Hora di bai	Hour of going
Hora de dor	Hour of pain
Dja'n q'ré	I wish
Pa el ca mantché	That it would not dawn!
De cada bêz	Each time
Que'n ta lembrâ	That I remember thee,
Ma'n q'ré	I would choose
Fica 'n morrê	To stay and die!

Translated in *Atlantic Islands* by Bentley Duncan (Chicago, 1972)

'Hora di Bai' is traditionally the last song, played at the end of the evening. You need the music and the dancing to appreciate the *morna*. As Archibald Lyall wrote:

> Properly to appreciate the work of Eugénio Tavares, it is necessary to see the humble people for whom he wrote gliding close-locked round the whitewashed, oil-lit room and to hear them, drugged for a few hours by his genius into forgetting their sorrows, singing softly to the strains of fiddle and guitar.

Tavares was primarily a composer – the words, it is said, took a couple of hours to invent after he had finished the music. But his lyrics struck deep in the hearts of his countrymen. Famous *mornas* of his include 'O Mar Eterno' (inspired by his love for an American woman who visited Brava on a yacht; her horrified father whisked her away one night and he never saw her again), and his lullaby, 'Ná ó menino ná'. When Tavares died in 1930, the whole of the island went to the funeral.

There above in planetary spheres
Shine brilliant and amazing stars:
But here on earth, one shines
For ever: Eugénio Tavares

One of the larger colonial houses on Praça Eugénio Tavares is the home of Brava's branch of the **Centrum Sete Sóis Sete Luas** (e info@7sois.org; w festival7sois. eu), an international Lusophone festival organisation. Check their website for occasional performances and exhibitions, usually in October and November, but sometimes at other times too.

FAJÃ D'ÁGUA

This is probably the most beautiful bay in Cabo Verde – a little village at the foot of the mountains, sheltered from the northeast winds and always with a bit of green, at least in parts. Above the bay, mango and papaya trees sway in the almost constant and welcome breeze. There is not much to do in the village, though swimming and fishing are possibilities. The surrounding area is great for hiking. This is a great place to relax, with your peace and quiet disturbed only by the bleating of a goat or the laughter of children playing. Or by what the locals refer to as 'the old-fashioned telephone', which is known elsewhere in the world as 'shouting to each other', a handy way of communicating across the *ribeira*.

Fajã is where the whaling boats used to anchor and here stands a monument to the passengers of the *Mathilde*. In 1943, a group of men – some American emigrants on a visit home, others young men who had never been out of Brava – bought the 55ft sloop. They all wanted to flee famine and go to New England. The *Mathilde* was in bad shape but this did not deter them; they made a few repairs and set sail on 21 August 1943. Their voyage was a clandestine one because there were wartime restrictions on maritime travel. To make matters worse, they had chosen the beginning of the hurricane season.

Just after the boat left the harbour, a 12-year-old boy on board noticed that it was leaking. He took fright, jumped overboard and swam for the shore, half an hour away. 'There,' says Ray Almeida, an American Cabo Verdean, 'he wept as he watched the sloop disappear over the horizon, carrying his compatriots to what he knew was certain death.' It is believed that the *Mathilde* went down in rough weather near Bermuda.

GETTING THERE AND AWAY A new alternative road into Fajã has been proposed at the time of writing, but until that transpires there is only one way in and out. In winter, if the island has the rare, double-edged blessing of heavy rain, landslides can block the road entirely, and have done so as recently as 2023. At these times the village is closed off from the world until the road can be cleared. It's a rare occurrence indeed, but one to keep in mind if visiting during September and October.

Look out, or ask around, for the one communal *aluguer*, which leaves Fajã for the *vila* at 07.00, returning at noon (250$). It is supposed to do an afternoon journey as well, leaving Fajã in the early afternoon and arriving back at 18.00, and occasionally there will be others. Ask around – there are always plenty of people hanging about. To charter an *aluguer* there or back costs around 2,500$. Fajã to Furna costs around 2,000$. Your accommodation can usually help with any transport needs.

WHERE TO STAY

Fajã Beach House (3 rooms) m 994 4394; e mirancolin@aol.com. A short walk south of town, overlooking the natural sea pools, this unexpectedly sleek low-slung house has 3 smartly furnished en-suite rooms (all with views, & all touchingly named for towns in Massachusetts). On-site restaurant-bar &, most unusually of all, a pool. **$$**

Pensão Sol na Baía (3 rooms) ☎ 285 2070; e solnabaia@caboverdesite.com, joandrade@hotmail.fr; w solnabaia.cv. Owned by José, a local who lived in France for many years, this imposing home has 2 neat, simple en-suite rooms looking directly over the sea with colonnaded balconies, & another with a view on to lush gardens. B/fast is taken by the water. Other meals & tasting of the house *grogue* & *ponche* by arrangement: 1,500$ for 3 courses (2,000$ for non-guests). **$$**

Bar dos Amigos (Manuel Burgo's place) (3 rooms) ☎ 285 1321. About midway along Fajã's only road, the 'hotel' consists of 3 rooms: very basic. **$**

Casa de Julia (1 room) m 985 0079. A brightly painted *casa* perched high above the bay, in the middle of the village, with 1 clean & spacious room. Quaint & inexpensive. **$**

Kaza di Zaza (3 apts) ☎ 285 5032; w kazadizaza.com. Set back up the hill, directly behind Burgo's, 3 rustic apartments among fruit trees with commanding views over the bay. Roof terrace with hammock. Guests can opt to eat with the English-speaking hosts, or use local fish & produce from their garden to cook for themselves. The hosts can organise boat & fishing trips with locals, community activities like helping out with the harvest or taking part in a football match, or suggest hiking trails. They also make their own fruit wines. Note, they close for a month in summer. **$**

Nós Raiz (2 rooms) m 977 9998; e nosraizcv@gmail.com. Big, if occasionally dark, rooms, clean bathrooms & a small terrace are nestled into a lushly planted garden with the mountains rearing up behind. **$**

WHERE TO EAT AND DRINK

The key to eating *anything* here is to order it in advance. Much of what is on offer is fresh fish, though chicken and goat dishes are also sometimes available. With minimal visitor numbers, nothing is bought in either hope or expectation. Call in at one of the places on the waterfront the night before, to order your lunch, or at lunchtime to order your dinner. Not much English is spoken, so have a pre-translated idea of what you might fancy at the ready. Opening hours are not given here because these usually will only reflect the prebookings of the day.

Bar Sodade At the entrance to the village. Pre-ordering should bring you the catch of the day. There are outdoor tables, but you might be asked to eat in the owner's own dining room, with its impressive range of ceramic chickens & other poultry-themed décor. **$$$**

Bar dy Nos At the entrance to the village. Overlooking the water, offering simple, well-cooked fish dishes at very reasonable prices. No mark-up on prices of drinks from the supermarket, either. **$$**

João da Alícia Near the natural pools; m 580 5397. Friendly crew serving fish & chicken dishes & generous sides. Great sea views from its rattan-shaded terrace. **$$**

WHAT TO SEE AND DO

Hiking A gentle walk to the disused airport is a must. You can also head a little further to the small black sand beach at Portéte, which takes around half an hour, but on a very steep coastal path (ask locally if it's currently safe to do so before setting off; note too that there is no mobile signal). It's also sometimes possible to organise a walk and lunch at a family home – ask at your accommodation. For longer hikes to or from the village, see page 266. Most accommodation owners can arrange drop-offs or pick-ups for one-way walks.

Natural pools The main road out of Fajã takes you past some impressive rocks jutting out of the sea and then onwards to some spectacular natural pools, around

1km from the village, just before you reach the airport. The pools become 'crowded' at weekends, when trucks from other parts of the island arrive to take advantage of one of Brava's few safe swimming options. If you're heading there at other times, do ask at your hotel about the day's waves and winds, as the pools can occasionally become dangerous.

Fishing and boat trips A different and less strenuous way of seeing Brava's coastal scenery is to engage one of the local fishermen for a half-day or longer to cruise the rocky coast or even go fishing. This is perhaps best arranged through Kaza di Zaza or one of the other guesthouses (page 259) as they may be able to find you an English-speaking boatman. Expect to pay about 7,000$ per boat, or 5,000$ per person, which includes the fuel and the time of the boatmen (usually two). Each boat can take four passengers, plus the crew.

A coastal trip will take you down past the airport and on to Tantum, where there is a single building and a beach with up to 30 fishing boats. Above the beach, you'll see a zig-zag path which leads to the village of Lomba, a settlement perched high on the ridge. Until relatively recently, the village womenfolk had to carry up the heavy loads of fish, perfectly balanced on their heads, so they could be collected and taken to sell in Vila Nova Sintra. But in 2015, a cable system was introduced, alleviating them of this onerous task.

When fishing, all fish caught from the boats on Brava is by hook and line. A reasonable catch might include grouper, snapper and tuna, plus a few other varieties.

OTHER PLACES TO VISIT

VINAGRE This village derives its name from the mineral water which still bubbles up here from deep below the mountains. There is not much going on here now – a few broken-down donkeys and some ancient farmers. The elaborate stone irrigation system and the extensive terracing are crumbling and largely overgrown. At the heart of the village is a bridge and a huge bougainvillea – a welcome splash of vermilion against the greys and browns.

On the left before the bridge is a majestic old water tank, fully equipped with gargoyle water spouts and large oval windows. Take a look inside to see how the water used to course through a carefully made tunnel under the road. To sample the water yourself, turn left just before the bridge, and follow the cobbled path down to where the piped spring water issues from a wall.

Further round on the left is the shell of a magnificent old house, inhabited within living memory. There are as many as four lime kilns around the settlement, once used to make whitewash for the houses – look out for their tall brick chimneys.

You can reach Vinagre by following a hike, or part of a hike (page 265).

NOSSA SENHORA DO MONTE This village was founded as a place of pilgrimage in 1826 and, within a decade, had become a bishop's palace. Earlier in the last century travellers said that the road from Nova Sintra to Nossa Senhora do Monte was as thickly populated as the Thames Valley. Now emigration has left just a couple of tiny villages.

DRIVES

Brava is very small, so small that in just half a day you can cover all the driveable roads by car or guided tour. This is well worth doing if you are pressed for time, but also to get a feel for the island – from its plunging mountains scored with deep *ribeiras* above Fajã d'Água, to the lively village at Lomba, and the dusty poverty at the end of the road in Cachaço.

Take the road west out of the *vila*. A sharp hairpin in the first kilometre takes you out of the *caldeira* and through the pretty village of **Cova Rodela**. Just past the telephone box in the heart of Cova, the road forks – the left-hand fork takes you round the rim of the crater, past **João de Nole**, to where the road ends at **Mato Grande**. It is worth a brief detour along this road: after about 700m, there is a viewing point (*miradouro*) looking out over Vila Nova Sintra towards Fogo.

Continuing from Cova, bear left at a second fork (the right fork will take you to Fajã d'Água) and descend beneath a hill where there is a large water tank – this is one of a series that serves all of Brava. If you look down the *ribeira* to your right at this point, you will see Fajã d'Água nestling in a bay far, far below. Below the water tank, you pass through the attractive village of **Cova Joana**, where one aspect of Brava's economy becomes apparent: while émigré money has allowed many of the houses to be restored, the others are just left to crumble away.

A hairpin bend brings you up out of the valley into **Nossa Senhora do Monte**. A turning to the left on the hairpin below the school will take you into the labyrinthine tracks and pathways that make up the villages of **Lima Doce** and **Mato**, further south. Standing over Mato is **Fontainhas** peak, which you will see if the mist is not down. At 976m, this is the highest peak on Brava. Nossa Senhora do Monte is a winding cobbled street between whitewashed houses, where the red flowers of the cardeal bushes spill down the walls. The village commands spectacular views down the *ribeiras* to the north, with the sea beyond. The village is more or less continuous with Tomé Barras, where the road divides. Take the left fork to continue on to Cachaço. At this point, the countryside seems to change, and it starts to feel wilder, emptier and drier. As the road weaves in and out among the ridges, note the rows of acacia trees – planted to maintain a semblance of green during the dry season.

Cachaço is where the road stops – less than 10km from Vila Nova Sintra. It is a disadvantaged place, and epitomises the economic problems besetting rural communities in many parts of Cabo Verde. Dependent exclusively on farming, it has been reduced almost to a ghost village. Although the volcanic soil is very fertile, increases in the price of seed and labour, and the unpredictability of the rains over a number of years are factors that have been felt keenly in Cachaço. Look about you and you will see traces of old field markings and terracing high up the slopes – all abandoned now – and shattered farmhouses left to the elements. However, perhaps the modern goat's cheese factory here offers some hope for the future. The tiny production runs are usually exported to Praia, hence the presence of passengers clutching cool boxes on the ferry. It is possible to visit, the best time being before 11.00.

Returning from Cachaço, take the left turning at Tomé Barras. After about 900m, a small turning on the left goes to the small settlement of **Campo Baixo**. Carrying straight on, you will arrive at the fishing settlement of **Lomba**, after about 3km. Although the cobbled road surface stops after about 1km, this journey is worth making just to marvel at the road engineering – in places the track has been cut through ridges of solid rock.

The village of Lomba is strung out along a thin, exposed ridge. Bravans have remarkably limited access to the sea because of the steepness of their volcano. If you have a good head for heights, and are prepared to crane your neck, you will see the fishing boats drawn up hundreds of metres below. Depending on the season, the catch might be bright-orange groupers, or swordfish and tuna which, from far off, look like slabs of silver. There is a single shop in the village, selling cold beers.

Lomba is a great place to watch the mist rolling down the *ribeiras*, or just to sit on the crumbling white rock of the ridge and try to see where the sea meets the horizon.

Returning along the road, pass the turning to Cachaço on your right, go through Tomé Barras, into Nossa Senhora do Monte and on towards the *vila*. Winding up out of Cova Joana, you will come to the turning to Fajã d'Água on your left. This is another spectacular road – completed only in 1989 – cut through living rock. Down to your right you will see several abandoned farms. You will reach Fajã after about 4km. It is a wild and beautiful place, a well-protected harbour where yachts frequently drop anchor beneath mountains which seem to stretch upwards forever.

A few houses line the waterfront, where, on really windy days, you will be wet by the spray. At 1km beyond the village there is the ill-fated Bravan airport, wedged in-between the mountains and the sea. Fickle crosswinds and a runway that is not quite long enough conspire to make the airstrip unsafe – one of the last planes to land here almost ended up in the sea. Talk of a new airport abounds, and some tentative ground-clearing has taken place near to Vila Nova Sintra, but the reality remains some way off from the dream.

On the road back out of Fajã look out for a turning on your left after about 3km. This road is not for the faint-hearted. After just over 2km, you will have to abandon your car, and continue to **Sorno** on foot, but it is well worth it (see page 267 for a description of Sorno).

HIKES   Colum Wilson (CW); Aisling Irwin (AI); Murray Stewart (MS)

Several of the hikes below pass through Mato Grande, and hikers can therefore mix and match parts of routes.

1 VILA NOVA SINTRA–MATO GRANDE–*MIRADOURO*–COVA RODELA–VILA NOVA SINTRA

Distance: 5km; time: 1½ hours; difficulty: 1 (MS)

This walk takes you up a steep path and then around the ring of hills to the south and west of Vila Nova Sintra on a well-surfaced, cobbled road. You are nearly always in sight of the *vila*, but you pass through the picturesque village of Mato Grande, clinging to the hillside, and on a clear day you get some excellent views of Fogo. The *miradouro* (viewing point) is the highlight of this walk, giving an amazing view of the *vila*, spread out beneath you like a map.

From the southeast corner of the main square, take the diagonal road out past the building labelled **Casa Teixeira**. After about 100m you will come to a crossroads, where you go straight on. Continue straight ahead again at a fork after a further 20m. After another 40m, the cobbled road turns sharp left. Go right on an unmade path that heads down to the bottom of the valley. After about 100m you will reach the valley floor.

Almost directly, go past a turning on your right leading up to a nearby white house. After another 50m, turn right up a *very* steep cobbled path in a gap in the stone wall. This climbs sharply between houses that seem to be built on platforms carved out of the hillside. After about 2 minutes, take a narrower dirt path off to the left with a wall on your right and the valley down to your left. From this point, and if the mist is not swirling around you, you get your first uninterrupted view of Fogo.

The path winds on around the hillside and after a few minutes crosses a small valley, then climbs sharply up the other side on a mixture of stone and rough steps. You pass a house on your right and reach a T-junction at which you turn right, following the cobbled path uphill with houses on your right and the valley down to your left.

Reaching a stone building, ignore the path that curves around to the left and take a wide-ish uphill cobbled path to the right of a disused water fountain. Immediately **before** crossing a valley traversed by a stone bridge, turn sharp left with a stone wall on your left and the valley on your right. A few hundred metres ahead is a rock face, but thankfully the path veers round to the left continuing upwards. Far down to your left you can see the *vila* football pitch. Now the path doubles back sharply to the right, continuing upwards between two stone walls, wending its way between abandoned houses. Reaching a 'Y' junction, take the left-hand fork across the top of the valley then immediately turn right and follow the cobbles as they twist right, left and right again and go in front of a large renovated two-storey house. Turn right at the end of the house to continue on a wide cobbled path with a concrete wall on your left and the second side of the house on your right. This road then curves to the left, with houses down below and deposits you at a sort of cobbled crossroads with a brightly painted discotheque incongruously in front of you and the unmarked and now rather tatty Centro Social de Mato Grande (the social centre) on your left.

Peer over the wall to the right of the disco, to see the village of **Garça** down in the valley and, close by, the white outline of one of a series of stone ships dotted around the mountainside. On the far ridge opposite is the village of **Baleia**, and at the east end of the ridge you will see a further ship.

On 24 June, it is these boats that are decorated with leaves and fruit to celebrate the festival of São João.

To continue the walk, leave the disco and social centre behind you and continue up the wide cobbled road with the valley and Garça down to your left. Soon, the *vila* appears again down to your right. Follow the road along the ridge, ignoring a path that leaves to the right and exit Mato Grande. After 1km (about 15–20 minutes), you will come to a cobbled road joining you from your right: this leads down to **João de Nole**, but ignore it and continue straight ahead.

Just 100m beyond this junction is a narrow, rough and steep path down on the right. (If you trust your knees, this is a quick way to descend to the *vila*.) Otherwise, the *miradouro* (viewpoint) is another 200m beyond this, and gives a breathtaking view over the *vila*.

Continuing beyond the viewpoint, pass a farm 'guarded' by three antique cannons and another 600m of walking downhill will bring you to a T-junction, in the pretty, often misty village of **Cova Rodela**. Turn right here and follow the winding, cobbled road back down to the *vila*. You will reach the western end of the main street after about 10 minutes and you turn left to take you back to the *vila*'s main square.

2 VILA NOVA SINTRA–MATO GRANDE–BALEIA–CASA EUGÉNIO TAVARES–BALEIA–MATO GRANDE–VILA NOVA SINTRA

Distance: 10km; time: 4 hours; difficulty: 3 (CW)

This walk south of the *vila* is a demanding sequence of ascents and descents, with spectacular views of Fogo out to the east. For much of this walk, the path is unmade and rough, and, particularly on the final steep zig-zag descent to the *casa*, care needs to be taken. Baleia is an attractive, if remote, spot to pause and gaze down vertiginous *ribeiras*. If you want to experience the unspeakable desolation of Brava's dryness, look no further than the *ribeira* where Tavares built his house.

Walk from the *vila* to Mato Grande (30 minutes) using the directions in the first four paragraphs of the previous walk.

In Mato Grande, looking south (with your back to the social centre and the disco on your left), take the small path directly in front of you, which leads down in the direction of **Garça**.

At Garça, you can take a detour along the ridge to visit the stone boat (*barco*), which looks like it has been stranded at the end of the ridge in some cataclysmic flood. The path continues up to **Baleia** on the next ridge, about 1km from Mato Grande. Immediately on entering the village, you will see a house on your left that sells biscuits and *grogue*.

Baleia has the feel of a bird's nest perched high on a windswept ridge. The village comprises a single cobbled street and a few houses huddled together against the mist and the ceaseless purring of the wind.

It takes 2 hours to get from here to Casa Eugénio Tavares and return. People in Baleia will readily point you towards the path to the *casa*. Follow the cobbled path along the ridge through Baleia. Just before you reach the last two houses, turn right and immediately start to descend on an unmade path.

After about 5 minutes, the path branches. Going left will bring you in a few minutes to Baleia's stone boat. Bear right for the *casa*, down the side of the ridge. After about 20 minutes, you will reach a few scattered houses, mostly ruined. At a fork in the path bear left. You will see some rudimentary crosses on a cairn some tens of metres up the right turning. This is a homemade chapel, and means that the locals do not have to hike over to Mato Grande every Sunday.

You are heading towards what looks like a ruin (but is actually inhabited). Cut close past the right side of this building (where the locals will point you in the right direction for Tavares's house), and descend a few hundred metres along the next ridge. If it is the dry season, you will enter a lunar landscape at this point, where there is nothing but rock and sand. The ruined huts look as if they have grown out of the landscape, rather than having been built by human hand.

After less than 10 minutes from the inhabited building, the path passes to the right through a small notch in a rocky ridge a few metres high. From here you will see the *casa* a long way below you on the other side of the valley. After a further 5 minutes, you will pass a ruin on your left. About 50m beyond this, there is a small (and easy-to-miss) turning on your right down the side of the *ribeira*. It is a very rough zig-zagging path, so watch your step. It will take you about 10 or 15 minutes.

The ruin of Eugénio Tavares's house is reached by a 5-minute scramble up from the floor of the *ribeira*. His house is surprisingly big – there are two storeys and outhouses. There is also a patio, and what looks like a small swimming pool, but was probably a water tank. In the dry season, you look out across a mind-numbing grey and brown panorama of splintered rock. But it clearly inspired Tavares and, apparently, a host of latter-day scribblers, who have left their poetic offerings all over the walls of the ruin.

Retrace your steps. For the return from Mato Grande to the *vila*, you can either go back the way you came (30 minutes) or go via the *miradouro* as described in the last part of the previous walk. The latter route takes about 1 hour.

3 VILA NOVA SINTRA–MATO GRANDE–MONTE FONTAINHAS–MATO–NOSSA SENHORA DO MONTE–COVA JOANA–VILA NOVA SINTRA

Distance: 9km; time: 3 hours 10 minutes; difficulty: 2 (CW)
This walk takes you to the heart of Brava, to its highest peak, from where you will get superb all-round views if you are not shrouded in mist. It is a steep ascent to Mato Grande, followed by a further steep ascent (on a cobbled path) from near Mato Grande up to the Fontainhas Plateau, where it is cool and green, and the air is heavy with sharp pine scents. Note: Mato Grande and Mato are different places.

Walk from the *vila* to Mato Grande (30 minutes) using the directions in the first four paragraphs of the Vila Nova Sintra–Mato Grande–*miradouro*–Cova Rodela walk.

For the 50-minute walk to **Fontainhas**, begin from the social centre in Mato Grande and take the road that leads up to the left of the tapstand. You will see Vila Nova Sintra below you on your right. After about 400m, you will pass a green church on your right, and, cresting a rise, you will see the path you are to take leading up from the left of the road about 200m in front of you. This is the beginning of a steep ascent on to the Fontainhas Plateau.

The path ascends the right side of a small valley. After about 200m, a path joins from the right. Your path bends round to the left at the top of the valley, and zig-zags upwards. Some 15 minutes after leaving the main road, the path flattens out and you pass to the right of a small peak with a large antenna on top. Directly after that, a small path joins on the left.

Five minutes after passing the antenna peak, take a right fork, and pass along the right edge of an undulating plateau, where the mist trails through spiky aloe vera and among the red flowers of the cardeal bushes. There are some farming huts, and occasional cattle grazing on the coarse grass. The air is sharp with the smell of pine.

After another 10 minutes, you reach a T-junction. The right turning heads down to **Mato**. Turn left, and very shortly you will pass a whitewashed house on your right. Bear right at a fork shortly after this. Follow the path upwards, and after less than 10 minutes, you will reach the peak. To get to Mato, which takes about 45 minutes, go back to the T-junction before the whitewashed house, but instead of turning right to retrace your steps, head straight on. After about 7 minutes of descending from the T-junction along a winding path, you will emerge on a low saddle, and will see the upper end of Mato down on your left.

Continue along the saddle for another 5 minutes, and then take a deeply worn path leading down on your left. After 5 minutes, this path will lead you past a concrete water tank on your left.

After another few minutes, the path becomes cobbled, and you are descending through the first of the houses in Mato. Five minutes later, you reach a T-junction with a telephone box on the right. From here, your aim is to reach the main road through Mato. Mato is criss-crossed by any number of small paths, and the best way to the main road is simply by asking.

Once on the road, follow it to the right, descending past a school on your left, and joining at last the main road to Nossa Senhora do Monte at a sharp hairpin.

Turn right on to the main road and walk for an hour, passing through **Cova Joana**, **Cova Rodela** and eventually reaching Vila Nova Sintra.

4 VILA NOVA SINTRA–SANTA BARBARA–VINAGRE–MATO GRANDE–JOÃO DE NOLE–VILA NOVA SINTRA

Distance: 5km; time: 2 hours 20 minutes; difficulty: 3 (CW)
In this walk, you descend almost to sea level by a steep zig-zagging cobbled path, and then climb back up again by a very rough (and in places precipitous) ridge path. It is not a walk to undertake if you have dodgy knees or don't like getting out of breath. Vinagre – a village nestling in the mouth of a *ribeira* – is the highlight of the walk, with its old lime kilns and air of decayed grandeur. The mineral waters that flow from a natural spring taste like a mild mixture of lemon juice and soapsuds, and have given the village its name. It is said that those who drink of the waters will never leave.

For the 40-minute walk to Vinagre, set out on the road east from the main square of the *vila*. After 5 minutes, you will reach the stone boat looking out towards Fogo.

Take the little cobbled path down to the left of the boat, and after just a short distance you will join the main road snaking its way down to Furna. Cross the road, and double back a few metres to pick up the cobbled path continuing its descent on the other side. Your path is actually the old road to Furna – watch out for the stray vehicles that still use this road. After 5 minutes descending, take a cobbled turning on your right towards **Santa Barbara**, which you will reach after another few minutes. About 10 minutes from the turning, staying on the same path, you will round an outcrop, and catch a glimpse of Mato Grande above you on the hill.

At this point, you will begin a series of sharp zig-zags down towards **Vinagre**, which you will reach after about 25 minutes.

The 1-hour hike from Vinagre to Mato Grande is a scramble, and some may prefer to turn round and retrace their steps up to Santa Barbara. The undaunted should cross over the bridge in Vinagre and follow the main path past a white house on the left with a brick kiln behind it. Immediately bear right up a rough path that looks as if it ends in a small rock quarry a few tens of metres from the main path. Pass through this area of broken rock, and, after a few minutes pass a ruin and follow the path as it doubles back up a ridge.

About 5 minutes after leaving the main path, you will pass an inhabited house on your left, and directly ascend past a ruin. The path is indistinct at this point, and does not look promising, but turn directly left behind the ruin, and you should be able to follow it.

This is the beginning of a very steep ascent on a rough path, where you will sometimes be looking for handholds. After about 20 minutes of arduous zig-zagging, you will emerge at a T-junction on a more major path, where you turn right along a contour. Following this path around the side of the hill will bring you to a small settlement after about 10 minutes. From here, you can see Mato Grande on the hill on your left.

Follow the path as it doubles back on itself through the settlement, and then follow the path up the hill under the phone line. After about 7 minutes, you cross over a small ridge, and your path improves. Three minutes later, you pass a water point with taps, where you turn left uphill.

After another 2 or 3 minutes, a path joins you from your right in front of a white, two-storeyed house. Go straight on, following the path uphill. Five minutes later, you cross a small valley, and then bear left at a fork. Two or 3 minutes later there is a white cross standing on a wall on your right beside a white house. Pass in front of the house on your right, and immediately turn right beside the house, following the path uphill. Within a couple of minutes you will reach a telephone box, and a larger cobbled path through Mato Grande. Turn left at the phone box, and after 5 minutes of ascending, you will reach the Centro Social de Mato Grande (social centre) on your left.

To get back to the *vila*, via **João de Nole**, takes about 40 minutes. From the social centre in Mato Grande, take the road up to the left of the tapstand. After about 1km, turn right at a T-junction.

After a further 400m, turn left down into João de Nole. After 100m, go straight across a small T-junction. After this, the cobbled path gets smaller as it starts to zig-zag sharply down towards the *vila*. About 10 minutes after the small crossroads, the path emerges on a cobbled street at the edge of town. Turn left on to the street.

5 VILA NOVA SINTRA–LEVADURA–FAJÃ D'ÁGUA
Distance: 6km; time: 2 hours; difficulty: 2 (AI)
This is a classic, downhill Cabo Verde *ribeira* walk, with your destination sparkling beside the sea during the brief glimpses you snatch as you descend. Before you reach it you have to negotiate a lot of superbly crafted cobbled paths, ghostly villages and

the echoey sides of the harsh valley walls. There is a short patch towards the end where there is no clear path and the going is slippery.

The first 25 minutes of the walk is on the road. From the town square head west on the town hall road. At the end of the street turn right up the Nossa Senhora do Monte road. Follow this for just over 20 minutes, passing through the village of **Cova Rodela**, with its superb dragon tree, on the way. Stop at a fork in the road: the high road continues to Nossa Senhora do Monte; to the right is the road to Fajã d'Água.

Walk for 2 minutes along the high road, then take a track to the right beside a sizeable tree. Follow this for about 5 minutes, ignoring another track up to the left, until you reach a crossroads of paths. To the right a track leads to a few houses on a nearby peak. Take the middle path, downhill, which leads you swiftly into a hidden valley of stark cliffs and, beyond them, the sea. Some 25 minutes from the crossroads you reach a water tank around which the path forks. The left path goes to the village of **Tomba Has**: take the right one instead. You are in a deep valley world of steep, stone-wall terracing and startling echoes.

Within a couple of minutes of leaving the water tank you will have your first proper view of Fajã d'Água, the archetypal nestling village, snug and green between the hostile brown Bravan mountains. Keep going, past two water tanks, through a settlement and, 15–20 minutes after the first water tank, past the quiet village of **Levadura** (to see it take a small detour on a path to the left). Now you are deep in the valley and the path is steep and winding.

Some 15 minutes from Levadura, when you are about level with a wood and a few houses on the other side of the valley, the path crosses a watercourse (generally dry) and a small dam, often full of water. Don't take the little path down to the left but go straight on, crossing, after a few minutes, a concrete barrier and following a path up through the houses ahead. In this jumbled settlement you will find someone who can lead you through to the other side where there is a well-trodden path the villagers all take down to Fajã d'Água. Beware: it is gravelly and slippery. For half an hour you descend on a path that is a mixture of rock, landslide and gravel, crisscrossing water channels, dams and stream beds and passing a big water tank, until you arrive at the road through Fajã d'Água.

6 VILA NOVA SINTRA–SORNO–SÃO PEDRO–VILA NOVA SINTRA
Distance: 9km; time: 4½ hours; difficulty: 2–3 (AI)

This spectacular walk encapsulates the essence of Brava: the remote valley hamlet of Sorno making miraculous use of its little stream to farm extensive green terraces up the mountainsides; the vivid, slightly menacing sea; the barren mountains; the ghost villages that are testament to livelier times; and, periodically, big brother Fogo looming from across the sea. The walk is suitable for any walker of average fitness, with just a very small slippery stretch to be negotiated. There is a 2-hour walk downhill, mainly along a road, and 2½ hours on a remote path that is steep but not difficult. There are no facilities in Sorno.

From Vila Nova Sintra walk for 25 minutes to the fork, as described in the first two paragraphs of the walk from Vila Nova Sintra to Fajã d'Água.

Take the right fork (the Fajã d'Água road), passing a big white water tank on the right after 20 minutes and, after a further 15 minutes, reaching a turning to the right. This road on the right is of much poorer quality and takes you past a small quarry and various houses. You may pass the odd person harvesting grass or loading it on to a donkey but soon you will leave even these few behind, and there is just you, the sea and the odd hawk. The dull brown of the mountains makes a huge contrast with the rich blue and harsh white of the sea.

Eventually one of the road's twists will reveal **Sorno** below, improbably tame below the ominous Brava slopes. The Sorno road takes 1½ hours to cover, dwindling to a path – slippery in places – some 20 minutes from the village and, all the while, the ingenious village reveals itself in the form of irrigation channels, neat water tanks and endless squares of tended terraces. Follow the path round to the front of a square white building and then follow your nose, and a set of stepped irrigation channels and water tanks, to the sea.

After a break on the beach, it is time for the ascent out of Sorno. Finding the path, which winds out of the other side of the valley from the side you entered, takes a little care. Use as your guide Sorno's first (more southerly) bay. With your back to the water and its twin-peak stacks behind you, gaze up the valley and look for the little path that mounts its left side. For the first 5 minutes it is a small dirty track,

WHALERS AND THE PACKET TRADE

For a young man with nothing but a peasant's struggle against hunger ahead of him, the prospect of a job on one of the New England whaling ships that pulled into Brava provided excitement and escape.

The first such boats arrived towards the end of the 18th century. Throughout most of the 19th century, a new vessel would arrive perhaps every three days so that the crew could resupply, drink and raise hell. Crucially, the whalers would also be searching for crew – as replacements for obstreperous crewmen who would be abandoned on Brava. The Cabo Verdeans were disciplined and took lower wages than their American counterparts, and developed great skill in the arts of whaling.

Stories of life aboard the whalers are full of excitement, courage and horror. The shot of the harpoon sinking into a 30m-long beast; the cries as the men rowed frantically to escape the thrashing of the whale's tail; the speed with which their little boats were towed through the ocean by the fleeing animal until they won control and sank a killer harpoon home. Men frequently died during these battles.

Some used the whaling ships as brief stepping stones to jobs in the USA – manual labour in the ports, in the cranberry bogs of southern New England and in the textile mills of New Bedford.

As steam replaced sail, the schooners and whalers could be bought or even 'inherited' for nothing. Cabo Verdeans in the USA took them over, did them up and began the era of the Brava Packet Trade – a regular link between the USA and the islands. The boats would take Bravans to work in the cranberry bogs and return loaded with goods and with *emigrantes* visiting their families. The Packet Trade became an independent link by which Cabo Verdeans could keep in contact with their families without depending on the transport system of another country.

There are plenty of dramatic tales about these ships – of charismatic captains, of tussles with disaster and of tragedy. The *Nellie May* was the first to begin a regular journey between the continents, in 1892. One of the longest recorded journeys of such a schooner was 90 days; the record for the shortest crossing was claimed to be 12 but was probably longer. World War II halted the trade, but afterwards one of the most legendary of the packet trade captains, Henrique Mendes, resurrected a sunken schooner and named her *Ernestina* (page 21).

but it then becomes paved and walled, if old and crumbly, soon crossing a concrete water channel and tank.

As you leave Sorno its colours dull and, after a good 20-minute walk, you turn to see its vivid greens already merging with the dull surrounding browns, its charm retreating. Half an hour of climbing out of Sorno brings you round into the next bay, a new set of jagged peaks ahead of you and, after entering a little wood, a turning to the right past a stack of dry stones. Take this and, in less than 5 minutes, you pass another prehistoric old home on the left – the path goes up and round behind it.

> **OTHER WALKS**
>
> There is also an easy path from Fontainhas to Cachaço; and there is said to be a more difficult (and poorly marked) path from Cachaço to Casa Eugénio Tavares. Enquire locally.

You are now entering the loneliest part of the walk, its stark remoteness made more poignant by the carefully crafted path, with its implication that someone once thought it would be useful. Some 50 minutes from the right turning at the stack of stones below, you reach the ghost village of **Tez Cova** – decaying old piles of stone houses from which folk used to try to farm the now-abandoned terraces. One half-expects the ghost of an old Bravan farmer to emerge from one of these hovels and share a thought on the fate of the island.

At Tez Cova you should walk through the village, broadly following the contour, rather than heading upwards and inland. The path dips shallowly and then climbs gently, passing on the left No 26, a building with a pale pink door. At the edge of Tez Cova, the final house is inhabited and you pass it on the left and go over a saddle, which reveals the vista of **São Pedro**, the busy overflow from Vila Nova Sintra. From here, it is half an hour to the *vila*, initially through a maze of paths (keep asking for the *praça*).

7 VILA NOVA SINTRA–FURNA
Distance: 3km; time: 50 minutes; difficulty: 1 (Al)

This walk follows the old, little-used cobbled road from Vila Nova Sintra to Furna. It is an easy descent, steep in places, and is a good alternative to being rattled around in the back of an *aluguer* when you are descending to the port for home.

Set out on the road east from the main square. After 5 minutes, you will reach the stone boat looking out towards Fogo. Take the little cobbled path down to the left of the boat, and after just a short distance, you will join the main road snaking its way down to Furna. Cross the road, and double back a few metres to pick up the cobbled path continuing its descent on the other side.

After 5 minutes descending, you pass a cobbled turning on your right towards Santa Barbara. Some 25 minutes later, the old road briefly joins the new road, but leaves it again after a short distance.

Just before entering Furna, you rejoin the new road for the last time.

8 FAJÃ D'ÁGUA–*CRUZ*– FAJÃ D'ÁGUA
Distance: 6km; time: 3 hours; difficulty: 2 (MS)

A steep climb from sea level, up the side of a *ribeira* to the *cruz*, followed by a descent of the cobbled road. Celebrate your efforts by hanging out with the locals sipping a glass of *grogue* in one of the seafront bars.

Start the walk on the right-hand side of the church. Follow this road up and at the first left-hand bend (after about 50m), take a narrow path that leads off to your right, climbing on cobbles. Continue on the path as it bends around to the

THE ILHÉUS DO ROMBO

These islands have been nature reserves since 1990 and are protected by law. The smaller ones are Ilhéu Luiz Carneiro, Ilhéu Sapado and Ilhéu do Rei.

The islets are, along with Raso and Branco islands near São Nicolau, the only home for the Cabo Verdean shearwater (*Calonectris edwardsii*). Bulwer's petrel (*Bulweria bulwerii*), known locally as *João-petro*, breeds here as well as on Raso. And the Madeiran storm petrel (*Oceanodroma castro*), known locally as the *jaba-jaba* or the *pedreirinho*, breeds only here and on Branco, Raso and islets off Boavista.

Until 2007, it was possible to visit the islets on a fishing boat from Fajã or Furna, which would do the round trip for a healthy fee. Most people chose to camp overnight, taking their own water and eating fish that they caught and grilled there. However, in 2007 the government tightened up on access to protected islands. Written ministerial permission is now required for foreigners, together with a modest payment, and is unlikely to be given. Fishermen could get hefty fines if discovered taking a tourist to the island. The restrictions may be relaxed in the future, so it is worth checking.

ILHÉU GRANDE Some 2km², Ilhéu Grande's highest point is Monte Grande, at 96m. It has a rounded shape. Seabirds used to breed here – the island is covered in thick layers of guano.

ILHÉU DE CIMA This long and narrow rock of 1.5km² is famous for its seabird colonies. It has a big lump sticking out of its southern end, 77m high, and some smaller rocky outcrops.

right. After 100m of climbing rough stone steps and cobbles, the path levels briefly before rejoining cobbles. Zig-zag upwards; in rainy times it can be a bit overgrown. To your right is the narrow, inhabited strip of Fajã d'Água, way down below. On reaching a Y-fork in the path, ignore the right-hand branch that leads to a water tank, keeping to the left and continuing to gently ascend. Ahead of you, up on the near horizon, is a stone building on a plateau; this is your initial goal. At one time, the town of Fajã had a narrow stretch of black-sand beach, but careless disposal of rocks during the construction of the ill-fated airstrip led to its disappearance. The upward path at one stage becomes a scramble over large boulders, though it is not dangerous. Although the stone building is your goal, at times it disappears from view and the zig-zags mean that at times you will be heading back, temporarily towards the sea. Cross a dry streambed and follow the path up to your right and cross the same streambed once again. The sea is now behind you, the steep *ribeira* way down to your right. Around 100m after this second crossing, continue on to find safe crossing into some bushes. (**Caution**: at this point, do not approach too close to the edge, as the cliff is prone to crumbling!) A steep, 5m cliff face will be immediately to your left once you're in these bushes, with a long drop-off to your right. The path turns left, along by the top of a stone wall. It then turns right, along a narrow ledge, parallel with the distant seashore. Turn slightly left, heading upwards to the stone building, now visible once again. Again you zig-zag upwards, until you pass the promontory with the ruined stone building just on your right. From here, across the *ribeira*, you will see the 20 or so abandoned houses of a village: the last resident left for the United States in 2013. Down below the village to its left, you can see the pumping station that pumps water up the hill for distribution to the whole of the island, somewhat resented by the Fajã d'Água residents and farmers, as it means less for their crops. Between November and July, the island often experiences not a single drop of rain. The path soon turns left up towards a steep rock face, then left again, heading briefly towards the ocean, and soon rejoins a section of path which is firm cobbles, with a low stone wall to your right. Then the path bends to the right, away from the sea and again towards the rock face. Continue the upward zig-zag, to reach the white *cruz* (cross) which is the venue for the 1 May festival of Cova Rodela village. This is the walk's highest point, at over 420m. On leaving the circular viewpoint, ignore the wide cobbles, instead choosing a narrower path to their left, and enter a wooded area. On exiting this 100m further on, look for a path that leaves to your right, then begin the steep, short descent to the road; on reaching it, follow it down to the left to reach Fajã d'Água around 45 minutes later – or cadge a lift, if you're lucky!

9

São Vicente

*Four o' clock in the dawning
São Vicente folk are there
To cry their sorrow
For sons who are sent away
To São Tomé*
           Mindelo lament

For many people Mindelo, the island's capital, *is* São Vicente. It's indeed a fine city, full of life and a certain grace. Some even consider it one of the most pleasant cities in West Africa. Mindelo's buzz contrasts with a dead hinterland – as dry as Sal but more extraordinary, as it has died at a younger age, while still covered in sweeping hills and mountain ranges. Hemmed in by mountains on one side and the ocean on the other, Mindelo has only one option: make music and party! The British called São Vicente the 'cinder heap'.

Wander outside the capital and those haunting questions evoked by the flatter islands return once again: 'How did people end up here? How have they survived?'

HIGHLIGHTS AND LOWLIGHTS

Many Cabo Verdean writers and thinkers were educated at the São Vicente *liceu* and Mindelo is proud of its intellectual and artistic tradition. It has a liveliness: visit for the music, for the occasional performance, for hanging around in the bars. Mindelo also houses a number of characterful restaurants. Cabo Verde's two most exuberant annual festivals take place on the island: the exuberant Carnival, a miniature Rio, in February or March and the beach music festival in August.

Also go for watersports, in particular windsurfing (if you have your own gear) but surfing, kitesurfing, diving and fishing as well. Or if you love desolate rocky coastlines and deserted beaches you will enjoy wandering here.

However, if you expect greenery, avoid São Vicente. For most of the year, much of the island is a desert. If you are on a tight schedule and long for the mountains you may regret having allocated time here. Swimming is treacherous on many beaches. There are some safe and pleasant sandy stretches but, at the time of writing, no real resort-style places of an international standard.

SUGGESTED ITINERARY AND NUMBER OF DAYS Wandering around Mindelo, including going up to the fort, takes most of a day, as does a trip by vehicle to the top of Monte Verde and back. If you want to make the most of the music, you may need to plan on a late, late night, with perhaps the following day to recover. To really get to know the city and its nightlife, though, try to stay for at least three nights, as one night out can lead to tips about how to spend the next. For those not interested in urban culture, a tour of the island taking in Baía das Gatas, Calhau and São Pedro can occupy a day. If the landscape's extremity appeals to you, there are a few hikes or wanderings that could occupy another day or two. If you just have a day on São Vicente, and you arrive early enough, you can visit Santo Antão, across the channel, and enjoy its glorious scenery by taking a trip along the mountain road to Ribeira Grande and back. Otherwise, if it is a clear day, then a walk or drive up to the top of Monte Verde is the most scenic activity; failing that go for a drive up Fortim for a grand view of Mindelo. For an easy day on the beach, stroll along Mindelo's seafront to Laginha or jump into a taxi and go to São Pedro or Baía das Gatas (page 295).

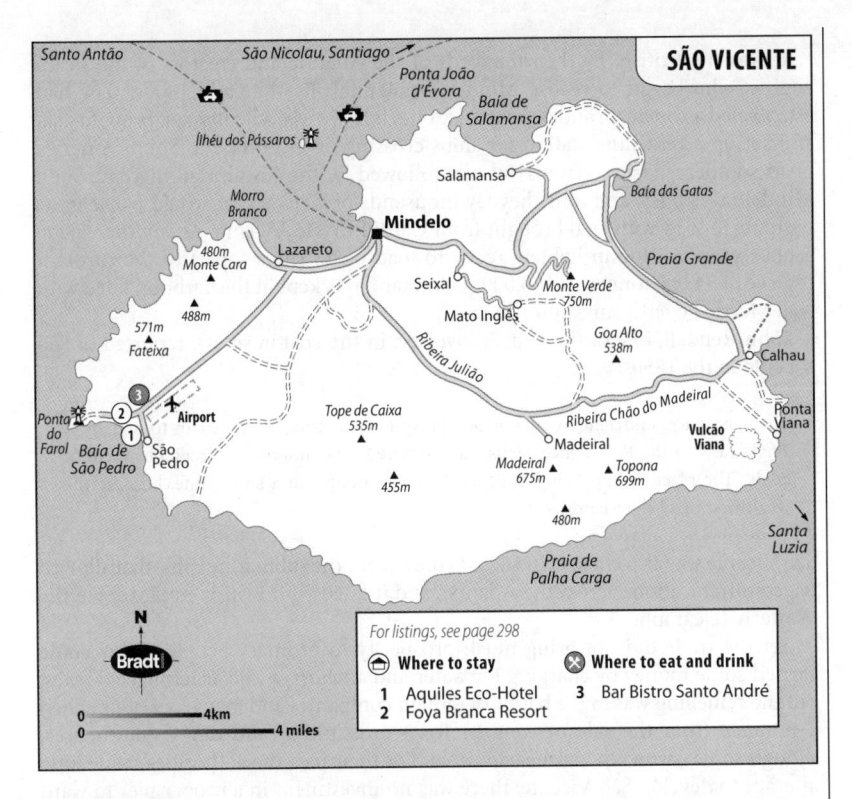

BACKGROUND INFORMATION

HISTORY This rock in the ocean was of little use to anyone before the end of the 18th century. After its discovery on 22 January 1462, and the traditional release of goats to prey on its delicate vegetation, humans forgot about it, except to land there occasionally with dogs and spend a night goat hunting. An attempt to populate the island was made in 1795, but it failed and just a few people remained, at the top of Monte Verde.

But São Vicente has one superlative natural resource. The island's harbour is a sweeping curve formed by a crater rim over whose northern side the sea has breached. A headland to the northeast of the harbour completes the protection while the ring of hills blocks wind from almost any direction. Thus Mindelo is a fine stopping point for ships crossing the Atlantic. When coal replaced wind as the main propellant, Mindelo became the ideal place for refuelling mid journey.

It was the British, by then the lords of the Atlantic and creators of the steam engine, who began to realise Mindelo's potential. By the early 1800s, they had established a consulate and depot there. One John Lewis, a lieutenant, brought coal and set up a refuelling station for ships crossing from Europe to South America or to southern Africa. His arrival was followed by the Royal Mail in 1850. Soon Mindelo was busy, and in its heyday thousands of ships a year would pause in its harbour to load with coal brought from Cardiff to São Vicente. At any time 5,000 tonnes were waiting in lighters ready to load on to ships – part of the constant reserve of 34,000 tonnes. A 100,000-gallon tank was kept in the harbour, filled with water ferried over from Santo Antão.

John Rendall, one of the British involved in the coal business, reported of São Vicente in the 1850s:

> There is space sufficient to anchor 300 vessels. Two steam packets run to and from England with the Post Office Mails, calling here every month for a replenishment of coals. The place is improving daily, and will no doubt, in a short time, become the wealthiest of all the islands.

São Vicente was also chosen, in 1875, as the site for the submarine cable that allowed telecommunications across the Atlantic, and it filled with British employees of the Western Telegraph.

Yet the trade did not bring much prosperity to ordinary people. Cabo Verde earned some money by charging for water and anchorage and exacting coal taxes, but the refuelling was in the hands of foreign companies and many locals scratched a pittance from the sale of rum, or from prostitution and dingy guesthouses, though some earned livings heaving coal. For their part the authorities made little attempt to develop São Vicente: there was no investment in a proper pier to ward off competition from Dakar, and little thought was given to the possibility of taking advantage of what was happening in the world beyond.

When Alfred Burdon Ellis visited in 1855, he wrote at length about the antics of the characters in his bawdy and squalid lodgings. On leaving, he concluded:

> Taken as a whole it is, perhaps, the most wretched and immoral town that I have ever seen; but what can be expected of a colony which is rated at such a low value that the salary of the governor is only four shillings and sixpence a day?

Thus, at the same time that it was the fourth-greatest coaling station in the world after Egypt's Port Said, Malta and Singapore, the city became a place of beggars, prostitutes, starving invalids and smugglers.

Unfolding world events continued to serve São Vicente a series of blows. The opening of the Suez Canal between the Mediterranean and the Red Sea in 1869 diminished the port's activity, though it bounced back after a while. Technology advanced and the cable connection became mechanised, so the employees of the Western Telegraph returned home. Ships' bunkers were built larger so they could carry enough coal for their entire journeys. Finally, oil replaced coal, drastically cutting the amount of labour required for refuelling. Drought and famine bit viciously and in 1941, the British consul at Mindelo, Captain J L Sands, reported on Mindelo's inhabitants:

> A large number are emaciated, worn out and have lost both heart and hope...the starving seem to accept the situation with an oriental fatalism. They do not press their

claims to live, they scarcely beg, may ask you for alms once or twice, and then simply stare at you as if resigned to what is to happen.

During this time, it was from Mindelo that the *contratados* were recruited in their thousands to go and labour on the plantations of São Tomé and Príncipe, the fellow Portuguese island colony to the south. The conditions there were akin to slavery and few ever returned.

At the same time, devastating cycles of drought meant that Mindelo saw many immigrants arrive from other islands, especially Santo Antão and São Nicolau. The earlier establishment of several educational institutions, including the Liceu Nacional Infante Dom Henrique, in the city, and the subsequent launch of the seminal cultural magazine *Claridade* (page 41), led to the city becoming the intellectual capital of the archipelago. That combination of despair and intellectual flourishing proved to be fertile ground for revolution (page 25).

SÃO VICENTE TODAY Mindelo, the island's capital, has an air of importance and blossoming, a sense of prosperity, even though that does not extend to all its inhabitants. *Emigrantes* return and invest, and the inward migration from other islands continues. Mindelo's marina is the country's largest and best equipped, and the island also has an international airport.

Much of Mindelo's terrain feels like a potential vast natural building site and, unsurprisingly, the island has not escaped the ubiquitous talk of mesmerising, huge foreign development plans. The latest grand scheme is Riviera Mindelo, a 350-hectare subdivision that will include a Jack Nicklaus-designed golf course, new maritime infrastructure, a conference and entertainment centre and luxury condominiums. A few years on from its 2021 proposal launch, it's still on the drawing board. Barefoot Luxury, a Belgian villa project around 10 minutes' drive from Mindelo, around the Ponta João d'Évora, is finished and the villas are on the market, but at the time of writing there was no indication as to whether they will end up being part of the island's tourist rental inventory. São Pedro Bay, another similar upmarket European project in São Pedro, in the south of the island, is at the same stage.

Far more relevant for visitors, as well as locals, the popular Laginha Beach area in the north of Mindelo has been beautified relatively recently, and continues to be lively and well used. Meanwhile, the boutique hotel concept has taken hold, and there are a number of new, forward-thinking and culturally nurturing cafés and shops.

GEOGRAPHY The island is 227km² and lies about 14km east of Santo Antão, its nearest occupied neighbour. It is extremely dry. Its highest peak, Monte Verde, is

FESTIVALS ON SÃO VICENTE

22 January	Municipality Day
February	Carnival
3 May	Santa Cruz
24 June	São João (St John)
29 June	São Pedro
8 August	Nossa Senhora da Luz
August full moon	Baía das Gatas music festival
September	Mindelact theatre festival

750m. There is irrigation in some of the principal valleys – Ribeira de Calhau and Ribeira da Vinha. Earlier this century there were irrigated plantations in Ribeira Julião. The island population is around 80,000, with up to 70,000 living in Mindelo. There have been many attempts at reafforestation, particularly along the road to the airport. The onset of the rains in July and August transforms the desert to green, before the island gradually begins to dry out again.

FLORA AND FAUNA São Vicente has one protected area: Monte Verde, which is a natural park. **Turtles** used to nest prolifically on São Vicente's beaches and one of their last remaining beaches, Praia Grande, runs between Baía das Gatas and Calhau. Here, as everywhere, hunting is a serious threat, as well as the illegal removal of sand for construction. The road running alongside the shore has storm drains running directly on to the beach and the rain will most likely sweep away any nests in their paths. The island does not harbour any **bird** specialities but there are plenty of interesting waders and migrant birds on the wet sand towards São Pedro, 1km from the airport, and on the sewage ponds 2km from the centre of town (reached by going south along the coastal road until just after the Shell oil storage terminals and following a track inland on the left).

SAFETY In terms of **crime**, begging by street children and indeed adults can be a nuisance and can verge on the aggressive. Daylight is no deterrent, though the threat feels greater after dark. The beggars are most common in Praça Amílcar Cabral and its side streets; around the Pastelaria Morabeza; along the coastal road, and in the streets just back from it. Sadly a confident '*não*' coupled with a determination to keep walking is not always enough to end the interaction. Watch out in general for pickpockets and don't go up to the fort on your own. Taking a taxi door-to-door after dark is strongly advised by locals, especially for solo women travellers. Violent muggings have been reported on the beach south of the Baía dos Gatos: exercise caution. The sea itself here can be dangerous as well, and at other swimming areas; take local advice. Laginha Beach is, however, almost always safe and is patrolled during busy periods.

GETTING THERE AND AWAY

BY AIR There are Cabo Verde Airlines flights to and from Sal and Praia, and the newish international airport also receives daily flights to and from Lisbon on TAP and a twice-weekly Cabo Verde Airlines service. Cabo Verde Airlines also offers a weekly direct flight to and from Paris, while Tranavia flies to Paris seasonally and offers flights to Marrakech weekly through the year. Named after Cabo Verde's late and great cultural icon, Cesária Évora, the airport has a small café, tourist information booth (✆ 231 1111; m 950 8475; ⊕ 08.00–19.00 daily, though take this with a pinch of salt), Cabo Verde Airlines (✆ 231 2400) and TAP (✆ 232 8050) ticket offices, gift shops and a music store, ATM, car-hire agency and free Wi-Fi (often out of service). Note that many of the offices and outlets will be closed when there are no flights due. For guidance on arriving at a Cabo Verdean airport from overseas, see page 58.

Taxis to town from the airport cost 1,000$ (1,200$ at night). It is 10km to Mindelo and 1km to São Pedro. Note, taxis to São Pedro will most likely charge the same rate as they do to Mindelo, despite the short distance.

BY FERRY Many people visiting Mindelo are in transit to Santo Antão, which cannot be reached by air. For further details of the reliable twice daily ferry services between Mindelo and Santo Antão, see page 305.

There is, theoretically, a CV Interilhas (w cvinterilhas.cv) bi-weekly ferry connection between São Vicente, Praia (Santiago) and São Nicolau, as well as a twice-weekly service to São Nicolau, then onwards to Boavista and Sal, but these may not appear on the schedule when they should and can still be cancelled or run horrifically late even if they do.

Cargo ships regularly go to Praia from São Vicente and, less regularly, to other islands. To find a place on one of these ships try the agents up towards the port and on Rua Cristiano de Sena Barcelos.

BY YACHT There is a modern marina (w marinamindelo.cv) at Mindelo, and the harbour and anchorage are excellent, offering protection from the northwest winds through to eastern and southern winds. There is fuel and water at the marina and ship repair is the best in the archipelago. They can confidently repair instruments here and are authorised for warranty work. There is also a chandlery with a range of equipment suitable for crossing the Atlantic.

Whether or not this is your first port of call in Cabo Verde, the procedure is to tie up at the marina and then walk to the Porto Grande and identify yourself to the *capitania* who will guide you through the other necessities such as the maritime police and the immigration police.

Mindelo Marina has a floating pontoon with a pleasant bar/restaurant. The other possible anchorage is at Baía de São Pedro, where it is best to anchor off the eastern end of the beach. Winds can occasionally be difficult there and there are no facilities. Watch the channel between São Vicente and Santo Antão, where winds can gust up to 40 knots, particularly between December and May.

For yacht services, try BoatCV (page 279).

GETTING AROUND

BY PUBLIC TRANSPORT Transcor buses (w transcor.cv) journey around Mindelo and its outskirts, even visiting Baía das Gatas during July and August. Buses gather at the square to the west of the Palácio do Povo (Presidential Palace). If you are staying for a few days, consider downloading the Transcor app for easier pre-paid options. Single tickets cost 43$ and can be bought on board; a physical or online *bilhete pré-pago* costs 315$ for five trips, or 530$ for ten, with one more for free. *Alugueres* gather in Praça Independéncia, connecting Mindelo with the rest of the island.

BY TAXI There are plenty of marked taxis cruising around central Mindelo. The municipality publishes official fares, so if in doubt, just ask your driver to show you the list. A typical journey within the city will cost about 250–500$. Taxis charge about 3,000$ for a return journey to the top of Monte Verde, 2,500$ return to Baía das Gatas and 2,500$ return to Calhau. It's 1,000$ to the airport and 1,200$ to São Pedro. Taxis can be hired for about 1,000$ per hour. Ask your hotel if you would like them to book you an English-speaking driver, but bear in mind that they can be rare. Fares at night are about 10% more than the daytime equivalents.

BY CAR There are many car-rental agencies in town. Many close for lunch between 12.30 and 14.30. In addition to those listed, any half-decent hotel receptionist will have rental agency details. Prices start from €35–55 per day for something basic. You might consider whether it is really worth hiring a car – it is certainly a one-day event, at most. After all, the island's mainly cobbled road network is hardly extensive and taking taxis to Baía das Gatas and Calhau at one side of the island, and São Pedro at the other, is easy to arrange.

Atlantic Car [282 F2] 102 Rua Baltazar Lopes da Silva, Mindelo; 231 7032; m 991 6229
Joel Evora 230 0303; m 993 4004/8110; e rentacarsv@joelevora.com

Transmello m 991 5784; e transmello@hotmail.com; w transmello.cv

WHERE TO STAY AND EAT

Virtually all hotels are in Mindelo. There are a couple of places in São Pedro, a well-respected hotel in Calhau, and a couple of budget places in Baía das Gatas. Just outside Mindelo, Lazareto has a few hotels, but it's hard to recommend either the hotels or the location. Mindelo's restaurant scene is booming, with everything from cute cafés serving breakfast and good coffee to reasonably upmarket places. Prices can be high but there's plenty of local and fast-food options for the budget-conscious. Outside the capital, most restaurants are geared to day-trip groups and are priced accordingly.

EXCURSIONS AND TOUR OPERATORS

There are several operators in Mindelo offering a variety of tours. The tourist information kiosk in front of the Pont d'Água complex has details of boat trips, walking tours and other excursions.

Atlantur [map, page 286] Rua d'António Aurélio Gonçalves; 231 2728; m 921 6229; e saovicente@atlantur.com; w atlantur.com. Tours include half-day island tours, lobster dinners, hikes, Sundays out which include both a mass & music/dancing, plus trips to Santo Antão. Also sells ferry & airline tickets & books hotels.
Barracuda Tours [282 F4] Rua Dr Baltazar Lopes da Silva; 232 5591; e geral@barracudatours.com; w barracudatours.com. Established family-owned agency that can organise inter-island travel & excursions.
vista verde tours [282 F3] Rua Dr Baltazar Lopes da Silva; 232 6671; m 993 0788; e office@vista-verde.com; w vista-verde.com; ⊕ year-round 08.00–noon Mon–Fri, plus Oct–Mar 10.00–13.00 Sat. Well-established, efficient travel agency specialising in socially & environmentally responsible tourism. The office is located east of the Praça Amílcar Cabral.

ACTIVITIES

WINDSURFING, KITESURFING AND SURFING São Vicente could be one of the world's greatest windsurfing and bodyboarding destinations. World windsurfing speed records have been set in São Pedro Bay. The wind there, at the southwest corner of the island, is the result of an unusual quirk in the landscape: the long straight valley behind the bay acts as a funnel concentrating the wind – a phenomenon known as the Venturi effect. The result is an unusually steady and strong breeze.

There are some good surfing spots around Calhau, including Praia Grande, around the headland to the north of Calhau, and Praia Branca, just south of Calhau and Sandy Beach. Frustratingly, however, equipment rental is hard to come by.

Itoma 00 43 699 195 28111; m 991 2852; e info@itoma.at; w itoma.at. This 23m motor catamaran is based in the marina & is booked mostly by groups from Europe for week-long

WINDSURFING AND SURFING

Surfers love some of the São Vicente beaches and, in 1997, Sandy Beach at Calhau was included in the European professional circuit. However, it is among windsurfers, who have reached bullet-like speeds here, that it has become famous.

For one young windsurfer, it was the channel between São Vicente and Santo Antão that posed the greatest challenge. He gazed longingly across the 14km stretch and promised himself that one day, when the winds were right, he would attempt the crossing. He waited a long time for the perfect day and then set out, just as the ferry pulled away from the pier for the same destination.

He raced across and arrived at Porto Novo before the ferry, much to the admiration of the rest of the windsurfing fraternity back in Mindelo. One man left unimpressed, however, was the local policeman, who promptly arrested him.

---

windsurfing (winter) or diving (summer) trips. The comfortable boat carries a range of sails & boards & offers a way to windsurf in places few people ever see. Takes 12–16 passengers. One-week cruise around €1,600 per person.
Sabura Surf Academy [map, page 286] Rua Unidade Africana, in the Luso Africana Galerias arcade; m 977 5681; e info@saburasurfacademy.com; w saburasurfacademy.com. Month-long surfing courses, for both board & bodysurfing, & private lessons. Rents surfboards, bodyboards, kitesurf equipment & SUPs, & provides transport to the island's best breaks.

SAILING As with much of Cabo Verde, but especially between São Vicente and Santo Antão, the seas can be rough and the winds very strong. Sailing to Santo Antão may be a nice idea, but trying to anchor in Porto Novo, Santo Antão's harbour, in a strong offshore wind can be very hairy and there is not the same level of support as can be found in the Canaries.

BoatCV (Kai Brossmann & Cesar Murais) [283 G6] \ 230 0382; e info@boatcv.com; w boatcv.com; ⊕ 09.00–noon & 15.00–18.00 Tue–Sat. Well-respected German & Cabo Verdean operation offering yacht support services & hiring out a variety of yachts, bare boat or captained.

FISHING The waters around São Vicente are internationally renowned for their blue marlin. The **Sport Fishing Centre** [282 B3] (m 993 1332; e caboverdefishingcentre@yahoo.it; w caboverdefishingcenter.com) is located by the Dokas restaurant and offers a full range of fishing experiences. For other operators, ask at the Mindelo Marina office or at the Marina Mindelo Floating Club.

DIVING Diving on São Vicente is undeveloped, but there are two diving centres, Haliotis [282 E3] (w haliotis.pt) at the Oásis Porto Grande hotel and Dive Tribe [282 B3] (w dive-tribe.com) by the ferry terminal near Dokas.

SWIMMING The best swimming is probably at the semi-artificial lagoon at Baía das Gatas and also at Baía de Salamansa. Then there's Praia da Laginha, the 'city beach' in the north of Mindelo, transformed with white sand said to be imported from Sal island, usually safe and sometimes manned with a lifeguard. A handful of city hotels have pools, some of them open to non-guests for a fee. These include Mansa Marina, Ouril Hotel Mindelo and Casamarel.

> **ENGLAND TO BARBADOS – AND LAS PALMAS TO ST LUCIA**
>
> *Murray Stewart*
>
> Mindelo was formerly one of the staging points for the OnDeck Atlantic Adventure, a race from Europe to Barbados. Crews were able to sign on for any of the individual legs, starting at Portsmouth and continuing to Lisbon, Madeira, São Vicente and Barbados. The São Vicente to Barbados leg – invariably the most popular leg – took around two weeks and was staged each November. The boats were half a dozen Farr 65s, sleek, thrilling ocean racers, with massive amounts of wind available to fill the spinnakers all the way downwind to the Caribbean. Creature comforts were not what these boats were about, yet crew members still had to pay around €2,000 for the adrenalin rush. Sadly, the race seems to have died out a few years ago.
>
> But in 2013, a spin-off from the Arc Rally, another long-running yacht rally, was announced, with a Cabo Verde stopover. Fifty yachts taking part in the Arc+ rally to St Lucia paused for breath at Mindelo and it has become a regular stopover ever since then, featuring most recently in the 2016 edition. It is hoped that the city will remain a regular fixture in the yachting calendar for many years to come. (See w worldcruising.com for more details.)

HIKING São Vicente is not one of the hiking islands but there are still several rewarding walks. It has a few small mountains and a breathtaking coastline of black rocks blasted by white foam, and white- or black-sand beaches.

You can walk up to the top of Monte Verde (following the cobbled road), or all the way along the coast from Baía das Gatas to Calhau. There are several walks in Calhau (page 296), ranging from 45 minutes to 3 hours. You can also walk from the Foya Branca Resort, in São Pedro, to the lighthouse at the end of the point (2 hours' round trip).

CULTURE Some Cabo Verdeans still laugh when Mindelo is described as the archipelago's 'capital of culture', but it has both the historical gravitas to make that claim and has also come on leaps and bounds since the early 2000s. It genuinely does feel like a place for new ideas and where tradition is honoured and reinvented. One very good reason for lingering on São Vicente has always been the music. At times it seems to simply pour out of every bar and restaurant, and the choice is wide. Live music does occur everywhere, especially at weekends, and there are also more formal events held at the various cultural centres in town. A mini surge of museum and gallery action has perked up the city's scene as well. Cesária Évora is properly commemorated in her hometown, as will soon be the city's maritime history. The Centro Cultural do Mindelo often has exhibitions, shows occasional films in its impressively sized auditorium and hosts music and other events, while the recently refurbished and expanded Centro Nacional de Arte, Artesanato e Design (CNAD; National Centre for Art, Crafts and Design; page 293) has temporary shows, a fascinating and important permanent collection and a delightful and occasionally lively bar/café. Just wandering around looking at the colonial-era and mid-century architecture is also a satisfying occupation.

SIGHTSEEING BY VEHICLE Several operators offer round-island excursions. Local operators can organise 'safari' trips around the island (page 278). Another good option is to hire a taxi with driver. They will happily wait for you as you stop to take photos or visit places of interest. Outside Mindelo there is not much traffic and, with a good map, it should not be problematic to guide yourself around the main sights. Go to Baía das Gatas, Calhau, Monte Verde and São Pedro.

MINDELO

The wide streets, cobbled squares and 19th-century European architecture all contribute to the sense of colonial history in Mindelo. Most things of interest lie not on the coastal road but on the next road back, which at the market end is called Rua Santo António and, after being bisected by the Rua Libertadores d'Africa (also known by its original name Rua de Lisboa), becomes Avenida 5 de Julho. Most road names in the centre of town have changed since independence, but many of the original signs linger and firms vary as to which street name they use, as do locals. Like most towns in Cabo Verde, street names are of limited use anyway, and mentioning them when talking to locals will often draw a blank stare. Taxi drivers can also be easily befuddled by street names, but are rarely stumped by the name of an actual establishment.

WHERE TO STAY Mindelo has a good number of hotels across all budgets, as well as a growing number of apartment rentals. Pleasingly, the standard is improving, with both locally- and European-owned boutique hotels beginning to dominate the scene, as well as a couple of reliable Portuguese chains. As with Platô in Praia, some of the more basic hotels are in old colonial buildings with central atriums, which means that a number of their rooms may be internal, with windows opening only on to a shaft. Budget choices, with a few exceptions, lack the charm and care of those on the more rural islands; if you're only staying a couple of nights perhaps plan to spend a little more here as the quality jumps significantly. At the time of writing there were sadly no hotel options overlooking Laginha beach, though a few Airbnbs do crop up there.

Casamarel [282 G4] (10 rooms) Alto Santo António 253; 232 1300; e info@casamarelhotel.com; w casamarelhotel.com. Perched atop the city in a calm, elevated neighbourhood. An expat couple have refashioned a 1910 pile once owned by a wealthy merchant from São Nicolau, & the public areas retain some of the stately old bones of what would have been a grand bourgeois home. Rooms are extremely comfortable & generous in size, with wide private terraces, linen-clad sofas, fridges & Nespresso machines (2 also have kitchenettes). All have extraordinary views. Also with a view, if more for languid paddles than laps, is a small pool. Restaurant, open to non-guests for both lunch & dinner, with occasional music nights. **$$$$$**

Ouril Hotel Mindelo [282 B3] (130 rooms) Av Marginal; 596 8640; e reservas.ourilmindelo@ourilhotels.com; ourilmindelo. Overlooking the marina & ferry port, this shiny, towering place has become the hotel of choice for Europeans en route to Santo Antão, for its great location but also its rooftop pool. Most of the smart rooms overlook the pleasant courtyard or neighbourhood, with only the heftily priced suites harbour-facing (some of these also have private balcony plunge pools). However, there are lots of nice public spaces to take in the view, including a breezy terrace restaurant. **$$$$–$$$$$**

Casa Branca [282 C3] (8 rooms) Alto São Nicolau; 231 6262; e info@casabrancahotel.com; casabrancaecochic. Rooms have either a great view over the bay or access to a private garden. Much use of wood, with a brown-&-white theme. AC, bar & restaurant. Gets mixed reviews & some maintenance issues, especially in bathrooms. Well located for the ferry. **$$$$**

Casa da Djedja [283 F5] (8 rooms) Rua Unidade Africana 13; 230 0739; e hello@casadadjedja.com; w casadadjedja.com. Central but on a broad,

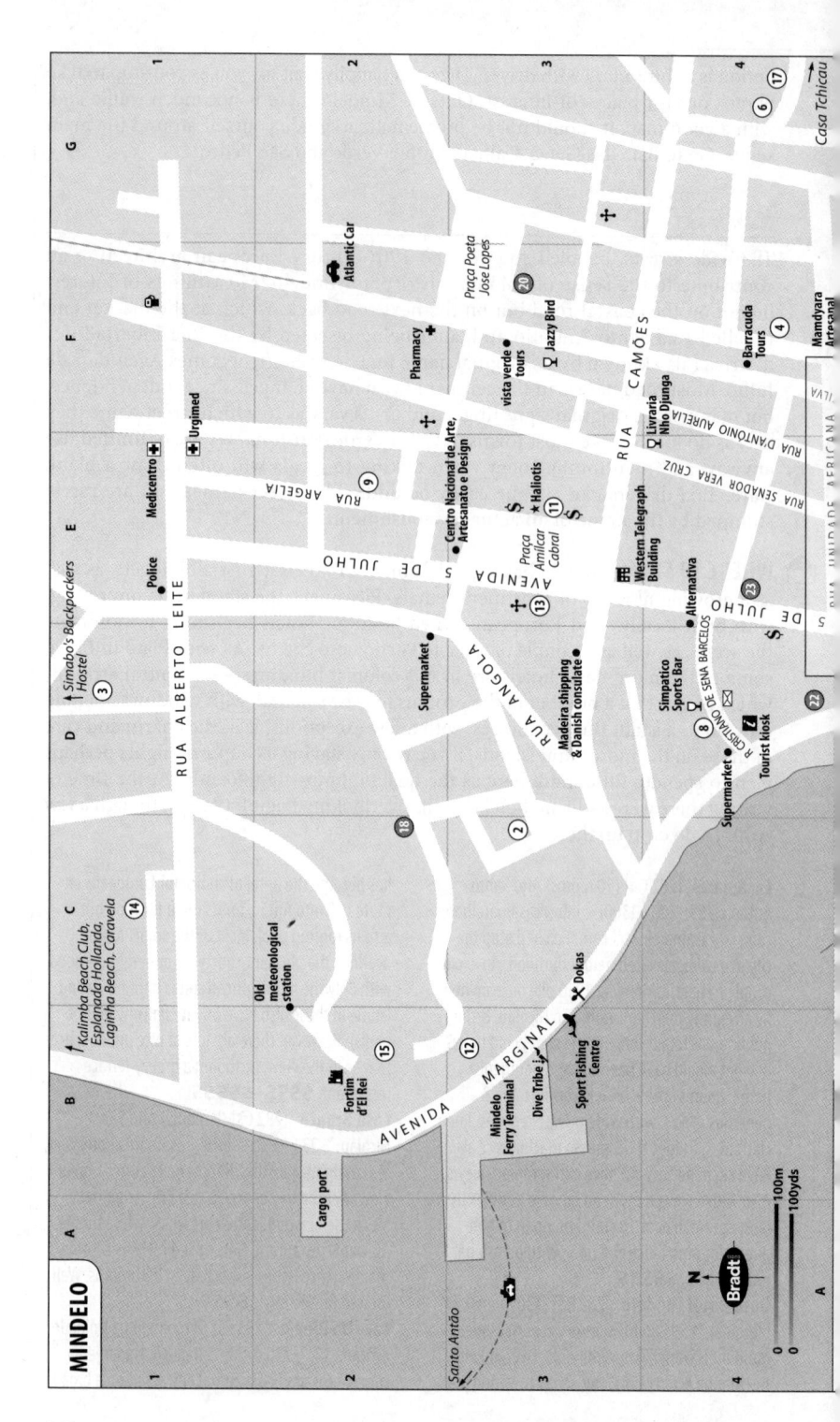

MINDELO

- Cargo port
- Santo Antão
- Kalimba Beach Club, Esplanada Hollanda, Laginha Beach, Caravela
- Fortim d'El Rei
- Old meteorological station
- Mindelo Ferry Terminal
- Dive Tribe
- Sport Fishing Centre
- Dokas
- AVENIDA MARGINAL
- RUA ALBERTO LEITE
- Simabo's Backpackers Hostel
- Police
- Medicentro
- Urgimed
- Pharmacy
- Atlantic Car
- RUA ANGOLA
- Supermarket
- Centro Nacional de Arte, Artesanato e Design
- RUA ARGELIA
- Haliotis
- Praça Amilcar Cabral
- 5 DE JULHO
- vista verde tours
- Jazzy Bird
- Praça Poeta Jose Lopes
- Madeira shipping & Danish consulate
- Western Telegraph Building
- Alternativa
- RUA CAMÕES
- Livraria Nho Djunga
- Barracuda Tours
- Mamdyara Artesanal
- Casa Tchicau
- Simpatico Sports Bar
- R CRISTIANO DE SENA BARCELOS
- Supermarket
- Tourist kiosk
- RUA SENADOR VERA CRUZ
- RUA D'ANTONIO AURELIA
- 5 DE JULHO
- RUA UNIDADE AFRICANA

0 100m
0 100yds

N

Bractt

São Vicente MINDELO

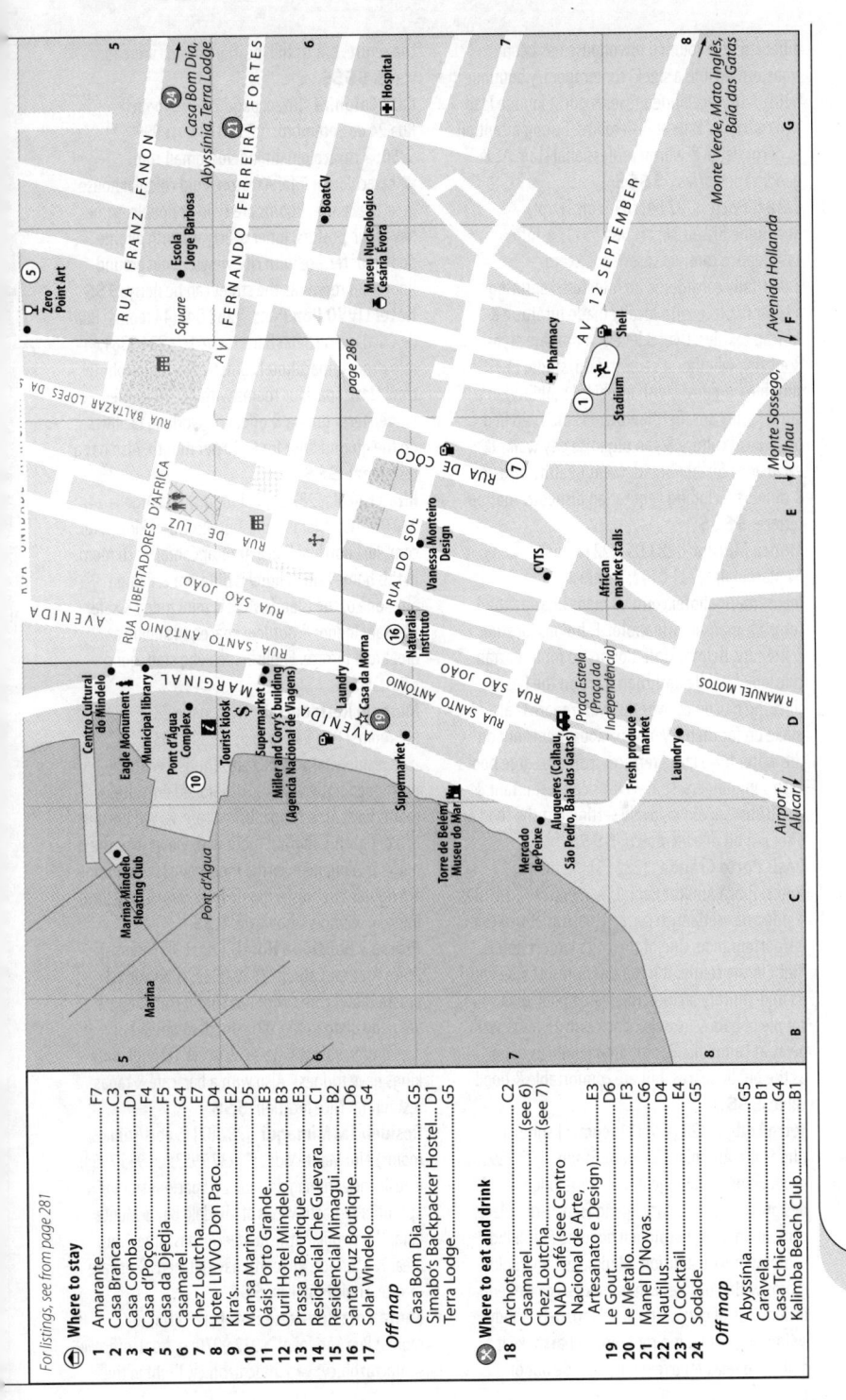

For listings, see from page 281

Where to stay

1. Amarante F7
2. Casa Branca C3
3. Casa Comba D1
4. Casa d'Poço F4
5. Casa da Djedja F5
6. Casamarel G4
7. Chez Loutcha E7
8. Hotel LIVVO Don Paco D4
9. Kira's E2
10. Mansa Marina D5
11. Oásis Porto Grande E3
12. Ouril Hotel Mindelo B3
13. Prassa 3 Boutique E3
14. Residencial Che Guevara C1
15. Residencial Mimagui B2
16. Santa Cruz Boutique D6
17. Solar Windelo G4

Off map

Casa Bom Dia G5
Simabo's Backpacker Hostel D1
Terra Lodge G5

Where to eat and drink

18. Archote C2
    Casamarel .... (see 6)
    Chez Loutcha .... (see 7)
    CNAD Café (see Centro
    Nacional de Arte,
    Artesanato e Design) E3
19. Le Gout D6
20. Le Metalo F3
21. Manel D'Novas G6
22. Nautilus D4
23. O Cocktail E4
24. Sodade G5

Off map

Abyssinia G5
Caravela B1
Casa Tchicau G4
Kalimba Beach Club B1

quiet street, a colonial townhouse has been transformed into a sleek, contemporary boutique hotel. A high-ceilinged foyer & guest lounge lead to a courtyard & its stylish rooms. Strong attention to décor detail & warm, professional staff. AC & good, varied b/fast. $$$$

Casa d'Poço [282 F4] (6 rooms, 1 apt) Rua Guiné Bissau 34; m 584 5911; e info@casadepoco.com; w casadepoco.com. Beautifully considered architecture capturing a spirit of place with locally made furniture & African textiles. Over 3 levels, rooms are stylish & earthy, whether it's a standard, studio (1 suitable for guests with impaired mobility) or a large family apt. German owners are switched on to local culture & can organise city walks & excursions further afield. Great healthy b/fasts & dinners including vegetarian dishes, & rooftop terrace. $$$$

Mansa Marina [283 D5] (22 rooms) Av Marginal; 231 0112; e info@mansamarinahotel.com; w mansamarinahotel.com; mansamarinahotel. Fabulous location & friendly, helpful staff. Rooms go for a spartan chic look & while bathrooms are on the basic side, the balconies over the water more than make up for them. More spacious rooms not on the water have large terraces instead. Large pool with sunloungers, spa, well-priced restaurant & bar. B/fast served in lovely setting but the food on offer is a bit of a let-down. $$$$

Oásis Porto Grande [282 E3] (48 rooms, 2 suites) Praça Amílcar Cabral; +351 217 524 100; e info@oasisatlantico.com; w oasisatlantico.com/en/portogrande. One of the city's largest hotels. Right in the centre, it has a classic resort vibe with its mid-century architecture, large pool, gym, couple of bars & its own beach club 15 mins' walk away at Langhina. Rooms aren't quite as glam as the public spaces, but are comfortable & good value. $$$$

Terra Lodge [283 G5] (11 rooms, 1 suite) 11 Alto Santo António, Rua Franz Fanon; 231 2919; e booking@terralodge.net; w terralodge.net. A design-conscious if easy-going French-run place, combining a pretty colonial building & striking contemporary extension. Minimalist fan-cooled rooms with balconies & hammocks. Eco credentials include use of grey water & solar panels. Shady swimming pool & fun roof terrace bar make it a place to relax for a few days. A little out of the centre, but its hill location affords it great views. $$$$

Casa Colonial [map, page 286] (9 rooms) Rua 24 de Setembro; 231 8760; m 999 5350; e casacolonialmindelo@gmail.com; w casacolonial.info. A restored old colonial house, near the centre. Rooms are twin or double, some have four-posters. Inner courtyard with plunge pool, roof terrace with city views. Avoid ground-floor front rooms as the street can be noisy. $$$

Hotel LIVVO Don Paco [282 D4] (44 rooms) Rua de Cristiano de Sena Barcelos 461; 231 9381; e info@thedonpacohotel.com; w thedonpacohotel.com. Neat, spacious rooms with AC. Welcomes longer-term guests & offers co-working facilities on the ground floor for €130 per month. Also has a restaurant. $$$

Kira's Hotel [282 E2] (11 rooms) Rua Argelia 24; 230 0274/5; e kiras@kirashotel.com; w kirashotel.com. Just north of Praça Amílcar Cabral, each room in this homey small hotel is different & named after one of the islands. AC, TV, mini fridge & safe; pleasant indoor & outdoor spaces, including a great roof terrace. English-speaking staff; good b/fast. $$$

Mindelo Residencial [map, page 286] (11 rooms) Rua São João 6; 230 0863; e m.residencial@gmail.com. This is a centrally positioned hotel with old-fashioned en-suite rooms with AC & fridge. B/fasts are served upstairs in a delightful, rooftop room with views over the harbour & inland over the mountains. Front rooms are lighter but noisier; some back rooms only have internal windows, however. $$$

Prassa 3 Boutique Hotel [282 E3] (9 rooms) Praça Amílcar Cabral; 230 0809; e booking@prassa3hotel.com; w prassa3hotel.com. Rooms verge on bling in this ultra-modern hotel, but are comfortable & have AC & sat TV (though only kings have fridges). Also with a bar-café & tapas restaurant. Nice location. $$$

Residencial Mimagui [282 B2] (5 apts/studios/rooms) Alto Monte Video; 232 7953; m 995 7954; e residencialmimagui@sapo.cv. Spacious studios & apts offer fantastic views of Mindelo Bay & Monte Cara. This popular little *residencial* has large living areas & a terrace. All rooms have kitchens & private terrace. English spoken. $$$

Santa Cruz Boutique Hotel [283 D6] (6 rooms) Rua São João; 972 9070; e front-office@santacruzbh.cv; w santacruzbh.cv. Right in the historic centre, this bright, stylish & fun boutique hotel is a wonderful city bolthole. There are a couple of standard rooms on offer, otherwise the rest are 'junior suites' & have variously a terrace, a balcony or a jacuzzi. All rooms have AC & flat screens with streaming. Rooftop terrace with views. Staff go that little bit extra & front desk is open 24 hours (handy in this location). $$$

Solar Windelo [282 G4] (9 rooms) Alto Santo António; 231 0070; e windelocapvert@gmail.com; w windelo.com. Located up a steep, short hill in a residential area, this is the former home of musician & composer Vasco Martins. Offers self-catering studio flats, rooms, suites & family rooms that can accommodate 6 guests, with simple, old-fashioned décor. B&B basis for rooms & suites. All have private baths & hot water & are cooled by fan, or AC for an extra charge. Some suites have balconies & great views – recommended. They can arrange excursions & give advice about wind- & kitesurfing. Dinner available on request, but it's also close enough to a few popular restaurants. $$$

Amarante [283 F7] (18 rooms) Av 12 Septembre; 231 3219; e gdamarante@cvtelecom.cv. Basic but tidy choice, with continental b/fast. Rooms are en suite, but have no hot water. Go for one with a balcony if available. $$

Casa Bom Dia [283 G5] (3 rooms) Rua Franz Fanon 14; m 527 4746; w casabomdiamindelo.com. Run by a resident multi-lingual Belgian family, this small & friendly guesthouse spread over 3 levels is a good-value choice if you don't want to be right in the centre. Fantastic communal rooftop, healthy b/fasts & helpful information. A 2-night minimum. $$

Casa Comba [282 D1] (7 rooms) Rua Dr Vicente Rendall Leite; m 597 7947; e comba@cvtelecom.cv. A warm Cabo Verdean welcome & popular roof terrace for b/fast in this good-value place at the top end of town. Pleasant rooms are cooled by fans. Easy walk to beach. $$

Chez Loutcha [283 E7] (24 rooms) Rua de Côco; 232 1636/1689; e chezloutcha@sapo.cv; w chezloutcha.com. Visitors either love or hate Chez Loutcha, located off Praça Estrela, & its rabbit warren of rooms are starting to look a little tatty (& note, some have interior windows). The proprietor offers free transport to his beachfront restaurant in Calhau where they have a large buffet, live music & dancing every Sun. $$

Residencial Che Guevara [282 C1] (12 rooms) Av Che Guevara 6; 232 2449; e cheguevara@cvtelecom.cv. A pleasant, quiet spot, located in the north of town along Rua Alberto Leite. Rooms all have fans, & private bathrooms with hot water (though not always). Also triples & family rooms. Free Wi-Fi in public areas, bikes for hire. Friendly French-speaking owner. $$

Pensão Chave d'Ouro [map, page 286] (21 rooms) Av 5 de Julho; 232 7050; w chavedouro.cv. Super-central position on the corner of Rua Libertadores d'Africa (Rua de Lisboa) & Av 5 de Julho. Supposedly, at more than 80 years of age, the oldest hotel in Mindelo. The better rooms have their original huge shuttered windows & are equipped with pitchers, but bathrooms are shared. Top-floor singles are little more than cupboards: avoid. Others do have a certain nostalgic charm. B/fast inc. Wi-Fi in restaurant only. $

Simabo's Backpacker Hostel [282 D1] (9 rooms) Av Vicente Rendall Leite 13, up the hill from Praia da Laginha. This brightly decorated & very cheap hostel has cold showers & only a couple of rooms with private bathrooms. Great roof terrace, some rooms with balconies. Communal kitchen & young guests mean it can be loud at night. The business helps finance a street dog charity & hosts volunteer vets. Cats stay on the premises, & dogs visit, so those with animal allergies should avoid. $

✕ WHERE TO EAT AND DRINK Mindelo is packed with restaurants, bars and cafés – this is only a small selection. One of the most appealing things about the city right now is its new generation of café, restaurant and bar owners who are focused on fostering local culture and community. While being meeting places for the city's creatively minded, they also welcome visitors with open arms. Examples of these listed below include Abyssínia, Café Verde, Kafé Djan Djan, as well as Bombu Mininu (page 289). For bread and pastries, the excellent **Pastelaria Morabeza** [map, page 286], with good coffee, snacks and free Wi-Fi, is on Rua Baltazar Lopes da Silva; there is also a beautifully original bakery on the Rua Senador Vera Cruz that has a steady queue of locals. The Fragata supermarket [283 D6] opposite the

MINDELO
Centre

For listings, see from page 281

🏠 **Where to stay**
1. Casa Colonial
2. Mindelo Residencial
3. Pensão Chave d'Ouro

✖ **Where to eat and drink**
4. Café Estrela
5. Café Royal
6. Café Verde
7. Casa Café Mindelo
   Chave d'Ouro (see 3)
8. Columbinho
9. Kafé Djan Djan
10. La Pergola
11. London
12. Pastelaria Algarve

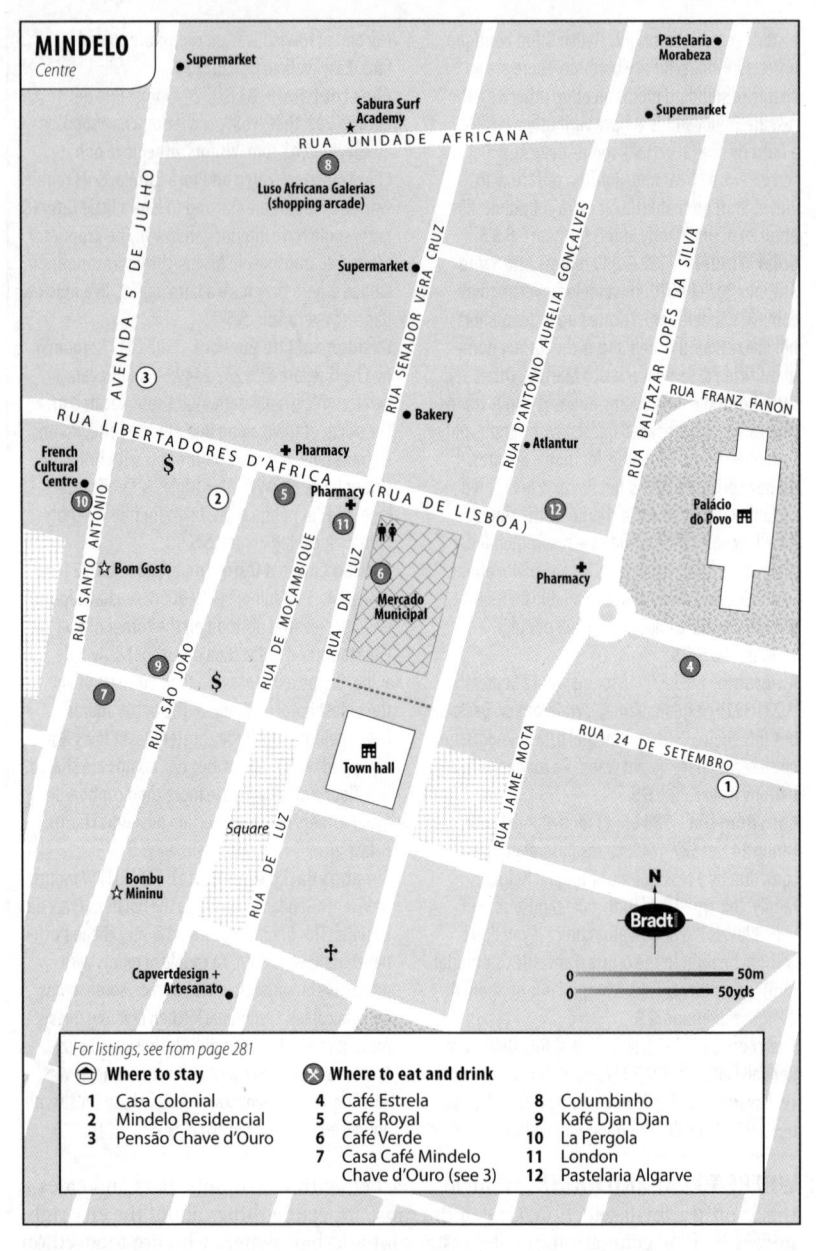

marina also has a bakery. Self-caterers should also try their luck for fresh fish at the daily open-air Mercado de Peixe [283 C7], along the waterfront next to the Belém tower, while other fresh produce can be found at both the Mercado Municipal [map, above] and Praça Estrela's open air stalls [283 D8].

Archote [282 C2] Rua Irmas do Amor de Deus]; 📞 232 3916; ⏱ noon–15.00 & 19.30–23.00 Sun–Thu, noon–15.00 & 19.30–midnight Sat. At the northern end of town, serving traditional Cabo

Verdean dishes & popular with locals. Good fish, & live music almost every night except Sun. $$$$$

Casamarel [282 G4] Page 281; ⏲ noon–21.00 daily. Non-guests welcome for lunch & dinner. Tables are set out on a hugely romantic terrace looking over the entire city. Interesting mix of local & international cooking (including a killer chicken satay). Wines by the glass are reasonably priced, but if you *are* after a big-budget bottle of something from Portugal, Italy or France, this is where you'll reliably find it. $$$$

Kalimba Beach Club [282 B1] Langinha beach, west side; m 586 2370; e info@ oasisatlantico.com; f kalimbabeachclub; ⏲ 09.00–midnight daily. Hotel Oásis Atlântico's pretty beach club is open to non-guests (& in fact feels nothing like a hotel bar). An airy blond wood pavilion sits right on the sand. Come for a post-swim glass of wine & a rare bowl of olives, or a grilled chicken or pasta lunch. Cocktails at sunset are worth the few extra escuodos for the wonderful view & atmosphere; DJs play sunset sets on summer Sats. Rents sunloungers & has free Wi-Fi. $$$$

Le Metalo [282 F3] Rua Capitão Heitor, up in Alto Miramar; m 996 2020; e info@metalo.cv; ☺ lemetalorestaurante; ⏲ 17.30–midnight Tue–Thu & Sun, 17.30–01.00 Fri & Sat. Cabo Verdean favourites – conch stew, seafood rice – as well as snacky options like burgers & panini. Good drinks list with cocktails & artisan *ponche* flavours, including *mancarra* (peanut). It's popular with locals, though that's much more about the music & the vibe at its bar, La Scène M (page 289), than the food. $$$$

Nautilus [282 D4] Av Marginal, across from the water; m 958 6622; f Nautilus.Mindelo; ⏲ 09.00–23.00 Sun–Thu, 09.00–midnight Fri & Sat. When the theme is 'age of sail' you can't expect a place to not be touristy. Huge people-pleasing menu of *tartares*, grills & rice dishes. $$$$

Café Estrela [map, opposite] Av Fernando Ferreira Fortes, opposite Palácio do Povo; ⏲ 19.00–21.00 Mon, noon–22.00 Tue–Sat. Its blank townhouse frontage is hard to spot unless it's open & a non-functioning phone makes booking impossible: just turn up, as there's usually a table. The delightful Lidia & her all-female team offer a choice of 2 dishes each night: lemon chicken perhaps, or a great *bitoque* (Portuguese-style steak & eggs). Wash it down with surprisingly good (& cheap) Portuguese wines. When you're done little cheese tartlets will arrive, or a papaya may be waved at you from the kitchen, awaiting your return gesture of yay or nay. The lovingly eccentric décor makes it all even more appealing. $$$

Caravela [282 B1] At the northern end of the Laginha Beach, just before the road bends away from the coast; ⏲ early–late daily. Usual variety of snacks, salads, fish dishes & good pizza. Popular on Sun lunchtimes, with a good mix of locals & visitors. Live music at w/ends, becoming a disco later on. $$$

Casa Café Mindelo [map, opposite] Rua Santo António; ⏲ 07.00–midnight daily. Relaxing place to enjoy a coffee or a drink, popular with expats. Fruit juices, snacks & cakes; mains can get expensive. Good b/fast option. $$$

Casa Tchicau [282 G4] Alto Solarino; m 951 5466; f casatchicauleonor; ⏲ 18.00–22.00 daily. At the top of the hill overlooking the city, this is great value, especially if you come hungry & with no other plans for the evening. The well-regarded kitchen turns out a multi-course feast for 1,500$ (drinks extra, but similarly inexpensive). The menu changes each night, but will include traditional mixed starters of croquettes & *pastel de atum*, fish or meat mains & dessert. A *morna* singer & a couple of musicians perform while you eat. Sometimes a little overwhelmed by French tour groups; service varies from perfunctory to warm. Closes in Aug. $$$

Chez Loutcha [283 E7] (page 285) ⏲ 07.00– 09.45, noon–15.00 & 19.30–23.30 Mon–Sat. On Sun the chef decamps to Calhau (page 297). Long-running restaurant on the ground floor of the hotel of the same name. Local & other West African dishes, including lobster & seafood. Service can be leisurely, & food can sometimes feel like they're resting on their laurels. Live music Wed & Fri, from 20.00. $$$

La Pergola [map, opposite] Part of the upstairs French Cultural Centre, Rua Santo António; m 982 7675; ⏲ 08.00–19.00 Mon–Fri, 08.00–15.00 Sat. This bar/restaurant feels oddly chaotic despite its pleasant courtyard setting. French expats come for pricey vegetarian dishes & seafood or just an afternoon juice or coffee. No Wi-Fi. Nightly acoustic act at 19.30. $$$

Le Gout [283 D6] Rua da Praia; ✆ 232 6100; ⏲ 10.00–midnight daily. On the seafront, Av Amílcar Cabral south end, upstairs in an old building. Has a good selection of meals, sometimes accompanied by live entertainment after 21.00 Wed–Sat. $$$

O Cocktail [282 E4] Av 5 de Julho; 232 7275; 08.00–midnight daily. Upstairs with simple food offerings – seafood, pizza, burgers, fresh juices. Live music from 20.00 Thu–Sun. $$$

Sodade [283 G5] Rua Franz Fanon 38; 230 3200. noon–15.00 & 18.00–23.00 daily. This rooftop restaurant offers an escape from the bustle of town, with an excellent panoramic view that is best before dark. Above the basic hotel of the same name. $$$

Abyssínia [283 G5] Alto Solarine, just off Rua Franz Fanon, on 1st street past the Terra Lodge pedestrian entrance; m 982 9739; abyssinia_mindel; 09.00–21.00 daily. This welcoming & atmospheric concept café, run by 2 sisters, is a little out of the way, but worth the uphill stroll for its home cooking & sense of community. Still a functioning *mercearia*, or corner store, it has a handful of tables to enjoy freshly made *tumberina* (tamarind) or *bissap* (hibiscus) juices, cake & coffee or a *prato do dia*, all showcasing traditional culinary culture. Music on Sat afternoons. $$

Café Royal [map, page 286] Rua Libertadores d'Africa (Rua de Lisboa); 353 1020; m 586 4562; 07.00–23.00 daily. Live music on Sat night is the main draw at this cavernous colonial-era place. Average food but an easy-going option if you can't snag a table elsewhere for dinner. $$

Café Verde [map, page 286] Rua Libertadores d'Africa (Rua de Lisboa) (inside the Mercado Municipal); & cafeverdemindelo; 09.00–16.00 Mon–Fri, 09.00–13.00 Sat. A stylishly boho space for sipping excellent Fogo-grown espresso & papaya smoothies each morning. Or come for a lunchtime grilled chicken & lentil salad, omelette or *cachupa* & finish with homemade cake. A friendly & convivial place in the middle of the market's own happy bustle. $$

Chave d'Ouro [map, page 286] Page 285; noon–13.00 & 19.00–22.00 daily. An old-fashioned restaurant upstairs in the hotel of the same name. The good-value menu gets mixed reviews, but the time-warp film-set surroundings are an experience in themselves. $$

CNAD Café [282 E3] In the Centro Nacional de Arte, Artesanato e Design; 231 7751; 09.00–21.00 Mon–Sat. Even if you're not visiting the city's art & design museum, its café has direct access from Praça Amílcar Cabral. Look for the canary yellow chairs & tables spilling out on to the terrace from its colonial-era interior. Café menu favourites are joined by authentic cakes (try the sweet goat's cheese tart), a 400$ hot *prato do dia*, good wine by the glass & artisan *grogue*. $$

Columbinho [map, page 286] Inside the small shopping arcade, Luso Africana Galerias, Rua Unidade Africana 08.30–23.30 Mon–Sat, 10.30–22.00 Sun. Open-air snack bar tucked away in an interior courtyard along a passageway that houses other businesses & boutiques. Popular with locals. Nightly live music. $$

Kafé Djan Djan [map, page 286] Rua São João; 974 1881; 08.30–16.30 Mon & Sat, 08.30–19.30 Tue–Fri, 08.30–14.30 Sun. Sunny, bustling spot for international café staples like açai & buddha bowls, or more locally leaning choices like a baked papaya b/fast dish. Coffee all day, wine in the afternoons. Encourages lingering with your laptop (free Wi-Fi) or pen & notebook. $$

Pastelaria Algarve [map, page 286] Rua Libertadores d'Africa (Rua de Lisboa); 231 8921; 09.00–22.00 Mon–Sat. Retaining some welcome old-world charm, a well-established place popular with middle-aged locals chewing the fat on its pleasant enclosed pavement terrace. Basic but good food. $$

London [map, page 286] Rua da Luz; 09.00–midnight Mon–Sat. Toasted panini for b/fast, burgers, shawarma & the like, day & night. $

Manel D'Novas [283 G6] Av Fernando Ferreira Fortes; m 991 5902; maneldnovas; noon–15.00 Mon–Sat. Usually a live music venue (see opposite), offering a ridiculously well-priced *prato do dia*, say rice & duck, for 500$, in an airy indoor-outdoor space. $

ENTERTAINMENT AND NIGHTLIFE Live music abounds in Mindelo. For those who don't fancy a really late night, most of the visitor-orientated restaurants have at least one Cabo Verdean evening with music, especially at weekends. Try Caravela and other venues at Laginha Beach just outside the centre of the city; Archote or the more central Café Royal, Le Gout (all from page 285) or **Casa da Morna** [283 D6], which opens around 19.00 and is owned by Tito Paris, one of Cabo Verde's most illustrious musicians. Or, just keep your ears open after 20.00 and follow the music. The clubs in Mindelo tend to open at about 22.30 or 23.00; people start arriving about midnight and they get lively by about 02.30, emptying at about 05.00. On a Sunday, people generally stop somewhere for some well-earned *cachupa* on their way home. Entry to most clubs costs around 500$. For a discussion of Cabo Verdean music and dancing, see page 43.

Bom Gosto [map, page 286] Rua Santo António; 09.00–midnight daily. Beamed-ceiling room with lots of terrace seating. Serves food but better for an early (or late) evening drink. Music most nights & big selection of *grogue* & *ponche*. Note, pay by cash, as cards attract a steep surcharge.

Bombu Mininu [map, page 286] Rua São João; m 595 0660; e bombumininu@gmail.com; & bombumininu; 10.00–18.00 Mon, 10.00–22.00 Tue–Thu, 10.00–midnight Fri, noon–midnight Sat. Bar, café, shop: Bombu is all of these, but much more. This vibrant, eclectically decorated shopfront space is a cultural centre, in every sense of the term. Owners & star local creatives Miriam Simas & António Tavares will welcome you for chat, a drink & later, performances, be they music, poetry or dance. Swing by during the day for cake & coffee & ask what's on.

Caravela [282 B1] (page 287) w/ends. Entry fee varies for this beachside restaurant which opens its downstairs disco on Fri & Sat nights.

Columbinho [map, page 286] (see opposite); 18.30–23.30 Mon–Wed, 18.30–01.00 Thu–Sat, 18.30–22.30 Sun. Super-authentic & casual courtyard bar that has a weekly calendar of musicians & w/end DJs.

Jazzy Bird [282 F3] w/ends. Local musicians often meet here for informal sessions. A good place for a laid-back night out & maybe catching a 'big name' player passing through. One of the city's longest-running cultural assets: taxi drivers may know it as 'Vou's', after the owner.

La Scène M [282 F3] Le Metalo (page 287); lascene_m; 11.00–midnight Mon–Sat, 17.00–midnight Sun. Metalo restaurant's courtyard hosts this excellent live music venue, with nightly acts ranging from local sounds, to R&B & jazz.

Livraria Nho Djunga [282 E4] Rua Senador Vera Cruz 8; NhoDjunga; 19.00–01.30 Tue–Sat. An interesting combo of bar/bookshop/ speakeasy. Musicians gather early on w/end evenings to have an impromptu jam. From Thu–Sat, scheduled acts appear later too, & are occasionally international, say Brazilian or *emigrantes* from Portugal or France. Drinks & snacks only.

Manel D'Novas [283 G6] (see opposite); 19.00–late Tue–Sat. Large performance space with calendar of musical events and parties.

Mansa Marina [283 D5] In the hotel (page 284); noon–23.00 daily. The hotel's 'secret bar' faces the pool & out over the harbour beyond, making its airy terrace a perfect (& surprisingly reasonably priced) place to have a drink or while away a few hours while waiting to jump on a ferry or plane. There's a good food menu, too.

Marina Mindelo Floating Club [283 C5] Av Marginal; 230 0032; marinamindeloclubfloatingbar; 08.00–22.00 Mon–Thu, 08.00–midnight Fri & Sat, 08.00–21.00 Sun. Absolute waterfront at this easy-going all-day bar floating right in the middle of city's marina. There's a full food menu with good basic dishes, but everyone is here for the huge G&Ts & sunset with a soundtrack of clinking masts. Gets lively on Fri & Sat nights with music later on.

Praça Amílcar Cabral [282 E3] At 20.00 on Sun, a different type of music: the municipal band strikes up.

Simpatico Sports Bar [282 D4] Rua Cristiano de Sena Barcelos; m 910 3030/2527; 09.00–23.00 daily. Popular sports bar/Irish pub, with supersized *caipirinhas* & mojitos for 500$. All the Euro matches & local leagues on the big screen, plus burgers & pizza. $$$

Terra Lodge [283 G5] (page 284) 15.00–22.00 daily. Extraordinary views, a good mix of locals, expats & travellers, plus well-mixed cocktails make this one of the city's best sunset drinks destinations. Snacks like cassava chips can keep you going until dinner, or stay on for a meal.

Zero Point Art [283 F5] 62 Rua Unidade Africa; 10.00–12.30 & 18.00–02.00 Wed–Sat; opening hours approx at best – check in person during the day if you plan on visiting at night. The downstairs gallery shows the work of late owner Alex de Silva, while upstairs there is an intimate bar with sofas. Locals also take drinks to the chairs on the footpath. Solo female travellers may sadly feel intimidated by bar staff, however, who have been known to demand a hefty extra 'donation' for 'viewing' the art.

SHOPPING A good array of Cabo Verdean products can be found at a stall inside the **Centro Cultural do Mindelo** (page 294), along with the bright shop in the Centro Nacional de Arte, Artesanato e Design (page 293). **Mamdyara Artesanal** [283 F5] (Rua Unidade Africana; m 994 4392; w mamdyara.com; ⏲ 09.00–13.00 & 15.00–19.00 Mon–Sat, noon–18.00 Sun) is the country's first natural skincare brand, and their Mindelo flagship shop carries all their beautiful products. Made using volcanic mud and local plants they're non-toxic and utilise recyclable packaging. They also do a specialist haircare range for those of African heritage. Lisbon-born but of joint Cabo Verdean and Guinea Bissauean lineage, the eponymous designer behind **Vanessa Monteiro Design** (page 294) has beautiful ceramics, textiles and objects for sale, while **Capvertdesign+ Artesanato** (12 Rua da Luz; m 976 0402; w capvertdesign.com; ⏲ 09.00–13.00 & 15.00–18.30 Mon–Sat) also showcases high-quality, Cabo Verdean-made crafts, homewares, postcards and T-shirts. Along Avenida 5 de Julho, heading north from its junction with Rua Cristiano de Sena Barcelos, **Alternativa** [282 E4] (on the first corner), stocks local books as well as local food items. The café/bar **Bombu Mininu** (page 289) has a fantastic collection of secondhand vinyl to browse, some of which is for sale, and **Abyssínia** (page 288) sells a range of iconic locally branded groceries that make fun souvenirs. Supermarkets are common; try the many branches of **Fragata**, for example opposite the marina or on Avenida 5 de Julho, which are open over lunch and late at night.

OTHER PRACTICALITIES

Banks There are many banks in the centre, nearly all with ATMs. There are also ATMs on Rua Libertadores d'Africa (Rua de Lisboa); and Avenida Amílcar Cabral, and at the two banks next to the Oásis Porto Grande hotel.

Banco Cómercial do Atlântico [282 E3] Praça Amílcar Cabral; ⏲ 08.00–14.30 Mon–Fri

Caixa Económica [282 D4] Av 5 de Julho, across from the basketball courts; ⏲ 08.00–15.00 Mon–Fri

Health care The municipal Hospital Baptista [283 G6] is in the southeast corner of town (📞 232 7355/231 1879). There are two modern private medical centres, both near the police station at the northern end of town and with good reputations: Urgimed [282 E1] (Rua Senegal; 📞 230 0170) and Medicentro [282 E1] (Rua Alberto Leite; 📞 231 8515). There are several pharmacies, including a large one at the top of Rua Libertadores d'Africa (Rua de Lisboa) [map, page 286].

Spas and therapies Mamdyara Artesanal [283 F5] (see above), offers a range of skin and hair treatments, though you will have to call or pop in to book as this currently can't be done online. **Naturalis Instituto** [283 D6] (Rua da Luz; m 588 2525; e naturalis.instituto@gmail.com; ⏲ 10.00–18.00 Mon–Sat) offers massages, facials, and nail and hair treatments.

The rest

Police [282 E1] At the north end of town on Rua Alberto Leite; 📞 231 4311. This is also where you can get your visa extended, if necessary (page 58).

Post office [282 D4] Rua Cristiano de Sena Barcelos; ⏲ 08.00–15.30 Mon–Fri
Public toilets [map, page 286] Inside the market on Rua Libertadores d'Africa (Rua de Lisboa)

Tourist information [282 D4] Av Marginal. This kiosk may have information, maps, postcards & a few souvenirs if you're lucky enough to find them open. It is not a municipal kiosk, however, so it may be focused on selling you excursions or souvenirs.

WHAT TO SEE AND DO Sturdy English-style architecture, with sloping roofs and the odd bow window, interspersed with pretty Pombaline and Neoclassical Portuguese flourishes, combine to tell the story of Mindelo's past. There is the **Miller and Cory's building**, now housing the Agencia Nacional de Viagens ('ANAV') office and Fragata supermarket; the old residence of the employees of Shell, now the **Portuguese consulate**; and the **Western Telegraph building** [282 E3] on the Praça Amílcar Cabral, often referred to simply as the Praça Nova. The square has an incredible grab bag of architectural history. There's the pleasing 19th-century villa that's home to **CNAD** (page 293) and its bold contemporary extension (2022), the elegant **Cinema Éden Park** (1922), and an archetypal 1930s Portuguese-style *quiosque* in the centre. The lines of the **Oásis Porto Grande** hotel (page 284) and several other buildings represent the mid-century. There are many examples of Mindelo's two short phases of urban development in the early years of the Estado Novo regime and in the 1960s, as well as some interesting old typeface, such as the original Art Deco *Luso Africana* signage on Rua Unidade Africana's 1960s *galerias* (small shopping arcade). The innovative Mindelo-based architecture firm Ramos Castellano has several buildings to see in the city, including the CNAD extension (page 293), Terra Lodge (page 284) and an apartment building, Casa Celestina on Avenida Baltazar Lopes da Silva (the group's Aquiles Hotel (page 298) is in São Pedro, and they also designed Mamiwata Eco Village (page 323) over on Santo Antão).

For those not keen to get ensconced in city life straight away, a wander could begin with a trip up to the fort, **Fortim d'El Rei** [282 B2], on the headland to the east of town (Alto São Nicolau). Be aware that there have been muggings in this area, so taxis are recommended. From there you can understand the layout of the city. This hilltop fortress became a prison in the 1930s. In 1934, the militia descended from Fortim on to a food riot incited by a famous carpenter, Ambrósio, who led the looting of the food stores in the customs house. His story is the subject of plays today. Many of São Vicente's notable rebels, including resistance fighters, were imprisoned in the fort in the 1960s before being deported to Angola.

Now the headland affords a more peaceful scene: the busy port and Mindelo beyond it, the hills curling round the magnificent harbour; the strange stump of 'Bird Island' poking out of the harbour; and Santo Antão. **Monte Cara**, or Face Mountain, on the other side of the harbour, is one of several places in the archipelago where the sharp erosion has sculpted a remarkable human profile out of the mountains. Beside the fort is the radio station, Mira D'Ouro.

On your return along the coast road, just after the port, is a **monument** surmounted by an eagle, commemorating the first air crossing of the southern Atlantic in 1922 by Sacadura Cabral and Gago Coutinho. They stopped here en route to Brazil, after their leg from the Canaries.

Follow Avenida Marginal south with its shady trees down the centre of the road. You will pass some fine old storehouses dating from the height of the shipping days: many of them have been transformed for new uses. Opposite the pier is the handsome **Old Customs House**, built in 1858 and extended in the early 1880s. It is now the **Centro Cultural do Mindelo**.

Keep going and you will pass, on your right, the **Torre de Belém** [283 D7], built in 1921 as a homage to the historic monument of the same name in Lisbon, and

WEAVING STORIES: MINDELO'S OLDEST NEW MUSEUM

Donna Wheeler

In the immediate post-independence fervour of 1976, the Mindelo-based artists Manuel Figueira, Luísa Queirós and Bela Duarte founded the Cooperativa Resistência. Their motto – *não deixar morrer a tecelagem!* – isn't the usual revolutionary cry, but the spirit of 'don't let the weaving die!' was in fact a key part of the radical reimaging of Cabo Verdean identity. It's one that continues to have a profound influence today.

The collection of the Centro Nacional de Arte, Artesanato e Design (National Centre for Art, Crafts and Design; CNAD; w cnad.cv) grew out of those heady early days, when the co-operative travelled from island to island documenting the techniques from master artisans of *pánu di téra* – traditional cloth (page 40) – including Nho Griga from Santo Antão and Nho Damásio from Santiago. They then, in 1977, founded CNAD's precursor, the National Crafts Centre (CNA) and established a permanent home in the historic Casa Senador Vera Cruz on Praça Amílcar Cabral.

As the first cultural institution created in the new nation, the CNA nurtured craft networks as well as collecting examples of material culture that would form the basis of Cabo Verdean visual and aesthetic identity. It was to broaden its brief in 2018, when it changed its name and created a programme of cross-disciplinary creative residencies, as well as announcing its new building plans.

Sitting at the northern apex of the elegant *praça*, CNAD today is both a literal and symbolic beacon of cultural innovation and preservation. The original building is a graceful example of 19th-century colonial architecture that is also a cultural

which housed the Portuguese governor from the 1920s. It was restored, thanks to the Portuguese, in 2002 and houses a small maritime museum (see opposite).

Ahead and in to the left lies the market and the **Praça Estrela**. One half of the square has been filled with permanent market stalls, and on the wall at the end of each row an artist has depicted a scene from the history of Mindelo, painted on to ceramic tiles. The pictures utilise photographs taken in the early 1900s. They allow us to imagine Mindelo at its economic height: great wooden piers, cranes and rail tracks forever hauling coal on shore to the storage bunkers; the grand and busy customs house; the ships' chandlers lining the front street. From there, head north towards the Palácio do Povo, passing through the **Praçinha de Igreja**, the oldest part of town where the first houses were built and where there is a pretty church, Nossa Senhora da Luz, the city's pro-cathedral, constructed in 1862.

After the church you will pass the **town hall** (*câmara municipal*). Built between 1850 and 1873, it initially housed the Águas de Madeiral water company founded by John and George Rendall.

In front of the town hall and facing on to Rua Libertadores d'Africa (Rua de Lisboa), is the **Mercado Municipal** [map, page 286], a beautifully light and airy two-storey building that was begun in 1784, extended in the 1930s with an obvious Portuguese aesthetic, and gently restored in the 1980s.

In the middle of town is the candy pink **Palácio do Povo** (Presidential Palace) [map, page 286], which is currently not open to the public. The ground floor was built in 1873 as a venue for official receptions. In the 1930s, the second storey was added as well as the exuberant white filigree. It is now the Supreme Court (Tribunal Judicial).

artefact in its own right, serving as colonial residence, an important secondary school and the studios of Rádio Barlavento, where Cesária Évora (page 44) first recorded and from where PAIGC members made revolutionary broadcasts in 1974. In 2022, CNAD reopened with both a sympathetic renovation of that hugely historic space, plus an entirely new wing.

Designed by the Mindelo-based firm Ramos Castellano Arquitectos, the extension utilises handcrafted construction techniques in a three-storey concrete, glass and wood pavilion. The result creates spaces that are both austere and textured, reflecting the islands' domestic architecture as well as the centre's focus on the makers' touch.

The extraordinary façade has an exterior skin of more than two thousand recycled barrel caps, blasted and painted by hand. These filter both light and air and their use also nods to the metal vessels of island trade and are a point of memory for the Cabo Verdean diaspora. Their colours conjure the bright palette of Mindelo's streetscapes but are not just decorative choices here: local composer Vasco Martins has 'scored' the building, each colour representing a musical note. The visual rhythm it creates pays homage to the city's intangible art of music, while providing shelter for its material cultural assets.

Permanent and temporary galleries show CNAD's carefully curated collections of textiles, ceramics and sculpture as well as contemporary art and design. A space is also dedicated to some of the founders' painting. There's a library, research centre, studios for artistic residencies, a shop and a café. The courtyard that connects the two spaces is used for performances, parties and other events, as well as serving as a place to observe the beauty of both buildings.

Behind the palace (ie: to the east) is the **Escola Jorge Barbosa** [283 F5] which has served a variety of purposes since its construction began in 1859. It has been an army barracks (the square was for parades), governor's office, army hospital and then, in the early 1920s, the influential grammar school, Liceu Nacional Infante D Henrique, important in fostering Cabo Verde's intellectual life and independence movement.

Museums

Centro Nacional de Arte, Artesanato e Design [282 E3] (CNAD; w cnad. cv; ⊕ 10.00–13.00 & 15.00–19.00 Tue–Fri, 10.00–14.00 & 18.00–21.00 Sat, 18.00–21.00 Sun; 500$) This art and design museum splits a permanent collection of rare Cabo Verdean crafts and temporary exhibitions of Modernist and contemporary art across its two beautifully designed and rendered buildings. There's also a terrace café/bar (page 288).

Museu do Mar [283 D7] (Inside the Torre Belem; ⊕ 09.00–18.00 Mon–Fri, 09.00–13.00 Sat; 200$) Spread over four floors, the exhibits include model ships and preserved fish in jars (!), with wall panels in English explaining Mindelo's maritime history and whaling in Cabo Verde. There is also reference to the connection with New Bedford and the schooner *Ernestina* (page 21). Slated for a museological overhaul in 2025.

Museu Nucleologico Cesária Évora [283 F6] (Rua Guerra Mendes 24; \262 3385; e nospatrimonio@gmail.com; w museus.cv; ⊕ 09.00–17.00 Mon–Fri,

09.00–13.00 Sat; 300$, cash only) A typical townhouse is dedicated to the barefoot diva, Mindelo's favourite daughter. Multi-lingual displays detail her life and loves: music, men, and a penchant for cognac. A couple of videos play including rare documentation of her state funeral, where the attendee list is a who's who of Cabo Verdean music. A few of her costumes and ephemera are also touchingly displayed and a soundtrack plays her haunting voice; you can listen to additional tracks through headphones.

Beaches Past the ferry terminal and port, to the north, is the long, sandy beach of Laginha, popular with the locals, safe for swimming and with an outdoor gym and a couple of bars and restaurants. It is also the place to go for some lively nightlife at weekends, with both live music and a disco.

Biblioteca Municipal [283 D5] (Rua Santo António; ⊕ 09.00–17.00 Mon–Fri) On the first floor of a building shared with Alliance Française, the Municipal Library has a fascinating collection of books on the history of Mindelo, including some on the British presence. A handsome building with an impressive wooden staircase.

Centro Cultural do Mindelo [282 D5] (CCM; \ 232 5840; e centroculturaldomindelo@gmail.com; f CCMindelo; ⊕ 09.00–21.00 Mon–Fri, 10.00–12.30 & 17.00–21.00 Sat, 17.00–21.00 Sun) Located in the Old Customs House on the coastal road, this ebullient cultural centre houses an auditorium, souvenir shop and a café, and hosts temporary exhibitions. Films, performances and music events also take place here.

Vanessa Monteiro Design [283 D7] (Rua da Moeda 22; e vanessamonteirodesign@gmail.com; ◙ & f vanessamonteirodesign; ⊕ 09.30–12.30 & 15.30–19.00 Mon–Fri, occasional Sat) A retail shop, yes, but also a fascinating exhibition space. Set in a beautiful wood-lined grocery store from the 1970s, it showcases both Monteiro's own work and collaborations with artists and designers from both Cabo Verde and the diaspora. While utilitarian, the objects and textiles – from reimagined 'house dresses' made from cotton experimentally farmed on Santiago to ceramics featuring goats – reflect on Cabo Verdean traditions and the country's current environmental challenges.

OTHER PLACES TO VISIT

Baía das Gatas and Calhau are the settings for weekend parties: vibrant on Saturdays and Sundays in high season, abandoned during the week. Monte Verde is stunning on a clear day but rather unexciting otherwise. A trip round the island is not a conventional aesthetic experience but can be a profound one.

MONTE VERDE A taxi costs 3,000$ return. To walk to the summit take a taxi or *aluguer* along the Baía das Gatas road for 8km as far as the right turn to Monte Verde's summit. A good cobbled road zig-zags up the north and east sides of the mountain to the top. You will see a big tank on the way up, on the left, a relatively recent project to gather the Monte Verde mist to irrigate the crops on the terracing below.

At the summit the mist may be down, in which case there is little to see but the radio antennae, guarded by a couple of soldiers and a cat.

On a clear day, however, the view is of a forest of black, misshapen crags, and the harbour beyond. Sunset beyond the forbidding peaks of Santo Antão is fabulous.

SALAMANSA Only 10 minutes' drive from the capital, in São Vicente terms this is a thriving place – people actually live here, drawing their livelihood from the sea, and there is a shop or two. Unless you're a windsurfer, there is really no overwhelming reason to visit other than to walk on the beautiful beach and muse on why this fishing village exists at all: it's too exposed for launching boats and most of the fishing fleet is drawn up some 5km away on the other side of the peninsula. The beach is not always safe for swimming but often has good conditions for kite- and windsurfing. There's one place to stay, **Kite House Salamansa**, only bookable on Airbnb. They can also help you out with kite hire. A couple of beach bars will welcome you, even if not much is going on. Bar Elvis has great views, not to mention crêpes with Nutella.

Alugueres from Mindelo cost 100$ one-way. During the week they are very few, so arrange your return in advance to avoid getting stuck. Otherwise a taxi costs around 1,000$ and can usually be prebooked to pick you up.

BAÍA DAS GATAS This resort is 12km from Mindelo town. During the week it has the feel of an English seaside resort out of season, with almost no-one to be seen. In front of rows of boarded-up bungalows, a pack of smooth-haired dogs trots along the wind-whipped sand. There's a children's play area with gaunt metal swings and slides, and at the extreme end of the bay, a low pier with powerful waves. However, at weekends the place is much more colourful, with families and groups of friends pitching their tents and playing football. Apart from that, it's a brilliant place to fish where you can easily pull in two-pounders from the shore and then light a fire and grill your own supper. It's also great for swimming because of a natural barrier that creates a huge lagoon.

During the full moon of August upwards of 10,000 people descend on Baía das Gatas for a three-day **festival** (f baiadasgatas) involving music, dancing, eating and general revelry. This venerable festival began as the best of them do – just a few musicians gathering for all-night jamming sessions; today bands come from all over the archipelago and abroad. The 40th event in 2024 featured a floating stage as well as a full programme of activities, including dance workshops and art exhibitions.

As you drive back out of the village there is a ruin on the shore on your left. This is the old fish-processing factory – it is here that the Salamansa fishermen draw their boats up. If the wind is in the right quarter you may be lucky enough to see them running home under full sail. They venture as far afield as the uninhabited island of Santa Luzia, returning with cold boxes full of snake-like moray eels, squid and grouper (like giant, bloated goldfish but tastier).

Getting there and away *Alugueres* from Mindelo cost 250$ one-way. During the week they are very few, so organise your return in advance to avoid getting stuck. A taxi costs around 2,500$ return.

Where to stay and eat Most people come on a day trip, so accommodation is limited. You can pitch a tent on the beach – not too close to anyone's barbecue, though, for fire safety reasons. With huge peaks and troughs in visitor numbers, restaurants appear and disappear very quickly. Those listed here are located on the seafront and seem to be the most resilient, though you will find others.

Residencial Átlanta (9 rooms) At the end of the main road, in front of the swimming lagoon; 232 7500; m 991 6211. Most rooms have private bath with hot water. Best to make enquiries or check in at the Restaurante Takeaway Átlanta, as the building with the rooms is a bit concealed. **$**

Restaurante Takeaway Átlanta On the seafront; ⏲ 10.00–18.00 daily. One of the 2 seafront options offering the usual meat & fresh fish dishes. Friendly owner. Usually open for drinks. $$$

Simpatico beach bar On the seafront, as you enter the town; ⏲ 10.00–21.00 daily. Serving a variety of fish dishes & snacks. Open later on w/ends, when there may be music. $$

CALHAU There's a more or less hourly *aluguer* for the 20-minute journey from Mindelo to the seaside town of Calhau (250$). A taxi will cost 2,500$ for a round trip. You could also walk there from Baía das Gatas, along the coast (2 hours).

A drive along the 18km 'scenic' road to Calhau is like a guided tour through all the ecological problems facing both the island and Cabo Verde as a whole. The road follows Ribeira Calhau, and takes just 25 minutes.

First the road passes through an area where there is a reafforestation programme. Then, as you continue southeast, you will see Monte Verde on your left. The little village on its western slopes is **Mato Inglês**. Lack of water has driven away all but one or two people.

A few kilometres further on is a right turn for **Madeiral**, a small village in the shadow of Topona Mountain. Old folk claim that the village was once supplied by water running down from the green slopes of the mountain above. Now the

THE BRITISH IN CABO VERDE

Golf, cricket and a smattering of English vocabulary were some of the lighter legacies left by the British in Cabo Verde. Their involvement with the archipelago was sporadic but widespread. It included the dominance of Maio in the heyday of its salt-collecting years; the brief 'ownership' of Santo Antão; the drastic sacking of Santiago by Francis Drake; and the monopolising of the orchil trade in several islands including Brava.

The British have also contributed to understanding the natural history of the islands. Charles Darwin spent three weeks recording fauna and flora on Santiago – his first initiation to the tropics on the famous voyage of the *Beagle*. As biographer Janet Browne writes, it was there that he 'caught a glimpse of his own powers and recognised a new kind of desire – the wish to make a contribution to the world of philosophical natural history'. Since Darwin, there have been others. T Vernon Wollaston visited in the 1870s and 1880s, and collected numerous beetles, moths and butterflies which are stored at the Natural History Museum in London. But it is in Mindelo that the British are now best remembered. They left a golf club that claims to be one of the largest non-grass courses in the world. Founded in 1893, it is the oldest sports association in Cabo Verde and hosted the first international golf championship, in 1906. It is situated just outside Mindelo, accessible from the road to Calhau. The turning is (badly) signposted on the right, a few hundred metres after the large cemetery on the left as you leave town. The clubhouse is fairly spartan, with a layer of dust and few facilities. They also left a feisty cricket team, which continued for many years.

English-derived words that have entered the Kriolu language were gathered by Frank Xavier da Cruz in 1950. Some rather telling, they include: *ariope* (hurry up), *blaquéfela* (black fellow), *bossomane* (boss man), *cachupa* (believed to have been derived from ketchup), *chatope* (shut up), *ovataime* (overtime), *tanquiu* (thank you), *fulope* (full up), *ovacote* (overcoat) and *salongue* (so long!).

mountain has the same scorched, dusty aspect as the rest of São Vicente. Madeiral, like the island's two or three other inhabited villages, is dependent on desalinated water, tankered in from Mindelo.

Past Madeiral the *ribeira* opens out and the valley floor is scattered with small squares of green. This is agriculture under siege – strong stone walls keep marauding goats out. The water that the windmills draw from the ground is becoming progressively saltier. In the search for sweet water, wells are pushed deeper, and windmills require stronger winds to keep the water flowing. In such precarious conditions, water-storage tanks are indispensable. Meanwhile the search for water goes on: the piles of earth across the valley floor mark the places where boreholes have been sunk but have struck only dry earth and rock.

It takes a particular kind of traveller to like Calhau. The village is a windswept wasteland of gravel and brown sand, protruding from which are the grey carcasses of half-finished breeze-block buildings. Brown peaks tower behind it while, in front, waves smash against the black, rocky coast. Nevertheless its proximity to the city makes it an option if you really can't stand the hustle and bustle of Mindelo; from here you can explore the rest of the island, occupy yourself with some interesting walks or just relax for a while. The land between the mountains and the sea is just asking to be built on. Down the southern part of the bay optimists have indeed built apartments and there is a boutique-style hotel.

A roundabout joining the tarmac road to Baía das Gatas tells you that you have reached the village. People live here still, and fish, but as with every other village, water is a problem. Calhau is alive and bustling at weekends, however, with city folk coming to their seaside retreats.

Where to stay and eat

Residencial Goa (10 rooms) Turn right at the roundabout; 232 9355; m 996 2696; e goacalhau@goa-mindelo.com; w goa-mindelo.com. This French-owned hotel has stark, Modernist-inspired architecture that fits well with the surrounding moonscape. The panoramic view encompasses Santo Antão, São Nicolau, Santa Luzia, Raso & Branco. Rooms are huge, stylishly decorated, with balconies on the 1st floor overlooking the sea. With its large living area & quiet location the hotel is good for families. B/fast is served on the seaside terrace or the inside courtyard, & dinner can be arranged. Charming hosts Stan & Raphaelle are very knowledgeable & will arrange excellent walks, excursions & fishing. Up for sale at time of writing; with luck its new owners will continue to provide such great service. **$$$**

Bar Restaurant Hamburg Turn left after the telecom tower & look for the building with black-&-white pebbles on the walls; 282 9309; 10.00–22.00 Mon–Sat, noon–19.00 Sun. Famous for its eel & other seafood, this little spot gets busy at the w/end. Occasionally feels like it's resting on its laurels. **$$$**

Chez Loutcha Page 285; 232 1636; 10.00–21.00 Mon–Sat, 13.00–17.00, Sun buffet. Clearly signposted down a rough track on the right as you enter Calhau (after the turning to the volcanoes), this is run by the proprietor of Chez Loutcha, the *pensão* in Mindelo, who cooks in Calhau on Sun. There is a buffet spread, with around 20 dishes; you can eat as much as you like for 1,950$, & live music, too. Free transport from Mindelo, if booked in advance. There are better options during the week. **$$$**

What to see and do There are various good fishing spots within easy access of the village, as well as surfing spots on Praia Grande, Sandy Beach and Topim Beach in the south. In summer turtles nest on the beach directly in front of Residencial Goa (do not go to the beach at night without asking advice as it is illegal to disturb them). There is a natural swimming pool at the foot of the volcano, offering some pleasant snorkelling.

There are also several walking trails. It takes about an hour to walk up to the Calhau volcano, to the north of the village. It takes 3 hours to do a circuit of the headland to the north (Panilinha). **Vulcão Viana**, to the south, can be ascended from a track that runs down its eastern side: the round trip from the track takes about 45 minutes. The oasis of Santa Luzia Terra can be reached in around 2 hours (you can, and should, arrange to be collected). You can also walk to Baía das Gatas, which also takes about 2 hours.

From Calhau you have a great view of uninhabited **Santa Luzia** and also the islets of Raso (page 361) and Branco, and even São Nicolau in the distance.

SÃO PEDRO A one-way *aluguer* from Mindelo will cost 200$ (taxi 2,000$) to São Pedro, which is just 1km past the airport. It is a little village with a shop and a few restaurants, colourful fishing boats drawn up on the beach and an air of tatty quaintness. The settlements here are on either side of the airport runway, but air traffic is very light.

Where to stay and eat *Map, page 273*

Aquiles Eco-Hotel (12 rooms) On the south side of the bay; 232 8002; e info@aquilesecohotel.com; w aquilesecohotel.com. Thoughtfully designed hotel. Organic b/fast, non-toxic cleaning products & recycled water support its 'eco' label, as does an unusual construction based heavily on responsibly sourced wood. Its spartan style will appeal to architecture fans, but is too simple for some. Rooms have balconies, though only the suite has a sea view. $$$

Foya Branca Resort (68 rooms, 6 villas) On the northwest side of the bay; 230 7400; e bookings.foyabranca@flaghotels.com. São Vicente's former star resort has fallen into disrepair; the large & once stylish rooms are now rather shabby. Go for seclusion, the grounds & the proximity to the sea, but don't expect it to live up to the 'resort' of its name. The beach in front is quiet during the week & more vibrant at w/ends when local families come down for the day. There's a regular, free shuttle bus to Mindelo. $$$

Bar Bistro Santo André Behind the Foya Branca Resort on São Pedro Beach; 231 5100; m 971 1765; ⊕ noon–22.00 Tue–Sun. This well-established, expanding & innovative restaurant owned by Swede Per Tamm has an excellent reputation. Relax on the terrace where you can enjoy their popular & famous suckling pig (Sun only) & a good range of dishes with some international touches. Also specialises in lobster, seafood & vegetarian options. $$$

What to see and do The beach is the main attraction, but there are unexpected currents in the sea so take local advice, stay close to the shore and don't swim alone.

You can also hike to the **Farol de Dona Amélia**, a 6km round trip, heading uphill just after the Foya Branca resort. It's challenging, with high winds, a narrow path, and sheer drops to the sea, so suitable only if you're wearing good shoes and have a head for heights.

SANTA LUZIA The smallest island of the archipelago (anything smaller is an islet), Santa Luzia is 35km^2 and uninhabited. Its highest peak, Topona, is 395m. It is extremely dry and barren. It has a rugged north coast and a south coast of scenic beaches and dunes. No seabirds are known to breed there any more.

Santa Luzia lay uninhabited until the 17th century, when it was granted to Luis de Castro Pireira. It has mainly been used for livestock raising when there has been rain. In the 19th century, about 20 people continued these activities. A family of goatherds lived there until the 1960s. Although it was once possible to visit the island, it now forms part of Cabo Verde's largest marine reserve where projects are underway to rebuild the fragile ecostructure. Visiting is therefore forbidden, except for scientists and volunteers, though in the long term there is a possibility of an ecologically sound visitor centre being constructed. Among the ongoing projects is the resettling of the endangered Raso lark here, to provide an additional habitat to Raso island. Happily, this translocated population is thriving in its new island digs, while the existing brown booby (*Sula leucogaster*) breeding community is also flourishing. A relatively recent influx of nesting red-footed boobies (*Sula sula*) has also joined them.

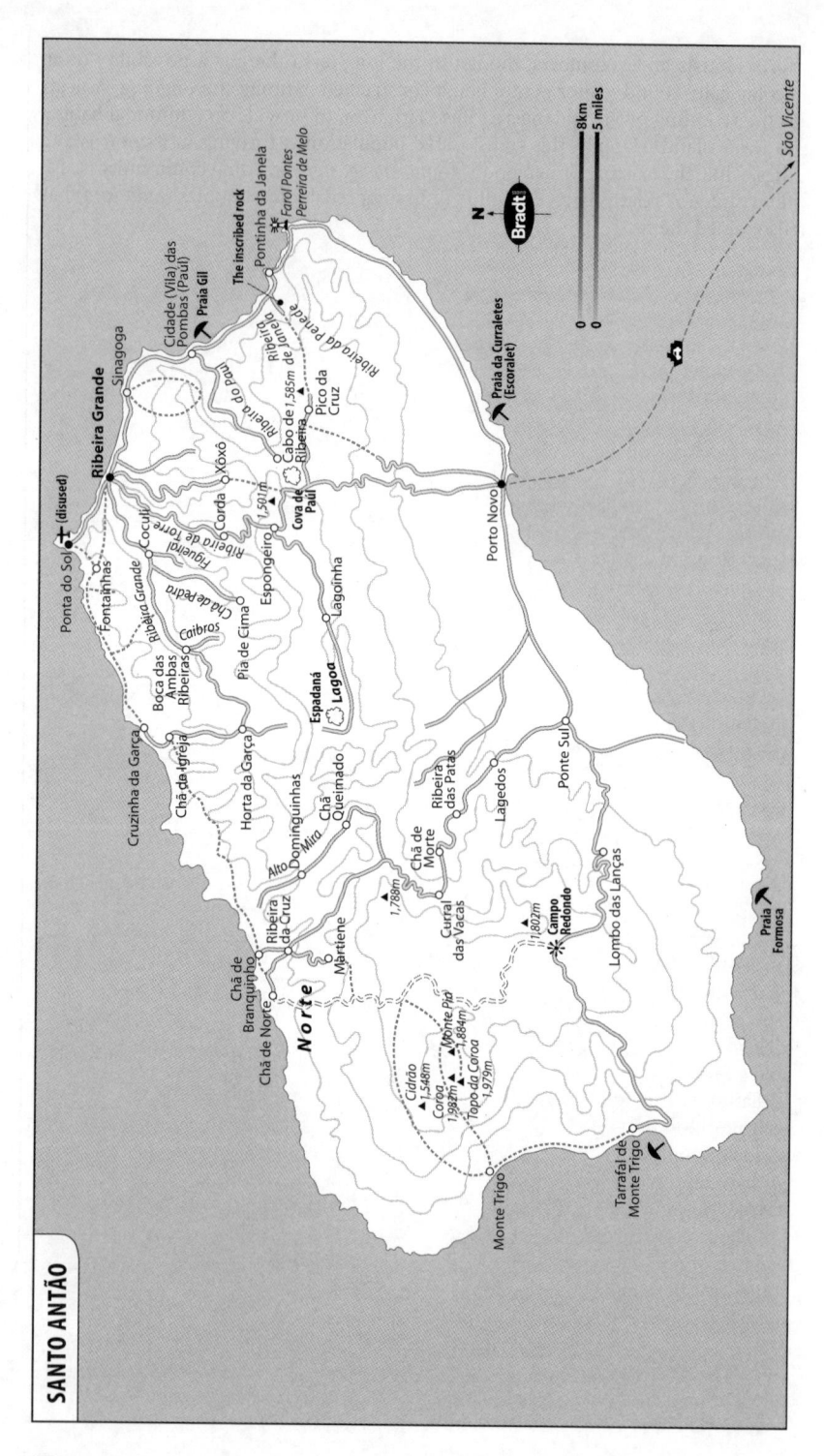

SANTO ANTÃO

10

Santo Antão

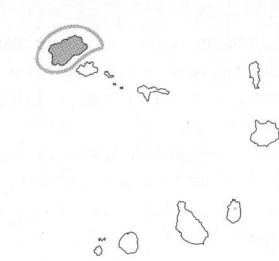

The rugged peaks and canyons of northeast Santo Antão are one of the world's great landscape dramas. Precarious roads trace the tops of its ridges giving sheer views on both sides down 1,000m cliffs. The people live in these deep valleys, their worlds enclosed by colossal volcanic walls. As you ascend the valleys on foot you discover in astonishment that their settlements reach high into the cliff sides, clinging to ledges and surrounded by banana trees and cassava. In the west of the island is an apocalyptic and inaccessible landscape of steep walls, jagged edges and harsh ravines.

There is a legend that Santo Antão's precipices defeated a bishop who, while visiting the more distant of his Cabo Verde flock, tried to reach Ribeira Grande from Paúl across the mountains. It is said that halfway through the journey, having scaled a terrifying cliff, he lost his nerve and could move neither forwards nor backwards. And so the bishop remained, supplied regularly by the more sure-footed of the island who would arrive with tents, food and clothing for him. He waited in a crevice until a road was built to conduct him away in safety.

HIGHLIGHTS AND LOWLIGHTS

There are two overwhelming attractions here: **hiking** the *ribeiras*, and a couple of impossibly remote but upmarket places to stay. Non-hikers can also appreciate the landscape from the spectacular **drives** over the ridges and along the *ribeira* floors. The mountain road from Porto Novo to Ribeira Grande is one of the highlights of a visit to Cabo Verde and is worth travelling along even if your schedule demands that you must return immediately to São Vicente. There are several rare **birds** to watch out for and **fishing** is possible with the locals. In Tarrafal de Monte Trigo, deliciously remote and with its own stark beauty, there are opportunities for **diving** and **snorkelling**.

Santo Antão would like to have a beach tourism industry but its ambitions are still a million miles away from the resort strips of Sal or Boavista. There are black, sandy beaches but many are hard to access and others disappear entirely in winter, with swimming only safe in the summer months. Watersports facilities are still scarce, though there is a dive centre in remote Tarrafal. Most accommodation, while perfectly adequate, characterful, clean and friendly, is not luxurious, though a clutch of new eco-resorts like Palmeira da Cruz and Mamiwata Eco Village have joined outliers like Pedracin Village in offering more upmarket options. Such authenticity, and the chance to relax, is a large part of the island's charm.

SUGGESTED ITINERARY AND NUMBER OF DAYS If you are interested in hiking, allow at least three clear days in which to tackle some of the classic Santo Antão walks: you could easily spend more than this if you are set on really exploring the island or wish to schedule rest days between the more demanding walks. If you are determined to visit the west of Santo Antão, allow plenty of time because roads are tricky and transport infrequent. If you are not into hiking, you could still fill at least a couple of days with sightseeing by vehicle and wandering through the valley of Paúl. A day trip is better than nothing, but ensure it is very well organised beforehand to avoid wasting valuable time in negotiations with local drivers or worse, getting stuck. Hiring a driver and his vehicle for a day will cost between 9,000$ and 12,000$.

BACKGROUND INFORMATION

HISTORY Fertile and green but mountainous and inaccessible, Santo Antão remained without much of a population for the first 90 years after its discovery on 17 January 1462. If people knew it in the 15th century it was because of its use in the mapping of an imaginary line down the Atlantic that divided Spanish and Portuguese colonial rights. The Treaty of Tordesillas in 1494 agreed that this north–south line would pass 370 leagues west of Santo Antão. Land to the west of that line was to belong to Spain. Land to the east – including the islands themselves and Brazil, which protrudes quite far into the southern Atlantic – was to belong to Portugal.

A series of people leased Santo Antão from the Portuguese Crown, the first in 1548. In the 1600s, its administration and ownership were granted to the Count of Santa Cruz. It was the son of the fourth Count of Santa Cruz, the Marquess of Gouveia, who was to add brief drama to Santo Antão from as far away as Europe. In Portugal, he kidnapped Mariana de Penha de França, the wife of a Portuguese nobleman, and escaped with her to England where, having run out of money, he mortgaged Santo Antão to the English in 1732. This went down very badly back in Cabo Verde and the Portuguese soon drove the English away.

After that excitement, the 18th century granted Santo Antão a little more recognition. Ribeira Grande achieved the status of *vila* in 1732 and, two decades later, Bishop Jacinto Valente chose to settle there, having rejected the crumbling and unhealthy capital of Santiago. It was to be another 120 years before Santo Antão was made capital of the Barlavento – it was the richest, most populated and least malarial of the northern islands at this time.

Perhaps it was the effect of living between the high and menacing walls of the *ribeiras*, but the people of Ribeira Paúl and the people of Ribeira Grande had a major argument in 1894 about their representation in Portugal. The people of Ribeira Grande decided to make war on their cousins down the road, armed themselves with guns, clubs and sticks and roared down the coast.

The people of Paúl were ready, though, and destroyed the road so that no-one could cross it. None, that was, but an athletic horse which leapt across the opening, whisking to safety a lucky inhabitant of Ribeira Grande who had been on the wrong side of the road. The people of Paúl fared the worst in the conflict – many of their men were later imprisoned and spent a lot of money regaining their freedom.

The island lost its position as Barlavento capital in 1934, when the seat of government was transferred to São Vicente. More recently, it lost its important role as supplier of water to its barren cousin across the channel, when a desalinisation plant was constructed on São Vicente. Santo Antão was plagued with an impenetrable interior and also the problem that its only good port – Tarrafal – was a long way from its agricultural area. In recent decades Porto Novo and the road that links it to Ribeira Grande and Tarrafal have improved the situation slightly.

FESTIVALS ON SANTO ANTÃO

The big festival of the year is São João Baptista on 24 June. It begins with a 20km procession of the cross from the mountains down into Porto Novo, done to the accompaniment of drumming. On arrival in Porto Novo, the people begin a party which lasts all week, with the statue of São João being paraded around town, again accompanied by drummers. Paúl's Municipality Day on 13 June is also a great festival, with a month-long build-up, horse races and dancing.

17 January	Municipality Day (Ribeira Grande)
3 May	Santa Cruz (Coculi)
13 June	Santa António das Pombas (Paúl)
24 June	São João Baptista
29 June	São Pedro (Chã de Igreja)
15 August	Nossa Sra da Piedade (Janela)
15 September	Nossa Sra da Graça (Ponta do Sol)
24 September	Nossa Sra do Livramento (Ponta do Sol)
7 October	Nossa Sra do Rosário (Ribeira Grande)
29 November	Santo André (Ribeira de Cruz)

SANTO ANTÃO TODAY Santo Antão has high unemployment and has its eyes fixed on tourism and agriculture as its principal routes to economic prosperity. There have been great plans for this mighty island, but the topography may yet prevent overdevelopment. There's long been talk about turning the east of Porto Novo into a tourist area, centred on Praia de Curraletes, often referred to as Escoralet, but this, like the rumours of reopening an airport, remain rumours. Local leaders prophesise tourist developments all along the new road to Tarrafal, though there is, as yet, thankfully little evidence of this. Whether all or any of the proposed development happens in the near future, many locals believe it won't be achieved without blighting Santo Antão's appeal. As the co-owner of Pedracin Village (page 318), businessman José Pedro Oliveira, once told *Iniciativa* magazine: 'I believe Santo Antão is one of the jewels of tourism in Cabo Verde, if we don't destroy it before. Building a big hotel in a valley or riverbed is the same as destroying it.' There has, however, been a number of small and eco-sensitive new hotels opening since the pandemic, all pointing hopefully to the idea that a gentler kind of tourism is possible here. Perhaps it will be Santo Antão's very remoteness which will serve to preserve its plentiful rustic charms for years to come.

GEOGRAPHY Santo Antão is second only to Santiago in size, at 779km^2, and second only to Fogo in the height of its greatest mountain – the volcano crater next to Topo da Coroa at 1,982m. It is the most northerly and the most westerly of the islands with a mountain range stretching from the northeast to the southwest.

The population is less than 50,000 and the island is divided into three municipalities: Porto Novo, covering the west and centred on the port town in the south; Paúl; and Ribeira Grande, which includes the town of that name (also known as Povoação) and the northern settlement of Ponta do Sol. The fertile areas are in the northeast, where there is often moisture on the peaks and intense agriculture, making use of permanent streams in two of the *ribeiras* – Paúl and Janela. The rest of the island is barren apart from around Tarrafal de Monte Trigo to the southwest where there is some water, which is used for irrigation.

Santo Antão's annual rainfall has plunged over the last century by about 45%. Engineers have been considering making better use of the island's one abundant source of water: the annual floods during storms between August and November, which can run off the mountains and into the sea in volumes of millions of cubic metres. Conservation dams in the upper mountains could store the run-off and be used for irrigation lower down the valleys.

FLORA AND FAUNA

Protected areas There are natural parks at Moroços, the area encompassing Cova, Ribeira Paúl and Ribeira Torre, and Topo da Coroa; there's a natural reserve at Cruzinha and a protected landscape at Pombas.

An old administrator on Santo Antão and captain of the Portuguese colonial army, Serafim Oliveira, introduced to Paúl a substantial number of plants and trees, most importantly *caneca* (sugarcane – the only ingredient of *grogue*), a type of mango tree and *jaqueira* (breadfruit tree), which grows to be very large and gives fruit all year.

Turtles nest here on the few remaining sandy beaches (almost all the sand has been removed illegally for construction), most notably in Cruzinha, where the small fishing community has undertaken a conservation programme with the assistance of the fisheries research institute, INDP, concentrating on preventing the removal of both sand and eggs.

ECONOMY Fishing, agriculture and the extraction of *pozzolana* (a volcanic dust used in cement making) are the economy's mainstays. But the island, which has the largest cultivated area of Cabo Verde, has in the past been frustrated in its desires to export agricultural products to the tourist islands of Sal and Boavista because of a 24-year embargo implemented as the result of millipede blight. This embargo was lifted for the majority of crops between 2008 and 2011, however, and it now provides mangoes, bananas, cassava and the like to other islands. There are small but growing industries producing *grogue* and its variants, herbs and jams. In fact, over three quarters of the arable land is planted with sugarcane, representing at least a third of the island's GDP.

SAFETY The water is calm for swimming at some beaches in the summer months (May–September) but the ocean is wild with a powerful undertow for the rest of the year. Take local advice.

During the rainy season and for some time thereafter, some roads may become impassable and some possibly dangerous. Driving during heavy rain should be avoided. The sea can be too rough for diving during some months and too cloudy during the rainy season (page 307). Flies can be a nuisance during and after the rains, so pack some repellent.

The west is very remote, waterless and hard to navigate. Hikers in that region should be well prepared and it is essential to take a local guide. Elsewhere, the principal walks, though punishingly steep at times, are mostly on cobbled footpaths which can lull your mind should you decide to explore elsewhere on your own. These are high mountains, remote at the top, with racing mists. Paths can fade into pebbly gullies, demanding a scramble. Between December and February temperatures drop to 10°C above 1,000m.

The hospital in Ribeira Grande is oversubscribed and may not be up to dealing with hiking injuries; for this kind of medical attention you would need to get the ferry to São Vicente.

GETTING THERE AND AWAY

BY AIR There are no flights to Santo Antão. The runway at Ponta do Sol suffers from dangerous crosswinds and has consequently been closed for years.

BY FERRY Everyone travelling to Santo Antão without their own boat takes the ferry from Mindelo (São Vicente) to Porto Novo and thankfully these ferries are far more reliable and punctual than other interisland routes.

The hour-long crossing is also beautiful, if you can avoid sea sickness: the view of São Vicente, with the forbidding mountains behind Mindelo, and its guardian rock erupting from the harbour, is stunning.

Porto Novo's **ferry terminal** has a café serving good coffee, an information centre which opens to greet the ferries, and an outlet of the local collective *grogue* shop Mestres Grogue (**w** mestresgrogue.com; ⊕ for ferries only), which also sells other local products and Cabo Verdean goods. Very rare for Cabo Verde, the terminal also has escalators to whisk passengers up to the waiting land transport. At the time of writing, two companies, CV Interilhas and Nosferry, each offered twice-daily crossings from Mindelo on the *Inter Ilhas* and *Mar d'Canal* respectively, with the boats leaving at 07.00, 08.00, 14.00 and 15.00, returning from Porto Novo at 10.00, 11.00, 15.00 and 16.00. A single passenger fare costs 1,500$. Only CV Interilhas currently offers online booking; you may have to pre-purchase Nosferry tickets at the terminal. Some car-hire firms may allow you to take your hire car between islands, but check when hiring.

BY YACHT The trip across from São Vicente can be hairy, with winds gusting up to 40 knots from December to May – they are channelled by the two islands, creating a Venturi effect. Porto Novo, the only harbour suitable for yachts, requires permission from Mindelo beforehand. There are no facilities for docking, rather a protected anchorage at up to 12m depth. It can be easier to visit Santo Antão by ferry, leaving a watchman back in Mindelo with your craft. Tarrafal is also a possible anchorage, offering total shelter from the trade winds but with a constant swell, making it hard to land with a dinghy or tender. Additionally, supplies on offer would only be basic (a few food items and water). Ponta do Sol is completely unsuitable for yachts.

GETTING AROUND

BY PUBLIC TRANSPORT *Alugueres* use the new, fast coastal road, so to travel the scenic, inland mountain route needs specifying to your driver. Expect to pay a much higher price for this option, but it's worth it. *Alugueres* are regular between Porto Novo and Ribeira Grande but many drivers time their trips according to the ferry timetables, when there is a frenzy of vehicles scrambling for passengers. Elsewhere they follow the usual principle, leaving villages for the town early in the morning and returning at midday or early afternoon. To access the west of the island it is best to stay in Porto Novo or arrive there early.

Aluguer drivers on Santo Antão are unlikely to overcharge you but they are likely to insist you have missed all public *alugueres* and should therefore hire them as taxis. Be sceptical and hang around for a bit. Cost follows the usual rule of thumb: charters cost ten times the price of a shared *aluguer*.

BY TAXI Taxis are either bright-blue saloon cars in Porto Novo, or chartered *alugueres* elsewhere.

BY CAR If you intend to take on the not inconsiderable challenge of heading west to Tarrafal or other remote areas, nothing other than a 4x4 will do. Contact **Pegaso** (📞584 0598; w pegaso.cv) or **Protur** (📞222 2896; see below).

WHERE TO STAY AND EAT

Nowhere on Santo Antão could currently be described as touristy, but the main venue for visitor accommodation is Ponta do Sol, attractive for its coastal aspect and colonial architecture. It also has a good range of restaurants, some with live music, and a few tourist services. There are several modest *pensões* and plenty of simple grill restaurants in the capital, Ribeira Grande (Povoação), while the more upmarket Pedracin Village Hotel is a few kilometres outside town along with other places up the actual *ribeira* itself. There is also accommodation, including the only really large hotel, in Porto Novo – not the beautiful side of the island but a good transport hub nonetheless, with several reasonable places to eat or buy food. A few *pensões* dot the valley of Paúl – if simplicity, embeddedness, a love of hiking and a cracking view are what you're after, these are for you. On Paúl's coast, between Vila das Pombas and Janela, you'll find plenty of traveller-orientated restaurants/bars. Atmospheric Tarrafal has a few *pensões*, as does Chã de Igreja, or at the other end of the spectrum, you can stay up above Cruzinha at one of the stylish ecolodges right on the coast, with unexpectedly glamorous set-menu dining at one. There are also some one-off venues elsewhere in the island, which are most useful for those trying to accomplish long hikes between distant outposts, along with homestays. Wherever you are, though, you'll almost always be able to find something to eat, but in the case of the smaller villages, it's best to ensure either you or your driver, guide or accommodation has called ahead to order a meal.

EXCURSIONS AND TOUR OPERATORS

Alsatour Paúl 📞223 1213; e alfred@alsatour. de; w alsatour.de. Alsatour runs a variety of programmes, mainly hiking. Website in German, but owner speaks English.

Atlantur [map, page 309] Porto Novo; 📞222 1991; e santoantao@atlantur.com. Excursions, fishing, hiking, airline/ferry tickets & transfers.
Protur 📞222 2896; e aviagenprotur@gmail.com. Provides tourist information & also rent cars.

ACTIVITIES

HIKING The grand *ribeiras* are where you'll find the iconic walks. You can either take transport up the main road and disembark for a steep descent, or you can walk or take transport along the coastal roads for a steep ascent. After torrential rains these *ribeiras* fill – take local advice about how to ascend them because there is usually an alternative path (see page 66 for safety advice).

The west of the island is unfrequented, a hidden world of ravines and cliffs cut into bizarre shapes by erosive winds. There are craters filled with lava flows and looming boulders of white pumice. Interspersed is the odd pool of greenery where irrigation has allowed cultivation. As more locals open their houses to guests, and paths are digitally mapped, the west is becoming slightly easier to explore. However, the area remains lonely, roads are sparse and traffic scarce. The landscape is also full of hidden dangers – landslides, sudden cliffs and lack of water. Even paths shown on the map can disappear in the rains. Plan well but most importantly, take a guide. Expect to pay around €50–100 per guide per day. Transport – if required – and lunch

> **BEST BEACHES**
>
> Note: the beaches listed all have black sand.
>
> **Praia de Curraletes (Escoralet)** Just 2km east of Porto Novo.
> **Praia Gil** Between Vila das Pombas and Janela.
> **Praia Formosa** In the southwest, inaccessible by road.
> **Sinagoga** Popular for swimming.
> **Tarrafal** The largest beach on Santo Antão.

will cost extra. Your accommodation should be able to provide recommendations and organise pick-ups and drop-offs if you're not going through a local agency, but try to do this in advance.

CANYONING Canyoning is centred on the Praia Gil beach, in the northeast. **Olivier Gilabert** (m 996 8218; e pelanoar@gmail.com; ⊕ Oct–Jun) speaks French and some English and will provide all equipment. The price of €80 per person for the half-day programme also includes lunch at a local's home. Canyoning can also be arranged through Mindelo-based outfit Cabo Mundo (w cabomundo.com).

CYCLING With the right kit, mountain biking is a rewarding activity – but don't underestimate the steepness of the hills or the heat of the day. Biking can be arranged through **Casa Espongeiro** (page 323). See also page 75 for the logistics of getting a bike to Cabo Verde.

DIVING There are canyons, lava tubes and tunnels, caves and rock bridges, all for exploration. For further information, contact **Green Turtle Diving Center** (m 979 5560; e info@greenturtledivingcenter.com; w greenturtledivingcenter.com), at the Santantao Art Resort or **Casa Baobab** in Tarrafal (page 326).

BEACHES AND SWIMMING Many beaches on Santo Antão disappear under the rougher water between October and May, and emerge, magically, to be enjoyed during the summer months of June to September. Likewise, the water is calmer for swimming during the summer but once winter starts the ocean is wild and there is a powerful undertow. You may make your own serendipitous discovery of beaches but there are a few suggestions above. Along the coast to the east of Cruzinha da Garça there are also several beaches (some black sand, some white).

FISHING From Cidade das Pombas, you can accompany local fishermen as they go out to catch sea eel, grouper, mackerel, octopus and lobster. In the west, Tarrafal offers similar possibilities, as does Cruzinha in the north. Your accommodation should be able to arrange it.

SURFING Jorge Viera Cortez (✆ 222 2725; m 986 5107; e info@surfariscaboverde.com; w surfariscaboverde.com) runs a surf school and can arrange accommodation in his Surf House in Tarrafal de Monte Trigo, or alternatively in Porto Novo. When not surfing, he also collects books, toys, etc, and distributes them to remote communities. With advance notice, you can join him.

CULTURE Some examples of traditional songs, generally inspired by toil, are 'Cantigas de Guarda Pardal' ('Songs of the Sparrow Watchman') and 'Cantigas de Currais de Trapiche' ('Songs to Encourage the Oxen as they Plod around the Trapiche'). Cordas do Sol is an internationally known band hailing from Paúl, and sing with a distinct Sant'anton accent; their 2010 release *Lume d'Lenha* ('Wood Fire') is particularly evocative. In high season at least, a few restaurants in most towns feature traditional music, as do the festivals listed on page 303.

SIGHTSEEING BY VEHICLE A lot of Santo Antão's beauty can be seen by vehicle, and an itinerary should include crossing from Porto Novo to Ribeira Grande by the mountain road, taking a detour at the top to see the Cova de Paúl and Pico da Cruz; driving up Ribeira do Paúl as far as Cabo de Ribeira; and driving up Ribeira Grande (the *ribeira*) through Coculi, Boca das Ambas Ribeiras, and round to Chã de Igreja and Cruzinha da Garça (refreshments at Pedracin Village or in Cruzinha). The road to Tarrafal is best enjoyed in an *aluguer* driven by someone used to the route, allowing you to take photos (page 324).

THE EAST

Destinations are listed in an anticlockwise order, starting with your point of arrival, Porto Novo.

PORTO NOVO In September 2005, this busy and windswept town was inaugurated as a city. As the sole entry and departure point to the island, its importance can't be disputed. It is full of smart new buildings paid for by Luxembourg as well as tended gardens and promenades overlooking the channel. The surprisingly flashy ferry terminal is a pride and joy and there is an impressive municipal headquarters and commercial centre to boast about. Porto Novo is *the* place to be during the São João festival. Just west of the ferry terminal is a sculpture by Luisa Domingos, a testament to the hardworking Cabo Verdean womenfolk. The poem translates as:

> So that she will forever be remembered
> In this rocky mass
> The noble figure beloved by us
> The lady of the Cabo Verde Islands
> Translated by Katie Donlan

An enjoyable evening can be spent here watching the sun set on the distant mountains of São Vicente and the glowing harbour of Mindelo. You can even see São Nicolau, no more than a timid relative beyond. There are one or two good restaurants, but as a point of arrival and departure, it rarely holds visitors for more than a day or two.

Getting there and away Most people's first experience of Porto Novo will be arriving by ferry. To get from Porto Novo to Ribeira Grande and beyond, choose from the many *alugueres* that queue up to meet the ferry from Mindelo. More likely, they will choose you – you may even be recruited as a passenger by a zealous tout on the boat. Many hotels will also pre-book a driver for you, making this process less overwhelming. Outside ferry times, hang around outside the port, or keep your eyes open as they are generally driving around town trying to find passengers. To get to Porto Novo from Ribeira Grande, find an *aluguer* in the main street. They run all day (contrary to what the drivers will tell you), though sporadically; the vast majority co-ordinate their trips with the ferry schedules.

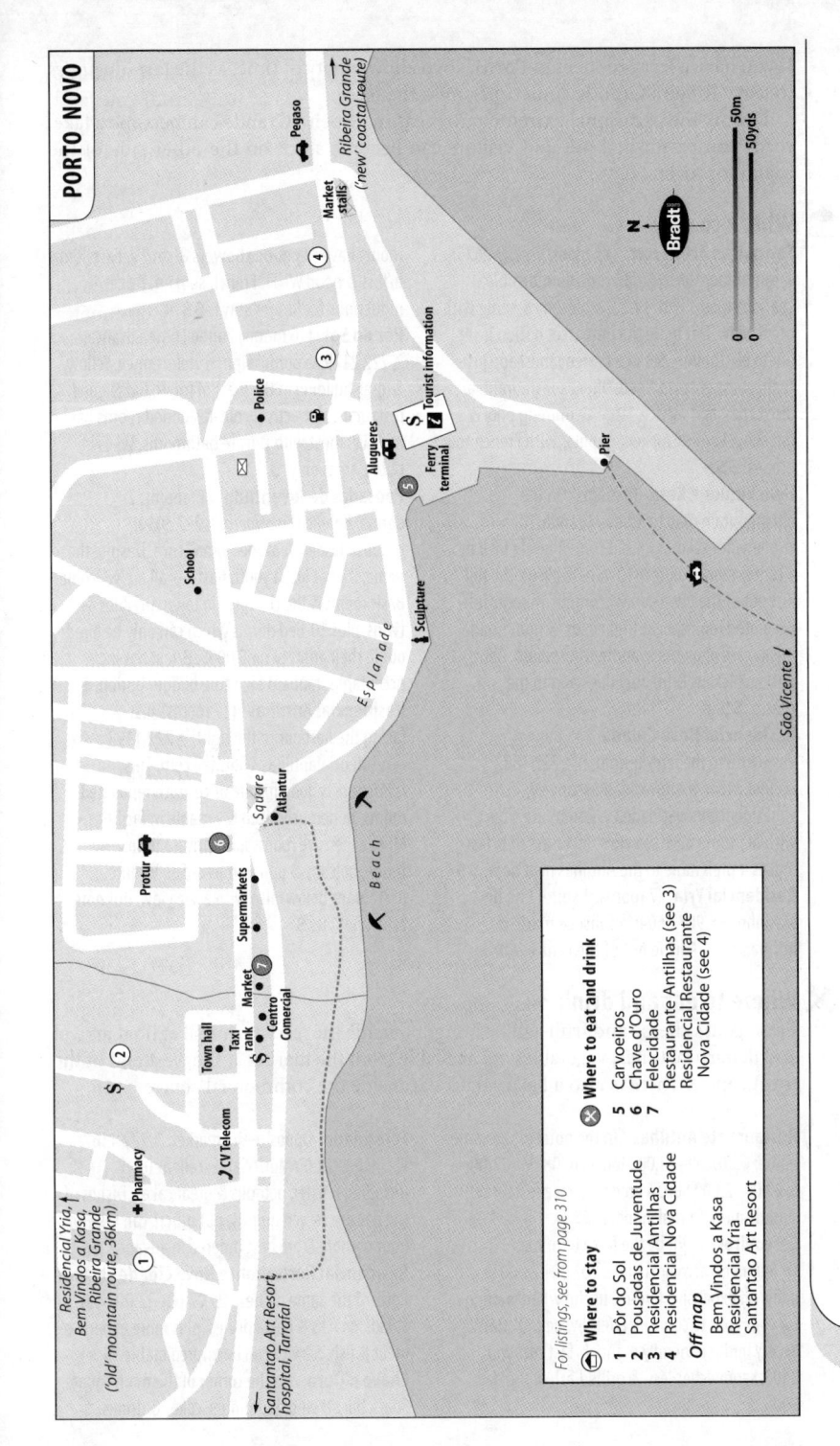

PORTO NOVO

For listings, see from page 310

Where to stay
1. Pôr do Sol
2. Pousadas de Juventude
3. Residencial Antilhas
4. Residencial Nova Cidade

Off map
Bem Vindos a Kasa
Residencial Yria
Santantao Art Resort

Where to eat and drink
5. Carvoeiros
6. Chave d'Ouro
7. Felcidade
Restaurante Antilhas (see 3)
Residencial Restaurante Nova Cidade (see 4)

Santo Antão THE EAST

10

If you have a ferry to meet in Porto Novo allow plenty of time, as the last *alugueres* to leave Ribeira Grande sometimes miss the ferry.

During the occasional extreme rainy season, Ribeira Grande can become a lake, roads can be washed out and visitors can become stuck on the other side of the island for several days.

Where to stay *Map, page 309*

Santantao Art Resort (73 rooms) 222 2675; e santantaoresort@gmail.com. Comfortable, spacious rooms with TV, AC & balcony & some with ocean view. Not quite the upmarket option it set out to be, though. Set in a barren landscape just to the west of Porto Novo. Offers a restaurant, a disco, massage service, large swimming pool & gift shop. English spoken; popular with French tour groups. **$$$**

Bem Vindos a Kasa (2 rooms) On the old mountain road to Ribeira Grande; e bemvindosakasa@gmail.com. A lovely B&B in a contemporary home, 10 mins' walk up the hill just out of the town sprawl. Simple, thoughtfully decorated rooms, beautiful views, & homemade meals care of owners Sandra & Armando. Goats, ducks, chickens & friendly dogs add to the charm. **$$**

Residencial Nova Cidade (15 rooms) Very close to the ferry terminal; 222 1882; m 998 2407; e rrnovacidade@sapo.cv; w residencialnovacidade.cv. Rooms are smart, with AC; some have sea view. Inclusion of b/fast makes it preferable to the Antilhas next door. **$$**

Residencial Yria (7 rooms, 1 suite) Chã de Matinho; m 987 6604; e fonseca.marie@hotmail.com. A little out of the centre. All rooms have AC, good showers & sat TV. Excellent b/fast & good Wi-Fi. French spoken. Price reductions for longer stays. **$$**

Pôr do Sol (16 rooms) Fundo Lomba Branca; 222 2179; e pordosolpn@cvtelecom.cv. Yellow-&-grey building in the west of town. Bar & good restaurant. Attractively old-fashioned rooms have AC & TV; most with private bathrooms. Wi-Fi in public areas only. **$**

Pousadas de Juventude (11 rooms, 2 dorms) Behind the *câmara*; 222 3010; e pousadasdejuventude@gmail.com. Despite the name, it's not just a youth hostel – all are welcome. Basic rooms & the cheapest in town. Doubles & twins, plus 10-bed dorms which can only be hired out in their entirety for 5,000$. B/fast not inc. Acceptable standard for a true budget option. **$**

Residencial Antilhas (17 rooms) Just facing the harbour to the right; 222 1193; e residencialantilhas@hotmail.com. This *residencial* is good for the price, with renovated rooms, generously sized & variable in facilities. More expensive rooms have private baths, AC, fridge, balcony & panoramas of São Vicente. Restaurant below, also with a sea view, but note b/fast not inc. **$**

Where to eat and drink *Map, page 309*

Fresh goat's cheese and fruit can be bought outside the ferry terminal at boat arrival and departure times; vegetables are available from the market at the west end of the town centre. There is also a basic snack bar inside the commercial centre.

Restaurante Antilhas In the hotel of the same name; 07.00–23.00 Mon–Sat, 08.00–17.00 & 20.00–23.00 Sun. A breezy terrace restaurant, slightly more formal indoors. **$$$**

Carvoeiros Right by the ferry terminal; w linktr.ee/carvoeiros.pn; 07.30–11.00 daily. An expansive terrace, useful when waiting for your boat to come in. Friendly, helpful staff & very budget-friendly menu: b/fast *cachupa* 350$, sandwiches less, & grilled fish of the day 900$. **$$**

Felecidade Opposite the market; 222 1167; 09.00–22.00 Mon–Sat. Excellent food including lobster, octopus & great cakes. Dishes of the day are served quickly, but others can take an hour or more & are best ordered in advance. **$$**

Residencial Restaurante Nova Cidade In the hotel of the same name; 07.00–23.00 daily. Salads, snacks & pasta dishes, plus more expensive meat & fish. Service can be unpredictable. **$$**

Chave d'Ouro On the corner of the main square. Snack bar serving doughnuts, cakes & drinks. **$**

Other practicalities
Banks There are two in town (⊕ 08.00–15.00 Mon–Fri), both with ATMs and Western Union. There's also a reliable ATM in the ferry terminal.

Health care The **hospital** is the huge grey and yellow building (❋ 222 1130) with an orange roof on the main road as it goes west out of town. There's also a pharmacy (❋ 222 1903) on the mountain road to Ribeira Grande.

Shopping Souvenirs (*grogue*, punch and pottery), island maps and guidebooks, postcards and stamps can be bought from the **shop/information centre** in the ferry terminal. The best-stocked supermarkets are all within 100m of the main square. A few women gather around the ferry terminal selling goat's cheese & mangoes, when in season, and others gather under a purpose-built shelter 200m to the east.

The rest
Police Near the post office; ❋ 222 1132
Post office From the port, follow the road 100m inland past the petrol station & it's on the left; ⊕ 08.00–15.30 Mon–Fri

Tourist information There is an office in the ferry terminal, though it closes soon after the ferries have arrived or departed

What to see and do Visit the little grey beach in town and watch the fishermen hauling up great tuna and the women selling it just a few metres away. Walk east for 25 minutes to Praia de Curraletes (Escoralet). Spend a night or two chilling out at one of the simple hotels, or, if you're here during the São João festival, join in the party!

FROM PORTO NOVO TO CIDADE DAS POMBAS (PAÚL)
Pontinha da Janela This small fishing town has two points of interest about it: the lighthouse and the inscribed rock.

A 3–4km walk along a coastal track from the town, **Farol Pontes Perreira de Melo** is a great viewpoint from which, on a clear day, you can see the entire northeastern coast of the island, and over to São Vicente, Santa Luzia and São Nicolau.

From Janela, a path up Ribeira da Peneda leads, after about 0.5km, to the **inscribed rock**, Pedra da Nossa Senhora. This large, free-standing rock bears some mysterious inscriptions and a cross. Researchers have thought it to be Aramaic, Phoenician, Malayalam or archaic Portuguese – it bears little resemblance to modern Portuguese or to Arabic, Hebrew, Berber or Tifnaq. Richard Lobban writes in the *Historical Dictionary of the Republic of Cape Verde*:

> The most fruitful investigation rests upon a comparison with the Portuguese inscription of a similar appearance, on a stone at Yellala Falls about 150km above the mouth of the River Congo. This was almost certainly inscribed by Diogo Cão in 1485 [and] appears to have two types of writing systems which range from archaic Portuguese, as well as letters which are in a distinctly different style which is the only form of writing in the case of Janela.

It was also common for the 15th-century Portuguese explorers to mark their landings and passages with stone inscriptions, especially with crosses; in short, the Janela inscription was most likely placed there by a 15th-century Portuguese. It is tempting to conclude that it was written by Diogo Gomes or by Diogo Afonso in the 1460s, or by Diogo Cão or his pilots in the 1480s.

> **TO THE END OF THE EARTH AND BEYOND** *Murray Stewart*
>
> The pick-up roars (briefly) out of town, but reaches little more than 40km/hour before the tarmac inevitably gives way to the more familiar, passenger-massaging cobblestones that are the trademark of Cabo Verde's road network. Cobblestones do not encourage speed, and our vehicle duly slows.
>
> For 30 minutes we wind upwards, our driver dropping through the gears until he can drop no more. We are now reduced to just above walking speed, and I am beginning to understand why it takes 2½ hours to cover the 26km from Porto Novo to Tarrafal de Monte Trigo. We come across a couple of cows, looking for something to munch: at an altitude of 1,200m, and at the end of the dry season, there's not much choice on their menu. In a month or so, the rains should come and the landscape will be transformed from desert to green. Life will be easier for the cows.
>
> Higher up, the cows give way to goats. We seem to be eyeball to eyeball with the craggy peaks of São Vicente, away to the southeast and an hour's ferry ride across the ocean from Santo Antão. But we have not finished our climb, not by far. After another 20 minutes of funereal progress, we turn a corner and we are no longer looking *across* at São Vicente's peaks, but *down* on the whole island, as if we were in an aeroplane. Front, back and both sides of the neighbouring island are visible. I ask the driver to stop for some photos and when he obliges, I realise for the first time that we have acquired an extra passenger from somewhere. Perched on the back of the truck is a middle-aged man, his feet wedged between a crate of beer and some plastic barrels. As well as being the passenger transport, we are also the Tarrafal delivery vehicle. We continue. Left hand only on the steering wheel, with his right hand our driver is tossing up a sealed package of pills he has collected from the pharmacy in Porto Novo, to deliver to someone in Tarrafal. The package is lobbed upward, then neatly caught, the pills seemingly rattling in perfect time to the seductive music washing over passengers from the dusty radio. An unusual percussive aid, I think to myself, but my admiration at our driver's dexterity and sense of rhythm is tempered by my preference for a 'both hands on the wheel' policy, as we negotiate yet another hairpin.
>
> Our next stop, even higher, is for another passenger to buy some fresh goat's cheese from a precariously situated dwelling. The mother goat plays with her two

CIDADE DAS POMBAS (VILA DAS POMBAS, PAÚL) A 15-minute drive south along the coast from Ribeira Grande is Cidade das Pombas, which marks the beginning of the majestic valley of Paúl. It has recently gained city status, but is still often referred to as 'Vila das Pombas' or even simply 'Paúl', though the latter is actually the name of the district, not the town. It's a long, strung-out town along the coast, the site of ambitious building projects, including a bridge at its southern end.

Getting there and away From Porto Novo, the new coastal road is a spectacular introduction to the stunning scenery of Santo Antão. Following the cliffs and with a tunnel or two hewn out of the rock, you will reach Cidade das Pombas (the *alugueres* will be marked Paúl) in 20 minutes. In Pombas the *alugueres* for Porto Novo currently leave from beside the bridge. Instead of waiting in the minibus for it to fill up, you can go to a café and ask the driver to collect you there.

From Ribeira Grande, the journey to Cidade das Pombas takes about 15 minutes and transport can be found around the mouth of Ribeira de Torre. In Pombas,

kids as the transaction completes. At this new altitude, I also have another startling discovery, for beyond São Vicente, the peaks of São Nicolau – the 'next-door island-but-one' – are now visible above a distant layer of white cloud. My fellow passengers tell me that they have even seen the volcanic cone of distant Fogo, on a clear day.

At a junction, the cobbles pass over the baton to a rutted dirt track and the discomfort increases. At last we are heading downward, a line of lonely telephone poles to guide us. The *ribeiras* are dry now, though will not remain so for long and I marvel at the deep troughs the previous year's rainwater has carved in the ground as it headed seawards. Bridges are often washed away, I am told, making it necessary to send up a vehicle from Tarrafal to meet another from Porto Novo, transferring goods by hand from one vehicle to the other, across the gap, to keep the town supplied.

There is no other road in.

We stop again, this time at a squat building, and we edge nervously on foot towards the nearby cliff. Tiny Tarrafal is below, perhaps 1,000m of descent. Before the dirt-track road was completed in the 1980s, this building was used to store goods brought from Porto Novo, and the townsfolk would have to carry everything down the steep cobbled path to town. It's actually quicker to walk from here, I am told, but I decline the opportunity. When our pick-up crawls for the remaining 30 minutes, I begin to believe it. I am looking at the sea ahead and wondering how we are going to descend so far in such a short distance. More hairpin bends provide the answer. Eventually we reach sea level and a wide black-sand beach is our reward as it ushers us into the town. For me, the journey is over. But our one silent passenger, a woman in her sixties, has yet further to go. Laden with fruit from Porto Novo, she has to wait for a boat to take her and her supplies up the coast to Monte Trigo, yet another hour away.

Or, if no boat appears, she has another 3 hours, on foot.

Fortunately for the west coast's residents, the sealed road to Tarrafal was completed in February 2021. The journey from Porto Novo now takes around 90 minutes, but is no less enthralling despite the relative comfort of its final descent.

it can be found by the road junction by O Veleiro restaurant (65$). To Cabo de Ribeira (up the Paúl Valley), transport can be found along the adjacent *avenida* in front of the carpentry workshop (170$).

Where to stay

Tienne del Mar (9 rooms) Located on the seafront; 352 3310; w tiennedelmar.com. Rooms are comfortable, decorated in earthy style, & all have balconies. Sea-view rooms are right on the water, with waves crashing below. Good open-air restaurant & b/fast. **$$$**

Aldeia Jerome (8 rooms, inc 2 suites & 1 apt) 223 2173; e aldeiajerome@gmail.com. Bright, clean, *pensão* set in a leafy, quiet location. All rooms are en suite & have fridges. Includes a suite for up to 4 people. English spoken. **$$**

Black Mamba (3 rooms) On the road heading north of town; m 980 3744. Glowing colours enliven the simple rooms here, as do the sea views if you nab one of those, as well as a private bathroom. Restaurant terrace overlooks the sea, with a reputation for good food, including vegetarian options. **$$**

Hotel Paúl Mar (19 rooms) 223 2300; e ilda.costa@sci.cv. Modern hotel with a high level of fittings. Rooms have private bathroom, TV, AC, good water pressure & hot water, but no Wi-Fi.

Balcony rooms are right by the waves. Buffet b/fast served in O Veleiro restaurant next door. **$$**
Pousada de Céu (3 rooms) Just 300m inland; ☎ 223 1695; e pousada@pousadaceu.com. A family homestay, small & popular. Rooms with private bath. Terrace, garden & mountain views. B/fast inc, evening meals by arrangement. **$$**
Casa Maracujá (2 rooms) Just 100m back from the pretty main square; ☎ 223 1000; m 955 3909. A couple of basic rooms, very inexpensive,

with a small communal plunge pool & pleasant terrace. Ask for details at the restaurant (see below). **$**
Residencial Mar & Sol (7 rooms) On the coastal road, towards the Ribeira Grande end of town; ☎ 223 1294. The owner, Noémia Melo, offers home cooking, & simple, authentic, spacious rooms, nearly all with private bathroom, others with a balcony & uninterrupted sea views. Prices vary accordingly. Courtyard for b/fast. **$**

✗ **Where to eat and drink** Several *mercearias* (small food shops) around the town also act as bars, where you can get a cold beer or shots of *grogue*. There is a municipal market opposite the *praça*, though it is often devoid of activity.

Atelier Opposite Hotel Paúl Mar; ⊕ 09.00–midnight daily. Bar & restaurant with nice outdoor setting & sun umbrellas. Small menu concentrates on a few freshly prepared dishes. Occasional live music at w/ends. **$$**
Casa Maracujá see above; ⊕ 09.00–23.00 daily. Pleasant upstairs terrace offering a different option: *carpaccios*, grilled cheese, salads. The *camoca* ice cream is also a draw on its own.

Occasional live music. English spoken; owner Hettie is also a guide. **$$**
Restaurante Atlântico On the main road towards Ribeira Grande, by the police station; m 959 7379; ⊕ 11.00–15.00 & 18.00–22.00 daily. Small veranda over the sea. Serving everything from a 20$ croquette to a 2,000$ lobster pizza, & much in between. Great-value *pratos do dia*; live music sometimes on Sat until 03.00. **$$**

Entertainment and nightlife At weekends, try the Atelier, Black Mamba, Maracujá or Atlântico (see page 313 and above) for live music.

Other practicalities There are two **banks**: a **BCA**, just past the main square, and **Caixa Económica**, next to Hotel Paúl Mar; both have ATMs. The **health centre** is in the central *praça* (☎ 223 1130). The **police** station (☎ 223 1292) is on the main road towards the Ribeira Grande end of town, and the **post office** can be found beyond the central *praça* on the right (☎ 223 1397; ⊕ 08.00–15.00 Mon–Fri).

What to see and do The main reason for being here is to travel up – or down – Ribeira do Paúl (see below) or to do neighbouring hikes such as that up Ribeirãozinho to Pico da Cruz. The statue of Santo António at the northern edge of the foot of the Paúl Valley is a 15-minute hike that will give you 180° views of the ocean and surrounding valleys. **Senhor Ildo's Trapiche**, to the right of the petrol station in Pombas, has bottled *grogue*, *ponche* and *mel*. The *senhor* has wised up to the tourist potential and charges a small fee to view his handsome *trapiche*, set behind some wooden doors in a courtyard of munching goats and indifferent cats.

RIBEIRA DO PAÚL A vast *ribeira* home to thousands of people and their agriculture – sugarcane, breadfruit and bananas – Paúl is renowned throughout the archipelago for its *grogue*, and one of its *trapiches* (sugarcane-juicing apparatus) is still driven by oxen. Highlights include Passagem, with its charming municipal park nestled among impressive almond trees and bougainvilleas. Beyond the villages of Lombinho and Cabo de Ribeira, up a steep incline, a panoramic view of the valley and ocean opens out. The road ends at Cabo de Ribeira, but a steep cobbled footpath continues to Cova, an impressive ancient crater now filled with verdant cultivation. Walk up or down, depending on your fitness and appetite for climbing; there are plenty of little shops and a few restaurants en route.

Getting there and away *Alugueres* travel from Cidade das Pombas all the way up to Paúl's Cabo de Ribeira for about 300$; private hire will be 2,000$–3,000$. Some *alugueres* do the full journey between Cabo de Ribeira and either Ribeira Grande or Porto Novo – the latter generally to meet the ferry from São Vicente.

Where to stay Accommodation is listed here in order of ascent up the valley. Most of the accommodation options can arrange transfers from Porto Novo in which you are dropped off at the head of Paúl and walk down to your accommodation, your bags continuing by vehicle. They will also give you help planning hikes. Alternatively, you can stay on the coast in one of the places listed under *Cidade das Pombas*, page 312.

Kasa d'Vizin (4 rooms) Eito, Val do Paúl; m +32 471 357473; w kasadvizin.com. Upmarket B&B with a stylish apartment for 4, a studio for couples, a large room with a double plus sofa bed, & a single. Communal sun terrace overlooking the village & lush sugarcane, mango, breadfruit & banana trees. Welcomes families (offers babysitting) & can cater for vegans/vegetarians. **$$$$**

Hotel Château Georgette (8 double bunks, 9 suites & 2 apts) m 351 2020; w hotelchateaugeorgette.com. Full of surprises, from its kookily elegant décor, including luxurious bunk rooms to lavish suites. Bunks can accommodate 2 & come with night lights, plugs & USB outlets & curtains. The basement hides a secret: a small pool & spa. B/fast from produce grown on their own nearby farm. **$$–$$$$**

Chez Hujo (12 rooms) Boca de Figueral, Val do Paúl; \352 2000; m 923 2515/954 3919; e jbeaudancaboverde1@gmail.com; w chez-hujo.cape-verdehotels.com. Pops of colour make this popular place up the valley easy to find. Rooms are nicely decorated. All with private bath; clothes washing available. Restaurant & bar. Family room available. **$$–$$$**

Casa das Ilhas (9 rooms) Lombo Comprido; \223 1832; m 996 7774; e casadasilhas@yahoo.fr; w casadasilhas.com. This Belgian-/Cabo Verdean-run *casa* is in fact a series of little houses built on the steep terracing of the mountainside, surrounded by fruit & vegetable planting – including sticks of sugarcane, from which their own *grogue* is made. Superb views, panoramic & full of the detail of valley life. Rooms are spartan but comfortable, all are en suite. Wi-Fi is reportedly fast enough to encourage long stays. At night great meals are served around a communal table where, during the day, the owners run a small local kindergarten – any contributions of children's clothes, pencils, etc, are welcome. Casa das Ilhas is reached by a 10min walk up a steep footpath from the road (the owners will send someone down to carry your bags or can pick you up in Porto Novo). English spoken. **$$**

Aldeia Manga (5 bungalows) \223 1880; e info@aldeia-manga.com; w aldeia-manga.com. Simply furnished bungalows perched on the side of a hill facing a steep cliff reaching up into the clouds, with spectacular views down the valley. The owner has made a great deal of effort to build in a sympathetic style & power is provided by solar panels. Natural swimming pool. A substantial buffet dinner is provided (order in advance). Jams are made with fruit from the garden. From here at least 6 unguided hikes are possible, including straight down to Vila das Pombas. Collection from the ferry can be arranged in advance. English & French spoken. **$$$**

Casa Cavoquinho (5 rooms) Cabo de Ribeira; \223 2065; m 998 9919; e info@cavoquinho.com; w cavoquinho.com. Run by a friendly Spanish couple, José & Belén, this house is wedged, vertiginously, into the mountainside & is easy to spot with its tangerine-toned exterior (the path off the main road reaches it from behind the old village water pump). Rooms are simple & attractive, each with a window affording a stunning view down the valley. There is also an evening bar/restaurant, along with a library. Wi-Fi in common areas only. José also leads guided treks & is very knowledgeable. English spoken. **$$$**

Chez Sandro (5 rooms, 1 apt) Cabo de Ribeira; 223 1941; m 921 7051; e sandro_lacerenza@yahoo.fr; w chezsandro.com. A French-Cabo Verdean operation, with simple but bright, clean & attractive rooms. Some are suitable for hiking groups, some have shared bathrooms. **Sandr'Arte**, the shop/bar below sells a huge array of souvenirs & local produce. HB available if prearranged. **$$**

✕ Where to eat and drink
Restaurants are listed in order of their ascent up the valley.

O Curral Chã João Vaz; 223 1213; ⏱ 10.00–18.00 Mon–Sat, 11.00–17.00 Sun. This café is perfect for taking a break from the long hike of Vale do Paúl. All organic, very inexpensive light meals & snacks. Try various kinds of spirits made by the ebullient owner, Alfred, buy some of his cheese & jams & chat to him about his latest ideas for the place. **$**

Cavoquinho Page 315; ⏱ daily by request. Innovative cuisine made from fresh fish & locally grown produce; 1 day's advance notice required for non-guests, & vegetarians can be catered for. Price is for a set 3-course meal. **$$$**

Sandr'Arte (see *Chez Sandro*, above) ⏱ 08.00–22.00 daily. This is a good place to stop for a drink. They also sell local crafts, *grogue* & coffee. **$$**

What to see and do Walking up or down the Paúl Valley is the chief activity and the sights along the way are described in the section on hikes on page 328. You can't fail to be fascinated by the everyday life of the valley.

RIBEIRA GRANDE (POVOAÇÃO) The mountain road from Porto Novo to Ribeira Grande pulls away past the outskirts of town where the inhabitants live among permanent, savage and sand-laden winds. It mounts through the cusps of the brown landscape. Already the achievement of the road builders seems extraordinary.

As it climbs higher and higher forest plantations begin to fill the higher valleys and a chill tinges the air. But you are still in the foothills – on and on you go until you reach the clouds and the eucalyptus and pine trees which thrive in the cold air. The road skates the ridges of the top of the island and sometimes there are breathless sheer drops on either side as you gaze down into the plunging *ribeiras*. Pinnacles, cliffs, and double bends around spires of rock, mark the descent into the verdant side of the island and you will see the puddle of Ribeira Grande long before you drop past the thatched stone houses to reach it.

The town, still known to many as Povoação, is a lively tangle of cobbled streets crammed into the space between the cliffs and the sea, and overflowing up the mouths of the two *ribeiras*: Ribeira Grande and Ribeira de Torre. For a place in such an awe-inspiring setting, the town is strangely lacking in places from which to appreciate the view, and the idea of ending a hard day's hike sipping a quiet beer

---

FROM CIDADE DAS POMBAS TO RIBEIRA GRANDE: SINAGOGA

Sinagoga lies on the point between Mão para Traz and Paúl. It is where a community of exiled Portuguese Jews from the Azores settled in the early 19th century. There are Jewish graves here as well as in Ponta do Sol. For more on Jewish history in Cabo Verde, see page 14. The synagogue that gave the town its name was used as a leper hospital after it had been abandoned. Today Sinagoga feels a little less remote, if still surrounded by ocean and mountains on all sides. It has a black-sand beach that's popular for swimming. There's also a fabulously located hotel, **RM Green Hotel** (w rmgreenhotel.com; **$$$**), with stylish wood and stone rooms and a pool overlooking the coast.

RIBEIRA GRANDE

← Ponta do Sol

Divin'Art,
Pedracin Village ←

Ribeira Grande

Paúl, Porto Novo (coastal road) →

Hospital,
Porto Novo
(mountain road),
Xôxô

For listings, see page 318

Where to stay
1 Residencial Bibi
2 Residencial Trópical
Off map
   Divin' Art
   Pedracin Village

Where to eat and drink
3 5 de Julho
4 Cantinho de Amizade
   Restaurante Trópical (see 2)
Off map
   Divin' Art (see Divin' Art)
   Pedracin Village
      (see Pedracin Village)

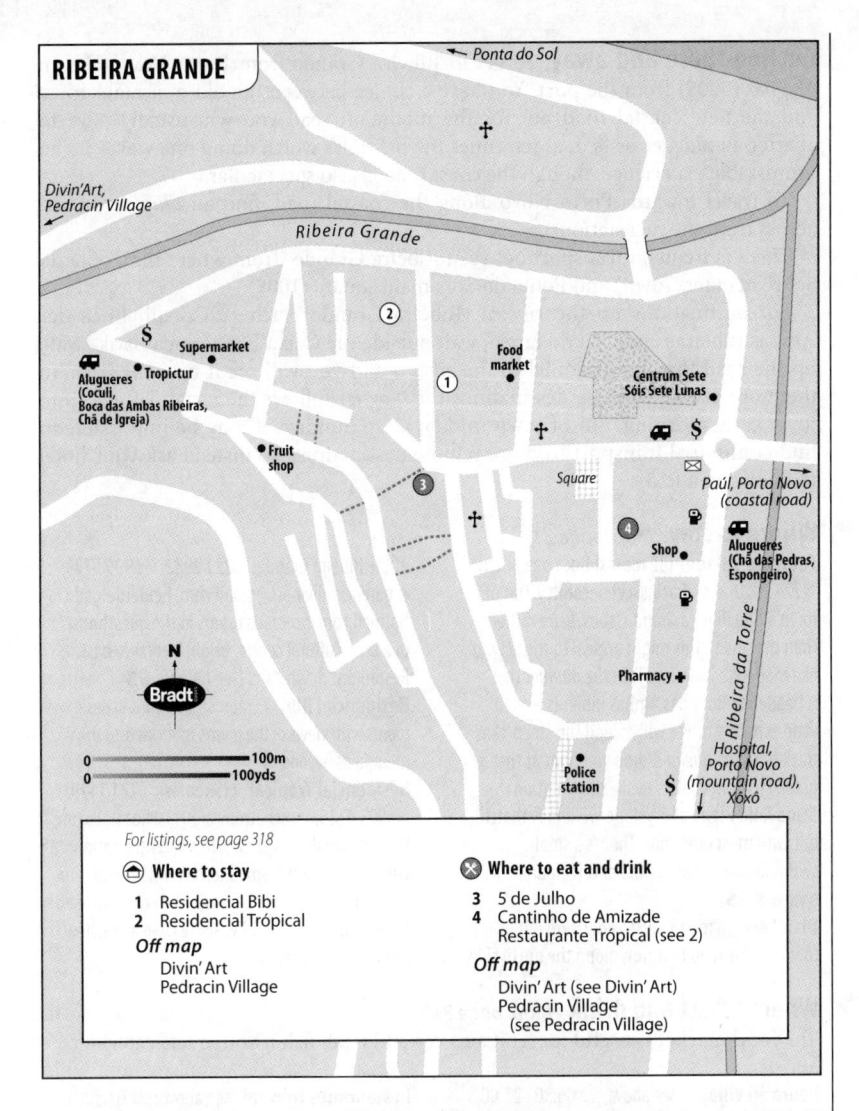

while gazing at some Atlantic panorama never quite materialises. Most people will pass through here without spending a night, especially with the more traveller-orientated Ponta do Sol accommodations and restaurants just up the road. It is a true transport hub: in low season you will be (gently) besieged by *aluguer* drivers ready to take you anywhere, if you have the money.

A church was first built in the town in 1595. Bishop Valente, who arrived in the mid 18th century, having abandoned Santiago, consecrated the large church of Nossa Senhora do Rosário in 1755. However, the transfer of the episcopal see to Santo Antão was never officially approved and it went instead, a while later, to São Nicolau. Each November, Ribeira Grande stirs into life for the international Sete Sóis Sete Luas music festival, which takes place outside by the Shell fuel station. For three days, musicians gather, sleeping in a purpose-built site [map, above]; curiously, it is not used the rest of the year, except for housing a few art works.

Getting there and away To get to Ribeira Grande from Porto Novo take an *aluguer* (500$) from the port. You have a choice between the old mountain route and the new coastal road but for the mountain road you will usually have to charter an *aluguer* or taxi, at ten times the price. It's worth doing one way – it's an unmissable experience, though the coast road is also spectacular.

To travel towards Porto Novo along the coastal road, find an *aluguer* or taxi across from the fuel stations.

There is frequent transport between Ribeira Grande (from where the Ponta do Sol road enters town) and Ponta do Sol's main square (100$).

For destinations up the *ribeira* (Ribeira Grande) such as Coculi, Boca das Ambas Ribeiras and Chã de Igreja, wait outside the Caixa Económica Bank (walk up the road that goes parallel to the *ribeira* and you will see it on your left). To the more distant of these destinations the *aluguer* follows the usual pattern (into town early morning, out of town midday). On Sundays it may be impossible to find communal transport to more remote destinations, so instead ask your hotel to book you a taxi.

Where to stay *Map, page 317*

Pedracin Village (32 rooms) Boca da Coruja; 224 2020; e pedracin@cvtelecom.cv. Out of town along Ribeira Grande (the *ribeira* rather than the town), this might appeal to those who like moderate isolation. Take the *aluguer* that is headed to Boca das Ambas Ribeiras – for a little extra the driver will ascend the steep 1km track from the *ribeira* & drop you right at the hotel. Pleasant chalets evoke the traditional Santo Antão style of drystone walling & thatch, but with most mod cons. There's a small swimming pool, solarium, bar & restaurant with a view. $$$

Divin' Art (5 rooms) Just under␣1km out of town, on the road that runs along the north side of the Ribeira Grande; 221 2832; m 999 5773; e gerencia.divinart@gmail.com, helderdelgado1@hotmail.com. Spacious rooms in the guesthouse of a busy cultural centre, bright but fairly basic. Restaurant downstairs (see below). $$

Residencial Bibi (3 rooms) 996 4659. Basic rooms with views of the town's rooftops & to the mountains beyond. $

Residencial Trópical (15 rooms) 221 1129; m 993 4116; e rochatropical2011@hotmail.com; w residencialtropical.cv. A town-centre option, with a restaurant & small terrace with some welcome shade (but no view). Most rooms are en suite with AC, fridge & TV. Some have a sea view, though no balcony. $

Where to eat and drink *Map, page 317*

The **food market** is useful for fruit and veg and fresh fish if you're self-catering.

Pedracin Village see above; ⊕ 06.30–23.00 daily. Out of town; a good restaurant with a spectacular view. $$$$

Cantinho de Amizade Near the petrol stations; 221 1392; ⊕ 08.00–22.00 daily. A spacious bar with restaurant & less formal area set in a courtyard. Fish, seafood, meat & goat dishes. A good place to while away an hour waiting for transport. $$$

Divin' Art see above. Breezy outdoors terrace & the usual range of fish, meat & seafood. Call ahead if you're coming in after a hike & your meal will be ready for you. Live music on Fri & other nights, when reservations are advisable. $$$

Restaurante Trópical see above; ⊕ 07.30–14.00 & 19.00–23.00 Mon–Sat. With both terrace & indoor (AC) seating. Nice old-fashioned place with occasional live music. $$$

5 de Julho In the town centre opposite the church; ⊕ 08.00–22.00 daily. Small, super-friendly café & restaurant with extensive menu (including vegetarian dishes), good coffee & a large, protected terrace with shaded seating overlooking the church and main drag. Wi-Fi. Also has basic rooms for rent (588 1971). $$

Entertainment and nightlife Ribeira Grande is not a music town, surprisingly, but **Trópical** occasionally has some on Saturdays, as does **Divin' Art** (see opposite).

Shopping Almost everything you need, including bread, can be found at the two petrol stations. There are also a number of small supermarkets in the town centre. For genuine Santo Antão souvenirs, **Divin' Art** (outside town; see opposite) sells a variety of crafts, wall-hangings, baskets and fridge magnets at reasonable prices.

Other practicalities
Banks BCA Bank, opposite the post office at the crossroads on the edge of town; **BCN**, down the side of Ribeira da Torre towards the hospital; and **Caixa Económica**, Rua Ponte Lavad (follow the road up the side of Ribeira Grande for a minute or so and it's on your left); all have ATMs (all ⊕ 08.00–15.00 Mon–Fri).

The rest
Hospital Off towards the Porto Novo mountain road; ☏ 221 1337
Pharmacy On the road towards the hospital; ☏ 221 1310
Police Go along the Porto Novo mountain road & turn right before the hospital; ☏ 221 1132

Post office At the end of the main street through town; ⊕ 08.00–15.30 Mon–Fri
Tourist information There is no tourist information point in Ribeira Grande, but try Tropictur, at the north end of town, for flight tickets & information

PONTA DO SOL A gracious town, built on a breezy peninsula, this is one of the oldest Barlavento settlements. It has a neat main square, beautiful town hall, decent restaurants and a tiny but lively harbour. It is increasingly popular with tourists and has been undergoing a mini construction boom for years, with apartments springing up on the surrounding hills, many of which are owned by *emigrantes*. Some appear forlorn and unfinished, others brightly painted and serving as short-term rental accommodation for tourists. From October to April – European high season – the numerous small hotels and restaurants can be at capacity, so advance booking for both is advisable. The listings that follow are not comprehensive: there are a few more pensões scattered about in the centre, and apartment rentals too.

Getting there and away Ponta do Sol is nearly at the end of the road. It is a 15-minute *aluguer* trip to get there from Ribeira Grande (50$), using transport that waits by the bridge over the Ribeira Grande itself. Transport out of Ponta do Sol leaves throughout the day, but is most common in the early morning. Taxis cost 500$.

In Ponta do Sol, private taxis leave from the square, at any time of day. To Fontainhas it costs 750$; to Paúl 1,500$; to Cruzinha 3,000$; to Porto Novo 4,500$; to Pico da Cruz 4,000$; and to Corda 2,000$. Change at Ribeira Grande for anywhere else, and for more frequent vehicles to most of the places listed above. Your hotel can book transport in advance, and may be able to negotiate better rates, especially for round trips. French-speaking drivers are relatively easy to find, but there are only a few who speak English.

Where to stay *Map, page 320*
Coração da Ponta do Sol (10 rooms) On the road into town from Ribeira Grande, before you descend into the square; ☏ 225 1048; m 924 9001; e hildevangelder@gmail.com; w coracaopontadosol.com. Renovated, extended & offering neatly decorated rooms, some with sea views. A small swimming pool is a welcome escape from post-hike heat & a rooftop terrace & jacuzzi

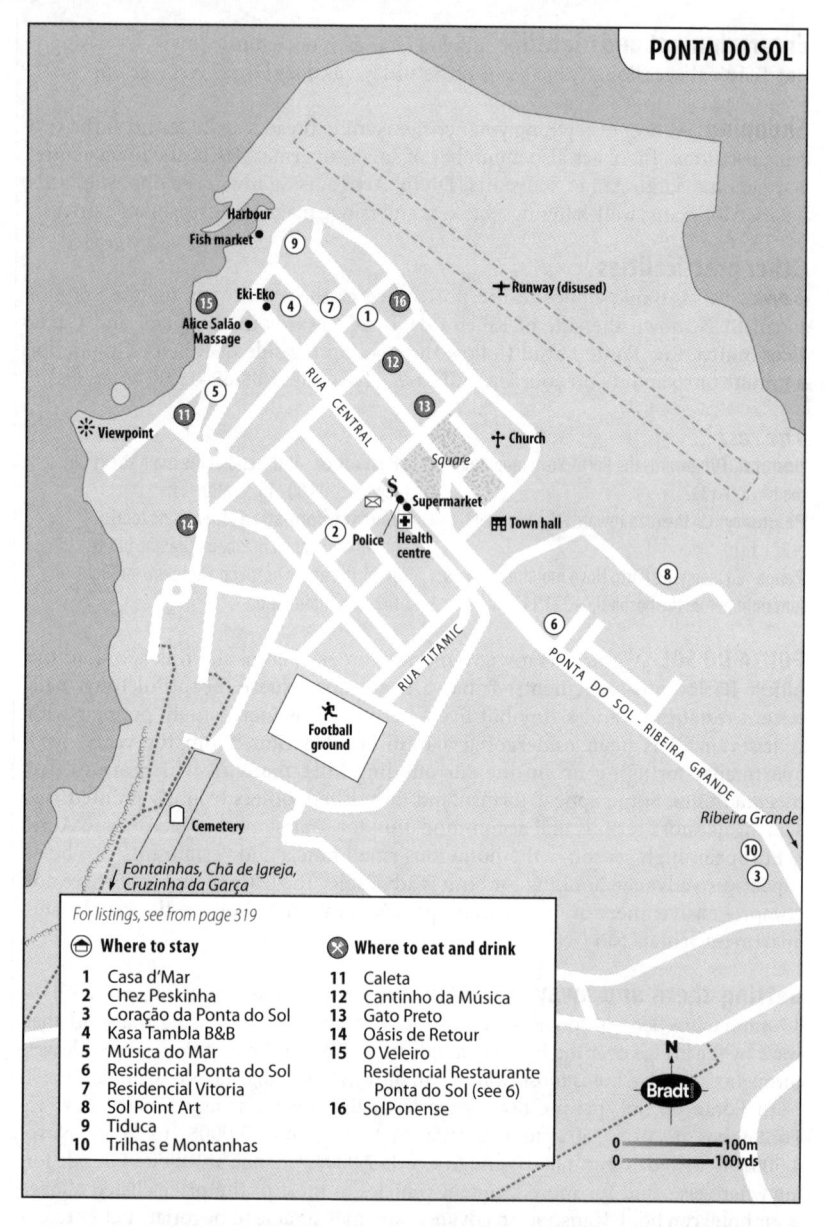

PONTA DO SOL

For listings, see from page 319

🛏 Where to stay
1. Casa d'Mar
2. Chez Peskinha
3. Coração da Ponta do Sol
4. Kasa Tambla B&B
5. Música do Mar
6. Residencial Ponta do Sol
7. Residencial Vitoria
8. Sol Point Art
9. Tiduca
10. Trilhas e Montanhas

🍴 Where to eat and drink
11. Caleta
12. Cantinho da Música
13. Gato Preto
14. Oásis de Retour
15. O Veleiro
    Residencial Restaurante
    Ponta do Sol (see 6)
16. SolPonense

---

are in the offing. Honesty bar. Belgian owners speak English, French & Dutch. Can advise on & organise trips & hikes. **$$$**

Música do Mar (5 rooms) Right on the harbourfront; ☏ 225 1121; e booking@musica-do-mar.com; w musica-do-mar.com. Cosy little place with welcoming staff & a small bar. Some rooms with balcony (sea view). Free Wi-Fi in bar. **$$$**

Tiduca Hotel (60 rooms) ☏ 225 1202; e tiduca. hotel@stu.cv; ⓕ tiducahotel. Controversial when built, this 6-storey port-side hotel is defiantly out of character. Rooms are large, modern & open-plan, if a little bland. Options at the front have balconies & particularly lovely, far-reaching sea views. If those aren't available, perhaps book elsewhere though, as some others only have an atrium outlook. **$$$**

Kasa Tambla B&B (10 rooms) `225 1526; m 982 5059; e kasatambla@gmail.com; w kasatambla.com. French-run establishment, close to the seafront, with a range of smartly decorated rooms, some with private balconies. Communal library & breezy terrace. B/fast service, courtyard & bar. **$$–$$$**

Casa d'Mar (4 rooms) `225 1390; m 951 2239; e casadmar.caboverde@gmail.com; w casadmar.blogspot.co.uk. Try to book the room (called 'Mar Azul') with the sea view & en-suite bathroom. Simple, clean rooms with furniture made by the owner's father in nearby Fontainhas. Good advice on restaurants & activities. French & English spoken. **$$**

Residencial Ponta do Sol (14 rooms) On the road towards Ribeira Grande; m 530 4660; e residencialpontadosol@gmail.com. All rooms are en suite with (mostly) hot water & fans. Some have a balcony from which, for top-floor rooms, there is a sea view. **$$**

Residencial Vitoria (5 rooms) `225 1075. Pleasant clean, spacious, well-lit rooms with AC, fridge & private bath. No Wi-Fi or TV. Prices are a bit lower than other places. **$$**

Sol Point Art (8 rooms) m 951 8927; e construplex.construplex@gmail.com. Located behind the town hall & close to the road that runs around the old landing strip, also known as your morning running track. Smartly furnished rooms, with TV & fridge & AC. **$$**

Trilhas e Montanhas (4 rooms) On the road into town from Ribeira Grande, before you descend into the square; `225 1313; m 950 7600; e geral@trilhasemontanhas.com; w trilhasemontanhas.com. A large modern building at the Ribeira Grande end of town. Pleasant rooms, some with balcony. Communal TV, Wi-Fi available only in public areas. **$$**

Chez Peskinha (7 rooms) `225 1091; w chez-peskinha.com. Simple, good-value place up a side street right in the centre. Can arrange extra beds for children. Rooftop terrace. **$**

✕ Where to eat and drink *Map, opposite*

Caleta Right on the seafront; `225 1561; ⏰ 11.00–23.00 daily. A tiny place with a big reputation. Offers fish, seafood, goat's cheese dishes, plus cocktails. Indoor & outdoor seating with really good cooking & a fantastic view over the ocean. **$$$**

Cantinho da Música m 977 0718; ⏰ 18.00–23.00 daily. This roof terrace restaurant & music bar can be very hard to get into – book ahead as it's one of the warmest & most fun places on the island. Owner Jackie's specialities include fish in a mango sauce & fried cassava, then flambéed bananas for dessert. Excellent live acts. **$$$**

Gato Preto (Black Cat) `225 1539; ⏰ 18.30–22.00 Tue–Sun. A well-regarded blend of Cabo Verdean & Swiss-French cooking. A popular place, which also has a *quintal fresca* (inner courtyard), & live music on Wed & Sun. Innovative dishes include seafood but also goat, pasta & fish. The 2- or 3-course menu is good value. **$$$**

O Veleiro m 971 3020; ⏰ 09.00–23.00 daily. Overlooks the sea & harbour – as close to the ocean as you can be. A good venue at sundown. Food a bit hit-&-miss; lobster available. **$$$**

Oásis de Retour m 959 5818; ⏰ 11.00–midnight Mon–Thu, 11.00–02.00 Fri & Sat, 16.00–midnight Sun. Welcoming space that feels like a private home. Good seafood dishes. **$$$**

Residencial Restaurante Ponta do Sol see above; ⏰ 07.00–22.00 daily. Terrace restaurant, as you head out of town, also known for its evening music. **$$**

SolPonense `225 1004; ⏰ 09.00–22.00 Mon–Sat. Push past the drinkers playing cards or *oril* in the tiny bar to find a quaint old-style dining area. You'll have to wait for food to arrive in this authentic place, so order & relax or take a stroll around town. Cheaper than most. No menu, so choice is limited. **$$**

Entertainment and nightlife There is not a lot of wild activity, but there is often live music somewhere in town. Calheta and Cantinho da Música, have the most frequent performances, with music also at Gato Preto (Wednesday and Sunday). Residencial Restaurante Ponta do Sol may also oblige. Less traditional music is often played on sound systems in the main square at weekends, with the promenading local teens a rather special sight.

Shopping Good crafts, gourmet goods and Mamdyara skincare products (page 290) from Mindelo are for sale at the excellent **Eki-Eko** [map, page 320] (⊕ 10.00–13.00 & 15.30–19.00 Mon–Sat), located just behind the Kasa Tambla B&B. All products – lamps, clothes, jams and other souvenirs – are sourced from Cabo Verde and some are even made on the premises. There's also a stylishly presented gift shop at the **Tiduca Hotel** (page 320), with artisan dolls and objects, stylish photographic titles about life on the island, and T-shirts. A couple of Senegalese shops are located down towards the harbour, selling both Cabo Verdean and African mainland products.

Other practicalities
Bank There is a BCA in the main square, with ATM.
Health centre ☏225 1130. Located in the handsome colonial building, with 2 sweeping staircases, to the east of the post office; limited facilities but there might be a duty doctor in town.
Massage Alice Salão; right on the main street near the port; m 999 0513. Alternatively, ask at your hotel as massage studios come & go.

Pharmacy The nearest is in Ribeira Grande.
Police Overlooking the main square; ☏225 1132
Post office Overlooking the main square, on the southern side; ⊕ 08.00–noon & 14.00–18.00 Mon–Fri
Tourist information Nothing official, but most accommodation will be able to organise excursions, transport, etc.

What to see and do Ponta do Sol is the embarkation point for hikes along the north coast and it is close enough to Ribeira Grande to be a useful setting-off point for hikes up its *ribeiras* (Torre and Grande). The town's port is worth a wander, with its small fleet and bustling harbour-side fish market. Locals use the deserted runway as an exercise circuit, but it's also fine for a pleasingly melancholy stroll too.

OTHER PLACES TO VISIT
Fontainhas Perched like a fairy-tale village on a high and precipitous spit of land above a deep *ribeira*, Fontainhas can be reached along a winding cobbled road from Ponta do Sol. Go up the hill, leaving the cemetery to your left, until you reach the cobbled road level with the end of the construction development, then turn right on to it. A spectacular walk on the road that heads west. It's about a 10km round trip.

Cruzinha da Garça This spectacularly sited coastal village, more usually known simply as Cruzinha, is more or less the end of the road that runs up Ribeira Grande before it turns north to hit the sea; it can also be accessed on foot from Fontainhas (page 329). There is a small fishing fleet that's the mainstay of the village, a couple of amiable restaurants, a small shop, one Airbnb, and back up the hill, just before the road to Chã de Igreja turns inland, two wonderful ecolodges.

🏠 *Where to stay and eat*
Palmeira da Cruz (9 rooms, 1 villa) m 973 9109; e palmeiradacruz@gmail.com; w en.palmeiradacruz.com. Architecturally elegant ecolodge on a wave-lashed headland with welcoming & engaged (& multi-lingual) Belgian hosts, Dany & Guy. Rooms are individually decorated with an artist's attention to detail, & have ultra-comfortable king beds. All have views & private terraces. Small solar-heated swimming pool facing out to sea. Generous b/fasts & the island's best coffee are served at your table. Dinners made from the hotel's own garden produce & fresh-caught fish are a treat: guests mingle at long tables over beautifully prepared 3 courses that include *grogue* & *ponche* tastings to finish (€22 pp). A special experience. Adults only. **$$$$**

Mamiwata Eco Village (14 rooms, 3 villas) 📞226 1122; e info@mamiwata-ecovillage.com; w mamiwata-ecovillage.com. Designed by Mindelo-based Ramos Castellano Arquitectos to take advantage of former agricultural terraces spectacularly stepping down a cliff, these stylish cabin-like rooms have extraordinary bird's-eye views & enclosed terraces. A bar, pool & restaurant welcome guests after a day out exploring. At the very start of the road to Chã de Igreja. German-run. Children by request. **$$$**

Pensão Só Na Fish (10 rooms) 📞226 1027; e sonafish@live.com. Large building in the village centre, overlooking the water. Rooms are very simple & only 1 is en suite. HB basis only. Bar & restaurant open to non-guests. **$**

Bar Crustáceo Up at the top of the village; m 582 2452; ⊕ lunch & dinner daily. This restaurant is bedecked in maritime murals & a tribute to Amílcar Cabral. Huge servings of whatever seafood you choose, all under 1,000$ (apart from lobster). **$$**

Pedra Balea On the main road into the village; ⊕ lunch & dinner daily. Beautiful views from a handful of wooden tables. Gorgeous Veronica will welcome you with a smile & cook up eel, fish or a simple egg & chips from scratch, including chipping & frying the potatoes to order. Don't dare leave without trying her famous chocolate *ponche* for afters. **$**

Espongeiro If arriving here after a walk (page 331), you might want to stay overnight at the lofty altitude of 1,370m.

Where to stay and eat Away from almost everything, Alain & Lucia run the small, recommended **Casa Espongeiro** (6 rooms; Ruta da Corda; m 981 1526/956 1364; e casaespongeiro@gmail.com; w casa-espongeiro.com; **$$**), offering a choice of private or shared facilities. Bike hire, guided walks and, for families with small children, donkey-assisted treks are also available, and there are meals on request.

Chã de Igreja This pretty village, with its smart white church and brightly painted houses, is built on a small promontory of land projecting from the west side of the *ribeira*. A good place to chill for a day. If intending to hike between Chã and Ponta do Sol, you can choose to do it in either direction, as accommodations are available in both places. To get there, take an *aluguer* up Ribeira Grande, through Coculi, Boca das Ambas Ribeiras, Horta de Garça and onwards. The best time to try for such transport is about 11.00–14.00: ask around near the fuel stations. You are unlikely to find public transport back on the same day, as it generally leaves early in the morning. The road up from Ribeira Grande winds up and down through some spectacular scenery, with great photo opportunities. Even if travelling *colectivo*, your driver will probably stop for a few snaps of towering crags and steep terraces. As you approach Chã, you'll suddenly reach a stretch of tarmac, a welcome break from bumpy cobbles. Soon you'll catch sight of a reservoir, then a dam, both opened in 2014. The old road used to go through the bottom of the *ribeira*, but the dam has greatly helped the area's agriculture.

There are beautiful, large beaches within 45 minutes of Chã de Igreja during the summer months (June to September) but for the rest of the year they are underwater.

Where to stay and eat There is a small shop in the village, and a couple of bars that serve food; meals can also be obtained from Residencial Mite e Banana.

Kasa d'Igreja (4 rooms, 4 tents) 1km from Chã de Igreja, on the road down to the sea; 📞352 6447; m 978 9090; e kasa-d-igreja@hotmail.com. Village-like collection of rooms, popular with those starting or finishing the coastal walk to Fontainhas. Tents contain proper beds & are somewhat cheaper, though have only cold water. Small swimming pool & much praised b/fasts & dinners. Some Anglophone guests find the language barrier with the current French owners a little difficult in such a remote setting, though as they were selling up at time of writing, that could change. **$$–$$$**

Residencial Mite e Banana (8 rooms) In the village centre; m 994 0759; e mitebanana@ hotmail.com. Occupying a newish building, with decent rooms, 2 with balcony. No frills, but they'll make you welcome & even do your laundry. Meals available 08.00–22.00 daily, though advance notice advisable. **$$**

Bar Tchiba Tucked behind the church; ⊕ Mon–Sat, or by request. This little rush-roof bar is perfect for a post-hike beer, but they can also feed you a fine fish dinner with a bit of notice. **$$**

THE WEST

The western part of Santo Antão is dominated by one vast volcano which reaches a height of 1,982m. Within its crater stands a younger cone, with a height of 1,979m. To its east, and almost as high, is Monte Pia, at 1,884m.

The west is largely inaccessible and underpopulated, although a number of mooted road-building projects west of Porto Novo could change this in the future. Currently there is a road from Porto Novo to Lagedos which runs northwest along a convoluted path through Chã de Morte, Curral das Vacas and on to Ribeira da Cruz in the northwest. From here it either heads west and then inland again, terminating at Monte Cebola, or continues down to the sea at Chã de Branquinho. When the rains are bad, whole sections of these roads may be impassable.

A network of hikes has been put together in the AB Kartenverlag map series (page 71), and there are others available via a number of hiking apps. Locals offer basic accommodation and meals at strategic points, making it more than possible to explore, but not without some forward planning. Either put yourself in the hands of a knowledgeable local operator such as Alsatour (page 306), quiz other hikers on social media/hiking apps for current contacts, or organise guides via your pre-booked accommodation in other parts of the island. Don't forget to cancel homestays well in advance if your plans change as your hosts might otherwise waste a day's journey to purchase food for your dinner and other supplies.

The views from the hike up and around Coroa are tremendous: down the steep western side of the volcano to Monte Trigo, and across to all the Barlavento islands when the weather is fine. The 1,000m ascent is not included in the hiking section because it's not the kind of hike that should be attempted without a guide. The paths are many and easily confused, there is no scattering of locals happy to put you right, and the landscape is hostile, with unexpected cliffs and no water.

TARRAFAL DE MONTE TRIGO This profoundly isolated spot on the west coast is definitely worth the effort. The road up, then down, from Porto Novo is spectacular (page 312), with breathtaking views over to São Vicente, Santa Luzia, São Nicolau and even Fogo, on a very clear day. It may not be passable in the rainy season, as bridges can be washed away. Your *aluguer* driver will probably stop if you want to take photos – and you undoubtedly will. The approach from the sea is also beautiful – a small spot of green colour among the brown-grey massifs of the mountains gradually resolves itself into the whites and pastels of this sleepy town. Around the black-sand shore – the longest stretch of beach on Santo Antão – fishermen relax, fierce games of *oril* click away under the trees, women wash clothes; and hens, pigs, goats and dogs go purposefully about their business. Sea eagles are common here, so keep an eye open for them plucking their dinner from the ocean. This is a great venue in which to do very little, a perfect place to relax at the beginning or end of a hiking holiday. Snorkelling and scuba-diving are both possibilities, as is

> **WARTIME BRITS IN TARRAFAL**
>
> When British merchant navy radio operator George Monk's ship, the *Auditor*, was torpedoed by a U-boat in 1941, most of the crew managed to escape into lifeboats. But what then? They had no navigational equipment, limited water and just a few cans of condensed milk to keep them going and they were bobbing up and down in the hostile Atlantic.
>
> Monk, now in his nineties, happened to have a diary in his pocket with navigational charts from which the crew worked out where they thought the Cabo Verde Islands might be. Then began traumatic days in which they rowed and rowed, all the time becoming fainter and more dehydrated. They rationed themselves to a few teaspoons of the milk each day.
>
> Finally, one morning, dawn rose on a distant mountain. 'It was vertical black lava rock going straight down into the sea,' says Monk. 'We couldn't land. We rowed for another six hours until we spotted the little village of Tarrafal.
>
> 'As we got near they spotted us and two of their fishing boats came out with carafes full of water. We just sat there, drinking water.'
>
> They eventually reached the beach and staggered into Tarrafal where they were cared for so kindly that Monk always yearned to return one day to say thank you.
>
> His dream came true in late 2007 when his story caught the imagination of Ron Hughes of Cape Verde Travel. Ron organised a trip for him, and the Cabo Verdean navy offered to take him to the remote village in western Tarrafal. As the ship approached the green puddle at the foot of the Tarrafal Mountains, Monk reminisced. 'I remember so well walking ashore here on this beach. It's so wonderful to come back,' he told me.
>
> He walked slowly up Tarrafal's main street in the heat of the midday sun and the word quickly spread. Before long a man of similar age, Germano Delgado, was coming along the street to meet him. Delgado had been one of his rescuers. The two 90-year-olds stood smiling at each other, nothing in common but a chance meeting 60 years before – and their age.
>
> 'I remember it quite well,' said Delgado. 'They were completely exhausted.'
>
> Then Monk and Delgado put their hands to their chests in Cabo Verdean greeting, shook hands like the British and went their separate ways.

fishing with the locals, which is best organised through the accommodation listed on page 326. In the last few years, especially since the final stage of the road was completed in 2021, this sleepy backwater has begun to waken itself. Electricity is now available all day, mobile-phone coverage has arrived and Wi-Fi is available in most of the guesthouses. Further improvements to the infrastructure are underway, for better or worse.

Getting there and away Several *aluguer* pick-up trucks leave Tarrafal for Porto Novo at an unhealthy 05.30 or 06.00 (700$), departing for the return journey at about 11.00. If you notify your driver the day before, he will pick you up at your *residencial*. The journey takes about 1½ hours, and winds along in parts. The trucks can be packed (a cushion is recommended, unless you manage to bag a much-coveted inside berth – again, try to reserve one with your driver the day before!). Generally the *alugueres* do not run on Sundays. There is also a Land Rover which can take eight passengers; ask your hotel for more information on this more luxurious option. But generally the *residencials* in Tarrafal will usually give you as much assistance as possible to plan your journey, including contacting the one or two local drivers on your behalf to arrange a private taxi. You could also charter a 4x4 in Porto Novo, which means you can stop to take in the unique landscape, perhaps several times, but at the very least at the *miradouro* of Campo Redondo, where the Norte plateau stretches before you. To find the Tarrafal *aluguer* in Porto Novo, ask around at the ferry terminal among the assembled drivers. Note, there is no ATM on this side of the island, so bring cash.

Where to stay and eat As accommodation is limited, it's best to book in advance. If you arrive without a booking, and everywhere is full, it's a long and expensive trip back to Porto Novo. Note that not all accommodation has hot water; that said, the water is never really cold. The following list is not exhaustive: there are simpler places like **Cantinho de Preta** (m 957 7325; e pousada.p.preta@gmail.com) and homestays such as **Marie-Alice's** (227 6002). Homestays can cost as little as 500$ per person a night, but it's thoughtful to offer more.

Although many people will eat at their chosen accommodation, an increase in visitor numbers has spawned a couple of restaurants by the beach, namely the **Mimina** and the **Café Casa Verde**, which you could check out should you fancy a change of scene.

Casa Baobab (6 rooms) 352 7049; w casabaobabtarrafal.com. Pretty, spacious rooms, some with large covered terraces, a couple with kitchenettes & 1 with bunks for children. Beautiful location looking straight over the beach & into the mountains. David, the French owner, can also assist you with diving arrangements (see below) & can provide advice about swimming & hikes. Book well ahead. **$$**

Marina d'Tarrafal (4 rooms) 227 6078; e info@marina-tarrafal.com; w marinatarrafal.com. Small coastal guesthouse in spacious grounds with charming hosts & simple rooms with views of the mountains, sugarcane fields & banana & coconut plantations. The owner used to be the ship's cook on the inter-island ferry & the cuisine is very good (available to non-guests, with notice, or you're welcome to take a drink or ice cream on their terrace). Hiking & snorkelling trips arranged. **$$**

Mar Tranquilidade (11 rooms) 227 6012; e info@martranquilidade.com; w martranquilidade.com. Run by Frank & Susi, a German-American couple who arrived here on their yacht in 1999 & decided to stay, this is an aesthetic little complex of vaulted-ceilinged, stone & thatch cottages, echoing the traditional architecture of the village. Rooms all have their own bathrooms but water is not heated. There's a shady terrace in front on which to hang out, & also Praça Tartaruga, a terrace on the beach which they have built as a place for

DIVING AND SNORKELLING

Snorkelling is possible with **Marina d'Tarrafal**. For diving, contact David Mückli, the French owner of **Casa Baobab**, who long ran the well-regarded Santo Antão Scuba Diving. He will again be operating a dive centre in Tarrafal in 2026, and has an excellent reputation, with PADI qualifications and naval and oil-rig diving experience, as well as good quality equipment. Rough seas prevent diving at times during December to March; while visibility can be poor in August and September, owing to the rains washing down into the ocean. At other times, though, you'll thrill to the underwater volcanic landscapes, with manta rays, occasional sharks and many other wonders. Beginners welcome for shore or boat dives.

SAY CHEESE: NORTE ON THE WORLD CULINARY STAGE

Donna Wheeler

In autumn 2017, Irineu da Luz travelled from her home in the arid rocky plateaus of Santo Antão's remote north to Bra, the centre of the Slow Food movement, in the rolling green hills of Piemonte. Her visit was a historic one for her community: she was there on behalf of Planalto Norte, a rural cooperative, and their raw milk goat's cheese, which had been nominated for a prestigious award.

'I never imagined that our product could one day be represented at one of the biggest events in the world,' she told the collected culinary press. In fact, Planalto Norte's flat–topped cylindrical cheese trumped 300 exhibitors from 23 different countries. The Slow Food committee was not just impressed by its milky white, pleasingly soft, elastic texture and gently tangy, herb-redolent flavour. What really grabbed their attention was the miracle that the cheese exists at all, and that it continues to be made with such care. As the judges declared, 'the difficult, arid environment, characterised by infrequent rains that fall on particularly sandy ground, could only be settled by determined, persevering people, the product of a multitude of different ethnic groups and histories, and by goats, the only animals able to survive on so little.'

Santo Antão and most of the other islands are dotted with makers that all produce notable cheeses. Along with the undoubtedly fine cheese, it was the 30-odd mountain herders' dedication to protecting their land and to resisting all short cuts, along with their impressive capacity to adapt to difficult environmental conditions, that found international recognition.

---

locals, & visitors, to congregate. They are very proud of their cuisine, which is available to non-guests with advance notice. Reliable Wi-Fi. Reservations are recommended as they are often full. **$$**

Vista Tarrafal (24 rooms) 227 6111; m 586 9623; w vistatarrafal.com. The largest place to stay on this side of the island. Neat, large & surprisingly flashy rooms. Restaurant & small swimming pool with sea view. **$$**

What to see and do Swim, dive, snorkel, fish from a local boat, play table tennis on the beach, chase a chicken, take the walk up the quebrada to the little waterfall. Bury yourself in the sand, which is reputed to have medicinal properties. Hike with a guide to Topo da Coroa. Read, sit and watch the waves. You can also buy authentic, artisanal soaps from **Kuruka**, based at the Marina d'Tarrafal (see opposite). They also sell other Cabo Verdean souvenirs.

You can also go by boat or on foot along the shore to **Monte Trigo**. If it's the latter, it's a 3- to 4-hour walk along the beach (defaulting to the dusty cliff track when the beach disappears in winter). This tiny fishing village is the island's westernmost settlement, making it also the westernmost inhabited place in Africa. For a less arduous day out, ask your hotel in Tarrafal about a one-way (1-hour) boat transfer to either drop you off or pick you up, or even to take you on a return journey. Staying the night (or longer) is possible, with a couple of well-run *residencials* to choose from. **Osvaldo Santos** (w casaosvaldomontetrigo.com; **$**) has three charming stone rooms, will feed you – a plate of fresh fish for 900$ or a lobster for 2,500$ – and can organise boat pickups and drop-offs from Tarrafal for around 5,000$. **Beira Mar** (**$$**) also has neat rooms and good food in a modern building right on the beach.

OTHER PLACES TO VISIT

Norte This region is remote and mostly inaccessible, which makes its landscape seem only more dramatic. Walkers are best accompanied with a guide, as services are few and far between and landslides frequent. It's also preferable to organise accommodation in advance. **Kasa Isabel Neves** (\222 3118; **$$**) offers simple rooms with the family who also offer guided trips up to Topo da Coroa. Isabel's son Fidel drives the *aluguer* from Porto Novo, so you can seek him out there if you've not pre-booked. In Chã de Feijoal, try booking with the **Residencial Casa do Planalto** (8 beds; m 992 0194; e limamoraisantonio@gmail.com; **$$**), run by the village co-operative.

Ribeira das Patas West and north of Porto Novo, the road passes through this village which is home to a co-operative (⊕ 09.00–noon & 14.00–18.00 daily). If passing through, it's a good chance to pick up a souvenir and support the local communities.

HIKES Colum Wilson (CW); Aisling Irwin (AI); Murray Stewart (MS)

If you have enough energy, the fourth and fifth hikes can be combined so that the walker goes up one *ribeira* and comes down the next.

1 VILA DE RIBEIRA GRANDE–COCULI–BOCA DAS AMBAS RIBEIRAS–CHÃ DE IGREJA
Distance: 12.5km; time: 5½ hours; difficulty: 2 (CW)

This is a spectacular walk, though not as green and cultivated as the other *ribeiras*. You can halve its length by taking transport from Ribeira Grande as far as Boca das Ambas Ribeiras. At the end of the walk you could turn round and walk back, or walk to Ponta do Sol (ie: the reverse of the next walk). Alternatively, you may be able to find an *aluguer* near the church that will take you to Ribeira Grande. If not, you may have to charter one.

Ribeira Grande is at the mouth of two *ribeiras*. The one that gives the town its name is the more northerly one. There's a wide, dusty track that leads up the *ribeira* from where the road to Ponta do Sol leaves town. The riverbed passes through scattered housing and cultivation and on the right, after about 20 minutes, an agronomy station. This was built by the Dutch under an aid scheme but is now run by the Cabo Verdeans. A tennis court was included in the package.

Some 45 minutes after setting out there is a large windmill on the left and a small shop which sells drinks. After another 10 minutes you reach the little village of **Coculi** with its prominent white church. This village marks the point where Ribeira Figueiral joins Ribeira Grande on the left. Bearing right at the fork just before the village, you will see that Ribeira Grande is joined almost immediately by another *ribeira* on the left, which leads up to **Chã de Pedra**.

The gentle ascent up Ribeira Grande continues and the land empties and becomes less lush, although a lot of sugarcane grows here. Two hours in, there's a slender aqueduct over the increasingly narrow *ribeira*. It was built by the Portuguese in 1956, and is still carrying water today.

Half an hour later is the small village of **Boca das Ambas Ribeiras**, or 'Mouth of Both Valleys' – the small valley of Ribeira dos Caibros leads up to the left. There are a couple of houses here and two prominent breadfruit trees. Breadfruit, which is in season in March, is considered a great delicacy. It has white flesh that is best cut into slices and boiled in salt water.

A cobbled road leads up the left side of Ribeira Grande, but the more interesting (and direct) route to **Chã de Igreja** is along a small path up the right (north) side of the valley.

You start climbing almost immediately, the path ahead repeatedly seeming to vanish as it curves steeply around the wrinkles of the sheer mountain face. Before long, the view of the valley floor far below is vertiginous, with farms and the occasional vehicle spread out like toys on a carpet. In places, there is nothing but a knee-high drystone wall separating you from a sheer drop of 500m. It was the same in the 19th century, when Alfred Burdon Ellis was prompted to write:

> Casualties…are not by any means uncommon, as the numerous wooden crosses that we passed on our way testified.

Watch out for Egyptian vultures (*Neophron percnopterus*) soaring on the thermals towards the head of the valley. They are unmistakable, with a black wing with a white leading edge, and a wingspan of up to 2m.

Finally, 1½ hours after leaving Boca, the path finds a nick in the mountain rim at a height of 830m. Over the saddle, look down on the tiny settlement of Selado do Mocho.

It is a hard descent (40 minutes) on a zig-zagging cobbled path to reach the edge of this remote village. Not long after passing around the head of a small valley into the village, the path cuts up to the top of a low ridge, where you find the village standpipe. Straight away, the path begins the descent into Ribeira Garça. Before long, you will catch your first glimpse of Chã de Igreja, on a small promontory of land projecting from the west side of the *ribeira*.

Descend into the deep cleft of the *ribeira*, and find a steep path up the seaward side of the village's promontory.

2 PONTA DO SOL–FONTAINHAS–FORMIGUINHAS–CHÃ DE IGREJA
Distance: 12km; time: 5 hours; difficulty: 2 (MS)

This coastal walk makes an interesting change from the *ribeiras*, passing through the village of Fontainhas, perched on a knife edge of rock, and with plenty of exposure to the sound and aroma of crashing waves. A lot of the walk is undulating with some steep parts and some level sections. Refreshments are available at all the places mentioned and there are a couple of bathing opportunities along the way, though care should be taken if the ocean is rough. At the end of the walk you can either stay the night in Chã de Igreja, or catch the *aluguer* that runs from near the church to Ribeira Grande. If you are forced to charter an *aluguer*, it should be about 3,000$. Some may prefer to do the walk in reverse, dropping their luggage at a hotel in Ponta do Sol, then taking transport to Chã and starting the walk back to their hotel from there.

From Ponta do Sol, head uphill and go past either side of the cemetery until you reach the wide, cobbled road. Turn right on to it. The cobbled road winds in and out among the folds of the steep mountains and finally affords you a fantastic view of **Fontainhas**, perched like a fairy-tale village on a high and precipitous spit of land above a deep *ribeira*. Some 40 minutes after setting out you will be on its extraordinary main street, built on the spine of the narrow promontory. The houses lining this higgledy-piggledy street have a sheer drop of several hundred metres behind them.

As you leave Fontainhas, and as the path climbs back towards the coast, there is a good view of the *ribeira* with its intricate terracing and ingeniously engineered irrigation channels running across the slopes. On the valley floor the wooden structure is a traditional *trapiche* – a mule-driven contraption used for pressing sugarcane in the all-important manufacture of *grogue*.

In the next *ribeira* the path weaves back inland towards the well-watered village of **Corvo**, 40 minutes from Fontainhas. Another 20 minutes brings you to the prettier village of **Formiguinhas**, where you descend to the shore.

The next stretch of the walk is the most impressive because much of the path has been hacked out of the massive, ancient rock formations. It is a spectacular but desolate walk, with the air full of the sound of the waves and the taste and smell of salt. At one point you emerge in a small, nameless settlement, where there are four houses and fields of rock. Here, there is no evidence of the passage of the centuries.

About 1½ hours from Formiguinhas the land opens out again and a broad *ribeira* leads up to the left. A small village (out of sight of the path) shelters in the mouth of this *ribeira*. After 15 minutes, cross a football pitch with metal goalposts and, 20 minutes later, you descend into the small fishing village of **Cruzinha da Garça**.

SANTO ANTÃO
Hiking

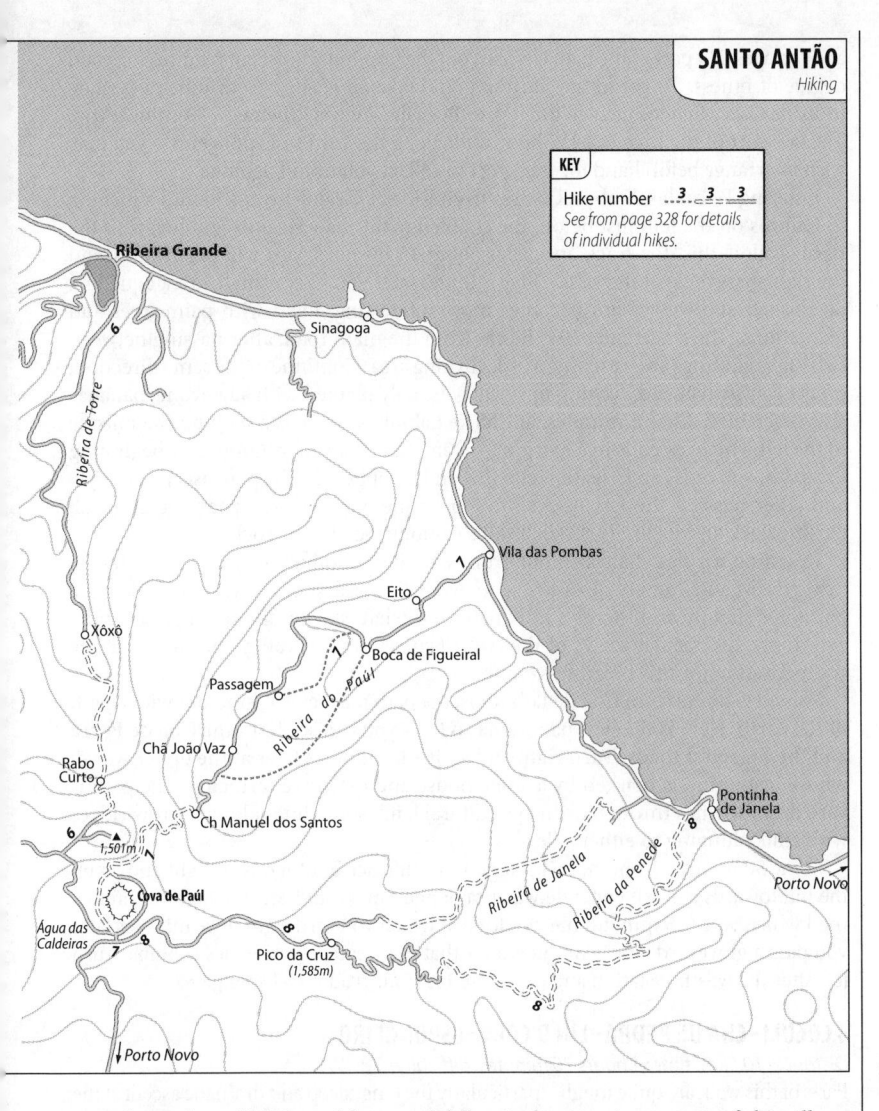

KEY
Hike number ---3---3---3
See from page 328 for details of individual hikes.

Pick up the cobbled road here and follow it for 10 minutes out of the village, seeing a cemetery high up on a hillside opposite. There's a track leading into the *ribeira* on the left. Follow it inland along the ridge rather than descending. The *ribeira* is dry and dramatic. There is nothing but the rustle of parched leaves and the rattle of pebbles falling from the sheer valley sides. Some 30 minutes after leaving Cruzinha, you arrive at a promontory projecting into the *ribeira* with a steep path up its side leading to **Chã de Igreja**.

3 BOCA DAS AMBAS RIBEIRAS–CAIBROS–CHÃ DE LOBINHOS–REAL–LAGOINHA–ESPONGEIRO
Distance: 14km; time: 5 hours; difficulty: 3 (Al)
This walk is a feast of ever more dramatic panoramas and, like the others leading from parallel *ribeiras*, takes you to an eerie, higher world away from the drama of canyons

and terraces. No part of the path is tricky, but the unremitting ascent requires a certain degree of fitness. To get to the starting point, take an *aluguer* from Ribeira Grande (outside Caixa Económica) all the way to **Boca das Ambas Ribeiras**, a 20-minute trip. The last part of the hike is a 1½-hour walk along the road to Espongeiro – you may wish to arrange beforehand for transport to collect you from Lagoinha.

Entering Boca das Ambas Ribeiras from Ribeira Grande, you will find a turning to **Caibros** on the left, just before the cobbled main road ascends and bends to the right. Follow this dirt track and, after about 15 minutes, you will begin to ascend the right-hand side of the valley. Five minutes later you pass a small, brick aqueduct on the left and the *ribeira* becomes more interesting, filled with palm trees and plantations. The track ends 30 minutes from the main road, after passing between two high buildings and reaching a little turning area. Continue in the same direction, on the footpath ahead, passing up a valley heavily planted with sugarcane, bananas and vegetables. After 5 minutes, at **Chã de Lobinhos**, there is a path up the hillside to the left which ascends in a hairpin for 20m. Less than 10 minutes after beginning this path, you cross an irrigation channel and a public tap. The path ascends steeply and, after passing the last house for some time, you will see your route ahead, darting back and forth, its cobbled walls camouflaged by the rock.

Reaching a ridge, half an hour from Chã de Lobinhos, you can see into the next *ribeira* and you are already eye to eye with the first of the craggy peaks. The path dips slightly and there's a little path to the left: stay on the main path for the ever more spectacular views of the two *ribeiras* – and of valleys beyond – ample compensation for this breathless climb.

Some 1½ hours from Chã de Lobinhos, the path reaches a T-junction with a path of red earth. Here is the best panorama so far – you can see both the Chã de Pedra and the Figueiral roads. Turn right and arrive 10 minutes later at the upper world, whose beginning is marked by a stone house and extensive terracing. The path is varied, sometimes through open agricultural land, sometimes along narrow ridges with cliffs plunging to either side.

Some 50 minutes from the last T-junction you reach another: turn right and go up the hill towards a green concrete water tank and tap. From here, the path becomes a road which, after 35 minutes meets a fork, at which you turn right. Five minutes later you pass a graveyard, and 5 minutes after that the weather station at **Lagoinha**. Turn left after the weather station and begin the 1½-hour trudge to **Espongeiro**.

4 COCULI–CHÃ DE PEDRA–LIN D'CORV–ESPONGEIRO

Distance: 10.5km; time: 4 hours 20 minutes; difficulty: 3 (CW)

Parts of this walk are quite tough – particularly the long, steep and dramatic ascent at the head of Chã de Pedra on an uncobbled path that can at times be akin to rock climbing. The approach to Lin d'Corv is across gently undulating agricultural land. To shorten the walk a little, you can try to catch a lift to Coculi and onwards, as far up Chã de Pedra as possible (it is possible to get a lift as far as Pia de Cima, if you are lucky).

From Coculi to Chã de Pedra takes 1½ hours. At **Coculi**, take the right fork, passing Coculi's church on your left, and after about 700m, take a turning on the left. The first part of this road up to **Chã de Pedra** is flat and not particularly interesting. It becomes livelier when it leaves the valley floor as it approaches **Pia de Cima**.

Through Pia de Cima, the road twists itself into mind-boggling contortions as it tackles unnerving inclines; it then deposits you in a rare flat area at the top of the village. Your path leads up to the left by the low wall beside the shop.

Ascending from Pia, you pass houses and the school. Even at the peak of the dry season, water may be rushing down the sides of the path from the pine-clad slopes above. Some 25 minutes after leaving Pia, you will crest a rise and find yourself looking down on the small settlement of **Agriões**. From where you are standing, you can see the path you will take weaving to and fro across the ridge that rises up behind the village.

Ten minutes will bring you down among the houses of Agriões. Carry on around a sharp hairpin between two houses and continue down to a *grogue* still. There are two forks here in quick succession: the first is of two narrow paths (turn left) and the second of two wider paths (turn left again). Your path crosses the valley floor, and after another few minutes leads you up the ridge. Ten minutes from the valley floor, the cobbled surface stops, and you will find yourself battling up a tough incline. To survive the next half-hour, up a steep and winding path, you need to be quite fit. The path will take you to the right at a fork, just above a small house. It is all worth it when you finally emerge on a breathtaking ridge, with a deep valley on either side and Agriões behind and below you. There is a small farmer's hut nearby, with arguably the best view in Cabo Verde.

Ten minutes from the ridge, turn left at a T-junction. From here, the path zig-zags up and up, affording great views to the north if you are lucky enough not to be caught in mist. Now you are facing the challenge of making your way up narrow paths of crumbling rock. At one point the path is so narrow and the walls so high that it is almost as if you are entering a cave. After 20 minutes, the path flattens out and, within a few minutes, goes up a shallow ridge towards a low thatched cottage. Bear right past the cottage and, after a few minutes, you will find yourself walking along the right side of a wide, low valley. Some 20 minutes beyond the thatched cottage you will emerge on a further, smaller ridge. Follow the path down towards the valley floor on your left.

After 10 minutes bear left at a fork. You are now in a desert-like area barren of greenery, the path at the mercy of shifting winds. The path may be hard to distinguish so confirm the route that follows with passing locals.

Five minutes after the previously mentioned fork bear right at a second fork and start ascending towards the road at **Lin d'Corv**, which you will reach after just over 10 minutes. There is not much at Lin d'Corv except a single house and a large area of the hillside concreted over and walled in to collect rainwater.

Turning left on to the road, it will take about 20 minutes to walk the 1.5km to **Espongeiro**. Wait here for a lift back down to Ribeira Grande. *Alugueres* run all day, though sometimes it can be an hour's wait.

5 ESPONGEIRO–LIN D'CORV–JOÃO AFONSO–CHÃ DE COELHO–FIGUEIRAL–COCULI
Distance: 10.5km; time: 3½ hours; difficulty: 3 (CW)

This hike involves a steep and spectacular descent into the head of João Afonso on a good, cobbled path. It can be shortened by getting transport to Coculi at Chã de Coelho. Get to the starting point by taking an *aluguer* along the Ribeira Grande–Porto Novo road as far as Espongeiro.

Standing on the main road from Ribeira Grande, take the turning at **Espongeiro**, known as the Lagoinha road. Walk for 1.5km until you reach **Lin d'Corv**, where there is a large area of hillside concreted over to collect rainwater. The path down João Afonso begins here. Be careful not to confuse it with the path to Chã de Pedra – the two paths meet at Lin d'Corv. It is important to pick up the right path, otherwise you will end up descending the wrong valley. Stand with your back to the tap at the bottom of the water catchment area, and then follow the path off to your right. The path will lead you down along the side of a low hill through a pine forest, and after about 10 minutes you will see a cottage at the top of a small rise. Take a small turning down to the right about 15m before reaching the cottage.

After less than 10 minutes you will reach a few houses at **Lombo de Pedra**. Pass through the settlement and, 5 minutes later, follow the white arrow painted on a rock to begin a series of zig-zags down the side of the mountain. From here, the path becomes dramatic, sometimes darting backwards and forwards, sometimes tracing down the knife edge of precipitous ridges, and sometimes carving across near-vertical slopes. After a vertiginous 35 minutes, you will pass a tapstand where clear water runs from the mountains above, and will be looking out over the village of **Fajã dos Cumes**.

Continuing the descent, another 30 minutes will bring you to the small village of **Caibros** (not to be confused with the *ribeira* of Caibros) and another 35 minutes beyond that, to **Chã de Coelho**. Passing through here and descending steeply for 10 minutes will bring you to the valley floor in João Afonso. From the point where you hit the valley floor, it will take about an hour to reach **Coculi**.

6 ÁGUA DAS CALDEIRAS–RIBEIRA DE TORRE–RIBEIRA GRANDE
Distance: 10km; time: 4 hours; difficulty: 2 (AI)

Torre is the most beautiful *ribeira* of them all: a descent from empty, misty pine forest through the clouds, down a steep rocky path with just the jagged peaks and the more adventurous birds for company, and finally through greenery and cultivation to sea level. Navigation is easy but the path is steep. To get to the start of the walk take an *aluguer* along the old Ribeira Grande–Porto Novo road to **Água das Caldeiras**. From Ribeira Grande this takes 40 minutes, and you should disembark at the first sign for the village on the right-hand side of the road. (To do this walk the other way round, leave Ribeira Grande on the Porto Novo road, passing the petrol station, and then the hospital, on the right. Torre is the great *ribeira* on the left.)

Take the cobbled road to the left, fenced off with a chain, and follow it uphill for 10 minutes enjoying the sharp coolness. Then take a wide stone track to the left and descend, always through forest. Pine trees were chosen for reforestation because their needles comb water from the clouds which drips down and moistens the soil.

After another 10 minutes there's a clearing. A footpath leads out of the far end. Take it and emerge at a vista of high craggy mountains dropping way below to patches of vivid green, tiny houses and, even this high, the sounds of barking dogs and voices echoing towards you. Two *ribeiras* lie before you – Torre is to the left and after 15 minutes of steep descent you realise you are firmly destined for it as you see the teeth-like crags that now separate you from next-door Paúl. The view is infinitely interesting: crazy terraces inserted into crevices; intriguing local paths disappearing into rock faces.

After 1½ hours you reach the first cultivation. After this, just continue downwards, through coffee and banana crops and past shallow shelving built to capture water. Sometimes the path follows a terrace – there are lots of people around by now so just ask for the footpath (*caminho*).

Ahead is the strange pinnacle of Torre, a rock that has defied the forces of wind and water to rise out of the middle of the *ribeira*. As you descend you pass the extraordinary hamlet of **Rabo Curto**, built on a ridge just wide enough for a row of one-room-thick houses and a footpath. About 2½ hours from the beginning, the path meets **Xôxô** (Chu Chu) village, green and damp, with dark cliffs on either side. It's another 1½ hours, or 6km, to **Ribeira Grande** along the road track down the *ribeira*. If you are lucky the *grogue* distillery 20 minutes down the road on the left will be in operation. Ten minutes before the end of the walk there is a glimpse of the sea through the crack in the mountains.

7 ILA DAS POMBAS–RIBEIRA DO PAÚL–EITO–PASSAGEM–COVA DE PAÚL

Distance: 9km; time: 4½ hours; difficulty: 3 (AI)

This is many people's favourite, in a huge, abundantly green valley cloistered among vast, cathedral-like cliff walls. It is so large that there are many villages on the way up, crammed on to every available ledge. Laughter, barks, clucks, arguments, drunkenness, car horns and radios resound through the valley so that even when you have left them below, and the clouds have intervened, their sounds pursue you into the peaks.

The starting point is **Cidade das Pombas** but you can cut over 1½ hours (and a lot of sweating) from this walk by taking transport up the *ribeira* – the road persists as far as Cabo de Ribeira. Perhaps a good compromise is to take transport beyond Eito as far as the drop-off point for Casa das Ilhas and pick up the hike from there.

From Pombas turn inland at the stadium to enter the valley. Reaching an aqueduct after 10 minutes, take the road up to the right, and leave the valley below, filled with cornfields and deep green trees. The road ascends through various villages including **Eito**, the biggest. Some 2.5km after entering the valley, and less than 1km after leaving Eito, the road bends back sharply to the right. Soon after this you will see a little sign, just after a shop, on the wall on the left, to the guesthouse Casa das Ilhas. Take this path, which leads you on a glorious route and cuts out a loop of the road.

You will pass Casa das Ilhas after about 15 minutes of steep ascent. Keep going, the only navigational challenge being a T-junction of paths with a wall in front of you, at which you turn left. The path continues, up and down, and eventually broadens into a road which takes you past flowing water, pools and verdant planting, up through Passagem. Half an hour after leaving Casa das Ilhas, you will reach the main road. Turn left to continue up the valley.

In **Passagem** there is a swimming pool filled with water every day during July and August (otherwise, with a day's notice, they'll refill it for you).

Keep going, through the villages of **Chã João Vaz** and **Chã Manuel dos Santos**. There are one or two places to stop for a drink (page 316). A couple of hours later you will finally leave the most vertiginous local house behind and follow the finely crafted cobbled path with its drystone walling, gazing upwards to wonder how it can possibly take you through the mountains above. Four hours from the start (assuming no stops), your lonely world of cold and cloud will push you over the top of the ridge and you will be gazing down into a fertile volcano crater filled with crops, orange trees, tomatoes and a few houses. Your exit from the crater is on the opposite side; reach it by following a stumbling path down to the right and into the crater, and then a track across it and out on to the road where, if you walk for a few seconds to the left, you find the final spectacle of the walk – the southern slopes of Santo Antão, Porto Novo and São Vicente beyond. Wait here for a lift back to town.

To go down the *ribeira* instead of up, take a lift along the main island road as far as **Cova**, which lies on the eastern side of the road and has two entrances – you want the one nearer to Ribeira Grande. As you enter Cova you will see the path you want leading up and out of the crater on the other side. Once you are on it, it's the same path down to the coast road.

8 PENEDO–RIBEIRA DO PENEDO–ESTÂNCIA DE PEDRA–PICO DA CRUZ–COVA

Distance: 14km; time: 5 hours 40 minutes; difficulty: 3 (CW)

Not for the unfit or faint-hearted, this long hike demands a high degree of fitness and takes you from sea level up to 1,600m in little more than 7km. After that, it is a less demanding 1-hour walk to the main road.

Reach the starting point by taking an *aluguer* along the coast road as far as the little village of **Penedo**, which lies at the mouth of the *ribeira* of the same name.

You strike up the *ribeira* on foot and the climb begins almost immediately, weaving among sugarcane plantations and the scattered houses. Follow the path up to the head of the valley and round to where it begins a tortuous zig-zagging ascent up an impossibly steep mountain face. If, as you pause for breath, you look back towards the coast, you will see the smaller Ribeira de Janela running parallel to Ribeira do Penedo, and slightly to the north.

There are small paths that lead off to the right and left but, sticking to the main path, you emerge on a narrow shoulder about 2 hours after setting out from Penedo. As you continue to ascend, it turns into a narrow ridge with staggering views first down one side, then the other, and a fantastic panorama to the south, east and north. If it is a clear day, **Pico da Cruz** can be seen ahead.

Even at this height (800m), the vegetation has changed – it is much greener here than on the ridges that lead, like dry ribs, to either side. Higher up it becomes cold and alpine with a sharp, resinous smell among the trees.

Along the ridge there are several houses. People have erected frames stretched across with gauze to allow the mist that boils over from the *ribeira* below to condense. After 1½ hours of walking along the ridge, you pass one of these frames and, at the same point, see the cobbled main road that snakes up from the valley towards the Pico. The road is slightly down to your left. Keep to the path, and, after 15 minutes, you join the road, and emerge, after another 40 minutes of steep hairpins, at a small group of houses in the shadow of the summit. Turn right on the road to Paúl past the old, white-painted house. Directly behind the house follow the very rough path which cuts up to the right. It's a 15-minute walk to the summit.

Retracing your steps from the summit to the small settlement, rejoin the road you arrived on and follow it straight on towards **Cova** (crater) and **Água das Caldeiras**. Following this road as it gently descends you will get your first glimpse of the crater about 45 minutes after leaving the summit. Ten minutes later you arrive at a crossroads. This is a good place to wait for a lift, or an *aluguer* back to either Porto Novo or Ribeira Grande.

9 CORDA–TERRINHA VERMELHA–COCULI
Distance: 6km; time: 2½ hours; difficulty: 2 (MS)

A delightful downhill walk, steep in places and with easy transport connections back to Ribeira Grande at the end. Steepish descents in places, tough on the knees, but otherwise not physically demanding.

To get to the start from Ribeira Grande, take an *aluguer* from outside the fuel stations to Corda (150$ if shared, 1,500$ if private hire, though try negotiating

> **LESS DEMANDING WALKS**
>
> The bases of many of the *ribeiras* provide flat walks with mighty views up the canyons. The best such walk is up Ribeira de Torre as far as Xôxô (Chu Chu) (page 334). Ribeira Grande provides a less interesting flat walk. All the *ribeiras* can be ascended quite far by vehicle, at which point you can walk back downhill. Ribeira do Paúl would be a particularly dramatic venue for this option. Finally, it is worth travelling up to Cova de Paúl for an easy wander around the crater (page 314).

down to 1,000$). The drive up to Corda, if you haven't already experienced it, is quite stunning. If you're in private hire, insist on photo stops.

Get the driver to drop you off at the **Mercearia Pecnin**, the small shop on the right where you can get drinks. Walk back 15m down the road and take the wide dirt road that veers off to the left, running parallel with the main road. After 200m, reach a fork at which you go left, with a primary school on your right. This wide road begins to descend fairly steeply, on a rocky base. Ahead of you is a bank of narrow terraces, built by slave labour under Portuguese colonial rule. The path narrows slightly, descending to a concrete-topped dam, but instead of crossing it, turn right to follow a rough cobbled path downwards, buildings on your left and more terraces on your right. Descending some rough stone steps, with the *ribeira* – often dry – on your left, you soon cross the *ribeira* to continue with a 2m-high stone wall on your left. Continue down with the watercourse now on your right. Soon the path leaves it far below and turns left under power lines, revealing the first of several stunning views down into the depths of the valley far below. The path now takes you around to the left. Continue down, ignoring a path that cuts back sharply to your right. You are now heading towards a rock pinnacle. After a period of descent on a particularly rocky path, you reach a grassy ledge beneath a rock face. Continue along the ledge and when the cliff reaches a corner, the path takes you sharp left. In front of you now, way below, are the villages of **Terrinha Vermelha** on your right and **Top D'Jock** on your left; slightly beyond you can see the buildings of your ultimate destination, Coculi, the main road and the dry bed of Ribeira Grande. The descent now takes you down a wide cobbled path; where the cobbles come to an end, at the top of a narrow *ribeira*, ignore a narrow path that leaves to your left. Continue right; the path then bends right and Coculi is directly in front of you, still some distance away. The path now temporarily levels out, and you continue along a narrow ledge beneath a cliff face. Terrinha Vermelha and Top D'Jock now loom larger below you. (The ledge becomes really narrow here at one point; if rain damage has made it impassable, you can return to the end of the cobbles, and take the path you ignored. This will eventually lead you down to the main road, though further up the Ribeira Grande.) Assuming it is passable, the path now begins its descent again on cobbles. On reaching the first building of Terrinha Vermelha (a small white square house), turn right to descend again on cobbles to reach a public washing area. Ahead of you now is a pretty, narrow passage between two rows of houses, but you turn down steps to the left immediately beyond the washing-up area. Continue to follow the wide path as it winds downwards, reaching a wider cobbled road at which you turn right and reach **Coculi** after 10 minutes. There are a couple of bars in the village and a church with (apparently) the largest bell in Cabo Verde. If you're lucky, meals might be available in one of the bars, but they should be able to rustle you up a sandwich in any event. Wait on the main road for a ride back to Ribeira Grande town (75$) if you've not pre-arranged a taxi pick-up.

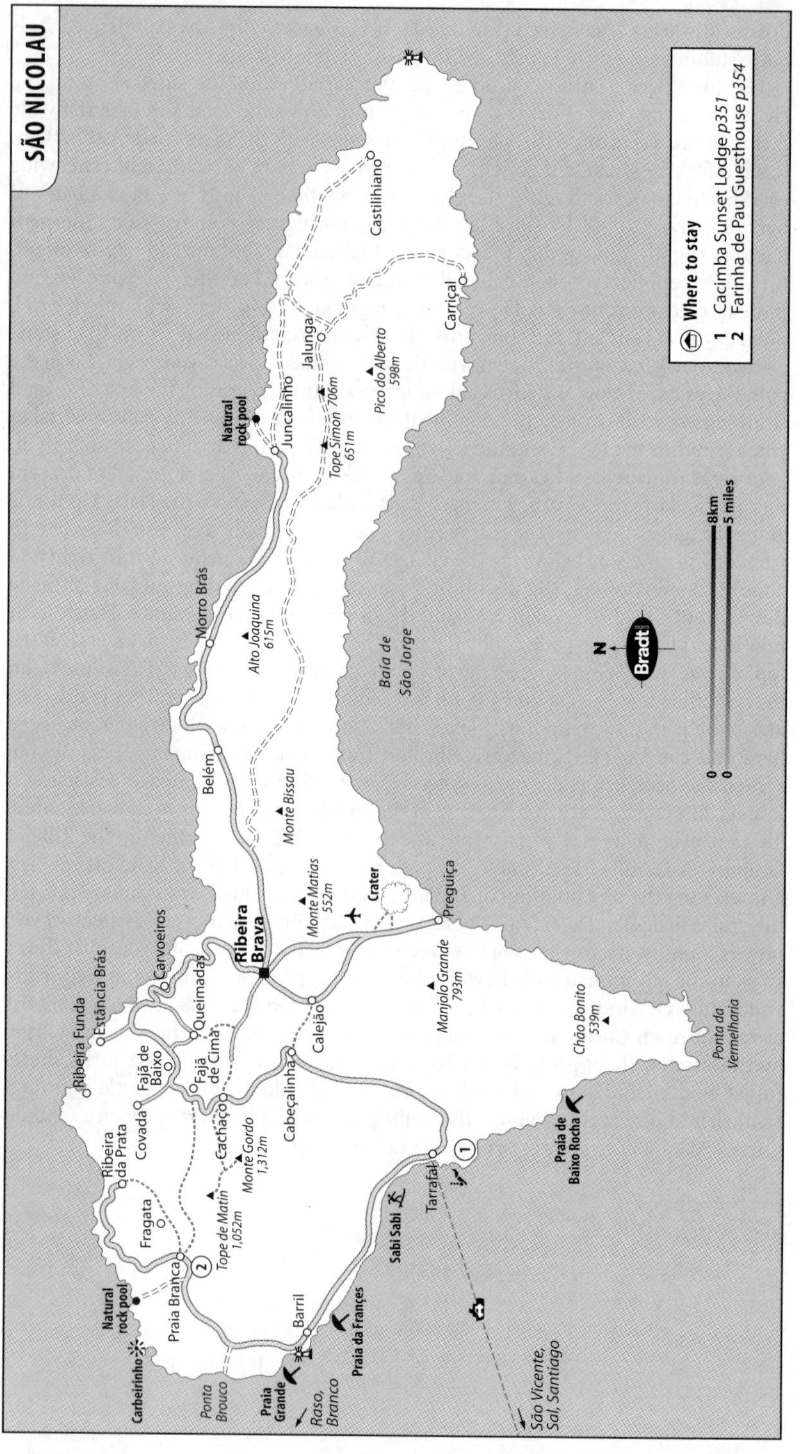
SÃO NICOLAU
Where to stay
1 Cacimba Sunset Lodge p351
2 Farinha de Pau Guesthouse p354
0 8km
0 5 miles
Bradt
N
Baía de São Jorge
Natural rock pool
Juncalinho
Jalunga
Castilhiano
Carriçal
Pico do Alberto 598m
Tope Simon 706m
651m
Morro Brás
Alto Joaquina 615m
Belém
Monte Bissau
Monte Matias 552m
Crater
Preguiça
Ribeira Brava
Carvoeiros
Estância Brás
Ribeira Funda
Queimadas
Fajã de Baixo
Fajã de Cima
Calejão
Manjolo Grande 793m
Chão Bonito 539m
Ponta da Vermelharia
Praia de Baixo Rocha
Cabeçalinha
Cachaço
Covada
Ribeira da Prata
Monte Gordo 1,312m
Tope de Matin 1,052m
Fragata
Praia Branca
Natural rock pool
Carbeirinho
Ponta Brouco
Barril
Praia da Françes
Praia Grande
Raso, Branco
Sabi Sabi
Tarrafal
São Vicente, Sal, Santiago

11

São Nicolau

Mother dear
I wanted to say my prayer
but I cannot:
my prayer sleeps
in my eyes, which cry for your grief
of wanting to nourish us but being unable to do so.

Baltasar Lopes, born on São Nicolau, quoted in *Fire: Six Writers from Azores, Madeira and Cape Verde* edited by Donald Burness (Three Continents Press, 1977)

It was in the shady valley of Ribeira Brava on São Nicolau and along the civilised cobbled streets of its town that, towards the end of the 19th century, the seeds of Cabo Verdean identity were planted. São Nicolau was for over 50 years the intellectual centre of the archipelago. Yet by 1931, its educational buildings had closed and the scholars had vanished to neighbouring São Vicente. Now Ribeira Brava, the capital, has an air of quiet dignity like a university town in the holidays. For all the island's austere beauty, it receives less than 1% of Cabo Verde's tourists and its population is declining. It is a victim, as Maio has been, of being the neighbour of a busy centre of commerce. But this can make São Nicolau a joy to visit. The *vila* is still pretty and there are several outstanding walks in the mountains, affording the visitor the opportunity to get close to village life.

HIGHLIGHTS AND LOWLIGHTS

This island has a little bit of everything the other islands have: an atmospheric main town with colonial architecture; long, deserted (black) beaches; villages frozen in time; dramatic cliffside roads; and some verdant mountains. Go for beautiful walks almost undisturbed by other tourists. Go for fishing: the island's waters are famed for their blue marlin. Go for diving, and discover a pristine marine ecosystem. Go to enjoy the daily routines of the local people, maybe joining them in one of their festivals where you may be a focus of their friendly curiosity. If you are not a hiker, you can still access some of São Nicolau's beauty by road though you will not be able to penetrate the Monte Gordo Natural Park.

There's a lot of potential for this to be an aquatic adventure destination, but its shore, breaks and dive sites remain remarkably unpeopled. There is now one dedicated dive outfit in Tarrafal, and perhaps more will follow. There are some prized, and accessible, beaches but it is far from a luxury flop-on-the-sand-type place and there are no resorts or high-end hotels. Surfers will need to bring their own boards, unless they can rustle up a loan from a local. The coast also offers other joys such as rocky, wave-lashed dramas and a couple of cliffside *lagoa* suitable for swimming.

Culturally, São Nicolau's interesting history has not yet been gathered together for presentation to the visitor, and there are no significant museums. On the flip side, as a lived culture, it remains more authentically itself than anywhere else in the country.

SUGGESTED ITINERARY AND NUMBER OF DAYS For hikers, Monte Gordo Natural Park, with its facilitation of guiding, advice and accommodation offers all sorts of interesting possibilities for walks across or around the centre of the island over several days. One could easily fill two or three full days with walks, with perhaps a day of sightseeing in-between. If you are a really committed hiker, then you could comfortably spend a lot longer here. If you are not, you could still fill two full days with perhaps a trip to Juncalinho's *lagoa*, and a drive through the island between Ribeira Brava and Ribeira da Prata, with many stops on the way.

BACKGROUND INFORMATION

HISTORY With a fertile hinterland and several almost permanent streams, São Nicolau was able to produce more agriculturally than the impoverished flat islands. It also has the widest bay of the archipelago, formed by the island's strange long finger that stretches to the east and affords a safe anchorage. Yet São Nicolau has always been overshadowed by others and so, apart from the brief flourishing of its seminary a century ago, it was never an island of importance.

It was discovered, along with the other windward islands, in 1461 – the date was probably St Nicholas's Day, 6 December. Families from Madeira and their Guinean slaves came to settle in the early 1500s. But the island was mountainous and inaccessible – indeed its lush interior is completely hidden from the outside – and so its productive agriculture and livestock potential did not attract more settlers until the 1600s. Even then, when the English sailor Dampier visited in 1683, he reported only 100 families on the island. He described the green interior, the vineyards producing good-quality wine, the abundance of wood and the great number of donkeys and goats. But even by 1731, there were only 260 inhabitants.

One great disadvantage of São Nicolau was the ease with which marauders could attack. Dutch, English and French pirates plagued the people, even after they retreated from their coastal settlement to Ribeira Brava, inland. It was not until a fortress was built in 1818 that security and a soaring population came to the island.

In 1805, the wealthy landowner who governed the island, José António Dias, had a son, Júlio José. He was a brilliant student but returned from his medical studies abroad to spend his life as a philanthropist on São Nicolau. Perhaps his greatest legacy came from his decision to move out of his large house in Ribeira Brava in 1866 and offer it to the three canons, three priests and three students who had arrived from Portugal to found a seminary on Cabo Verde. This prevented them leaving for Santo Antão, having despaired of finding a building on São Nicolau.

The *liceu* attached to the seminary flourished, offering the same subjects as high schools in Portugal. Suddenly the brightest Cabo Verdean children were able to learn subjects as varied as the classics, chemistry and political economy. This education groomed them for careers in either the Church or the Portuguese civil service. In this way Cabo Verde became the centre for evangelisation of Portuguese West Africa, along with its politicisation.

The impact created by the generations that passed through the Seminário-Liceu de São Nicolau should not be underestimated, for they spread abroad, used by the Portuguese as an interface between themselves and their West African territories.

They were articulate and intelligent, wedded to the idea of Cabo Verde being part of Portugal, but nevertheless, deeply concerned with the lot of their people. As teachers and administrators they had influence over the next generation, which took their ideas and moulded them into more radical form. The prime example of such a two-generation process was Juvenal Cabral, the seminary-educated teacher who fought for better conditions for Cabo Verde and whose son was Amílcar Cabral, the leader of the revolution and one of the most revered political thinkers of the 20th century.

But the life of the seminary was all too brief. It was a victim of the difficult relationship that emerged between the Catholic Church and the government in the democratic republic of Portugal after the Church was separated from the state in 1911. This separation led to the splitting of the seminary – with its precious *liceu* relocated to Mindelo.

The seminary closed in 1917, reopened in 1923, and shut forever in 1931. For the next couple of years it was used to accommodate around 400 political prisoners from an uprising in Madeira, and subsequently from mainland Portugal. The Bishop of Cabo Verde, rumoured to be terrified by 'hordes of deported revolutionaries and anti-clericals', fled to São Vicente. All that remained was a highly educated peasant population, joined by many of the prisoners who, once released, decided to stay on. One visitor in the 1930s was astonished when a local boy, prompted by a reference in Kriolu to a rose, quoted: '*Rosa, vita tua diuturna non est.*'

The 20th century brought desperate **droughts** to São Nicolau, in 1921, 1940 and the 1950s. There was some light, though. In the late 1960s, or so the story went, the 20th century also brought synthesisers to the island. In a now debunked tale, a ship transporting the latest Moog and Korg keyboards set out for Brazil but instead

FESTIVALS ON SÃO NICOLAU

Festivals draw on the strong Cabo Verdean tradition of music and dancing. Carnival is an exhilarating, exhausting three-day party (page 346). New Year is also cause for big celebration, as is Epiphany on 5 January. In April there is Pascoela, celebrated in Fajã – mass followed by games, horse races and processions. There are many festivals through the summer, including one lasting two days in Juncalinho, as well as São Pedro which is best seen in Ribeira Brava where horses are raced recklessly along the dry riverbed. Festival dates are as follows:

February or March (variable date)	Carnival
April (variable date)	Pascoela (Fajã)
13 April	Santo António (Preguiça)
Early May (variable date)	Nossa Sra do Monte (Cachaço)
24 June	São João (Praia Branca, with horse racing)
29 June	São Pedro (*vila* and Fajã Lompelado, with horse racing)
Sunday following 29 June	São Pedrinho (Prainha beach, near the *vila*)
August	Music festival (Praia da Tedja, Tarrafal)
September	Sweet Water festival (Ribeira da Prata)
1st Sunday in October	Nossa Sra do Rosário (in the *vila*)
1st Sunday in December	São Francisco (Tarrafal)
6 December	Municipality Day

> ### THE MONTE GORDO NATURAL PARK
>
> Although there are 47 protected areas in Cabo Verde, enshrined in law, all but Monte Gordo have an Achilles heel: their precise, mapped boundaries have not been legalised. This leaves them vulnerable. On Boavista, for example, there are several areas where land originally allocated for protection has been reallocated for tourism development instead.
>
> On São Nicolau, however, the boundaries of its beautiful heart were officialised in 2007. Much work has been done and more is still underway to create a park that is compelling for tourists and might enhance the prosperity of the people who live there.
>
> The park occupies some 952ha in the northwest of the island, and includes the peak of Monte Gordo.
>
> It's an important area ecologically because of its rich biodiversity. The unique conditions that have generated this interesting ecology set it apart, not just from the rest of the island but also from the rest of Cabo Verde. At the heart of these differences is climate, which affects not just life in the area but also landscape. In the south and southeast there are humid and semi-humid regions. In the north and northwest it is arid.
>
> A key aim of the park is to develop a thriving local economy predicated on conservation of the area: over 2,000 people live within the park boundaries. This is why a lot of thought has gone into training guides (who are salaried), and training local people to be useful to visitors, for example by making handicrafts. There is a good park office (page 346) where you can get information and purchase handicrafts made exclusively on the island. The park certainly has potential, yet to be fulfilled.

disappeared, its cargo washing up on one of the west coast's beaches (page 347). Whatever the truth, the banned *funaná* did become electrified, even if it wasn't via this unlikely cargo, and the story serves to illuminate the tenacity and creativity that characterise this very special island, not to mention the deeply mystical undercurrent that many claim to feel here.

SÃO NICOLAU TODAY Agriculture, and the port at Tarrafal, are the economic mainstays. Catching and canning tuna keeps the occupants of Tarrafal busy, though the second factory at the remote, eastern village of Carriçal closed some time ago. The island hopes to eventually develop ecotourism and beach tourism, though these are still in their infancy. The domestic airline woes of 2024 (page 73) hit São Nicolau hard, with a lack of flights meaning many cancellations and even fewer visitors than usual. The island's small band of tourism operators is, at the time of writing, lobbying the government hard to find solutions, especially the possibility of installing airport lighting to allow for night arrivals and departures.

GEOGRAPHY At 343km^2, the island is mainly barren rock with a large semi-humid valley in its centre, cultivated with maize and beans on the higher slopes, and sugarcane and banana below. In the west is a range of mountains with the highest, Monte Gordo, reaching 1,312m. This peak is the meeting point of two ranges – one runs north–south and the other out to the northwest. The eastern finger of land is a long ridge of barren mountains. Between the central mountains and the western coast are stony plains. Desertification seems to have hit São Nicolau particularly hard – its orange groves and coffee plantations are long gone and the old folk reminisce about verdant mountainsides that are now bare – in fact the lines of stone walls that used to divide fields can be traced impossibly high up the mountainsides. There is evidence of much reafforestation. The population is currently about 13,300.

FLORA AND FAUNA
Flora There are 46 endemic species of plant on São Nicolau, of which 32 can be found in the Monte Gordo Natural Park. One of these, Macela do Gordo (*Nauplussmithii*), is native to Monte Gordo and 17 are on the list of endangered species for the island of São Nicolau.

The fairy-tale dragon tree (*Dracaena draco*), locally known as *dragoeiro*, is almost abundant on this island – this is about the only place in the archipelago where the endangered species grows naturally. It can reach about 10m high and its flattened top and grey gnarled branches give the landscape the feel of an ancient world – it is said the trees can live for 1,000 years. The 'blood' of the dragon tree has been used in traditional medicines to relieve pain and is also used to colour *grogue*. The tree grows mainly on northeast-facing slopes at altitudes of between 500m and 900m, but the lazy way to see it at its finest is to walk from the main road up the access road to the Monte Gordo Park office. Some fine specimens line the route. Conservationists are trying to use it more in reafforestation programmes. The dragon tree is an endemic species of Macaronesia – it grows in the Canary Islands and in Madeira, where it is also endangered.

Birds BirdLife International currently lists 30 Important Bird Areas in Cabo Verde, of which the islets of Raso and Branco are two and the central mountain range around Monte Gordo is another. This last area, running roughly between Fajã de Baixo and Praia Branca, is an important breeding area for the Cape Verde petrel (*Pterodroma feae*); there were thought in 1998 to be about 30 pairs, making its status 'near-threatened'. As recently as 2022, though, there were 84 pairs. Park guides may show you where they can be found, though you are more likely to hear rather than see them.

Other birds thought to frequent São Nicolau are the Cape Verde little shearwater (*Puffinus assimilis boydi*); the Cape Verde buzzard (*Buteo 'buteo' bannermani*); the rare endemic Cape Verde peregrine (*Falco peregrinus madens*); the spectacled warbler (*Sylvia conspicillata*); the blackcap (*Sylvia atricapilla*); and the endemic Cape Verde swift (*Apus alexandri*). Most people accept that the Cape Verde red kite

> **A CHANCE FIND**
>
> The endangered Cape Verde warbler (*Acrocephalus brevipennis*) was until recently thought to inhabit only Santiago. Then, in 1970, someone found a specimen of the bird stored at Centro de Zoologia, Lisbon. It was reported as having come from São Nicolau, so ornithologists decided to scour the island in the hope of finding some more. They were rewarded – by 1998, their surveys had identified eight territories in the northwest of the island although they believe the bird's long-term prospects there are poor. The bird is brown with a creamy throat, a long-pointed black beak and black feet. On São Nicolau it inhabits the forested areas of the park and nests in small, dense stands of cane (*Arundo donax*) along dry riverbeds.

(*Milvus milvus fasciicauda*) is now extinct on São Nicolau. For birds on Raso (such as the Cape Verde shearwater), see page 361.

SAFETY Some of the walks in this chapter are steep, especially in and out of Ribeira Brava, and the descents can be hard on older knees, no matter how fit their owners are. This is indicated in the text, but do heed local advice if you are concerned.

Swim in the *lagoas* only when the water is calm. Crime is almost unheard of, apart from the clandestine hunting of turtles.

GETTING THERE AND AWAY

BY AIR São Nicolau is served by twice-weekly direct Cabo Verde Airlines flights from either Sal, Mindelo or Praia. In a land of dramatic scenery, the descent into São Nicolau is one of the best. As it nears land, the plane veers suddenly between a jagged ridge and a volcano crater. In winter, flights can be cancelled at short notice, due to high winds. The tiny airport is a 10-minute drive from the main town.

From the airport to Ribeira Brava it costs 350$ in an *aluguer*. You might be able to charter one as a taxi, which will cost 1,000$.

BY FERRY The inter-island ferry service has been improved by the increase in the network provided by **CV Interilhas** (w cvinterilhas.com), though currently there are only twice-weekly services to Sal and São Vicente each. Flying is still the preferable way of getting there and away, due to the distance, rough sea conditions and regular delays or cancellations. From São Nicolau (Tarrafal) to Sal takes 8 or more hours (5,000$) and to São Vicente about 5 hours (2,850$). Buy tickets online at least a couple of hours before expected departure. Some cargo boats also take a limited number of passengers from Tarrafal to São Vicente.

BY YACHT The best anchorage is at the harbour of Tarrafal, and it's where you report to the marine police. There's no marina and there are no buoys. Should there be northeast winds rushing down the ravines towards you, it can be impossible to shuttle to land. There's also Preguiça – for a long time São Nicolau's main harbour – which is more exposed. Carriçal is a tiny, remote village with a pretty bay and shelter from the northeast winds. Anchor outside the cove.

GETTING AROUND

BY PUBLIC TRANSPORT *Alugueres* ply the road between the main square in Ribeira Brava and Tarrafal (50 minutes, sometimes longer; 500$). They travel intermittently all day, but are more frequent leaving Tarrafal before 08.30 and leaving Ribeira Brava between 09.30 and noon. Near the check-in time for plane departures, around 2 hours before, you'll find *alugueres* destined for the airport waiting in Ribeira Brava's square.

Alugueres also travel along the eastern ridge as far as Juncalinho (250$) and, very infrequently, on to Carriçal (800$). They go from Tarrafal north up the coast as far as Ribeira da Prata (around 450$). These follow the principle: into Ribeira Brava in the early morning, out of town around lunchtime, but you can usually pick up transport until nightfall. On Sundays, it's more difficult. Drivers are very keen for tourists to hire them as taxis, at roughly ten times the price. To avoid this, hang around nonchalantly until you are part of a group rather than approaching an empty minibus or truck, or simply insist that you will only travel *colectivo*. A new road has made travelling to Tarrafal much easier, although heavy rain can cause landslides in the wet season.

BY TAXI 'Taxis' are obtained by simply chartering an *aluguer*: Ribeira Brava to Tarrafal 3,200$; to Preguiça 1,000$. A day's hire might be as much as 12,000$.

BY CAR To reach outlying places accessed by dirt tracks, it is best to enquire about a jeep and driver from the *aluguer* drivers or at the town hall. A day's hire without a driver will cost around 6,500$, usually a little more for a 4x4. The latter is strongly recommended if heading off the main road or east to Carriçal.

Agência e Transporte Santos & Santos
[map, page 349] Ribeira Brava; 235 1830;
e fsantos57@hotmail.com. Car hire with or without driver.
Monte Gordo Rent a Car [map, page 349]
Ribeira Brava; 235 1280; m 992 8877;

e montegordorentacar@gmail.com. Based in an office upstairs in the Municipal Market.
Rotxa Skribida Tarrafal; 236 1827;
e rotxaskribida@gmail.com

BY BOAT A fishing boat can take you from Preguiça to Carriçal and from Carriçal to visit caves down the coast, though you may have to bargain hard to keep the cost under 12,000$ for the 2-hour journey.

WHERE TO STAY AND EAT

The two main centres are Ribeira Brava (*vila*) and Tarrafal. Hikers tend to stay in Ribeira Brava and anglers, divers and surfers in Tarrafal. There is a modest guesthouse in Preguiça and a decent one in Juncalinho. Praia Branca also has a good place, with the option for various activities. Both main centres have a small selection of restaurants, with fresh fish and seafood being ubiquitous in Tarrafal.

EXCURSIONS AND TOUR OPERATORS

For the services of a guide for a full day's hike, you could expect to pay between €80 and €140 (per guide, not per person), depending on your transport/lunch requirements.

Agência e Transporte Santos & Santos
[map, page 349] Ribeira Brava; 235 1830;
e fsantos57@hotmail.com. Organises trips & car hire (see above).
Paulinho Juncalinho; m 996 6191. An English speaker with a 4x4 who can do island tours or guided hikes.

Rotxa Skribida Tarrafal; 236 1827;
m 994 5146; e rotxaskribida@gmail.com;
w hikingsaonicolau.com. Guided hikes or tours by vehicle. Features hikes in the Juncalinho area; the owner, Toi d'Armanda, has very good spoken English. Can also arrange boat trips around Raso, if enough notice is given – permission is needed from the government.

ACTIVITIES

HIKING Hiking and fishing are the two big attractions of São Nicolau. Some walks are described on page 357. The mixture of verdant agricultural land, vertiginous *ribeiras*, craggy peaks and dry, arid landscapes all in such an unfrequented place is what makes São Nicolau so special. By far the most beautiful walks are in the mountainous interior, though we include one or two others as well. The walks can be divided, roughly, into two: those that are based on several steep and beautiful paths in and out of the *vila*; and those that lie west of the main road that runs through Fajã and Cachaço. Since this road runs in a horseshoe shape through the centre of the walking areas, you can alter some walks to suit: you can use local transport to shorten walks or to enable you to walk only downhill or only uphill – or you can sandwich several walks together. Rotxa Skribida (page 345) is one agency which does walks to the east of Ribeira Brava, among others.

The **Monte Gordo Natural Park** (page 342 encompasses many good walks and its visitors centre, Casa do Ambiente, can be found in Cachaço (\ 237 1582; e pnmonte. gordo@hotmail.com; park admission 300$, free on weekends). It is a new-looking building about 200m uphill along a track from the main Ribeira Brava to Tarrafal road. Here you can obtain information about the park and about hikes, collect a brochure/map, arrange a trained multi-lingual guide, and look at the little endemics garden. You can also arrange for lunch to be prepared for you when you've done your walk (approximately 600$ per person), book into the rooms or campsite, and buy some artisanal products or books on flora and fauna. There are plans to further increase facilities for tourists here, including setting up permanent café facilities and a shop.

The principal hikes within the park are signposted. Staff can find you homestay accommodation in Cachaço. The park regards itself as a resource for the whole of São Nicolau and may therefore be of assistance with walks that lie outside its boundaries.

> **SÃO NICOLAU CARNIVAL**
>
> If you ever catch yourself wondering how people on this quiet island entertain themselves then here is the answer: Carnival. It may last just three days but arguably the other 362 in the year are spent preparing for it.
>
> There is the music, for a start. Songs are written specially for the festival, dispersed, learned and rehearsed. But that's nothing compared with the costumes. The Carnival King's and Queen's outfits cost around 100,000$ (around €1,000) each to produce – and they look correspondingly spectacular. Anyone who wants to have a costume made, dance in the procession for all three days and get into the sponsored parties must budget for around 7,000$. The costumes are designed according to the theme of the year. Fittings are conducted blindfold so that the wearer has no idea what he or she is dressed as until the big day.
>
> By the first day of the festival the island has divided into two rival groups who spend 4 or 5 hours dancing and singing their way along different routes into the main square. Festivities continue into the next morning – the two rival, post-procession parties don't begin until around 03.00. After sleeping until mid-afternoon, the second day of festivities begins: pretty much a repeat of the first. Then there is a day of rest. On the third day of the festival (Fat Tuesday), many onlookers emerge in their own costumes. Even outside Carnival times, the evidence of this giant party is there to be seen: you may suddenly be confronted by the figurine of a full-size, papier-mâché elephant, starfish or even Donald Duck, abandoned in someone's garden – relics of the previous year's festivities. After all the work in creating them, it is sometimes too painful to destroy them.

FISHING The quality of the deep-sea fishing is high, particularly for blue marlin and barracuda. Off the island's southern bank, ten-plus blue marlin releases in a single day are not unheard of. Chartering a boat for blue marlin fishing requires a bit of planning because they generally have to come across from São Vicente. It is best to book beforehand. In the UK, for example, **Big Fish Charters** (w bigfishcharters.co.uk) has a boat moored in Mindelo that will do marlin runs off São Nicolau for around €600 a day. You could ask around Tarrafal, but if you do find someone, expect to pay no less than the European charters. The season runs from March to July.

BOAT TRIPS Local fishermen can be hired at Tarrafal for day trips. At Preguiça, you could also head down the coast, for example to caves, beaches or to the village of Carriçal.

DIVING The island is the best in Cabo Verde for shore dives. **São Nicolau Diving** (page 353) offers those and a range of other options.

BIRDWATCHING Birdwatching rates along with fishing and hiking as one of São Nicolau's prime attractions. For some of the birds that can be found on the island, see page 343.

Visits to Ilhéu Raso, to view, among others, the Raso lark, have been banned since 2007, after a clampdown by the government. As the island forms part of a marine reserve, this situation is unlikely to change. It is possible only to hire a fishing boat for around €100 per day and circle the island and its companion Ilhéu Branco.

As a consolation, it is worth visiting scenic Carbeirinho (page 354), where many of the migratory birds found on Raso also visit, and which some ornithologists believe should be given protected status.

TURTLES Loggerhead turtles nest here and are particularly abundant on beaches north and south of Tarrafal, Porto da Lapa and Carriçal. Sadly, turtles are still hunted for their meat on São Nicolau. The town halls in both Tarrafal and Ribeira Brava have turtle-conservation programmes in which you may be able to participate, though no 'turtle walks' are offered at present. Ask around at the town hall in Ribeira Brava, in case the situation changes. **São Nicolau Diving** (page 353) may also help you see them.

BEACHES If you wander the coast of São Nicolau you may make some discoveries of your own. There are beaches up the west coast from Tarrafal – for example Praia Grande, Praia Branca and Praia Francês. Porto da Lapa has a beautiful beach which is accessible either by fishing boat from Preguiça or by hiking from south of Juncalinho (you will need a guide). There's also a beach at Carriçal and Praia de Baixo Rocha is a pretty cove and important turtle-nesting beach a 1-hour walk south of Tarrafal. Be warned, however: beaches can temporarily disappear in bad weather.

SURFING There can be good surf on the coast north of Tarrafal. Sabi Sabi is probably the best-known place to start – it's a reliable, long right-hander point break, sheltered from strong winter winds, and varying from 1 to 3 footers. There is no equipment hire in Tarrafal, nor any surf camps or organised tours. You could, however, ask for advice from the owner of Farinha de Pau Guesthouse (page 354), who is a keen surfer.

HORSERIDING São Nicolau has a proud horse-racing tradition and horses are brought from other islands for the big races of the year at the festivals of São João and São Pedro. Riding for tourists is in its infancy, though you may be able to organise something through Daniel Cabral (m 981 6516) or his colleague Fernando (m 918 1449). Horses are fully equipped, but there are no riding hats, etc, for riders. Expect to pay around €20 per hour. The Cabo Verdean horses are slight in build, so would not suit heavier riders.

SIGHTSEEING BY VEHICLE One of the most spectacular roads in Cabo Verde is the road from Ribeira Brava to Tarrafal. This 26km route pulls out of Ribeira Brava and negotiates a series of deep creeks cut into the mountainside of the northern coast before turning inland to the lush Fajã Valley. Mountain ranges spike the right-hand side and you ascend gently through Fajã de Baixo (Lower Fajã) and Fajã de Cima (Upper Fajã), almost completely encircled by a ring of mountains. Then the road turns to the southwest and you enter the stony plains that lead down towards Tarrafal. After Tarrafal the land is flat and brown but it is worth following the odd signposted track down to the coast on the left to witness the beaches or the striking rock formations. Finally the road bends inland to Praia Branca and out in a semicircle, finishing in Ribeira da Prata. Many sights to see on the way are described on the following pages.

RIBEIRA BRAVA

Known as *Stancha*, or *Stanxa* to the locals, this is a pretty town with houses of ochre, green and blue, and neat gardens blooming with plants and flowers. It is wedged into the steep sides of a *ribeira*, leading to a charming chaos of steep, interlocking streets in some parts of town. Narrow cobbled streets lead away from the large *praça* – the Largo do Terreiro – and an imposing cathedral visited by the old women of the town every day. They have first claim to the wooden benches in the square, by the way. Lining the streets are surprisingly well-stocked, old-fashioned shops with quaint wooden counters in dim, shuttered interiors. The *ribeira* – green even in the dry season – towers above and cuts the town deeply in two, its narrow floor functioning as an extra road for much of the year, and an impromptu racetrack for horses during festivals. There is a charming statue of the town's famous poet, Baltasar Lopes da Silva, in the smaller square to the west of the main *praça*. Especially in low season, there are few restaurant options.

WHERE TO STAY Map, opposite
Accommodation is all of a good standard, budget to mid-range but limited, meaning it is sometimes booked up in high season. Reserve ahead.

Pensão Residencial Jardim (10 rooms) Up the hill at the southern end of town; ╲235 1117/1950; e pensaoresidencialjardim@hotmail.com. A sparkling white *pensão* with eccentric old-world charm, & a friendly, helpful owner & family. A terrace offers a shady retreat, with sweeping views down on to the pastels of the town below. Rooms have AC, TV & private bathrooms with hot water. There are 2 mini apartments with kitchenettes & options for families via interconnecting doors.

A rooftop restaurant (page 350) serves lunch & dinner, available on request. It's in a steep part of town, accessed along a short, uphill alleyway. French spoken, some English. **$$**

Pensão Santo António (15 rooms) Just east of the Largo do Terreiro gardens; ╲235 2200; e mcdossantos@cvtelecom.cv; pensaosantoantonio. This easy-to-spot pastel blue building has a bright, fresh feel with large rooms, some of which overlook the square, & a shared living room with TV. Rooms have private bathrooms, AC & TV, & some have a fridge. Free Wi-Fi in public areas. On-site restaurant for b/fast only. **$$**

Bela Sombra (20 rooms) Near the Igreja Nossa Senhora do Rosário; \235 1830; e fsantos57@ hotmail.com. The biggest in town & fairly new. Rooms are fine: 10 of them have AC, some with balcony, all with hot water. Corridors are a bit gloomy. Room facilities vary, as do prices, so ask to see what you're getting. Will organise car hire. **$**

Pousada Mana Guimara (6 rooms) Near the roundabout petrol station; \235 1830. Rooms all have minibars & TV; those at the front can be a little noisy. French-speaking owner is happy to organise excursions. **$**

WHERE TO EAT AND DRINK *Map, right*

Finding much choice here at times can seem quite a challenge, especially in low season. Having said that, fresh fish arrives daily from the coastal villages, announced by the tooting of pick-up truck horns, so it's well worth finding. Order several hours beforehand if you want something other than the dish of the day. The São Nicolau speciality is *molho* or *modje* – goat meat, potatoes and onions with cornmeal and rice – fairly rustic, if truth be told. In addition to the places listed here, there are a few rough-and-ready places on the road up to the old seminary. Fresh bread can be bought from the **bakery** on a little road off the post office square; vegetables are available from the municipal **market** (⊕ early–late daily), a gathering place for locals, selling cheap snacks and maybe some super-cheap fried fish portions, on the street running down to the *ribeira*. Ask around in the market and someone will find someone who will sell you some fresh goat's cheese.

Caverna A street back up from Largo do Terreiro; \235 2200; ⊕ 19.00–22.00 Mon–Sat. Tiny entrance & cellar-like corridor, leading up to a smart dining room with elaborate, throne-like chairs. Belongs to the Pensão Santo António; standards are good. **$$$**

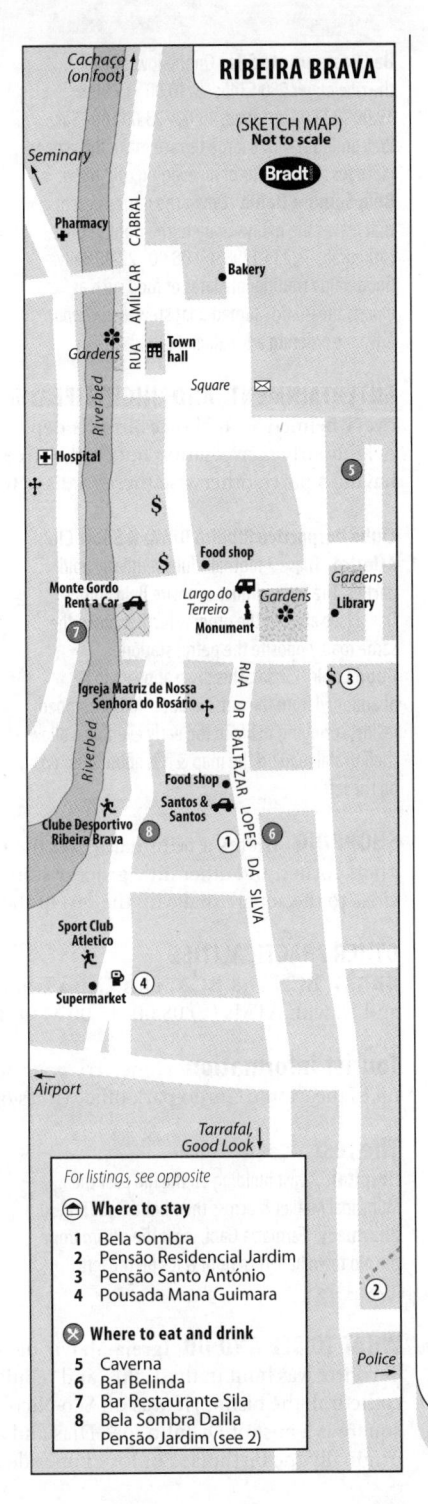

RIBEIRA BRAVA

(SKETCH MAP)
Not to scale

For listings, see opposite

Where to stay
1. Bela Sombra
2. Pensão Residencial Jardim
3. Pensão Santo António
4. Pousada Mana Guimara

Where to eat and drink
5. Caverna
6. Bar Belinda
7. Bar Restaurante Sila
8. Bela Sombra Dalila
   Pensão Jardim (see 2)

São Nicolau RIBEIRA BRAVA

11

349

Bar Restaurante Sila On the low side of the *ribeira*; m 980 5345; ⊕ 10.00–15.00 & 19.00–22.00 Sun–Wed, 10.00–23.00 Thu–Sat. Welcoming staff & a large terrace make this a good place for simple grills or an evening *caipirinha*. $$
Bela Sombra Dalila Down the narrow street that leaves the main square to the right of the cathedral; ☏ 235 1298; ⊕ 08.00–22.00 daily. Good-value traditional plates of food such as *modje*, the island's famed goat stew, & *cachupa*. Advance ordering advisable. $$

Pensão Jardim Page 348; ☏ 235 1117; ⊕ 07.30–22.00 daily; lunch when ordered, 19.00 onwards for dinner. Rooftop restaurant serving lunch & dinner, with a mostly traditional menu. Above the hotel of the same name. Lunch & dinner should be ordered in advance. $$
Bar Belinda On the main road in from Tarrafal; m 995 5409; ⊕ 08.00–22.00 Mon–Sat, 09.00–15.30 Sun. Popular with locals. Normally has a few very good-value & filling daily dishes & b/fast *cachupa*. Covered courtyard & inside tables. $

ENTERTAINMENT AND NIGHTLIFE The population of Ribeira Brava is not overwhelmed with choices in this department; entertainment is normally a bit of neighbourly conversation out on the streets. One of the two football clubs might be having a party, otherwise there's a disco to the south of the town centre.

Clube Desportivo Ribeira Brava & Sport Club Atletico These 2 football clubs regularly hold parties. The 1st is almost opposite Bela Sombra Dalila (see above), the other is further down the same road, opposite the petrol station.
Good Look ⊕ Sat. This disco appears to be abandoned from the outside but is fully equipped inside, springing to life in the early evening. Follow the Tarrafal road off the map & it is about 50m up, on the left.

Largo do Terreiro On Sat & Sun nights the town becomes very lively as people go to the *praça* to hang out & listen to a DJ or traditional music. In the old-fashioned way rarely seen on other islands any more, entire families arrive to chat, dance, play & socialise – young & old mixing, & everyone keeps an eye out for everyone else's kids. It's a lively crowd.

SHOPPING There's a minimarket on the road going north that has the BCA Bank on its corner, and other little grocery stores around the centre. A few Chinese shops close to the square make up the rest of the options.

OTHER PRACTICALITIES
Banks BCN and BCA, plus **Caixa Económica**, are all just off Largo do Terreiro and all with ATMs (⊕ 08.00–15.00 Mon–Fri).

Tourist information None. Try your accommodation choice or, for hiking, go up to the Monte Gordo park office (if it's open).

The rest
Hospital A vast building on the hill past the Municipal Market & across the ribeira; ☏ 235 1130
Pharmacy Farmácia Gabi; cross the *ribeira* from the old town hall, turn right & it's on the left; ☏ 235 1173

Police On the airport side of town, out beyond Pensão Jardim; ☏ 235 1152
Post office Opposite the back of the town hall; ⊕ 08.00–16.00 Mon–Fri

WHAT TO SEE AND DO Igreja Matriz de Nossa Senhora do Rosário, on Largo do Terreiro, was built in the 1700s, and rebuilt between 1891 and 1898 to become the cathedral: the bishopric was on São Nicolau between 1866 and 1940. In the main square is a bust of Dr Júlio José Dias and also the library, in the building that was originally the birthplace of José Lopes de Silva, one of Cabo Verde's major poets.

The **seminary** (page 340), is on Rua Seminário, a little way up the road away from the pharmacy, on the right. You can ask the priest's permission to explore its rambling buildings and courtyards and one of the knowledgeable priests in attendance may explain some of its rich history.

AROUND RIBEIRA BRAVA

FAJÃ DE BAIXO AND FAJÃ DE CIMA At the heart of the lush interior of São Nicolau, these villages have nothing specific to seek out but do offer some pleasant meandering and their verdant surrounds provide good photo opportunities.

CACHAÇO Here can be found more beauty, the office for the natural park, two viewpoints (*miradouros*) and a few small grocery stores, one of which sells a particularly fine goat's cheese: mild and perfect for a packed lunch.

Cachaço is the confluence of the main road, the track up into the natural park and two hiking paths, one from Fajã de Baixo and one up from Ribeira Brava.

There's also a small track to a viewpoint at the little church, Senhora do Monte. There's also another designated viewpoint just over 0.5km south down the main road, on the left.

Homestays in Cachaço can be organised through park office and visitors centre (page 346) and are very good value (**$**). Breakfast is included and other meals can be arranged. You can also stay at a **campsite** about 1.5km inside the park (Monte Gordo Natural Park; 5 rooms, 7 pitches for tents; organise through the park office; ☎ 237 1582/1829; **$**), where there are also basic twin and double rooms, some with private bathrooms. There is no hot water, but you can use the communal kitchen, which has a gas cooker, fridge, etc. Bring your supplies up from Cachaço (or Ribeira Brava, for a bigger range).

TARRAFAL

This impoverished port town lies at the base of stony, barren hills that betray little about São Nicolau's lush interior. The town feels parched and can reach 40°C in the summer. It is strung out along a very long coastal road. At the southern end of this road is the port. A block inland from the port is the long, main square. Plans to turn Tarrafal into a marina have not progressed to date, though there is still talk of transforming not just the harbour but also the main street.

WHERE TO STAY

Cacimba Sunset Lodge [map, page 338] (7 rooms) Around 15 mins' walk south of town; m 993 3581/983 7917; e info@cacimbasunset. com; w cacimbasunset.com. Peaceful & right on the water, with sea-facing pool & roof terrace. Simple, bright, ultra-clean rooms have en suites, & 1 has a balcony, for which it's worth paying the small extra. As the lodge of São Nicolau Diving (page 353), it attracts a good community of divers, watersports enthusiasts & the odd marine biologist. Along with dives & SUP rental, they can organise hikes, cooking classes, beach BBQs & shark sightings. B/fast inc, other meals by request. Solar powered. **$$**

Casa Patio (6 rooms) To the south of town, in Alto Calheta, overlooking the sea; m 973 7027; e info@casa-patio.de; w casa-patio.de. Welcoming B&B with a helpful owner who has good advice on hiking trails. Rooms have good-quality finishes & furniture, en suites & sea view. Some have balconies. **$$**

Edificio Magico (10 rooms) Overlooking Praia de Tedja beach; ☎ 236 1941; m 982 0301; e edimagico.com; w edificiomagico.com. Aparthotel with varying sizes of well-equipped if dated units, all with private bathrooms, fridges & basic cooking facilities & TV, some with AC. B/fast not inc but is available. Try for an upper unit: they're brighter. Sometimes closes in Jun. **$$**

Pensão Tocely (formerly Tonecas) (10 rooms, 2 apts) ✆ 236 1040; m 993 1398; e tonecas1959@ hotmail.com. Large, en-suite rooms, some with AC & all with hot water. Restaurant upstairs for guests only, Wi-Fi in public areas. **$$**

Residencial Alice (18 rooms) On the coast road, north of the port; ✆ 236 1187 m 598 6963; e aliceresidencial3@gmail.com. This family-run place has been an institution in Tarrafal for many years. Lots of old-world charm. Most rooms have a balcony with a view of the sea, & most have AC, private bathroom & hot water. Roof terrace. Ask for an upper room, if available: they're much lighter & brighter. **$$**

Zena Star Apartments (5 apts) On the right-hand side of the dry *ribeira*; m 976 2464;

e info@zenastar.com; w zenastar.com. Italian-owned, well-kept mini apartments ideal for those who want to self-cater. Sea views & great terrace. **$$**

Regina B&B (4 rooms) On the northern outskirts of town; ✆ 236 1860. Clean, tiled rooms with bathrooms (no hot water), balconies & basic kitchens. Views of the sea, & while quiet, still lots of local life around in the evening. B/fast €5 extra, despite the name. Friendly. **$**

Residencial Natur (7 rooms) ✆ 236 1178. Going north along the coast road, go past Residencial Alice, turn right just before the football pitch (the walled one on land, not the one on the beach) & then left – the hotel is on your right. Spacious, bright & simple, en-suite rooms have fans. Roof terrace with great views both inland & seaward. B/fast available, but not inc. About the cheapest in town, especially if you forego the hot water! **$**

✕ WHERE TO EAT AND DRINK

Casa de Pasto Alice (see Residencial Alice, above); ⊕ noon–23.00 daily. Thought by many to be the best eatery in Tarrafal, this is a large living room-type space serving traditional foods. It's wise to book in advance for anything beyond the *prato do dia*. **$$$**

Black Fish Club ⊕ noon–late daily. In front of a handsome former *residencial* building, which it shares with the delightfully kooky fishing museum. A few basic dishes, including pizza & fish, served on a pleasant terrace overlooking the beach & fishing boats. **$$**

Golfinho Opposite Pensão Tocely; ⊕ 08.00–22.00 daily. Standard fare, good-value *prato do dia*. Shady & breezy terrace, pub-like interior. Wi-Fi available. **$$**

Restaurant Bia Right down by the port; ✆ 236 1138; ⊕ 09.00–22.00 daily. Bright dining room in a colonial shopfront. Feels like eating with family: huge serves of sides, flash-grilled fish & kindness. **$$**

Restaurant Casa do Pescador North of the town, right on the beach; m 987 0297; ⊕ 11.00–midnight Mon–Wed, 11.00–02.00 Thu–Sat. Huge breezy outdoor terrace strung with fairy lights. Standard fish dishes & pizza. Great for a sunset cocktail. Reportedly stays open *super* late on weekends. **$$**

Gelateria Leon m 972 4256; ⊕ 09.30–22.00 Mon–Sat. Beyond Pensão Tocely, just before you reach the port. Cones as well as creative sundae cups. **$**

ENTERTAINMENT AND NIGHTLIFE Tarrafal does not have too much to offer in terms of nightlife, and locals advise against the Esplanada on the Praia de Tedja beach at night: it has a 'bad ambience'. If you're very lucky, you might find some live music in one of the restaurants listed.

OTHER PRACTICALITIES

Banks Caixa Económica and BCA (both ⊕ 08.00–15.00 Mon–Fri), both with ATMs, are both near the central mini roundabout.

Ferries Information and tickets for CV Fast Ferry are available from agency Praia d'Tedja (✆ 236 1155) up near the *câmara* building. The schedule is at best once weekly, fairly unreliable and subject to change. Occasionally, other boats come calling.

> **MEDICINAL SAND**
>
> Some of the black-sand beaches around Tarrafal and Barril, further north, are reputed to have healing powers, particularly in the alleviation of the symptoms of arthritis. It is thought they are high in iodine and titanium. Sufferers tend to bury themselves in the sand and lie there; some claim they have subsequently achieved relief for many months. The effective period is June to August.

The rest

Hospital Behind Praia de Tedja; 236 1130
Police 236 1132

Post office At the top of the main square; 08.00–16.00 Mon–Fri

WHAT TO SEE AND DO

Beaches A pretty and busy black-sand beach, **Praia de Tedja** is located just south of town. Locals swim near the fishing boats off the calm, main beach, the **Praia Campo Pedrada**. The **Praia de Baixo Rocha** is a 1½-hour walk south of Tarrafal. This beautiful pale sand cove is a wonderful, tranquil place to swim, as well as an important place for nesting turtles – the sticks you see in the summer are marking nests in the hope that people won't inadvertently destroy the eggs. It's a lonely walk over a landscape like burned fudge with dramatic views of the mountains beyond. Cross the town's southern cove (Praia de Tedja) and find the track leading south from it. You pass a yellow building on the left. You are making for a cove that lies between the furthest headland you can see and the second-furthest – a much lower, smaller headland. The trick is to avoid all the bulges of tiny headlands between you and the cove and stick to the main track. The route is possible in a 4x4 or can be done in a fisherman's boat for around 10,000$.

Diving South of town, **São Nicolau Diving** (m 975 4656; e info@saonicolaudiving.com; w saonicolaudiving.com) is a five-star PADI dive centre, the first on the island. They offer a number of boat (€50 pp) and shore dives (€40 pp) each day, with all equipment provided. Courses – including open water and divemaster training – free-diving, and SUP guided tours and rental can also be arranged. Well regarded, they also are dedicated to ocean conservation and scientific exploration of the island's marine environment.

NORTH OF TARRAFAL

The road northwest of Tarrafal follows fairly close to the shoreline until Barril, after which it cuts inland to Praia Branca, heads north out towards the coast again and then bends east, finishing in Ribeira da Prata. Along the coastal part of this road are several beautiful parts of coastline, including the beaches of Praia Grande and Praia da Françes, and Carbeirinho (all signposted), the last with its spectacular rock formations. Across the ocean you will see the outline of three of Cabo Verde's uninhabited islands, Raso, Branco and then Santa Luzia.

PRAIA DA FRANÇES A pleasant sandy beach just south of Barril. It's signposted, and also rumoured to be a great surfing spot.

PRAIA GRANDE Another attractive beach, with a rare backdrop of trees for shade. It's a beautiful place to watch the sunset and is known for its good beach fishing.

CARBEIRINHO After Barril, turn left off the road and follow the signposted but dusty and desolate track over the rocks, stopping short of the coast. This is a stretch of dramatic rock formations and undulating expanses of smooth black rock on which to sit and gaze at the crashing waves and abundant white foam. There are some steps carved into sandy rock down to the drama below. To the right of them is a deep inlet with stunning rock formations (be careful walking its circumference on the high side as there is a sharp overhang). Well worth detouring off the main road for this experience: it's considered one of the seven wonders of Cabo Verde, after all. If, after descending the steps, you head south, you will find after a few minutes a little *lagoa* in which you can swim when the weather is calm.

PRAIA BRANCA An attractive hillside town, known as the home of the late Armando Zeferino Soares, composer of iconic *morna* hit 'Sodade' (page 44). The village, marked by a stone entrance arch, has a few typical shops, bars, cafés and one accommodation and activities option. Just south of town, take the rough track down to the right, marked Boca Ribeira. This is an area popular with donkeys and goats, which is why much of the agriculture is fenced off. When you reach the ocean, 200m off to your right is a **natural rock pool**, suitable for a dip (the sea beyond is too rough).

Where to stay and eat Map, page 338

Farinha de Pau Guesthouse (3 rooms) m 915 3916; e contact@farinhadepau.com; w farinhadepau.com. Coming from Tarrafal, it's the 1st house on the right, just after the Boca Ribeira signpost to the left. Brazilian Sergio & his Cabo Verdean wife Simone offer 3 very basic rooms in their eco-conscious establishment. Simone made the bricks & Sergio used them to make the walls! Excellent meals available with the hosts, inc vegetarian & vegan options. Superb b/fasts. Sergio can advise on hikes, surfing & snorkelling (though no equipment is supplied). He also has 2 good-quality bikes for hire. Airport transfers (extra cost), or public transport available from Ribeira Brava. **$$**

RIBEIRA DA PRATA Driving up from Praia Branca, the road ends in a bottleneck, where you have to leave your car and walk up cobbled streets to this beautiful scenic village – well worth the effort. Ribeira da Prata will give you the feeling of having stepped back in time.

People visit mainly in order to see **Rotcha Scribida**, the 'writing on the rock'. Ask for directions at the top of the village: it is a 2-minute scramble up the other side of the *ribeira*. There you will see a stratum of rock where localised erosion has revealed some intricate darker lines – or, if you must, rock that bears words written by an ancient people who knew the island long before the Portuguese. Historians have plumped for the former explanation; some locals prefer the latter.

There is infrequent public transport between Tarrafal and Ribeira da Prata (300$ one-way). There are several shops selling water, biscuits, bread and *grogue*.

SOUTH OF RIBEIRA BRAVA

PREGUIÇA From the road Preguiça does not look much – a few half-built houses, a football pitch, a signpost. The bulk of the village is out of sight, clinging to the steep slope above the shoreline. A precipitous cobbled street winds down among colourful houses past an old church, to a crumbling pier where sizeable boats used to berth with cargo from Mindelo. But Preguiça has not fared well since independence: politicians favoured then tiny Tarrafal as the port of choice, and as its western neighbour prospered, so Preguiça declined in importance. It now receives no cargo, and has to content itself with fish. To the right of the pier you can swim in the shingly bay where the bright fishing boats are drawn up on the beach. Fishermen used to dive from boats to catch lobsters by hand at a depth of 10–15m. They wore masks and breathed compressed air piped from the surface, allowing them to stay down for up to an hour at a time.

On the other side of the village is the Portuguese fort, built in the early 1800s, with several cannons. The two memorials (one erected by the Portuguese, the other by the Cabo Verdeans) commemorate the voyage of Pedro Álvares Cabral, who in 1500 passed this point on his way to discovering the coast of Brazil.

Attempts by the Ribeira Brava town hall to protect turtles have been less successful in Preguiça than elsewhere. Those involved in the programme believe that much of the meat makes its way, either by boat or plane, to Praia, where it attracts a high price.

The town's paved seafront is pretty, but there's not too much to see or do here. That said, it's worth taking the short journey if you have a spare couple of hours. To get there, take an *aluguer* from the main square in the *vila* – they leave intermittently (250$), or you can just walk and hitchhike the 8km. Before dark you should be able to find *colectivo* transport back quite easily, though a chartered vehicle will cost at least 1,000$.

Fishing with local fishermen; boat trips up and down the coast to isolated beaches such as Porta da Lapa (a black-sand beach popular with turtles) or to Carriçal; hanging out – some people love this fishing village as a place in which to do very little very pleasantly.

THE EAST

The eastern part of São Nicolau is mostly an arid, boulder-strewn desert. It is hard to believe that just 70 years ago it was well populated and farmed using dryland techniques that yielded crops of corn and manioc. Now, however, just two populated villages remain: Juncalinho and Carriçal. The area has a raw, desolate beauty that will move some and depress others.

JUNCALINHO Juncalinho lies along the eastern ridge, which is almost entirely devoid of vegetation, but which is characterised by jagged rock formations and deep *ribeiras*. The effects of rain and the lack of it can be seen on the journey here. First of all, hundreds of disused terraces and a scattering of abandoned dwellings bear witness to a time when water and agriculture – and people – were far more numerous. Secondly, the damage to the road caused by heavy rains can take years to properly repair. In places, it can get entirely washed away. It is a disadvantaged, humble village on a plain littered with boulders. Only the cemetery and the football pitch have been cleared of stones. It has its desolate charm, though. A sign indicates the currently Instagram-famous *lagoa*, just ahead of the tiny volcano.

Getting there and away *Alugueres* depart from Ribeira Brava for Juncalinho at around 10.00, taking about 25 minutes to get there. They depart from Juncalinho for Ribeira Brava approximately between 14.00 and 16.00.

Where to stay and eat Homestays can be arranged via some of the island's best guides, for example Toi d'Armanda (page 345).

Jardim (4 rooms) 235 2800; m 996 6191 (or through Pensão Jardim in Ribeira Brava). A distinctive, 2-storey house with a tower-like construction at the front, this is run by a branch of the Jardim family who run the *pensão* in Ribeira Brava. Rooms are pleasant & spacious & all have recently renovated private baths with hot water. Amalia & English-speaking Paulinho can often be found in their restaurant, 100m further into Juncalinho on the main road on the right. $$

Jardim On the right of the main road; ⊕ 07.30–22.00 daily. A local eatery-cum-shop owned by the Jardim family (page 355). Should always be able to serve up a *prato do dia*, but otherwise order a few hours ahead. $$

Lanchonette Caminha d'Lagoa Off the main road on the route down to the *lagoa*, on the left. $

What to see and do

Lagoa You can drive the 5 minutes to the coast, or walk for 15 minutes past circular, stone pig-pens, and gaze down at the crater – black rock lashed with white foam. On a calm day the *lagoa* lies just beyond the reach of the swell, full of beautiful blue-green water, and is a scenic place to bathe or picnic, despite the rather incongruous cement steps. If you are keen to swim, and are coming from Ribeira Brava, check with the *aluguer* drivers in the *vila* who usually have a good idea about the state of the sea on any given day. In August, the *lagoa* is the somewhat unlikely but spectacular venue for a well-established traditional music festival, with artists attending from all over the island. You can see the stage at the western end of the cliff.

Coastal walk and volcanic crater To the east of the *lagoa*, pick your way carefully along the cliff top to see some fine volcanic rock formations adorning the ocean inlets as the swell crashes against them. Down below, you may see some seasoned fishermen using a simple line, bait and stone-weight combination to haul in sizeable *pica* and other fish suitable for either supper or sale. Head inland, crossing the dry *ribeira*, and you can enter the distinctive crater of a modest volcano. Rather than scramble up the 100m or so of steep climb, circle around to its southern (inland) side where the crater wall has collapsed and you can gain effortless access. Afterwards, continue south for a few hundred metres to find the cobbled road that will take you back to Juncalinho after 10 minutes' walk.

Hike to Carriçal There are two hiking routes to Carriçal. The first is along the road. It is a magnificent walk. The road turns right after Juncalinho and climbs in

---

GREENING SÃO NICOLAU

Fajã and its environs are lush and green thanks to technology and a lot of effort. It began in 1980 when, with French aid, the people built a 2km tunnel into the mountainside to tap into water there. The pipe did not just transform Fajã's agriculture but also became the source of water for outlying dry areas such as Juncalinho. Initially it gushed 1,000m^3 per day but this has now subsided to 400m^3. To see the tunnel ask for 'Galeria de Fajã'.

Engineers and educationalists have been working hard to introduce new farming techniques to the area. The key has been to expand the use of traditional irrigation channels (if you are interested, it's worth wandering around the heavily planted terraces of Fajã to see how endless terraces of crops are kept watered by the judicious opening and closing of channels). Some of the water is supplied by boreholes and pumped uphill from where it can descend to do its irrigation.

A second technique, microirrigation, or 'drip drip', is slowly gaining acceptance and can be found in the area too.

a series of precipitous bends high into the mountains inland, over the ridge and down to the sea again. The terrain is dark brown, with heaps of earth and rock, and a frothy coastline.

The second route is along a path that heads directly south out of Juncalinho village, climbs steeply into the mountains, traverses the heights for around an hour and then descends into Ribeira de Palhal and the abandoned village of Urzeleiros (named after the indigo lichen urzela which was farmed here; page 16). The latter path takes around 5 hours and is known as the Caminho de Cinta. It is poor quality and hard to navigate in places. We suggest you either take a guide (who you could probably pick up in Juncalinho) or use the hike description given in the AB Kartenverlag 1:50,000 map of São Nicolau (page 71). Not a place to be caught short of water. The road may be nearby, but traffic is sparse.

CARRIÇAL Carriçal is a pretty village located on the unusually greenery-fringed Baia Gombeza. It's probably one of the most isolated in the archipelago, and a place of notable disadvantage. Most families are crammed into two-roomed, concrete houses with hens, pigs, dogs and cats bustling outside. Below the houses lies a tree-filled *ribeira*, a pretty beach and a cluster of boats. You can pay a fisherman to take you out to net a pile of moray eels and bright-orange groupers, or to go up the coast to explore the coves and caves.

By the steps down to the shore is a deserted factory. Before it closed some years ago, huge pans of tuna were boiled on wood fires and then canned in tins pressed on the premises. Turtle hunting was popular and lucrative here until it was made illegal, but education programmes run by the Ribeira Brava municipality (see page 347 for information on turtles) have been largely successful in stopping this.

There is a small shop where you can buy drinks and snacks and it is possible to arrange a room for the night if you ask around.

Getting there and away In a 4x4, it will take 35 minutes to get to Carriçal from Juncalinho. Check, however, that the road to Carriçal is open – it is sometimes impassable because of landslides. The road veers inland at Juncalinho, then continues east, before branching off south. When it is passable, it is spectacular, offering views all the way down the north coast.

Alugueres leave Ribeira Brava for Carriçal at around midday, and depart Carriçal for Ribeira Brava early in the morning. You might find a later one, depending on whether anyone has some fish to bring to town. If the road is impassable (which it often is in the rainy season), a fisherman might be persuaded to take you by boat from Preguiça.

HIKES *Colum Wilson (CW); Aisling Irwin (AI); Murray Stewart (MS)*

HIKES IN AND OUT OF RIBEIRA BRAVA
1 Ribeira Brava–Calejão–Ribeira Brava
Distance: approximately 4km; time: 2½ hours; difficulty: 1 (CW)
Leave Ribeira Brava on the airport road, ascending past the needles on your left. Bear right at the first junction (the left turn goes to Morro Brás and Juncalinho). After a short distance, bear right again on the road towards the cemetery, which you pass 25 minutes after setting out. The road winds for a short distance in the plantations in the bottom of the *ribeira* before leading you up the other side to rejoin the airport road. Follow it away from the edge of the *ribeira* to the airport, which you will reach 35 minutes after the cemetery.

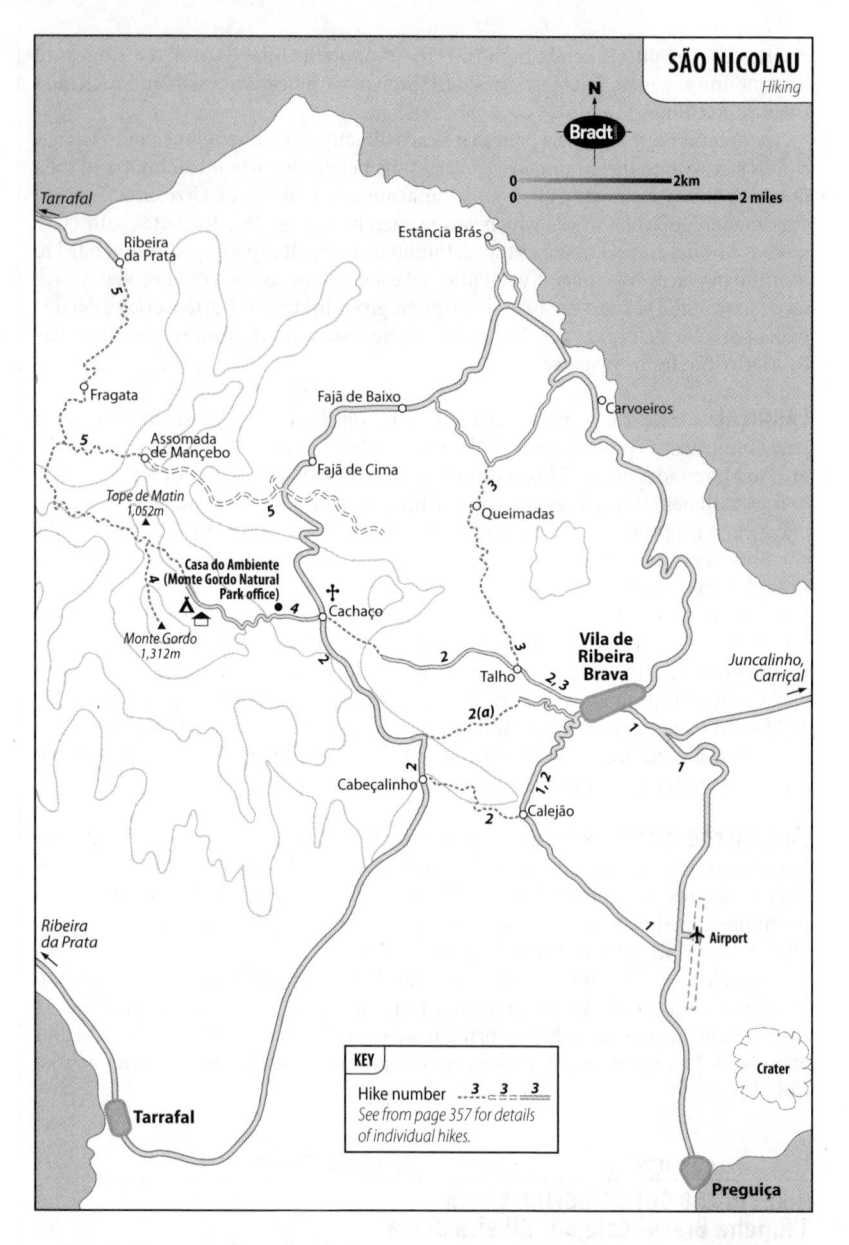

Some 400m past the airport, there is a signposted turning to the right down to **Calejão**, which lies on the lower slopes of the mountain range.

It is a quiet village, strung out along the old road. After 3km you will pass a path on your left – the descent from Cabeçalinho (described in the next hike, opposite) which joins your path opposite a graffiti-decorated stone on the right. There's a shop, which may be open to sell you water, biscuits and soft drinks. The impressive, ochre-coloured building on the hill to the left is the old orphanage and bishop's residence.

The road continues, straight at first, and then begins a superb descent into Ribeira Brava along a series of S-bends. There is an excellent view up the valley. The track emerges in the São João area of town beside the old seminary.

2 Ribeira Brava–Cachaço–Cabeçalinho–Calejão
Distance: approximately 11km; time: at least 4 hours, not allowing for stops en route; difficulty: 2–3 (MS)

This is one of the best walks; at least 4 hours with a steep ascent and descent. You should allow extra time if you want to wander into the Monte Gordo Natural Park, even if it's only to see the dragon trees or to get information on the further hikes available from there (page 346). From town, simply follow the cobbled road up the right-hand side of the *ribeira* – a fascinating walk through the villages. On the outskirts of town you'll see carpenters busy in their workshops. You may be accompanied by schoolchildren of all ages, who presumably make part of this journey on an almost daily basis. If they know two foreign words then they are 'pen' and its French equivalent 'stilo!' Keep to the cobbles and with average fitness you pass some lofty crags to arrive in the first buildings of **Cachaço**. To the right the road winds up to a wonderfully positioned white church, nestled at the foot of a rocky outcrop, but carry on a further 100m to reach the main road of the island where there are a couple of shops selling bread, biscuits and drinks (and, if you are lucky, fresh goat's cheese – ask for *queijo de cabra*). There is also a small museum of water, though there are plans to convert it into an environment interpretation centre.

Around here, the landscape is green, with plenty of perfectly shaped dragon trees. Turn left on the main road for a fantastic view of Ribeira Brava; 100m along the road you reach the entrance road for the Monte Gordo Natural Park. Peer down the gullies where vehicles have been known to tumble – and look up at the mountain on your right down which rocks often fall on to the road. There's a great view of the path you took up the *ribeira* and of the spine of mountains out to the east and you can also see both sides of the barren peninsula protruding to the east. Eventually the road turns to the right and you begin to see the gentler slopes that lead down to Tarrafal.

Some 40 minutes after leaving Cachaço the road takes a sharp right turn, just before a blue house. The track off to the left (see (a), below) is an option for returning to Ribeira Brava, but you can also continue on the main road for another 5 minutes until you reach a white concrete water tank on the right, in front of a large, new building – this is the entrance to **Cabeçalinho**. Take the left track opposite the water tank, veering diagonally before ascending on to a wider, visible path for 10 minutes to reach a panorama over the southern mountains and sea. Now there's half an hour of steep, zig-zagging descent – not for bad knees. This path is less used and not well maintained, at times becoming a rocky streambed where the cobbles have been destroyed during the rains. Care is needed to avoid twisting an ankle. Soon the path veers to the right, along the side of a stone wall, leaving the streambed and eventually reaching a T-junction, opposite a graffiti-covered stone. Turn left here and from here it is about 40 minutes back to town along the zig-zag cobbled road described in the previous walk.

(a) An alternative is to descend the first track to Ribeira Brava. On this track it takes about 40 minutes less to reach the *vila*. Leave the main road between Alto António Miguel and Morro Cone Rocha and go uphill for about 100m as far as the pass. Soon you will find yourself in Palso. Follow the path on the ridge to the *vila*.

3 Ribeira Brava–Queimadas

Distance: approximately 5.5km; time: 1½ hours; difficulty: 2 (CW)

Follow the cobbled road out of town and up the right-hand side of the *ribeira*. After 30 minutes you reach the small village of **Talho**. At the village standpipe (on a small concrete platform with a telephone box next to it), turn right up a small cobbled track. Very soon the cobbles give way to dust and the path begins to look far less

TRAILS IN THE MONTE GORDO NATURAL PARK

With thanks to Silvino Brito and José Monteiro of the Monte Gordo Natural Park office

These are three of the first trails delineated in the natural park. These and two others are detailed on the map issued by the park office.

SOUTHERN VIEW TRAIL This hike begins and ends at the entrance to the park. You begin by going along the main recreational trail, observing the plentiful endemic flora and fauna, the *caberinos* where local community members tend their fields, alongside the imposing peak of Monte Gordo to Assomada de Ribeira Calhaus. Here you encounter beautiful volcanic rock formations and have a splendid view of the valley below. You make your way down into the green, watery Ribeira Calhaus, and slowly begin to wind your way up the mountainside. You will see the endemic *saio* growing out of the rock walls. The hike is a bit steep and rocky, but well worth the effort for the views. After peaking, you come down along the cliffside and make your way to the village of Hortela after passing more wonderful volcanic rock formations. In Hortela, you can enjoy traditional foods for lunch, or continue to make your way back into the park.

RECREATIONAL TRAIL This hike takes you from the entrance of the park along the main recreational trail, past magnificent collections of *tortolhos*, through community farms, alongside Monte Gordo peak, winding your way to Assomada de Ribeira Calhaus. You then make your way down through volcanic rocks into a green oasis where you can sometimes see running water. Traverse traditional abandoned homes with views of the cliffs on both sides. You make your way back to Assomada and take the trail off to your left which winds down and along the edge of the farms in Cachaço, giving you great views of this rural village along with the valley below where Fajã lies. You end by making your way back to the park entrance.

WESTERN LOOP From Assomada de Ribeira Calhaus going westward, this loop passes over the top of Mont Desert with breathtaking views of Canto Fajã and the Fajã Valley. The ridge also passes over the mountain village of Fragata (where *grogue* is still produced in the traditional manner) before you descend past Tope de Matin and Tope Moka to the old settlement of Ribeira de Calhaus. Stay awhile to enjoy the freshwater spring and also enjoy shaded relief from the sun under the grand eucalyptus trees. Continuing along the loop you will make a climb back up to Assomada de Ribeira Calhaus along the old trail which was amazingly cut into the hillside. There are also spectacular views of the surrounding islands of Raso, Branco, Santa Luzia and, if you are lucky, you will be able to also see São Vicente and Santo Antão.

> **OTHER HIKES**
>
> The park staff may be able to advise on other classic São Nicolau hikes. One of these runs north from Tarrafal, past Carbeirinho and on to Praia Branca, then turns inland towards Fragata, and on across the Monte Gordo Natural Park to Cachaço. Another is to descend from Hortela to Tarrafal.

promising. Keep following it up the hillside, resisting the temptation to take an easier, wider path which heads left after a few minutes.

As you ascend, the path swings to the left and, 30 minutes from the phone box, you emerge on a saddle. Looking back over the *ribeira*, Monte Gordo is to the right – the massive humpbacked mountain surmounted by radio masts. Turning around and looking over into the next *ribeira* you can see **Queimadas** in the valley. Fajã is through a gap in the range above it.

It is a pleasant, though steep, descent to the village. It is well worth (slightly) provoking any dog you see just to hear the extraordinary echo in this amphitheatre of a valley. At the T-junction by the old school turn left for Fajã to find transport back.

HIKES TO THE WEST OF THE MAIN ROAD
4 Fajã de Baixo–Fragata–Ribeira da Prata
Distance: approximately 6km; time: 3 hours; difficulty: 3 (CW)

This is a magnificent walk with some steep ascents. The only problem is finding transport from Ribeira da Prata back to Tarrafal at the end of the walk: there are only two *aluguer* drivers resident in Ribeira da Prata and you may find yourself in a one-sided negotiation in which you end up chartering a vehicle for an exorbitant sum. Minimise hassle by beginning this walk early in the morning so you can try hitching back from Prata or picking up the mid-afternoon school run. Alternatively, take the midday *aluguer* from Tarrafal to Ribeira da Prata and do the walk in reverse. Take an *aluguer* to Cachaço. After Fajã and before Cachaço, there's a large sign on the right for Pico Agudo Canto Fajã. Take this and, after about 50m, bear left. You will see a prominent finger of rock in the saddle ahead. After about 15 minutes, you reach a T-junction with a small grave marked by a white cross on a mound nearby. Turn left and follow the track as it winds towards the saddle and then becomes a path which ascends steeply. You will reach the saddle about 50 minutes after setting out.

From the saddle, descend on a beautifully cobbled hairpin track. After about 20 minutes, you reach **Fragata**, with houses built on fantastic ledges and outcrops with sheer drops on either side. The track leads you round the head of the *ribeira* and then begins the descent towards **Ribeira da Prata**. From the saddle to the village is approximately a 2-hour walk. Crops here include sugarcane, cassava, bananas and maize, and coarse tobacco (*erva*). It is smoked in pipes by the old folk, who spurn cigarettes as a lightweight invention.

RASO AND BRANCO

Just 7km², Raso has sheer cliffs, which rise out of the water to a plateau no more than 164m high. It has the familiar stony plains but also grassy areas. To the south are colonies of sea petrels and shearwaters, red-billed tropicbirds and brown boobies – but Raso's most celebrated occupant is the Raso lark (*Alauda razae*), known locally as *calhandra do Ilhéu* and one of the rarest birds in the world, if also one of

A TASTE FOR BABY SHEARWATERS

Catch a young shearwater while it is still in the nest and eating mostly grass – and you have a creature whose ounce of flesh will fetch a lot of money. This was the reason for the annual hunt of shearwaters (*Calonectris edwardsii*), known locally as *cagarra*, on Ilhéu Raso, during which tens of thousands were harvested and, it is claimed, many were hidden among cargoes of fish and shipped to the Netherlands to satisfy the demands of the Cabo Verdean community there.

It should have been easy to prevent. The fishermen who hunted the birds came from just one village, in Santo Antão; the cull happened during the same, predictable, short period each year, and it was strictly illegal. Yet it continued year after year, which eventually became a problem even for the fishermen because numbers started to plummet. In 2007, they managed to catch only 18,000 chicks compared with the previous year's catch of 27,000.

If left to their own devices, shearwaters live for about 40 years, according to Tommy Melo, founder of Cabo Verde's first environmental organisation, Biosfera 1. But they lay only one egg annually.

Eating shearwaters was originally a tradition anchored in famine. During World War II, when imports were difficult, they became a food source. Later, they became a symbolic dish eaten during annual October celebrations to mark the end of famine.

By 2008, Melo was resolute that the hunting should stop and now, indeed, it has. He initially visited the fishermen to explain about the problem and gathered the resources to police the island during October. To convince the Cabo Verde government that there was a problem, Melo even made a video about the cull, which can be seen on YouTube; it is not, however, for the squeamish or faint-hearted.

'My despair is knowing that the Cape Verde shearwater, the Raso lark and the Raso lizard are endemic species that exist nowhere else in the world and that in a matter of years they may no longer exist even in Cabo Verde if we don't stop hunting them for food or raising them as pets,' said Melo back in 2007. Thankfully, thanks to the sterling efforts of Melo and others, the cull was stopped in 2008. During nesting season, a team stays permanently on the island, which is estimated to be home to 75% of the bird's total population, simply to protect them. It seems that the shearwaters have been saved, especially as a number of international conservation plans are now in effect, including those in co-operation with Madeira, the Azores and the Canaries, the shearwater's other Macaronesian habitats. Another threat has emerged, however, as overfishing by factory boats off West Africa has disrupted the marine food chain and forced the birds to travel for up to 12 days to find food. During the lengthy absences, their chicks can face starvation or threats from predators.

the world's most ordinary-looking. The forbidding island was their only home for 500 years and they are rated 'critically endangered' on the international Red List of threatened species. Drought conditions and predators saw a perilous decline in their population in 2004, when it fell to less than 100. This trend however reversed from 2010 onwards, and by 2017, there were up to 1,000 mature birds.

This was seen as a rare window of opportunity to ensure the species' survival. After a programme to eradicate introduced predators on the larger island of Santa

Luzia, around 30 larks were carefully taken from Raso by boat in 2018, and in 2019 the population was further reinforced. It's in fact a return as well as a translocation; there's significant fossil evidence to suggest there was a lark population on Santa Luzia in the distant past. There's cautious optimism that the project has been a success. In 2023, the original Raso population was estimated to be around 1,500, while on Santa Luzia numbers had reached around 600. Raso is also known for its endemic Raso lizards.

Branco is even smaller than Raso at just $3km^2$. It is, however, taller, at 327m, and has one small water source. Tiny as it is, it's one of the most important sites in Cabo Verde for breeding seabirds and is blindingly white from their guano deposits. The island was the unlikely host to 30 human inhabitants in 1833 – prisoners who were dumped there and left to survive or die.

Branco was, until 1940, the last outpost of the Cape Verde giant skink, a delightful lizard-like creature coloured a mottled white and brown and with a big, heavy tail. It was the second-largest skink in the world, reaching 65cm in length and lived among the rocks eating the seeds of plants and occasionally augmenting this diet with bird eggs. Their numbers began plummeting when the prisoners arrived. After that, they were the sporadic victims of local fishermen who trapped them to eat, and their skins were popular as shoe material. The final blow was the series of droughts in the early 20th century. A luckier creature is the giant gecko (*Tarentola gigas*). The smaller *Tarentola gigas brancoensis* lives along the rocky coast of Branco. Their cousins, *Tarentola gigas gigas*, live in the pits and fissures of rock over on Raso.

The two islands were defined as nature reserves in 1990. Despite this, until tougher legislation was passed in 2008, Raso was swamped each year with fishermen from Santo Antão, there to sate their hunger for baby shearwaters (see opposite).

Appendix 1

LANGUAGE

If you are serious about learning a language before going to Cabo Verde then the big decision is whether to choose Portuguese or Kriolu. Kriolu can be learned from the online app Speak Kriolu or a number of websites. If you have access to a Cabo Verdean community, someone may happily give lessons. If you plan to spend some time there and need to win the confidence of people other than professionals and officials, it will be essential to learn Kriolu, and learning Portuguese may turn out to have been a confusing waste of time. For short-term visitors, the warmth you will generate and smiles you will receive by learning one or two phrases of Kriolu will justify the effort. And if you want to choose one phrase? Make it *'Tudu dret?'* (How are you?). It does not matter if you don't understand the reply! A thumbs up in reply will be well understood.

In the absence of Kriolu, having some Portuguese is of huge help, especially for negotiating written information. Combined with a smattering of French, to make what might be called 'Fraughtuguese', you'll get by. English speakers are becoming more common and you can usually find someone who speaks either French or English.

PORTUGUESE The biggest barrier to the swift acquisition of some Portuguese is pronunciation – it really takes many weeks to master it before learning any words. After that, the rudiments are reasonably simple and English speakers will recognise a large number of words, particularly in written form.

Pronunciation The following are basic rules, although there are a lot of exceptions:

- If a word carries an acute (´) or circumflex (^) accent then stress the syllable that carries it. Otherwise stress the second-last syllable.
- Vowels that carry a tilde (~) on the top, and vowels followed by 'm' are nasalised.
- Many vowels disappear, for example an 'e', 'a' or 'o' at the end of a word; and many 'e's at the beginning of words. Tone down unstressed vowels.
- Double vowels are pronounced as two separate vowels.

s = 'sh' at the end of the word; 'z' in the middle; soft 'c' at the beginning
z = 'sh' at the end of a word
c = soft 'c' if there's a cedilla underneath or if it's before an 'i' or an 'e'
g = soft 'j' if before an 'i' or an 'e'
j = soft 'j'
rr = rolled
r = only rolled at the beginning of a word

lh = 'ly'
ch = 'sh'
qu = 'kw', before an 'a'; 'k' before an 'e' or an 'i'
nh = 'ny'
x = 'sh' or 's' – the rules are complicated – just take a chance
a = as in 'father' when stressed; as in 'air' when unstressed
e = as in 'jet' when stressed; as in the second 'e' of 'general' when unstressed
i = as in 'seen' but shorter
o = as in 'not' or 'note' when stressed; as in 'root' when unstressed
u = usually as in 'root'
h = don't pronounce

Grammar The most basic way of making something plural is by adding -s or -es to the end. The most basic verb endings are as follows:

I buy	compr-o	We buy	compr-amos
You buy (singular)	compr-as	You buy (plural)	compr-ais
You/he/she buys	compr-a	They buy	compr-am

Address all but intimates in the third person (literally: 'could he help me'). You don't need to bother with personal pronouns (I, you, he) unless you want to emphasise them (eg: *I* am talking to *you*).

Common compound verbs
be   ser (I am: *sou*/you are, he is: *é*/we are: *somos*/they are: *são*)
give dar (I give: *dou*/you give, he gives: *dá*/they give: *dão*)
go   ir (I go: *vou*/you go, he goes: *vai*/let's go: *vamos*)
have ter (I have: *tenho*/you have, he has: *tem*/we have: *temos*/they have: *têm*)
like gostar de (I like = *gosto de*)

Greetings
good morning   bom dia
good afternoon (after midday)   boa tarde
good evening (after 18.00)   boa noite
goodbye   até logo ('until later')
how are you?   como está?
I am well/everything's fine   estou bem ('shtoe beyng')

Questions, answers and useful phrases
What is your name?   Como se chama?
Do you speak English?   Fala inglês?
Is it possible…?   É possível…?
How much does it cost?   Quanto custa?
What is this called?   Como se chama isso?
Can you help me?   Pode me ajudar?
Pardon?   Como?
Where?   Onde?
When?   Quando?
How?   Como?
Why?   Porquê?
What?   Quê?

Appendix 1 LANGUAGE

A1

365

Do you have a spare room?	Tem um quarto vago?
You're welcome	De nada ('it's nothing')
I am from London	Sou de Londres
My name is…	Chamo-me…
Where is…?	Onde fica…?
I don't know	Não sei
I don't understand	Não compreendo
Straight on	Em frente
On the right	À direita
On the left	À esquerda
More slowly	Mais devagar
I have to go	Tenho de ir
To have coffee	Tomar café
To have breakfast	Tomar o café de manhã
There is…	Há…
There is no…	Não há…
Too much	Demais
That's enough!	Basta!
More or less	Mais ou menos

Menu items

fish stew	cozido de peixe
grilled squid	lula grelhada
shellfish cooked with rice	arroz de marisco
generally wahoo, a white, hard fish steak	peixe serra
dried cod	bacalhau
dried cod and chips fried together	bacalhau à Brás
maize, beans, chicken, other meat	cachupa rica
maize, beans	cachupa pobre
a chicken dish	djagacida or jag
a soup	conj
corn bread	gufong
a milk pudding, rather like crème caramel	pudim de leite
sponge impregnated with coconut, like steamed pudding	tarte de coco

Food and drink

bean	feijão
beef	carne de vaca
beer	cerveja
bread	pão
cake	bolo
cassava	mandioca
cheese	queijo
chicken (as food)	frango
chips	batatas fritas
coffee	café
dessert	sobremesa
eel	moreia
eggs	ovos
haricot beans	congo
lobster	lagosta
maize	milho
meat	carne
milk	leite
octopus	polvo
potato	batata
rice	arroz
rum (local)	grogga
shrimp/prawn	camarão
sweet potato	batata doce

tea	*chá*	veal	*vitela*
tuna	*atum*	water	*água*
turkey	*peru*	wine	*vinho*

Days and months

Sunday	*domingo*	Wednesday	*quarta-feira*
Monday	*segunda-feira* (second day)	Thursday	*quinta-feira*
		Friday	*sexta-feira*
Tuesday	*terça-feira*	Saturday	*sábado*

January	*janeir*	July	*julho*
February	*fevereiro*	August	*agosto*
March	*março*	September	*setembro*
April	*abril*	October	*outubro*
May	*maio*	November	*novembro*
June	*junho*	December	*dezembro*

Numbers

1	*um/uma*	16	*dezasseis*
2	*dois/duas*	17	*dezassete*
3	*três*	18	*dezoito*
4	*quatro*	19	*dezanove*
5	*cinco*	20	*vinte*
6	*seis* ('saysh')	30	*trinta*
7	*sete*	40	*quarenta*
8	*oito*	50	*cinquenta*
9	*nove*	60	*sessenta*
10	*dez* ('desh')	70	*setenta*
11	*onze*	80	*oitenta*
12	*doze*	90	*noventa*
13	*treze*	100	*cem*
14	*catorze*	1,000	*mil*
15	*quinze*	a million	*um milhão*

Other common words

aeroplane	*avião* ('avi-ow')	boarding house	*pensão*
after	*depois de*	book	*livro*
also	*também*	boy	*rapaz*
and	*e*	breakfast	*pequeno almoço* ('pekaynalmoss')
at	*a*		
bad	*mau, má*	brother	*irmão*
baggage	*bagagem*	bus	*autocarro*
bakery	*padaria*	buy	*comprar*
bank	*banco*	candle	*vela*
bathroom	*casa de banho*	car	*carro*
battery	*pilha*	casualty department	*banco de socorros*
beach	*praia*	cat	*gato*
beautiful	*lindo/a*	change	*troco*
bed	*cama*	cheap	*barato/a*
before	*antes de*	chicken	*galinho*
big	*grande*	church	*igreja*

cinema	*cinéma*
city	*cidade*
closed	*fechado*
condom	*camisinha*
cow	*vaca*
customs	*alfândega*
day	*dia*
diarrhoea	*diarréia*
difficult	*difícil*
dinner	*jantar*
doctor	*médico/a*
dog	*cão*
drink (to)	*beber*
drink	*bebida*
early	*cedo*
eat	*comer*
English	*inglês*
enough	*bastante*
exchange (to)	*trocar*
father	*pai*
fever	*febre*
film	*película*
flight	*vol*
girl	*rapariga*
goat	*cabra*
good	*bom/boa*
he	*ele*
heavy	*pesado/a*
high	*alto/a*
hill	*colina*
hospital	*hospital*
hot	*quente*
hotel	*hotel*
house	*casa*
hurt (to)	*doer*
husband	*marido*
I	*eu*
ill	*doente*
in	*em*
key	*chave*
lagoon	*piscina*
leave	*partir*
letter	*carta*
light	*luz* ('loosh')
little (ie: 'not much')	*pouco/a*
lorry	*camião*
low	*baixo/a* ('baysho')
lunch	*almoço*
magazine	*revista*
man	*homem*
market	*mercado*
matches	*fósforos*
money	*dinheiro*
mosquito net	*mosquiteiro*
mother	*mãe*
mountain	*montanha*
much	*muito/a*
never	*nunca*
newspaper	*jornal*
night	*noite*
nightclub	*boite*
no	*não*
nothing	*nada*
now	*agora*
of	*de*
old	*velho*
open	*aberto/a*
path	*caminho*
pen	*caneta*
perhaps	*talvez*
pharmacy	*farmácia*
pillow	*almofada*
please	*faz favor*
police	*policia*
post office	*correio*
rain	*chuva*
rest	*descansar*
restaurant	*restaurante*
road	*rua*
room	*quarto*
room for a couple	*quarto casal*
room for one	*quarto individual*
room for two	*quarto duplo*
salt	*sal*
school	*escola*
sea	*mar*
sell	*vender*
send	*enviar*
she	*ela*
sheet	*lençol*
shop	*loja*
shower	*chuveiro*
sister	*irmã*
small	*pequeno/a*
sorry	*desculpe*
speak	*falar*
spouse	*esposo/a*
square (town)	*praça*
sun	*sol*
supermarket	*supermercado*
swim	*nadar*
telephone	*telefone*

thanks (as in 'much obliged')	obrigado/a	village	aldeia
that	esse	visa	visto
they	eles/elas	we	nós
this	este	wind	vento
ticket	bilhete	with	com
to	para ('pra')	woman	mulher
today	hoje	work	trabalhar
toilet	sanitário	yes	sim
toilet paper	papel higiênico	yesterday	ontem
tomorrow	amanhã	you (polite masc)	o senhor
town	vila	you (polite fem)	a senhora
town hall	câmara	you (familiar)	você
travel	viajar	you (polite masc pl)	os senhores
very	muito/a	you (polite fem pl)	as senhoras

KRIOLU *São Vicente Kriolu translations by 10th-grade pupils at the José Augusto Pinto School in Mindelo, São Vicente, with help from their teacher, Keith West. Santiago translations and introductory material by Steven Maddocks.*

The Kriolu language varies widely across the archipelago, to the extent that people from São Vicente profess not to be able to understand their compatriots from Santiago. Although every island has its own version, the greatest difference is between the Barlavento Kriolu spoken in the north of Cabo Verde, and Sotavento Kriolu, spoken in the south.

São Vicente Kriolu is slightly more Portuguese than Santiago, or Badiu, Kriolu – the latter contains more African words. Generally speaking, Barlavento Kriolu is more clipped and staccato, and Sotavento Kriolu is more open, with rounded vowels, and spoken more aggressively. There are differences in vocabulary, with each using its own slang. Among the biggest differences are subject pronouns, 'You' (singular) is *bu* in Sotavento Kriolu and *bo* in Barlavento Kriolu. 'You' (plural) is *nhos* and *bzot*, respectively. An 'a' in Sotavento Kriolu often comes out as an 'o' in Barlavento, as in 'work' (*trabadju/trabodj*) or 'ill-mannered' (*malkriadu/malkriod*).

In Santiago they tend to pronounce the whole word. Consequently it is much easier for the beginner to understand what is being said. In São Vicente whole syllables – both in the middle and at the ends of words – may be left out. So for example the *-adu* at the end of words in Sotavento Kriolu becomes *-od* in Barlavento Kriolu – so *Kansadu* would be pronounced *Kansod*. In Santiago Kriolu, *v* changes to *b* and *lh* becomes *dj*, so the word for red – *vermelho* in the north – is pronounced *burmedju* in the south. For more about the current status of Kriolu and Portuguese, see page 37.

Here, the Santiago translation is given first, followed by the São Vicente version. The two different versions of Kriolu have been represented as simply as possible for a novice. All of the sounds correspond roughly to their English equivalents. Peculiarities are as follows:

tx represents the 'ch' in 'cherry'
dj represents the 'j' in 'Jerry'
x is the 'sh' of 'sham'

j is the 'z' of 'pleasure'
k is hard, as in 'kick'
s is soft, as in 'sick'

The only accents used here are to draw attention to stress. For verbs, in Sotavento Kriolu stress is always on the penultimate syllable, in Barlavento on the last syllable. This has been represented by an accented final a, e, or i.

Grammar 'You' has familiar and polite, singular and plural forms, as well as gender. It would be rude to address an elderly stranger with the familiar form.

	Sotavento Kriolu	Barlavento Kriolu
you (singular, familiar)	*bu* (except *bo e*, you are)	*bo*
you (singular, polite)	*nho* (masc), *nha* (fem)	*bosé* (masc and fem)
you (plural, familiar)	*nhos*	*bzot*
you (plural, polite)	*nhos*	*bosés*

Shopping

Excuse me, where is the shop?	*Undi ki e loja, pur favor?*	*Ondé k'e loja, d'favor?*
Do you have bottled water?	*Nhos tem agu di garafa?*	*Bzot tem agua d'garafa?*
How much does this cost?	*Keli e kantu?*	*Keli tonté?*
It's too expensive	*Kel e karu dimas*	*Kel e txeu kor*
I'm not paying that. It's a rip-off!	*N ka kre kumpra'l. Kel e robo!* (strong)	*N ka kre kompra'l. Bo ti ta ingana'm!*

Airport

What time will the flight leave?	*Ki ora ki avion ta sei?*	*Kazora k'aviau ta sei?*
Is there a telephone here?	*Li tem telefon?*	*Li tem t'lefon?*
I'm very upset because my baggage has not arrived	*N sta mutu xatiadu pa modi nha bagagem ka ben*	*N ta txeu xatiod mod nha bagagem ka ben*
I'm in a hurry	*N sta ku presa*	*N ta k'pres*

Taxi

Please take me to Hotel X	*Pur favor, leba'm ti Hotel X*	*D'favor, leva'm té Hotel X*

Hotel

Do you have a vacant room?	*Nhos tem kuartu?*	*Bzot tem um kuart?*
May I see the room first?	*N kre odja kuartu purmeru?*	*N ta gostá d'oia kel kuart primer?*
What time is breakfast?	*Ki ora ki e ora di kafé?*	*Kazora k'e kafé?*

Bank

Where is the bank?	*Undi ki e banku?*	*Ondé k'e bonk?*
What is the exchange rate?	*Kal ki e kambiu di oji?*	*Tonté k'e kambiu?*
When does the bank close/open?	*Ki ora ki banku ta fitxa/ta abri?*	*Kazora k'bonk t'f'txá/t'abrí?*

Hiking

Where is the path to the peak?	*Undi ki e kaminhu pa piku?*	*Ondé k'e kamin pa piku?*
Is this the path to get there? (hiker points)	*Ekeli ki e kaminhu pa la?*	*Keli k'e kamin pa la?*

Where can I buy water?	Undi ki N podi kumpra agu?	Ondé k'n podé kompra agua?
How far is it to the valley floor?	Falta txeu pa nu txiga fundu rubera?	Tont temp këgent t'levá pa txigá la na fund?
How many hours to the road?	Kantu tenpu falta pa nu txiga strada?	Tont temp k'falta'm pa'n txigá strada?
Go left at the fork	Na dizviu toma skerda	Na skina bo t'v'rá pa skerda
Go right at the crossroads	Na kruzamentu vira a direta	Na kruzament bo t'v'ra pa dreta
Can you show me on the map?	Bu podi mostra'm li na napa?	Bo podé mostra'm li na mapa?
I need a guide	N mesti um guia	N presiza d'um guia
I want to go to the *grogue* distillery	N kre ba ti trapixe	N kre bai pa trapixe
No more *grogue* or I'll get drunk	Si n toma mas grogu n ta fika moku	Se n tomá mas grog, n ta fuxká
Is it possible to walk along that path? (point)	N podi anda na kel kaminhu?	N podé anda la na kel kamin?
I want to go to the crater	N kre ba ti kratera	N kre bai pa kratera
Is there public transport?	Tem transport?	Tem transport?

Restaurant

Could you bring me the menu, please?	Traze'm ementa, pur favor?	Traze'm imenta, d'favor
We've been here a long time	Dja dura ki nu txiga li	Diaza k'nu ta li
Could I have the bill, please?	Traze'm konta, pur favor?	Traze'm konta, d'favor
Do you have any change?	Bu tene troku?	Bo tem trok?

Greetings and personal communication

Hello	Oi/Ola	Oi
Goodbye	Txau	Txau
Yes	Sim	Sim
No	Nau	Nau
Do you speak English?	Bu ta papia ingles?	Bo t'falá ingles?
Which island are you from?	Bo e di ki ilha?	Bo e d'kual ilha?
What is your name?	Modi ki e bu nomi?	Mané k'e bo nom?
My name is...	Nha nomi e...	Nha nom e...
Can you help me?	Bu podi djuda'm?	Bo podé isda'm?
What is this called?	Modi ki e nomi di kel kuza li?	Mané k'e nom d'es kosa?
I don't understand	N ka ta entendi	N ka ti ta entende'b
Please speak more slowly	Papia mas dibagar, pur favor	Falá mas d'vagar, d'favor
I don't have any money	N ka tene dinheru	N ka tem d'nher
That's enough	Dja txiga	Ta bom

Miscellaneous

English		
If	Si	Se
Often	Txeu bes	Txeu vez
Already	Dja	Ja
Still	Inda	Inda
Now	Gosi	Grinhasim
Other	Otu	Ot
Sorry	Diskulpa'm	Diskulpa'm
How are you?	Modi ki bu sta?	Manera bo ta?
General greeting	Tudu bon? Tudu dretu?	Tud dret?
Excuse me	Kon lisensa	Ko l'sensa
I'm here on holiday	N sta li di feria	N ta d'feria
I'm from London/England/America	Ami e di Londres/Inglatera/Merka	Mi e d'Londres/d'Inglater/d'Merka
Collective *aluguer* (often a Toyota Hiace)	Ias	Ias
Bad/damaged/broken/ill/mistaken	Mariadu	no single word covers the same range
Good/excellent/cool/fine	Fixe	Kul
Good/tasty/delicious/fun	Sabi	Sab
That's not on	Keli ka ta da	Keli ka ta dret
There's a power cut	Lus dja bai	Lus ja bai
I don't eat meat	N ka ta kumé karni	N ka ta k'mé karn

Appendix 2

FURTHER INFORMATION

BOOKS There is little about Cabo Verde on the shelves of British bookshops, but books can be found online, whether new or from secondhand retailers. The British Library (**w** bl.uk) also has many of the books below; membership is free and open to all, though you will have to register and obtain a library card to order books up from the stacks. Mindelo and Praia's municipal libraries also can be accessed onsite, as well as the university libraries of each city. For a comprehensive digest of Cabo Verdean literature published in English pre-1990, consult the *World Bibliographical Series*, volume 123, Cape Verde, by Caroline Shaw (Clio Press, 1991).

Activities
Cabo Verde, Santo Antão, Guia dos Circuitos Turísticos. A detailed, if now dated, guide to hikes in Santo Antão, each with a foldout, high-quality map to show the route. Although written in Portuguese, it is of great value even without the text. It might still be available on Santo Antão; otherwise, try online Portuguese bookshops.

Hammick, Anne and Heath, Nicholas *Atlantic Islands: Azores, Madeira, Canary and Cape Verde Islands* Imray, Laurie, Norie and Wilson, 2004. An essential practical guide for yachties, with loads of ultra-detailed, non-perishable information.

Cabo Verde library collections
The Arquivo Historico Nacional (*CP 321, Chã d'Areia, Praia, Santiago, Cape Verde*; **w** arquivonacional.cv) was founded in 1988 and now comprises a large collection of historic and recent books as well as documents of the colonial administration concerning such issues as customs, emigration and Church matters, among many other subjects.

The Cape Verdean Special Collection in the James P Adams Library, Rhode Island College (600 Mount Pleasant Av, Providence, RI 02908; +1 401 456 9653; **w** library.ric.edu). In this collection you will find books, newspapers, tapes of Cabo Verdean television and radio programmes, photographs and various private Cabo Verdean collections. There is at least 40 linear feet of material.

Culture
Baker, George *Cape Verde Art and Culture: Custom, Tradition and Environment* CreateSpace IPP, 2016

Hurley-Glowa, Susan *Songs for Cabo Verde; Norberto Tavares's Musical Visions for a New Republic* University of Rochester Press, 2021

de Miranda, Mónica and Schofield Cardoso, César *ATLANTICA: Contemporary Art from Cabo Verde, Guinea Bissau, São Tomé and Príncipe and their Diasporas* Hangar Books (2021)

Okeke-Agulu, Chika and Underwood, Joseph L *African Artists From 1882 to Now* Phaidon Press, 2021

Economy and politics

Africa South of the Sahara Europa Publications. A reference book that is updated every year.
Europa World Year Book, by the same publisher. Another reference book; Cabo Verde is covered less extensively.
Fernandes Pilgrim, Aminah and Resende-Santos João (eds.) *Economic Growth and Democracy in Post-Colonial Africa: Cabo Verde, Small States, and the World Economy* Lexington Books, 2022. Essays gathered here from both academics and policy practitioners explore Cabo Verde's history of good governance and social peace, alongside its political and institutional evolution, foreign affairs and development policies.
Foy, Colm *Cape Verde: Politics, Economics and Society* Pinter, 1988. A penetrating if dated guide to the working of government in post-independence Cabo Verde.

Health

Wilson-Howarth, Jane *Healthy Travel: Bites, Bugs and Bowels* Cadogan, 2009
Wilson-Howarth, Jane and Ellis, Matthew *Your Child Abroad: A Travel Health Guide* Bradt Guides, 2014

History and sociology

Araújo, Américo C *Little Known: The European Side of the Cape Verde Islands* DAC Publishers, 2000. Documents European connections with the islands and includes translations of some poems of Jorge Barbosa.
Balla, Marcelo Gomes *António's Island: Missing Pages of History for Blacks and Hispanics* Braiswick, 2002. An idiosyncratic collection of articles about Cabo Verde's history.
Berger Coli, Waltraud and Lobban, Richard A *The Cape Verdeans in Rhode Island: A Brief History*. On the same theme as Halter (see below).
Brito-Semedo, Manual *Cabo Verde – Ilhas Crioulas* Rosa de Porcelana Editora, 2023. One of the country's most respected, if often controversial, thinkers, his most recent book is both a history of Cabo Verdean identity and a socio-cultural analysis of how the country currently imagines itself.
Carreira, António *People of the Cape Verde Islands* Hurst, 1982. A detailed analysis of one of the fundamental forces of Cabo Verdean society: emigration, both forced and voluntary. It is an academic work by a respected Cabo Verdean historian.
Davidson, Basil *No Fist is Big Enough to Hide the Sky: The Liberation of Guinea-Bissau and Cape Verde* Zed Press, 1981. A lively account of the armed struggle in Guinea-Bissau.
Davidson, Basil *The Fortunate Isles* Hutchinson, 1989. A one-volume history of the islands by Britain's foremost historian of Africa. The book is a very readable, personal account of the emergence of a much-loved nation from the bonds of colonialism. There is also a detailed and interesting analysis of Cabo Verde's socialist policies in the last third of the book.
Duncan, Bentley *Atlantic Islands: Madeira, the Azores and the Cape Verdes in 17th Century Commerce and Navigation* University of Chicago Press, 1972. A formidable mass of information about the slave and other trades, spilling over into other centuries and with plenty of interesting titbits.
Green, Toby *A Fistful of Shells* Allen Lane, 2019. While only touching on Cabo Verde in passing, this radically different approach to understanding the history of West Africa is great background reading, by a respected professor of both precolonial West Africa and global inequality.
Halter, Marilyn *Between Race and Ethnicity: Cape Verdean American Immigrants 1860–1965* University of Illinois Press, 1995. Written as part of a larger project to understand American

immigrants from a variety of countries, this book mixes fascinating accounts of the lives of Cabo Verdeans in the US with a history of the home left behind during a key time in the country's diasporic formation.

Lobban, Richard *Cape Verde: Crioulo Colony to Independent Nation* Westview Press, 1995. An excellent book with a broad sweep, by a seasoned Cabo Verde watcher.

Lobban, Richard and Saucier, Paul Khalil *The Historical Dictionary of the Republic of Cape Verde* Scarecrow Press, 2007. Very readable, this book is ideal for answering a broad spectrum of questions about Cabo Verde.

Ludtke, Jean *Atlantic Peeks: An Ethnographic Guide to the Portuguese-Speaking Islands* Christopher Publishing House, 1989. Recommended; may be available secondhand.

Rodney, Walter *How Europe Underdeveloped Africa* Verso, 2018. Originally published in 1970, and a continuation of Rodney's earlier work that explores the Atlantic slave trade on both Cabo Verde and the mainland coast, this is a classic text of African studies and a meticulously researched exposé of imperial extraction across the continent.

Serels, Mitchell *The Jews of Cape Verde* Sepher-Hermon Press, 1997. A history of the Jewish presence in Cabo Verde from the 15th century to the early 20th century.

Tomás, António *Amílcar Cabral: The Life of a Reluctant Nationalist* Oxford Academic, 2021. A revised English version of Tomás's 2007 biography in Portuguese; thoughtfully describes Cabral's formation as a revolutionary leader, as well as the complexities of Lusophone Africa's various liberation movements, including that of Cabo Verde.

History titles in Portuguese

Carreira, António *Cabo Verde: Formação e Extinção de uma Sociedade Escravocrata* Centro de Estudos da Guiné Portuguesa, 1972. This is an important work on the Cabo Verdean slave economy.

Germano Lima, António *Ilha de Capitães* Spleen, 1997. An account of the history of Boavista.

Lopes, Jose Vicente *Cabo Verde: Os Bastidores da Independencia* Spleen, 1996. An exhaustive, vivid and polyphonic history of Cabo Verde from 1910 to 1981, but with a focus on the immediate post-independence years; explores the identity-building nature of literature, music and language as well as the politics of those years.

Language

Gonçalves, Manuel da Luz and Andrade, Lelia Lomba de *Pa Nu Papia Krioulu* Mili Mila, 2010. A lively book that uses poetry, recipes and cultural articles to teach Kriolu to non-speakers, and teach Kriolu speakers how to read and write the language.

Literature and poetry

Burness, Donald *Fire: Six Writers from Angola, Mozambique and Cape Verde* Three Continents Press, 1977. This devotes some time to the exposition of Baltasar Lopes's novel *Chiquinho*.

Clew Parsons, Elsie *Folk Lore from the Cape Verde Islands* American Folklore Society, 1923. In British libraries. A fascinating accumulation of tales she collected from American *emigrantes* in the early 1900s.

Hamilton, Russell *Voices from an Empire: A History of Afro-Portuguese Literature* University of Minnesota Press, 1975. Includes an in-depth examination of leading Cabo Verdean writers and poets of the 20th century.

Leite, Ana Mafalda, *Cape Verde: Language, Literature and Music* Portuguese Literary and Cultural Studies, 2002

Leite, Vicente Rendal *The Booklet (A Caderneta)* Instituto Caboverdiano do Livro. Translation of the story by Baltasar Lopes.

Strathern, Oona *Traveller's Literary Companions* In Print, 1994. Devoted to Cabo Verdean poetry.

Classic Cabo Verdean works
In translation
Almeida, Germano *The Last Will and Testament of Senhor da Silva Araujo* New Directions 2004. Drawing comparisons to Calvino and Svevo, Almeida's 1989 novel is a tragicomedic tour de force, chronicling the life of a Mindelo merchant via his literal legacies.

Arena, Joaquim *Under Our Skin* Unnamed Press, 2022. Taking the historical figure of Joao de Sá Panasco glimpsed in a painting on a museum wall as a starting point, Arena explores his own fractured identity and the foundational stories of the enslaved people of his homeland.

Fortes, Corsino *Selected Poems of Corsino Fortes* Archipelago Press, 2015. A beautiful collection of work in translation from across the entire career of one of the country's most well-known poets.

Lopes, Baltasar *Chiquinho: A Novel of Cabo Verde* Tagus Press 2019. The seminal Cabo Verdean novel written in 1947 in its first English translation, also a key text in the literature of Lusophone Africa.

Pereira, Celia *Estória, Estória: Do Tambor a blimundo*. Children's book and audiobook, in Italian, Portuguese and English, including the story of the liberated ox, Blimundo, and an assortment of Cabo Verdean sayings.

Salústio, Dina *The Madwoman of Serrano* Dedalus Africa, 2020. The first novel published by a woman in Cabo Verde, in 1998, and the first to be translated into English, is a magical realist tale of village life and considered the country's foremost postcolonial and feminist work.

Varela, Dai *Tufas, the Creole Princess – Learning the Magic Words* (2017) and *Tufas, the Creole Princess – the apology box* (2018), JOVEMTUDO Cabo Verde

No current translation
Lopes, Manuel *Chuva Braba* (Wild Rain) and *Flagelados do Vente Leste* (Victims of the East Wind). The latter novel was the basis for the first Cabo Verdean-produced feature-length motion picture, which has the same title and was shot on Santo Antão.

Romano, Luís *Negrume/Lzimparin* Leitura, 1973. This book of short stories and poems – the title means 'dusk' in English – was published in both Portuguese and Kriolu, one of the first to do so.

de Sousa, Henrique Teixeira *Ilhéu de Contenda* Editorial O Seculo, 1978. A novel of the class conflict and the winds of change on the Fogo of 1964, made into a film of the same name in 1995. The film's soundtrack features Cesária Évora.

Natural history
Birdwatchers should try these:

Aves de Cabo Verde This useful little orange booklet includes colour drawings of most of the important birds, their local and Latin names and a short explanation in English. Available from CVI (Cape Verde Investments) in Praia.

Bannerman, David and Mary *History of the Birds of the Cape Verde Islands* Oliver and Boyd, 1968. An entertaining book which combines distinguished ornithology with genial accounts of their times in Cabo Verde.

Clarke, Tony, Orgill, Chris and Disley, Tony *A Field Guide to the Birds of the Atlantic Islands: Canary Islands, Madeira, Azores, Cape Verde* Helm Field Guides, 2006.

Garcia Del Rey, Eduardo *Field Guide to the Birds of Macaronesia* Lynx, 2011

Hazevoet, Cornelis *The Birds of the Cape Verde Islands* British Ornithologists' Union, 1995. Order from the Natural History Book Service (2–3 Wills Rd, Totnes, Devon TQ9 5XN, UK; 01803 865913; e customer.services@nhbs.co.uk; w nhbs.co.uk).

Hazevoet, Cornelis Sixth report on birds from the Cabo Verde Islands, including records of 25 taxa new to the archipelago. Available for download from w africanbirdclub.org.

Plantas Endémicas A small guide to the country's vegetation, it has been translated into English and is also available from CVI (see opposite).

Personal accounts There are many fascinating accounts written by British sailors, civil servants and entrepreneurs who have passed through the archipelago. They include:

Burdon Ellis, Alfred *West African Islands* Chapman and Hall, 1855. Entertaining and irritating by turns.

Dampier, William *A New Voyage Round the World* Adam and Charles Black, 1937. This is an account of the sailor's visit in 1683, complete with pirates, bandits and a generally unfavourable impression of the Cabo Verdean people.

Lyall, Archibald *Black and White Make Brown* Heinemann, 1938. An intelligent and highly entertaining account of the journey this journalist made to both Cabo Verde and Portuguese Guinea.

Rendall, John *A Guide to the Cape Verde Islands* C Wilson, 1856. Frustratingly lacking in detail given the promise of the title, but fascinating nevertheless.

Roberts, George *Account of a Voyage to the Islands of the Canaries, Cape de Verde and Barbadoes, in 1721* can be found within *A New General Collection of Voyages and Travels, Vol I*, collected by Thomas Astley Frank Cass, 1968 – another lively set of adventures.

Valdez, Francisco Travassos *Six Years of a Traveller's Life in Western Africa, vol 1* Hurst and Blackett, 1861. An unusually positive account by a Portuguese man sent to report on the islands for the government.

ONLINE MEDIA AND OTHER WEBSITES

w **africanbirdclub.org** Information about birdlife.

w **africanews.com** and **allafrica.com** News stories on Cabo Verde.

w **anacao.cv** Cabo Verdean weekly newspaper site, based in Praia.

w **asemana.cv** Cabo Verdean weekly newspaper site, based in Praia. One of the largest circulations in the country.

w **brava.news** Online newspaper for Brava, but with full English language site geared to the Bravan diaspora.

w **cabowork.com** Government-run information portal for digital nomads, start-ups, entrepreneurs and remote workers, with cultural information and occasional news updates.

w **capeverdetips.co.uk** Aimed largely at people who are buying or already own property on Sal. It includes plenty of advice about travel and life in Sal and can advise on wedding blessings there. Also has a useful link to British Embassy Information for British Nationals in Cabo Verde.

w **expressodasilhas.cv** Cabo Verdean weekly newspaper site, based in Praia.

w **governo.cv** The official government website, in Portuguese, but with some official documents in English.

w **protectedplanet.net/country/CPV** Details Cabo Verde's protected areas.

w **rtc.cv** and **radiomorabeza.cv** Streaming radio shows and podcasts.

w **scvz.org** Zoological Society of Cabo Verde, with some English-language information.

w **visit-caboverde.com** Cabo Verde's tourism board's official site, with good inspirational content but sadly scarce practical advice.

Index

Entries in **bold** indicate main entries; entries in *italics* indicate maps.

Acacia americana 6
accessible travel 69
accidents 66–7
accommodation 77–9 *see also*
  places by name
  Boavista 140
  Brava 253
  Fogo 228
  Maio 211
  Sal 100–1
  Santiago 167–8
  Santo Antão 306
  São Nicolau 345
  São Vicente 278
Achada Leite (Santiago) 192
Achada Santo António
  (neighbourhood, Praia) 170,
  172–3, *174–5*, *177–8*, *179–80*
Afonso, Diogo 12
African Market (Assomada) 190
African Plate 3
agriculture 31–3
Agriões (Santo Antão) 333
Água das Caldeiras (Santo Antão)
  334, 336
aid 30
AIDS/HIV 35–6
air travel
  getting to/from Cabo Verde
    59–60
  inter-island flights 72–4
  airports 60
Alcatraz (Maio) 220
Alexander's kestrel 165, 217
Alexander's swift 226
Almada, José Luís Hopffer 41
Almeida, Elida 47
Almeida, Germano 40, 41–2, 376
alphabet, Kriolu 37, 39
alugueres 74, 75, **76–7** *see also*
  public transport
Andrade, Mayra 45, 46
Angola 25, 34
animal bites 67
animal welfare 89–90
animals *see* flora and fauna
anti-fascists 196
apartments, self catering 118–19,
  168, 215
architecture
  contemporary 291, 292, 322–3
  Gothic 185, 186
  Manueline 185
  18th-century 212

19th-century 181, 228, 230,
  236, 291–2
20th-century 291–2
vernacular 187, 191, 236
area 2, **3**
Aristides Pereira International
  Airport (Boavista) 139
Armed Forces Movement
  (Portuguese) 26
arretos (small stone walls) 32
art, contemporary 42, 181, 293,
  373–4
arts, the 84 *see also* culture
Assomada (Santiago) **188–92**, 204
  accommodation 189
  what to see and do 190–2
Atlantic Music Expo 50, 164
Atlantic telecommunications
  cable 274
ATMs 71–2

Badiu (Sotavento identity,
  language) 37, **39**, 84, 86, 369
Badius (community, Santiago) 191
Badius (historical) 24, 39
Baía das Gatas (Boavista) 154
Baía das Gatas (São Vicente) 295
Baía da Murdeira (Sal) 111, **126**
Baía Varandinha (Boavista) 142
Baixo, Praia (Santiago) 169, **197**
Baixo de João Leitão (reef,
  Boavista) 142
Baixo Rocha, Praia de (São
  Nicolau) 347, 353
Baleia (Brava) 263, 264
Balejas, Praia dos (Boavista) 155
Baluarte (Boavista) 135
Bana 46, 49
Bangaeira (Fogo) 238
banks 71–2
Barbosa, Eileen 23
Barbosa, Jorge **41**, 131, 162, 164
Barbosa, Shauna 43
Barlavento islands 3
Barragem Poilão (Santiago) 187–8
Barreiro (Maio) 220
batuku (dancing) 46
batuku (music style) 43, 46–7
Bau 46
beaches 53 *see also by name*
  Boavista 142, 143
  Fogo 229–30
  Maio 211–12
  Sal 102–6

Santiago 169–77, 182
Santo Antão 307
São Nicolau 347, 353
São Vicente 279, 294
begging 67, 86
Ben'Oliel graves (Sal Rei) 152
Bettencourt, Fátima 41
Biblioteca Municipal (Mindelo)
  294
Bird Island (Mindelo) 291
birds 6–7
  Boavista 135, 137
  Brava 252, 270
  Fogo 226
  Maio 209
  Sal 96
  Santiago 165
  São Nicolau 343–4, 347, 361–3
  São Vicente 276
Bius 45, 47
black-winged stilt 96, 209
blackcap 343
Blue Sharks (national football
  team) 48–9
Boa Entrada (Santiago) 190–1
Boa Esperança (nature reserve,
  Boavista) 135, 153
Boa Esperança (township,
  Boavista) 138
Boavista 56, **131-60**, *132*
  accommodation 140–1
  activities 141–5
  drives 144–5
  excursions 141
  festivals 134
  geography 134–5
  highlights and lowlights 131
  history 132–4
  natural history 132–8
  safety 138
  suggested itinerary and
    number of days 131–2
  travel agents, tour operators
    141
  transport 139–40
Boca das Ambas Ribeiras (Santo
  Antão) 328
Boca Fonte (Fogo) 245
Bofareira (Boavista) 153
Botanical gardens
  Sal 107
  Santiago 187, **188**
boxing 189
Branca, Praia (São Nicolau) 347, **354**

378

Branco 7, 9, **361–3**
'Brasil' (neighbourhood, Praia) *see* Achada Santo António
Brava 57, **248–71**
　accommodation 253
　activities 253–4
　drives 260–3
　festivals 251
　geography 252
　highlights and lowlights 248–9
　hiking 253, 259, 262–71
　history 249–51
　natural history 252
　safety 252
　suggested itinerary and number of days 249
brick factory (Boavista) 157
British (historical) 17, 207, 274, **296**, 325
Brito, António de Paula 37
brown booby 6, 7, 155, 165
budgeting 71
Bulimundo 48, 49
Bulwer's petrel 7, 96, 270
Buracona (Sal) 127
bus travel 74 *see also* taxis, public transport
business travellers 58

Cabeçalinho (São Nicolau) 359
Cabeço das Tarafes (Boavista) 160, 155
Cabo Verde Creole (CVC) *see* Kriol/Kriolu
Cabral, Amílcar **25–6**, 181, 192, 375
　museum (Praia) 181
Cabral, Juvenal 25, 341
Cabral, Praia de (Boavista) 143, 147, 152
Cabral, Sacadura 291
Cachaço (Brava) 261, 269
Cachaço (São Nicolau) 346, **351**, 359, 361
cachupa (food) 79, 80, 296
Ca'da Mosto, Alvise 11
Caibros (Santo Antão) 331–2, 334
Calejão (São Nicolau) 357–9
Calhau (São Vicente) 278–9, **296–8**
Calheta (Maio) 212, **218–19**
Calheta de São Miguel (Santiago) **196–7**, 201–2
Calheta Funda (Sal) 106, 107, **126**
camping 79
　Maio 212
Campo Baixo (Brava) 261
Campo Redondo (Santo Antão) 326
Canary Current 5
canyoning (Santo Antão) 307
Cão, Diogo 311
Cape Verde (animals) buzzard 165, 343
　cane warbler 7, 165, 226
　giant skink 7, 363
　little shearwater 165, 226, 343
　peregrine 165, 226, 343
　petrel 7, 96, 137, 154, 226, 270, 343
　purple heron 7, 165, 190, 192
　red kite 7

shearwater 7, 165, 226, 252, 270, 343, 362
sparrow 137
swift 96, 165, 343
warbler 252, 343
capitãos see social structure, historical
car rental 75
　Boavista 140
　Brava 253
　Fogo 228
　Maio 211
　Sal 100–1, 108
　Santiago 167
　Santo Antão 306
　São Nicolau 345
　São Vicente 277–8
Carbeirinho (São Nicolau) 353, **354**, 361
Cardoso, César Schofield 42, 373
Cardoso, Pedro (also known as 'Afro') 41
Carnation Revolution 26, 196
Carnival 51, 83
　São Nicolau 51, **346**
　São Vicente 51, **272**
Carriçal (São Nicolau) 347, 356, **357**
Casa da Memória (Sal Rei) 152
Casa da Memória (São Filipe) 236
Casa do Ambientes (visitors centres/park offices)
　Serra Malagueta, Santiago 192–3, 199
　Monte Gordo, São Nicolau 346, 351
Casa Teixeira (Brava) 262
Cascabulho (Maio) 219
Cassard, Jacques 171, 183, 185
Castro Pireira, Luis de 298
cathedral, ruins (Cidade Velha) 185
Catholicism 35, 38, 82, 191
caves (Fogo) 230, 246
Centro Cultural do Mindelo 290, 294
Centro Nacional de Arte, Artesanato e Design (CNAD; Mindelo) 292–3
Cesária Évora International Airport 276
Chã (wine cooperative, label) 241
Chã d'Areia (neighbourhood, Praia) 170, *172–3*
Chã das Caldeiras (Fogo) 223, 225, **237–42**, *237*, **243–6**
　accommodation 239–40
　eating and drinking 240
　what to see and do 240–2
Chã de Coelho (Santo Antão) 333–4
Chã de Igreja (Santo Antão) **323–4**, 328–31
Chã de Lobinhos (Santo Antão) 331–2
Chã de Morte (Santo Antão) 324
Chã de Pedra (Santo Antão) 328, 332–3
Chã João Vaz (Santo Antão) 316, 335
Chã Manuel dos Santos (Santo Antão) 335

Chantre, Teófilo 46
Chão Bom (Santiago) 169, 196, 199 *see also* concentration camp
charities 88
Chaves, Praia de (Boavista) 140, 142, 143, 149, 157
China, investment and aid 28, 30, 187
Chu Chu (Santo Antão) *see* Xôxô
Churchill, Winston 21
Cicília (wreck) 142
Cidade das Pombas (Santo Antão) 312–14
　accommodation 313–14
　eating and drinking 314
　practicalities 314
Cidade do Porto Inglés (Maio) 212–18, *213*
　accommodation 213–15
　eating and drinking 215–16
　entertainment and nightlife 216
　practicalities 216
　shopping 216
　what to see and do 216–18
Cidade Velha (Santiago) 162, 170–1, **182–7**, *183*
　accommodation 184
　eating and drinking 184
　history 12, 182–3
　practicalities 184
　what to see and do 184–7, 203
citizenship, Cabo Verdean 58
Claridade (publication) 10, 25–6, 41, 275
climate 4
　when to visit 51
cloth *see* craft, *panos/panú*
clothing, what to take 70
CNAD *see* Centro Nacional de Arte, Artesanato e Design
coal, coaling stations (São Vicente) 20, 273–4, 292
Coculi (Santo Antão) 318, 328, 332–4, 336–7
coffee 31, 81, 221, 242
coladeira (traditional music style) 43, 45, 49
Columbus, Christopher 133
communications 85
communism 23, 25, 41
Compania Nacional de Cabo Verde e Guiné 18
concentration camp (Tarrafal) 196
conservation **5–10**, 89–90
　Boavista 135, 136, 137
　Fogo 226
　Maio 208, 209
　Sal 96, 97, 98
　Santiago 165
　Santo Antão 304
　São Nicolau 343, 344
Convento e Igreja de São Francisco 185, 186
convicts, Portuguese 14, 20, 24, 196, 223, 341, 363
Corda (Santo Antão) 336–7
Cordas do Sol 46, 308
Coroa (Santo Antão) *see* Topo da Coroa
corruption, lack of 86

379

Corvo (Santo Antão) 330
Costa da Fragata (Sal) 96, **129**
Costa de Boa Esperança (Boavista) 153
Coutinho, Gago 291
Cova de Paúl (Santo Antão) 308, 335
Cova Joana (Brava) 261, 262, 264–5
Cova Rodela (Brava) 261, 262–3, 264–5, 270
co-working spaces 58–9, 181, 284, 377
craft 84, 144, 151, 168, 179, 184, 190, 191, 290, 292–3, 294, 322 *see also panos/panú*
cream-coloured courser 137, 208, 217
credit cards 71
Creole culture, creolification 18, 19, 23, 24, 34, 38–9
Creole language *see* Kriol/Kriolu
cricket 296
crime 36, **69–70**, 86, 138, 165, 276
Criol, Criolu *see* Kriol/Kriolu
cruising
    cruise ships 60
    yachts **55**, 277
Cruzinha da Garça (Santo Antão) 306, 307, **322–3**, 329–31
Cuba 28
culture 38–50
Curral Velho, Praia de (Boavista) 155
Curralinho, Praia de (Boavista) 155–6
churches
    Convento e Igreja de São Francisco (Cidade Velha) 185, 186
    Igreja de Nossa Senhora do Rosário (Cidade Velha) 185, 187
    Igreja Matriz de Nossa Senhora do Rosário (São Nicolau) 350
    Igreja Nossa Senhora da Conçeição (Cidade Velha) 186
    Igreja Nossa Senhora de Fátima (Boavista) **152**, 159
    Nossa Senhora do Monte (Brava) 260, 261
    Nossa Senhora do Socorro chapel (Fogo) 243
    Pró-catedral Nossa Senhora da Graça (Praia) 181
    Pró-catedral Nossa Senhora da Luz (Mindelo) 292
    Sé catedral (Cidade Velha) 185
Curral das Vacas (Santo Antão) 324
Curral Velho (Boavista) 135, 143, **155**
currency 2, 71
cycling 77–6
    Fogo 229
    Maio 215
    Sal 106
    Santiago 170, 195
    Santo Antão 307
Cruz, Bishop Francisco da 185
Cruz, Frank Xavier da 296

Dampier, William 94, 221, 340, 377
dance 39, **43–7**, 84
Darwin, Charles 168, 171, 296
Davidson, Basil 10, 20, 92, 374
de Noli, António 11–12, 94, 163, 182
degredados ('the exiled'/convicts) *see* social structure, historical
dehydration 64
Delgado, Germano 325
dengue fever 65
Depression era 20
desalination 115, 154
design *see* craft
development work 89
diarrhoea 62, 63
Dias, José António 340
Dias, Júlio José 340, 350
diaspora 34–5, 37
digital nomads 59
diphtheria 61
disability, travelling with a 69
diving 53–4
    Boavista 141
    insurance 61
    Maio 212
    Sal 105–6
    Santiago 169, 195
    Santo Antão 307, 326
    São Vicente 279
    shipwrecks 12–13, 142
dogs 89
Domingos, Luísa 308
dragon trees 5, 252, 343, 359
Drake, Francis 171, 183, 197, 205, 207, 250
drip irrigation 33, 226
driving 75 *see also drives by place*
    Boavista 144–5
    Brava 260–3
    Santiago 170
    Santo Antão 308
    São Nicolau 348
    São Vicente 280–1
Dromadaire (wreck) 142
droughts 3, 4, 20, 21, 25, 27, 32, 113, 251, 274–5, 341
drugs 36, 47, 68
    drug trade 36, 165
    prescription drugs 61–2
Duarte, Abílio 25–6
Duarte, Bela 292
Duarte, Vera 41
dust storms *see* harmattan
Dutch, the (historical) 17, 43, 223
DVT (deep vein thrombosis) 62

EASE portal, for visa exemptions 58
eco-lodges 140, 228, 291, 322
economy 2, **29–33**
education 37, 38
Egyptian vultures 329
Eito (Santo Antão) 335
elections 28–9
electricity
    supply 32, 70
    voltage 2, 70
Ellis, Alfred Burdon 274, 329
embassies and consulates 59
emigration 20, 25, 27, **34–5**
energy resources 32–3

entertainment 84 *see also places by name*
entry requirements 58–9
environmental projects 89
Ernestina (schooner) **21**, 268
erosion 3, 32–3, 336
    control of 32–3
Ervatão (Boavista) 135
Escola Jorge Barbosa (Mindelo) 293
Espargos (Sal) **109–11**, *109*
    accommodation 110
    eating and drinking 110
    practicalities 111–17
Espingueira (Boavista) 153
Espongeiro (Santo Antão) **323**, 331–4
Estância de Baixo (Boavista) 160
Estoril (beach, Boavista) 139, 147–51
Estrela Square (Mindelo) *see* Praça Estrela
etiquette 86–8
European Union 29, 31, 33
Evans, Christopher 186
Évora, Cesária 27, **44**, 46, 48, 84, 280, 293
    Museu Nucleologico Cesária Évora (Mindelo) 293–4
exchange rate 2, 71

Fajã d'Água (Brava) 54, 252, **258–60**, 261, 266–71
Fajã de Baixo and Fajã de Cima (São Nicolau) 348, 351
Fajã dos Cumes (Santo Antão) 334
family history, Cabo Verdean 22
famines *see* droughts
farol *see* lighthouses *or by name*
Farol Dona Maria Pina (Praia) 182
Farol Pontes Pereira de Melo (Santo Antão) 311
fascism, Portuguese 23, 24, 26, 196
fauna 6–9 *see also* flora and fauna *for individual islands*
Fazenda (neighbourhood, Praia) 170, *172*–3
Fea's petrel 226
Feijoal (Fogo) 246
ferries, inter-island 53, **74–5**
    Boavista 139
    Brava 252–3
    Fogo 227, 235
    Maio 210
    Sal 99, 111
    Santiago 166
    Santo Antão 305
    São Nicolau 344
    São Vicente 276–7
festivals 51, **82–3**
    Boavista 134
    Brava 251
    Fogo 225
    Maio 207
    Sal 95, 124
    Santiago 164
    Santo Antão 303
    São Nicolau 341, 346
    São Vicente 272, 275, 295
fidalgos (noblemen) *see* social structure, historical
Figueira, Manuel 292

Figueira da Horta (Maio) 220
Figueira das Naus (Santiago) 199–200
Finaçon (band) 49
fishing (leisure) 51, **54**
  Brava 254, 260
  Boavista 143
  Fogo 231
  Maio 212
  Sal 105
  Santiago 169
  Santo Antão 307
  São Nicolau 347
  São Vicente 279
fishing industry 8–9, **30–1**
flag 2, **27**
Flamengos de Baixo (Santiago) 201
flora 5–6 *see also* flora and fauna *for individual islands*
flora and fauna
  Boavista 135–7
  Brava 252
  Fogo 225–7
  Maio 209–10, 216–17
  Sal 96–8
  Santiago 165
  Santo Antão 304
  São Nicolau 343
  São Vicente 276
fog collectors 33, **202**
Fogo 57, **221–47**, *222 see also places by name*
  accommodation 228
  activities 229–30
  coffee farms 242
  excursions 229
  festivals 225
  geography 225
  highlights and lowlights 221
  history 223–4
  natural history 224
  safety 227
  suggested itinerary and number of days 222–3
  tour operators and travel agents 229
  transport 227–8
  wine 82, 245
  wineries 236, 240–1
folklore 50
Fonseca, Jorge Carlos 28, 41, 43
Fontainhas (Santo Antão) 319, **322**, 329
Fontainhas, Monte (Brava) 252, 261, 264–5
Fontes, Margarida 42
Fontona (Sal) 126
food and drink 79–82
football 48, 181
forced labour 20
foreign investment 29–32
Formiguinhas (Santo Antão) 329, 330
Fortes, Corsino 41, 43, 376
forts
  Fortim d'El Rei (Mindelo) 291
  Forte da Preguiça (São Nicolau) 355
  Forte de São José (Cidade do Porto Inglés) 212
  Forte Duque de Bragança (Sal Rei) 152–3

Forte Real do São Filipe (Cidade Velha) 184–5
Fragata (São Nicolau) 360, 361
Francês, Praia da (São Nicolau) 353
freed population, historical 19–20
French, the (historical) 17, 19, 35, 40, 57, 59, 86, 291
French Revolution 19
funaná (music style) 43–9, 84
Fundo das Figueiras (Boavista) 153
Furna (Brava) **254**, 269
further information 373–7

Gama, Vasco da 182
Gamboa, Praia de (beach/neighbourhood, Praia) 164, 166, *172–3*, 174, 182
Garça (Brava) 263–4
gay and lesbian travellers, *see* LGBTQIA+ travellers
GDP (gross domestic product) 2, **29**, 30, 31, 304
genealogy 22
geography 3–4
  Boavista 140
  Brava 253
  Fogo 227
  Maio 209–10
  Sal 102
  Santiago 170
  Santo Antão 299
  São Nicolau 336
  São Vicente 276
geology **3–4**, 11
  Fogo 11, 223–5, 226
geothermal energy 30, 225
giant gecko 363
giving back 88–90, 108, 285
golf **107**, 275
  minigolf 117
Gomes, Diogo 12, 94, 163, 181, 311
Gomez, Jewelle 43
Gouveia, Marquess of 302
government 2, **28–9**, 377
greater hoopoe lark 209
green turtles 135
greetings 87, 371
grey-headed kingfisher 5, 7, 226
grogue (alcoholic spirit) 81, **82–3**
grogue, distilleries and production 31, 304, 314, 329, 334, 360
grumettas (mercenary bodyguards) *see* social structure, historical
Gruta da Fonte do Monte Inhuco *see* caves
Gruta do Monte Preto *see* caves
Guevara, Mynda 47
guides, hiring 68
Guinea-Bissau (former Portuguese Guinea) 25–8, 34, 47, 60, 166, 204

Hanno 11
harassment
  Santa Maria street vendors 88, 98, **122**
  sexual 69
harmattan 4, 51, 193
Hartwell (wreck) 13, 142
hawksbill turtles 135
health 61–9

heat exhaustion 64
heat stroke 64
helmeted guineafowl 7
Henrique, Yuran 42
Henry the Navigator 11
hepatitis A and B 61
hikes, hiking **51**, 57
  accidents and safety 66–7, 68–70, 304
  Boavista 139, 144, **158–60**
  Brava 253, 259, **262–71**
  Fogo 229, 240, **243–7**
  Maio 211
  Sal 129–30
  Santiago 169, 195, **198–203**
  Santo Antão 301, 304, 306–7, 324, **328–37**, *330–1*
  São Nicolau 345–6, 356–7, **357–61**
  São Vicente 280
hissing 87
history **10–28**
  Boavista 132–3
  Brava **249–50**, 268
  Fogo 223–4
  Maio 207
  Sal **93–4**, 112, 127
  Santiago **163–4**, 170–1, 182–3, 196
  Santo Antão 302
  São Nicolau 340–2
  São Vicente 273–5
hitchhiking 75, 210
Holy Spirit Congregation 191
homestays 57, **78–9**, 184, 193, 326, 351, 355
horseriding
  Sal 107
  São Nicolau 348
Hortelão (Santiago) 187, 198–9
Hospital Agostinho Neto (HAN; Praia) 181–2
Hospital Central Dr Baptista de Sousa ('Hospital Baptista', Mindelo) 290
Hospital do Sal (Espargos) 111
hospitals *see health care by place*
hotels *see accommodation by place*
Hughes, Ron 325
humpback whales 9, 54, 96, 135, 137, 143, 212
Hurricane Beryl (1982) 251
hydroponics 33, 149–50

Iago sparrow 158, 165, 217
igreja see churches
Ilhéu de Cima (Brava) 270
Ilhéu de Curral Velho (Boavista) 137, 155
Ilhéu do Sal Rei (Boavista) 55, 133, 135, 143, **152–3**
Ilhéu Grande (Brava) 270
Ilhéu Raso 7, 252, 347, **361–3**
Ilhéus do Rombo (Brava) 7, 252, **270**
IMF (International Monetary Fund) 29
immunisations 61
independence movement **23–7**, 181, 196, 292, 293
inheritance, land ownership 22
inscribed rock (Santo Antão) *see* Pedra da Nossa Senhora

381

insect bites 62
insurance 58, 61
international telephone code 2
internet access 85
itineraries 56-7
    Boavista 131-2
    Brava 249
    Fogo 222-3
    Maio 206-7
    Sal 93
    Santiago 163
    Santo Antão 301-2
    São Nicolau 340
    São Vicente 272-3
Islam 38

Jann, Beatrice 138
Jean Piaget University 38, 186
Jewish history and immigration 14-15, 24, 152, 316, 375
jiggers 62
João de Nole 263, 265-6
João Galego (Boavista) 153-4
João Valente seamount 136
Johnson, Piran 13
Juncalinho (São Nicolau) 340, 347, 355-6
Jurado, Luis Felipe Lopez 136

Kabuverdianu *see* Kriol/Kriolu
kasubodi see crime
kayaking
    Boavista 143
    Santiago 193
Kebra Kanela (beach/ neighbourhood, Praia) *172-3*, 177, 179, 182 *see also* beaches and places in Praia
Kennedy, Patrick 35
Kentish plover 96, 208, 209, 217
Kite Beach (Sal) 97, 104
kitesurfing *see* windsurfing
kitesurfing champions 103
Kriol/Kriolu 2, 25, 36, **37-9**, 41, 43, 46, 71, **86-7**, 296, 364, **369-72**

Lacação, Praia de (Boavista) 135, 137, **155**
ladinos (baptised slaves) *see* social structure, historical
Laginha, Praia da (Mindelo) 279, 288, 294
lagoa (lake), in Cimidor (Maio) 209
lagoa (lake), in Juncalinho (São Nicolau) 355-6
Lagoa, town (Maio) 222
Lagoinha (Santo Antão) 331-2
lançados ('outcasts'/traders) *see* social structure, historical
language 2, **36**, 92-3
    Kriolu **37**, 369-72
    English-derived words 296
    Portuguese 364-9
Larsson, Henrick 49
lemon sharks *see* sharks
leprosy, leper colonies 8, 133, 316
Lewis, Lieutenant John 274
LGBTQIA+ travellers 69
life expectancy 2, 29, 35
lighthouses
    Boavista 53, 153, 154
    Sal 130

Santiago 169, 182, 195, 202
Santo Antão 311
São Vicente 280
Lima Doce (Brava) 261
Lin d'Corv (Santo Antão) 332-3
Lindbergh, Charles and Anne Morrow 171
literacy 29, 35
literature 25, 26, **40-3**, 185-6, 275
Lusophone 37, 41, 375-6
living and working in Cabo Verde 58-9 *see also* co-working
Lobban, Richard 311, 374
Lobo, Ildo 49
location 3
loggerhead turtles 8, 53, 96-7, 135-7, 143-4, 217, 227, 347 *see also* turtles
Lomba (Brava) 260, 261-2
Lombo de Pedra (Santo Antão) 334
Lopes, Baltasar 36, 41, 339, 375
Lopes, James 22
Lopes, Manuel 41
Lumi, Djeison 47
Lura (Maria de Lurdes Assunção Pina) 46
Luso-British Commission 133, 152
Luz, Irineu da 327
Lyall, Archibald 94, 111, 248, 254, 257, 377

Madeiral (São Vicente) 296
Madeiran storm petrel 7, 270
magnificent frigatebird 6, 7, 139, 155
Main Square (Praia) *see* Praça Alexandre Albuquerque
Maio 56, **205-20**, *206 see also places by name*
    accommodation 211
    activities 211-12
    festivals 207
    geography 208-9
    highlights and lowlights 205-6
    history 16, **207**
    natural history 209-10
    safety 210
    suggested itinerary and number of days 206-7
    transport 210-11
malaria 62
malaria-free status 65
mammals 7
Manuel I, King of Portugal 14
maps 71
marine archaeology 12-13, 181
marine life **7-9** *see also individual species*
    Boavista 136-7
markets 123, 149, 190, 195, 286
Martins, Manuel António 94, 112
Mascarenhas, António Manuel 28
Mathilde (wreck) 258
Mato Grande (Brava) 261, 262-6
Mato Inglês (São Vicente) 296
media 85-6
medical
    kit 61-2
    problems 62-7
medicinal sand (São Nicolau) 353
Melo, Tommy 362
melon-headed whales 96

Mendes, Henrique 21, 268
Mendes brothers 49
Mercado Municipal *see* markets
mestiços (African and European heritage, historical term) 18, 19, 25
Miller and Cory's building (Mindelo) 291
Mindelo (São Vicente) 272, **281-94**, *282-3*, *286*
    accommodation 281-5
    eating and drinking 285-8
    entertainment and nightlife 288-90
    history 20, 275, 291
    practicalities 290-1
    shopping 290
    what to see and do 291-4
mobile phones 85-6
Modernism
    architecture 181, 280, 291, 297
    art 293
    literature 42
money 71-2
Monk, George 325
monopolies, Crown 18, 24
monsoon, southwest 4
Monte Caçador (Boavista) 135
Monte Cebola (Santo Antão) 324
Monte Estância (Boavista) 135
Monte Genebra (Fogo) 243
Monte Gordo (São Nicolau) 342, 343
Monte Gordo Natural Park (São Nicolau) 339, 340, **342**, 343, 346, 351, 359
    trails 360
Monte Grande (Sal) 96
Monte Leão (Sal) 96, **126**, 130
Monte Leste (Sal) 127
Monte Pia (Santo Antão) 324
Monte Santo António (Boavista) 135
Monte Trigo (Santo Antão) 324, 327
Monte Verde (São Vicente) 275, 276, 280, 294
Monte Xota (Santiago) 187, 200
Montebarro (Fogo) 245-6
Monteiro, Mitu 103
Monteiro, Vanessa 292, 294
Montinho (Fogo) 224, 246
Montrond, Alberto 241
Montrond, David 241
Montrond, Duc François Louis Armand Fourcheut de 238, **241**
Montrond, Michel 47
Mormons 38
morna (traditional music style) 40-1, 43-50, **156**, 256, 257
Moroços (Santo Antão) 304
Morrinho (Maio) 212, 219
Morrinho do Açúcar (Sal) 96
Morrinho do Filho (Sal) 96
Morro (Maio) 209, 218
Morro de Areia (Boavista) 135
Morro Negro Lighthouse (Boavista) 154
Mosteiros (Fogo) 240, 242-3, 245-7
Mozambique 23
MpD (Movimento para a Democracia, political party) 2, 28

murals *see* street art
Murdeira Bay (Sal) *see* Baía da Murdeira
Murdeira Village (Sal) 111
museums 84
　Casa da Memória (Sal Rei) 152
　Casa da Memória (São Filipe) 236
　Casa Museu Eugénio Tavares (Brava) 257
　Centro Nacional de Arte, Artesanato e Design (Mindelo) 292–3
　Museu Amílcar Cabral (Santiago) 181
　Museu da Resistência *see* Museu do Campo de Concentração
　Museu de Arqueologia (Praia) 181
　Museu de Arqueologia da Boavista (Boavista) 152
　Museu de Tabanka (Santiago) 190
　Museu do Campo de Concentração (Santiago) 196
　Museu do Mar (Mindelo) 293
　Museu Etnográfico da Praia 181
　Museu Municipal de São Filipe 236
　Museu Nucleologico Cesária Évora (Mindelo) 292–3
　Palácio da Cultura Ildo Lobo (Praia) 181
music **43–50**, 84 *see also individual music styles*
　music industry, Lusophone 48–50, 84, 164
Mussolini, Benito 94

Nani (Luís Carlos Almeida da Cunha) 49
Napoleon 19
National Assembly 27
nationalism 23–7
natural history **5–10**, 296, 376–7 *see also* flora and fauna *for individual islands*
natural resources 32
Nazarenes 38
Nellie May (whaler) 268
Nenny (Marlene Fernanda Cardoso Tavares) 47
Néuza 47
Neves, José Maria Pereira 28, 37
Nho Lobo (lazy wolf,) 48 *see also* folklore
nightlife 56 *see also* places by name
Nissah (Nissah Barbosa) 47
Norte (Santo Antão) 328
nuclear power, proposed 33
nurse sharks *see* sharks

Oasis of Santo Tirso (Boavista) 155
Old Customs House (Mindelo) 291
older travellers 69
Olho de Mar (Boavista) 155, 160
Oliveira, Bento 42
Oliveira, José Pedro 303
Oliveira, Serafim 304

Olympians, Cabo Verdean 189
opening hours 84–5
orchil dye 16, 17, 296
Organisation of African Unity 26
Os Tubarões 49
Osório, Oswaldo 41

packet trade 21, 268
packing 70–1
Pai António (Fogo) 242, 245–6
PAICV (Partido Africano da Independência de Cabo Verde, political party) 28
PAIGC (Party for the Independence of Guinea and Cape Verde, historical political party) 25–7, 293
Palácio da Cultura Ildo Lobo (Santiago) 42, 181
Palácio do Povo (Mindelo, São Vicente) 292
Palmarejo (neighbourhood, Praia) 170, *172–3*, 175, 178, 179–80
Palmeira (Sal) 55, 108, 126–7
pan-Africanism 26, 41
panos/panú (six-banded cloth) **40**, 181, 292
　trade in 16–18
Paris, Tito 48, 49, 288
Parque Natural do Fogo 226, 230, *237*
Parque Natural Monte Gordo *see* Monte Gordo Natural Park
Parque Natural Monte Verde *see* Monte Verde
Parque Natural Serra Malagueta *see* Serra Malagueta
Passagem (Santo Antão) 314, 335
Pássaros (Boavista) 135, 137, 154
Paúl (Santo Antão) *see* Cidade das Pombas
PCD (Partido da Convergencia Democratica, political party) 28
Pede Pranta (Fogo) 246
Pedra Badejo (Santiago) 169, 197
Pedra da Nossa Senhora (Santo Antão) 311
Pedra de Lume (Sal) 127–8
Pedro Vaz (Maio) 219–20
Pelourinho (monument, Cidade Velha) 185
Penedo (Santo Antão) 335–6
Penha de França, Mariana de 302
Penoso (Maio) 220
people 34–6
Pereira, Aristides **25**, 27, 133
Pereira, Luis de Castro 250
pests, agricultural 33
pests, medical risks 62–3
Pettingall, Charles 152
Pettingall, Julia Maria 159
Phoenicians 11, 311
photography
　collections 42, 152
　etiquette 88
　opportunities 252, 323, 326, 337, 351, 355
Pia de Cima (Santo Antão) 332
Pico (volcano, Fogo) *see also* Chã das Caldeiras
　eruption, geology 223–4, 225
　hiking 222, 240, **243–4**

Pico da Cruz (Santo Antão) 308, 314, 335–6
Pico Forçado (Boavista) 135
Pina, Agostinho da 47
Pina, Daniel David Varela de 189
Pires, Jorge 14
Pires, Pedro 28
Planalto Norte (cheesemakers, Santo Antão) 327
planning tips 51–7, 58–9, 61–7, 70–2
Platô (or Plateau; neighbourhood, Praia) 162, 170, 174, 175–7, *176*, 181
poetry 40–3, 375–6
　readings 184, 289
polio, immunisation 61
politics 28–30, 374
ponche (liquor) 81, **82–3**
Ponta Antónia (Boavista) 143, 153
Ponta da Parede (Sal) 126
Ponta do Roque (Boavista) 155
Ponta do Sol (Boavista) 135, 153, 158
Ponta do Sol (Santo Antão) **319–22**, *320*, 329
　accommodation 319–21
　eating and drinking 321
　entertainment and nightlife 321
　practicalities 322
　shopping 322
　what to see and do 322
Ponta Preta (Maio) 210, 211, 212, **217–18**
Ponta Preta (Sal) 103, **104**, 106, **125–6**, 130
Ponta Sino (Sal) 103
Pontinha da Janela (Santo Antão) 311
population 2, 29, **34–5**
Portela (Fogo) 238, 244–5
Porto Novo (Santo Antão) 303, **308–11**, *309*
　accommodation 310
　eating and drinking 310
　practicalities 311
Porto Rincão (Santiago) 190
Portuense, Bishop Vitoriano 185
Portugal
　African colonies 18, 19, 23–7
　Carnation Revolution 26
　colonial rule 11–27
　debt to, financial 30
　discovery and settlement 11–17
　Estado Novo dictatorship 24–6, 196
　independence from 26–7
Portuguese consulate (Mindelo) 291
Portuguese Guinea 14–17, 23, 25–6, 40, 196
Portuguese language 36–5, 364–9
post offices 85
poverty 29, 86, 88
Povoação (Santo Antão) *see* Ribeira Grande
Povoação Velha (Boavista) 133, 151, **156–7**, 160
Praça Alexandre Albuquerque (Santiago) 181
Praça Estrela (Mindelo) 286, 292

383

Pracinha de Igreja (Mindelo) 292
Praia (Santiago) 162, **170–82**,
     172–3, *176*
   accommodation 174–5
   eating and drinking 175–8
   entertainment and nightlife
      178–9
   history 170–1 *see also* Cidade
      Velha
   practicalities 180–1
   shopping 179–80
   what to see and do 181–2
Praínha (beach/neighbourhood,
     Praia) *172–3*, 174, 177–8, 182
Preguiça (São Nicolau) 344, 345,
     354–5
Presidential Palace *see* Palácio
     do Povo (Mindelo, São
     Vicente)
pretos (free Africans) *see* social
     structure, historical
prices 72, 77–82
   food and drink 79–82
prickly heat 64
Princess Louisa (wreck) 13
Príncipe *see* São Tomé and
     Príncipe
Prior of Crato 183
Project Biodiversity (Sal) **97**, 108
Protestantism 38
proverbs 50
public holidays 2, 82–3
public transport (*alugueres*) 74–5
   Boavista 140
   Brava 253, 258
   Fogo 228
   Maio 210–11
   Sal 99, 100
   Santiago 167
   Santo Antão 305
   São Nicolau 334–5
   São Vicente 277
Punta Lembje (Sal) 104

quad bikes
   Boavista 144, 145
   issues with 8, 97, 98, 136,
      137, 145
   Sal 108
Quebra Canela (neighbourhood
     of Praia, Santiago) *see* Kebra
     Kanela
Queimadas (São Nicolau) 360–1
Queirós, Luísa 292
Quintal da Música (Praia) 170,
     175, **179**

rabies 66, 67
Rabil (Boavista) 144, **157**
Rabil Lagoon (Boavista) 136, 137,
     144, 158, 159–60
Rabo Curto (Santo Antão) 334
radio 85
rainfall **4–5**, 32, 51
Ramos Castellano Arquitectos 291,
     292, 323
Ramsar sites (Boavista) 135–6
Raso *see* Ilhéu Raso
Raso lark 7, 299, 347, 361–3
reafforestation 198, 200, 276
real estate on Sal 118
real estate purchase, visa 58

384

Rebelados (community, Santiago)
     191
   rebelados, historical ('rebels',
      escaped slaves) 163
red tape 58–9
red-billed tropicbird 6, 7, 96,
     129, 165
refuelling station, historical
     (Mindelo) 274
religion 2, 38
remittances 29, 30–1, 35
Rendall, John 94, 274, 292
rendeiros (farm workers) *see* social
     structure, historical
renewables, renewable energy
     30, 32–3
residency, Cabo Verdean 58
Resistance Museum (Tarrafal)
     see Museu do Campo de
     Concentração
restaurants 79–82 *see also* places
     by name
Ribeira Brava (São Nicolau) 339,
     348–51, *349*
   accommodation 348–9
   eating and drinking 349–50
   entertainment and nightlife 350
   hikes to and from 357–61
   practicalities 350
   what to see and do 350–1
Ribeira da Barca (Santiago) 166,
     192
Ribeira da Cruz (Santo Antão) 324
Ribeira da Prata (Santiago) 195,
     199–200
Ribeira da Prata (São Nicolau)
     354, 361
Ribeira das Patas (Santo Antão)
     328
Ribeira de Janela (Santo Antão)
     303, 336
Ribeira de João (Maio) 220
Ribeira de Torre (Santo Antão)
     312, 316, 334
Ribeira do Paúl (Santo Antão) 303,
     308, **314–16**, 335, 336
   accommodation 315–16
   eating and drinking 316
Ribeira do Penedo (Santo Antão)
     335–6
Ribeira Garça (Santo Antão) 329
Ribeira Grande (Santiago) *see*
     Cidade Velha
Ribeira Grande (Santo Antão)
     316–19, *317*, 323, 330, 332
   accommodation 318
   eating and drinking 318
   getting there and away 318
   practicalities 304, 319
Ribeira Ilhéu (Fogo) 247
Ribeira Principal (Santiago) 169,
     198, 199
Rocha Estância (Boavista) 135,
     156, 160
Romano, Luís 41, 376
Rotcha Scribida (Santo Antão) 354
Rua Banana (Cidade Velha,
     Santiago) 187
Rui Vaz (Santiago) 187

safety 66, 67–70
sailing *see* yachts, yachting

Sal 56, **92–130**, *93 see also* places
     by name
   accommodation 100–1, 113, 118
   activities 102–8
   festivals 95, 124
   geography 96
   highlights and lowlights 92–3
   hiking 129–30
   history 93–4, 112, 127
   natural history 96–8
   safety 98
   sightseeing tours 108
   suggested itinerary and
      number of days 93
   tour operators and travel
      agents 101–2
   transport 98–100
Sal Rei (Boavista) **145–53**, *146*
   accommodation 145–8
   eating and drinking 148–50
   entertainment and nightlife
      151
   hikes from 158, 159
   practicalities 151
   what to see and do 152–3
Sal Rei Bay (Boavista) 142
Salamansa (São Vicente) 295–6
Salazar, António de Oliveira 26,
     40, 196
Salinas do Porto Inglês (Maio)
     209–10, **216–17**
Salineiro (Santiago) 203
salt production and trade 15,
     18, 296
   Boavista 133, 138
   Maio 205, 207–8, 216–17, 219
   Sal 93–4, 112, 127–8
Salústio, Dina 41, 42, 376
Sampadjudu (Barlavento identity,
     language) 37, 39, 86, 369
Sancho (folkloric monkey) 10, 50
sand fleas 62–3
Sands, J L 274
Santa Barbara (Brava) 266
Santa Cruz, Counts of 302
Santa Luzia 2, 3, 5, 7, **298–9**, 362–3
Santa Maria (Sal) **111–25**, *114*, *116*
   accommodation 113–19
   eating and drinking 119–21
   entertainment and nightlife
      121
   practicalities 123–5
Santa Maria (wreck) 138, 139,
     153, 158–9
Santa Maria Bay (Sal) **102–3**, 104
Santa Maria Salina (Sal) 96, **125**
Santa Mónica, Praia de (Boavista)
     141, 143, **155–6**, 160
Santiago 57, **162–206**, *163*
   accommodation 167–8
   activities 169–70
   festivals 164
   geography 164
   highlights and lowlights 162–3
   hiking 169, **198–203**
   history 12–19, 24, 26, 163–4,
      170–1, 182–3
   natural history 165
   safety 165
   sightseeing tours 168, 197
   suggested itinerary and
      number of days 163

tour operators and travel
   agents 168
transport 166–7
Santiago, Dino D' 47
Santo Antão 56, **300–37**, *300 see
   also places by name*
   accommodation 306
   activities 306–8
   festivals 303
   geography 303–4
   highlights and lowlights 301
   hiking 302, **328–37**, *330–1*
   history 302
   natural history 304
   safety 304
   sightseeing tours 302
   suggested itinerary and
      number of days 301–2
   tour operators and travel
      agents 306
   transport 305–6
São Domingos (Santiago) **187–8**,
   200
   accommodation 187, 188
   what to see and do 188
São Filipe (Fogo) 223, **230–7**, *232*
   accommodation 231–4
   eating and drinking 234–5
   entertainment and nightlife 235
   practicalities 235
   what to see and do 236–7
São Francisco (Santiago) 197–8
São Jorge (Fogo) 243, 247
São Jorge dos Orgãos (Santiago) 188
São Nicolau 56, *338*, **339–63**
   see also places by name
   accommodation 345
   activities 344–8
   festivals 341, 346
   geography 342–3
   highlights and lowlights
      339–40
   hiking 345–6, 356, **357–61**, *358*
   history 340–2
   natural history 343–4
   safety 344
   sightseeing tours 340
   suggested itineraries and
      number of days 333–4
   tour operators and travel
      agents 345
   transport 344–5
São Pedro (Brava) 269
São Pedro (São Vicente) 275, 277,
   280, **298**
São Tomé and Príncipe,
   immigration 23, 24, 274, 373
São Vicente 56, **272–99**, *273 see
   also places by name*
   accommodation 278
   activities 278–81
   festivals 275
   geography 275–6
   highlights and lowlights 272
   history 19, **273–5**
   natural history 276
   safety 276
   sightseeing tours 278
   suggested itinerary and
      number of days 272–3
   tour operators and travel
      agents 278

transport 276–8
scams *see* street vendors
Sé Catedral *see* churches
sea travel
   by cargo boat 75
   by cruise ship 60
   by yacht 55, 60–1
   inter-island *see* ferries
seamounts 136
Seminário-Liceu de São Nicolau
   see seminary (Ribeira Brava)
seminary (Ribeira Brava) 23,
   340–1, 351
Serra do Pico do António
   (Santiago) 164, 165, 169, 197
Serra Malagueta (Santiago) 33, 163,
   165, 169, **192–3**, 198–9, 202
Serra Negra (Sal) 96, 128–9, 129
sexual harassment 69
sharks
   lemon sharks 128, 137
   nurse sharks 135, 137, 144, 153
   shark fishing 54, 105, 217
   shark watching
      Sal 101, 106
Shigella 63, 69
shipping industry 20, 21, 30,
   268, 274
shipwrecks 12–13, 181 *see also
   individual wrecks by name*
   Boavista 142
shopping 83–4
Assomada (Santiago) 190
Chã das Caldeiras (Fogo)
   241–2
Cidade do Porto Inglês (Maio)
   216
Espargos (Sal) 111
Mindelo (São Vicente) 290
Ponta do Sol (Santo Antão) 322
Porto Novo (Santo Antão) 311
Praia (Santiago) 179–80
Sal Rei (Boavista) 151
Santa Maria (Sal) 122–3
São Filipe (Fogo) 235
Vila Nova Sintra (Brava) 256–7
Silva, Alex de 42, 289
Silva, Dany 49
Silva, Filinto Elísio 41
Silva, José de 44
Silva, José Lopes de 142, 350
Silva, Ulisses Correia e 28
Silveira, Onésimo 41
SIM cards 85–6
Sinagoga (Santo Antão) 14, 307,
   316
skin infections 64–5
slave trade 13–19, 24, 40, 182–3,
   185, 374–5
   end of 19
Slow Food (Italian culinary culture
   organisation) 327
small talk 87
snorkelling
   Boavista 144
   Sal 106
   Santiago 195
   Santo Antão 324, 326
   São Nicolau 354
   São Vicente 297
sobrado (architectural style) 57,
   228, 230, 236

social interaction 87
social issues 35–6
social structure, historical 24
sodade, concept of 40–1, 45
'Sodade', song 44, 354
solar energy 32–3
Solidade, Jennifer 47
Sørensen, Marie Louise Stig 186
Sorno (Brava) 262, 267–9
Sotavento islands 3
Souza, Carmen 47
Spanish (historical) 14, 17, 19
spectacled warbler 226, 343
Spingueira *see* Espingueira
Spínola, António de 26, 27
street art 42, 179, 181–2
street vendors 88
   on Sal 98, 122
Suez Canal 274
sugarcane 31, 82, 304
sunburn 64
sunshine, hours of 4
surfing 54–5
   Boavista 143
   Maio 212
   Sal 104–5
   Santiago 169, 195
   Santo Antão 307
   São Nicolau 347, 354
   São Vicente 278–9
Sousa, Tutu 182
swimming 53
   Boavista 139, 143
   Brava 254, 259–60
   Fogo 229–30, 236–7, 243
   Maio 211–12, 218
   safety 66, 98, 227, 252
   Sal 106, 125
   Santiago 169–70, 182, 193
   Santo Antão 307, 316, 327
   São Nicolau 347, 353, 354, 356
   São Vicente 279, 294, 295,
      297, 298
syncretism 82–3, 191
Szekely, Tamas 209

tabanka (folk theatre) 48, 164, 170
   museum (Assomada, Santiago)
      190
Talho (São Nicolau) 360
tamarisk palms 5
Tarrafal (Santiago) 175, 176,
   193–6, 205
   accommodation 193–4
   eating and drinking 194
   entertainment and nightlife
      194–5
   practicalities 195
   what to see and do 195–6
Tarrafal (Santo Antão) *see* Tarrafal
   de Monte Trigo
Tarrafal (São Nicolau) **351–3**
   accommodation 351–2
   eating and drinking 352
   entertainment and nightlife
      352
   practicalities 347
   what to see and do 353
Tarrafal de Monte Trigo (Santo
   Antão) 307, 299, **324–8**
Tartaruga, Reserva Natural
   (Boavista) 135

385

Tavares, Eugénio 27, 36, 45, 156, 248, 250, 254, **257**
　Casa Museu Eugénio Tavares **257**, 263–4, 269
Tavares, José Luiz 42
Tavares, Noberto 46, 190
taxis 75 *see also* public transport
　Fogo 228
　Mindelo 277
　Porto Novo 305
　Praia 167
Tcheka 46, 48
tectonic plates 3
Tedja, Praia de (São Nicolau) 351, 352, 353
telephones 85–6
television 85
temperatures 4–5
Terra Branca (neighbourhood, Praia) 181–2
terrain 3–4
Terrinha Vermelha (Santo Antão) 336–7
tetanus 61
Tez Cova (Brava) 269
thalassotherapy 128
theft *see* crime
Thomas, Charles 133
ticks 63
time zone 2
Tira Chapeú (neighbourhood, Praia) 170, *172–3*
Tomba Has (Brava) 267
Top d'Jock (Santo Antão) 337
Topo da Coroa (Santo Antão) 303, 327–8
Tordesillas, Treaty of 302
Torre de Belém (Mindelo) 291, 293
tour operators, international 57–8, 113
tour operators, local
　Boavista 141
　Fogo 229
　Sal 101–2
　Santiago 168
　Santo Antão 306
　São Nicolau 345
　São Vicente 278
tourism 31
town halls (*câmara municipal*)
　Mindelo 292
　São Filipe 236
trade
　historical 13–22
　contemporary 29–31
transport, inter- and intra-island 72–7
　Boavista 139–40
　Brava 252–3
　Fogo 227–8
　Maio 210–11

Sal 98–100
Santiago 166–7
Santo Antão 305–6
São Nicolau 344–5
São Vicente 276–8
transport, international 59–61
travel clinics, pretravel 62
travel insurance 61, 68, 70
tuna fishing 51, 30–1
turtles 8–9
　Boavista 135, **136–7**, 143–4, 159
　Fogo 227
　Maio 208, 210, 217
　Sal 96–8, 108
　Santo Antão 304
　São Nicolau 347, 353, 355
　São Vicente 276, 297
typhoid 61, 66

Ultratrail (Boavista) 144
unemployment 29
United States, connection to aid 27
　remittances 30
　Cabo Verdean immigration 34–5, 251, 268

Valente, Bishop 302
Varela, João Manuel 41
vegetarian food 79, 119
vehicles *see also* transport by place
　accidents 66
　rental 75
Veiga, Carlos Alberto Wahnon de Carvalho 15, 28, 29
Velhinho, Vadinho 41
Verandinha, beach (Boavista) 157
Viana Desert (Boavista) 157
Vieira Brothers 49
Vieira, Arménio 41, 42
Vieira, Nancy 47, 48
Vieira, Paulino 49
Vila das Pombas (Santo Antão) *see* Cidade das Pombas
Vila do Maio *see* Cidade do Porto Inglês
Vila Nova Sintra (Brava) 254–60, 255
　accommodation 254–6
　eating and drinking 256
　hikes from 262–9
　practicalities 256–7
　what to see and do 257–8
Vinagre (Brava) **260**, 265–6
visas 58
volcanic activity 3–4
　Fogo 221, 223, 223–4
　Brava 250
volunteering 89–90
Voz de Cabo Verde 46, 49

Vulcão Viana (São Vicente) 298
Vynckier family 115

War of Spanish Succession 19
water
　drinking 62, 82
　supplies 87, 154, 202, 218
wave technology 33
websites 377
weddings 377
Western Telegraph 274
　building (Mindelo) 291
wetlands (Boavista) 96, 135
whale watching
　Boavista 137, 138, 143
　Maio 212
　Sal 92, 96
whales 9, **138**
whaling, historical 20, 22, 293
　Brava 248, 250, 258, **268**
white-faced storm petrel 137, 154
Wi-Fi 85
windsurfing 56
　Boavista 141–3
　Sal 102–5
　São Vicente 278–9, 295
wine 82, 245
wineries (Fogo)
　Adega Cooperativa de Chã das Caldeiras (Chã label) 240–1
　Adega de Monte Barro (Maria Chaves label) 236
Wollaston, T Vernon 296
women
　demographics 34–5
　travellers 69
World Bank 30
World Trade Organization 29
World War II 20–1, 325, 268

Xavier, Bishop António José 185
Xôxô (Santo Antão) 334, 336

yachts, yachting 60–1, 75
　Boavista 140
　Brava 253
　Fogo 227
　Maio 210
　Sal 99, 102
　Santiago 166
　Santo Antão 305
　São Nicolau 344
　São Vicente 277, 279, 280
yellow fever, immunisation certificate 61
yoga (Sal) 108

Zika virus 65
zoo, petting (Sal) 107

INDEX OF ADVERTISERS

Archipelago Choice inside front cover
Camara Municipal de Santa Cruz second colour section
Hotel Morabeza second colour section
Wanderlust 372